Webster's

21ST CENTURY

Dictionary

Webster's

21ST CENTURY

Dictionary

Walter C. Kidney, Editor
Prepared under the direction
of Laurence Urdang

THOMAS NELSON PUBLISHERS
Nashville

Published in Nashville, Tennessee, by Thomas Nelson, Inc., Publishers
and distributed in Canada by Lawson Falle, Ltd., Cambridge, Ontario.

Printed in the United States of America.

Library of Congress Cataloging-in-Publication Data

Webster's 21st century dictionary.
 Webster's 21st century dictionary / Walter C. Kidney, editor ;
prepared under the direction of Laurence Urdang.
  p. cm.
 Originally published: Webster's new compact dictionary. 1991.
 ISBN 0-8407-3427-1 (PB)
 I. Kidney, Walter C. II. Urdang, Laurence. III. Title.
PE1628.W55685 1992
423—dc20   91–45457
                                                          CIP

2 3 4 5 6 7 8 9 10 — 99 98 97 96 95 94 93 92

FOREWORD

Nelson's *Webster's 21st Century Dictionary* is the perfect reference companion for everyone whose work may need a quick check for accuracy. Executives, secretaries, proofreaders, students—anyone can have ready answers to common language problems in spelling, hyphenation, and pronunciation.

This compact volume was written specifically to provide the information in an easy-to-use format. Its small size makes it easy to keep within hand's reach on desktop or in drawer. It can be tucked into a briefcase or book bag for work on the go.

This edition has been revised to include new words being introduced into the language, spelling and division guides, brief definitions, and parts of speech are included with each entry. Phonetic spellings have also been added for words which may be difficult to pronounce, such as *negligee,* or where a word may be pronounced in more than one way, such as minute (min′ət) and minute (mī nyo̅o̅t′). Now you can know quickly whether stationary or stationery is the word you want, whether effect or affect is the right choice. In addition, this practical handbook includes weights and measures equivalents, and U.S. states and their capitals.

A convenient size and accessible format makes Nelson's *Webster's 21st Century Dictionary* the primary choice of anyone who wants an accurate working knowledge of the English language.

PRONUNCIATION KEY

Symbol	Key Word	Symbol	Key Word
ă	băt	ŏ	ŏbject
ā	cāpe	ō	ōak
â	târt	ô	ôrb
à	pàrāde	ȯ	ȯf
a͞u, a͞w	a͞utumn,	oͤi	spoͤil
	paͤwn	ōo	ōoze
ä	äwful	o̯o	co̯ok
		oͧu	oͧur
ĕ	pĕck	oͧw	noͧw
ē	mēal	oͤy	loͤyal
ê	têrm		
ė	rėply	ŭ	pŭn
eͤw	neͤws	ū	trūe
		û	bûrn
ĭ	tĭc		
ī	nīce	ÿ (ē)	merrÿ
î	stîr	y̆ (ĭ)	gly̆cerine
ï	skï	ȳ (ī)	tȳpe
		ẏ (ĭ)	tẏpical

ə (roughly "uh") can symbolize any vowel. Always appears in an unstressed syllable, for instance, *cynicism* (sin′ə siz″əm), *island* (ī′lənd).

A

Ă, a, *n.* **1.** first letter of the English alphabet. **2.** best grade.

ă, *indef. art.* **1.** one. **2.** any single.

ăb′á·cŭs, *n.* calculating device using sliding beads.

á·băft′, *adj., adv. Nautical.* nearer the stern.

á·băn′dŏn, *v.t.* **1.** leave permanently. **2.** give up. —*n.* **3.** freedom from self-restraint. —**a·ban′don·ment,** *n.*

á·băn′dŏned, *adj.* **1.** left or given up permanently. **2.** without self-restraint; shameless.

á·bāse′, *v.t.,* **abased, abasing.** degrade; humble. —**a·base′ment,** *n.*

á·băsh′, *v.t.* embarrass; shame. —**a·bashed′,** *adj.* —**a·bash′ed·ly,** *adv.*

á·bāte′, *v.t., v.i.,* **abated, abating.** lessen; diminish. —**a′bate·ment,** *n.*

ăb·át·töir′, *n.* slaughterhouse.

ăb·bé, *n. French.* abbot; priest.

ăb′bĕss, *n.,* nun directing a convent.

ăb′bĕy, *n., pl.* **ab′beys.** monastery or convent.

ăb′bŏt, *n.* monk directing a monastery.

ăb·brē′vĭ·āte″, *v.t.,* **-ated, -ating.** shorten to essentials. —**ab·bre′vi·a′tion,** *n.*

ăb′dĭ·cāte″, *v.t.,* **-cated, -cating.** give up, as office or power. —**ab″di·ca′tion,** *n.*

ăb′dŏ·mĕn, *n.* **1.** part of the human body between the chest and hips. **2.** part of an animal body in a similar location. —**ab·dom′in·al,** *adj.*

ăb·dŭct′, *v.t.* carry away, esp. by force. —**ab·duc′tion,** *n.* —**ab·duc′tor,** *n.*

á·bēam′, *adv., adj.* across a ship or boat.

á·bĕd′, *adv.* in bed.

ăb″êr·rā′tion, *n.* deviation from what is considered normal.

á·bĕt′, *v.t.,* **abetted, abetting.** aid or encourage. —**a·bet′tor, a·bet′ter,** *n.*

á·bĕy′ance, *n.* suspension of activity.

ăb·hŏr′, *v.t.,* **abhorred, abhorring.** regard with horror or disgust. —**ab·hor′rence,** *n.* —**ab·hor′rent,** *adj.*

á·bīde, *v.,* **abode** or **abided, abiding.** *v.i.*

1. remain. **2.** dwell. —*v.t.* **3.** wait for. **4.** *Informal.* tolerate.

á·bīd′ĭng, *adj.* enduring; steadfast.

á·bĭl′ĭ·tў, *n., pl.* **-ties. 1.** power. **2.** talent; aptitude.

ăb′jĕct, *adj.* **1.** downcast. **2.** contemptible. —**ab·ject′ly,** *adv.*

ăb·jĕc′tion, *n.* abject state.

ăb·jūre′, *v.t.,* **-jured, -juring.** renounce formally. —**ab″ju·ra′tion,** *n.*

ăb′lá·tĭve, *n.* grammatical case of origin, means, location, etc. —**ab′la·tive,** *adj.*

á·blāze′, *adv., adj.* afire.

ā′ble, *adj.,* **abler, ablest. 1.** with the power to do a certain thing. **2.** competent. —**a′bly,** *adv.*

ăb·lū′tion, *n.* washing; cleansing.

ăb′nĕ·gāte, *v.t.,* **-gated, -gating.** deny or renounce for oneself. —**ab″ne·ga′tion,** *n.*

ăb·nôr′măl, *adj.* not normal. —**ab″nor·mal′i·ty,** *n.*

á·bôard′, *adv.* **1.** onto a ship, train, etc. —*prep.* **2.** on a ship, train, etc.; on board.

á·bōde′, *n.* **1.** home; dwelling. **2.** brief term of residence.

á·bŏl′ĭsh, *v.t.* do away with. —**ab″o·li′tion,** *n.*

ăb″ŏ·lĭ′tion·ĭst, *n.* person in favor of the abolition of something.

Ā bŏmb, *n.* atomic bomb.

á·bŏm′in·á·ble, *adj.* disgusting; loathsome. —**a·bom′in·a·bly,** *adj.*

á·bŏm′in·āte″, *v.t.,* **-nated, -nating.** hate or loathe. —**a·bom″in·a′tion,** *n.*

ăb″ŏ·rĭg′ĭ·năl, *adj.* **1.** primitive; original. —*n.* **2.** aborigine.

ă″bŏ·rĭg′in·ē, *n.* original inhabitant, esp. a savage.

á·bôr′tion, *n.* **1.** termination of pregnancy before full development of a fetus. **2.** wretched piece of work. —**a·bor′tion·ist,** *n.*

á·bôr′tive, *adj.* (of a hope or attempt) frustrated at an early stage.

á·bōund′, *v.i.* to have or offer something in abundance.

á·bōut′, *prep.* **1.** concerning; regarding. **2.** around. **3.** near by. **4.** on the point of. —*adv.* **5.** nearly; approximately. **6.** in all directions. **7.** in the opposite direction.

á·bóve′, *prep.* **1.** higher than. **2.** greater

1

than. —*adv., adj.* **3.** to or in a higher place. **4.** in a previous part of a text.

a·bóve'bôard'', *adj., adv.* without deception or disguise.

a·brāde', *v.t.*, -braded, -brading. scrape or rub. —**a·brā'sion**, *n.* —**a·brā'sive**, *adj., n.*

a·brĕast', *adv., adj.* **1.** alongside. **2.** side by side.

a·brĭdge', *v.t.*, -bridged, -bridging. shorten; abbreviate. —**a·bridg'ment**, *n.*

a·brŏad', *adv., adj.* **1.** outside one's own country. **2.** outdoors. **3.** over a broad area.

ăb'rò·gāte'', *v.t.*, -gated, -gating. end or revoke, as a law. —**ab''ro·ga'tion**, *n.*

ab·rŭpt', *adj.* **1.** sudden. **2.** steep. —**ab·rupt'ly**, *adv.* —**ab·rupt'ness**, *n.*

ăb'scĕss, *n.* area filled with pus.

ăb·scŏnd', *v.i.* leave secretly and hurriedly.

ăb·sĕnt, *adj.* not present. —*v.t.* remove. —**ab'sence**, *n.* —**ab'sent·ly**, *adv.*

ăb''sĕn·tēe', *n.* absent person. —**ab''sen·tee'ism**, *n.*

ăb'sĕnt-mīnd'ĕd, *adj.* **1.** not paying attention. **2.** forgetful.

ăb'sò·lūte, *adj.* **1.** perfect. **2.** pure; unqualified. **3.** unrestricted. —*n.* **4.** that which is perfect, pure, or unmodified. —**ab''so·lute'ly**, *adv.*

ăb·sŏlve', *v.t.*, -solved, -solving. free from blame or guilt. —**ab''so·lu'tion**, *n.*

ăb·sôrb', *v.t.* **1.** take in, as a fluid. **2.** get the attention of; fascinate. —**ab·sorb'ent**, *adj., n.* —**ab·sorp'tive**, *adj.* —**ab·sorp'tion**, *n.*

ăb·stāin', *v.i.* refrain. —**ab·sten'tion**, **ab'sti·nence**, *n.* —**ab'sti·nent**, *adj.*

ăb·stē'mĭ·òus, *adj.* abstaining from excess.

ăb·străct, *adj.* **1.** reduced to essentials. **2.** non-material; non-specific. —*n.* **3.** summary; abridgment. —*v.t.* (ăb·străct') **4.** remove, esp. in a theft. **5.** summarize; abridge. **6.** cause attention to wander. —**ab·strac'tion**, *n.*

ăb·strŭse', *adj.* hard to understand.

ăb·sùrd', *adj.* nonsensical. —**ab·surd'ly**, *adv.* —**ab·surd'i·ty**, **ab·surd'ness**, *n.*

a·bùn'dánce, *n.* great supply. —**a·bun'dant**, *adj.* —**a·bun'dant·ly**, *adv.*

a·būse', *v.t.*, -bused, -busing, *n. v.t.* **1.** use or treat wrongly. —*n.* **2.** wrong use or treatment. **3.** insult. —**a·bus'ive**, *adj.*

a·bùt', *v.i.*, -butted, -butting. meet at an edge or end; border.

a·bùt'mĕnt, *n.* construction touching or helping to support another construction.

a·bўs'măl, *adj.* measureless in depth; bottomless.

ă·bўss', *n.* **1.** great depth; chasm. **2.** hell.

a·cā'cià, *n.* tropical plant with white or yellow flowers.

ăc''à·dĕm'ĭc, *adj.* **1.** pertaining to scholarship. **2.** unconnected with actuality; theoretical.

a·căd'ĕ·mў, *n.* **1.** school. **2.** cultural organization. —**a·ca''de·mi'cian**, *n.*

ăc·cēde', *v.i.*, -ceded, -ceding. consent.

ăc·cĕl'ĕr·āte'', *v.* -ated, -ating. *v.t., v.i.* increase in speed. —**ac·cel''er·a'tion**, *n.*

ăc·cĕl'ĕr·ā''tòr, *n.* vehicle speed control.

ăc'cĕnt, *n.* **1.** emphasis. **2.** national or regional manner of pronouncing. —*v.t.* (ăc·cent') **3.** emphasize; stress.

ăc·cĕn'tù·āte'', *v.t.*, -ated, -ating. emphasize; stress. —**ac·cen·tu·a'tion**, *n.*

ăc·cĕpt', *v.t.* **1.** receive or take willingly. **2.** agree to. —**ac·cept'a·ble**, *adj.* —**ac·cept'a·bly**, *adv.* —**ac·cept''a·bil'i·ty**, *n.* —**ac·cept'ance**, *n.*

ăc'cĕss, *n.* **1.** means or way of approach. **2.** right of approach. **3.** outburst; attack.

ăc·cĕs'si·blĕ, *adj.* readily approached or reached. —**ac·ces''si·bil'i·ty**, *n.*

ăc·cĕs'sion, *n.* **1.** increase or addition. **2.** assumption of office or position.

ăc·cĕs'sô·rў, *n., pl.* -ries. **1.** additional working part, decorative object, etc. **2.** companion in a crime.

ăc'ci·dĕnt, *n.* unexpected event, usually undesirable. —**ac''ci·den'tal**, *adj.* —**ac''ci·den'tal·ly**, *adv.*

ăc·clāim', *v.t.* **1.** applaud; cheer. —*n.* **2.** applause. —**ac''cla·ma'tion**, *n.*

ăc'cli·māte'', *v.t.*, -ated, -ating. accustom to a new environment. Also, **ac·clim'a·tize''**.

ăc·clĭv'ĭ·tў, *n., pl.* -ties. upward slope.

ac·cŏm'mo·dāte'', v.t., -dated, -dating. 1. provide with food, lodging, etc. 2. adjust to existing conditions. 3. help with a loan, favor, etc. —ac·com''mo·da'tion, n. —ac·com'mo·dat''ing, adj.

ac·cŏm''mo·dā'tions, n., pl. lodgings, esp. temporary ones.

ac·cŏm'pà·nï·mĕnt, n. 1. something used with another thing; accessory. 2. music used to supplement that of a singer, soloist, etc.

ac·cŏm'pà·nist, n. player of a musical accompaniment.

ac·cŏm'pà·nÿ, v.t., -nied, -nying. 1. travel with. 2. provide a musical accompaniment for.

ac·cŏm'plĭce, n. associate, especially in crime.

ac·cŏm'plĭsh, v.t. succeed in doing. —ac·com'plish·ment, n.

ac·cŏm'plĭshed, adj. 1. completed. 2. highly skilled.

ac·côrd', v.t. 1. grant, as a favor. 2. cause to be in agreement or harmony. —v.i. 3. be in agreement or harmony. —n. 4. agreement; harmony. 5. consent. —ac·cord'ance, n. —ac·cord'ant, adj.

ac·côrd'ĭng, adj., adv. 1. in accordance. 2. according to, a. in accordance with. b. as stated by.

ac·côrd'ĭng·lÿ, adv. 1. as is indicated or prescribed. 2. therefore.

ac·côr'dï·ŏn, n. reed instrument with keyboard and bellows. —ac·cor'di·on·ist, n.

ac·cŏst', v.t. approach and catch the attention of.

ac·coūnt', v.t. 1. regard as. —v.i. 2. account for, a. explain or interpret. b. justify. c. be condemned or punished for. —n. 3. story; narrative. 4. explanation. 5. justification. 6. importance. 7. set of business transactions involving one client or customer. 8. business record.

ac·coūnt'à·ble, adj. answerable; responsible.

ac·coūnt'ĭng, n. keeping or interpretation of business accounts. —ac·count'ant, n. —ac·count'an·cy, n.

ac·coū'têr·mĕnt, n. piece of clothing or equipment carried on the person.

ac·crĕd'ĭt, v.t. 1. certify as competent or valid. 2. attribute. —ac·cred''it·a'tion, n.

ac·crē'tion, n. growth, esp. by accumulation.

ac·crūe', v.i. be added, esp. in a regular way. —ac·cru'al, n.

ac·cū'mū·lāte'', v., -lated, -lating. v.t., v.i. gather; collect. —ac·cu''mu·la'tion, n. —ac·cu'mu·la''tive, adj. —ac·cu'mu·la''tor, n.

ăc'cû·rate, adj. correct; truthful. —ac'cu·ra·cy, ac'cu·rate·ness, n.

ac·cûrs'ĕd, adj. 1. under a curse. 2. damnable.

ac·cū'sà·tĭve, n. grammatical case for direct object of verb. —ac·cu'sa·tive, adj.

ac·cūse', v.t., -cused, -cusing. denounce; blame. —ac·cus'er, n. —ac''cu·sa'tion, n.

ac·cŭs'tŏm, v.t. cause to become used to something.

ac·cŭs'tŏmed, adj. usual; customary.

āce, n. 1. playing card with one pip. 2. leading expert.

à·cĕr'bï·tÿ, n. harshness of temper or speech.

ăc'ė·tāte'', n. fiber or fabric derived from cellulose.

à·cĕt'ÿ·lēne, n. highly inflammable gas.

āche, v.i., ached, aching, v.i. 1. suffer dull pain. —n. 2. dull pain.

à·chiēve', v.t., -chieved, -chieving. succeed in reaching, finishing, or fulfilling. —a·chieve'ment, n.

ăc'ĭd, n. 1. chemical compound reacting with base to form salt. 2. sour substance. —adj. 4. pertaining to acids. 5. sour. —a·cid'i·ty, n. —a·cid'ic, adj.

à·cĭd'ū·loŭs, adj. containing or suggesting acid.

ac·knŏwl'ĕdge, v.t., -edged, -edging. 1. admit as true or valid. 2. show appreciation or gratitude for. —ac·knowl'edg·ment, n.

ăc'mē, n. summit.

ăc'nē, n. skin complaint.

ăc'ò·lÿte, n. priest's assistant; altar boy.

ā'côrn, n. nut of an oak tree.

à·coūs'tĭc, adj. pertaining to transmission or reception of sound through air, etc. Also, a·cous'ti·cal. —a·cous'ti·cal·ly, adv.

à·coūs'tĭcs, n. 1. sing. science of transmission of sound through air, etc. **2.** *pl.* acoustic properties.

ac·quaint', *v.t.* **1.** make known. **2.** make familiar. —**ac·quain'tance**, *n.*

ăc''qui·ĕsce', *v.i.*, -esced, -escing. consent or comply. —**ac''qui·es'cence**, *n.* —**ac''qui·es'cent**, *adj.*

ac·quīre', *v.t.*, -quired, -quiring. obtain; get.

ăc'qui·sĭ'tion, *n.* **1.** act or instance of acquiring. **2.** something acquired.

ac·quĭs'i·tĭve, *adj.* **1.** pertaining to acquisition. **2.** greedy, grasping.

ăc·quĭt', *v.t.*, -quitted, -quitting. **1.** release from blame or detention. **2.** conduct; behave. —**ac·quit'tal**, *n.*

ā'cre, *n.* land area equal to 43,560 square feet or 4,047 square meters. —**a'cre·age**, *n.*

ăc'rid, *adj.* harsh and bitter.

ăc'ri·mō''nў, *n.* harshness of manner or expression. —**ac''ri·mo'ni·ous**, *adj.*

ăc'rȯ·băt'', *n.* gymnastic entertainer, esp. one performing high above the ground. —**ac'ro·bat'ic**, *adj.*

ăc''rȯ·nўm, *n.* word formed from the initial letters of a phrase or title, as *NASA.*

a·crŏss', *prep.* **1.** from one side to the other of. **2.** on the other side. —*adv.* **3.** from one side to the other.

ăct, *n.* **1.** something done. **2.** law. **3.** one of the main divisions of a play, etc. —*v.i.* **4.** do something. **5.** conduct oneself. **6.** have an effect on something. **7.** perform in a play or plays.

ăct'ĭng, *n.* **1.** the profession of one who performs in plays. —*adj.* **2.** temporarily performing a specified function.

ăc'tion, *n.* **1.** state of being active. **2.** something done. **3.** *Informal.* interesting activity. **4.** combat. **5.** lawsuit.

ăc'ti·vāte'', *v.t.*, -vated, -vating. cause to be active. —**ac''ti·va'tion**, *n.*

ăc'tĭve, *adj.* **1.** performing actions. **2.** having an effect. **3.** *Grammar.* pertaining to verbs whose subjects act rather than being acted on. —**ac'tive·ly**, *adv.*

ăc·tĭv'i·tў, *n.*, *pl.* -ties. action, esp. one of a number performed in a sequence.

ăc'tȯr, *n.* person, especially a man performing in plays. Also, *fem.*, **ac'tress**.

ăc'tū·ȧl, *adj.* **1.** really existing. **2.** presently existing. —**ac''tu·al'i·ty**, *n.*

ăc'tū·ȧl·lў, *adv.* **1.** really. **2.** presently. **3.** in fact; nevertheless.

ăc'tū·ār''ў, *n.*, *pl.* -aries. mathematician for an insurance company. —**ac''tu·ar'i·al**, *adj.*

ăc'tū·āte', *v.t.*, -ated, -ating. cause to act.

à·cū'mĕn, *n.* sharpness of mind.

à·cūte', *adj.* **1.** sharp. **2.** mentally keen. **3.** highly sensitive or perceptive. **4.** severely threatening or distressing. —**a·cute'ly**, *adv.* —**a·cute'ness**, *n.*

ăd'ȧge, *n.* old saying.

à·dä'gïō, *adj. Music.* slow.

ăd'à·mȧnt, *adj.* unyielding.

à·dăpt', *v.t.* change to suit conditions. —**a·dapt'a·ble**, *adj.* —**a''dap·ta'tion**, *n.*

ădd, *v.t.* **1.** join to another or others. **2.** compute as a total. —*v.i.* **3.** constitute an addition. —**ad·di'tion**, *n.* —**ad·di'tion·al**, *adj.* —**ad·di'tion·al·ly**, *adv.*

ȧd·dĭct', *v.t.* **1.** make dependent on a drug, etc. —*n.* (a'dikt) **2.** addicted person. —**ad·dic'tion**, *n.*

ăd'dle, *v.t.*, -dled, -dling. confuse; muddle.

ȧd·drĕss', *n.* **1.** speech; oration. **2.** location of a business, residence, etc. **3.** skill. —*v.t.* **4.** speak to formally. **5.** direct as a message. **6.** apply. —**ad''dres·see'**, *n.*

ȧd·dūce', *v.t.*, -duced, -ducing. offer as a reason, proof, or example.

ăd'é·noīd'', *n.* normal growth in the throat behind the nose.

à·dĕpt', *adj.* **1.** skilled. —*n.* **2.** skilled person; expert.

ăd'é·quȧte, *adj.* suitable or sufficient. —**ad'e·quate·ly**, *adv.* —**ad'e·qua·cy**, *n.*

ăd·hēre', *v.i.*, -hered, -hering. **1.** cling. **2.** be loyal or obedient. —**ad·her'ent**, *adj.* —**ad·her'ence**, **ad·he'sion**, *n.* —**ad·he'sive**, *adj.*, *n.*

ăd''-hŏc'', *adj.* for one special purpose.

a·dieu' (a dyōō'), *interj.*, *n.*, *pl.* -dieux. *French.* good-bye.

ăd'i·pōse'', *adj.* fatty.

ȧd·jā'cĕnt, *adj.* near or adjoining.

ăd'jĕc·tĭve, *n.* word qualifying a noun. —**ad''jec·tiv'al**, *adj.*

ȧd·jōīn', *v.t.* be next to.

ȧd·joŭrn', *v.t.* **1.** suspend operations of (a meeting, court, etc.). —*v.i.* **2.** suspend operations. —ad·journ'ment, n.

ad·jŭdge', v.t., -judged, -judging. 1. decide or declare formally. 2. award by legal process.

ad·jūd'ĭ·cāte'', v.t., -cated, -cating. pass judgment regarding. —ad·jud''i·ca'tion, n.

ăd'jŭnct, n. something added.

ad·jūre', v.t., -jured, -juring. 1. command formally. 2. request solemnly.

ad·jŭst', v.t. 1. cause to fit or function properly. 2. settle. —v.i. 3. adapt oneself. —ad·just'a·ble, adj. —ad·just'er, ad·just'or, n. —ad·just'ment, n.

ăd'jŭ·tánt, n. assistant to military commander.

ăd''-lĭb', v., -libbed, -libbing. Informal. improvise while talking.

ăd·mĭn'ĭs·têr, v.t. 1. direct or manage. 2. give, esp. according to prescribed rules.

ăd·mĭn''is·trā'tion, n. 1. act or process of administering. 2. term of office. 3. officials directing or managing. —ad·min'is·tra''tive, adj. —ad·min'is·tra''tor, n.

ăd'mi·răl, n. naval officer of the highest rank.

ăd'mi·răl·tў, n., pl. -ies. naval administrative department.

ăd·mīre', v.t., -mired, -miring. regard with great respect or pleasure. —ad'mir·a·ble, adj. —ad''mi·ra'tion, n. —ad·mir'er, n.

ad·mĭs'si·ble, adj. 1. proper for admission. 2. allowable.

ad·mĭs'sion, n. 1. act or instance of admitting. 2. confession. 3. permission for one to enter a theater, etc.

ăd·mĭt', v.t., -mitted, -mitting. 1. allow to enter. 2. confess or concede. —ad·mit'tance, n.

ăd·mĭx'tûre, n. something added to create a mixture.

ăd·mŏn'ĭsh, v.t. 1. urge, esp. as a warning. 2. reproach. —ad''mo·ni'tion, n. —ad·mon'i·to''ry, adj.

à·do', n. fussy talk or action.

à·dō'bē, n. dried, unfired brick.

ăd''o·lĕs'cĕnce, n. youth between puberty and physical maturity. —ad''o·les'cent, adj., n.

à·dŏpt', v.t. take as one's own. —a·dop'tion, n.

à·dôre', v.t., -dored, -doring. worship.

—a''do·ra'tion, n. —a·dor'a·ble, adj.

à·dôrn', v.t. decorate. —a·dorn'ment, n.

à·drĕn'à·lĭn, n. hormone promoting vigorous bodily action.

à·drĭft', adj., adv. drifting.

à·drŏĭt', adj. clever. —a·droit'ly, adv. —a·droit'ness, n.

ăd''ū·lā'tion, n. excessive praise or respect.

à·dŭlt', n. 1. physically mature person or animal. —adj. 2. physically mature. —a·dult'hood, n.

à·dŭl'têr·āte'', v.t., -ated, -ating. add undesirable ingredients to. —a·dul'ter·a''tion, n.

à·dŭl'têr·êr, n. committer of adultery. Also, fem., a·dul'ter·ess.

à·dŭl'têr·ў, n., pl. -ies. n. infidelity of a spouse. —a·dul'ter·ous, adj.

ăd·vănce', v., -vanced, -vancing, n., adj. v.t. 1. move forward. 2. suggest for consideration. 3. pay before earned. —v.i. 4. move forward. —n. 5. motion forward. 6. act intended to secure favor or friendship. 7. improvement. 8. sum to be repaid in money or work. 9. promotion. —adj. 10. early. —ad'vance'ment, n.

ăd·văn'tàge, n. 1. more favorable situation. 2. benefit. —ad''van·ta'geous, adj.

ăd'vĕnt, 1. arrival. 2. Advent, a. coming of Christ. b. period before Christmas.

ăd''vĕn·tĭ'tioŭs, adj. coming or happening by accident.

ăd·vĕn'tûre, n., v., -tured, -turing. n. 1. risky undertaking. 2. thrilling or exciting experience. —v.t. undertake with risk. —v.i. 4. seek adventures. —ad·ven'tur·er, n. —ad·ven'tur·ous, adj.

ăd'vĕrb, n. Grammar. word modifying a verb. —ad·ver'bi·al, adj.

ăd'vêr·sār'ў, n., pl. -saries. opponent or enemy.

ăd·vêrse', adj. opposing or unfavorable. —ad·verse'ly, adv.

ăd·vêr'sĭ·tў, n., pl. -ties. difficulty or misfortune.

ăd'vêrt', v.i. refer.

ăd''vêr·tīse, v., -tised, -tising. v.t. 1. call attention to in order to elicit a public response. —v.i. 2. request something

publicly. —ad'ver·tis''er, *n.* —ad''
ver·tise'ment, *n.* —ad'ver·tis''
ing, *n.*

ad·vice', *n.* **1.** opinion urging choice or rejection of a course of action. **2.** piece of information.

ad·vis'a·ble, *adj.* to be advised; desirable. —ad·vis''a·bil'i·ty, *n.*

ad·vise', *v.t.*, -vised, -vising. **1.** urge to choose or reject a course of action. **2.** recommend. **3.** give information. —ad·vis'er, ad·vis'or, *n.* —ad·vi'so·ry, *adj.*

ad·vise'ment, *n.* thought; consideration.

ad'vo·cate, *n.* **1.** person arguing one side of a dispute, esp. a lawyer. —*v.t.* **2.** ad'vo·cate, to argue in favor of. —ad'vo·ca·cy, *n.*

adz, *n.* long-handled tool for dressing wood. Also, **adze.**

ae·gis, *n.* sponsorship.

ae'on, *n.* extremely long time.

āer'āte, *v.t.*, -ated, -ating. expose to air.

āer'i·al, *adj.* **1.** in or of the air. **2.** pertaining to aviation. —*n.* **3.** antenna for sending or receiving radio waves.

ā'e·rō''bĭcs, *n.* exercises to strengthen circulation and respiration.

āer''ō·dȳ·năm'ĭcs, *n.* study of the dynamics of gases in motion. —aer''o·dy·nam'ic, *adj.*

āer''ŏ·näu'tĭcs, *n.* science of flying. —aer''o·nau'ti·cal, *adj.*

āer'ŏ·sŏl, *n.* liquid applied by spraying from a pressurized container.

āer'ō·spāce'', *n.* all space, including the earth's atmosphere.

aĕs'thēte'', *n.* person sensitive to art or beauty.

aĕs·thĕt'ĭc, *adj.* **1.** pertaining to beauty. **2.** sensitive to art or beauty. —*n.* **3.** aes·thet'ics, study of art or beauty.

à·fâr', *adv.* at a great distance.

af'fà·ble, *adj.* cordial; pleasant. —af''fa·bil'i·ty, *n.*

af·fâir', *n.* **1.** business matter. **2.** event. **3.** amorous relationship.

af·fĕct', *v.t.* **1.** have influence on. **2.** move emotionally. **3.** make an affectation of.

af''fĕc·tā'tion, *n.* pretentious mannerism.

af·fĕct'ĕd, *adj.* **1.** characterized by affectation. **2.** moved emotionally.

af·fĕct'ĭng, *adj.* emotionally moving.

af·fĕc'tion, *adj.* **1.** love. **2.** sickness.

af·fĕc'tion·āte, *adj.* loving.

af''fĭ·dā'vĭt, *n.* sworn written statement.

af·fĭl·ĭ·āte, *v.t.*, -ated, -ating, *n. v.t.* **1.** combine, as independent businesses for mutual benefit. —*n.* **2.** af·fĭl'ĭ·āte, affiliated business, etc. —af·fil'i·a'tion, *n.*

af·fĭn'ĭ·tȳ, *n., pl.* -ties. **1.** attraction. **2.** similarity.

af·fĭrm', *v.t.* **1.** state emphatically. **2.** confirm; ratify. —af''fir·ma'tion, *n.* —af·fir'ma·tive, *adj.*

af·fĭx', *v.t.* attach.

af·flĭct', *v.t.* trouble. —af·flic'tion, *n.*

af'flū·ėnt, *adj.* prosperous. —af'flu·ence, *n.*

af·fôrd', *v.t.* **1.** have enough money or other resources. **2.** supply; provide.

af·frāy', *n.* fight.

af·frŏnt', *v.t.* **1.** insult or challenge openly. —*n.* **2.** open insult or challenge.

à·fīre', *adv., adj.* on fire. Also, **a·flame'.**

à·flōat', *adv., adj.* floating.

à·fŏot', *adv., adj.* **1.** on foot. **2.** in action or in progress.

à·fôre'said, *adj.* previously said.

à·frāid', *adj.* **1.** full of fear. **2.** unable because of fear. **3.** regretful, as because of inability.

à·frĕsh', *adv.* from the beginning again.

ăft, *adv., adj. Nautical.* toward or at the stern.

af'têr, *prep.* **1.** behind. **2.** later than. **3.** lower in rank or importance. **4.** in search or pursuit of. **5.** in imitation of. —*adv.* **6.** behind. **7.** later.

af'têr·éf·fĕct'', *n.* later consequence.

af'têr·măth'', *n.* consequence, usually unfavorable.

af''têr·nōon', *n.* period after noon and before evening.

af'têr·thôught'', *n.* belated thought.

af'têr·wàrd, *adv.* later. Also, **af'ter·wards.**

à·gain', *adv.* **1.** once more. **2.** besides.

à·gainst', *prep.* **1.** toward or into contact with. **2.** opposed or hostile to.

āge, *n., v.,* aged, aging. *n.* **1.** remoteness in time of birth or origin. **2.** distinctive period of history, geology, etc. **3. of age,** legally mature. —*v.t.* **4.** bring or allow to come to ripeness or maturity. —*v.i.* **5.** become old.

ā'gĕd, *adj.* **1.** of a specified age. **2. the aged,** old people.

āge''ĭs·m, *n.* discrimination against the elderly.

āge'lĕss, *adj.* unaffected by time or age.

ā'gĕn·cÿ, *n., pl.* **-cies. 1.** office handling business for others. **2.** government office. **3.** active force. **4.** means.

à·gĕn'dă, *n., pl.* business matters to be dealt with.

ā'gĕnt, *n.* **1.** person handling business for others. **2.** government official. **3.** active force or substance.

àg·glŏm'êr·āte, *v.,* **-ated, -ating.** *n., adj., v.t., v.i.* **1.** gather into a mass. —*n.* **2. àg·glŏm'êr·āte,** mass of miscellaneous things. —*adj.* **3.** gathered into a mass. —**ag·glom''er·a'tion,** *n.*

àg·grăn'dīze, *v.t.,* **-dized, -dizing,** increase in power, status, wealth, etc. —**ag·gran'dize·ment,** *n.*

ăg'grà·vāte'', *v.t.,* **-vated, -vating. 1.** make worse. **2.** annoy. —**ag''gra·va'tion,** *n.*

ăg'grē·gāte'', *v.,* **-gated, -gating,** *adj., n. v.t., v.i.* **1.** collect or gather. —*adj.* **ăg'grē·gàte. 2.** total; collective. —*n.* **3.** sum; total. —**ag''gre·ga'tion,** *n.*

àg·grĕs'sion, *n.* hostile act or policy. —**ag·gres'sor,** *n.*

àg·grĕs'sĭve, *adj.* **1.** disposed to commit aggressions. **2.** forceful, as in business.

àg·griēve', *v.t.,* **-grieved, -grieving.** wrong or offend seriously.

à·ghăst', *adj.* horrified.

ă'gīle, *adj.* nimble; deft. —**a·gil'i·ty,** *n.*

ă'gĭ·tāte'', *v.t.,* **-tated, -tating. 1.** shake violently. **2.** disturb emotionally. —**a''gi·ta'tion,** *n.*

à·glōw', *adj., adv.* glowing.

ăg·nŏs'tĭc, *n.* person regarding the existence of God as unknowable.

à·gō', *adj., adv.* in the past.

à·gŏg', *adj.* eager and excited.

ăg'ō·nīze, *v.t.,* **-nized, -nizing.** put in agony.

ă'gō·nÿ, *n., pl.* **-ies.** intense suffering.

à·grăr'ĭ·àn, *adj.* pertaining to farming or the country.

à·grēe', *v.* **agreed, agreeing.** *v.i.* **1.** consent or promise. **2.** be of the same opinion. **3.** be harmonious or in accord. **4.**

match exactly. —*v.t.* **5.** concede as true. —**a·gree'ment,** *n.*

à·grēe'à·ble, *adj.* **1** pleasant. **2.** reacting favorably. —**a·gree'a·bly,** *adv.*

ăg'rĭ·cŭl''tûre, *n.* science or occupation of farming. —**ag''ri·cul'tur·al,** *adj.*

à·groūnd', *adj., adv.* (of a ship) in water too shallow for floating.

à·hĕad', *adv., adj.* **1.** in front. **2.** with an advantage over competitors.

āid, *n., v.* help.

āide-de-cămp, *n., pl.* **aides-de-camp.** assistant military officer.

ĀIDS, acquired immune deficiency syndrome.

āil, *v.t.* distress or sicken. —**ail'ment,** *n.*

āil'êr·ŏn, *n.* the part of an airplane wing that controls rolling.

āim, *v.t.* **1.** point, as for shooting. **2.** intend. —*v.i.* **3.** point a gun, etc. —*n.* **4.** act of pointing a gun, etc. **5.** intention or goal.

āim'lĕss, *adj.* without a goal or purpose.

āin't, *v.i., Dialect.* am, is, or are not.

āir, *n.* **1.** gas compound surrounding the earth. **2.** appearance as derived from action, facial expression, etc. **3.** song or melody. **4. airs,** affectations. —*v.t.* **5.** ventilate.

āir'bôrne'', *adj.* flying.

āir côn·dĭ''tion·ĭng, treatment of air to control purity, temperature, and humidity. —**air conditioner,** *n.* —**air' con·di''tion,** *v.t.*

āir'crăft, *n., pl.* **-craft.** flying craft.

āir'fīeld'', *n.* field for taxiing, takeoff, and landing of airplanes.

āir fôrce, flying fighting force.

āir'līne, *n.* company operating regularly scheduled aircraft flights. —**air'lin''er,** *n.*

āir'plāne, *n.* heavier-than-air flying craft with wings.

āir'pôrt'', *n.* airfield with terminal, storage, and service buildings.

āir'shĭp'', *n.* lighter-than-air flying craft.

āir'tīght'', *adj.* **1.** preventing passage of air. **2.** unable to be disproven, as an argument.

āir'ÿ, *adj.,* **airier, airiest. 1.** open to air or breeze. **2.** loftily situated. **3.** impermanent as air. **4.** flippant; thoughtless. —**air'i·ly,** *adv.* —**air'i·ness,** *n.*

aīsle, *n.* **1.** passageway, esp. among seats

as in a theater. **2.** a division of a church, esp. between pillars.

a·jär′, *adj., adv.* partly open, as a door.

a·kim′bō, *adj., adv.* with hands on hips and elbows out.

a·kin′, *adj.* **1.** of the same family. **2.** of the same sort.

â′′là carte′, with each dish ordered and paid for separately.

a·lăc′ri·tÿ, *n.* willing readiness.

â′′là mōde′, **1.** in fashion. **2.** with ice cream.

a·lärm′, *n.* **1.** emergency signal. **2.** occasion for fear. **3.** fear —*v.t.* **4.** startle or frighten.

a·lăs′, *interj.* exclamation of regret.

äl·bē′ĭt, *conj.* even though.

ăl·bī′nō, *n., pl.* **-nos.** person or animal without skin pigmentation.

ăl′bŭm, *n.* **1.** blank book for mounting photographs, stamps, etc. **2.** blank book for sketching. **3.** booklike container for phonograph records.

ăl·bū′mèn, *n.* egg white or similar substance.

ăl′chè·mÿ, *n.* pre-scientific chemistry. —**al′che·mist**, *n.*

ăl′cò·hŏl′′, *n.* colorless liquid used as fuel, intoxicant, etc.

ăl′′cò·hŏl′ĭc, *adj.* **1.** pertaining to alcohol. —*n.* **2.** person addicted to alcohol.

ăl′cōve, *n.* place set back from a larger adjoining space.

äl′dêr, *n.* small tree of the birch family.

äl′dêr·măn, *n.* city ward representative.

āle, *n.* strong beerlike drink.

a·lêrt′, *adj.* **1.** watchful. —*v.t., n.* **2.** alarm. —**a·lert′ly**, *adv.* —**a·lert′ness**, *n.*

ăl′′făl′fà, *n.* fodder plant.

ăl·gaē, *n. pl.; sing.* **al′ga.** one-celled water plants.

ăl′gè·brà, *n.* mathematical system based on symbols, not numbers. —**al′′ge·bra′ic**, *adj.*

āl′ĭ·ás, *adv.* **1.** otherwise known as. —*n.* **2.** assumed name.

ăl′ĭ·bī, *n., pl.* **-bis.** legal plea of absence from the scene of a crime.

āl′ĭ·èn, *adj.* **1.** from outside; foreign. —*n.* **2.** foreigner.

āl′ĭ·èn·āte′′, *v.t.*, **-ated, -ating. 1.** deprive someone of. **2.** act so as to lose the friendship of. —**al′′i·en·a′′tion**, *n.*

āl′ĭ·èn·ĭst, *n.* specialist in mental illness.

a·līght′, *v.i.* **1.** descend, as from a vehicle or animal. —*adv., adj.* **2.** lighted. **3.** afire.

a·līgn, *v.t.* line up. —**a·lign′ment**, *n.*

a·līke′, *adj.* **1.** of the same kind or form. —*adv.* **2.** in the same way.

ăl′′ĭ·mèn′tà·rÿ, *adj.* pertaining to food or nourishment.

ăl′ĭ·mō′′nÿ, *n.* allowance paid to one divorced spouse by the other.

a·līve′, *adj.* **1.** living. **2.** vigorous or lively. **3.** teeming.

ăl′kà·lī′′, *n., pl.* **-lis.** acid-neutralizing chemical. —**al′ka·line′′**, *adj.*

ăl′kà·lŏīd′′, *n.* bitter, alkali-containing chemical.

ăll, *adj.* **1.** every. **2.** the whole of. —*n., pron.* **3.** everything or everybody. —*adv.* **4.** entirely.

Äl′läh, *n.* Muslim name for God.

ăl·lāy′, *v.t.* calm or soothe.

ăl·lĕge′, *v.t.*, **-leged, -leging.** assert, esp. without proof. —**al′′le·ga′tion**, *n.* —**al·leg′ed·ly**, *adv.*

ăl·lē′giánce, *n.* loyalty.

ăl′lè·gō′′rÿ, *n., pl.* **-ies.** story or display using symbols. —**al′′le·gor′i·cal**, *adj.*

ăl′lêr·gÿ, *n., pl.* **-gies.** excessive sensitivity to some substance. —**al·ler′gic**, *adj.*

ăl·lē′vï·āte, *v.t.*, **-ated, -ating.** relieve; mitigate. —**al·le′vi·a′′tion**, *n.*

ăl′lēy, *n., pl.* **-leys. 1.** narrow service street. **2.** garden walk.

ăl·lī′ánce, *n.* **1.** combination of independent nations, etc. **2.** treaty for such a combination. **3.** organization or club. **4.** marriage.

ăl·līed′, *adj.* **1.** joined in an alliance. **2.** closely related.

ăl′′li·gā′′tör, *n.* broad-snouted reptile of the southeastern U.S.

ăl·lĭt′′êr·ā′tion, *n.* use of the same sound to start several succeeding words.

ăl′lò·cāte′′, *v.t.*, **-cated, -cating.** assign or allot. —**al′′lo·ca′tion**, *n.*

ăl·lŏt′, *v.t.*, **-lotted, -lotting. 1.** distribute to sharing parties. **2.** assign. —**al·lot′ment**, *n.*

ăll′ōut′, *adj.* without reservation; total.

ăl·lōw′, *v.t.* **1.** permit. **2.** give or grant. **3.**

grant to be true. —**al·low'a·ble**, *adj.*
—**al·low'ance**, *n.*

al·loy', *v.t.* **1.** mix. **2.** weaken; dilute.
—*n.* **3.** **ăl'loy**, metal or metals with admixtures.

all'spīce'', *n.* spice made from a West Indian berry.

al·lūde', *v.i.*, **-luded, -luding.** make reference to. —**al·lu'sion**, *n.* —**al·lu'sive**, *adj.*

al·lūre', *v.t.*, **-lured, -luring**, *n. v.t.*
1. attract temptingly. —*n.* **2.** quality of attraction or temptation. —**al·lure'ment**, *n.*

al·lū'vĭ'um, *n.* soil deposited by moving water. —**al·lu'vĭ·al**, *adj.*

al·lȳ', *v.*, **-lied, -lying**, *n.*, *pl.* **-lies.** *v.t.*, *v.i.* **1.** unite for a common purpose. —*n.* **2.** person, country, etc. joined in an alliance.

ălmà mätêr, one's college or secondary school.

ăl'mà·năc'', *n.* annual publication including a calendar and diverse useful information.

al·mīght'ў, *adj.* **1.** totally powerful. —*n.* **2. the Almighty**, God.

ăl'mŏnd, *n.* edible nut from a tree.

ăl'mōst, *adv.* nearly.

ălms, *n.*, *pl.* **alms.** charitable gift or money.

a·lŏft', *adv.*, *adj.* up high.

a·lōne', *adj.*, *adv.* **1.** by oneself or itself. **2.** only.

a·lŏng', *prep.* **1.** in the lengthwise direction of. —*adv.* **2.** together with another or others. **3.** steadily forward or into the future.

a·lŏng'sīde'', *prep.* **1.** beside. —*adv.* **2.** to or at the side.

ă·lōōf'', *adv.* **1.** at some distance. —*adj.* **2.** showing no interest or concern. —**a·loof'ness**, *n.*

a·lŏŭd', *adv.* **1.** in the normal volume of voice. **2.** loudly.

ăl'phà·bĕt'', *n.* all the letters of a language in a customary order. —**al''pha·bet'i·cal**, *adj.* —**al'pha·bet·ize''**, *v.t.*

ăl·rĕad'ў, *adv.* **1.** before a stated time. **2.** so soon.

ăl'sō, *adv.* additionally.

ăl'tàr, *n.* block or table used for religious ceremonies.

ăl'têr, *v.t.*, *v.i.* change. —**al''ter·a'tion**, *n.*

ăl''têr·cā'tion, *n.* quarrel; dispute.

ăl·têr·nāte, *v.*, **-nated, -nating**, *adj.*, *n.* *v.i.* **1.** act, appear, etc. in turns. —*v.t.* **2.** employ in turns. —*adj.* **3.** **ăl'ter·nàte**, acting, appearing, etc. in turns. —*n.* **4.** someone or something that acts, appears, etc. in turns. —**al''ter·na'tion**, *n.*

ăl·têr'nà·tĭve'', *n.* **1.** other choice. —*adj.* **2.** available as another choice.

ăl·thōugh', *conj.* even though.

ăl·tĭm'ĕ·têr, *n.* gauge for measuring altitude.

ăl'ti·tūde, *n.* height, esp. when considerable.

ăl'tō, *n.*, *pl.* **-tos. 1.** musical range between soprano and tenor. **2.** singer, instrument or part with this range.

ăl''tó·gĕth'êr, *adv.* **1.** completely. **2.** in general.

ăl'trŭ·ĭsm, *n.* concern for others, not oneself. —**al''tru·is'tic**, *adj.* —**al'tru·ist**, *n.*

ăl'ŭm, *n.* astringent used in medicine.

a·lū'mĭ·nŭm, *n.* lightweight metal.

a·lŭm'nŭs, *n.*, *pl.* **-ni.** school graduate. Also, *fem.*, **a·lum'na**, *pl.* **-nae.**

ăl'wȧys, *adv.* **1.** all of one's life. **2.** forever. **3.** continually.

ăm, *v.* first person present singular indicative of *be*.

a·măl'gàm, *n.* a mixture.

a·măl'gàm·āte'', *v.*, **-ated, -ating**, *v.t.*, *v.i.* form a combination or mixture. —**a·mal''ga·ma'tion**, *n.*

a·măss', *v.t.* gather.

ăm'a·têur, *n.* **1.** non-professional participant. **2.** admirer of an art. —*adj.* **3.** by or for non-professional participants.

ăm'a·têur''ĭsh, *adj.* without professional competence.

ăm'a·tô''rў, *adj.* pertaining to love or sex.

a·māze', *v.t.*, **-mazed, -mazing.** stun with surprise. —**a·maz'ing**, *adj.* —**a·maze'ment**, *n.*

ăm·băs'sa·dôr, *n.* senior diplomat. —**am·bas''sa·do'ri·al**, *adj.* —**am·bas'sa·dor·ship''**, *n.*

ăm'bêr, *n.* **1.** fossil resin. —*adj.* **2.** yellow-brown.

ăm'bêr·grĭs, *n.* whale secretion used for perfume.

ăm''bi·dĕx'troŭs, *adj.* equally able

with both hands. —**am″bi·dex·ter′i·ty,** *n.*

ăm′bï·ènce, *n.* quality or mood of an environment. Also, **am′bi·ance.** —**am′bi·ent,** *adj.*

ăm·bĭg′ū·oŭs, *adj.* having more than one possible meaning. —**am″bi·gu′i·ty,** *n.*

ăm·bĭ′tion, *n.* **1.** strong desire for success. **2.** thing whose attainment is strongly desired. —**am·bi′tious,** *adj.*

ăm′ble, *v.i.,* **-bled, -bling,** *n. v.i.* **1.** move easily and slowly. —*n.* **2.** easy, slow walk.

ăm·brō′sïä, *n.* divine food.

ăm′bū·lànce, *n.* vehicle for the sick.

ăm′bū·là·tō″rÿ, *adj.* able to walk.

ăm′bŭsh, *n.* **1.** concealment for attackers. **2.** attack from a concealed position. —*v.t.* **3.** attack from a concealed position.

à·mēl′iō·rāte″, *v.t.,* **-rated, -rating.** improve. —**a·mel″io·ra′tion,** *n.*

ā·mĕn′, *interj.* so be it.

ā·mēn′à·ble, *adj.* agreeable.

à·mĕnd′, *v.t.* **1.** alter. **2.** improve. —*n.* **3.** amends, compensation for damage, injury, etc. —**a·mend′ment,** *n.*

à·mĕn′ï·tÿ, *n., pl.* **-ties.** something agreeable or polite.

Â·mĕr″ĭ·cä′nä, *n. pl.* literature, artifacts, etc. having to do with U.S. history or culture.

Â·mĕr′ĭ·càn·ĭsm, *n.* **1.** partiality to things identified with the U.S. **2.** something characteristic of the U.S.

ăm′ė·thÿst, *n.* **1.** violet quartz or corundum. **2.** shade of violet.

ā′mï·à·ble, *adj.* creating friendly feelings. —**a′mi·a·bly,** *adj.* —**a″mi·a·bil′i·ty,** *n.*

ă′mï·cà·ble, *adj.* without hostility or resentment. —**a′mi·ca·bly,** *adv.*

à·mĭd′, *prep.* among. Also, **a·midst′.**

à·mĭss, *adj.* **1.** not right. —*adv.* **2.** not in the right way.

ăm′ï·tÿ, *n.* friendship.

àm·mō′nïä, *n.* pungent, water-soluble gas.

ăm″mū·nĭ′tion, *n.* projectiles, together with their charges of gunpowder, etc. fired esp. from guns.

ăm·nē′sïä, *n.* loss of memory.

ăm′nĕs·tÿ, *n., pl.* **-ties.** general pardon by a government, esp. for political crimes.

à·mŏk′, *adv.* amuck.

à·mŏng′, *prep.* **1.** surrounded closely by. **2.** in the company or society of. Also, **a·mongst′.**

ā·môr′àl, *adj.* without a sense of right or wrong.

ăm′ôr·oŭs, *adj.* expressing love, esp. sexual love.

à·môr′phoŭs, *adj.* shapeless or formless.

ă′môr·tīze″, *v.t.,* **-tized, -tizing.** pay off gradually. —**am″or·ti·za′tion,** *n.*

à·moūnt′, *n.* **1.** total. **2.** quantity. —*v.i.* **3.** add up.

à·mour′, *n.* love affair.

ăm′pēre, *n.* unit for measuring electric current. —**am′per·age,** *n.*

ăm·phĭb′ï·àn, *n.* **1.** animal able to live on land and water. —*adj.* **2.** Also, **am·phib′i·ous.** able to live on land and water.

ăm′phi·thē″à·têr, *n.* arena or stadium with tiers of seats surrounding the central area. Also, **am′phi·the″a·tre.**

ăm′ple, *adj.,* **ampler, amplest. 1.** copious. **2.** sufficient. —**am′ply,** *adv.*

ăm′plï·fÿ″, *v.t.,* **-fied, -fying. 1.** increase in size. **2.** increase in strength, as an electronic signal. —**am′pli·fi″er,** *n.* —**am″pli·fi·ca′tion,** *n.*

ăm′plï·tūde″, *n.* **1.** breadth or extent. **2.** abundance.

ăm′pū·tāte″, *v.t.,* **-tated, -tating.** remove, as a limb of a body. —**am″pu·ta′tion,** *n.* —**am″pu·tee′,** *n.*

à·mŭck′, *adv.* in a condition of murderous insanity.

ăm′ū·lėt, *n.* magical charm worn on the person.

à·mūse′, *v.t.,* **-mused, -musing. 1.** be funny to. **2.** entertain. —**a·muse′ment,** *n.*

ăn, *indef. art.* variant of *a,* used when the following word begins with a vowel.

à·năch′rŏn·ĭsm, *n.* something outside its proper historical period. —**a·nach″ron·is′tic,** *adj.*

ăn′à·grăm″, *n.* word formed from the letters spelling another word.

ā′nàl, *adj.* pertaining to the anus.

ăn″à·lŏg, *n.* represented by physical variables.

à·năl′ò·gÿ, *n., pl.* **-gies.** *n.* comparison

of an unfamiliar thing to a more familiar one. —a·nal′o·gous, *adj.*

á·năl′ỹ·sis, *n., pl.* -ses. 1. separation into component parts. 2. summary of such a separation. 3. psychoanalysis. —an′a·lyst, *n.* —an′′a·lyt′ic, an′′a·lyt′ic·al, *adj.* —an′a·lyze′′, *v.t.*

ăn·âr′chỹ, *n.* 1. society without rulers. 2. political or organizational chaos. —an′ar·chism′′, *n.* —an′ar·chist, *n.*

á·năth′e·má, *n.* 1. solemn curse. 2. something hated and despised.

á·năt′ó·mỹ, *n.* 1. study of the composition of animals and plants. 2. composition of an animal or plant. —an′′a·tom′i·cal, *adj.*

ăn′′cĕs·tŏr, *n.* forebear; one from whom a person descends. Also, *fem.*, an′′ces·tress. —an′′ces·try, *n.*

ăn′′chŏr, *n.* 1. device for mooring a ship or boat. —*v.i.* 2. to secure by anchor.

ăn′chō′′vỹ, *n., pl.* -vies. tiny, salty, herringlike fish.

ān′ciėnt, *adj.* 1. of the oldest period of human history. 2. very old. —*n.* 3. person, esp. an author or philosopher, of the ancient period. 4. very old person.

ănd, *conj.* 1. along with. 2. *Informal.* used instead of the infinitive *to*.

ănd′ī′′rŏn, *n.* horizontal iron support for firewood, used in pairs.

ăn′ĕc·dōte′′, *n.* true short story.

á·nē′mĭ·á, *n.* shortage of hemoglobin or red cells in the blood. —a·ne′mic, *adj.*

ăn′′ĕs·thē′sĭä, *n.* lack of sensation induced by a gas or drug. —an′′es·thet′ic, *adj., n.* —an·es·the·tize′′, *v.t.*

á·nĕw′, *adv.* once more.

ān′gĕl, *n.* messenger or attendant of God. —an·gel′ic, *adj.*

ăn′gêr, *n.* 1. strong annoyance. —*v.t.* 2. make angry.

ăn·gī′ná pĕc′tó·rĭs, painful heart condition.

ăn′gle, *n., v.i.,* -gled, gling. *n.* 1. divergence of two lines or surfaces that meet. —*v.i.* 2. fish. 3. *Informal.* use stratagems for personal gain. —an′gler, *n.*

ăn′gle·wŏrm′′, *n.* earthworm.

Ăn′glĭ·căn, *n.* 1. member of the Church of England or churches in communion with it, e.g. the Episcopal Church. —*adj.* 2. pertaining to the Church of England or churches in communion with it. —An′gli·can·ism, *n.*

Ăn′glō-Săx′ŏn, *n.* 1. person descended from the Angles and Saxons in England. 2. person of English ancestry. —*adj.* 3. pertaining to or characteristic of the Anglo-Saxons.

ăn′grỹ, *adj.* -grier, -griest. 1. seriously annoyed. 2. suggesting human anger by action, appearance, etc. —an′gri·ly, *adv.*

ăn′guĭsh, *n.* intense suffering.

ăn′gū·lár, *adj.* 1. having angles. 2. conspicuous for angles. —an′′gu·lar′i·ty, *n.*

ăn′i·lĭne, *n.* benzene derivative used for dyes.

ăn′′i·măd·vêrt′, *v.i.* comment disapprovingly. —an′′i·mad·ver′sion, *n.*

ăn′ĭ·mál, *n.* 1. living thing other than a plant or bacterium. 2. any such thing other than a human being. —*adj.* 3. pertaining to animals.

ăn′i·māte, *v.t.,* -mated, -mating, *adj. v.t.* 1. give life to. 2. make lively. —*adj.* 3. ăn′i·máte, having life. —an′′i·ma′tion, *n.*

ăn′′ĭ·mŏs′ĭ·tỹ, *n., pl.* -ties. hostility. Also, an′i·mus.

ăn′i·sēed′, *n.* aromatic seed of the anise plant.

ăn′kle, *n.* joint between the foot and the leg.

ăn′nàls, *n., pl.* historical records.

án·nĕx′, *v.t.* 1. join to a larger existing part. —*n.* 2. ăn′nĕx, a part so joined. —an′′nex·a′tion, *n.*

án·nī′hĭl·āte′′, *v.t.,* -ated, -ating. destroy utterly. —an·ni′′hil·a′tion, *n.*

ăn′′nĭ·vêr′sár·ỹ, *n., pl.* -ries. same day of the year as that on which something occurred.

ăn′nó·tāte′′, *v.t.,* -tated, -tating. explain or elaborate with notes. —an′′no·ta′tion, *n.*

án·nōunce′, *v.t.,* -nounced, -nouncing. make known, esp. publicly. —an·noun′cer, *n.* —an·nounce′ment, *n.*

án·nŏy′, *v.t.* trouble, esp. so as to provoke dislike. —an·noy′ance, *n.*

ăn′nū·ál, *adj.* 1. yearly. 2. living only one year, as a plant. —*n.* 3. something published once a year. 4. annual plant. —an′nu·al·ly, *adv.*

ăn·nū′i·tỹ, *n., pl.* -ties. annual income bought from an insurance company.

án·nŭl′, *v.t.,* -nulled, -nulling. make legally void. —an·nul′ment, *n.*

An·nŭn''cı̇̈·ā'tion, *n.* announcement to the Virgin Mary of the impending birth of Christ; celebrated March 25.

ăn'ȯ·dȳne, *n.* pain reliever.

a·noı̇̈nt', *v.t.* put oil, etc. on as part of a ceremony of consecration. —a·noint·ment, *n.*

a·nŏm'a·lÿ, *n., pl.* -lies. something inconsistent or abnormal. —a·nom'a·lous, *adj.*

a·nŏn', *adv.* soon.

a·nŏn'ÿ·moŭs, *adj.* written or spoken by someone whose name is unknown or unpublished. —an''o·nym'i·ty, *n.*

an·ȯth'êr, *adj.* **1.** one more. **2.** different. —*n.* **3.** one more. **4.** a different one.

ăn'swêr, *n.* **1.** reply to a question. **2.** solution to a problem. **3.** action provoked by something competing. —*v.t.* **4.** reply to. —*v.i.* **5.** give an answer. **6.** be matching or well-suited. **7.** be accountable or responsible.

ăn'swêr·a·ble, *adj.* **1.** able to be answered. **2.** accountable; responsible.

ănt, *n.* small social insect.

ăn·tăg'ȯ·nĭsm, *n.* hostility. —an·tag'ȯ·nist, *n.* —an·tag''o·nis'tic, *adj.* —an·tag'o·nize'', *v.t.*

Ănt·ârc'tĭc, *n.* **1.** southernmost zone of the earth. —*adj.* **2.** pertaining to this zone.

ăn''te·cē'dĕnt, *adj.* **1.** coming before. —*n.* **2.** something coming before.

ăn''te·dāte'', *v.t.,* -dated, -dating. precede in time.

ăn''te·di·lū'vı̇̈·an, *adj.* **1.** before the Flood. **2.** from remotest antiquity.

ăn'te·lōpe'', *n.* deerlike animal.

ăn·tĕn''na, *n., pl.* —nae (for 1), —nas (for 2). **1.** feeler on the head of an insect. **2.** aerial; conductor for sending or receiving radio waves.

ăn·tē'rı̇̈·or, *adj.* **1.** previous. **2.** at the front end.

ăn''te·rōōm'', *n.* room preceding a major room.

ăn'thĕm, *n.* hymnlike song.

ăn·thŏl'ō·gÿ, *n.* book of literary selections.

ăn'thra·cīte'', *n.* hard coal.

ăn''thrȯ·poı̇̈d'', *adj.* **1.** resembling humanity. —*n.* **2.** anthropoid animal.

ăn''thrȯ·pŏl'ō·gÿ, *n.* study of mankind. —an''thro·pol'o·gist, *n.*

ăn''tı̇̈·bī·ŏt'ĭc, *n.* substance for destroying or weakening microorganisms.

ăn''tı̇̈·bŏd''ÿ, *n., pl.* -ies. blood ingredient that fights foreign substances, e.g. bacteria.

ăn'tĭc, *n.* ridiculous or peculiar action.

ăn·tĭc'ı̇̈·pāte'', *v.t.,* -pated, -pating. **1.** look forward to, esp. with pleasure. **2.** use forethought to deal with. **3.** predict. —an·tic''i·pa'tion, *n.*

ăn''tı̇̈·clī'măx, *n.* disappointment of increasing expectations. —an''ti·cli·mac'tic, *adj.*

ăn''tı̇̈·dōte'', *n.* substance to counteract a poison.

ăn''tı̇̈·hı̇̈s'ta·mı̇̈ne, *n.* substance to counteract allergic reaction.

ăn·tĭp'a·thÿ, *n., pl.* -thies. dislike. —an·tip''a·thet'ic, *adj.*

ăn''ti·quar'ı̇̈·an, *n.* student of antiquities.

ăn·ti·quar'ÿ, *n., pl.* -quaries. *n.* collector or student of antiquities.

ăn·ti·quat''ĕd, *adj.* obsolete.

ăn·tīque, *n.* **1.** old manufactured object, esp. a valuable one. —*adj.* **2.** ancient.

ăn·tĭq'ui·tÿ, *n., pl.* -ties. **1.** ancient times. **2.** something antique.

ăn''tı̇̈·sĕp'tĭc, *n.* **1.** substance for destroying harmful bacteria. —*adj.* **2.** destroying harmful bacteria.

ăn''tı̇̈·sō'cial, *adj.* **1.** hostile to society. **2.** shunning society.

ăn·tĭth'ė·sı̇̈s, *n., pl.* -ses. direct opposite. —an''ti·thet'i·cal, *adj.*

ăn''tı̇̈·tŏx'ı̇̈n, *n.* substance for counteracting plant, animal, or bacterial toxin.

ănt'lêr, *n.* horn of a deer, moose, etc.

ăn'tȯ·nÿm'', *n.* word meaning the opposite.

ā'nŭs, *n.* opening at lower end of alimentary canal.

ăn'vı̇̈l, *n.* object on which iron, etc. is rested while being hammered.

ănx·ī·ė·tÿ, *n., pl.* -ies. **1.** fear of possible harm. **2.** eagerness to act. —anx'ious, *adj.* —anx'ious·ly, *adv.*

an'ÿ, *adj.* **1.** someone, as readily as all others. **2.** every. —*n.* **3.** any person or persons.

an'ÿ·bŏd''ÿ, *pron.* some one person, as readily as all others. Also, **an'y·one''.**

an'ÿ·hŏw'', *adv.* **1.** in any way. **2.** whatever the situation is. Also, **an'y·way''.**

an'ÿ·thı̇̈ng'', *pron.* **1.** some one thing, as

readily as all others. —*n.* **2.** something, whatever or how much it may be.

an′y·whĕre″, *adv.* in or into any place. Also, **an′y·place″**.

ā·ôr′tà, *n., pl.* **-as, -ae.** blood vessel from the heart. —**a·or′tic**, *adj.*

à·pârt′, *adv.* **1.** to pieces. **2.** separately.

à·pârt′heid, *n.* racial segregation, esp. in the Union of South Africa.

à·pârt′mĕnt, *n.* series of rooms forming a separate dwelling in a building.

ă′pà·thў, *n.* lack of feeling or emotion. —**a″pa·thet′ic**, *adj.* —**a″pa·thet′ic·al·ly**, *adv.*

āpe, *n., v.t.,* **aped, aping.** *n.* **1.** large animal of the monkey family. —*v.t.* **2.** imitate.

ăp′êr·tûre, *n.* opening.

ā′pĕx, *n.* peak.

ăph′o·rĭsm, *n.* brief statement of a truth. —**aph″o·ris′tic**, *adj.*

ăph″rò·dĭs′ĭ·ăc, *n.* drug promoting sexual excitement.

ā′pĭ·ār″ў, *n., pl.* **-ries.** bee farm.

à·pīēce′, *adv.* for each.

à·plŏmb′, *n.* self-possession.

À·pŏc′à·lўpse, *n.* revelation to St. John the Apostle. —**a·poc″a·lyp′tic**, *adj.*

À·pŏc′rў·phà, *n. pl.* biblical books not accepted by Protestants and Jews.

à·pŏc′rў·phàl, *adj.* highly dubious.

ăp′ò·gēe″, *n.* furthest distance of a satellite from its planet.

à·pŏl″ò·gĕt′ĭc, *adj.* confessing oneself to be at fault.

à·pŏl′ò·gīze″, *v.i.,* **-gized, -gizing.** confess oneself to be at fault and seek forgiveness.

à·pŏl′ò·gў, *n., pl.* **-gies. 1.** confession of a fault in search of forgiveness. **2.** statement defending one's actions, etc.

ăp′ò·plĕx″ў, *n.* bursting of blood vessel with consequent loss of bodily function. —**ap″o·plec′tic**, *adj.*

à·pŏs′tāte″, *n.* renouncer of one's professed faith, etc. —**a·pos′ta·sy**, *n.*

à·pŏs′tle, *n.* **1.** one of the twelve disciples of Christ sent to preach. **2.** preacher of a new faith. —**a″pos·tol′ic**, *adj.*

à·pŏs′trò·phē, *n.* **1.** a sign, ', used to indicate possessives, omitted letters, plurals involving numerals or initials, etc. **2.** remark made to or as if to some individual in the course of a speech, etc.

à·pŏs′trò·phīze″, *v.t.* **1.** spell with an apostrophe. **2.** address in an apostrophe.

à·pŏth′ė·cār″ў, *n., pl.* **-ies.** druggist.

ăp·päll′, *v.t.* put in a state of horror or fear. Also, **ap·pal′.** —**ap·pall′ing**, *adj.*

ăp″pà·rā′tŭs, *n.* **1.** instruments, etc. required for an experiment, job, etc. **2.** organizational structure.

ăp·păr′ĕl, *n.* **1.** clothes. —*v.t.* **2.** clothe.

ăp·păr′ĕnt, *adj.* **1.** clear; obvious. **2.** as judged from appearances. —**ap·par′ent·ly**, *adv.*

ăp″pà·rī′tion, *n.* ghost or phantom.

ăp·pēal′, *n.* **1.** request for help, mercy, etc. **2.** request for reconsideration. **3.** attractiveness. —*v.t.* **4.** request to have reconsidered. —*v.i.* **5.** make an appeal. **6.** have appeal.

ăp·pēar′, *v.i.* **1.** come into sight. **2.** seem. —**ap·pear′ance**, *n.*

ăp·pēase′, *v.t.,* **-peased, -peasing.** satisfy when hostile or demanding. —**ap·pease′ment**, *n.*

ăp·pĕl′lànt, *n.* person who appeals, esp. in law.

ăp·pĕl′làte, *adj.* handling appeals, as a court.

ăp″pĕl·lā′tion, *n.* name given to something or someone.

ăp·pĕnd′, *v.t.* add; join. —**ap·pend′age**, *n.*

ăp″pĕn·dĕc′tò·mў, *n., pl.* **-ies.** surgical removal of an appendix.

ăp·pĕn″di·cī′tis, *n.* inflammation of the appendix.

ăp·pĕn′dĭx, *n., pl.* **-dixes, -dices. 1.** supplementary portion at the end of a book, etc. **2.** blind branch of the intestine.

ăp′pêr·tāin″, *v.i.* belong.

ăp′pė·tīte″, *n.* desire, as for food. —**ap′pe·tiz″er**, *n.* —**ap′pe·tiz″ing**, *adj.*

ăp·plaud′, *v.t.* show approval of, as by applause.

ăp·plause′, *n.* **1.** indications of approval of a dramatic performance, etc. **2.** public recognition and approval.

ăp″ple, *n.* common, crisp fruit, generally red or green.

ăp·plī′ance, *n.* machine, etc., esp. for home use.

ăp′plĭ·cà·ble, *adj.* able to be applied.

ăp·plў′, *v.,* **-plied, -plying.** *v.t.* **1.** place, as on an object or surface. **2.** put to use, as a theory or rule. **3.** devote to a task. —*v.i.* **4.** make a formal request. **5.** be relevant. —**ap″pli·ca′tion**, *n.* —**ap′pli·cant**, *n.*

ap·point′ *v.t.* **1.** choose and designate. **2.** provide; furnish. —**ap·poin′tive,** *adj.* —**ap·point″ee′,** *n.*

ap·point′ment, *n.* **1.** meeting at a stated time. **2.** selection, as for public office. **3.** provision or furnishing.

ap·pôr′tion, *v.t.* divide into shares. —**ap·por′tion·ment,** *n.*

ăp′po·sīte, *adj.* appropriate.

ap·prāise′, *v.t.,* -praised, -praising, estimate the value of. —**ap·prais′er,** *n.* —**ap·prais′al,** *n.*

ap·prē′cĭ·a·ble, *adj.* **1.** sufficient to be noted. **2.** worthy of note; considerable.

ap·prē′cĭ·āte″, *v.,* -ated, -ating. *v.t.* **1.** be grateful for. **2.** value truly. —*v.i.* **3.** gain in value. —**ap·pre″ci·a′tion,** *n.* —**ap·pre′ci·a·tive,** *adj.*

ăp′′pre·hĕnd″, *v.t.* **1.** fear. **2.** understand. **3.** capture and arrest. —**ap″pre·hen′sion,** *n.*

ăp′′pre·hĕn′sĭve, *adj.* fearful.

ap·prĕn′tĭce, *n., v.t.,* -ticed, -ticing. *n.* **1.** assistant learning a trade. —*v.t.* **2.** enroll as an apprentice. —**ap·pren′tice·ship″,** *n.*

ap·prīse′, *v.t.,* -prised, -prising. inform; notify. Also, **ap·prize′.**

ap·prōach′, *v.t.* **1.** come close to. **2.** propose business to. —*v.i.* **3.** come close. —*n.* **4.** act or instance of coming close. **5.** way of coming close. **6.** manner of taking action.

ap·prōach′a·ble, *adj.* willing to be talked with.

ăp′′prō·bā′tion, *n.* approval.

ap·prō′prĭ·āte, *adj., v.t.,* -ated, -ating. *adj.* **1.** useful or proper. —*v.t.* **2. ap·prō′prĭ′āte″,** reserve for a purpose, as money. **3.** take for oneself. —**ap·pro′′pri·a′tion,** *n.*

ap·prove′, *v.,* -proved, -proving. *v.t.* **1.** state to be good or suitable. **2.** think favorably of. —*v.i.* **3.** regard favorably. —**ap·prov′al,** *n.*

ap·prŏx′ĭ·māte, *adj., v.t.,* -ated, -ating. *adj.* **1.** reasonably accurate but not precise. —*v.t.* **2.** amount to as an approximate figure, etc. —**ap·prox′i·mate·ly,** *adv.* —**ap·prox′′i·ma′tion,** *n.*

ap·pûr′te·nance, *n.* additional device or feature; accessory.

ă′prĭ·cŏt″, *n.* orange-colored peachlike fruit.

Ā′pril, *n.* fourth month.

ā′prŏn, *n.* covering worn over a dress or trouser front when working.

ăp·rŏ·pōs′, *adv.* **1. apropos of,** with regard to. **2.** at the right time. —*adj.* **3.** to the point; relevant.

ăpt, *adj.* **1.** displaying a tendency. **2.** likely. **3.** able; intelligent. —**apt′ly,** *adv.* —**apt′ness,** *n.*

ăp′tĭ·tūde″, *n.* talent or ability.

ăq′′uà·mà·rīne′, *n.* pale bluish-green.

à·quär′ĭ·ŭm, *n.* tank, bowl, etc., usually with glass walls, used for displaying live fish, etc.

à·quăt′ĭc, *adj.* of the water.

ăq′ue·dŭct, *n.* engineering structure for conducting water.

ă′que·oŭs, *adj.* like, of, or created by water.

ăq′ui·līne″, *adj.* pertaining to or suggesting eagles.

ăr′à·ble, *adj.* good for producing crops.

ăr′bĭt·êr, *n.* judge of controversial matters.

âr′bĭ·trār″y̆, *adj.* **1.** unreasonable or unjustified. **2.** admitting no discussion or complaint. **3.** chosen at random as a basis for discussion. —**ar″bi·trar′i·ly,** *adv.*

âr′bĭ·trāte″, *v.t.,* -trated, -trating. **1.** adjudicate after hearing disputants. **2.** submit for adjudication. —**ar″bi·tra′tion,** *n.* —**ar′bi·tra″tor,** *n.*

âr′bòr, *n.* shaded walk or garden.

âr·bō′rē·àl, *adj.* of or inhabiting trees.

âr·bŭ′tŭs, *n.* **1.** shrub with dark green leaves and red berries. **2.** trailing plant with white or pink blossoms.

ârc, *n.* **1.** segment of a circle. **2.** light formed by electricity jumping between electrodes.

âr·cāde′, *n.* **1.** row of arches. **2.** covered walk, esp. one between shops.

ârch, *n.* **1.** curved structure resisting compressive forces. —*v.i.* **2.** bend as an arch does. —*adj.* **3.** chief. **4.** cheerfully mischievous. —**arch′way″,** *n.*

âr·chā′ĭc, *adj.* **1.** out of date. **2.** ancient.

ârch·ăn·gĕl, *n.* chief angel.

ârch′bĭ′shŏp, *n.* superior bishop.

ârch′dūke′, *n.* Austrian royal prince. Also, *fem.,* **arch′duch′ess.**

âr′′chē·ŏl′o·gy̆, *n.* study of ancient cultures through their artifacts. —**ar′′che·ol′o·gist,** *n.* —**ar″che·o·log′i·cal,** *adj.* Also, **archaeology.**

ärch′êr, *n.* user of a bow and arrow. —**arch′er·y,** *n.*

** är″chĭ·pĕl′a·gō,** *n., pl.* **-gos, -goes. 1.** group of closely spaced islands. **2.** area of water surrounding such a group.

är′chĭ·tĕct″, *n.* designer of buildings.

är′chĭ·tĕc″tûre, *n.* **1.** art of designing buildings. **2.** a style of building. —**ar″chi·tec′tur·al,** *adj.*

är·chīves, *n. pl.* official records.

Ârc′tĭc, *n.* **1.** northernmost zone of the earth. —*adj.* **2.** pertaining to this zone.

âr′dėnt, *adj.* eager. —**ar′dent·ly,** *adv.*

âr′dör, *n.* eagerness; zeal.

âr′du·oŭs, *adj.* difficult or tedious.

âre, *v.* present indicative plural of *be.*

âr′ē·à, *n.* **1.** surface measure. **2.** region.

ārēä cōde, three-digit code used in telephoning indicating a region.

à·rē′nà, *n.* large space for athletic contests and spectators.

âr′gŏn, *n.* chemical element, an inert gas.

âr′gó·sў, *n., pl.* **-sies.** *Poetic.* large merchant ship or merchant fleet.

âr′gūe, *v.,* **-gued, -guing.** *v.i.* **1.** express a difference or differences of opinion. **2.** offer reasons for or against something. —*v.t.* **3.** present as true or valid. **4.** express differences of opinion over. —**ar′gu·ment,** *n.* —**ar″gu·men·ta′tion,** *n.*

âr″gū·mĕn′ta·tĭve, *adj.* given to argument or quarreling.

à′rĭ·à, *n.* song, as in an opera.

ā′rĭd, *adj.* dry. —**a·rid′i·ty,** *n.*

à·rīse′, *v.i.,* **arose, arisen, arising. 1.** get up. **2.** happen.

ār″is·tŏc′rà·cў, *n., pl.* **-cies. 1.** government by a small hereditary or select class. **2.** such a class. —**a·ris′to·crat,** *n.* —**a·ris″to·crat′ic,** *adj.*

à·rĭth′mė·tĭc, *n.* calculation with numerals. —**ar″ith·met′i·cal,** *adj.*

ârk, *n.* **1.** vessel of Noah. **2.** wooden chest.

ârm, *n.* **1.** upper human limb. **2.** anything suggesting this by form, position, or function. **3.** weapon. **4. arms,** the military profession. —*v.t.* **5.** equip with weapons.

âr·mâ′dà, *n.* fleet of fighting ships or airplanes.

Âr″mà·gĕd′dòn, *n.* major decisive battle.

ârm″à·mėnt, *n.* weapons with which a ship, airplane, etc. is equipped.

ârm′chāir″, *n.* chair with arm supports.

ârm′fŭl″, *n., pl.* **-fuls.** amount that can be held in one or both arms.

âr′mi·stice, *n.* suspension of hostilities; truce.

âr′mör, *n.* material, usually metal, protecting against weapons and missiles. —**ar′mored,** *adj.*

âr′mör·ў, *n., pl.* **-ies. 1.** building for military activities and equipment storage. **2.** place for storing weapons.

ârm′pĭt″, *n.* area beneath the arm at the shoulder.

âr′mў, *n., pl.* **-mies. 1.** land military force. **2.** large number of persons.

à·rō′mà, *n.* scent; odor. —**ar″o·mat′ic,** *adj.*

à·round′, *prep.* **1.** on all sides of. **2.** in any or all areas of. —*adv.* **3.** on all sides. **4.** in any or all areas. **5.** *Informal.* **a.** nearby. **b.** idly or aimlessly.

à·rouse′, *v.t.,* **aroused, arousing. 1.** awaken. **2.** call into activity. —**a·rous′al,** *n.*

àr·rāign, *v.t.* **1.** bring to court as a defendant. **2.** accuse. —**ar·raign′ment,** *n.*

àr·rānge′, *v.,* **-ranged, -ranging.** *v.t.* **1.** put in order. —*v.t., v.i.* **2.** plan; prepare. —**ar·range′ment,** *n.*

âr′rànt, *adj.* utter; downright.

àr·rāy′, *v.t.* **1.** arrange. **2.** dress. —*n.* **3.** order or arrangement. **4.** clothing.

àr·rears′, *n. pl.* things overdue, esp. payments.

àr·rĕst′, *v.t.* **1.** seize because of the commission of a crime. **2.** stop. —*n.* **3.** act or instance of arresting. **4.** state of being arrested.

àr·rīve′, *v.i.* **1.** come to a place. **2.** happen. —**ar·riv′al,** *n.*

ăr′ró·gànt, *adj.* proud and insolent. —**ar′ro·gant·ly,** *adv.* —**ar′ro·gance,** *n.*

ăr′ró·gāte″, *v.t.,* **-gated, -gating.** claim or seize unjustly. —**ar″ro·ga′tion,** *n.*

ăr′rōw, *n.* missile shot from a bow.

àr·rōў′ò, *n., pl.* **-os.** *Southwest U.S.* gully.

âr′sė·năl, *n.* place for making or storing weapons.

âr′sė·nĭc, *n.* silvery-white poisonous chemical element.

âr′sŏn, *n.* crime of burning buildings, etc. —**ar′son·ist,** *n.*

ârt, *n.* **1.** activity of creating things that arouse the emotions through one or more senses. **2.** things so created. **3.** skill or profession. **4.** cunning.

âr'tër·ÿ, n., pl. -ies. 1. major blood vessel. 2. main line of travel or communication. —ar·te'ri·al, adj.

âr·tē·sï'an wĕll, n. well whose opening is lower than the head of water supplying it.

ârt'fŭl, adj. cunning.

âr·thrī'tĭs, n. inflammation of a joint of the body. —ar·thrit'ic, adj.

âr'ti·chōke, n. edible flower head of thistlelike plant.

âr'tĭ·cle, n. 1. object for use. 2. writing on a factual subject. 3. Grammar. a, an, or the.

âr·tĭc'ū·lâte, adj., v., -lated, -lating. adj. 1. readily understood. 2. able in speech. 3. jointed. —v.t. (âr tĭc'ū lāte″) 4. express clearly. 5. arrange in a clear and orderly manner. 6. assemble with joints. —v.i. 7. speak clearly. —ar·tic″u·la'tion, n.

âr'tĭ·fīce, n. 1. cunning. 2. cunning action. 3. insincere behavior.

âr'tĭf·i·cêr, n. craftsman.

âr″tĭ·fĭ'cial, adj. 1. manufactured, esp. in imitation. 2. contrived or affected. —ar″ti·fi'cial·ly, adv. —ar″ti·fi·ci·al'i·ty, n.

âr·tĭl'lêr·ÿ, n. 1. guns or other devices for shooting large missiles. 2. army branch handling such devices.

âr'tĭ·sàn, n. craftsman.

ârt'ĭst, n. practitioner of an art. —ar·tist'ic, adj. —ar'tist·ry, n.

ârt'lĕss, adj. unaffected; natural.

ârt'ÿ, adj., -ier, -iest. feigning artistic sensitivity.

ăs, adv. 1. equally. 2. for example. 3. if and when. —conj. 4. equally to. 5. in the manner that. 6. while. 7. because; since. 8. though. —pron. 9. that. —prep. 10. in the guise of.

ăs·bĕs'tòs, n. fibrous mineral used in fireproofing.

à·cĕn'dàn·cÿ, n. 1. domination. 2. rise to power. Also, as·cen'den·cy.

à·cĕnd', v.t., v.i. climb or rise. —as·cent', n. —as·cen'dent, adj.

Ás·cĕn'sion, n. ascent of Christ into heaven, celebrated 40 days after Easter.

ăs'cêr·tāin, v.t. find out.

às·cĕt'ĭc, adj. 1. without pleasure or self-indulgence. —n. 2. one who lives an ascetic life. —as·cet'i·cism, n.

às·crībe', v.t., -scribed, -scribing. relate to a supposed cause. —as·crip'tion, n.

ā·sĕp'sis, n. absence of disease producing germs. —a·sep'tic, adj.

ăsh, n., pl. ashes. 1. remainder of something not fully burnt. 2. tree of the olive family. —ash'tray″, n.

à·shāmed', adj. feeling shame.

à·shôre', adj., adv. on or onto the shore.

à·sīde', adv. 1. at or to the side. 2. apart. 3. in reserve.

ăs'i·nīne″, adj. silly. —as″i·nin'ity, n.

ăsk, v.t. 1. seek to know. 2. seek information of. 3. seek, as a favor. 4. invite. —v.i. 5. seek a favor, information, etc.

à·skănce', adv. with suspicion or disapproval.

à·skĕw', adv., adj. slanted or twisted out of position.

à·slēep', adj., adv. in or into a state of sleep.

 às·pâr'à·gùs, n. plant with edible shoots.

ă″spär·tāme, n. a synthetic sweetener.

ăs'pĕct, n. 1. way of interpreting or understanding something. 2. appearance or manner. 3. face or side toward a certain direction.

ăs'pĕn, n. type of poplar tree.

às·pêr'ĭ·tÿ, n., pl. -ties. roughness of manner or speech.

às·pêr'sion, n. hostile or accusing remark.

ăs'phält, n. black tarlike material.

ăs·phÿx'ĭ·āte″, v.t., -ated, -ating. harm through deprivation of oxygen. —as·phyx″i·a'tion, n.

às·pīre', v.i. -pired, -piring. have ambitious intentions. —as″pi·ra'tion, n. —as·pir'ant, n.

ăs'pĭ·rĭn, n. white crystalline drug used to relieve minor pain and fever.

ăss, n. 1. donkey. 2. silly person.

às·sāil', v.t. attack. —as·sail'ant, n.

às·săs'sĭn, n. murderer, esp. of a statesman. —as·sas'sin·ate″, v.t. —as·sas″sin·a'tion, n.

às·säult', n., v.t. attack.

ăs·sāy', n. 1. chemical evaluation, as of an ore. —v.t. 2. perform an assay upon.

às·sĕm'ble, v.t., v.i., -bled, -bling. gather. —as·sem'blage, as·sem'bly, n.

às·sĕnt', v.i. 1. agree; consent. —n. 2. agreement; consent.

às·sêrt', v.t. 1. declare. 2. claim. 3. assert oneself, present one's claims, demands, etc. boldly. —as·ser'tion, n. —as·ser'tive, adj.

as·sèss′, *v.t.* evaluate. —**as·sess′ment, as·ses′sor,** *n.*

ăs′sĕt, *n.* something contributing to a profit or advantage.

as·sĭd′ū·oŭs, *adj.* devoted to a task. —**as·sid′u·ous·ly,** *adv.* —**as″si·du′i·ty,** *n.*

as·sīgn′, *v.t.* **1.** give out as a task or responsibility. **2.** appoint. **3.** transfer possession or enjoyment of. —*n.* **4.** *Law.* person to whom possession or enjoyment of something is transferred. —**as·sign′ment,** *n.* —**as·sign′a·ble,** *adj.* —**as″sign·ee′,** *n.*

as·sĭm′ĭ·lāte″, *v.t.*, **-ated, -ating. 1.** absorb. **2.** make like some larger entity. —**as·sim″i·la′tion,** *n.*

as·sĭst′, *v.t.* help in a task or occupation. —**as·sist′ant,** *n.* —**as·sist′ance,** *n.*

as·sō′cĭ·āte, *v.t.*, **-ated, -ating,** *adj.*, *n. v.t., v.i.* **1.** join in a social or business relationship. —*v.t.* **2.** connect in one's mind. —*adj.* **3.** joined in a social or business relationship. —*n.* **4.** someone or something so joined. —**as·so″ci·a′tion,** *n.*

as·sôrt′, *v.t.* classify. —**as·sort′ment,** *n.*

as·sôrt′ĕd, *adj.* **1.** of various kinds. **2.** classified.

as·suāge, *v.t.*, **-suaged, -suaging.** relieve, as suffering.

as·sūme′, *v.t.*, **-sumed, -suming. 1.** suppose without knowing. **2.** take upon oneself. **3.** take or receive from another. **4.** begin to cultivate, as a role or affectation. **5.** feign.

as·sŭmp′tion, *n.* **1.** act or instance of assuming. **2. the Assumption,** ascent of the Virgin Mary to heaven, celebrated August 15.

as·sūre′, *v.t.*, **-sured, -suring. 1.** state emphatically. **2.** convince. **3.** make certain or safe. **4.** reassure. —**as·sur′ance,** *n.* —**as·sured′,** *adj.*

ăs′tēr, *n.* daisylike flower.

ăs′tēr·ĭsk, *n.* a sign, *, used for footnote references, etc. in print.

a·stêrn′, *adv. Nautical.* backwards.

ăs′tēr·oīd″, *n.* **1.** small planetlike body. **2.** resembling a star.

ăsth′mà, *n.* respiratory disorder. —**asth·mat′ic,** *adj., n.*

a·stĭg′mà·tĭsm, *n.* eye defect which causes imperfect focusing. —**a″stig·mat′ic,** *adj.*

a·stĭr′, *adj., adv.* full of diverse action.

as·tŏn′ĭsh, *v.t.* surprise greatly. —**as·ton′ish·ment,** *n.*

as·toŭnd′, *v.t.* surprise very greatly.

a·strāy′, *adv., adj.* away from guidance or control.

a·strīde′, *prep., adv., adj.* straddling.

a·strĭn′gĕnt, *adj.* **1.** constrictive, styptic. —*n.* **2.** substance which causes contraction of body tissues.

as·trŏl′ō·gў, *n.* study of stars and planets as influences on events. —**as″tro·log′i·cal,** *adj.* —**as·trol′o·ger,** *n.*

ăs′trò·naŭt″, *n.* person exploring or traveling through outer space.

ăs″trò·nŏm′ĭ·càl, *adj.* **1.** pertaining to astronomy. **2.** fantastic, as a number of quantity.

ăs·trŏn′ò·mў, *n.* study of planets, stars, etc. and space. —**as·tron′o·mer,** *n.*

as·tūte′, *adj.* shrewd. —**as·tute′ness,** *n.*

a·sŭn′dêr, *adv., adj.* in parts.

a·sў′lŭm, *n.* home for persons needing protection, e.g., the insane.

ăt, *prep.* in, on, or near (used to specify time, place, or rate).

ā′thē·ĭsm, *n.* belief that no god exists. —**a′the·ist,** *n.* —**a″the·is′tic,** *adj.*

ăth·lēte″, *n.* a person who engages in athletics.

ăth·lĕt′ĭcs, *n. pl.* sports involving vigorous bodily exercise. —**ath·let′ic,** *adj.*

a·thwart′, *adv., prep.* from side to side.

ăt′làs, *n.* book of maps.

ăt′mós·phēre″, *n.* **1.** air closest to the earth. **2.** prevailing mood. —**at″mos·pher′ic,** *adj.*

ăt′ŏll, *n.* ring of coral islands or reefs.

ă′tòm, *n.* smallest unit constituting a distinct chemical element. —**a·tom′ic,** *adj.*

a·tŏmĭc bŏmb, bomb acting through atomic energy created by fission. Also, **atom bomb.**

a·tŏmĭc ĕnêrgў, energy created through fission or fusion of the nuclei of certain atoms.

ăt′óm·īz″êr, *n.* device creating a fine spray.

a·tōne′, *v.i.* **-atoned, atoning.** make right or show regret for a wrong one has done. —**a·tone′ment,** *n.*

a·tŏp′, *prep., adv.* on top of.

a·trō′cioŭs, *adj.* **1.** vicious; outrageous. **2.** wretchedly bad. —**a·troc′i·ty,** *n.*

ă″trŏ·phў, *n.* **1.** a wasting away. —*v.i., v.t.* **2.** to waste away.

at·tach′, *v.t.* **1.** fasten to something. **2.** bind by ties of affection. **3.** assume legal possession of, as to settle a bad debt. —**at·tach′ment**, *n.*

at″ta·ché′, *n.* special member of an embassy staff.

at·tack′, *v.t.* **1.** act against with physical violence, harsh words, etc. **2.** commence to solve, work out, etc. with vigor. —*n.* **3.** act or manner of attacking.

at·tain′, *n.* arrive at. —**at·tain′a·ble**, *adj.* —**at·tain′ment**, *n.*

at·tar′, *n.* scent extracted from flowers.

at·tempt′, *v.t.*, *n.* try.

at·tend′, *v.t.* **1.** be present at. **2.** accompany. **3.** care for. —*v.i.* **4.** be present at a meeting, etc. **5.** give heed. —**at·ten′dance**, *n.*

at·tend′ant, *n.* **1.** minor assistant. —*adj.* **2.** accompanying.

at·ten′tion, *n.* **1.** heed. **2.** care, esp. medical care.

at·ten′tive, *adj.* paying heed or care. —**at·ten′tive·ly**, *adv.*

at·ten′u·āte′, *v.t.*, -ated, -ating. **1.** thin. **2.** weaken or dilute. —**at·ten″u·a′tion**, *n.*

at·test′, *v.t.* bear witness; certify. —**at″tes·ta′tion**, *n.*

at″tic, *n.* unfinished floor space beneath the roof of a house.

at·tīre′, *v.t.*, -tired, -tiring, *n.* *v.t.* **1.** dress, esp. showily. —*n.* **2.** clothes, esp. showy ones.

at′ti·tūde″, *n.* **1.** opinion or feeling. **2.** posture.

at·tōr′nēy, *n.*, *pl.* -eys. lawyer.

at·tract′, *v.t.* **1.** pull toward oneself. **2.** draw by evoking interest, allure, etc. in. —**at·trac′tive**, *adj.* —**at·trac′tive·ly**, *adv.* —**at·trac′tive·ness**, *n.* —**at·trac′tion**, *n.*

at·trib′ūte, *v.t.*, -uted, -uting, *n.* *v.t.* **1.** name something as the cause for. —*n.* (ăt′trib·ūte) **2.** distinguishing quality or feature. —**at″tri·bu′tion**, *n.*

at·tri′tion, *n.* wearing-down.

at·tūne′, *v.t.*, -tuned, -tuning. put in harmony.

au′būrn, *n.* reddish-brown.

auc′tion, *n.* **1.** public sale to the highest bidder for each item. —*v.t.* **2.** sell at an auction. —**auc″tion·eer′**, *n.*

au·dā′cious, *adj.* daring. —**au·da′ci·ty**, *n.*

au′di·ble, *adj.* able to be heard. —**au′di·bly**, *adv.* —**au″di·bil′i·ty**, *n.*

au′di·ence, *n.* **1.** group attending a play, concert, lecture, etc. **2.** persons reached by a book, etc. **3.** formal interview.

au′di·ō″ *adj.* pertaining to electronic reproduction of sound.

au′dit, *v.t.* **1.** examine financial accounts. —*n.* **2.** examination of financial accounts. —**au′dit·or**, *n.*

au·di′tion, *n.* **1.** trial of ability for an actor, musician, etc. —*v.t.* **2.** give an audition to. —*v.i.* **3.** perform at an audition.

au″di·tō′ri·ŭm, *n.* room for an audience.

au′di·tō″ry, *adj.* pertaining to hearing.

au′ger, *n.* drill.

aught, *n.*, *Archaic*. **1.** anything. **2.** zero. —*adv.* **3.** in any way.

aug·ment′, *v.t.* add to. —**aug″men·ta′tion**, *n.*

au′gur, *v.t.* **1.** predict. —*n.* **2.** prophet. —**au′gu·ry**, *n.*

au·gŭst′, *adj.* **1.** grand; majestic. —*n.* **2.** August, eighth month.

aunt, *n.* sister of a father or mother, or wife of an uncle.

au′rà, *n.* quality emanating from a particular place or person.

au′ràl, *adj.* pertaining to hearing.

au′rē·ōle″, *n.* halo.

au re·voir (ō″rə vwahr′), *French*. until I see you again; good-bye.

au′ri·cle, *n.* **1.** outer ear. **2.** upper chamber of the heart. —**au·ric′u·lar**, *adj.*

au·rĭf′êr·oŭs, *adj.* gold-bearing.

aus·pĭce, *n.*, *usually pl.* sponsorship.

aus·pĭ′cioŭs, *adj.* favorable; promising.

aus·tēre′, *adj.* **1.** severe in manner. **2.** characterized by abstention. —**aus·ter′i·ty**, *n.*

au·then′tĭc, *adj.* true or genuine. —**au″then·tĭ′ci·ty**, *n.*

au·then′tĭ·cāte″, *v.t.*, -ated, -ating. prove the authenticity of. —**au·then″tĭ·ca′tion**, *n.*

au′thor, *n.* creator, esp. of a written work. Also, *fem.*, **au′thor·ess**. —**au′thor·ship″**, *n.*

au·thôr″i·tār′i·ǎn, *adj.* characterized by excessive show or use of authority. —**au·thor″i·tar′i·an·ism**, *n.*

au·thôr′i·tā″tive, *adj.* **1.** confirmed by competent authority. **2.** having authority.

au·thôr′i·ty, *n.*, *pl.* -ties. **1.** official power. **2.** person having such power. **3.**

proof for a statement. **4.** expert. **5. the authorities,** persons with legal power.

au·thor·ize, *v.t.*, **-ized, -izing.** give official consent to. **—au·thor·i·za·tion,** *n.*

au·to, *n.* automobile.

au·to·bi·og·ra·phy, *n.*, *pl.* **-ies.** story of one's own life. **—au·to·bi·o·gra·phi·cal,** *adj.*

au·toc·ra·cy, *n.*, *pl.* **-cies.** government by one absolute ruler. **—au·to·crat,** *n.* **—au·to·crat·ic,** *adj.*

au·to·graph, *n.* one's name in one's handwriting.

au·to·mat, *n.* restaurant with coin-operated serving machines.

au·to·mat·ic, *adj.* controlled by machinery, etc. rather than humans. **—au·to·mat·ic·al·ly,** *adv.*

au·to·ma·tion, *n.* replacement of human beings as controlling elements by automatic devices.

au·tom·a·ton, *n.*, *pl.* **-ta.** manlike self-controlled machine; robot.

au·to·mo·bile, *n.* self-propelled passenger vehicle.

au·to·mo·tive, *adj.* pertaining to self-propelled road vehicles.

au·ton·o·my, *n.* self-government. **—au·ton·o·mous,** *adj.*

au·top·sy, *n.*, *pl.* **-sies.** examination of a corpse to determine the cause of death.

au·tumn, *n.* season between summer and winter. **—au·tum·nal,** *adj.*

aux·il·i·a·ry, *adj.*, *n.*, *pl.* **-ries.** *adj.* **1.** serving to assist. **2.** supplementary. **—n. 3.** something that assists or supplements. **4.** *Grammar.* verb used in connection with the principal verb of a sentence.

a·vail, *v.t.* **1.** avail oneself, take advantage. **—v.i. 2.** be of help or use. **—n. 3.** advantage or benefit.

a·vail·a·ble, *adj.* able to be used or acquired. **—a·vail·a·bil·i·ty,** *n.*

av·a·lanche, *n.* sudden descent down a slope of a mass of snow, rock, etc.

av·a·rice, *n.* greed. **—av·a·ri·cious,** *adj.*

a·vast, *interj. Nautical.* stop.

a·venge, *v.t.*, **-avenged, avenging.** take revenge for. **—a·veng·er,** *n.*

av·e·nue, *n.* **1.** major street. **2.** approach road.

av·er·age, *n.*, *adj.*, *v.*, **-aged, -aging.** *n.* **1.** number representing the sum of a group of added figures divided by the

number of figures. **—adj. 2.** typical. **3.** revealed by an average. **—v.t. 4.** find the average of. **—v.i. 5.** form an average.

a·verse, *adj.* opposed; reluctant. **—a·verse·ly,** *adv.*

a·ver·sion, *n.* strong dislike.

a·vert, *v.t.* **1.** prevent. **2.** turn away, as the eyes.

a·vi·ar·y, *n.*, *pl.* **-ries.** place for captive birds.

a·vi·a·tion, *n.* practice of flying aircraft.

a·vi·a·tor, *n.* person who flies aircraft. Also, *fem.*, **a·vi·a·trix.**

av·id, *adj.* eager. **—a·vid·i·ty,** *n.*

a·vo·ca·do, *n.*, *pl.* **-dos.** pear-shaped tropical fruit.

av·o·ca·tion, *n.* spare-time pursuit; hobby.

a·void, *v.t.* keep oneself away or safe from. **—a·void·a·ble,** *adj.* **—a·void·ance,** *n.*

av·oir·du·pois, *n.* system of weights using a pound of 16 ounces.

a·vow, *v.t.* confess. **—a·vow·al,** *n.* **—a·vowed,** *adj.*

a·wait, *v.t.* wait for.

a·wake, *v.*, **awoke** or **awaked, awaking,** *adj. v.t.*, *v.i.* **1.** Also, **a·wak·en,** wake. **—adj. 2.** not asleep.

a·ward, *v.t.* **1.** bestow, as a prize, favor, etc. **—n. 2.** something awarded.

a·ware, *adj.* conscious or perceptive. **—a·ware·ness,** *n.*

a·wash, *adj.*, *adv.* just below water level; flooded.

a·way, *adv.* **1.** to or in another place or direction. **2.** from a place. **3.** out of one's possession. **4.** continuously. **—adj. 5.** absent. **6.** at a specified distance.

awe, *n.*, *v.t.*, **awed, awing.** *n.* **1.** overwhelming respect, reverence, etc. **—v.t. 2.** fill with awe. **—awe·some,** *adj.*

aw·ful, *adj.* **1.** bad. **2.** awe-inspiring.

aw·ful·ly, *adv.* **1.** in an awful manner. **2.** *Informal.* very.

a·while, *adv.* for a short time.

awk·ward, *adj.* **1.** clumsy. **2.** embarrassing. **3.** dangerous or difficult. **—awk·ward·ly,** *adv.* **—awk·ward·ness,** *n.*

awl, *n.* pointed tool.

awn·ing, *n.* device for shading windows, porches, etc. usually made of canvas.

a·wry, *adv.*, *adj.* **1.** twisted. **2.** not right.

ax, *n.*, *pl.* **axes.** broad-bladed chopping tool. Also, **axe.**

ăx′ĭ·òm, *n.* statement accepted as a basic truth. —ax′′i·o·mat′ic, *adj.*

ăx′ĭs, *n.*, *pl.* axes. line on which something is centered or rotates. —ax′i·al, *adj.*

ăx′le, *n.* shaft on which a wheel turns.

aў′′à·tōl′làh, *n.* Shi′ite Muslim religious leader.

aўe, *adv.*, *n.* yes, esp. in voting.

à·zāl′eà, *n.* flowering shrub.

ăz′ūre, *n.* sky blue.

B

B, b, *n.* 1. second letter of the English alphabet. 2. second-best grade.

băb′ble, *v.*, -bled, -bling, *n.* *v.t.*, *v.i.* 1. speak unclearly or meaninglessly. —*n.* 2. unclear or meaningless spoken words or sounds. —bab′bler, *n.*

bābe, *n.* baby.

bā′boōn, *n.* large monkey.

bā′bў, *n.*, *pl.* -bies, *v.t.*, -bied, -bying. *n.* 1. very young child. 2. infantile person. —*v.t.* 3. treat with excessive care or indulgence. —ba′by·ish, *adj.* —ba′by·hood, *n.*

băc′cà·läu′rē·àte, *n.* bachelor's degree.

băch′e·lör, *n.* 1. unmarried man. 2. person holding the lowest academic degree. —bach′e·lor·hood′′, *n.*

bà·cĭl′lùs, *n.*, *pl.* bacilli (bà·cil′ī). rodshaped bacterium.

băck, *n.* 1. part of a person opposite the face. 2. uppermost part of an animal. 3. side of an object opposite that usually faced; rear. 4. spine. —*adj.* 5. at the rear. 6. related to the past. —*adv.* 7. toward the rear. 8. into the past. 9. in return. —*v.t.* 10. sponsor; support. —*v.t.*, *v.i.* 11. move backwards. —back′er, *n.* —back′ing, *n.*

băck′bīte′′, *v.t.*, *v.i.* slander, esp. someone absent. —back′bit′′er, *n.*

băck′bōne, *n.* 1. spine. 2. strength of character.

băck′fīre, *v.i.* 1. fire prematurely, as an engine. 2. have adverse results, as a plan. —*n.* 3. premature firing of an engine.

băck′groūnd, *n.* 1. area at the rear of a scene. 2. information generally useful in a given situation. 3. origin, experience, or environment.

băck′lăsh, *n.* sudden or sharp reaction.

băck′lŏg′′, *n.* accumulation.

băck′slīde′′, *v.i.*, -slid, -slidden or -slid, -sliding. forget good resolutions. —back′slid′′er, *n.*

băck tălk, *Informal.* insolent reply.

băck′wàrd, *adv.* Also, back′wards. 1. toward the rear. 2. back foremost. 3. toward the past. —*adj.* 4. toward the rear or the past. 5. not sufficiently advanced. —back′ward·ly, *adv.* —back′ward·ness, *n.*

băck′woŏds′, *n.* *pl.* region of sparsely settled forest. —back′woods′man, *n.*

bā′còn, *n.* cured meat from the back and sides of a hog.

băc·tēr′ĭ·à, *n.*, *pl.* of bacterium. microscopic vegetable organism. —bac·te′ri·al, *adj.* —bac·te′ri·al·ly, *adv.*

băc·tē′′rĭ·ŏl′ò·gў, *n.* study of bacteria. —bac·te′′ri·ol·og′i·cal, *adj.* —bac·te′′ri·ol′o·gist, *n.*

băd, *adj.* worse, *n.*, *adj.* 1. unfavorable evil, or unacceptable. —*n.* 2. condition or realm of that which is bad. —bad′ly, *adv.* —bad′ness, *n.*

bădge, *n.* object worn as a symbol of authority or distinction.

băd′gêr, *n.* 1. burrowing animal. —*v.t.* 2. torment.

băd′′ĭ·nàge′, *n.* teasing conversation or banter.

băd′mĭn·tòn, *n.* game played with rackets and shuttlecocks.

băf′fle, *v.t.*, -fled, -fling, *n.* *v.t.* 1. confuse. —*n.* 2. passage made to divert or stop sound, light, etc. —baf′fling, *adj.* —baf′fling·ly, *adv.*

băg, *n.*, *v.*, bagged, bagging. *n.* 1. flexible container open at one end. 2. purse. 3. suitcase. —*v.t.* 4. put into bags. 5. kill, esp. in sport. —*v.i.* 6. bulge.

băg′gàge, *n.* containers for things taken on a journey.

băg′gў, *adj.* irregularly bulging. —bag′gi·ness, *n.*

băg′pīpe′′, *n.*, *often pl.* reed musical instrument played with air under pressure in a bag. —bag′pip′′er, *n.*

bāil, *n.*, *v.* *n.* 1. security for temporary release of a prisoner. 2. suspension handle. —*v.t.* 3. have released temporarily by putting up security. **4.** empty of water with a vessel. —*v.i.* **5. bail out**, escape, often by parachute. —**bail'a·ble,** *adj.*

bāil'ĭff, *n.* **1.** deputy sheriff. **2.** officer keeping order in a court.

bāil'ĭ·wĭck, *n.* **1.** area of a bailiff's authority. **2.** any area of authority or competence.

bāit, *n.* **1.** something used as an attraction in trapping or fishing. —*v.t.* **2.** supply with bait. **3.** harass, as with dogs.

bāke, *v.,* **-ked, -king.** *v.t., v.i.* cook or harden with dry heat. —**bak'er,** *n.*

bāk'êr·ў, *n., pl.* **-eries. 1.** place for baking food made with flour, etc. **2.** place where such food is sold.

băl'ánce, *n., v.,* **-anced, -ancing.** *n.* **1.** state of rest due to equal leverage around a point or line. **2.** state of harmony, stability, etc. **3.** weighing device. **4.** remainder from a subtraction. —*v.t.* **5.** put in balance. **6.** compare or contrast. **7.** review, as accounts. —*v.i.* **8.** come into or be in balance.

băl'cò·nў, *n., pl.* **-ies. 1.** floor area projecting from a building. **2.** interior floor area overlooking a lower floor.

băld, *n.* **1.** without hair. **2.** without disguise or mitigation. —**bald'ly,** *adv.* —**bald'ness,** *n.*

bāle, *n., v.t.,* **baled, baling.** *n.* **1.** large compressed or tied bundle. —*v.t.* **2.** make into bales.

bāle'fŭl, *adj.* hostile; evil. —**bale'ful·ly,** *adv.* —**bale'ful·ness,** *n.*

bälk, *v.i.* **1.** refuse to act. **2.** be daunted. —*v.t.* **3.** obstruct. —*n.* **4.** obstruction. —**balk'y,** *adj.*

băll, *n.* **1.** evenly rounded object; sphere. **2.** game or games played with such an object. **3.** an entertainment of dancing. —*v.t.* **4.** form into spheres.

băl'lăd, *n.* **1.** narrative song or poem. **2.** sentimental song.

băl'lást, *n.* **1.** weighty material used for stability. —*v.t.* **2.** supply with ballast.

băll bēarĭng, machinery bearing rotating on steel balls.

băl''lé·rĭ'na, *n.* leading female ballet dancer.

băl·let', *n.* entertainment by dancers, esp. one acting out a story.

băl·lĭs'tĭcs, *n.* study of the motion and

behavior of projectiles. —**bal·lis'tic,** *adj.*

băl·lōon', *n.* **1.** lighter-than-air bag with no engine or steering mechanism. —*v.i.* **2.** travel in balloons. —**bal·loon'ist,** *n.*

băl'lŏt, *n.* **1.** paper for indicating a vote. **2.** collective vote for a candidate, proposal, etc.

băll'rōōm, *n.* room for social dancing.

băl'lў·hōō'', *n. Informal.* ostentatious publicity.

bälm, *n.* **1.** healing or soothing substance. **2.** anything that heals or soothes.

bälm·ў, *adj.,* **balmier, balmiest.** soothing or refreshing. —**balm'i·ness,** *n.*

băl·sà, *n.* lightweight wood of a tropical American tree, used for model-making, etc.

băl'sám, *n.* aromatic resin from certain trees. —**bal·sam'ic,** *adj.*

băl'ŭs·têr, *n.* columnlike support for a railing.

băl'ŭs·trāde'', *n.* railing supported by balusters.

băm'bōō, *n.* tall tropical grass with hollow woodlike stems.

băm·bōō'zle, *v.t. Informal.* mystify or cheat.

băn, *v.t.,* **banned, banning.** *n. v.t.* **1.** forbid. —*n.* **2.** act or instance of forbidding.

bà·nāl', *adj.* boringly ordinary. —**ba·nal'i·ty,** *n.*

bà·năn'à, *n.* **1.** treelike tropical plant. **2.** fruit from this plant.

bănd, *n.* **1.** strip of binding material. **2.** stripe. **3.** group of wind and percussion musicians. **4.** informal group, esp. of armed persons. —*v.t.* **5.** mark with bands. —*v.i.* **6.** gather or unite. —**band'mas''ter,** *n.* —**bands'man,** *n.* —**band'stand'',** *n.*

bănd'áge, *n., v.t.,* **-aged, -aging.** *n.* **1.** strip of cloth, etc., esp. for covering a wound. —*v.t.* **2.** tie with a bandage.

băn·dăn'ná, *n.* printed cloth for the head or neck. Also, **ban·dan'a.**

băn'dĭt, *n.* armed robber. —**ban'ditry,** *n.*

bănd'wăg''òn, *n.* **1.** wagon for the musicians in a circus parade. **2.** obviously winning side of a controversy.

băn'dў, *v.t.,* **-died, -dying,** *adj. v.t.* **1.** exchange rapidly, as words. **2.** send

back and forth rapidly, as a tennis ball.
—*adj.* **3.** bowed, as legs.

bāne, *n.* evil or destructive influence.

băng, *n.* **1.** loud noise, as from an explosion or collision. **2.** Often, **bangs,** short hair across the forehead. —*v.i.* **3.** make a loud noise. **4.** strike.

băn'gle, *n.* decorative band for the wrist or ankle.

băn'ĭsh, *v.t.* drive away; exile. —**ban'ish·ment,** *n.*

băn'ĭstêr, *n.* stair railing.

băn'jō, *n.* plucked stringed instrument with circular body. —**ban'jo·ist,** *n.*

băngk, *n.* **1.** shore of a river or lake. **2.** slope. **3.** long mound. **4.** tilt, as a vehicle or its supporting surface at a turn. **5.** organization for the saving and lending of money. —*v.t.* **6.** heap up. **7.** tilt while turning. **8.** put into a bank. **9.** cover partly, as a fire. —*v.i.* **10.** have a bank account.

băngk'êr, *n.* proprietor or officer of a bank.

băngk'ĭng, *n.* **1.** operation of a bank or banks. —*adj.* **2.** pertaining to the activities of banks.

băngk'rŭpt'', *adj.* **1.** unable to pay debts. **2.** without resources. —*n.* **3.** bankrupt person. —*v.t.* **4.** make bankrupt. —**bank'rupt·cy,** *n.*

bănns, *n. pl.* notice of marriage to be performed. Also, **bans.**

băn'quĕt, *n., v.i.,* **-queted, -queting.** *n.* **1.** formal dinner or luncheon. —*v.i.* **2.** participate in a banquet. —**ban'quet·er,** *n.*

băn'tàm, *n.* **1.** small fowl. —*adj.* **2.** miniature; tiny.

băn'têr, *n.* **1.** teasing. —*v.i.* **2.** exchange teasing remarks. —**ban'ter·er,** *n.*

băp'tĭsm, *n.* rite of initiation, as into a church. —**bap·tis'mal,** *adj.*

băp'tīze, *v.t.,* **-ized, -izing.** initiate into a church, esp. by sprinkling with or immersion in water.

bâr, *n., v.t.,* **barred, barring,** *prep. n.* **1.** long round object, used in an enclosure as a lever, etc. **2.** stripe. **3.** obstruction. **4.** drinking place. **5.** counter for serving drinks. **6.** division of a musical composition. **7.** legal profession. —*v.t.* **8.** secure with a bar. **9.** exclude. **10.** obstruct. —*prep.* **11.** except for.

bârb, *n.* **1.** sharp projection. —*v.t.* **2.** furnish with barbs.

bâr·bâr·ĭ·àn, *n.* uncivilized person; savage. —**bar·bar'i·an·ism,** *n.*

bâr·bâr·ĭc, *adj.* typical of or suggesting barbarians. —**bar·bar'i·cal·ly,** *adv.*

bâr'bâr·ĭsm, *n.* barbaric act or state.

bâr·bâr·ĭ·tÿ, *n., pl.* **-ities. 1.** cruelty. **2.** barbaric state.

bâr·bâr·oŭs, *adj.* **1.** cruel. **2.** uncivilized. —**bar'bar·ous·ly,** *adv.* —**bar'bar·ous·ness,** *n.*

bâr'bē·cūe, *n.* **1.** to cook outdoors over an open fire. **2.** fireplace or grill used for cooking outdoors. **3.** meal cooked over an open fire. **4.** meat cooked and basted with sauce.

bârbed, *adj.* **1.** having sharp projections. **2.** harsh, as a remark; caustic.

bâr·bĭ·tū·ràte, *n.* sedative.

bârd, *n.* **1.** Celtic poet. **2.** any minstrel or poet. —**bard'ic,** *adj.*

bāre, *adj.,* **barer, barest,** *v.t.,* **bared, baring.** *adj.* **1.** uncovered or unconcealed. **2.** unfurnished. **3.** mere. —*v.t.* **4.** strip of covering or concealment. —**bare'ness,** *n.*

bāre'băck'', *adv., adj.* without a saddle.

bāre'fāced'', *adj.* **1.** shameless. **2.** with an uncovered face.

bāre'lÿ, *adv.* **1.** by the smallest possible amount. **2.** nakedly.

bâr'gaĭn, *n.* **1.** business agreement. **2.** advantageous purchase. —*v.i.* **3.** reach or attempt to reach a business agreement. —**bar'gain·er,** *n.*

bârge, *n., v.,* **barged, barging.** *n.* **1.** slow freight-carrying boat. **2.** ceremonial boat carrying royalty, etc. —*v.t.* **3.** carry by barge. —*v.i.* **4.** barge in, *Informal.* intrude. —**barge'man,** *n.*

bâr'ĭ·tōne'', *n.* **1.** musical range between tenor and bass. **2.** singer, instrument or part with this range.

bârk, *n.* **1.** short utterance of a dog. **2.** covering of the stem of a tree or shrub. **3.** sailing vessel square-rigged on all but the last of three or more masts. —*v.t.* **4.** utter in a barklike tone. **5.** utter a bark. **6.** strip bark from. **7.** skin by accident.

bâr'lēy, *n.* grass with edible grain.

bârn, *n.* building for crop storage, keeping of cows, etc. —**barn'yard'',** *n.*

bar'na·cle, *n.* shellfish that clings to ship bottoms, whales, etc.

ba·rŏm'e·têr, *n.* device for measuring atmospheric pressure and thus foretelling weather changes. —**bar''o·met'ric, bar''o·met'ri·cal,** *adj.*

băr'ŏn, *n.* low-ranking noble. Also, *fem.,* **bar'on·ess.** —**bar'on·age,** *n.* —**ba·ro'ni·al,** *adj.*

băr'ŏn·ėt, *n.* titled British commoner. —**bar'on·et·cy,** *n.*

Ba·rōque', *n.* florid style in architecture, etc. in the 17th century. Also, **ba·roque'.**

băr'ráck, *n.* **1.** Usually, **barracks,** dormitory for soldiers. —*v.t.* **2.** house in barracks.

băr·rà·cu'dà, *n., pl.* **-da, -das.** pikelike tropical fish.

bàr·räge, *n.* defensive barrier of artillery fire, captive balloons, etc.

băr'rėl, *n., v.,* **-reled, -reling.** *n.* **1.** container, usually wood, with circular ends and bulging sides. **2.** measure of about 31 gallons. —*v.t.* **3.** put into barrels. —*v.i.* **4.** *Informal.* move at high speed.

băr'rĕn, *adj.* **1.** unable to support plant life. **2.** unable to bear children. **3.** profitless. —**bar'ren·ness,** *n.*

băr'rĭ·cāde'', *n., v.t.,* **-caded, -cading.** *n.* **1.** obstruction, as to military advance. —*v.t.* **2.** defend or shut off with a barricade.

băr'rĭ·êr, *n.* obstruction.

bàr'rĭng, *prep.* excepting; aside from.

băr'rōw, *n.* **1.** hand-held frame for carrying loads. **2.** wheelbarrow.

bâr'têr, *n., v.t., v.i.* trade with goods or services alone.

ba·sält', *n.* dark volcanic rock. —**ba·sal'tic,** *adj.*

bāse, *n., v.t.,* **based, basing,** *adj. n.* **1.** part on which a thing rests or stands. **2.** basis. **3.** principal ingredient. **4.** center of military operations. —*v.t.* **5.** give a basis or foundation to. —*adj.* **6.** contemptible. **7.** inferior, as a metal. —**base'ly,** *adv.* —**base'ness,** *n.*

bāse'bǎll'', *n.* **1.** game played in a diamond-shaped field with a batted ball. **2.** ball used in this game.

bāse'lĕss, *adj.* unfounded in fact.

bāse'mėnt, *n.* **1.** lowermost part of a building. **2.** cellar.

băsh, *v.t. Informal.* hit, as with a club.

băsh'fŭl, *adj.* shy. —**bash'ful·ly,** *adv.* —**bash'ful·ness,** *n.*

bās'ĭc, *adj.* **1.** most important or significant; essential. —*n.* **2. basics,** most important or significant features. —**bas'i·cal·ly,** *adv.*

bās'il, *n.* herb of the mint family.

bā'sĭn, *n.* **1.** shallow bowl for liquids. **2.** pool. **3.** area drained by a river.

bā'sĭs, *n., pl.* **-ses. 1.** something on which a thing depends. **2.** main ingredient.

băsk, *v.i.* **1.** lie in warmth. **2.** enjoy favor, etc.

băs'kėt, *n.* container of woven wood, wire, etc.

băs'kėt·bǎll'', *n.* **1.** game in which a ball is tossed over a hoop into a suspended net. **2.** ball used in this game.

bāss, *n.* **1.** lowermost musical range. **2.** singer, instrument, or part with this range. **3. băss,** *pl.* **basses, bass.** spiny-finned edible fish.

băs''sĭ·nĕt', *n.* basketlike bed for a baby.

bàs·sōōn', *n.* bass woodwind. —**bas·soon'ist,** *n.*

băs'tàrd, *n.* **1.** person born out of wedlock. **2.** *Informal.* harsh or malicious person. —*adj.* **3.** born out of wedlock. **4.** not authentic. —**bas'tard·y,** *n.*

bāste, *v.t.,* **basted, basting. 1.** sew temporarily. **2.** cover with juices, etc. while cooking. —**bast'ing,** *n.*

băt, *n., v.,* **batted, batting.** *n.* **1.** club used for striking a ball, as in baseball or cricket. **2.** nocturnal flying mammal. —*v.t.* **3.** hit with a bat. —*v.i.* **4.** have a turn batting.

bătch, *n.* quantity of material prepared or gathered at one time.

băth, *n., pl.* **baths. 1.** complete washing or immersion. **2.** liquid for immersion or washing. —**bath'room'',** *n.* —**bath'tub'',** *n.*

bāthe, *n.,* **bathed, bathing.** *v.i.* **1.** take a bath. **2.** go swimming, esp. in an ocean or lake. —*v.t.* **3.** give a bath to. —**bath'er,** *n.*

bā'thŏs, *n.* **1.** ridiculous anticlimax. **2.** insincere sentimentality.

băth'rōbe, *n.* robe used before and after bathing.

ba·tŏn', *n.* staff used for directing musicians, as a badge of office, etc.

băt·tăl'ión, *n*. subdivision of a military division.

băt'tèn, *n*. **1.** thin strip of wood. —*v.t.* **2.** secure or cover with battens. —*v.i.* **3.** thrive.

băt'têr, *v.t.* **1.** hit or attack repeatedly. —*n*. **2.** person who bats. **3.** cake mixture.

băt'têr·ў, *n., pl.* -ies. *n*. **1.** device for storing electricity. **2.** group of cannons used together. **3.** group of any machines, etc. used together. **4.** *Law.* illegal beating.

băt'tĭng, *n*. fiber packed in sheets.

băt'tle, *n., v.,* -tled, -tling. *n*. **1.** major military encounter. **2.** warfare. —*v.t., v.i.* **3.** fight. —bat'tle·field'', *n*.

băt'tle·mėnt'', *n*. defensive wall with openings for shooting.

băt'tle·shĭp'', *n*. warship with heavy guns and armor.

bäu'ble, *n*. trinket.

bäwd'ў, *adj.,* -ier, -iest. obscene. —bawd'i·ness, *n*.

bäwl, *v.i.* **1.** yell. **2.** weep loudly.

bāy, *n*. **1.** distinct area of a wall. **2.** broad inlet, esp. of a sea. **3. at bay, a.** unable to escape. **b.** unable to attack. —*v.i.* **4.** give prolonged howls.

bāy'ò·nĕt'', *n., v.t.,* -netted, -netting. *n*. **1.** sharp thrusting weapon attached to a gun muzzle. —*v.t.* **2.** stab with a bayonet.

baŷ'oū, *n*. marshy area of a river or lake, esp. in Louisiana.

bāy wĭndōw, *n*. window jutting from a building, esp. a window with its own foundations.

bà·zäar', *n*. **1.** Near Eastern salesplace. **2.** temporary sale, esp. for charity.

bē, *v.i.,* was or were, been, being. **1.** exist: often refers to an adjective describing the subject. **2.** occur. **3.** continue. **4.** (Used variously as an auxiliary verb).

bēach, *n*. **1.** flat shore, esp. a sandy one. —*v.t.* **2.** haul onto a beach.

bēach'cōmb''êr, *n*. seaside scavenger.

bēa'còn, *n*. **1.** signal light. **2.** navigational radio station.

bēad, *n*. **1.** small decorative ball. **2.** small drop. **3. draw a bead on,** take aim at.

bēad'ў, *adj.,* -ier, -iest. beadlike; small and shiny.

bēak, *n*. **1.** pointed mouth, esp. of a bird. **2.** projection suggesting this.

bēam, *n*. **1.** horizontal structural member. **2.** shaft of light. **3.** steady radio or radar signal. **4.** width of a ship. —*v.t.* **5.** send as a radio or radar beam. —*v.i.* **6.** shine. **7.** smile kindly.

bēan, *n*. any of various edible seeds.

bēar, *v.t.* **1.** carry. **2.** endure. **3.** suffer. **4.** give birth to. **5.** produce. —*v.i.* **6.** head or move in a stated direction. **7. bear with,** be patient with. —*n*. **8.** large shaggy mammal. **9.** speculator in the fall of stock prices. —bear'er, *n*. —bear'a·ble, *adj*.

bēard, *n*. **1.** hair on the lower jaw, etc. —*v.t.* **2.** intrude upon and confront. —beard'ed, *adj*.

bēar'ĭng, *n*. **1.** posture or attitude. **2.** support for a rotating part. **3. bearings,** orientation.

bēast, *n*. **1.** large animal. **2.** cruel or uncouth person.

bēast'lў, *adj.,* -lier, -liest. nasty. —beast'li·ness, *n*.

bēat, *v.,* beat, beaten, beating, *n. v.t.* **1.** hit with force. **2.** win against. **3.** move vigorously back and forth, as arms or wings. —*v.i.* **4.** throb, as the heart. —*n*. **5.** marked rhythm. **6.** unit of such a rhythm. **7.** regular round, as that of a policeman.

bē''à·tĭf'ĭc, *adj*. **1.** blissful. **2.** imparting blessings.

bēat'ĭng, *n*. **1.** act or instance of hitting, esp. a person or animal. **2.** defeat.

beau, *n., pl.* beaus, beaux. suitor.

beaū'tĭ·fŭl, *adj*. having beauty. Also, beau'te·ous. —beau'ti·ful·ly, *adv*.

beaū'tĭ·fŷ'', *v.t.,* -fied, -fying. make beautiful. —beau''ti·fi·ca'tion, *n*.

beaū'tў, *n., pl.* -ties. **1.** quality sensed in that which is in perfect harmony. **2.** beautiful woman.

bēa'vêr, *n*. broad-tailed, dam-building rodent.

bè·câlm', *v.t.* halt from a lack of wind in sails.

bè·cāuse', *conj*. **1.** for the reason that. **2. because of,** as a result of.

bĕck'ón, *v.i.* **1.** make a summoning gesture. —*v.t.* **2.** summon with a gesture.

bè·còme', *v.,* -came, -come, -coming. *v.i.* **1.** come to be as specified. —*v.t.* **2.** be suitable to.

bė·cóm′ĭng, *adj.* **1.** suitable; seemly. **2.** attractively appropriate, as clothing. —be·com′ing·ly, *adv.*

bĕd, *n.*, *v.*, **bedded, bedding.** *n.* **1.** object to lie upon. **2. to bed,** to rest in a lying position. **3. into bed,** beneath the upper bedclothes of a bed. **4.** layer of rock, etc. **5.** layer of surface soil, as for flowers. **6.** foundation for machinery. **7.** bottom of a body of water. —*v.t.* **8.** put into a bed. —*v.i.* **9.** go to or into bed. —bed′cov′′er, *n.* —bed′fel′′low, *n.* —bed′room′′, *n.* —bed′side′′, *n.*, *adj.* —bed′spread′′, *n.* —bed′spring′′, *n.* —bed′time′′, *n.*

bė·dăz′zle, *v.t.*, -zled, -zling. dazzle; amaze.

bĕd′clōthes′′, *n. pl.* sheets, covers, etc. for a bed.

bĕd′dĭng, *n.* all movable objects used with a bed.

bė·dĕv′ĭl, *v.t.*, -iled, -iling. harass; torment. —be·dev′il·ment, *n.*

bĕd′lăm, *n.* chaotic situation.

bė′′drăg′gle, *v.t.*, -gled, -gling. soil as by dragging through mud.

bĕd′rĭd′′dèn, *adj.* confined to bed by permanent illness or feebleness. Also, **bed′fast′′.**

bĕd′rŏck′′, *n.* uppermost layer of solid rock.

bĕd′stĕad′′, *n.* framework for bedding.

bēe, *n.* **1.** four-winged, pollen-gathering insect. **2.** social meeting for joint work or competition. —bee′hive′′, *n.* —bee′keep′′er, *n.* —bee′keep′′ing, *n.* —bees′wax′′, *n.*

bēech, *n.* hardwood tree.

bēef, *n.*, *pl.* **beeves** or **beefs. 1.** meat from cows, steers, etc. **2.** any such animal. —beef′steak′′, *n.*

bēef′′ÿ, *adj.*, -ier, -iest. muscular; brawny.

bēe′līne′′, *n.* straight route.

bēer, *n.* **1.** drink of fermented malt, hops, etc. **2.** any of various soft drinks made from plants.

bēet, *n.* plant with an edible root.

bēet′le, *n.* **1.** insect with hard wings. **2.** large mallet. —*adj.* **3.** Also, **beet′ling.** overhanging. —bee′tle-browed′′, *adj.*

bė·fäll′, *v.i.*, -fell, -fallen. happen.

bė·fĭt′, *v.t.*, -fitted, -fitting. be suitable to. —be·fit′ting, *adj.* —be·fit′ting·ly, *adv.*

bė·fôre′, *prep.* **1.** at an earlier time than. **2.** in front of. **3.** in preference to. —*adv.* **4.** at an earlier time. **5.** in front. —*conj.* **6.** earlier than the time that something happens. **7.** rather than.

bė·fôre′hănd′′, *adv.* **1.** in advance. —*adj.* **2.** ahead of time.

bė·fōul′, *v.t.* make foul.

bė·friĕnd′, *v.t.* act as a friend to.

bĕg, *v.*, **begged, begging.** *v.t.*, *v.i.* ask as a favor.

bĕg′gàr, *n.* **1.** person who asks strangers for his livelihood. —*v.t.* **2.** impoverish. **3.** render inadequate, esp. any description of a thing. —beg′gar·y, *n.*

bĕg′gàr·lÿ, *adj.* miserably inadequate.

bė·gĭn′, *v.*, **began, begun,** *v.t.*, *v.i.* start, commence. —be·gin′ning, *n.*

bė·gĭn′nêr, *n.* **1.** person who begins. **2.** completely inexperienced person.

bė·grŭdge′, *v.t.*, -grudged, -grudging. resent another's having or receiving. —be·grudg′ing·ly, *adv.*

bė·guīle′, *v.t.*, -guiled, -guiling. **1.** charm. **2.** while away pleasantly. —be·guile′ment, *n.*

bė·hälf′, *n.* in or **on behalf of, a.** in the name of. **b.** in support of.

bė·hāve, *v.*, -haved, -having. *v.i.* **1.** conduct oneself properly —*v.t.* **2.** conduct in a specified way. **3.** conduct properly. —be·hav′ior, *n.*

bė·hĕst′, *n.* command; urging.

bė·hīnd, *prep.* **1.** at the rear of. **2.** at or to the far side of. **3.** too late or slow for. **4.** in defense or support of. **5.** concealed by. —*adv.* **6.** at the rear. **7.** into a state of lateness or slowness.

bė·hōld′, *v.t.*, -held, -holding. see; look at. —be·hold′er, *n.*

bė·hŏld′ĕn, *adj.* indebted.

bė·hōōve′, *v.t.*, -hooved, -hooving. obligate.

bē′ĭng, *n.* **1.** existence. **2.** essential nature. **3.** something alive.

bė·lā′bör, *v.t.* attack by or as if by beating.

bė·lāt′ĕd, *adj.* later than expected or desirable. —be·lat′ed·ly, *adv.*

bĕlch, *v.i.* **1.** emit stomach gas through the mouth. *v.t.* **2.** emit violently, as smoke. —*n.* **3.** act or instance of belching.

bė·lēa′guêr, *v.t.* harass, as by a siege.

běl·frў, *n., pl.* **-fries.** tower or turret for bells.

bè·līe', *v.t.,* **-lied, -lying. 1.** represent deceptively. **2.** prove as false.

bè·līēve', *v.,* **-lieved, -lieving.** *v.t.* **1.** accept as true or truthful. **2.** guess to be so. —*v.i.* **3.** have faith. **4.** accept the existence of something. —**be·lief',** *n.* —**be·liev'er,** *n.* —**be·liev'able,** *adj.*

bè·līt'tle, *v.t.,* **-tled, -tling.** treat as of minor importance. —**be·lit'tle·ment,** *n.*

běll, *n.* **1.** hollow instrument, usually metal, that sounds when struck. **2.** something having the characteristic flared shape of this. **3.** *Nautical.* half-hour unit of time.

bělle, *n.* attractive woman.

bělles''lět'très, *n. pl.* literature as an art.

běl'lĭ·cōse'', *adj.* warlike. —**bel'li·cos''i·ty,** *n.*

běl·lĭg'êr·ėnt, *adj.* **1.** eager to fight. **2.** at war. —*n.* **3.** nation, etc. at war. —**bel·lig'er·ence, bel'lig'er·en·cy,** *n.*

běl'lōw, *v.t., n.* **1.** shout or roar. *n.* **2.** **bellows,** device for pumping air to a hearth.

běl'lў, *n., pl.* **-lies,** *v.i.,* **-lied, lying.** *n.* **1.** stomach. **2.** human abdomen. **3.** animal's underside. —*v.i.* **4.** swell.

bè·lŏng', *v.i.* **1.** be property. **2.** be a member, citizen, etc. of something. **3.** be appropriate.

bè·lŏng'ĭngs, *n., pl.* possessions.

bè·lŏv'ėd, *adj.* **1.** loved. —*n.* **2.** loved one.

bè·lōw, *prep.* **1.** lower than; under. **2.** inferior in worth or amount to. —*adv., adj.* **3.** to or in some lower place. **4.** later, as in a book. **5.** *Nautical.* on or to a lower deck.

bělt, *n.* **1.** strap worn around the waist, over the chest, etc. **2.** long, narrow region, road, etc. **3.** strap for driving machinery. **4.** *Informal.* **a.** hit violently. **b.** sing emphatically.

bè·mōan', *v.t.* lament.

bè·mūse', *v.t.,* **-mused, -musing.** put in a thoughtful or bewildered frame of mind.

běnch, *n.* **1.** broad seat or stool. **2.** massive worktable. **3.** judge's seat. **4. the bench,** jurisprudence. —*v.t.* **5.** put on a bench.

běnd, *v.,* **bent, bending,** *n.* *v.t.* **1.** form as a curved or angled shape, esp. by force. **2.** bow or stoop. **3.** submit oneself. —*n.* **4.** bent section. **5.** curve, as in a road or river.

bè·nēath', *prep.* **1.** under. **2.** unworthy of. —*adj., adv.* **3.** underneath.

běn'ė·dĭc'tion, *n.* blessing.

běn''ė·făc'tion, *n.* act or instance of charity.

běn''ė·făc''tör, *n.* conferrer of benefactions. Also, *fem.,* **ben'e·fac''tress.**

bè·něf'ĭ·cėnt, *adj.* doing good. —**be·nef'i·cence,** *n.* —**be·nef'i·cent·ly,** *adv.*

běn''ė·fī'ciȧl, *adj.* useful; advantageous. —**be''ne·fi'cial·ly,** *adv.*

běn''ė·fī'cī·ār·ў, *n., pl.* **-aries.** enjoyer of a benefit.

běn'ė·fĭt, *n., v.t.,* **-fitted, -fitting.** *n.* **1.** advantage. **2.** entertainment to raise funds for charity, etc. **3.** payment from insurance, etc. —*v.t.* **4.** be of advantage to.

bè·něv'ȯ·lėnt, *adj.* kindly; well-intentioned. —**be·nev'o·lent·ly,** *adv.* —**be·nev'o·lence,** *n.*

bè·nīght'ėd, *adj.* **1.** lacking enlightenment. **2.** hampered or surrounded by darkness.

bè·nīgn', *adj.* **1.** friendly; well-intentioned. **2.** *Medicine.* not malignant. —**be·nign'ly,** *adv.* —**be·nig'ni·ty,** *n.*

bè·nĭg'nȧnt, *adj.* **1.** benevolent. **2.** beneficial.

bè·quēath', *v.t.* transfer to heirs. —**be·quest',** *n.*

bè·rāte', *v.t.,* **-rated, -rating.** scold.

bè·rēave', *v.t.,* **-reft, -reaving. 1.** leave sorrowful, esp. by dying. **2.** deprive; strip. —**be·reave'ment,** *n.*

bè·ret', *n.* soft, flat, visorless cloth cap.

bêrm, *n.* earth embankment. Also, **berme.**

běr'rў, *n., pl.* **-ies. 1.** juicy cover for a seed or seeds. **2.** dried seed of a coffee plant, etc.

bêr·sêrk', *adv., adj.* in violent frenzy.

bêrth, *n.* **1.** shelflike bed. **2.** job. **3.** ship's mooring place.

bêr·ўl, *n.* class of hard stone: includes emeralds and aquamarines.

bè·sēech', *v.t.,* **-sought,** or **-seeched, seeching.** request earnestly. —**be·seech'ing·ly,** *adv.*

bė·sĕt', *v.t.*, -set, -setting. harass.

bė·sĕt'tĭng, *adj.* obsessive, as a sin.

bė·sīde', *prep.* 1. at the side of. 2. compared with. 3. added to. 4. irrelevant to.

bė·sīdes', *adv.* 1. in addition; else. —*prep.* 2. in addition to; other than.

bė·sīēge', *v.t.*, -sieged, -sieging. 1. lay siege to. 2. distract repeatedly.

bė·smîrch', *v.t.* mark or soil.

bė·spēak', *v.t.*, -spoke, -spoken or -spoke, -speaking. 1. speak for ahead of time; reserve. 2. be eloquent of; reveal.

bĕst, *adj.* 1. superlative of *good*. 2. major; greater. —*adv.* 3. superlative of *well*. 4. that which is best. 5. one's utmost.

bĕs'tĭ·ăl, *adj.* savage. —bes''ti·al'i·ty, *n.*

bė·stîr', *v.t.*, -stirred, -stirring. rouse to action.

bĕst măn, groom's ring bearer at a wedding.

bė·stōw, *v.t.* give or grant. —be·stow'al, *n.*

bĕt, *n.*, *v.*, betted, betting. *n.* 1. guess on the unpredictable outcome of an event, made to gain money, etc. 2. money, etc. put up to back one's guess. 3. possible guess or action regarding an unpredictable matter. —*v.t.* 4. put up to back one's bet. 5. guess in betting. —*v.i.* 6. make a bet.

bė·trāy', *v.t.* 1. be treacherous to. 2. reveal, as a secret. 3. seduce with a false promise of marriage. 4. reveal involuntarily. —be·tray'al, *n.*

bė·trŏth'ăl, *n.* engagement to marry.

bė·trŏthed', *n.* fiancé or fiancée.

bĕt'têr, *adj.* 1. comparative of *good*. 2. major; greater. —*adv.* 3. comparative of *well*. —*n.* 4. social superior. 5. that which is better. 6. Also, bet'tor, person who bets.

bĕt'têr·mĕnt, *n.* improvement.

bė·twēen', *prep.* 1. with two specified persons or things, one on each side. 2. involving or relating two persons or things. 3. as a result of two specified causes. 4. from either one of, in choosing. 5. as a secret shared by two persons.

bĕv'ĕl, *n.* 1. outer edge formed as a diagonal. —*v.t.* 2. form as such a diagonal.

bĕv'êr·ăge, *n.* something to drink other than water.

bė·wāre', *v.*, *v.i.* 1. be cautious. —*v.t.* 2. be cautious of.

bė·wĭl'dêr, *v.t.* confuse, esp. with surprise. —be·wil'der·ment, *n.*

bė·wĭtch', *v.t.* 1. cast a spell on. 2. charm with delight.

bė·yŏnd', *prep.* 1. on the far side of. 2. too late or advanced for. 3. outside the power or domain of. 4. after; past. —*adv.* 5. further away.

bī·ăn'nū·ăl, *adj.* twice a year. —bi·an'nu·al·ly, *adv.*

bĭb, *n.* apronlike cloth to catch dribbles.

bĭb''lī·ŏg'rà·phÿ, *n.*, *pl.* -phies. list of books, articles, etc. used, recommended, or in existence. —bib''li·og'ra·pher, *n.* —bib''li·o·graph'i·cal, *adj.*

bĭb'ū·loŭs, *adj.* fond of alcoholic beverages.

bī·căm'êr·ăl, *adj.* composed of two legislative chambers.

bĭck'êr, *v.i.* quarrel about trifles. —bick'er·er, *n.*

bī'cÿ·cle, *n.* two-wheeled vehicle for a balancing rider. —bi'cy·clist, bi'cy·cler, *n.*

bĭd, *n.*, *v.*, bid or (for 4 and 6) bade, bid or (for 4 and 6) bidden, bidding. *n.* 1. offer for an auctioned item. 2. offer to fulfill a contract for a stated sum. 3. attempt to gain victory, favor, notice, etc. —*v.t.* 4. command or ask. 5. offer for an auctioned item. 6. express, esp. a good-bye. —*v.i.* 7. make a bid. —bid'der, *n.*

bier, *n.* support for a coffin.

bī'fō''cäls, *n.* *pl.* spectacles whose lenses have two areas apiece, each with two focuses.

bĭg, *adj.*, bigger, biggest. 1. great in size or amount. 2. full-grown. 3. elder. 4. important. —big'ness, *n.*

bĭg'à'mÿ, *n.* marriage to two spouses in a single period. —big'a·mous, *adj.* —big'a·mist, *n.*

bĭg'ŏt, *n.* person with strong, intolerant, unreasoning attitudes. —big'ot·ry, *n.* —big'ot·ed, *adj.*

bīke, *n. Informal.* bicycle.

bī·lăt'êr·ăl, *adj.* 1. involving two sides or factions. 2. reciprocal; mutual. —bi·lat'er·al·ly, *adv.*

bī·lĭn'guàl, *adj.* 1. familiar with two lan-

guages. **2.** expressed in two languages.
bĭl´iŏus, *adj*. ill-tempered.
bĭlk, *v.t*. cheat.
bĭll, *n*. **1.** itemized list or statement. **2.** written request for payment. **3.** printed announcement. **4.** piece of paper currency. **5.** beak of a bird. —*v.t*. request payment from in writing.
bĭll´bôard´´, *n*. large board for advertising posters.
bĭl´lĕt, *n*. **1.** job; position. **2.** order to house a soldier. **3.** accommodation obtained with such an order. —*v.t*. **4.** house with such an order.
bĭl´´lĕt-doūx´, *n*., *pl*. **billets-doux.** love letter.
bĭll´fōld´´, *n*. wallet.
bĭl´liȧrds, *n*. game using hard balls propelled by a cue.
bĭl´lĭng, *n*. public listing of entertainers on a program.
bĭl´´liŏn, *n*. **1.** *U.S.* thousand million. **2.** *Great Britain*. million million. —**bĭl´lionth,** *adj*.
bĭll ȯf fāre, menu.
bĭl´lōw, *n*. **1.** swelling mass, as of water or smoke. —*v.i*. **2.** appear in billows. —**bil´low·y,** *adj*.
bī·mȯnth´lў, *adj*. **1.** every two months. **2.** twice a month.
bĭn, *n*. large container for loose storage.
bī´´nā·rў, *adj*. of or pertaining to the mathematical base 2.
bīnd, *v.*, **bound, binding.** *v.t*. **1.** tie or fasten together. **2.** obligate. **3.** reinforce, as with tape. —*v.i*. **4.** stick fast or together. —**bind´er,** *n*. —**bind´ing,** *n*.
bĭn´nȧ·cle, *n*. housing for a ship's compass.
bĭn·ŏc´u·lȧr, *n*. **1.** **binoculars,** twin telescopelike glasses, one for each eye. —*adj*. **2.** pertaining to both eyes.
bī´´ō·chĕm´ĭs·trў, *n*. study of life processes as an aspect of chemistry.
bī´´ō·dė·grād´ȧble, *adj*. readily decomposed by bacteria.
bī·ŏg´rȧ·phў, *n.*, *pl*. **phies.** story of a person's life or career. —**bi´´o·graph´i·cal,** *adj*. —**bi·og´ra·pher,** *n*.
bī·ŏl´ȯ·gў, *n*. study of animals and plants. —**bi´´o·log´i·cal,** *adj*. —**bi·ol´o·gist,** *n*.
bī·ŏ´nĭcs, *n*. the study of living systems for application to mechanical or electronic systems.

bī´´ō·phўs´ĭcs, *n*. study of biological phenomena as related to physics. —**bi´´o·phys´i·cal,** *adj*. —**bi´´o·phys´i·cist,** *n*.
bī´pĕd, *n*. two-footed animal.
bîrch, *n*. hardwood tree with smooth bark.
bîrd, *n*. warm-blooded, feathered, flying animal.
bîrd's-eȳe, *adj*. taken from high above, as a view.
bîrth, *n*. **1.** emergence from a womb, egg, etc. **2.** heredity. **3.** origin or beginning —**birth´mark´´,** *n*. —**birth´place´´,** *n*. —**birth´rate´´,** *n*. —**birth´right´´,** *n*.
bîrth´dāy´´, *n*. anniversary of one's birth.
bĭs´cuĭt, *n.*, *pl*. **-cuits, -cuit. 1.** small hard-baked cookie or cracker. **2.** breadlike lump eaten esp. with gravy.
bī´sĕct, *v.t*. divide in two parts, esp. equal ones.
bĭsh´ȯp, *n*. **1.** clergyman overseeing a number of local churches or parishes. **2.** chessman moving diagonally an unlimited number of squares. —**bish´op·ric,** *n*.
bī´sȯn, *n*. shaggy, large North American mammal.
bĭt, *n*. **1.** small piece or amount. **2.** boring tool. **3.** metal mouthpiece for controlling a horse. **4.** (computers) one binary digit or piece of data.
bĭtch, *n*. **1.** female dog. **2.** *Informal*. disagreeable woman. —**bitch´y,** *adj*.
bīte, *v.*, **bit, bitten, biting,** *n*. *v.t*. **1.** close one's jaws firmly upon. **2.** cut or eat into. —*v.i*. **3.** make a biting motion. —*n*. **4.** wound from being bitten. **5.** snack. **6.** ability to wound or disturb one's feelings.
bīt´ĭng, *adj*. wounding to the feelings. **-bit´ing·ly,** *adv*.
bĭt´tĕr, *adj*. **1.** harsh-tasting. **2.** causing much suffering. **3.** extremely resentful. —**bit´ter·ly,** *adv*. —**bit´ter·ness,** *n*.
bĭt´tĕr·sweēt´´, *adj*. **1.** causing both sadness and pleasure. **2.** low-sugar chocolate.
bĭtūmĭnŏus cōal, soft coal, yielding tar when burned.
bī´vȧlve´´, *n*. mollusk with two hinged shells.
bĭv´ou̅·ȧc, *n.*, *v.i.*, **-acked, -acking.** *n*.

1. temporary encampment. —*v.i.* **2.** camp in a bivouac.

bī·wēek'lȳ, *adj., adv.* every two weeks.

bī·zârre', *adj.* odd; grotesque.

blăb, *v.,* blabbed, blabbing, *n. v.t., v.i.* **1.** reveal, as a secret. —*v.i., n.* **2.** chatter.

blăck, *n.* **1.** perfectly dark color, opposite to white in shading. **2.** something that is black, e.g. clothes. **3.** person of central African descent; negro. —*adj.* **4.** of the color black. **5.** negro. **6.** dejected or sullen. **7.** evil. —**black'ness,** *n.*

blăck'băll'', *v.t.* exclude or prevent from being a member.

blăck bĕlt, belt denoting highest skill in karate or judo.

blăck'bĕr''rȳ, *n., pl.* **ries.** dark berry of various types of bramble.

blăck'bîrd'', *n.* bird whose male has black plumage.

blăck'bōard'', *n.* board of slate or other material for writing on with chalk.

blăck'ĕn, *v.t.* **1.** make black. **2.** defame. —*v.i.* **3.** become black.

blăck eȳe, **1.** discoloration around the eye from a blow. **2.** something causing disrepute.

blăck'jăck'', *n.* **1.** small, flexible club. **2.** card game.

blăck'lĭst, *n.* **1.** list of persons out of favor. —*v.t.* **2.** put on such a list.

blăck'māil'', *n.* **1.** extortion by threats, esp. to reveal harmful information. —*v.t.* **2.** practice blackmail on. —**black'mail''er,** *n.*

blăck mârk, something unfavorable recorded against one.

blăck mârkĕt, unlawful system for selling legally restricted goods. —**black marketeer.**

blăck'ōut'', *n.* **1.** putting out of lights, as in a play or during an air raid. **2.** sudden loss of consciousness.

blăck shēep, disreputable member, esp. of a family.

blăck'smĭth'', *n.* person who forges iron by hand.

blăd'dêr, *n.* **1.** sac for collecting and discharging body fluids. **2.** any of various bags for air or liquid.

blāde, *n.* **1.** metal part with a cutting edge or point. **2.** leaf, esp. of grass.

blāme, *v.t.,* blamed, blaming, *n. v.t.* **1.** accuse for a fault. **2.** put the responsibility for on someone. **3.** fail to sympathize with or understand. —*n.* **4.** responsibility. —**blame'less,** *adj.* —**blame'less·ly,** *adv.* —**blame'less· ness,** *n.* —**blame'wor''thy,** *adj.*

blănch, *v.t., v.i.* **1.** turn pale or white. **2.** scald.

blăn'dĭsh, *v.t.* flatter or coax. —**blan' dish·ment,** *n.*

blănk, *adj.* **1.** free of marks, as paper. **2.** without thought, expression, etc. **3.** unmitigated. —*n.* **4.** blank piece of paper. **5.** blank space. **6.** cartridge without a missile. **7.** lapse of awareness. —**blank'ly,** *adv.* —**blank'ness,** *n.*

blănk'ĕt, *n.* **1.** warm bedcover. **2.** broad or thick cover. —*v.t.* **3.** cover or obscure, as if with a blanket. —*adv.* **4.** covering all or many possibilities.

blāre, *v.,* blared, blaring, *n. v.i., v.t.* **1.** sound loudly and harshly. —*n.* **2.** loud, harsh sound. **3.** ostentation.

blâr'nĕy, *n.* wheedling, flattering talk.

blă·sé', *adj.* bored from over-familiarity.

blăs·phēme', *v.t.,* -phemed, -pheming. speak sacrilegiously of. —**blas·phem'· er,** *n.* —**blas'phem·y,** *n.* —**blas'phem· ous,** *adj.*

blăst, *v.t.* **1.** shatter, as with lightning or explosives. **2.** criticize harshly. —*v.i.* **3.** blow violently. —*n.* **4.** explosion or explosive force. **5.** violent rush of air. **6.** loud sound, as on a trumpet.

blăst fûrnàce, furnace for smelting iron, using a blast of air for draft.

blăst'ŏff'', *n.* departure of a rocket.

blā'tànt, *adj.* shamelessly obvious. —**bla'tant·ly,** *adv.* —**bla'tan·cy,** *n.*

blāze, *v.,* blazed, blazing, *n. v.t.* **1.** indicate the route of, esp. by cutting the bark of trees. —*v.i.* **2.** burn brightly. —*n.* **3.** bright fire. **4.** brilliant display. **5.** cut made on tree bark in blazing a trail.

blāz'êr, *n.* jacket in a solid color, often with the badge of a school, etc.

blēach, *v.t., v.i.* **1.** make or become light in color. —*n.* **2.** something used for bleaching.

blēach'êrs, *n. pl.* tiers of benches for spectators.

blēak, *adj.* **1.** barren and gloomy. **2.** unpromising; without hope. —**bleak'ly,** *adv.* —**bleak'ness,** *n.*

blēar'ў, *adj.,* **-ier, -iest.** blurred, as the eyes.

blēat, *v.i.* **1.** utter a light cry, as a goat or calf. —*n.* **2.** cry made by such an animal.

blēed, *v.,* **bled, bleeding,** *v.i.* **1.** lose blood. **2.** feel sympathetic grief. —*v.t.* **3.** cause to lose blood. **4.** practice embezzlement or extortion upon.

blĕm'ĭsh, *n.* **1.** skin flaw. **2.** flaw or defacement. —*v.t.* **3.** make or form a blemish upon.

blĕnch, *v.i.* **1.** become pale. **2.** flinch.

blĕnd, *v.,* **blended, blending,** *n. v.t.* **1.** mix. **2.** shade into each other. —*v.i.* **3.** mix. **4.** harmonize. —*n.* **5.** mixture. —**blend'er,** *n.*

blĕss, *v.t.,* **blessed, blessing. 1.** invoke divine favor for. **2.** approve heartily. **3.** confer happiness upon. —**bles'sed,** *adj.* —**bles'sed·ly,** *adv.* —**bles'sed·ness,** *n.*

blĕs'sĭng, *n.* **1.** invocation of divine favor. **2.** approval. **3.** favorable event or circumstance.

blīght, *n.* **1.** plant disease. **2.** deterioration. **3.** source of deterioration. —*v.t.* **4.** put a blight on.

blĭmp, *n.* lighter-than-air vehicle without a rigid frame.

blīnd, *adj.* **1.** without eyesight. **2.** without perception. **3.** closed at the end or rear. **4.** hidden. **5.** beyond human reason or control. —*n.* **6.** device for shutting out light or view. **7.** deceptive ruse. —*v.t.* **8.** make blind. —**blind'ly,** *adv.* —**blind'ness,** *n.*

blīnd'fōld'', *n.* **1.** device to prevent a person temporarily from seeing. —*v.t.* **2.** put a blindfold on.

blĭnk, *v.i.* **1.** wink repeatedly. **2.** go on and off repeatedly, as a light. —*v.t.* **3.** cause to blink.

blĭss, *n.* intense, tranquil happiness. —**bliss'ful,** *adj.*

blĭs'têr, *n.* **1.** raised area of skin enclosing watery matter. **2.** anything similar in form. **3.** form blisters on. —*v.i.* **4.** become blistered.

blīthe, *adj.* cheerful. —**blithe'ly,** *adv.* —**blithe'ness,** *n.*

blĭtz, *n.* sudden, massive attack.

blĭz'zàrd, *n.* heavy storm of snow and wind.

blōat, *v.t.* swell abnormally.

blŏb, *n.* small, round form.

blŏc, *n.* group of organizations or persons united in a common interest.

blŏck, *n.* **1.** thick, short piece of material. **2.** auctioneer's platform. **3.** Also, **blockage,** obstruction. **4.** urban area bounded by streets. —*v.t.* **5.** obstruct.

blŏck·āde', *n., v.t.,* **-aded, -ading.** *n.* **1.** barrier to navigation, created by warships, etc. —*v.t.* **2.** impose such a barrier on.

blŏck'hĕad'', *n.* stupid person.

blŏck'hŏuse'', *n.* fortified retreat.

blŏnd, *adj.* **1.** having light hair and skin. —*n.* **2.** blond person. Also, *fem.,* **blonde.**

blŏod, *n.* **1.** fluid in the arteries of animals. **2.** lineage. **3.** temperament. **4.** kinship. **5.** bloodshed. —**blood'less,** *adj.*

blŏod'cûrd''lĭng, *adj.* horrifying.

blŏod'hŏund'', *n.* large hound tracking by scent.

blŏod'shĕd'', *n.* killing.

blŏod'shŏt'', *adj.* reddened from broken veins, as the eyes.

blŏod'thîrst''ў, *adj.* eager to kill. —**blood'thirst''i·ness,** *n.*

blŏod'ў, *adj.* **-ier, -iest. 1.** covered with blood. **2.** involving much bloodshed.

blōom, *v.i.* **1.** put forth flowers. **2.** be full of health or youth. —*n.* **3.** flower. **4.** period or state of flowering.

blŏs'sòm, *n.* **1.** flower, esp. of a fruit. —*v.i.* **2.** put forth blossoms.

blŏt, *n., v.,* **blotted, blotting.** *n.* **1.** stain, as from ink. **2.** something that mars or discredits. —*v.t.* **3.** stain. **4.** efface **5.** dry, as writing in ink. —*v.i.* **6.** make blots.

blŏtch, *n.* **1.** skin discoloration. —*v.t.* **2.** mark with blotches. —**blotch'y,** *adj.*

blŏt'têr, *n.* **1.** sheet for blotting up excess ink. **2.** log of events, esp. in a police station.

blŏuse, *n.* loose shirt.

blōw, *v.,* **blew, blown, blowing,** *n. v.i.* **1.** move, as wind. **2.** exhale with force. **3. blow over, a.** pass by, as a storm. **b.** cease to be troublesome, as a scandal. —*v.t.* **4.** drive with wind or breath. **5.** cause to sound with the breath, as a horn. **6. blow up, a.** inflate. **b.** explode. **c.** enlarge. —*n.* **7.** stroke, as with a fist or club. **8.** saddening shock. —**blow′er,** *n.*

blōw′ōut′′, *n.* rupture of an automobile tire.

blōw′tôrch′′, *n.* lamp for burning or melting.

blŭb′bèr, *n.* **1.** whale fat. —*v.i.* **2.** weep noisily. —**blub′ber·y,** *adj.* —**blub′ber·er,** *n.*

blŭd′geȯn, *n.* **1.** short club. —*v.t.* **2.** beat with a bludgeon. **3.** coerce.

blūe, *n.* **1.** primary color, that of a clear sky. **2. blues, a.** jazz tune with a slow tempo, and words, and a certain harmonic pattern. **b.** mental depression. —*adj.* **3.** of the color blue. **4.** sad.

blūe′bèr′′rÿ, *n., pl.* **-ries.** shrub with blue-black berries.

blūe′blȯod′′, *n.* person of distinguished ancestry. —**blue′blood′′ed,** *adj.*

blūe′-cȯl′làr, *adj.* pertaining to manual workers.

blūe′jāy′′, *n.* blue North American bird.

blūe lāw, law restricting commerce or recreation on a quasi-religious basis.

blūe′prĭnt′′, *n.* **1.** photographic reproduction of a measured drawing, appearing as white on blue. **2.** any plan or project. —*v.t.* **3.** reproduce or present as a blueprint.

blūe′stȯck′′ĭng, *n.* female pedant.

blŭff, *v.t.* **1.** deceive with an air of frankness or assurance. —*adj.* **2.** frank or abrupt in manner. **3.** rising steeply. —*n.* **4.** steep cliff or ridge. **5.** act or instance of bluffing.

blŭn′dȇr, *n.* **1.** avoidable error. —*v.i.* **2.** make such an error. **3.** move unthinkingly or awkwardly. —**blun′der·er,** *n.*

blŭnt, *adj.* **1.** with a dull edge. **2.** plainspoken. —*v.t.* **3.** dull the edge of. —**blunt′ly,** *adv.* —**blunt′ness,** *n.*

blûr, *v.,* **blurred, blurring,** *n. v.t.* **1.** cause to lose sharpness or clarity. —*v.i.* **2.** become indistinct. —*n.* **3.** something that blurs; smear. **4.** indistinct image or impression. —**blur′ry,** *adj.* —**blur′ri·ness,** *n.*

blûrt, *v.t.* say impulsively.

blŭsh, *v.i.* **1.** become red in the face with embarrassment or anger. **2.** be ashamed. —*n.* **3.** redness in the face. **4.** pink tone.

blŭs′tȇr, *v.i.* **1.** roar, as the wind. **2.** pretend rage, bravery, etc. —*n.* **3.** pretense

of rage, bravery, etc. —**blus′ter·er,** *n.*

bōar, *n.* **1.** ungelded male pig. **2.** wild hog.

bōard, *n.* **1.** long, flat piece of wood. **2.** sheet of fibrous material. **3.** meals as part of one's accommodations. **4.** administrative group. **5. on board,** on or onto a ship, airplane, train, etc. —*v.t.* **6.** go on or onto, as a ship. **7.** pay for the accommodations, with meals, of. —*v.i.* **8.** live as a boarder. —**board′er,** *n.*

bōardĭng hȯuse, house offering lodgings with board.

bōast, *v.i.* **1.** talk to excess about one's merits or accomplishments. —*n.* **2.** boasting remark. **3.** something boasted about. —**boast′er,** *n.* —**boast′ful,** *adj.* —**boast′ful·ly,** *adv.* —**boast′ful·ness,** *n.*

bōat, *n.* **1.** small vessel or craft. **2.** loosely, any ship. **3.** container with curved sides converging at the ends. —*v.i.* **4.** travel in a boat, esp. for recreation. —**boat′man,** *n.*

boat·swain, (bō′sun), *n.* petty officer in charge of a deck crew.

bŏb, *v.,* **bobbed, bobbing,** *n. v.t.* **1.** cut in a short hairdo. —*v.i.* **2.** sink, then rise again quickly. —*n.* **3.** short hairdo. **4.** quick sinking and rising movement. **5.** weight hung from a line or pendulum.

bŏb′slĕd′′, *n., v.i.,* **sledded, sledding.** *n.* **1.** long high-speed sled. —*v.i.* **2.** ride in such a sled.

bŏck, *n.* dark beer.

bōde, *v.t.,* **boded, boding. bode ill** or **well;** foretell bad or good events.

bŏd′ĭ·lÿ, *adj.* **1.** pertaining to the body. —*adv.* **2.** physically.

bŏd′ÿ, *n., pl.* **-ies.** *n.* **1.** physical part of a man or animal. **2.** corpse. **3.** part of a vehicle that encloses passengers or freight. **4.** distinct area of water or land. **5.** object in outer space. **6.** group or organization. **7.** richness or favor.

bŏd′ÿ·guârd′′, *n.* person or group protecting against attack.

bŏg, *n., v.* **bogged, bogging.** *n.* **1.** marshy or spongy area. —*v.t., v.i.* **2.** sink into a bog. **3.** slow or halt, as in accomplishing something. —**bog′gy,** *adj.*

bŏg′gle, *v.i.,* **-gled, -gling. 1.** overwhelmed. **2.** hesitate.

bō′gŭs, *adj.* false.

bo′gy·măn″, *n.*, *pl.* -men. imaginary demon. Also, bo′gey·man″.

boil, *v.t.* 1. heat in water that bubbles from being heated. 2. heat to bubbling. —*v.i.* 3. be heated in either of these ways. 4. seethe, as with rage. —*n.* 5. enough heat for boiling. 6. inflamed, pus-filled swelling.

boil′êr, *n.* 1. container for boiling things. 2. container for making steam or heating water.

bois′têr·oŭs, *adj.* 1. rowdy. 2. stormy. —bois′ter·ous·ly, *adv.*

bōld, *adj.* 1. daring. 2. presumptuous. 3. conspicuous. —bold′ly, *adv.* —bold′ness, *n.*

bo·lō′gnä, *n.* smoked sausage.

bōl′stêr, *n.* 1. long pillow. —*v.t.* 2. prop up.

bōlt, *n.* 1. fastener with a thread; screw. 2. sliding device for securing a door, etc. 3. arrow for a crossbow. 4. stroke of lightning. 5. sudden dash. 6. roll, as of cloth. —*v.t.* 7. fasten or secure with a bolt. 8. swallow hastily. —*v.i.* 9. flee or start suddenly.

bŏmb, *n.* 1. explosive or incendiary device. —*v.t.* 2. destroy or attack with bombs.

bŏm·bärd′, *v.t.* 1. attack with bombs or shells. 2. direct atomic particles against the nuclei of. —bom·bard′ment, *n.*

bŏm″bàr·dïer′, *n.* person who bombs from an airplane.

bŏm′bäst, *n.* grandiose, empty language. —bom·bas′tic, *adj.*

bŏmb′êr, *n.* 1. military plane for dropping bombs. 2. person who plants bombs.

bŏmb′shĕll″, *n.* 1. bomb. 2. someone or something sensational.

bōnä fīde, in good faith.

bo·nän′zà, *n.* source of prosperity.

bŏn′bŏn″, *n.* piece of candy.

bŏnd, *n.* 1. something that binds. 2. business obligation. 3. certificate of money lent at interest to an organization. 4. monetary guarantee from a bailed prisoner, employee, etc.

bŏnd′àge, *n.* servitude.

bōne, *n.*, *v.t.*, boned, boning, *n.* 1. part of a skeleton. —*v.t.* 2. remove the bones from.

bŏn′fīre″, *n.* large outdoor fire.

bon mot (bâw″ mō′), *pl.* bons mots. witty or pithy remark.

bŏn′nĕt, *n.* woman's cloth hat with a chin strap.

bō′nŭs, *n.*, *pl.* -nuses. payment in addition to that customary.

bon voyage (bâw vwah yahj′) good journey; said to someone departing.

bŏn′ÿ, *adj.*, -ier, -iest. with bones much in evidence. —bon′i·ness, *n.*

bōō, *inter.*, *n.*, *pl.* boos, *v.t.*, booed, booing. *interj.*, *n.* 1. sound made to startle or show disapproval. —*v.t.* 2. disapprove of with boos.

bōō′bÿ, *n.*, *pl.* -bies. fool. Also, boob.

bŏŏk, *n.* 1. long piece of writing, etc., published or kept as a distinct entity. 2. major subdivision of such a piece. 3. libretto. 4. books, business accounts. 5. something suggesting a bound book in form. —*v.t.* 6. record. 7. make a reservation for. —book′bind″er, *n.* —book′bind″ing, *n.* —book′case″, *n.* —book′keep″er, *n.* —book′keep″ing, *n.* —book′let, *n.* —book′shelf″, *n.* —book′shop″, book′store″, *n.*

bŏŏk′ĕnd″, *n.* device for holding books upright on a shelf.

bŏŏk′māk″êr, *n.* person who takes bets. Also, *Informal*, book′ie.

bŏŏk′wŏrm, *n.* person fond of reading.

bōōm, *n.* 1. loud, deep, hollow sound. 2. spar hinged at one end. 3. flurry of business or industrial activity. —*v.i.* 4. make a booming noise. 5. enjoy a boom, as a town or industry.

bōōm′êr·ăng″, *n.* 1. Australian throwing stick that returns to the thrower. —*v.i.* 2. be harmful to the originator, as a plot.

bōōn, *n.* favor or blessing.

bōōn′dŏg″gle, *n.* piece of meaningless, contrived work.

bôor, *n.* uncouth person. —boor′ish, *adj.*

bōōst, *v.t.* 1. lift from below. 2. add to the power of. 3. speak in praise of. —*n.* 4. act or instance of boosting.

bōōt, *n.* 1. shoe with tall sides. —*n.*, *v.t.* 2. kick. —*v.t.* 3. (computers) to load operating system software.

bōōth, *n.* small shelter or enclosure.

bōōt′lĕg″, *v.*, -legged, -legging, *adj.* *v.t.* 1. make or sell unlawfully, esp. liquor. —*v.i.* 2. act as a bootlegger. —*adj.* 3, made or sold by bootleggers. —**boot′leg″ger**, *n*.

boo′ty̆, *n.*, *pl.* **-ties.** plunder; spoils.

booze, *n.*, *v.i.*, **boozed, boozing.** *Informal. n.* **1.** liquor. —*v.i.* **2.** drink liquor heavily.

bo′ră̆x, *n.* **1.** crystalline salt. **2.** *Informal.* cheap, showy furniture.

bôr′dêr, *n.* **1.** edge. **2.** special area along an edge. **3.** political boundary. —*v.t.* **4.** give a border to. **5.** adjoin the edge of. —*v.i.* **6. border on, a.** adjoin. **b.** nearly belong to. —**bor′der·land″**, *n.* —**bor′der·line″**, *n.*

bôre, *v.*, **bored, boring.** *n. v.t., v.i.* **1.** penetrate with a rotating movement. —*v.t.* **2.** dig by boring. **3.** weary by being uninteresting. **4.** cylindrical hollow, e.g. in the barrel of a cannon. **5.** uninteresting person or thing. **6.** petty annoyance. —**bore′dom**, *n.*

bŏr′ough, *n.* incorporated town.

bŏr′row, *v.t.* **1.** take and later return. **2.** take for use in one's own creative work. —**bor′row·er**, *n.*

bŏs′ŏm, *n.* **1.** human breast, esp. as the seat of emotion. **2.** midst.

bŏss, *n.* **1.** employer or manager. **2.** rounded projection. —*v.t.* **3.** *Informal.* order or control firmly.

bŏs′sy̆, *adj.*, *Informal.* domineering.

bo′sŭn, *n.* boatswain.

bŏt′à·ny̆, *n.* study of plants. —**bo·tan′i·cal, bo·tan′ic**, *adj.* —**bot′a·nist**, *n.*

bŏtch, *v.t.* **1.** ruin, as work. —*n.* **2.** clumsy or ineffectual work.

bŏth, *adj.*, *pron.* **1.** one and the other. —*conj.*, *adv.* **2.** equally.

bŏth′êr, *v.t.* **1.** annoy or worry. —*v.i.* **2.** take the trouble to do something. —*n.* **3.** source of annoyance or worry. —**both′er·some**, *adj.*

bŏt′tle, *n.*, *v.t.*, **-tled, -tling.** *n.* **1.** container, usually glass and with a stoppable narrow outlet, for liquids and gases. **2.** capacity of such a container, used as a measure. —*v.t.* **3.** put into a bottle. —**bot′tler**, *n.*

bŏt′tle·nĕck″, *n.* obstruction to a flow of work, traffic, water, etc.

bŏt′tŏm, *n.* **1.** lowermost part. **2.** ground under a body of water. **3.** cause or meaning. —**bot′tom·less**, *adj.*

bou·doir′, *n.* woman's private sitting room or bedroom.

bough, *n.* limb of a tree.

bouil·lŏn, *n.* clear broth.

boul·dêr, *n.* large, rounded stone.

boul·è·vârd″, *n.* major city street, often tree-lined.

bounce, *v.*, **bounced, bouncing.** *n. v.i.* **1.** jump in a new direction after striking a hard surface. —*v.t.* **2.** cause to jump in this way. —*n.* **3.** act or instance of bouncing. **4.** ability to bounce.

bound, *v.i.* **1.** jump. **2.** run with jumping steps. **3.** bounce. —*v.t.* **4.** adjoin or determine the boundaries of. —*n.* **5.** act or instance of jumping or bouncing. **6. bounds,** limits. —*adj.* **7.** tied or joined. **8.** obligated. **9.** certain. **10.** headed for a specified goal. —**bound′less**, *adj.*

bound′à·ry̆, *n.*, *pl.* **-ries.** border of an area of land.

bou·quet′, *n.* **1.** bunch or arrangement of flowers. **2.** aroma of wine.

bour·bŏn, *n.* American whiskey made from corn mash.

bour·geois (boor′zhwah), *n.*, *pl.* **-geois,** *adj. n.* **1.** member of the bourgeoisie. —*adj.* **2.** concerned with money, possessions, social conventions, etc. **3.** pertaining to the bourgeoisie.

bour·geoi·sie (boor″zhwah zē), *n.*, *sing.* or *pl.* social class of merchants, businessmen, professionals, clerks, etc.; middle class.

bout, *n.* **1.** fight or contest. **2.** period or spell.

bou·tique, *n.* small shop for fashionable goods.

bow (bō for 1–3, 6; bou for 4, 5, 7–9). *n.* **1.** springy length of wood for shooting arrows. **2.** length of wood for playing various stringed instruments. **3.** Also, **bow knot,** knot with two loops. **4.** front part of a ship, etc. **5.** forward bend of the upper body as a mark of respect or acceptance. —*v.t.* **6.** play with a bow. **7.** cause to stoop, as beneath a burden. —*v.i.* **8.** bend the upper body forward. **9.** agree or submit.

bŏw′ĕl, *n.* **1.** intestine. **2. bowels,** inner depths.

bōwl, *n.* **1.** deep, wide-topped container. —*v.t.* **2.** roll with an underhanded motion. **bowl′er**, *n.*

bōw′lĕg″gĕd, *adj.* with legs curved outward at the knees.

box 34

bŏx, *n.* **1.** container, usually rectangular and with a lid. **2.** compartment suggesting this in form. **3.** blow of the hand. —*v.t.* **4.** put into a box. **5.** have a fistfight with. —**box′er,** *n.*

bōy, *n.* young male. —**boy′hood′′,** *n.* —**boy′ish,** *adj.*

bōy′cŏtt, *n.* **1.** refusal to deal or associate with a person or persons in order to coerce them. —*v.t.* **2.** practice a boycott on.

brāce, *v.t.,* **braced, bracing,** *n.* *v.t.* **1.** stiffen. **2.** prepare for an emotional shock. **3.** stimulate. —*n.* **4.** stiffening device. **5.** pair. **6.** hand tool for drilling with a bit.

brāce′lĕt, *n.* decorative armband.

brăck′ĕt, *n.* **1.** brace for a corner. **2.** horizontally projecting support. **3.** classification —*v.t.* **4.** support with brackets.

brăd, *n.* thin, small-headed nail.

brăg, *v.i.,* **bragged, bragging,** *n.* *v.i.* **1.** boast. —*n.* **2.** boasting talk. —**brag′ger, brag′gart,** *n.*

brāid, *n.* **1.** interweaving of three strands of fiber. —*v.t.* **2.** make into a braid.

brāin, *n.* **1.** organ of thought, control of actions, etc. **2. brains, a.** intelligence. **b.** cleverness. —**brain′y,** *adj.*

brāin′stôrm, *n.* *Informal.* sudden idea or impulse.

brāin′wăsh′′, *v.t.* change the attitudes or beliefs of through psychological conditioning.

brāise, *v.t.,* **braised, braising.** brown, then simmer, esp. meat.

brāke, *n.,* *v.,* **braked, braking.** *n.* **1.** device for slowing or stopping machinery. —*v.t.,* *v.i.* **2.** slow down or stop with a brake.

brāke′măn, *n.* assistant to a railroad conductor.

brăm′ble, *n.* prickly shrub.

brăn, *n.* grain husks separated from flour in milling.

brănch, *n.* **1.** woodlike extension from the body of a tree, etc. **2.** anything derived or extending from a main body, system, etc. —*v.i.* **3.** put forth branches. **4.** extend as a branch.

brănd, *n.* **1.** identifying mark or symbol of a company's merchandise. **2.** merchandise so identified. **3.** identifying mark burned into hide or skin. **4.** piece

of burning wood. —*v.t.* **5.** put a brand on.

brăn′dĭsh, *v.t.* wave, as a sword or club.

brănd-nĕw, *adj.* wholly new.

brăn′dў, *n.,* *pl.* **-dies,** *v.t.,* **-died, -dying.** *n.* **1.** distilled grape or other wine. —*v.t.* **2.** preserve in brandy.

brăsh, *adj.* **1.** hot-headed. **2.** noisy and uncouth. —**brash′ness,** *n.*

brăss, *n.* **1.** alloy of copper and zinc. **2. brasses,** wind instruments of brass. **3.** *Informal.* high military officers.

brás·sière′, *n.* supporter for women's breasts.

brăt, *n.* ill-behaved child.

brá·vâ′dō, *n.* false courage or confidence.

brāve, *adj.,* *n.,* *v.t.,* **braved, braving.** *adj.* **1.** courageous. **2.** fine-looking. —*n.* **3.** American Indian warrior. —*v.t.* **4.** encounter defiantly. —**brave′ly,** *adv.* —**brav′er·y, brave′ness,** *n.*

brâ′vō, *interj.* well done!

brá·vū′rá, *n.* brilliance or daring.

brăwl, *v.i.* **1.** fight noisily. —*n.* **2.** noisy fight. —**brawl′er,** *n.*

brăwn, *n.* muscular strength. —**brawn′y,** *adj.*

brāy, *n.* **1.** cry of a donkey. —*v.i.* **2.** make this or a similar sound.

brā′zĕn, *adj.* **1.** made of brass. **2.** shameless. **3.** strident. —**bra′zen·ly,** *adv.* —**bra′zen·ness,** *n.*

brēach, *n.* **1.** opening broken through. **2.** violation. **3.** rift, as in a friendship. —*v.t.* **4.** make a breach in or through.

brĕad, *n.* **1.** food of baked flour, water, etc. **2.** livelihood. —*v.t.* **3.** coat before cooking with bread crumbs.

brĕadth, *n.* **1.** width. **2.** range, as of knowledge.

brĕad′wĭn′′nêr, *n.* sole support of a family.

breāk, *v.,* **broke, broken, breaking,** *n.* *v.t.* **1.** force to divide into pieces. **2.** put out of repair. **3.** terminate. **4.** violate. **5.** end of the effectiveness of. **6.** reduce in health, wealth, rank, etc. —*v.i.* **7.** force one's way. **8.** end a relationship. **9.** appear or begin suddenly. **10.** pause in activity. **11.** be broken. **12. break down, a.** fail in health or operation. **b.** abandon self-restraint. —*n.* **13.** act or instance of breaking. **14.** stroke of luck or mercy. **15.** pause in activity. **16.**

change. —**break′age,** n. —**break′a·ble,** adj.

break dănc·ĭng, n. style of dancing characterized by acrobatic spins and robotic movement.

break′dōwn′′, n. **1.** failure of health or operation. **2.** detailed analysis.

break′êr, n. **1.** wave that breaks on the shore. **2.** device or person that breaks.

brĕak′făst, n. morning meal.

break′nĕck′′, adj. reckless, as speed.

break′throūgh′′, n. **1.** act or instance of forcing a way against opposition. **2.** major accomplishment or discovery.

break′wâ′′têr, n. wall for breaking the force of waves.

brĕast, n. **1.** upper forward part of the body. **2.** this part regarded as the seat of emotions. **3.** female milk-secreting gland. —v.t. **4.** oppose or head into forcefully. —**breast′bone′′,** n. —**breast′-feed′′,** v.t.

brĕath, n. **1.** air going into and out of the lungs. **2.** manner of breathing. **3.** ability to breathe readily. —**breath′less,** adj. —**breath′less·ly,** adv. —**breath′y,** adj.

brĕathe, v., **breathed, breathing.** v.i. **1.** move air into and out of the lungs. —v.t. **2.** speak or sing, esp. quietly.

brĕath′tāk′′ĭng, adj. astonishing or exciting.

brēech, n. **1.** buttocks. **2.** loaded end of a gun. **3. breeches,** trousers.

brēed, v., **bred, breeding,** n. v.t. **1.** give birth to. **2.** raise, as animals. **3.** be a source of. —v.i. **4.** give birth to offspring. **5.** emerge or proliferate. —n. **6.** strain, as of animals. **7.** type, esp. of person. —**breed′er,** n.

brēed′ĭng, n. **1.** act of one who breeds. **2.** manners or character.

brēeze, n., v.i., **breezed, breezing.** n. **1.** light wind. —v.i. **2.** become a breeze. **3.** move briskly or jauntily. —**breez′y,** adj.

brĕth′rĕn, n. Archaic. **1.** brothers. **2.** monks.

brĕv′ĭ·tў, n. briefness.

brēw, v.t. **1.** make by fermenting malt and hops, as beer. **2.** make by any of various means, as beverages or other liquids. **3.** plot. —v.i. **4.** begin to appear or take shape. —n. **5.** something brewed. —**brew′er,** n.

brēw′êr·ў, n., pl. **-ies.** place for brewing malt beverages.

brīár, n. brier.

brībe, v.t., **bribed, bribing,** n. v.t. **1.** pay to abuse a position of trust. —n. **2.** payment offered for this. —**brib′er·y,** n.

brĭc′-à-brăc′′, n. miscellaneous decorative objects.

brĭck, n. **1.** oblong object of baked or unbaked clay, etc., used in construction. **2.** oblong object of any material. —v.t. **3.** enclose or cover with brickwork. —**brick′lay′′er,** n. —**brick′work′′,** n.

brīde, n. woman at the time of her wedding. —**brid′al,** adj. —**brides′maid′′,** n.

brīde′grōōm′′, n. man at the time of his wedding.

brĭdge, n., v.t., **bridged, bridging.** n. **1.** structure for crossing a stream, valley, etc. **2.** any of various connecting structures, etc. **3.** control post of a ship. **4.** card game for four players. —v.t. **5.** cross with or as with a bridge.

brĭdge′hĕad′′, n. fortified position of invaders.

brī′dle, n., v.t., **-dled, -dling.** n. **1.** harness for a horse's head. **2.** means of restraint. —v.t. **3.** put a bridle on. **4.** restrain.

brĭef, adj. **1.** short or concise. —n. **2.** legal summary —v.t. **3.** supply with useful information. —**brief′ly,** adv. —**brief′ness,** n. —**brief′ing,** n.

brĭef′cāse, n. handle-held case for business papers.

brī′êr, n. thorny bush.

brĭg, n. **1.** two-masted square-rigged ship. **2.** navy or marine position.

brĭ·gāde′, n. **1.** military unit formed of battalions. **2.** pseudo-military organization.

brĭg′à·dīer gĕnêrȧl, military officer between a colonel and a major general. Also, **brig′′a·dier′.**

brĭght, adj. **1.** shedding or reflecting much light. **2.** intelligent or mentally active. **3.** cheerful. **4.** promising. —**bright′ly,** adv. —**bright′ness,** n. —**bright′en,** v.t., v.i.

brĭl′liȧnt, adj. very bright. —**bril′liant·ly,** adv. —**bril′liance, bril′lian·cy,** n.

brĭm, n., v.i., **brimmed, brimming.** n.

1. rim. —*v.i.* 2. run or run over with liquid.

brĭn′dled, *adj.* gray or tawny with darker spots. Also, **brin′dle.**

brīne, *n.* salty water.

brĭng, *v.t.,* **brought, bringing. 1.** carry or escort to a place. **2.** cause as a consequence. **3. bring about,** cause. **4. bring out,** make apparent. **5. bring up,** raise, as children.

brĭnk, *n.* edge or verge.

brĭsk, *adj.* **1.** lively or abrupt. **2.** forceful, as the wind. —**brisk′ly,** *adv.* —**brisk′ness,** *n.*

brĭs′kĕt, *n.* breast meat.

brĭs′tle, *n., v.i.,* **-tled, -tling.** *n.* **1.** stiff hair, as on a pig. **2.** fiber on the head of a brush. —*v.i.* **3.** stand up stiffly. **4.** be tense with annoyance, etc.

brĭt′tle, *adj.* easily shattered. —**brit′tle-ness,** *n.*

brōach, *v.t.* bring forth as a subject of discussion.

brôad, *adj.* **1.** wide. **2.** diverse. **3.** not strict. **4.** not detailed. —**broad′ly,** *adv.* —**broad′ness,** *n.* —**broad′en,** *v.t., v.i.*

brôad′căst′′, *v.t.,* **-cast,** or (for 1) **-casted, -casting,** *n. v.t.* **1.** send by radio or television. **2.** scatter widely. —*n.* **3.** radio or television program. —**broad′cast′′er,** *n.*

brôad′-mīnd′′ĕd, *adj.* not strict or opinionated. —**broad′′-mind′ed·ly,** *adv.* —**broad′′-mind′ed·ness,** *n.*

brō·chûre′′, *n.* pamphlet.

brōgue, *n.* Irish accent, esp. in speaking English.

brōĭl, *v.t.* cook with direct heat from a fire, etc. —**broil′er,** *n.*

brōke, *adj. Informal.* without money; bankrupt.

brŏk′ĕn, *adj.* **1.** past participle of *break,* used adjectivally. **2.** deprived of spirit, health, etc. **3.** badly pronounced, as by a foreigner. **4.** discontinuous. —**brok′en·ly,** *adv.*

brŏk′êr, *n.* agent for buying and selling. —**brok′er·age,** *n.*

brŏn′cō, *n., pl.* **-cos,** wild or half-wild horse of the West. Also, **bron′cho.**

brŏn′tò·saŭr′′ŭs, *n.* large herbivorous dinosaur.

brŏnze, *n., v.t.* **bronzed, bronzing.** *n.* **1.** alloy of copper and tin. **2.** reddish-brown. —*v.t.* **3.** color like or coat with bronze.

brōoch, *n.* large ornamental pin.

brōod, *n.* **1.** group of children or baby chickens. —*v.i.* **2.** worry or sulk at length.

brōok, *n.* **1.** small stream. —*v.t.* **2.** endure.

brōom, *n.* bundle of straws, etc. attached to a stick and used for sweeping. —**broom′stick′′,** *n.*

brŏth, *n.* soup from boiled meat.

brŏth′ĕl, *n.* house of prostitution.

brŏth′êr, *n.* **1.** son of one's father. **2.** fellow-human as an object of love, etc. **3.** fellow-member of a religious order, lodge, etc. —**broth′er·hood,** *n.* —**broth′er·ly,** *adj.*

brŏth′êr-ĭn-läw′′, *n., pl.* **broth′ers-in-law′′. 1.** brother of a spouse. **2.** husband of a sister or sister-in-law.

brŏw, *n.* **1.** eyebrow. **2.** forehead. **3.** edge of a cliff.

brŏw′bēat′′, *v.t.,* **-beat, -beaten, -beating.** bully.

brŏwn, *n.* **1.** color combining red, yellow, and black. —*v.t., v.i.* **2.** make or become brown.

brŏwse, *v.i.,* **browsed, browsing.** look idly through things for sale. —**brows′er,** *n.*

brūise, *v.,* **bruised, bruising,** *n. v.t.* **1.** injure the skin or surface of with a blow or pressure. **2.** hurt, as the feelings. —*v.i.* **3.** become bruised. —*n.* **4.** mark made by bruising.

brŭnch, *n. Informal.* meal part-breakfast, part-lunch.

brū·nĕt′, *n.* person with dark hair, esp. when with dark eyes. Also, *fem.,* **bru-nette′.**

brŭnt, *n.* shock or stress, as of an attack.

brŭsh, *n.* **1.** device for cleaning, painting, etc. consisting of bristles on a handle. **2.** act or instance of brushing. **3.** something suggesting a brush in form. **4.** Also, **brush′wood′′,** underbrush. —*v.t.* **5.** remove or apply with a brush. **6.** apply a brush to. **7.** graze lightly in passing.

brŭsh′ŏff′′, *n. Informal.* tactless act of dismissing or ignoring someone.

brŭsque, *adj.* abrupt in manner. —**brusque′ly,** *adv.* —**brusque′-ness,** *n.*

brū′tȧl, *adj*. extremely cruel or harsh. —**bru·tal′i·ty**, *n*.

brū′tȧl·īze, *v.t.*, **-ized, -izing. 1.** make brutal. **2.** treat brutally. —**bru″tal·i·za′tion**, *n*.

brūte, *adj*. **1.** beastlike, esp. in force or lack of intelligence. —*n*. **2.** beast. **3.** brutal person. —**brut′ish**, *adj*.

bŭb′ble, *n*., *v.i.*, **-bled, -bling.** *n*. **1.** void or body of gas surrounded by a liquid. **2.** something bubblelike in roundness and thinness. **3.** something insubstantial. —*v.i*. **4.** give off bubbles. —**bub′bly**, *adj*.

bŭc″cȧ·nēer′, *n*. pirate, esp. in the Caribbean Sea.

bŭck, *n*. **1.** grown male deer, goat, etc. **2.** act or instance of bucking. **3.** *Informal*. dollar. —*v.t*. **4.** oppose with force. —*v.i*. **5.** rear upward, as a horse.

bŭck′ĕt, *n*. open watertight container.

bŭck′le, *n*., *v*., **-led, -ling.** *n*. **1.** fastener for two ends of a belt, etc. —*v.t*. **2.** fasten with a buckle. **3.** cause to bulge or bend, as sheet metal. —*v.i*. **4.** bulge or bend.

bŭck′tōōth″, *n*. projecting front tooth. —**buck′toothed′**, *adj*.

bŭck′whēat″, *n*. wheat with triangular seeds.

bū·cŏl′ĭc, *adj*. pastoral; serene and countrylike.

bŭd, *n*., *v.i.*, **budded, budding.** *n*. **1.** swelling from which a flower, leaf, etc. grows. —*v.i*. **2.** put forth such swellings.

bŭdge, *v*., **budged, budging.** *v.t.*, *v.i.* move by or because of force.

bŭdg′ĕt, *n*. **1.** allotment of money, time, etc. for various purposes. —*v.t*. **2.** submit to a budget. —**budg′et·ar″y**, *adj*.

bŭff, *n*. **1.** dull tan color. —*v.t*. **2.** polish with a soft surface.

bŭf′fȧ·lō, *n*., *pl*. **-loes. 1.** any of various wild oxen. **2.** American bison.

bŭf′fêr, *n*. something that prevents or lessens the shocks of collision.

bŭf·fet′, *n*. **1.** sideboard. **2.** meal for eaters helping themselves.

bŭf·fōōn′, *n*. clownish person. —**buf·foon′er·y**, *n*.

bŭg, *n*., *v.t.*, **bugged, bug·ging.** *n*. **1.** insect. **2.** (computers) an error in programming. *v.t*. **3.** *Informal*. **a.** plant listening devices in. **b.** pester.

bŭg′gÿ, *n*., *pl*. **-gies. 1.** light one-horse carriage. **2.** baby carriage.

bū′gle, *n*. trumpetlike brass instrument. —**bu′gler**, *n*.

build, *v*., **built, building**, *n*. *v.t*. **1.** assemble, as a structure. **2.** found or base. **3.** bring into being or develop. —*v.i*. **4.** establish or base something. **5.** accumulate. —*n*. **6.** frame of the body. —**build′er**, *n*.

build′ing, *n*. habitable construction.

built′-ĭn′, *adj*. integral or inherent.

built′-ŭp′, *adj*. made from a number of parts.

bŭlb, *n*. **1.** any of various underground plant stems, roots, or buds. **2.** something swelling toward the end. —**bulb′ous**, *adj*.

bŭlge, *n*., *v.i.*, **bulged, bulging.** *n*. **1.** swelling. —*v.i*. **2.** swell.

bŭlk, *n*. **1.** size or weight. **2.** greater or principal part. —*v.i*. **3.** be massive or important. —*adj*. **4.** shipped without containers. —**bulk′y**, *adj*.

bŭll, *n*. **1.** male ox, elephant, etc. **2.** speculator in the rise of stock prices. **3.** papal decree. —**bul′lish**, *adj*.

bŭll′dŏg″, *n*. small, heavy-built fighting dog.

bŭll′dōze″, *v.t.*, **-dozed, -dozing. 1.** push or level earth. **2.** *Informal*. force with aggressiveness. —**bull′doz·er**, *n*.

bŭl′lĕt, *n*. pointed projectile from a firearm. —**bul′let-proof″**, *adj*.

bŭl′lė·tĭn, *n*. **1.** announcement, esp. of news. **2.** official publication.

bŭl′liŏn, *n*. ingots of precious metal.

bŭlls′eÿe″, *n*. **1.** center of a target. **2.** direct hit.

bŭl′lÿ, *n*., *pl*. **-lies**, *v.t.*, **-lied, -lying**, *n*. **1.** person who injures or threatens weaker persons. —*v.t*. **2.** act as a bully toward.

bŭl′wârk, *n*. defensive wall or barrier.

bŭm, *n*., *v*., **bummed, bumming.** *n*. **1.** poor person who refuses to work. —*v.i*. **2.** live as a bum. —*v.t*. **3.** obtain by begging.

bŭm′ble·bēe″, *n*. yellow-and-black bee.

bŭmp, *v.t*. **1.** collide with, esp. not violently. —*v.i*. **2.** move over a bumpy surface. **3.** bump into, **a.** collide with. **b.** *Informal*. meet by chance. —*n*. **4.** act or instance of bumping or of being bumped. **5.** surface unevenness or swelling. **—bump'y,** *adj.*

bŭmp'êr, *n.* **1.** device to receive the shock of collisions. **—***adj.* **2.** especially abundant, as a crop.

bŭmp'tioŭs, *adj.* annoyingly self-assertive. **—bump'tious·ly,** *adv.*

bŭn, *n.* small baked roll.

bŭnch, *n.* **1.** small cluster. **2.** *Informal.* group of persons. **—***v.t., v.i.* **3.** gather into a bunch.

bŭn'dle, *n., v.t.,* **-dled, -dling.** *n.* **1.** group of things bound or wrapped together. **—***v.t.* **2.** make into a bundle.

bŭn'gȧ·lōw'', *n.* one-storied cottage.

bŭn'gle, *v.,* **-gled, -gling,** *n. v.t., v.i.* **1.** do or act stupidly. **—***n.* **2.** act or instance of bungling. **—bun'gler,** *n.*

bŭn'iȯn, *n.* inflamed swelling at the joint of the big toe.

bŭnk, *n.* **1.** flat frame serving as a bed, esp. in barracks, camps, or ships. **2.** *Informal.* false statements. **—***v.i.* **3.** sleep in a bunk. **—bunk'house'',** *n.*

bŭnk'êr, *n.* **1.** storage space for coal, etc. **2.** underground shelter against bombs or shells.

bŭn'nў, *n., pl.* **-nies.** *Informal.* rabbit.

bŭn'tĭng, *n.* cloth for making flags or flaglike decorations.

bŭoў, *n.* **1.** floating signal or marker. **2.** life preserver. **—***v.t.* **3.** lift up, as the spirits. **4.** keep afloat.

bŭoў'ȧnt, *adj.* **1.** a tendency to float. **2.** cheerful or optimistic. **—buoy'an·cy,** *n.*

bŭr, *n.* **1.** seed capsule with sharp, clinging extensions. **2.** burr.

bŭr'dėn, *n.* **1.** heavy load. **2.** theme. **3.** chorus or refrain. **—***v.t.* **4.** put a load upon. **—bur'den·some,** *adj.*

bū'reau, *n., pl.* **-reaus, -reaux. 1.** official agency or department. **2.** chest of drawers.

bū·reâu·crȧ·cў, *n., pl.* **-cies. 1.** government by officials. **2.** government departments as a source of political power, obstruction to progress, etc. **—bu'reau·crat'',** *n.* **—bu''reau·crat'ic,** *adj.*

bŭr'glȧr, *n.* person who breaks into buildings, esp. to steal. **—bur'gla·ry,** *n.* **—bur'glar·ize'',** *v.t.*

bŭr'ï·ȧl, *n.* burying of the dead.

bŭr'lăp, *n.* coarse jute or hemp cloth.

bŭr·lĕsque', *n., v.t.,* **-lesqued, -lesquing.** *n.* **1.** sexually allusive vaudeville. **2.** satirical parody. **—***v.t.* **3.** make the subject of a burlesque.

bŭr'lў, *adj.,* **-lier, -liest.** big and strong. **—bur'li·ness,** *n.*

bûrn, *v.,* **burned** or **burnt, burning.** *v.t.* **1.** use as fuel. **2.** damage with heat. **3.** create or finish with fire or intense heat. **4.** damage with acids, etc. **—***v.i.* **5.** be on fire. **6.** give out light or heat. **7.** be damaged by heat. **8.** be full of eagerness or passion. **—***n.* **9.** burned place **—burn'a·ble,** *adj.*

bûrn'êr, *n.* device for applying intense heat.

bûr'nĭsh, *v.t.* rub to a polish.

bûrn''ōut, *n.* lethargy resulting from excess stress.

bûrp, *n., v.i. Informal.* **1.** belch **—***v.t.* **2.** cause to burp.

bûrr, *n.* **1.** rough edge on cut metal. **2.** rough trilling of the sound *r,* as by a Scot

bûr'rōw, *n.* **1.** hole of a digging animal. **—***v.i.* **2.** dig deep holes. **3.** hide in or as if in a burrow.

bûrst, *v.,* **burst, bursting,** *n. v.i.* **1.** be torn apart, as from pressure. **2.** make a sudden and vehement beginning into song, tears, etc. **—***v.t.* **3.** cause to be torn apart. **—***n.* **4.** act or instance of bursting. **5.** sudden show of energy. **6.** volley of shots.

bŭrў, *v.t.,* **-ied, -ying. 1.** put under earth or other material. **2.** entomb. **3.** put out of sight or notice. **4.** immerse, as in work.

bŭs, *n., pl.* **-es, -ses,** *v.t.,* **-ed** or **-sed, -ing** or **-sing.** *n.* **1.** vehicle for many passengers. **2.** (computers) a circuit for connecting two components. **—***v.t.* **3.** transport by bus.

bŭsh, *n.* **1.** low, spreading woody plant. **2.** land overgrown with bushes. **—bush'y,** *adj.*

bŭsh'ėl, *n.* dry measure of 4 pecks or 32 quarts.

bus'i·ly (bĭz'ĭ·lў), *adv.* in a busy manner.

busi'ness (bĭz'nės), *n.* **1.** type of work or commerce. **2.** duty or task. **3.** rightful concern. **4.** commerce. **5.** event or affair. **6.** mean business, have earnest intentions. **—busi'ness·man,** *n.* **—busi'ness·wom''an,** *n.*

busi′ness·like″ (bĭz′nes·līk″), *adj*. efficient.

bŭst, *n*. **1.** head, neck, and upper part of the chest. **2.** sculpture of these parts. **3.** *Informal*. **a.** failure. **b.** bankruptcy. —*v.t., v.i.* **4.** *Informal*. break or burst.

bŭs′tle, *n., v.i.,* -tled, -tling. *n*. **1.** activity, as of a crowd. —*v.i.* **2.** move hurriedly.

bus′y (bĭz′ÿ), *adj.,* -ier, -iest, *v.t.,* -ied, -ying. *adj*. **1.** with much to do. **2.** in action or use. **3.** full of distracting elements, as a decoration. —*v.t.* **4.** cause to be busy. —**bus′y·ness,** *n*.

bus′y·bod″y (bĭz′ÿ·bŏd″ÿ), *n., pl.* -ies. gossipy or meddlesome person.

bŭt, *prep*. **1.** except for. —*conj*. **2.** and yet. **3.** on the other hand. —*adv*. **4.** only; merely. **5.** just; only.

bŭtch′êr, *n*. **1.** slaughterer or seller of meat. —*v.t.* **2.** slaughter. —**butch′er·y,** *n*.

bŭt′lêr, *n*. head male house servant.

bûtt, *n*. **1.** thick end. **2.** remnant of a smoked cigarette or cigar. **3.** target. **4.** act or instance of butting. —*v.t.* **5.** ram with the head. **6.** join without overlapping.

bŭtte, *n*. steep hill isolated in flat land.

bŭt′têr, *n*. **1.** solid product made from churned cream. —*v.t.* **2.** spread with butter. **3.** butter up, *Informal*. ingratiate oneself with. —**but′ter·fat″,** *n*.

bŭt′têr·flÿ″, *n., pl.* -flies. slenderbodied four-winged insect.

bŭt′têr·mĭlk″, *n*. liquid remaining after butter is made of cream.

bŭt′têr·sčotch″, n. candy of brown sugar, butter, etc.

bŭt′tŏcks, *n., pl*. part on which one sits.

bŭt′tŏn, *n*. **1.** broad object passed through holes or loops in cloth as a fastener. **2.** object pushed to operate a control mechanism. **3.** large badge with a slogan, etc. —*v.t.* **4.** fasten with buttons. —**but′ton·hole″,** *n*.

bŭt′trĕss, *n*. **1.** heavy mass resisting a thrust, as that of an arch. —*v.t.* **2.** give stability or support to.

bŭx′ŏm, *adj*. attractively plump.

buÿ, *v.t.,* bought, buying, *n. v.t.* **1.** get in return for money. **2.** *Informal*. accept as true or wise. —*n*. **3.** *Informal*. something cheap at the price. —**buy′er,** *n*.

bŭzz, *v.i.* **1.** make a deep, rough hum.

—*n*. **2.** hum of this sort. —**buzz′er,** *n*.

bŭz′zârd, *n*. **1.** type of slow hawk. **2.** type of vulture.

bÿ, *prep*. **1.** close to. **2.** past. **3.** a multiplier or other dimension being. **4.** in measures or units of. **5.** after. **6.** during the time of day or night. **7.** not later than. **8.** through the agency of. **9.** according to. **10.** by way of, **a.** past or through. **b.** as a means or form of. **11.** in readiness. **12.** aside. **13.** past. —**by′stand″er,** *n*.

bÿ′gŏne″, *adj*. in the past.

bÿ′läw″, *n*. rule for an organization's internal affairs.

bÿ′līne, *n*. printed line identifying author of news story, article, etc.

bÿ′pǎss″, *n*. route, etc. serving as an alternate way between two points.

bÿ′-prŏd′ŭct, *n*. product incidental to a main one. Also, **by′prod″uct.**

bÿte, *n*. (computers) a group of eight bits of data.

C

C, c, *n*. **1.** third letter of the English alphabet. **2.** third best grade or rating. **3.** centigrade.

cǎb, *n*. **1.** chauffeured vehicle for hire. **2.** shelter for the operator of a locomotive, etc.

cà·bǎl′, *n*. **1.** group of intriguers. **2.** intrigue of such a group.

cǎb·à·ret (kab″à·rā′), *n*. restaurant with musical entertainment.

cǎb′bàge, *n*. vegetable with a head of thick leaves.

cǎb′ĭn, *n*. **1.** primitive house. **2.** passenger room on a ship. **3.** passenger space in an airplane.

cǎb′ĭ·nèt, *n*. **1.** boxlike piece of furniture. **2.** body of officials reporting to a head of state. —**cab′i·net·mak″er,** *n*. —**cab′i·net·work″,** *n*.

cā′ble, *n., v.t.,* -bled, -bling. *n*. **1.** heavy rope. **2.** heavy electric wire. **3.** cablegram. —*v.t.* **4.** send a cablegram to.

cā′ble·grǎm″, *n*. transoceanic telegraph message.

ca·boose′, *n.* car for the conductor and brakemen of a freight train.

cache, *n.*, *v.t.*, **cached, caching.** *n.* **1.** hiding place, esp. for food and supplies. **2.** goods hidden in such a place. —*v.t.* **3.** put in a cache.

căck′le, *v.i.*, **-led, -ling,** *n.* *v.i.* **1.** make henlike noises. —*n.* **2.** henlike noise. **3.** *Informal.* busy, meaningless talk.

ca·cŏph′o·nÿ, *n.*, *pl.* **-nies.** harsh, disagreeable sound. —**ca·coph′o·nous,** *adj.*

căc′tŭs, *n.*, *pl.* **-tuses, -ti.** prickly desert plant.

căd, *n.* violator of a gentlemanly code. —**cad′dish,** *adj.*

ca·dăv′êr, *n.* corpse. —**ca·dav′er·ous,** *adj.*

căd′diē, *n.* person who carries a golfer's clubs. Also, **cad′dy.**

cā′dênce, *n.* **1.** rise and fall of a speaking voice. **2.** marching rhythm. **3.** end of a musical phrase.

ca·dĕt′, *n.* **1.** military student. **2.** trainee.

cădge, *v.*, **cadged, cadging.** *v.t.*, *v.i.* **1.** beg. —*v.t.* **2.** get by begging. —**cadg′er,** *n.*

că′drē, *n.* organizational nucleus, esp. of military officers.

ca·fe (ka fā′), *n.* small restaurant. Also, **ca·fé′.**

căf′′e·tē′rï·à, *n.* self-service restaurant.

căf·fēine′, *n.* stimulant in coffee or tea. Also, **caf·fein′.**

cāge, *n.*, *v.t.*, **caged, caging.** *n.* **1.** openwork structure for confinement. **2.** openwork structure of any kind. —*v.t.* **3.** confine in a cage.

ca·hoots′, *Informal.* **in cahoots with, in** a conspiracy with.

cais′son, *n.* **1.** watertight chamber for work under water. **2.** ammunition wagon.

ca·jōle′, *v.t.*, **-joled, -joling.** coax or wheedle. —**ca·jol′er·y,** *n.*

cāke, *n.*, *v.*, **caked, caking.** *n.* **1.** sweetened piece of baked dough. **2.** flat piece of food, fried, or baked. **3.** piece of soap. —*v.t.*, *v.i.* **4.** cover with or form a solid crust.

ca·lăm′ï·tÿ, *n.*, *pl.* **-ties.** disaster. —**ca·lam′i·tous,** *adj.*

căl′cū·lāte′′, *v.*, **-lated, -lation.** *v.t.* **1.** ascertain through rational means. **2.** plan methodically. —*v.i.* **3.** reckon. **4.** rely. —**cal′cu·la′′tor,** *n.* —**cal′′cu·la′tion,** *n.* —**cal′cu·la·ble,** *adj.*

căl′cū·lāt′′ėd, *adj.* intended to produce the actual result.

căl′cū·lāt′′ĭng, *adj.* scheming.

căl′cū·lŭs, *n.* method used in higher mathematics.

căl′dròn, *n.* large kettle.

căl′ėn·dár, *n.* **1.** printed object or device for determining the day of the month, etc. **2.** system for reckoning the years. **3.** schedule of agenda.

căl′ėn·dêr, *n.* **1.** machine for giving a smooth finish. —*v.t.* **2.** smooth in a calender.

călf, *n.*, *pl.* **calves.** *n.* **1.** young cow or bull. **2.** fleshy part of the lower leg. —**calf′skin′′,** *n.*

căl′ĭ·bêr, *n.* **1.** diameter of a bullet, gun bore, etc. **2.** quality of character. Also, **cal′i·bre.**

căl′ĭ·brāte′′, *v.t.*, **-brated, -brating.** **1.** establish the scale of measurements of. **2.** determine the caliber of. —**cal′′i·bra′tion,** *n.*

căl′ĭ·cō′′, *n.*, *pl.* **-coes, -cos.** printed cotton.

căl′ĭ·pêr, *n.* device for measuring outside or inside diameters. Also, **cal′i·pers.**

căl′′ĭs·thĕn′ĭcs, *n. pl.* athletic exercises.

cälk, *v.t.* caulk.

căll, *v.t.* **1.** utter loudly. **2.** summon. **3.** name or describe. **4.** telephone. **5.** awaken. —*v.i.* **6.** make an order or request. **7.** impose a demand. **8.** make a visit. **9.** cry, as an animal. **10.** shout. —*n.* **11.** act or instance of calling. **12.** urge or appeal. —**call′er,** *n.*

căl·lĭg′′rá·phÿ′′, *n.* handwriting, penmanship, often ornamental.

căll′ĭng, *n.* vocation.

căl·lī′ò·pē′′, *n.* organ of steam whistles.

căl′loŭs, *adj.* insensitive to the sufferings of others. —**cal′lous·ly,** *adv.* —**cal′lous·ness, cal·los′i·ty,** *n.*

căl′lōw, *adj.* immature or inexperienced. —**cal′low·ness,** *n.*

căl′lŭs, *n.*, *pl.* **-luses.** hard thickening on the skin.

cälm, *adj.* **1.** without strong emotion. **2.** undisturbed. —*n.* **3.** state of quiet. —*v.t.* **4.** make quiet or tranquil. —**calm′ly,** *adv.* —**calm′ness,** *n.*

căl′ṓ·riē, *n.* unit of heat measurement.

căl′ŭm·nÿ, *n.*, *pl.* **-nies.** slander.

căm, *n.* rotating machine part producing reciprocating motion.

câ″mȧ·râ′dē·riē, *n.* cheerful companionship.

căm′bêr, *n.* shallow upward curve.

căm′brĭc, *n.* fine linen or cotton.

căm′côr·dêr, *n.* combined portable video camera and recorder.

căm′ĕl, *n.* desert animal storing water in one or two humps.

căm′ē·ō, *n.*, *pl.* **-os.** gem of contrasting layers of stone.

căm′êr·ȧ, *n.* **1.** boxlike device for taking photographs, shooting movie film, etc. **2.** optical device for copying a view. **—cam′er·a·man,** *n.*

căm·óu·flāge, *n.*, *v.t.* **-flaged, -flaging.** *n.* **1.** paintwork, etc. making something hard to see or interpret. **—v.t. 2.** apply camouflage to.

cămp, *n.* **1.** temporary residence in the open. **2.** recreation area in the country. **—v.i. 3.** establish or live in a camp. **—camp′fire″,** *n.* **—camp′site″,** *n.* **—camp′er,** *n.*

căm·pāign′, *n.* **1.** series of operations to attain a planned goal. **—v.i. 2.** act in a campaign. **—cam·paign′er,** *n.*

căm′phŏr, *n.* aromatic crystalline substance.

căm′pŭs, *n.*, *pl.* **-puses. 1.** open area of lawn and trees, esp. the grounds of a school. **2.** academic community.

căn, *v.i.*, past tense **could** for 1 and 2, **canned, canning** for 3, *n. v.i.* **1.** be able or know how to. **2.** have the right to. **3.** preserve in sealed cans or jars. **—n. 4.** metal container sealed to preserve food, etc. **5.** cylindrical container, esp. of sheet metal. **—can′ner,** *n.*

cȧ·năl′, *n.* artificial waterway.

cȧ·nârd′, *n.* rumor, esp. a malicious one.

cȧ·nār′ÿ, *n.*, *pl.* **-ies.** yellow songbird.

căn′cĕl, *v.t.*, **-celed, -celing. 1.** cover with marks, esp. in order to invalidate. **2.** invalidate or terminate. **3.** *Math.* remove from both sides of an equation. **—can″cel·la′tion,** *n.*

căn′cêr, *n.* spreading malignant tumor. **—can′cer·ous,** *adj.*

căn″dè·lâ′brŭm, *n.*, *pl.* **-bra.** branched candlestick.

căn′dĭd, *adj.* **1.** frank. **2.** unposed, as a snapshot. **—can′did·ly,** *adv.* **—can′dor, can′did·ness,** *n.*

căn′dĭ·dāte″, *n.* competitor for public office, an honor, etc. **—can′di·da·cy,** *n.*

căn′dle, *n.*, *v.t.*, **-dled, -dling.** *n.* **1.** cylinder of wax, etc. with a central wick for burning. **—v.t. 2.** inspect against a light, as eggs.

căn′dle·stĭck″, *n.* holder for candles.

căn′dÿ, *n.*, *pl.* **-dies,** *v.t.*, **-died, -dying.** *n.* **1.** flavored sweet. **—v.t. 2.** cook in sugar. **3.** form into sugar crystals.

cāne, *n.*, *v.t.*, **caned, caning.** *n.* **1.** hollow, jointed plant stalk. **2.** stick held while walking. **—v.t. 3.** stretch with split rattan, as a chair seat. **4.** beat with a cane.

cā′nīne, *adj.* **1.** pertaining to dogs. **2.** pertaining to wolves or foxes. **—n. 3.** dog, wolf, or fox. **4.** sharp human tooth.

căn′ĭs·têr, *n.* small storage can used in a kitchen.

căn′kêr, *n.* ulcerous sore.

căn′nêr·ÿ, *n.*, *pl.* **-ries.** plant for canning food.

căn′nĭ·bȧl, *n.* person or animal that eats its own kind. **—can′ni·bal·ism,** *n.*

căn′nĭ·bȧl·īze″, *v.t.*, **-ized, -izing.** strip in order to reuse parts.

căn′nòn, *n.*, *pl.* **-nons, -non.** heavy gun.

căn″nòn·āde′, *n.* continuous firing of cannon.

căn·nŏt′, *v.i.* can not.

căn′nÿ, *adj.*, **-nier, -niest.** shrewd. **—can′ni·ly,** *adv.* **—can′ni·ness,** *n.*

cȧ·noe (kȧ·nōō′), *n.*, *v.i.*, **-noed, -noing.** *n.* **1.** narrow paddled boat. **—v.i. 2.** travel by canoe.

căn′ón, *n.* **1.** basic principle or law. **2.** church official. **3.** official list of writings. **—ca·non′i·cal,** *adj.*

căn′ōn·īze″, *v.t.*, **-ized, -izing.** declare to be a saint. **—can″on·i·za′tion,** *n.*

căn′ō·pÿ, *n.*, *pl.* **-pies. 1.** light, rooflike covering supported by poles. **2.** rooflike projection, as over a window.

cănt, *n.* **1.** hypocritical jargon. **2.** slang or jargon of a group. **—v.t., v.i. 3.** slant.

căn·tăn′kêr·oŭs, *adj.* ill-tempered.

càn·tâ′tȧ, *n.* setting of a narrative for chorus.

căn·tēen′, *n.* **1.** portable container for

water. **2.** recreation center, as for soldiers.

căn′têr, *n.* easy gallop.

căn′tĭ·lē′′vêr, *n.* **1.** projecting structural member secured at one end. —*v.t.* **2.** support with or treat as a cantilever.

căn′tō, *n.,* *pl.* **-tos.** division of a long poem.

căn′tör, *n.* singer at a Jewish service.

căn′văs, *n.* **1.** tightly woven heavy cloth of hemp, cotton, etc. **2.** painting on canvas.

căn′văss, *v.t., v.i.* solicit for votes, opinions, sales orders, etc.

căp, *n., v.t.,* **capped, capping.** *n.* **1.** soft, close-fitting hat. **2.** anything for capping. —*v.t.* **3.** cover the upper end of.

cā′pà·ble, *adj.* **1.** competent. **2. capable of,** with the ability, personality, etc. for. —**ca′′pa·bil′i·ty,** *n.* —**ca′pa·bly,** *adv.*

cà·pā′cioŭs, *adj.* spacious.

cà·păc′ĭ·tў, *n., pl.* **-ties. 1.** ability to contain a quantity of material, number of persons, etc. **2.** amount that can be produced. **3.** role or function. **4.** capability.

cāpe, *n.* **1.** cloak. **2.** projection of land seaward.

cā′pêr, *v.i.* **1.** leap about playfully. —*n.* **2.** playful leap.

căp′ĭl·lār′′ў, *adj.* pertaining to the attraction of liquids in narrow tubes to above normal levels.

căp′ĭ·tàl, *n.* **1.** location of a national or state government. **2.** money for investing or lending. **3.** upper feature of a column or pier. **4.** letter of the form used to begin a sentence or proper name. —*adj.* **5.** excellent. **6.** large, as letters. **7.** pertaining to the death penalty.

căp′ĭ·tàl·ĭsm, *n.* economic system based on investment or lending at interest of privately owned money. —**cap′i·tal·ist,** *n.* —**cap′′i·tal·is′tic,** *adj.*

căp′ĭ·tàl·īze′′, *v.,* **-ized, -izing.** *v.t.* **1.** spell with an initial capital. **2.** use as or change into capital (2). **3.** furnish with capital (2). —*v.i.* **4. capitalize on,** exploit. —**cap′′i·tal·i·za′tion,** *n.*

căp′ĭ·tòl, *n.* legislative building.

cà·pĭt′ū·lāte, *v.i.,* **-lated, -lating.** cease to fight or resist. —**ca·pit′′u·la′tion,** *n.*

cà·prīce′, *n.* whim or whimsy. —**ca·pri′cious,** *adj.*

căp′sīze, *v.,* **-sized, -sizing.** *v.t., v.i.* overturn, as a boat.

căp′stàn, *n.* upright drum for winding cables.

căp′sŭle, *n.* sealed container.

căp′taĭn, *n.* **1.** military or naval officer. **2.** master of a ship. **3.** leader. —**cap′tain·cy,** *n.*

căp′tiŏn, *n.* title, explanation, etc. for a printed picture.

căp′tioŭs, *adj.* argumentative or faultfinding. —**cap′tious·ly,** *adv.* —**cap′tious·ness,** *n.*

căp′tĭ·vāte′′, *v.t.,* **-vated, -vating.** fascinate, as with charm. —**cap′′ti·va′tion,** *n.*

căp′tĭve, *n.* captured person or animal. —**cap·tiv′i·ty,** *n.*

căp′tör, *n.* person who takes a captive.

căp′tûre, *v.t.,* **-tured, -turing.** *n.* *v.t.* **1.** prevent from fleeing, fighting, etc. by force. **2.** express through art or speech. —*n.* **3.** act or instance of capturing.

câr, *n.* **1.** automobile. **2.** wheeled vehicle of any kind. **3.** elevator compartment.

cà·răfe′, *n.* bottle for serving beverages, usually water or wine.

căr′à·měl, *n.* **1.** burnt sugar, used as a flavor or color. **2.** type of candy.

căr′àt, *n.* **1.** unit of 200 milligrams for weighing gems. **2.** karat.

căr′à·văn′′, *n.* group of travelers, beasts of burden, etc. in a desert.

câr′bīne, *n.* **1.** short-barreled rifle. **2.** light automatic military rifle.

câr′′bò·hў′drāte, *n.* starch or sugar.

câr′bŏn, *n.* nonmetallic element found in organic compounds.

câr′bŭn·cle, *n.* **1.** subcutaneous inflammation. **2.** type of gem.

câr′bŭ·ret′′ôr, *n.* device for making explosive mixtures of air and gasoline.

câr′cáss, *n.* **1.** dead animal body. **2.** rough frame or shell, as of a building.

cârd, *n.* **1.** stiff paper bearing writing, etc. **2.** one of such papers used in games. **3.** postcard. **4. cards,** game played with cards.

cârd′bôard′′, *n.* thick, papery sheeting.

câr′dĭ·ăc′′, *adj.* pertaining to the heart.

câr′dĭ·gàn, *n.* sweater buttoning in front.

câr′dĭ·nàl, *n.* **1.** Roman Catholic ecclesiastic second to the pope. **2.** red American songbird. **3.** cardinal number. —*adv.* **4.** primary.

câr′dĭ·năl nŭmbêr, basic number, as 1, 2, 3, etc.

câr′dĭ·ō·grăm′′, *n.* electrocardiogram. —**car′di·o·graph′′,** *n.*

câr′′dĭ·ŏl′ō·gÿ, *n.* branch of medicine concerned with the heart.

câre, *n., v.,* **cared, caring.** *n.* **1.** responsibility. **2.** charge or protection **3.** caution or heed. **4.** worry. —*v.i.* **5.** have responsibility. **6.** feel liking or desire. **7.** feel affection. **8.** feel concern. —*v.t.* **9.** have as a subject of concern.

câre′fŭl, *adj.* **1.** cautious. **2.** with attention to accuracy.

câre′lĕss, *adj.* not properly careful.

cà·rĕss′, *v.t.* **1.** touch lightly and affectionately. —*n.* **2.** gesture or touch indicating affection.

câr′gō, *n., pl.* **-goes, -gos.** freight.

căr′ĭ·cà·tûre′′, *n., v.t.,* **-tured, -turing.** *n.* **1.** exaggerated rendering of a person's peculiarities. —*v.t.* **2.** render in caricature. —**car′i·ca·tur′′ist,** *n.*

căr′ĭēs, *n.* decay of teeth or bones.

câr′ĭl·lŏn, *n.* set of bells tuned to a scale. —**car′′il·lon·neur′,** *n.*

câr′mĭne, *n.* purplish red or crimson.

câr′nàge, *n.* slaughter.

câr′năl, *n.* pertaining to the body or its appetites.

câr′nĭ·văl, *n.* **1.** time of merrymaking before Lent. **2.** fair with entertainments.

câr′nĭ·vōre′′, *n.* flesh-eating animal or plant. —**car·niv′o·rous,** *adj.*

căr′ŏl, *n., v.,* **-oled, -oling.** *n.* **1.** song of praise, esp. at Christmas. —*v.i., v.t.* **2.** sing exuberantly. —**car′ol·er, car′ol·ler,** *n.*

cà·rōuse′, *v.i.,* **-roused, -rousing,** *n. v.i.* **1.** drink together boisterously. —*n.* **2.** Also, **ca·rous′al,** period of carousing.

cà′′roŭ·sĕl′, *n.* merry-go-round.

cârp, *v.i., n., pl.* **carp** or **carps.** *v.i.* **1.** find fault unjustly. —*n.* **2.** edible freshwater fish. —**carp′er,** *n.*

câr′pèn·têr, *n.* builder in wood. —**car′pen·try,** *n.*

câr′pèt, *n.* **1.** cloth floor covering. —*v.t.* **2.** cover with or as if with a carpet. —**car′pet·ing,** *n.*

câr′pôrt′′, *n.* open-ended shelter for an automobile.

căr′rĭage, *n.* **1.** large animal-drawn passenger vehicle. **2.** any of various moving and carrying devices. **3.** posture.

căr′rĭ·êr, *n.* **1.** thing or person that carries. **2.** aircraft carrier.

căr′rĭ·òn, *n.* dead, decaying flesh.

căr′rót, *n.* vegetable with an edible orange root.

căr′rÿ, *v.,* **-ried, -rying.** *v.t.* **1.** support or suspend. **2.** take the weight of and move. **3.** transmit. **4.** win or attain. **5.** prosecute or develop. —*v.i.* **6.** be transmitted.

cârt, *n.* **1.** small wagon. —*v.t.* **2.** transport in a small wagon.

câr·tĕl′, *n.* monopolistic association of businesses.

câr′tĭ·làge, *n.* tough, elastic skeletal tissue.

câr′tón, *n.* cardboard or plastic box.

câr′tōōn′, *n.* **1.** amusing or satirical drawing. **2.** motion picture of such drawings. **3.** artist's design for a fresco, tapestry, etc. —**car·toon′ist,** *n.*

câr′trĭdge, *n.* **1.** unit of ammunition for a handgun, rifle, etc. **2.** any unit loaded or fitted into a machine.

cârt′whēel′′, *n.* sidewise handspring.

cârve, *v.t.,* **carved, carving. 1.** form by cutting parts from. **2.** cut into parts, as meat. —**carv′er,** *n.* —**carv′ing,** n.

căs·cāde′, *n., v.i.,* **-caded, -cading.** *n.* **1.** chain of shallow waterfalls. —*v.i.* **2.** falling or as if in a cascade.

cāse, *n., v.t.,* **cased, casing.** *n.* **1.** box. **2.** instance. **3.** predicament. **4.** rational argument. **5.** form of a noun, etc. that shows its role in a sentence. —*v.t.* **6.** put in a case.

cāse′mént, *n.* window hinged on one side.

căsh, *n.* **1.** money as opposed to checks, etc. **2.** money or check given in payment. —*v.t.* **3.** exchange for money, as a check or coupon.

căsh·ĭêr′, *n.* **1.** person in charge of cash in a bank, etc. —*v.t.* **2.** dismiss, as from the military.

căs′ĭng, *n.* outer cover.

cà·sĭ′nō, *n., pl.* **-nos. 1.** place for dances, entertainments, etc. **2.** place for gambling.

căsk, *n*. barrel for liquids.

căs′kėt, *n*. **1.** box for jewels, etc. **2.** ornate coffin.

căs′sė·rōle′′, *n*. **1.** dish for baking. **2.** food baked in such a dish.

căs·sĕtte′, *n*. a compact, ready-to-use case containing audio or video tape.

căs′sŏck, *n*. clergyman's long, loose garment.

căst, *v.t.*, **cast, casting**, *n*., *v.t.* **1.** throw. **2.** directs or projects. **3.** form in a mold. —*n*. **4.** act or instance of casting. **5.** something formed in a mold. **6.** casing of a broken limb. **7.** group performing a play, etc. **8.** air or appearance.

căst′à·wāy′′, *n*. shipwrecked person.

căste, *n*. rigid social division, esp. in India.

căst′êr, *n*. **1.** small wheel supporting a furniture leg, etc. **2.** table pitcher for vinegar, etc. Also, **cast′or**.

căs′tǐ·gāte′′, *v.t.*, **-gated, -gating**. rebuke severely. —**cas′′ti·ga′tion**, *n*. —**cas′ti·ga′′tor**, *n*.

căst′ǐng, *n*. something cast in a mold.

căs′tle, *n*. **1.** heavily fortified residence. **2.** chess rook.

căst′-ŏff′′, *adj*. discarded.

căs′trāte, *v.t.*, **-trated, -trating**. remove the testicles of. —**cas·tra′tion**, *n*.

căs′ū·àl, *adj*. **1.** occurring by chance. **2.** not regular. **3.** informal. **4.** relaxed. —**cas′u·al·ly**, *adv*. —**cas′u·al·ness**, *n*.

căs′ū·àl·tў, *n*., *pl*. **-ties**. **1.** victim of an accident or military action. **2.** serious accident.

căs′ū·ist·rў, *n*., *pl*. **-tries**. sophistry. —**cas′u·ist**, *n*.

căt, *n*. **1.** small, furry, four-footed animal. **2.** any feline.

căt′à·clŷsm, *n*. sudden, drastic change. —**cat′′a·clys′mic**, *adj*.

căt′à·cōmb′′, *n*. underground passage with burial places.

căt′à·lŏg, *n*., *v.t.*, **-loged, -loging**. *n*. **1.** list of things acquired, to be sold, etc. —*v.t.* **2.** list in a catalog. Also, **cat′a·logue′′**.

căt′à·lŷst, *n*. something that affects the speed of a chemical reaction without being altered in the process. —**cat′′a·lyt′ic**, *adj*.

căt′′à·mà·răn′, *n*. boat with two parallel hulls.

căt′à·pŭlt′′, *n*. **1.** machine for hurling missiles, launching airplanes, etc. —*v.t.* **2.** hurl or launch from or as if from a catapult.

căt′à·răct′′, *n*. **1.** large waterfall. **2.** opacity in the eye causing blindness.

că·târrh′, *n*. inflammation of mucous membranes in the nose or throat.

cà·tăs′trò·phē, *n*. major disaster. —**cat′′a·stroph′ic**, *adj*.

căt′căll′′, *n*. shrill noise expressing contempt.

cătch, *v.*, **caught, catching**, *n*. *v.t.* **1.** capture or seize. **2.** discover or surprise. **3.** become infected with. —*v.i.* **4.** become caught or entangled. **5.** take or retain hold. —*n*. **6.** act or instance of catching. **7.** number of things caught, esp. fish. **8.** something for catching hold. **9.** desirable spouse or acquaintance. **10.** *Informal*. drawback. **catch′er**, *n*.

cătch′äll′′, *n*. place, category, etc. for miscellaneous things.

cătch′ǐng, *adj*. **1.** contagious. **2.** attractive.

cătch′ŭp, *n*. ketchup.

cătch′ў, *adj*. **-ier, -iest**. memorable, as a tune.

căt·è·chǐsm (kat′ə kism), *n*. set of questions and answers, esp. on religious doctrine.

căt′é·chīze′′, *v.t.*, **-chized, -chizing**. question in detail. Also, **cat′e·chise′′**.

căt′′è·gôr′ǐ·càl, *adj*. **1.** pertaining to categories. **2.** specific, as a statement. —**cat′′e·gor′i·cal·ly**, *adv*.

căt′è·ġo·rīze′′, *v.t.*, **-rized, -rizing**. put into categories.

căt′è·gô′′rў, *n*., *pl*. **-ries**. classification.

cā′têr, *v.t.* **1.** supply food, drink, tableware, etc. to parties for a fee. **2.** be overly accommodating. —**ca′ter·er**, *n*.

căt′ér·côr′′nered, *adj.*, *adv*. on diagonally opposite corners. Also, **cat′er·cor′′ner** or **cat′ty·cor′′ner**.

căt′êr·pǐl′′làr, *n*. crawling larva of a butterfly, moth, etc.

căt′gŭt′′, *n*. tough string made from dried intestines of sheep, etc.

cà·thâr′sǐs, *n*. purging, esp. of morbid emotions.

cà·thâr′tǐc, *n*. **1.** medicine for clearing the bowels. —*adj*. **2.** pertaining to cathartics. **3.** pertaining to a catharsis.

că·thē′drȧl, *n.* church in which a bishop normally officiates.

căth′o·lĭc, *adj.* **1.** universal. **2.** Catholic, pertaining to the Roman Catholic Church. —*n.* **3.** Catholic, member of the Roman Catholic Church. —**cath″o·lic′i·ty,** *n.* —**Ca·thol′i·cism,** *n.*

căt′năp″, *n., v.i.,* -napped, -napping. *n.* **1.** brief nap. —*v.i.* **2.** take such a nap.

căt′s′-păw″, *n.* person used by another as a tool.

căt′sŭp, *n.* ketchup.

căt′tle, *n. pl.* cows, bulls, etc. —**cat′tle·man,** *n.*

căt′wǎlk″, *n.* narrow elevated walk, esp. for industrial workers.

cau′cŭs, *n., v.i.,* -cused or -cussed, -cusing or -cussing *n.* **1.** business meeting of political leaders. —*v.i.* **2.** meet in a caucus.

caul′drȯn, *n.* caldron.

cau′li·flow″êr, *n.* edible white head of a vegetable of the cabbage family.

caulk, *v.t.* make watertight, esp. a seam.

cau′sȧl, *adj.* pertaining to or involving the relation of cause and effect. —**cau·sal′i·ty,** *n.*

cause, *n., v.t.,* caused, causing. *n.* **1.** something to which a later event or condition is attributed. **2.** reason or motivation. **3.** goal or purpose, esp. political or religious. **4.** case for advocacy. —*v.t.* **5.** be the cause of. —**caus′er,** *n.* —**caus′a·tive,** *adj.*

cause′wǎy″, *n.* raised roadway.

caus′tĭc, *adj.* **1.** burning. **2.** bitterly sarcastic.

cau′têr·īze″, *v.t.,* -ized, -izing. *Medicine.* burn or sear, as the flesh of a wound, to seal it. —**cau″ter·i·za′tion,** *n.*

cau′tion, *n.* **1.** care, as to avoid danger. **2.** warning. —*v.t.* **3.** warn. —**cau′tion·ar″y,** *adj.*

cau′tioŭs, *adj.* careful to avoid danger.

căv′ȧl·cāde″, *n.* procession, esp. on horseback.

căv″a·lier′, *n.* **1.** horseman, esp. a knight. **2.** gallant. —*adj.* **3.** casual. **4.** arrogant.

căv′ȧl·rў, *n., pl.* -ries. *n.* **1.** fighting force on horseback. **2.** fighting force in motor vehicles. —**cav′al·ry·man,** *n.*

cāve, *n., v.,* caved, caving, *n.* **1.** covered opening in the earth. —*v.i., v.t.,* **2.** cave in, collapse. —**cave′-in″,** *n.*

căv′êrn, *n.* spacious cave. —**cav′ern·ous,** *adj.*

căv′ï·âr″, *n.* roe, esp. that of sturgeon. Also, **cav′i·are″.**

căv′ĭl, *n., v.i.,* -iled, -iling. quibble. -**cav′il·er, cav′il·ler,** *n.*

căv′ï·tў, *n., pl.* -ities. hollow place.

cȧ·vȯrt′, *v.i.* frolic.

caў·ěnne′, *n.* extremely hot red pepper.

caў·ūse′, *n.* small cowboy horse.

cēase, *v.,* ceased, ceasing. *v.i., v.t., n.* stop. —**cease′less,** *adj.*

cē′dȧr, *n.* type of fragrant pine.

cēde, *v.t.,* ceded ceding. yield possession of.

cēil′ĭng, *n.* **1.** structure or surface forming the upper part of a room, etc. **2.** upper limit.

cěl′e·brāte″, *v.,* -brated, -brating. *v.t.* **1.** perform ritually. **2.** mark or commemorate with festivity. **3.** do honor to. —*v.i.* **4.** have festivities. —**cel″e·bra′tion,** *n.* —**cel′e·brant,** *n.* —**cel′e·brat″ed,** *adj.*

cè·lěb′rĭ·tў, *n., pl.* -ties. **1.** fame. **2.** currently famous person.

cè·lěr′ï·tў, *n.* swiftness.

cěl′êr·ў, *n.* plant with edible leaf stalks.

cè·lěs′tiȧl, *adj.* pertaining to heaven or outer space.

cěl′ï·bȧte″, *n.* **1.** unmarried person. **2.** sexually abstinent person. —*adj.* **3.** pertaining to celibates or celibacy. —**cel′i·ba·cy,** *n.*

cěll, *n.* **1.** unit of protoplasm. **2.** unit of space. **3.** habitable space in a prison, monastery, etc. **4.** electric battery. **5.** local unit of an organization. —**celled,** *adj.* —**cel′lu·lar,** *adj.*

cěl′lȧr, *n.* **1.** basement. **2.** storage space totally or partly underneath a building. **3.** collection of wine.

cěl′lo·phāne″, *n.* transparent wrapping material.

cěl·lō (chellō), *n., pl.* -los. large stringed instrument. —**cel′list,** *n.*

Cěl′lū·loīd″, *n. Trademark.* plastic made from nitrocellulose and camphor.

Cěl′sïŭs, *adj.* centigrade.

cē·měnt′, *n.* **1.** mixture of burned lime and clay, used for building. **2.** adhesive substance. —*v.t.* **3.** join with cement. **4.** cover with cement.

cĕm'ė·tĕr''ў, *n.*, *pl.* -ies. area of land for burying the dead.

cĕn'sör, *n.* **1.** person who eliminates unauthorized material from writings, etc. **2.** official who criticizes the state of government, society, etc. —cen'sor·ship'', *n.*

cĕn·sô'rĭ·oŭs, *adj.* given to harsh criticism.

cĕn'sûre, *n.*, *v.t.*, -sured, -suring. *n.* rebuke or condemnation. *v.t.* **2.** rebuke or condemn.

cĕn'sŭs, *n.* counting and analysis of population, etc.

cĕnt, *n.* hundredth part of a dollar.

cĕn'täur'', *n.* *Greek Mythology.* creature with the body of a horse and the head and trunk of a man.

cĕn''tė·năr'ĭ·ản, *n.* person 100 years old.

cĕn'tė·năr'ў, *adj.*, *n.*, *pl.* -ies. centennial.

cĕn·tĕn'nĭ·ål, *adj.* **1.** pertaining to or marking a period of 100 years. —*n.* **2.** hundredth anniversary. **3.** celebration of such an anniversary.

cĕn'tĕr, *n.* **1.** point or area equidistant from all outer points. **2.** place of concentration. **3.** area of political moderation. —*v.t.* **4.** put or concentrate at a center.

cĕn'tĭ·grāde'', *adj.* pertaining to a system of temperature measurement in which the range between the freezing and boiling points of water is 100 degrees; Celsius.

čĕn'tĭ·grăm'', *n.* hundredth part of a gram. Also, cen'ti·gramme''.

cĕn'tĭ·mē''tĕr, *n.* hundredth part of a meter. Also, cen'ti·me''tre.

cĕn'tĭ·pēde'', *n.* many-legged crawling insect.

cĕn'trål, *adj.* **1.** located at the center. **2.** accessible from all points. **3.** fundamental; basic. —cen'tral·ly, *adv.*

cĕn'trål·īze'', *v.t.*, -ized, -izing. **1.** unite under or control from a single authority. **2.** place at a center. —cen''tral·i·za'tion, *n.*

cĕn·trĭf'ŭ·gål fôrce, force tending to pull a mass away from a point around which it moves.

čĕn·trĭp'ė·tål fôrce, force tending to pull a mass toward a point around which it moves.

cĕn'tû·rў, *n.*, *pl.* -ries. **1.** period of 100 years. **2.** such a period as a unit, reckoned from A.D. **1.**

cė·răm'ĭc, *n.* **1.** ceramics, making of objects from baked clay or similar materials. **2.** object so made. —*adj.* **3.** pertaining to ceramics. **4.** made as a ceramic.

cē'rē''ål, *n.* **1.** grain used as food. **2.** food manufactured from such grain. —*adj.* **3.** pertaining to grain.

cėr·ė'brål, *adj.* reasoned rather than felt.

cĕr''ė·mō'nĭ·ål, *adj.* **1.** formal. —*n.* **2.** ceremony.

cĕr'ė·mō''nў, *n.*, *pl.* -nies. **1.** ordered set of actions for a formal occasion. **2.** formality. —cer''e·mo'ni·ous, *adj.*

cĕr'tản, *adj.* **1.** without doubt. **2.** without error. **3.** inevitable. **4.** unspecified. —cer'tain·ly, *adv.* —cer'tain·ty, *n.*

cĕr·tĭf'ĭ·căte, *n.* document that certifies.

cĕr'tĭ·fў'', *v.t.*, -fied, -fying. **1.** declare formally to be competent, valid, true, etc. **2.** issue a certificate to. —cer''ti·fi·ca'tion, *n.*

cĕr'tĭ·tūde'', *n.* inevitability.

cĕs·sā'tion, *n.* stop.

cĕs'sion, *n.* act or instance of ceding.

cĕss'poōl, *n.* receptacle for plumbing wastes.

chāfe, *v.*, chafed, chafing. *v.t.* **1.** wear by rubbing. **2.** warm by rubbing, as the skin. —*v.i.* **3.** become restless and annoyed.

chăff, *n.* **1.** waste from threshed grain. **2.** worthless stuff. —*n.* *v.i.* **3.** banter.

chăfĭng dĭsh, metal dish with a heating lamp underneath.

chà·grĭn', *n.*, *v.t.*, -grined, -grining. *n.* **1.** embarrassment at failure or disappointment. —*v.t.* **2.** cause chagrin in.

chāin, *n.* **1.** flexible length formed of connected pieces. **2.** related series of events, arguments, etc. **3.** chains, bondage. —*v.t.* **4.** fasten with a chain.

chāin rĕăction, series of reactions each caused by one immediately previous.

chāir, *n.* **1.** seat with a back. **2.** official post or position, esp. a chairmanship or professorship. **3.** chairman. —*v.t.* **4.** preside over as chairman.

chāir'măn, *n.* person who presides over

a meeting. —**chair'man·ship''**, *n*. Also, **chair'per''son**.

chāise longue, *pl*. **chaise longues**. daybed with a chairlike back at one end. Also, **chaise lounge**.

cha·let (sha lā'), *n*. Swiss farmhouse with a low, jutting roof.

chǎl'ĭce, *n*. wine goblet used in religious communions.

chälk, *n*. **1**. soft white limestone. **2**. white or dyed stonelike material for writing or drawing. —*v.t*. **3**. write or mark with chalk. —**chalk'y**, *adj*.

chǎl'lĕnge, *v.t*., **-lenged, -lenging**, *n*. *v.t*. **1**. call upon to fight, compete, or act bravely. **2**. demand identification of. **3**. demand proof from or for. **4**. reject as a juror. —*n*. **5**. act or instance of challenging. **6**. demand for one's best effort. —**chal'leng·er**, *n*.

chăm'bêr, *n*. **1**. room, esp. a bedroom. **2**. enclosed space, as in a machine, gun, or part of the body. **3**. legislative or official body. **4**. **chambers**, judge's office. —**cham'bered**, *adj*. —**cham'ber·maid''**, *n*.

chāmbêr mūsĭc, music written for small groups and intended for small gatherings.

cha·mē·lē·ŏn (ká mē'lē ŏn), *n*. lizard able to change the color of its skin.

cham·ois (sham'ē), *n*. **1**. small European mountain antelope. **2**. Also, **cham'my**, soft leather of a chamois or other animal, used for polishing.

chămp, *v.t*., *v.i*. bite or chew noisily.

chăm·pāgne, *n*. sparkling white wine, originally from northern France.

chăm'pĭ·ŏn, *n*. **1**. person who fights in another's behalf. **2**. athlete winning or getting first place in a series of competitions. **3**. advocate of a cause. —*v.t*. **4**. defend or advocate. —**cham'pi·on·ship''**, *n*.

chănce, *n*., *adj*., *v*., **chanced, chancing**. *n*. **1**. possibility of becoming, doing, or getting something desired. **2**. the unpredictable. **3**. unpredictable event. **4**. risk. **5**. lottery ticket. —*adj*. **6**. accidental. —*v.t*. **7**. risk. —*v.i*. **8**. transpire or come by accident.

chăn'cĕl, *n*. area of a church around the altar.

chăn'cĕl·lór, *n*. high government or aca-demic official. —**chan'cel·lor·ship''**, *n*.

chănc'ў, *adj*., **-ier, -iest**. risky or uncertain.

chăn''dė·liēr', *n*. lighting fixture suspended from a ceiling.

chănd'lêr, *n*. supplier, esp. to ships. —**chand'ler·ry**, *n*.

chānge, *v*., **changed, changing**, *n*. *v.t*. **1**. make into a different form. **2**. give up one for the other, as articles of clothing, vehicles, etc. **3**. give lower denominations of money in exchange for. —*v.i*. **4**. become different. **5**. leave one vehicle for another. —*n*. **6**. act or instance of changing. **7**. variety. **8**. money returned from that offered in payment. **9**. money in small denominations, esp. coins. —**change'less**, *adj*. —**change'a·ble**, *adj*.

chăn'nĕl, *n*., *v.t*., **-neled, -neling**. *n*. **1**. deeper part of a watercourse. **2**. body of water linking two larger ones. **3**. groove. **4**. *Television and radio*. frequency band. **5**. **channels**, offices in an official sequence for a given purpose. —*v.t*. **6**. send through or as through a channel. **7**. make grooves in.

chănt, *n*. **1**. sung liturgical music. **2**. heavily rhythmical song or speech. —*v.t*. **3**. sing or utter in a chant.

chăn'tĕy, *n*., *pl*. **-teys**. rhythmical work song of a sailor. Also, **chan'ty**.

chā·ŏs (kā'os), *n*. utter disorder. —**cha·ot'ic**, *adj*.

chăp, *v*., **chapped, chapping**. *v.t*., *v.i*. roughen or crack, as the skin or lips.

chăp'ĕl, *n*. **1**. small church. **2**. private church, as in a school or house.

chăp'êr·ōn (shap'êr ōn), *n*., *v.t*., **-oned, -oning**. *n*. **1**. person who accompanies young unmarried persons to ensure propriety. —*v.t*. **2**. accompany as a chaperon. Also, **chap'er·one''**.

chăp'laĭn, *n*. **1**. clergyman employed by an institution, military force, etc. **2**. clergyman attached to a chapel.

chăps, *n*., *pl*. leather leggings worn by cowboys.

chăp'têr, *n*. **1**. division of a book. **2**. local branch of an association. **3**. council of a religious community.

châr, *v*., **charred, charring**. *v.t*., *v.i*. **1**. burn on the surface. **2**. burn to charcoal.

chăr´ăc·têr, *n.* **1.** personality. **2.** moral strength. **3.** person as judged by his actions. **4.** eccentric or conspicuous person. **5.** reputation. **6.** person in a work of fiction. **7.** any symbol used in forming writing.

chăr´´ăc·têr·ĭs´tĭc, *adj.* **1.** typical. —*n.* **2.** typical or distinguishing quality. —**char´´ac·ter·is´tic·al·ly,** *adv.*

chăr´ăc·têr·īze´´, *v.t.,* **-ized, -izing. 1.** attribute or give characteristics to. **2.** be characteristic of. —**char´´ac·ter·i·za´tion,** *n.*

chá·rāde´, *n.* pantomime offering clues to guessing a secret word.

chär´cōal´´, *n.* wood partially burned in the absence of air.

chârge, *v.,* **charged, charging,** *n.* *v.t.* **1.** supply or load. **2.** electrify. **3.** accuse. **4.** make responsible. **5.** ask as a price or fee. **6.** enter as a debt. **7.** attack with swift movement. **8.** require payment. **9.** move swiftly in an attack. —*n.* **10.** act or instance of charging. **11.** that with which something is charged. **12.** care or responsibility. **13.** object of one's care or responsibility. —**charge´a·ble,** *adj.*

chăr´ĭ·ŏt, *n.* two-wheeled horse-drawn vehicle. —**char´´i·o·teer´,** *n.*

chá·rĭs´má (ká riz´má), *n.* quality of leadership derived from the personality. —**char´´is·mat´ic,** *adj.*

chăr´ĭ·tà·ble, *adj.* **1.** kindly. **2.** generous. **3.** pertaining to charities.

chăr´ĭ·tỹ, *n.,* *pl.* **-ties. 1.** love for mankind. **2.** generosity to the needy. **3.** organization for helping the needy. **4.** kindness in judging others.

chär·lá·tán (shahr´lá tán), *n.* perpetrator of frauds. —**char´la·tan·ism, char´la·tan·ry,** *n.*

chârm, *n.* **1.** attractive or delightful quality. **2.** trinket. **3.** magic spell. —*v.t.* **4.** exercise charm or a charm upon. —**charm´er,** *n.* —**charm´ing,** *adj.*

chârt, *n.* **1.** map, esp. for navigation. **2.** graph or table. —*v.t.* **3.** make a chart of. **4.** map or plan.

chär´têr, *n.* **1.** license or franchise. **2.** statement of fundamental organizational principles. **3.** hire of a vehicle. —*v.t.* **4.** grant a charter to. **5.** hire, as for a trip.

chár´ỹ, *adj.* **-ier, -iest. 1.** cautious. **2.** sparing.

chāse, *v.,* **chased, chasing,** *n.* *v.t.* **1.** go after to overtake or capture. **2.** drive away. **3.** hunt. **4.** engrave, as metal. —*v.i.* **5.** *Informal.* rush. —*n.* **6.** pursuit. **7.** hunting of game.

chăsm (kas´m), *n.* abyss.

chăs·sĭs (chas´ē), *n., pl.* **-sis.** frame and running gear of an automobile, not including the engine.

chāste, *adj.* **1.** pure, esp. of sexual desire or activity. **2.** tastefully restrained. —**chas´ti·ty,** *n.*

chăs´tĕn, *v.t.* correct or subdue, esp. by punishment or scolding.

chăs·tīse´, *v.t.,* **-tised, -tising.** punish or scold.

chăt, *n.,* *v.i.,* **chatted, chatting.** *n.* **1.** light, informal conversation. —*v.i.* **2.** have such a conversation.

chă·teau´, *n., pl.* **-teaux, -teaus.** castle or country house in France. Also, **châ·teau´.**

chăt´tĕl, *n.* piece of movable personal property.

chăt´têr, *v.i.* **1.** make rapid sounds with the voice. **2.** talk foolishly. **3.** make rapid clashing sounds, as the teeth of a chilled person. —*n.* **4.** chattering noise. **5.** foolish talk.

chauf·feŭr´, *n.* person hired to drive an automobile.

chau´vĭn·ĭsm, *n.* fanatical devotion to one's country, etc. —**chau´vin·ist,** *n.* —**chau´´vin·is´tic,** *adj.*

chēap, *adj.* **1.** low in price. **2.** low in worth. **3.** despicable. **4.** *Informal.* stingy. —*adv.* **5.** at low cost. —**cheap´ly,** *adv.* —**cheap´ness,** *n.* —**cheap´en,** *v.t., v.i.*

chēat, *v.t.* **1.** deceive, esp. for money. **2.** evade. —*v.i.* **3.** be deceptive. —*n.* **4.** deception. **5.** deceiver.

chĕck, *n.* **1.** precaution. **2.** inspection. **3.** halt or frustration. **4.** identification slip. **5.** document transferring money. **6.** bill, as in a restaurant. **7.** square in a checkered pattern. **8.** *Chess.* danger to a king. —*v.t.* **9.** halt or restrain. **10.** verify or investigate. **11.** place with another for shipment or storage. —**check´book´´,** *n.* —**check´room´´,** *n.*

chĕck´êr, *n.* **1.** person or thing that checks. **2. checkers, a.** pattern of squares in alternating colors. **b.** game played on a board with this pattern. **3.** disk used in playing checkers. —**check′ er·board″,** *n.*

chĕck′māte″, *n.,* **-mated, -mating.** *n.* **1.** *Chess.* inevitable capture of a king. **2.** total defeat or ruin. —*v.t.* **3.** impose a checkmate on.

chĕck′ŭp″, *n.* medical examination.

chĕd′dàr, *n.* hard cheese, often sharp.

chēek, *n.* **1.** side of the face below the eye. **2.** impudence.

chēer, *n.* **1.** happiness. **2.** shout of delight, encouragement, etc. **3.** food and entertainment. —*v.i.* **4.** shout cheers. **5.** become less unhappy. —*v.t.* **6.** encourage, etc. with cheers. **7.** make less unhappy. —**cheer′ful,** *adj.* —**cheer′ less,** *adj.*

chēese, *n.* food made from milk curds.

chēese′bŭrg″êr, *n.* hamburger cooked with cheese.

chēese′cāke″, *n.* cake made with cheese.

chēese′clŏth″, *n.* loosely woven cotton.

chĕf, *n.* cook, esp. a supervising cook.

chĕm′ĭ·càl, *adj.* **1.** pertaining to, or produced or operated by, chemistry. —*n.* **2.** substance produced by or used in chemistry. —**chem′i·cal·ly,** *adv.*

chė·mīse′, *n.* loose-fitting woman's dress or slip.

chĕm′ĭs·trÿ, *n.* study of substances and their production or conversion. —**chem′ist,** *n.*

chė·nĭlle′, *n.* fabric woven from a soft, tufted yarn.

chĕr′ĭsh, *v.t.* regard as dear or precious.

chĕr′rÿ, *n.,* *pl.* **-ries.** tree bearing a small, red fruit.

chĕr′ŭb, *n.,* *pl.* **-ubs, -ubim.** angel often shown as a chubby, winged child. —**che·ru′bic,** *adj.*

chĕss, *n.* game played on a checkerboard with 16 pieces on each of two sides. —**chess′board″,** *n.* —**chess′man,** *n.*

chĕst, *n.* **1.** any of various boxlike containers for storage. **2.** part of the body within the ribs.

chĕst′nŭt, *n.* tree of the beech family with an edible nut.

chĕv′rŏn, *n.* sign like a V or inverted V, used for military insignia, heraldry, etc.

chēw, *v.t.* reduce with the teeth, as for swallowing. —**chew′y,** *adj.*

Chi·an·ti (kē ähn′tē), *n.* dry red table wine.

chĭc, *n.* elegance; smartness.

chī·cān′êr·ÿ, *n.,* *pl.* **-ries.** trickery.

chī·cä″nō, *n.,* *fem.* a person of Mexican descent.

chĭck, *n.* young bird, esp. a chicken.

chĭck′ĕn, *n.* hen or rooster.

chĭck′ĕn-heârt″ėd, *adj.* cowardly.

chĭck′en pŏx, contagious virus disease of children.

chĭck′pēa″, *n.* edible seed of a bushy plant.

chĭc′ó·rÿ, *n.* plant with leaves used in salad and roots used as a coffee substitute.

chīde, *v.,* **chided** or **chid** or **chidden, chiding.** *v.t., v.i.* scold; rebuke.

chiĕf, *n.* **1.** principal person —*adj.* **2.** main. —**chief′ly,** *adv.*

chiĕf′tàin, *n.* leader of a tribe or clan.

chif·fo·nier (shif″ȯ nēr′), *n.* chest of drawers. Also, **chif″fon′nier′.**

Chi·hua·hua (tshĭ wä′wä), *n.* small dog.

chīld, *n.,* *pl.* **children. 1.** human before puberty. **2.** offspring. —**child′birth″,** *n.* —**child′hood″,** *n.* —**child′less,** *adj.* —**child′like″,** *adj.*

chīld′ĭsh, *adj.* characteristic of children, esp. as regards behavior or judgment.

chĭl′ĭ, *n.* dish of beef, red pepper, etc. Also, **chili con car′ne.**

chĭll, *n.* **1.** perceptible cold. **2.** shiver from cold. —*adj.* **3.** chilly. —*v.t.* **4.** cause to be cold. —*v.i.* **5.** become cold.

chĭll′ÿ, *adj.,* **-ier, -iest.** cold.

chīme, *n.,* *v.,* **chimed, chiming.** *n.* **1.** bell, esp. in a clock. **2.** chimes, tuned bells. —*v.t., v.i.* **3.** sound with chimes.

chī·mē′rá (kĭ mē′rȧ), *n.* fantastic, imaginary thing. —**chi·mer′i·cal,** *adj.*

chĭm′nēy, *n.,* *pl.* **-nies.** passage for smoke or heat.

chĭm″păn·zēe′, *n.* medium-sized ape.

chĭn, *n.* part of the face at the lower jaw.

chī′nȧ, *n.* **1.** porcelain. **2.** vitrified earthenware. **3.** dishes, etc. Also, **chi′ na·ware.**

chĭnk, *n.* **1.** narrow crack. **2.** clinking sound.

chĭntz, *n.* printed cotton, usually glazed.

chĭp, *n.,* *v.,* **-ped, -ping.** *n.* **1.** small cut or broken piece. **2.** token used in gambling, etc. **3.** (computers) the basic component of miniaturized electronic circuitry. —*v.t.* **4.** knock chips from. —*v.i.* **5.** break into chips.

chĭp'mŭnk'', *n.* small North American squirrel.

chĭp'pêr, *adj.* lively in spirit.

chī·rŏp'ŏ·dў, *n.* podiatry. —**chi·rop'o·dist**, *n.*

chī''rŏ·prăc'tĭc, *n.* treatment of illness through manipulation of the joints. —**chi'ro·prac''tor**, *n.*

chîrp, *v.i.* make short, shrill, birdlike noises.

chĭs'ĕl, *n.*, *v.t.*, **-eled** or **-eling**. *n.* **1.** cutting tool narrow at one end. —*v.t.* **2.** cut with a chisel. —*v.i.* **3.** *Informal.* cheat, esp. on small matters. —**chis'el·er**, *n.*

chĭt'chăt'', *n.* light conversation or gossip.

chĭt'têr·lĭngs, *n. pl.* small intestines of pigs as a food. Also, **chit'lins, chit'lings.**

chĭv'ăl·rў, *n.* **1.** medieval institution of knighthood. **2.** courage, gallantry, etc. —**chiv·al'ric**, *adj.* —**chiv'al·rous**, *adj.*

chlō·rīne (klō'rēn), *n.* greenish chemical used for disinfection. —**chlo'ri·nate''**, *v.t.*

chlô'rŏ·fôrm'', *n.* **1.** volatile liquid anaesthetic. —*v.t.* **2.** kill or anaesthetize with chloroform.

chlô'rŏ·phўll, *n.* green substance in plants. Also, **chlo'ro·phyl.**

chŏck, *n.* **1.** wedge stopping wheels from rolling. —*v.t.* **2.** stop with chocks.

chŏck'-fŭll', *adj.* absolutely full.

chŏc'ŏ·lăte, *n.* **1.** dark-brown substance made from or flavored with cacao seeds. **2.** reddish brown.

choīce, *n.*, *adj.*, **choicer, choicest.** *n.* **1.** fact or instance of choosing. **2.** thing chosen. —*adj.* **3.** superior in quality.

choir (kwīr), *n.* **1.** chorus, esp. one singing religious music. **2.** part of a church for such a chorus.

chōke, *v.*, **choked, choking**, *n.* *v.t.* **1.** cut off the breath of. **2.** clog. —*v.i.* **3.** suffer from the cutting-off of breath. —*n.* **4.** act, instance, or sound of choking.

chŏ·lĕs·têr·ōl, *n.* solid found in bile, etc.

chōōse, *v.*, **chose, chosen, choosing.** *v.t.* **1.** decide upon as best to take, do, etc. —*v.i.* **2.** make a choice.

chōōs'ў, *adj.*, **-ier, -iest.** *Informal.* taking great care or trouble over purchases, etc. Also, **choos'ey.**

chŏp, *v.*, **chopped, chopping**, *n. v.t.*, *v.i.* **1.** cut with small blows. —*n.* **2.** small cutting blow. **3.** meat cut from the rib, shoulder, or loin. **4.** small, distinct waves of water. **5.** chops, mouth and lower cheeks. —**chop'per**, *n.* —**chop'py**, *adj.*

chŏp'stĭcks'', *n. pl.* twin sticks used in eating, esp. in the Far East.

chŏp sū'ĕy, meat, bean sprouts, bamboo shoots, etc.

chó·răle', *n.* **1.** hymn tune. **2.** choral composition. **3.** chorus or choir.

chor·al (kōr'əl), *adj.* pertaining to or for a chorus.

chord (kōrd), *n.* **1.** combination of musical tones. **2.** straight line intercepting an arc at two points.

chôre, *n.*, routine or hard task.

chor·e·og·ra·phy (kōr''ē ahg'ra fē), *n.* art of planning or executing ballets or dances. —**chor''e·o·graph'ic**, *adj.* —**chor'e·o·graph''**, *v.t.* —**chor''e·og'ra·pher**, *n.*

chôr'tle, *v.*, **-tled, -tling.** *v.i.*, *v.t.* speak with chuckles.

cho·rus (kō'rus), *n.* **1.** singing group. **2.** composition for such a group. **3.** repeated part of a song composed in stanzas. **4.** unison. —*v.t.* **5.** utter in chorus.

chŏw, *n.* **1.** medium-sized dog. **2.** *Informal.* food.

chŏw'dêr, *n.* soup of milk, clams, fish, etc.

chow mein (chŏw mān), fried noodles, meat, bean sprouts, etc.

chrĭs'tĕn, *v.t.* **1.** baptize. **2.** name formally. —**chris'ten·ing**, *n.*

Chrĭs'tĕn·dŏm, *n.* Christian part of the world or of humanity.

Chrĭs'tiǎn, *n.* **1.** believer in Christ. —*adj.* **2.** pertaining to believers in Christ or to their churches. **3.** consistent with the teachings of Christ, esp. regarding charity or salvation. —**Chris'ti·an'i·ty**, *n.*

Chrĭstiǎn nāme, *n.* name given to a person, as at baptism.

Chrĭst'măs, *n.* celebration of the birth of Christ, usually December 25.

chrō·măt'ĭc, *adj.* **1.** pertaining to color. **2.** *Music.* composed of semitones, as a scale.

chrōme, *n., adj., v.t.,* **chromed, chrom-ing.** *n.* **1.** chromium or a chromium al-loy. —*adj.* **2.** made with chromium. —*n.* **3.** plate with chrome.

chrō'mĭ·ŭm, *n.* corrosion-resistant me-tallic element.

chrō'mö·sōme'', *n.* gene-bearing body.

chrŏn'ĭc, *adj.* **1.** long-lasting or recur-rent. **2.** suffering from a chronic ail-ment. —**chron'i·cal·ly,** *adv.*

chrŏn'ĭ·cle, *n., v.t.,* **-cled, -cling.** *n.* **1.** chronological record. —*v.t.* **2.** put into such a record. —**chron'i·cler,** *n.*

chrŏ·nŏl'ŏ·gÿ, *n., pl.* **-gies. 1.** measure-ment of time. **2.** recording of events in order of occurrence. **3.** dating of event. —**chron''o·log'i·cal,** *adj.*

chrŏ·nŏm'ĕ·têr, *n.* highly accurate time-piece.

chrÿs'ȧ·lĭs, *n.* pupa or cocoon of a butter-fly.

chrÿs·ăn'thĕ·mŭm, *n.* showy late-blooming flower.

chŭb'bÿ, *adj.* **-bier, -biest.** plump.

chŭck, *v.t.* **1.** toss. **2.** tap, esp. under the chin. —*n.* **3.** neck and shoulder cut of beef. **4.** act or instance of chucking.

chŭck'le, *v.i.,* **-led, -ling,** *n. v.i.* **1.** laugh softly. —*n.* soft laugh.

chŭg, *n., v.i.,* **chugged, chugging.** *n.* **1.** sound of an engine exhaust. —*v.i.* **2.** move with chugs.

chŭm, *n. Informal.* friend. **chum'my,** *adj.*

chŭmp, *n. Informal.* person with bad judgment.

chŭnk, *n.* thick fragment.

chŭnk'ÿ, *adj.* **-ier, -iest.** short and thick.

chûrch, *n.* **1.** religious organization. **2.** religious building. **3.** whole commu-nity of Christians. —**church'go''er,** *n.* —**church'ly,** *adj.* —**church'man,** *n.*

chûrch'yârd'', *n.* grounds of a church, esp. when used as a cemetery.

chûrl, *n.* surly, ill-mannered person. —**churl'ish,** *adj.*

chûrn, *n.* **1.** device for shaking cream to form butter. —*v.t., v.i.* **2.** stir or shake.

chūte (shōōt), *n.* slide for transferring materials, etc.

chŭt'nēy, *n.* Indian relish.

chutz·pah (hŏŏtz'pȧh), *n. Yiddish.* im-pudence; audacity. Also, **chutz'pa.**

cī·cā·dȧ (si kā'dȧ), *n.* large insect mak-ing a shrill rasping sound; often called a locust.

cī'dêr, *n.* apple juice, usually fermented.

cī·gâr', *n.* rolled tobacco for smoking.

cĭg''ȧ·rétte', *n.* tobacco rolled in paper for smoking.

cĭnch, *n.* **1.** *Informal.* something easy. **2.** strap for securing a saddle.

cĭn'dêr, *n.* ash.

cĭn'ė·mȧ, *n.* motion picture or pictures. —**cin''e·mat'ic,** *adj.*

cĭn'nȧ·môn, *n.* East Indian spice.

cī'phêr, *n.* **1.** code. **2.** zero.

cîr'cȧ, *prep.* around; used with dates.

cîr'cle, *n., v.t.,* **-cled, -cling.** *n.* **1.** closed two-dimensional curve with one center. **2.** something formed like such a curve. **3.** group of friends, persons with com-mon interests, etc. —*v.t.* **4.** go around in a circle.

cîr'cuĭt, *n.* **1.** continuous path of move-ment. **2.** regular round of professional visits. **3.** path of an electric current.

cîr·cū'ĭ·toŭs, *adj.* roundabout.

cîr·cuĭt·rÿ, *n.* components of an electri-cal circuit.

cîr'cŭ·lȧr, *adj.* **1.** shaped like a circle. —*n.* **2.** pamphlet, etc. for general dis-tribution.

cîr'cŭ·lȧr·īze'', *v.t.,* **-ized, -izing. 1.** so-licit from or notify by means of circu-lars. **2.** make circular.

cîr'cū·lāte'', *v.,* **-ated, -ating.** *v.i.* **1.** move in a closed, continuous path. **2.** move from person to person or place to place. —*v.t.* **3.** cause to move in either of these ways. —**cir'cu·la·to''ry,** *adj.*

cîr''cū·lā'tion, *n.* **1.** act or instance of circulating. **2.** normal movement of blood. **3.** readership of a periodical.

cîr'cŭm·cīse'', *v.t.,* **-cised, -cising.** cut away the foreskin of. —**cir''cum·ci'sion,** *n.*

cîr''cŭm'fêr·ence, *n.* dimension along the line of a circle. —**cir·cum'fer·en''tial,** *adj.*

cîr''cŭm·lō·cū'tion, *n.* wordy, evasive speech.

cîr''cŭm·năv'ĭ·gāte, *v.t.,* **-gated, gat-ing.** sail or fly entirely around.

cîr'cŭm·scrībe'', *v.t.,* **-scribed, -scribing. 1.** draw a circle around. **2.** confine.

cîr''cŭm·spĕct'', *adj.* cautious. —**cir''cum·spec'tion,** *n.*

cîr·cŭm·stănce", *n.* **1.** accompanying condition. **2.** chance. **3.** **circumstances,** state of material welfare.

cîr''cŭm·stăn'tial, *adj.* **1.** pertaining to circumstances or circumstance. **2.** pertaining to legal evidence implying but not proving something. **3.** detailed.

cîr'cŭm·vĕnt'', *v.t.* prevent or overcome with cunning. —cir''cum·ven'tion, *n.*

cîr'cŭs, *n.* **1.** traveling show of animals, acrobats, etc. **2.** ancient show of human and animal combats, etc.

cîr'rŭs, *n.* feathery cloud formation.

cĭs'têrn, *n.* tank for water storage.

cĭt'à·dĕl, *n.* fortress, esp. in a city.

cīte, *v.t.,* **cited, citing. 1.** mention as a scholarly authority. **2.** mention as an example. **3.** mention officially as meritorious. **4.** summon before a court. —ci·ta'tion, *n.*

cĭt'ĭ·zèn, *n.* member of a state or other political entity. —cit'i·zen·ry, *n.* —cit'i·zen·ship'', *n.*

cĭt'rŏn, *n.* lemonlike fruit whose rind is candied.

cĭt''rŏn·ĕl'lá, *n.* oil used to repel mosquitoes, etc.

cĭt·rŭs, *adj.* of or pertaining to lemons, oranges, limes, etc. —cit'ric, *adj.*

cĭt'ў, *n., pl.* -ies. **1.** large community. **2.** government of such a community.

cĭv'ĭc, *adj.* pertaining to cities or their citizens.

cĭv'ĭcs, *n., pl.* study of the relation of citizens to political entities.

cĭv'ĭl, *adj.* **1.** not military or religious. **2.** polite. —ci·vil'i·ty, *n.*

cĭvĭl ĕngĭnēerĭng, engineering of public works or the like. —civil engineer.

cĭ·vĭl'ià n, *n.* person outside any military or police organization.

cĭv''ĭ·lĭ·zā'tion, *n.* **1.** lawful, orderly state of society. **2.** society characterized by order. **3.** civilized part of the world.

cĭv'ĭ·līze'', *v.t.,* -ized, -izing. cause to adopt civilization.

cĭvĭl sêrvĭce, non-military, non-police government service. —civil servant.

cĭvĭl war, war between factions of the same nation.

clăd, *adj.* dressed.

clăim, *v.t.* **1.** designate for oneself. **2.** assert as true. **3.** require. —*n.* **4.** act or instance of claiming. **5.** something claimed. —claim'ant, claim'er, *n.*

clāir·vŏy'ànce, *n.* sensitivity to things not usually seen, esp. the supernatural. —clair·voy'ant, *adj., n.*

clăm, *n.* bivalve mollusk.

clăm'bêr, *v.i.* climb laboriously.

clăm'mў, *adj.,* -mier, -miest. cold and moist.

clăm'ŏr, *n.* **1.** loud outcry. —*v.i.* **2.** make such an outcry, as in demanding or complaining. —clam'or·ous, *adj.*

clămp, *n.* **1.** mechanical device for holding things together. —*v.t.* **2.** fasten with a clamp.

clăn, *n.* group of families with a common ancestor. —clans'man, *n.*

clăn·dĕs'tĭne, *adj.* secret; stealthy.

clăng, *n.* loud ringing noise.

clăng'ŏr, *n.* clanging, as of bells.

clănk, *n.* dull metallic sound.

clăn'nĭsh, *adj.* sociable together but excluding others.

clăp, *v.t.,* **1.** strike together, as the palms of the hands. —*v.i.* **2.** clap the palms together. —*n.* **3.** sound of clapping. **4.** act or instance of clapping.

clăp·bôard (klə'bərd), *n.* board used as a siding for buildings.

clăp'pêr, *n.* object for striking a bell.

clăque, *n.* group for the purpose of applauding a performer, esp. for pay.

clăr'ĕt, *n.* dry red table wine.

clăr'ĭ·fў'', *v.t.,* -fied, -fying. make clear. —clar''i·fi·ca'tion, *n.*

clăr''ĭ·nĕt', *n.* reed woodwind instrument. —clar''i·net'ist, *n.*

clăr'ĭ·tў, *n.* clearness, esp. to the understanding.

clăsh, *v.i.* **1.** strike together violently. **2.** be in violent disagreement. —*n.* **3.** act or instance of clashing.

clăsp, *n.* **1.** folding fastener. **2.** embrace. **3.** grasp, as of the hand. —*v.t.* **4.** hold with or in a clasp.

clăss, *n.* **1.** category or grade. **2.** social or economic level. **3.** *Informal.* stylishness. **4.** group of students taught or graduating together. —*v.t.* **5.** classify. —class'less, *adj.* —class'mate'', *n.* —class'room'', *n.*

clăs'sĭc, *adj.* **1.** excellent of its kind. **2.** completely typical. **3.** harmonious. **4.** pertaining to Greco-Roman antiquity or art. —*n.* **5.** something excellent of its kind. **6.** Greek or Roman author.

clăs'sĭ·càl, *adj.* **1.** pertaining to Greco-

Roman antiquity or art. 2. *Music*. serious and of permanent value. 3. traditional.

clăs′sĭ·cĭsm, *n*. adherence to forms or principles deemed classic. **clas′si·cist,** *n*.

clăs′sĭ·fy″, *v.t.,* **-fied, -fying. 1.** put into meaningful categories. **2.** designate officially as secret. **clas″si·fi·ca′tion,** *n*.

clăt′ter, *n*. **1.** loud rattling noise. —*v.i.* **2.** make a clatter. —*v.t.* **3.** cause to clatter.

clause, *n*. **1.** unit of a sentence. **2.** unit of a document.

claus″trŏ·phō′bĭ·à, *n*. morbid fear of enclosure. —**claus″tro·pho′bic,** *adj*.

clăv′ĭ·chôrd″, *n*. pianolike keyboard instrument.

clăv′ĭ·cle, *n*. collarbone.

claw, *n*. **1.** hooked paw or foot. —*v.t., v.i.* **2.** scratch or grasp with or as with a claw.

clay, *n*. earth in a readily molded state.

clean, *adj*. **1.** free of dirt, germs, impurities, etc. **2.** keeping things clean. **3.** irreproachable. **4.** thorough. —*v.t.* **5.** make clean. —**clean′er,** *n*. —**clean′up″,** *n*.

clean′ly, *adj., -lier, -liest*. free of or avoiding dirt, etc. —**clean′li·ness,** *n*.

cleanse, *v.t.,* **cleansed, cleansing**. make clean.

clear, *adj*. **1.** perfectly transparent. **2.** lucid. **3.** unambiguous. **4.** obvious. **5.** unobstructed. **6.** free of blame, danger, debt, etc. —*adv*. **7.** clearly. —*v.t.* **8.** make clear. **9.** pass without colliding with. **10.** net a profit of. —**clear′ly,** *adv*. —**clear′ness,** *n*.

clear′ánce, *n*. **1.** space between two obstructions. **2.** official approval to proceed.

clear′ĭng, *n*. forest area free of trees.

cleat, *n*. object attached to a surface to improve traction, give reinforcement, etc.

cleave, *v.,* **cleaved** or (for 1) **cleft** or **clove, cleaved** or (for 1) **cleft** or **cloven, cleaving.** *v.t., v.i.* **1.** split. —*v.i.* **2.** adhere or be faithful. —**cleav′er,** *n*. —**cleav′age,** *n*.

clef, *n*. *Music*. symbol establishing pitch.

cleft, *n*. narrow opening; crack.

clĕm′ént, *n*. **1.** merciful. **2.** mild, as the weather. —**clem′en·cy,** *n*.

clĕnch, *v.t.* press or bind firmly together.

clêr′gy, *n., pl*. **-gies.** priests, ministers, and other religious leaders. —**cler′gy·man,** *n*.

clêr′ĭ·càl, *adj*. **1.** pertaining to clerks. **2.** pertaining to clergy.

clêrk, *n*. **1.** record keeper. **2.** retail employee.

clĕv′êr, *adj*. able in understanding, contriving, etc. —**clev′er·ly,** *adv*. —**clev′er·ness,** *n*.

cli·ché, *n*. trite metaphor or phrase.

clĭck, *n*. **1.** sharp noise from striking, buckling, etc. —*v.t., vi*. **2.** move with a click.

clī′ént, *n*. person who buys professional services.

clī″én·tēle′, *n*. clients of a professional merchant, etc.

clĭff, *n*. abrupt rise of land.

clī·măc′têr·ĭc, *n*. critical period of life, esp. in middle age.

clī·māte, *n*. characteristic weather. **cli·mat′ic,** *adj*.

clī′măx, *n*. point of greatest interest, emotion, tension, etc. —**cli·mac′tic,** *adj*.

clĭmb, *v.t.* **1.** move upward upon or within. —*v.i.* **2.** climb something. **3.** grow or become higher. —*n*. **4.** act or instance of climbing. **5.** something climbed. —**climb′er,** *n*.

clĭnch, *v.t.* **1.** establish firmly. **2.** bend to secure firmly, as a driven nail. —*n*. **3.** act or instance of clinching.

clĭng, *v.i.,* **clung, clinging. 1.** hold firmly. **2.** stay close.

clĭn′ĭc, *n*. **1.** session of medical treatment as a form of instruction. **2.** association of medical specialists. **3.** place for treating outpatients.

clĭn′ĭ·càl, *adj*. **1.** pertaining to clinics. **2.** pertaining to medical education and treatment involving actual cases. **3.** impersonally analytical.

clĭnk, *n*. **1.** high, muted ringing. —*v.i.* **2.** make such a sound. —*v.t.* **3.** strike so as to make such a sound.

clĭnk′êr, *n*. lump of coal ash, etc.

clĭp, *v.,* **clipped, clipping.** *v.t.* **1.** cut, as with scissors. **2.** fasten. **3.** *Informal*. hit sharply. —*v.i.* **4.** move swiftly. —*n*. **5.** fastener. **6.** *Informal*. sharp blow.

clĭp'pêr, *n.* **1.** fast sailing vessel. **2. clippers,** device for cutting hair.

clĭp'pĭng, *n.* article cut from a periodical.

clĭque, *n.* exclusive social group. —**cliqu'ish,** *adj.*

clōak, *n.* **1.** long, loose garment worn over the shoulders. —*v.t.* **2.** cover with a cloak. **3.** obscure.

clŏb'bêr, *v.t. Informal.* beat.

clŏck, *n.* **1.** machine for measuring time. **2.** narrow sock ornament. —*v.t.* **3.** time. —**clock'work",** *n., adj.*

clŏck'wīse", *adv., adj.* as the hands of a clock move, i.e. from left to right through 12 o'clock.

clŏd, *n.* **1.** lump of earth. **2.** *Informal.* stupid person.

clŏg, *v.,* **clogged, clogging,** *n. vt.* **1.** stop flow through; choke. —*v.i.* **2.** become stopped up. —*n.* **3.** act or instance of clogging. **4.** thick-soled shoe.

clŏis'têr, *n.* **1.** covered walk in a monastery, etc. **2.** monastic institution.

clōne, *n., v. Biology.* a genetic duplicate of an organism.

clōse, *v.,* **closed, closing,** *adj.,* **closer, closest,** *n. v.t.* (klōz) **1.** block or fill, as with a door. **2.** move so as to block or fill. **3.** deny public access to. **4.** conclude. —*v.i.* **5.** become closed. —*n.* **6.** conclusion. —*adj.* (klōs) **7.** near; not far. **8.** confined. **9.** intimate. **10.** stuffy. **11.** careful. **12.** secretive. —**close'ly,** *adv.* —**close'ness,** *n.* —**clo'sure,** *n.*

clŏs'ĕt, *n.* **1.** small storage room. —*v.t.* **2.** put in a small room for privacy.

clōse'-ŭp", *n.* photograph at close range.

clŏt, *n., v.i.,* **clotted, clotting.** *n.* **1.** lump, esp. of coagulated blood. —*v.i.* **2.** form a clot.

clŏth, *n., pl.* **cloths. 1.** material of interwoven fibers. **2.** piece of such material. **3. the cloth,** the clergy.

clōthe, *v.t.,* **clothed, clothing. 1.** put clothes on. **2.** give clothes to.

clōthes, *n., pl.* things to cover the human body. Also, **cloth'ing.**

clŏud, *n.* **1.** mass of vapor in the sky. **2.** mass of airborne material. **3.** something marring happiness, reputation, etc. —*v.t.* **4.** make indistinct, as from vapor. **5.** mar. —*v.i.* **6.** become cloudy. —**cloud'less,** *adj.* —**cloud'y,** *adj.*

clŏud'bûrst", *n.* sudden, violent rainstorm.

clŏut, *n.* **1.** blow. —*v.t.* **2.** hit.

clōve, *n.* **1.** tropical spice. **2.** section of a head of garlic, etc.

clō'vĕn, *adj.* divided or split.

clō'vêr, *n.* three-leafed herb.

clō'vêr-lēaf", *n.* system of curved ramps between roads crossing at different grades.

clŏwn, *n.* **1.** entertainer with funny antics. —*v.i.* **2.** act like a clown.

clŏy'ĭng, *adj.* repulsively sweet, sentimental, etc.

clŭb, *n., v.* **clubbed, clubbing.** *n.* **1.** stick, etc. for striking blows. **2.** similar object used in exercises or sports. **3.** social group. **4.** suit of playing cards. —*v.t.* **5.** strike with a club. —*v.i.* **6.** unite for a purpose. —**club'foot",** *n.* —**club'house",** *n.*

clŭck, *n.* **1.** henlike sound. —*v.i.* **2.** make such a sound.

clūe, *n.* **1.** indication of the solution to a puzzle.

clŭmp, *n.* cluster, as of trees.

clŭm'sÿ, *adj.,* **-sier, -siest.** without skill or care. —**clum'si·ly,** *adv.* —**clum'si·ness,** *n.*

clŭs'têr, *n.* **1.** loose group. —*v.t., v.i.* **2.** gather in a group.

clŭtch, *v.t., v.i.* **1.** grasp violently. —*n.* **2.** grasp. **3. clutches,** unrightful possession or power. **4.** device for engaging a machine with its mover.

clŭt'têr, *v.t.* **1.** fill with unwanted things. —*n.* **2.** disorderly accumulation.

cōach, *n.* **1.** enclosed horse-drawn carriage. **2.** bus. **3.** railroad passenger car. **4.** trainer, as in sports or performing arts. —*v.t.* **5.** train, rehearse, or prompt. —**coach'man,** *n.*

cō·ăg'ū·lāte", *v.,* **-ated, -ating.** *v.i., v.t.* turn from a liquid to a semi-solid. —**co·ag"u·la'tion,** *n.* —**co·ag'u·lant,** *n.*

cōal, *n.* **1.** combustible mineral. **2.** ember. —*v.t.* **3.** supply with coal.

cō"ȧ·lĕsce', *v.i.,* **-lesced, -lescing.** unite. —**co"a·les'cence,** *n.*

cō"ȧ·lī'tion, *n.* act of uniting for a specific purpose.

cōal oīl, kerosene.

côarse, *adj.* **1.** composed of large grains, fibers, etc. **2.** roughly made. **3.** unrefined, as manners or language.

—**coarse′ly**, *adv.* —**coarse′ness**, *n.*
—**coars′en**, *v.t.*, *v.i.*

cōast, *n.* **1.** land by a sea, etc. —*v.i.* **2.** move by gravity or momentum. **3.** sail along a coast. —**coast′al**, *adj.* —**coast′line′′**, *n.*

cōast′êr, *n.* **1.** person or thing that coasts. **2.** mat or stand for wet glasses. **3.** ship on a coastal run.

cōat, *n.* **1.** cold-weather garment. **2.** jacket. **3.** Also, **coat′ing**, layer of material. —*v.t.* **4.** cover with a coat.

cōat òf ârms, *Heraldry.* arms of a person, state, etc.

cōax, *v.t.*, persuade with flattery or wheedling.

cō·ăx′ĭ·àl, *adj.* having a common axis.

cŏb, *n.* corncob.

cŏb′ble, *v.t.*, -**bled**, -**bling**, *n.* **1.** repair, as shoes. **2.** assemble clumsily. —*n.* **3.** Also, **cob′ble·stone′′**, large pebble used for paving.

cŏb′blêr, *n.* **1.** person who cobbles. **2.** fruit-filled pastry.

cō′brà, *n.* poisonous Asian and African snake.

cŏb′wĕb′′, *n.* web of a spider.

cō·cāine,′, *n.* narcotic from the coca plant.

cŏck, *n.* **1.** rooster. **2.** faucet. —*v.t.* **3.** tilt. **4.** make ready for firing, as a gun.

cŏck·āde′, *n.* hat badge or ribbon.

cŏck′à·tōō′′, *n.* crested East Indian parrot.

cŏckêr spăniel, small, droopy-eared spaniel.

cŏck′eȳed′′, *adj. Informal.* awry; wrong.

cŏck′le, *n.* edible shellfish.

cŏck′nēy, *n.*, *pl.* -**nies**. **1.** native of London's East End. **2.** dialect of such a native.

cŏck′pĭt′′, *n.* **1.** place for a cockfight. **2.** space for an airplane crew.

cŏck′rōach′′, *n.* crawling insect found in buildings.

cŏck′sūre′′, *adj.* foolishly self-assured.

cŏck′tāil′′, *n.* **1.** mixed alcoholic drink. **2.** mixed appetizer.

cŏck′y̆, *adj.*, -**ier**, -**iest**. *Informal.* showily self-assured.

cō′cōa, *n.* drink made from roasted cacao powder.

cō′cò·nŭt, *n.* fruit of a palm tree, whose flesh and juice are consumed. Also, **co′coa·nut**.

cò·cōōn′, *n.* case of certain insect pupas, made of a thread.

cŏd, *n.*, *pl.* **cod, cods**. edible northern saltwater fish. Also, **cod′fish′′**.

cŏd′dle, *v.t.*, -**dled**, -**dling**. **1.** cook in water just below boiling. **2.** take excessive care of; pamper.

cōde, *n.*, *v.t.*, **coded, coding**. *n.* **1.** set of laws or principles. **2.** formula for secret messages. **3.** formula for transcription by telegraph, wigwag, etc. —*v.t.* put into code.

cō′dēine, *n.* pain reliever derived from opium. Also, **co′dein**.

cŏd′ĭ·cĭl, *n.* appendix to a will.

cŏd′ĭ·fȳ′′, *v.t.*, -**fied**, -**fying**. put into systematic form, esp. in writing. —**cod′′i·fi·ca′tion**, *n.*

cō′-ĕd′′, *n. Informal.* woman in a coeducational school. Also, **co′ed′′**.

cō·ĕd′′ū·cā′tion, *n.* enrollment of men and women in the same school. —**co·ed′′u·ca′tion·al**, *adj.*

cō′′ĕf·fĭ′cient, *n.* multiplier.

cō·êrce′, *v.t.*, -**erced**, -**ercing**. compel by force or threats. —**co·er′cion**, *n.*

cō·ē′vàl, *adj.* at or of the same age.

cō′′ĕx·īst′, *v.i.* **1.** exist together. **2.** live together without dispute. —**co′′ex·ist′ence**, *n.*

cŏf′fēe, *n.* drink made from the roasted seed of a tropical shrub.

cŏf′fêr, *n.* chest for valuables.

cŏf′fĭn, *n.* burial chest.

cŏg, *n.* gear tooth.

cō·gĕnt, *adj.* forcefully convincing, as an argument. —**co′gen·cy**, *n.*

cŏg′ĭ·tāte′′, *v.*, -**tated**, -**tating**. *v.t.*, *v.i.* ponder. —**cog′′i·ta′tion**, *n.* —**cog′i·ta′′tor**, *n.*

co·gnac (kōn′yăk), *n.* a French brandy.

cŏg′nāte′′, *adj.* **1** related. —*n.* **2.** someone or something related.

cŏg·nĭ′tion, *n.* knowledge or perception. —**cog′ni·tive**, *adj.*

cŏg′nĭ·zănce, *n.* official notice. —**cog′ni·zant**, *adj.*

cŏg·nō′mèn, *n.* nickname.

cŏg′whēel′′, *n.* gear wheel, esp. in a clock, toy, etc.

cō·hăb′ĭt, *v.i.* live together, esp. out of wedlock. —**co·hab′′i·ta′tion**, *n.*

cō·hēre′, *v.i.*, -**hered**, -**hering**. **1.** stick

together. **2.** be rationally connected. —co·her'ent, *adj.* —co·her'ence, *n.*

co·hē'sion, *n.* tendency of particles, etc. to hold together. —co·he'sive, *adj.*

cŏif·fūre', *n.* hair style.

coīl, *n.* **1.** spiral or helix. —*v.t.*, *v.i.* **2.** wind into a coil.

coīn, *n.* **1.** piece of metal used as money. **2.** metal money. —*v.t.* **3.** stamp as money. **4.** invent as a new expression. —coin'age, *n.*

cō''ĭn·cīde', *v.i.*, -cided, -ciding. **1.** happen at the same time. **2.** be in the same space. **3.** be in agreement. —co·in'ci·dence, *n.* —co·in''ci·den'tal, co·in'ci·dent, *adj.*

cō·ĭ'tŭs, *n.* sexual intercourse. Also, co·i'tion, *n.*

cōke, *n.* **1.** fuel derived from coal. **2.** slang for cocaine.

cŏl'ăn·dêr, *n.* large strainer.

cōld, *adj.* **1.** having a temperature lower than normal or working temperature. **2.** having a relatively low temperature. **3.** feeling a lack of warmth. **4.** unemotional. **5.** hostilely unexpressive. **6.** *Informal.* **a.** unprepared. **b.** unconscious. **c.** fully memorized. —*n.* **7.** cold conditions, weather, etc. **8.** illness associated with cold weather. —cold'ly, *adv.* —cold·ness, *n.*

cōld'bloōd''ĕd, *adj.* **1.** having blood the temperature of the environment. **2.** without emotion, conscience, etc.

cōld wâr, prolonged hostile situation without fighting.

cōle'släw'', *n.* salad of shredded raw cabbage.

cŏl'ĭc, *n.* abdominal cramp.

cŏl·lăb'ō·rāte'', *v.i.*, -rated, -rating. **1.** work together, as on a project. **2.** assist the invaders of one's country. —col·lab''o·ra'tion, *n.* —col·lab'o·ra''tor, *n.* —col·lab''o·ra'tion·ist, *n.*

cŏl·lăpse', *v.*, -lapsed, -lapsing, *n. v.i.* **1.** fall because of weakness. **2.** fold when not in use. **3.** fail suddenly in bodily or mental health. —*v.t.* **4.** cause to collapse. —*n.* **5.** act or instance of collapsing. —col·laps'i·ble, *adj.*

cŏl'lär, *n.* **1.** band worn around the neck. **2.** band of material applied to a shaft, etc. —*v.t.* **3.** seize by the neck. **4.** put a collar on.

cŏl'lär·bōne'', *n.* bone between the breastbone and shoulder blade; clavicle.

cŏl·lăt'êr·ăl, *n.* **1.** security for a loan. —*adj.* **2.** accompanying. **3.** related through a remote ancestor.

cŏl'lēague, *n.* professional associate.

cŏl·lĕct', *v.t.*, *v.i.* **1.** gather together. —*v.t.* **2.** acquire to enjoy permanently. **3.** enforce payment of. —*adv.*, *adj.* **4.** with the receiver paying the charges. —col·lect'a·ble, col·lect'i·ble, *adj.*, *n.* —col·lect'or, *n.* —col·lec'tion, *n.*

cŏl·lĕct'ĕd, *adj.* with one's emotions under control.

cŏl·lĕc'tĭve, *adj.* **1.** involving cooperation. —*n.* **2.** collective enterprise or workplace. —col·lec'tive·ly, *adv.*

cŏl·lĕc'tĭv·ĭsm, *n.* adoption of collective working methods. —col·lec'tiv·ist, *n.*, *adj.* —col·lec'tiv·ize'', *v.t.*

cŏl'lēge, *n.* **1.** generalized institution of higher learning. **2.** specialized school. **3.** official organization. —col·le'giate, *adj.*

cŏl·līde', *v.i.*, -lided, -liding. strike together with direct impact. —col·li'sion, *n.*

cŏl'liē, *n.* large, long-haired dog.

cŏl·lō'quĭ·ăl, *adj.* pertaining to or used in informal conversation only. —col·lo'qui·al·ism, *n.*

cŏl·lō'quў, *n.*, *pl.* -quies. discussion.

cŏl·lū'sion, *n.* unlawful conspiracy. —col·lu'sive, *adj.*

cȯ·lōgne', *n.* perfumed toilet water.

cō'lŏn, *n.* **1.** part of the large intestine. **2.** punctuation mark written thus : .

colo'nel (kêr'nĕl), *n.* military officer between a lieutenant colonel and a brigadier general. —colo'nel·cy, *n.*

cŏl'ȯ·nīze, *v.*, -nized, -nizing. *v.t.* **1.** establish colonies in. —*v.i.* **2.** settle in or as a colony.

cŏl''ȯn·nāde', *n.* row of columns, esp. before a porch.

cŏl'ȯ·nў, *n.*, *pl.* -nies. **1.** region in the possession of a foreign nation. **2.** community of settlers. **3.** group of social insects, etc. —co·lon'i·al, *adj.*, *n.* —col'on·ist, *n.*

cŏl'ör, *n.* **1.** property deriving from specific wavelengths of light. **2.** pigment. **3.** vividness. **4.** colors, **a.** national flag. **b.** uniform, badge, etc. distinctively colored. —*v.t.* **5.** give color to. —*v.i.* **6.**

blush. —**col″or·a′tion,** *n.* —**col′or·ful,** *adj.* —**col′or·ing,** *n.*

còl″ór·à·tū′rà, *n.* soprano capable of brilliant effects.

còl′ör·lĕss, *adj.* not vivid.

co·lŏs′sàl, *adj.* gigantic; enormous.

co·lŏs′sŭs, *n., pl.* **-si, -suses.** something gigantic.

cōlt, *n.* young male horse.

cŏl′ŭmn, *n.* **1.** narrow, upright structural support. **2.** stack of printed or written lines read together. **3.** regular series of articles by a journalist. **4.** file of troops. —**col′um·nist,** *n.*

cō′mà, *n.* pathological unconsciousness. —**co′ma·tose″,** *adj.*

cōmb, *n.* **1.** pronged device for arranging the hair or other fibers. **2.** crest of a rooster, etc. **3.** honeycomb. —*v.t.* **4.** use a comb on. **5.** search exhaustively.

cŏm′băt, *n., v.t.,* **-bated, -bating.** *n.* **1.** battle. —*v.t.* (kəm bat′) **2.** fight or oppose. —**com·bat′ant,** *n., adj.* —**com·bat′ive,** *adj.*

cŏm″bĭ·nā′tion, *n.* **1.** act or instance of combining. **2.** group of successive settings of a lock dial that open the lock.

cŏm·bīne, *v.t., v.i.* **1.** join together. —*n.* (cŏm′bīne) **2.** machine that harvests and threshes grain. **3.** syndicate.

cŏm′bō, *n., pl.* **-bos.** *Jazz.* small instrumental group.

cŏm·bŭs′tion, *n.* act of burning. —**com·bus′ti·ble,** *adj.*

cóme, *v.i.,* **came, come, coming,** *interj.* *v.i.* **1.** move to this place. **2.** attend; be present. **3.** occur; happen. —*interj.* **4.** be truthful, reasonable, etc.

co·mē′dĭ·àn, *n.* humorous performer. Also, *fem.,* **co·me″di·enne′.**

cŏm′e·dў, *n., pl.* **-dies. 1.** drama with a happy ending. **2.** amusing situation.

cóme′lў, *adj.,* **-lier, -liest.** physically attractive.

co·mĕs′tĭ·ble, *n., adj.* edible.

cŏm′ét, *n.* cloud of fine dust in orbit around the sun.

cóm′fört, *n.* **1.** feeling of physical well-being. **2.** consolation. —*v.t.* **3.** console or reassure.

cóm′fört·à·ble, *adj.* **1.** enjoying comfort. **2.** promoting comfort. —**com′fort·a·bly,** *adv.*

cóm′fört· êr, *n.* **1.** source of comfort. **2.** quilt.

cŏm′ĭc, *adj.* **1.** Also, **com′i·cal,** amusing. **2.** pertaining to comedy. **3. comics,** comic strip. —*n.* **4.** comedian. —**com′i·cal·ly,** *adv.*

cóm′ĭng, *adj.* **1.** on the way. **2.** destined for preeminence. —*n.* **3.** approach or arrival.

cŏm′mà, *n.* a mark, used especially to separate phrases or clauses in a sentence.

còm·mănd′, *v.t.* **1.** order or direct. **2.** have authority over. **3.** have the use or enjoyment of. **4.** overlook. —*n.* **5.** order. **6.** authority or control.

cŏm′măn·dănt″, *n.* commanding officer.

cŏm″màn·dēer′, *v.t.* take control of by authority or force.

còm·măn′dêr, *n.* naval officer between a lieutenant commander and a captain in rank.

còmmăndêr ĭn chiĕf, *n., pl.* **commanders in chief.** supreme military commander.

còm·mănd′mènt, *n.* order, esp. a standing one from a deity.

còm·măn′dō, *n., pl.* **-dos, -does.** member of a raiding force.

còm·mĕm′ó·ráte″, *v.t.,* **-rated, -rating.** honor or preserve the memory of. —**com·mem″o·ra′tion,** *n.* —**com·mem′o·ra·tive,** *adj.*

còm·mĕnce′, *v.,* **menced, -mencing.** *v.t., v.i.* begin.

còm·mĕnce′mènt, *n.* **1.** beginning. **2.** high-school graduation ceremony.

cóm·mĕnd′, *v.t.* **1.** praise. **2.** recommend. **3.** entrust. —**com′mend′a·ble,** *adj.* —**com″men·da′tion,** *n.* —**com·mend′a·to″ry,** *adj.*

còm·mĕn′sûr·à·ble, *adj.* able to be measured or evaluated in the same way.

còm·mĕn′sû·ráte, *adj.* equal or in proportion.

cŏm′mĕnt, *n.* **1.** remark or remarks on something observed. **2.** opinion or explanation regarding something. —*v.i.* **3.** make a comment.

cŏm′mèn·tār″ў, *n., pl.* **-ries.** set of explanatory notes.

cŏm′mèn·tā″tör, *n.* person who comments on current events.

cŏm′mêrce, *n.* purchasing and sale of merchandise.

cóm·mêr′ciàl, *adj.* **1.** pertaining to commerce. —*n.* **2.** television or radio advertisement.

cŏm·mêr'ciȧl·ĭsm, *n.* emphasis on ready mass saleability rather than on quality, taste, etc.

cŏm'mêr'ciȧl·īze'', *v.t.,* **-ized, izing.** make, sell, etc. for maximum profit.

cŏm·mĭn'gle, *v.,* **-gled, -gling.** *v.t., v.i.* blend.

cŏm·mĭs'êr·āte'', *v.t.* **-ated, -ating.** feel sympathetic sorrow. **—com·mis''er·a'tion,** *n.*

cŏm''mĭs·sār'ĭ·ȧt, *n.* military department in charge of food.

cŏm'mĭs·sār''ÿ, *n., pl.* **-ries.** *n.* **1.** military food shop. **2.** factory canteen.

cŏm·mĭs'sion, *n.* **1.** entrusted task. **2.** formal authorization. **3.** military officership. **4.** committee. **5.** salesman's percentage of the amount of a sale. —*v.t.* **6.** entrust or authorize. **7.** put in service, as a ship.

cŏm·mĭs'sion·êr, *n.* head of a municipal department or commission.

cŏm·mĭt', *v.t.* **-mitted, -mitting. 1.** obligate. **2.** state the position of in a controversy. **3.** do, esp. a crime. **4.** send for confinement. **—com·mit'ment,** *n.* **—com·mit'al,** *n.*

cŏm·mĭt'tēe, *n.* chosen group of persons with specified responsibilities. **—com·mit'tee·man,** *n.* **—com·mit'tee·wom''an,** *n.*

cŏm·mōde', *n.* **1.** chest of drawers. **2.** water closet.

cŏm·mō'dĭ·oŭs, *adj.* roomy.

cŏm·mŏd'ĭ·tÿ, *n., pl.* **-ties.** *Commerce.* material or article, as opposed to a service.

cŏm'mȯ·dôre'', *n.* **1.** naval officer ranking between a captain and a rear admiral. **2.** head of a yacht squadron.

cŏm'mȯn, *adj.* **1.** pertaining to many or to all. **2.** not unusual. **3.** low in rank or status. **4.** vulgar. —*n.* **5.** area of public land in a village. **—com'mon·ly,** *adv.*

cŏm'mȯn·êr, *n.* citizen not of the nobility.

cŏmmȯn lăw, law based on custom and court decision.

cŏm'mȯn·plāce'', *adj.* **1.** completely or tritely familiar. —*n.* **2.** something commonplace.

cŏmmȯn sĕnse, ordinary good judg-

ment. **—com'mon-sense'', com''mon·sen'si·cal,** *adj.*

cŏm'mȯn·wēal'', *n.* general good.

cŏm'mȯn·wĕalth'', *n.* **1.** federation of states. **2.** state.

cŏm·mō'tion, *n.* uproar.

cŏm·mū'nȧl, *adj.* pertaining to or shared by a community or group.

cŏm·mūne', *v.i.,* **-muned, -muning,** *n.* *v.i.* **1.** be in intimate communication or sympathy. —*n.* (kom'yōōn) **2.** community sharing goods, responsibilities, etc.

cŏm·mūn'ĭ·cȧ·ble, *adj.* **1.** able to be communicated. **2.** able to be transferred, as an illness.

cŏm·mūn'ĭ·cȧnt, *n.* partaker of the Eucharist.

cŏm·mūn'ĭ·cāte, *v.,* **-cated, -cating.** *v.t.* **1.** make understood to others. —*v.i.* **2.** exchange messages. **3.** be in communion. **4.** be connected, as rooms. **—com·mun''i·ca'tion,** *n.*

cŏm·mūn'ĭ·cȧ·tĭve, *adj.* talkative or confiding.

cŏm·mūn'ion, *n.* **1.** state of intimacy. **2.** *Christianity.* sharing of bread and wine in remembrance of Christ. **3.** religious denomination.

cŏm·mūn''ĭ·qué, *n.* official message or news release.

cŏm'mū'nĭsm, *n.* **1.** political theory demanding public ownership of economic resources. **2. Communism.** socialism derived from the theories of Karl Marx. **—com''mu·nis'tic,** *adj.* **—com'mu·nist,** *n., adj.*

cŏm·mūn'ĭ·tÿ, *n., pl.* **-ties. 1.** town, etc. **2.** group with common interests, etc. **3.** sharing in common.

cŏm·mūte', *v.,* **-muted, -muting.** *v.t.* **1.** alter, as a prison sentence. —*v.i.* **2.** travel regularly, as between home and work. **—com·mut'er,** *n.* **—com''mu·ta'tion,** *n.*

cŏm·păct', *adj.* **1.** occupying a minimal space. **2.** succinct. —*n.* (kom'pakt) **3.** small cosmetic case. **4.** small-bodied car. **5.** mutual agreement. **—com·pact'ly,** *adv.* **—com·pact'ness,** *n.*

cŏm·păn'ion, *n.* **1.** person who keeps one company. **2.** one of a pair or set. **—com·pan'ion·ship'',** *n.*

cŏm·păn'ion·ȧ·ble, *adj.* willing to keep one company.

cóm·pǎn'ión·wāy'', *n.* stair in a ship.

cóm'pá·nÿ, *n., pl.* **-nies. 1.** fellowship; companionship. **2.** group of persons. **3.** group of persons assembled for social purposes. **4.** guests. **5.** business organization or association. **6.** military unit.

cǒm'pá·rà·ble, *adj.* allowing comparison.

cóm·pār'à·tǐve, *adj.* **1.** involving comparison. **2.** in comparison to other cases. **—com·par'a·tive·ly**, *adv.*

cóm·pāre', *v.*, **-pared, -paring,** *n.* *v.t.* **1.** examine for similarities and differences. **2.** regard or describe as similar. **—v.i. 3.** be similar to, esp. in worth. **—n. 4. beyond compare,** without equal.

cóm·pār'ĭ·són, *n.* **1.** act or instance of comparing. **2.** similarity.

cóm·pârt'mĕnt, *n.* division of a larger space.

cóm'pàss, *n.* **1.** instrument for establishing or indicating direction. **2.** scope. **3. compasses,** instrument for drawing circles.

cóm·pǎs'sión, *n.* sympathy, esp. with suffering or weakness. **—com·pas'sion·ate**, *adj.*

cóm·pǎt'ǐ·blè, *adj.* **1.** content together. **2.** logically consistent. **—com·pat''i·bil'i·ty**, *n.*

cóm·pā'trǐ·ót, *n.* fellow national.

cóm·pĕl', *v.t.*, **-pelled, -pelling.** force.

cóm·pĕn'dǐ·ŭm, *n., pl.* **-ums, -a.** detailed summary. **—com·pen'di·ous**, *adj.*

cŏm'pĕn·sāte'', *v.*, **-sated, -sating.** *v.t.* **1.** pay, as for work or damage. **—v.i. 2.** serve to offset or make up for something else. **—com''pen·sa'tion**, *n.* **—com'pen'sa·to''ry**, *adj.*

cóm'pēte', *v.i.*, **-peted, -peting.** act in rivalry. **com''pe·ti'tion**, *n.* **—com·pet'i·tive**, *adj.* **—com·pet'i·tor**, *n.*

cŏm'pĕ·tĕnt, *adj.* **1.** normal in mental ability. **2.** able to work, etc. adequately. **3.** adequately done. **4.** legally authorized. **—com'pe·tent·ly**, *adv.* **—com'pe·tence, com'pe·ten·cy**, *n.*

cóm·pīle', *v.t.*, **-piled, -piling.** gather or publish together, as documents. **—com·pil'er**, *n.* **—com''pi·la'tion**, *n.*

cóm·plā'cén·cÿ, *n.* satisfaction, esp. with oneself. **—com·pla'cent**, *adj.*

cóm·plāin', *v.i.* **1.** discuss one's griev-

ance with others. **—v.t. 2.** state as a grievance. **—com·plain'er**, *n.*

cóm·plāint', *n.* **1.** act or instance of complaining. **2.** wording in which one complains. **3.** distressing illness.

cóm·plāi'sànt, *adj.* willing or eager to please. **—com·plai'sance**, *n.*

cŏm'plĕ·mĕnt, *n.* **1.** something that completes. **2.** wholeness. **—v.t. 3.** complete. **—com''ple·men'ta·ry**, *adj.*

cóm·plēte', *adj., v.t.*, **-pleted, -pleting.** *adj.* **1.** entire; with nothing missing. **2.** accomplished. **3.** utter. **—v.t. 4.** perfect. **5.** finish. **—com·plete'ly**, *adv.* **—com·plete'ness**, *n.* **—com·ple'tion**, *n.*

cóm·plĕx', *adj.* **1.** not readily analyzed or understood. **—n.** (kom'pleks) **2.** something complex. **3.** *Psychology.* **a.** group of impulses controlling behavior. **b.** obsessive attitude. **—com·plex'i·ty**, *n.*

cóm·plĕx'ión, *n.* color and texture of the skin.

cŏm'plǐ·cāte'', *v.t.*, **-cated, -cating. 1.** make difficult to do or understand. **2.** make unnecessarily complex. **—com''pli·ca'tion**, *n.*

cóm·plǐc'ǐ'tÿ, *n., pl.* **-ties.** association, esp. in crime.

cŏm'plǐ·mĕnt, *n.* **1.** expression of praise. **—v.t. 2.** pay a compliment to.

cŏm''plǐ·mĕn'tàr·ÿ, *adj.* **1.** serving as a compliment. **2.** granted free of charge.

cóm·plÿ', *v.i.*, **-plied, -plying.** act as ordered or urged. **—com·pli'ance**, *n.* **—com·pli'ant**, *adj.*

cóm·pō'nént, *n.* **1.** part of a whole. **—adj. 2.** serving as a component.

cóm·pôrt', *v.t.* conduct or behave. **—com·port'ment**, *n.*

cóm·pōse', *v.t.*, **-posed, -posing. 1.** create or organize artistically. **2.** constitute. **3.** put in order. **4.** make calm.

cóm·pōsed', *adj.* apparently calm.

cóm·pǒs'ĭte, *adj.* made of many constituents.

cŏm''pǒ·sǐ'tion, *n.* **1.** something composed. **2.** method of composing. **3.** nature, as of constituents or traits.

cŏm'pōst, *n.* decayed matter for use as fertilizer.

cóm·pō'sûre, *n.* apparent calm.

cŏm'pōte'', *n.* dish of stewed fruits.

cŏm'pŏund, *adj.* **1.** not simple; complex. **—n. 2.** substance of mixed elements. **3.** building enclosure. —*v.t.* (cŏm·pound´) **4.** mix or make by mixing. **5.** permit unlawfully.

cŏm´´pre·hĕnd´, *v.t.* **1.** have a conception or understanding of **2.** include —com´´pre·hen´sion, *n.* —com´´pre·hen´si·ble, *adj.*

cŏm´´pre·hĕn´sĭve, *adj.* including all or most elements. —com´´pre·hen´sive·ly, *adv.* —com´´pre·hen´sive·ness, *n.*

cŏm·prĕss´, *v.t.* **1.** press to lessen volume. **2.** put under pressure. —*n.* (kahm´ pres) **3.** pad of cloth applied as an aid to medicine. —com·pres´sion, *n.* —com·pres´sor, *n.*

cŏm·prīse´, *v.t.*, -prised, -prising. **1.** include. **2.** consist of.

cŏm´pro·mīse´´, *n.*, *v.*, -mised, -mising. *n.* **1.** expedient but not fully satisfactory agreement. **2.** something with disparate elements. —*v.i.* **3.** make a compromise. —*v.t.* **4.** endanger in reputation, etc.

cŏmp·trŏl´lêr, *n.* financial manager.

cŏm·pŭl´sion, *n.* act or instance of compelling. —com·pul´sive, *adj.* —com·pul´so·ry, *adj.*

cŏm·pŭnc´tion, *n.* uneasy, guilty feeling.

cŏm·pūte´, *v.t.*, -puted, -puting. determine by calculation. —com´´pu·ta´tion, *n.*

cŏm·pūt´êr, *n.* electronic device for rapid calculation or data comparison. —com·put´er·ize, *v.t.* —com·put´´er·i·za´tion, *n.*

cŏm´răde´´, *n.* **1.** close friend. **2.** associate. —com´rade·ship´´, *n.*

cŏmsăt, *n.* communications satellite.

cŏn, *v.t.*, conned, conning, *adj.*, *n. v.t.* **1.** survey carefully. —*n.* **2.** person or argument opposed. —*v.t.* **3.** swindle. —*n.* **4.** convict.

cŏn·cāve´, *adj.* curving inward. —con·cav´i·ty, *n.*

cŏn·cēal´, *v.t.* hide or keep secret. —con·ceal´ment, *n.*

cŏn·cēde´, *v.t.*, -ceded, -ceding. **1.** admit as true. **2.** acknowledge defeat in. **3.** grant.

cŏn·cēit´, *n.* **1.** excessive pride. **2.** fanciful idea or expression.

cŏn·cēit´ĕd, *adj.* full of conceit.

cŏn·cēive´, *v.*, -ceived, -ceiving. *v.i.* **1.** form an idea. **2.** become pregnant.

—*v.t.* **3.** imagine as possible or true. **4.** become pregnant with. —con·ceiv´a·ble, *adj.* —con·ceiv´a·bly, *adv.*

cŏn´cĕn·trāte´´, *v.*, -trated, -trating, *n. v.t.* **1.** focus. **2.** increase in strength. —*v.i.* **3.** focus attention or effort. —*n.* **4.** something concentrated. —con´´cen·tra´tion, *n.*

cŏn·cĕn´trĭc, *adj.* having a common or identical center.

cŏn´cĕpt, *n.* idea of something possible. —con·cep´tu·al, *adj.*

cŏn·cĕp´tion, *n.* act or instance of conceiving.

cŏn·cêrn´, *v.t.* **1.** be the business of. **2.** cause care or anxiety in. **3.** have as a subject. —*n.* **4.** business or affair. **5.** care or anxiety. **6.** business organization. **7.** importance.

cŏn·cêrned´, *adj.* **1.** anxious. **2.** interested. **3.** engaged in political or social problems.

cŏn·cêrn´ĭng, *prep.* on the subject of.

cŏn´cêrt, *n.* **1.** series of musical compositions performed at one time. **2.** harmony.

cŏn·cêrt´ĕd, *adj.* performed in an agreed manner.

cŏn´´cêr·tī´nà, *n.* small accordion.

cŏn·cer·to (kŏn chĕr´tō), *n.*, *pl.* -tos, -ti. orchestral composition, usually with soloists.

cŏn·cĕs´sion, *n.* **1.** act or instance of conceding. **2.** something conceded. **3.** trade conducted on another person's property.

cŏn·cĕs´sion·āire´´, *n.* person allowed to engage in trade on another's property.

cŏn·cĭl´ĭ·āte´´, *v.t.*, -ated, -ating. pacify or appease. —con·cil´i·a´´tor, *n.* —con·cil´i·a·to´´ry, *adj.* —con·cil´´i·a´tion, *n.*

cŏn·cīse´, *adj.* confined to essentials, as a piece of writing. —con·cise´ly, *adv.* —con·cise´ness, *n.*

cŏn´clāve, *n.* private meeting.

cŏn·clūde´, *v.*, -cluded, cluding. *v.t.* **1.** end. **2.** reach an opinion or decision. —*v.i.* **3.** bring a meeting, etc. to an end. —con·clu´sion, *n.*

cŏn·clū´sĭve, *adj.* compelling a certain opinion or decision.

cŏn·cŏct´, *v.t.* **1.** make of varied ingredients. **2.** devise. —con·coc´tion, *n.*

cŏn·cŏm´ĭ·tànt, *adj.* **1.** accompanying.

—*n.* **2.** something that accompanies. —con·com'i·tant·ly, *adv.*

cŏn'côrd, *n.* harmonious agreement.

còn·côrd'ànce, *n.* list of occurrences in a book of certain words, etc.

cŏn'côurse, *n.* **1.** crowd. **2.** space or hall for accommodating crowds.

cŏn·crēte, *adj.* (kon krēt') **1.** real; material. **2.** specific. —*n.* (kon'krēt) **3.** material of cement and stone, etc. —*v.t., v.i.* **4.** solidify. —con·cre'tion, *n.*

cŏn'cŭ·bīne'', *n.* mistress.

cŏn''cū·pĭs'cénce, *n.* lust. —con''cu·pis'cent, *adj.*

còn·cûr', *v.i.*, -curred, -curring. **1.** agree. **2.** cooperate. **3.** coincide. —con·cur'rent, *adj.* —con·cur' rence, *n.*

còn·cŭs'sion, *n.* **1.** shock, as from a blow. **2.** malfunctioning of the mind or body from a blow.

còn·dĕmn', *v.t.* **1.** disapprove of strongly. **2.** reject as unfit. **3.** acquire by legal authority. **4.** sentence, as to prison. —con''dem·na'tion, *n.*

còn·dĕnse', *v.,* -densed, -densing, *v.t., v.i.* **1.** turn from a gas to a liquid. —*v.t.* **2.** put in succinct form. —con''den·sa' tion, *n.* —con·dens'er, *n.*

cŏn''de·scĕnd', *v.i.* **1.** show patronizing affability to an inferior. —*v.t.* **2.** do with a good grace despite superior status. —con''de·scen'sion, *n.*

cŏn'dĭ·mĕnt, *n.* flavor or seasoning.

còn·dĭ'tion, *n.* **1.** state of health, repair, etc. **2.** good state of health, etc. **3.** something necessary or required. —*v.t.* **4.** put in condition. **5.** accustom.

còn·dĭ'tion·àl, *adj.* subject to certain conditions.

còn·dōle', *v.i.*, -doled, -doling. express sorrowful sympathy. —con·dol'ence, *n.*

cŏn''dó·mĭn'ĭ·ŭm, *n.* **1.** multi-unit group of privately owned dwellings. **2.** territory under a joint rule.

còn·dōne', *v.t.*, -doned, -doning. to voluntarily fail to forbid or disapprove.

còn·dūce', *v.i.*, -duced, -ducing. tend or lead. —con·duc'ive, *adj.*

còn·dŭct', *v.t.* **1.** lead or direct. **2.** transmit. **3.** behave. —*n.* (kahn' duct) **4.** behavior.

còn·dūc'tŏr, *n.* **1.** leader of a band or orchestra. **2.** person in charge of a train,

etc. **3.** thing that transmits electricity, heat, etc.

còn'duĭt, *n.* channel for wiring or fluids.

cōne, *n.* **1.** solid generated by rotating an isosceles triangle around its centerline. **2.** fruit of an evergreen.

còn·fĕc'tion, *n.* food made with sugar. —con·fec'tion·er, *n.* —con·fec'tion· er·y, *n.*

còn·fĕd'êr·à·cў, *n., pl.* -cies. alliance.

còn·fĕd'êr·àte, *n., adj., v.,* -ated, -ating. *n.* **1.** ally or accomplice. —*adj.* **2.** allied. —*v.t., v.t.* (còn·fĕd'êr·āte'') **3.** ally. —con·fed''er·a'tion, *n.*

còn·fêr', *v.,* -ferred, -ferring. *v.t.* **1.** bestow. —*v.i.* **2.** consult or discuss. —con· fer'ment, *n.* —con'fer·ence, *n.*

còn·fĕss', *v.t.* **1.** admit as true. **2.** profess belief in. **3.** hear the confession of.

còn·fĕs'sion, *n.* **1.** act or instance of confessing. **2.** admission of sins by a penitent. **3.** creed or sect.

còn·fĕs'sion·àl, *n.* place where a priest hears confessions.

còn·fĕs'sŏr, *n.* priest who hears confessions.

còn·fĕt'tĭ, *n.* finely chopped colored paper thrown about in celebration.

cŏn'fĭ·dànt'', *n.* person in whom one confides. Also, *fem.,* con'fi·dante''.

còn·fīde', *v.,* -fided, -fiding. *v.i.* **1.** place trust, esp. by relating secrets. —*v.t.* **2.** entrust to someone's care or hearing.

còn'fĭ·dénce, *n.* **1.** trust. **2.** self-assurance. —con'fi·dent, *adj.* —con'fi· dent·ly, *adv.*

cŏn''fĭ·dĕn'tiàl, *adj.* **1.** to be kept a secret. **2.** entrusted with secrets. —con'' fi·den'tial·ly, *adv.*

còn·fĭg''ŭ·rā'tion, *n.* outline or contour.

cŏn·fīne', *v.t.*, -fined, -fining. *n. v.t.* **1.** keep within limits or boundaries. **2.** keep as if a prisoner. —*n.* **3.** confines (khan'fīnz), boundaries. —con·fine' ment, *n.*

còn·fĭrm', *v.t.* **1.** certify as true. **2.** approve formally. **3.** admit fully to a church. —con''fir·ma'tion, *n.*

cŏn'fĭs·cāte, *v.t.*, -cated, -cating. seize by authority. —con''fis·ca'tion, *n.*

cŏn''flà·grā'tion, *n.* fire causing major damage.

cŏn·flĭct, *n.* (kahn'flikt) **1.** fight. **2.** disagreement. **3.** emotional malaise or quandary. —*v.i.* (kən flikt′) **4.** be hostile or in disagreement.

còn·flū·ence, *n.* place where two rivers, etc. meet.

còn·fôrm′, *v.i.* **1.** form one's appearance, manners, etc. according to prevailing standards. **2.** act or be in accordance with a law, rule, etc. **3.** be similar. —*v.t.* **4.** cause to conform. —**con·form′i·ty,** *n.*

còn·fôrm′ĭst, *n.* person who conforms unquestioningly.

còn·fŏund′, *v.t.* confuse.

còn·frónt′, *v.t.* **1.** approach or face hostilely. **2.** to force to meet. —**con′′fron·ta′tion,** *n.*

còn·fūse′, *v.t.,* **-fused, -fusing. 1.** hamper in the powers of perception, analysis, decision, etc. **2.** embarrass. **3.** mistake for another. —**con·fu′sion,** *n.*

còn·fūte′, *v.t.,* **-futed, -futing.** show as wrong. —**con′′fu·ta′tion,** *n.*

còn·gēal′, *v.t., v.i.* thicken or freeze. —**con·geal′ment,** *n.*

còn·gēn′ĭ·àl, *adj.* agreeable. —**con·gen′′i·al′i·ty,** *n.*

còn·gĕn′ĭ·tàl, *adj.* from the time of birth. —**con·gen′i·tal·ly,** *adv.*

còn·gĕst′, *v.t.* fill to excess. —**con·ges′tion,** *n.*

còn·glŏm′êr·āte′′, *v.,* **-ated, -ating.** *adj., n. v.t., v.i.* **1.** form into a mass. —*adj.* (còn glŏm′êr āte) **2.** formed as a mass. —*n.* **3.** mass of small elements. **4.** corporation composed of diverse subsidiaries. —**con·glom′′er·a′tion,** *n.*

còn·grăt′ù·lāte′′, *v.t.,* **-lated, -lating.** show sympathetic pleasure, as for success or good luck. —**con·grat′′u·la′tion,** *n.* —**con·grat′u·la·to′′ry,** *adj.*

cŏn′grè·gāte′′, *v.,* **-gated, -gating.** *v.t., v.i.* gather into a group or assembly. —**con′′gre·ga′tion,** *n.* —**con′′gre·ga′tion·al,** *adj.*

cŏn′grĕss, *n.* **1.** legislative body. **2.** formal gathering. —**con·gres′sion·al,** *adj.*

Cŏn′grĕss·măn, *n.* member of the U.S. Congress, esp. the House of Representatives.

còn·grŭ·ènt, *adj.* in correspondence or harmony. —**con′gru·ence,** *n.*

cŏn′grŭ·oŭs, *adj.* **1.** congruent. **2.** appropriate. —**con·gru′i·ty,** *n.*

cŏn′ĭc, *adj.* **1.** Also, **con′i·cal,** cone-shaped. **2.** derived from a cone.

cŏn′ĭ·fêr, *n.* tree or shrub bearing cones. —**co·nif′er·ous,** *adj.*

còn·jĕc′tûre, *n., v.* **-tured, -turing.** *n., v.t., v.i.,* guess. —**con·jec′tur·al,** *adj.*

còn·jōĭn′, *v.t., v.i.* join together.

cŏn′jŭ·gàl, *adj.* marital.

cŏn′jŭ·gāte′′, *v.t.,* **-gated, -gating.** give the inflections of a verb. —**con′′ju·ga′tion,** *n.*

còn·jŭnc′tion, *n.* **1.** union or combination. **2.** coincidence. **3.** word linking others in a sentence. —**con·junc′tive,** *adj.*

còn·jŭnc′tûre, *n.* combination of events.

cŏn′jûre, *v.t.,* **-jured, -juring.** cause to appear as by magic. —**con′jur·er, con′jur·or,** *n.*

còn·nĕct′, *v.t.* **1.** join. —*v.i.* **2.** adjoin. —**con·nec′tor, con·nec′ter,** *n.* —**con·nec′tive,** *adj.* —**con·nec′tion,** *n.*

còn·nīve′, *v.i.,* **-nived, -niving. 1.** conspire. **2.** permit crime, etc. to occur by ignoring it. —**con·niv′er,** *n.* —**con·niv′ance,** *n.*

còn′′nois·sêur′, *n.* person with refined knowledge.

cŏn·nōte′, *v.t.,* **-noted, -noting.** imply through wording, etc. —**con′′no·ta′tion,** *n.*

còn·nū′bĭ·àl, *adj.* marital.

cŏn′quêr, *v.t.* overcome, as in war. —**con′quer·or,** *n.*

cŏn′quĕst, *n.* **1.** act or instance of conquering. **2.** something conquered.

cŏn′′săn·guĭn′ĭ·tỹ, *adj.* blood relationship.

cŏn′sciĕnce, *n.* inner prompting to do good or repent evil. —**con′′sci·en′tious,** *adj.*

cŏn′scioŭs, *adj.* **1.** aware of the surrounding world. **2.** aware of some specific thing. **3.** deliberate. —**con′scious·ness,** *n.*

còn·scrĭpt′, *v.t.* **1.** enroll forcibly in an army, labor force, etc. —*n.* **2.** conscripted person. —**con·scrip′tion,** *n.*

cŏn′sè·crāte′′, *v.t.,* **-crated, -crating.** dedicate, as to deity. —**con′′se·cra′tion,** *n.*

còn·sĕc′ŭ·tĭve, *adj.* one after the other. —**con·sec′u·tive′ly,** *adv.*

còn·sĕn′sŭs, *n.* general agreement on a question.

còn·sĕnt', *n.* **1.** permission. **2.** agreement. —*v.i.* **3.** give permission.

cŏn'sė·quĕnce'', *n.* **1.** result. **2.** importance.

cŏn'sė·quĕnt, *adj.* resulting.

cŏn''sė·quĕn'tial, *adj.* **1.** important. **2.** consequent.

còn·sêrv'à·tĭve, *n.* **1.** person skeptical of change. **2.** pertaining to conservatives. **3.** avoiding excesses. —**con·serv'a·tive·ly**, *adv.* —**con·serv'a·tism**, *n.*

cŏn·sêr'và·tô''rÿ, *n.*, *pl.* -ries. **1.** greenhouse. **2.** art or music school.

còn·sêrve', *v.t.*, -served, -serving. keep from decaying, being squandered, etc. —**con''ser·va'tion**, *n.* —**con''ser·va'tion·ist**, *n.*

còn·sĭd'êr, *v.t.* **1.** think of the importance, implications, etc. of. **2.** regard; believe. **3.** be considerate of.

còn·sĭd'êr·à·ble, *adj.* extensive or significant.

cŏn·sĭd'êr·àte, *adj.* respectful of the feelings of others.

còn·sĭd''êr·ā'tion, *n.* **1.** state of being considerate. **2.** act of considering. **3.** something to be considered. **4.** fee.

còn·sīgn', *n.* **1.** deliver. **2.** entrust. —**con'sign'ment**, *n.*

còn·sĭst', *v.i.* **1.** be composed. **2.** have essential nature.

còn·sĭs'tĕn·cÿ, *n.* **1.** agreement with something already done, stated, or implied. **2.** ability to hold together, as of a liquid. —**con·sis'tent**, *adj.* —**con·sis'tent·ly**, *adv.*

còn·sōle', *v.t.*, -soled, -soling, *n.* *v.t.* **1.** soothe or cheer in grief or annoyance. —*n.* (kahn'sōl) **2.** television set, etc. standing on the floor. **3.** instrument panel. —**con''so·la'tion**, *n.*

còn·sŏl'ĭ·dāte'', *v.*, -dated, -dating. *v.t.*, *v.i.* unite into a solid; whole. —**con·sol''i·da'tion**, *n.*

cŏn'sŏm·mé'', *n.* soup based on a clear meat broth.

cŏn'sò·nànt, *adj.* **1.** in harmony. —*n.* **2.** speech sound other than a vowel. —**con'so'nance**, *n.*

cŏn·sôrt', *v.i.* **1.** be in company or association. —*n.* (kahn'sort) **2.** spouse of a sovereign.

còn·sôr'tĭ·ŭm, *n.*, *pl.* -tia. international business alliance.

còn·spĭc'ū·oŭs, *adj.* **1.** readily observed. **2.** compelling observation. —**con·spic'u·ous'ly**, *adv.* —**con·spic'u·ous·ness**, *n.*

còn·spīre', *v.t.*, -spired, -spiring. plan secretly as a group. —**con·spir'a·cy**, *n.* —**con·spir'a·tor**, *n.*

cŏn·stà·ble, *n.* policeman. —**con·stab'u·lar''y**, *n.*

cŏn'stànt, *adj.* **1.** continual. **2.** faithful. —*n.* **3.** unvarying element. —**con'stant·ly**, *adv.* —**con'stan·cy**, *n.*

cŏn''stĕl·lā'tion, *n.* pattern of stars.

cŏn''stêr·nā'tion, *n.* horrified shock.

cŏn'stĭ·pāte'', *v.t.*, -pated, -pating. impair the movement of the bowels. —**con''sti·pa'tion**, *n.*

còn·stĭt'ū·ėnt, *adj.* **1.** forming an essential part. **2.** electing. —*n.* **3.** voter. **4.** constituent thing. —**con·stit'u·en·cy**, *n.*

cŏn·stĭ·tūte'', *v.t.*, -tuted, -tuting. **1.** combine to form. **2.** be tantamount to.

cŏn''stĭ·tū'tion, *n.* **1.** act or instance of constituting. **2.** fundamental law. **3.** body, esp. as regards health.

cŏn''stĭ·tū'tion·àl, *adj.* **1.** pertaining to a constitution. **2.** permitted by a constitution. **3.** pertaining to health. —*n.* **4.** health-promoting walk.

còn·strāin', *v.t.* **1.** compel. **2.** restrain. —**con·straint'**, *n.*

còn·strĭct', *v.t.* force to be narrow. —**con·stric'tion**, *n.*

còn·strŭct', *v.t.* build. —**con·struc'tor**, *n.* —**con·struc'tion**, *n.*

còn·strŭc'tĭve, *adj.* useful or helpful.

còn·strūe', *v.t.*, -strued, -struing. interpret.

cŏn'sŭl, *n.* government agent in a foreign city who assists his nationals there. —**con'sul·ar**, *adj.* —**con'sul·ate**, *n.*

còn·sŭlt', *v.t.* **1.** seek advice or information from. —*v.i.* **2.** discuss business matters. —**con''sul·ta'tion**, *n.*

còn·sŭl'tànt, *n.* **1.** person who is consulted. **2.** person who seeks advice.

còn·sūme', *v.t.*, -sumed, -suming. **1.** use up in the process of living, etc. **2.** destroy, as by fire.

còn·sūm'êr, *n.* person who uses goods or services for himself rather than in business.

cŏn·sŭm'màte, *adj.*, *v.t.* -mated, -mating. *adj.* **1.** perfect. —*v.t.* (kahn sәm āt') **2.** complete, esp. the state of marriage by sexual intercourse. —con''sum·ma'tion, n.

còn·sŭmp'tion, n. 1. act or instance of consuming. 2. tuberculosis of the lungs. —con·sump'tive, adj.

cŏn'tăct, n. 1. touch. 2. communication. 3. connection.

còn·tā'gioŭs, adj. distributed by personal contact, as disease. —con·ta'gion, n.

còn·tāin', n. 1. enclose; include. 2. restrain. —con·tain'er, n.

còn·tăm''ĭn·āte'', v.t., -ated, -ating. spoil the purity of. —con·tam''in·a'tion, n. —con·tam'in·ant, n.

cŏn'tĕm·plāte'', v.t., -plated, -plating. 1. regard or think of intently. 2. anticipate. —con''tem·pla'tion, n. —con·tem'pla·tive, adj.

còn·tĕm'pò·rār''ў, adj., n., pl. -ries, adj. 1. Also, con·tem''po·ra'ne·ous, of the same time. 2. modern. —n. 3. person or thing of the same age.

còn·tĕmpt', n. 1. disapproval involving a feeling of one's own superiority. 2. defiance, as of a court order. —con·tempt'i·ble, adj.

còn·tĕnd', v.t. 1. assert forcibly. —v.i. 2. fight or be in opposition. —con·tend'er, n.

cŏn'tĕnt, n. 1. something contained. 2. meaning or message. (còn·tĕnt') 3. contentment. —adj. 4. satisfied. 5. willing. —v.t. 6. satisfy. —con·tent'ed, adj. —con·tent'ed·ly, adv. —con·tent'ed·ness, n.

còn·tĕn'tioŭs, adj. quarrelsome.

còn·tĕnt'mĕnt, n. contented state.

còn'tĕst, n. 1. competition or fight. —v.i. (còn·tĕst') 2. dispute. 3. fight to gain or hold. —con·test'ant, n.

cŏn'tĕxt, n. circumstances giving exact meaning. —con·tex'tu·al, adj.

cŏn·tĭg'ŭ·oŭs, adj. 1. in touch. 2. adjacent. —con''ti·gu'i·ty, n.

cŏn'tĭ·nĕnt, n. 1. major land mass. 2. the Continent, European mainland. —adj. 3. exercising restraint. —con''ti·nen'tal, adj. —con'ti·nence, n.

còn·tĭn'gèn·cў, n., pl. -cies. chance occurrence.

còn·tĭn'gént, adj. 1. depending on chance. —n. 2. chance occurrence. 3. group of recruits.

còn·tĭn'ū·ȧl, adj. 1. repeated without pause. 2. continuous. —con·tin'u·al·ly, adv.

con·tĭn'ūe, v., -ued, -uing. v.t., v.i. 1. not stop. 2. recommence. 3. extend. —v.i. 4. remain. —con·tin''u·a'tion, con·tin'u·ance, n.

còn·tĭn'ū·oŭs, adj. uninterrupted. —con·tin'u·ous·ly, adv. —con''tin·u'i·ty, n.

còn·tôrt', v.t. twist out of shape. —con'tor'tion, n.

cŏn'toûr, n. outline of a form.

cŏn'trȧ·bănd'', n. 1. goods unlawful to import or export. —adj. 2. constituting such goods.

cŏn''trȧ·cĕp'tion, n. prevention of pregnancy. —con''tra·cep'tive, adj., n.

cŏn'trăct, n. 1. formal business agreement. —v.t. (con·tract') 2. undertake or establish by contract. 3. be afflicted with. 4. make smaller. —v.i. 5. make a contract. 6. become smaller. —con·trac'tion, n.

cŏn'trăc·tŏr, n. 1. person who undertakes work by contract. 2. builder.

cŏn''trȧ·dĭct', v.t. 1. declare to be falsely stated. 2. declare to have not spoken the truth. 3. be inconsistent with. —con''tra·dic'tion, n. —con''tra·dic'to·ry, adj.

còn·trăl'tō, n., pl. -tos. lowest female singing voice.

còn·trăp'tion, n. Informal. gadget.

cŏn·tră·ry, n., pl. ries, adj. n. 1. (con'tra ry) something opposite. —adj. 2. opposite. 3. (con tra'ry) stubborn; perverse. —con·trar'i·ly, adv.

còn·trăst', v.t. 1. show the differences of from another or others. —v.i. 2. reveal differences from another or others. —n. (con'trast) 3. act or instance of contrasting. 4. something notably different.

cŏn'trȧ·vēne'', v.t., -vened, -vening. act in violation of. —con''tra·ven'tion, n.

còn·trĭb'ūte, v., -uted, -uting. v.t., v.i. give toward a desired total. —con·trib'u·tor, n. —con''tri·bu'tion, n. —con·trib'u·to''ry, adj.

còn·trīte', adj. repentant. —con·trite'ness, con·tri'tion, n.

còn·trīve', v.t., -trived, -triving. 1. devise or invent. **2.** bring about. —con·triv'ance, *n.*

con·trol', *v.t.*, -trolled, -trolling, *n. v.t.* **1.** govern or direct. **2.** restrain. —*n.* **3.** ability to control. **4.** Often, **controls,** means of controlling. —con·trol'la·ble, *adj.*

con·trol'ler, *n.* financial manager.

con'tro·ver''sy, *n., pl.* -sies. earnest debate. —con''tro·ver'sial, *adj.*

con'tro·vert'', *v.t.* **1.** dispute. **2.** debate.

con·tu'me·ly, *n., pl.* -lies. scornful abuse.

con·tu'sion, *n.* bruise.

co·nun'drum, *n.* riddle answered with a pun.

con''ur·ba'tion, *n.* area of urban density resulting from unchecked growth.

con'va·lesce'', *v.i.*, -lesced, -lescing. become better after illness. —con''va·les'cent, *n., adj.* —con''va·les'cence, *n.*

con·vec'tion, *n.* movement of heated or cooled gases or liquids.

con·vene', *v.*, -vened, -vening. *v.i., v.t.* assemble in a meeting.

con·ven'ience, *n.* **1.** ease or handiness. **2.** something promoting this. —con·ven'ient, *adj.*

con'vent, *n.* community of nuns.

con·ven'tion, *n.* **1.** assembly of a political party, professional association, etc. **2.** something customary.

con·ven'tion·al, *adj.* **1.** ordinary. **2.** customary.

con·verge', *v.*, -verged, -verging. *v.t., v.i.* to come together. —con·ver'gence, *n.* —con·ver'gent, *adj.*

con·ver'sant, *adj.* familiar; skilled.

con''ver·sa'tion, *n.* **1.** informal talk. **2.** ability to carry on such talk. —con''ver·sa'tion·al, *adj.* —con''ver·sa'tion·al·ist, *n.*

con·verse', *v.i.*, -versed, -versing, *adj., n. v.i.* **1.** carry on a conversation. —*adj.* (con'verse) **2.** in reverse order or position. —*n.* **3.** something converse. —con·verse'ly, *adv.*

con·vert', *v.t.* **1.** change from one thing or state to another. **2.** acquire a new religion. —*v.i.* **3.** be converted. —*n.* (con'vert) **4.** person with a new religion. —con·vert'er, con·vert'or, *n.* —con·vert'i·ble, *adj.*

con·vex', *adj.* curving outward. —con·vex'i·ty, *n.*

con·vey', *v.t.* **1.** transport. **2.** transmit. **3.** succeed in expressing. —con·vey'er, con·vey'or, *n.* —con·vey'ance, *n.*

con·vict', *v.t.* **1.** find guilty. —*n.* (con'vict) **2.** person found guilty.

con·vic'tion, *n.* **1.** act or instance of convicting or being convicted. **2.** strongly held belief.

con·vince', *v.t.*, -vinced, -vincing. cause to believe.

con·viv'i·al, *adj.* **1.** fond of company. **2.** festive.

con·voke', *v.t.*, -voked, -voking. call to an assembly. —con'vo·ca''tion, *n.*

con''vo·lu'tion, *n.* **1.** twist, fold, etc. **2.** formation of these.

con'voy, *n.* **1.** ships, etc. with a protective escort. **2.** protective escort. **3.** several military, etc. vehicles traveling together. —*v.t.* (con voy') **4.** escort protectively.

con·vulse', *v.t.*, -vulsed, -vulsing. **1.** agitate. **2.** rack with laughter or anger. —con·vul'sion, *n.* —con·vul'sive, *adj.*

coo, *v.i.*, cooed, cooing. **1.** make a dovelike sound. —*n.* **2.** dovelike sound.

cook, *v.t.* **1.** prepare (food) by heating. —*v.i.* **2.** act as a cook. **3.** become cooked or heated. —*n.* **4.** person who cooks. —cook'er·y, *n.* —cook'book'', *n.*

cook'ie, *n.* small baked sweet biscuit.

cool, *adj.* **1.** slightly cold; not warm. **2.** not adding to body heat. **3.** showing no emotion. **4.** unenthusiastic. —*n.* **5.** cool condition. —*v.t.* **6.** make cool. —*v.i.* **7.** become cool. —cool'er, *n.* —cool'ly, *adv.* —cool'ness, *n.*

coon, *n.* racoon. —coon'skin'', *n.*

coop, *n.* **1.** shelter for chickens, etc. —*v.t.* **2.** confine.

coop'er, *n.* barrel maker.

co''öp'er·ate'', *v.i.*, -ated, -ating. act in harmony or together with others. Also, co''-op'er·ate''. —co''op''er·a'tion, *n.*

co''öp'er·a·tive, *adj.* **1.** willing to cooperate. **2.** jointly owned by the users. —*n.* **3.** cooperative store, apartment house, etc. Also, co''-op'er·a·tive.

co·ôr'di·nate, *adj., n., v.t.*, -nated, -nating. *adj.* **1.** equal in importance. **2.**

pertaining to coordination. —*n*. **3.** something coordinate. *v.t.* (kō''or'də nāt'') **4.** put in proper interaction. **5.** make coordinate.

cō''ôr'dĭ·nā''tion, *n*. **1.** act or instance of coordinating. **2.** proper interaction, esp. of the limbs or muscles.

cŏp, *n., v.t.,* **copped, copping.** *Informal*. *n*. **1.** policeman. **2.** arrest. —*v.t.* **3.** seize. **4.** inform.

cōpe, *v.i.,* **coped, coping.** attack and overcome a problem or emergency.

cōp'ĭng, *n*. uppermost course of an un-roofed masonry wall.

cō'pĭ·oŭs, *adj*. abundant.

cŏp'pêr, *n*. reddish metallic element.

cŏp'pêr·hĕad'', *n*. poisonous North American snake.

cŏpse, *n*. thicket. Also, **cop'pice.**

cŏp'ŭ·lāte'', *v.i.,* **-lated, -lating.** have sexual intercourse. —**cop''u·la'tion,** *n*.

cŏp'ÿ, *n., pl.* **-ies,** *v.t.,* **-ied, -ying.** *n*. **1.** imitation of an original. **2.** individual published book. **3.** words to be printed. —*v.t.* **4.** make or be a copy of. —**cop'y·ist,** *n*.

cŏp'ÿ·rīght'', *n*. **1.** exclusive right to publish a book, etc. or license its publication. —*v.t.* **2.** obtain a copyright for.

cō·quëtte', *n*. flirtatious woman.

cŏr'ăl, *n*. **1.** hardened skeletons of a marine animal. **2.** yellowish red.

côrd, *n*. **1.** strong string. **2.** electric wire. **3.** 128 cubic feet of chopped wood.

côr'dĭàl, *adj*. **1.** warmly friendly. —*n*. **2.** liqueur. —**cor'dial·ly,** *adv*. —**cor''di·al'i·ty,** *n*.

côr'dŏn, *n*. **1.** circle of guards. —*v.t.* **2.** put a cordon around.

côr'dó·vàn, *n*. soft, dark leather.

côr'dù·rŏÿ'', *n*. **1.** ribbed cotton. **2.** felled tree trunks used as a paving.

côre, *n., v.t.,* **cored, coring.** *n*. **1.** central part or element. —*v.t.* **2.** remove the core from.

côrk, *n*. **1.** bark of an oak tree. **2.** stopper made of this bark. —*v.t.* **3.** stop with a cork.

côrk'screw'', *n*. augerlike device for pulling corks.

côrn, *n*. **1.** American plant with kernels on a cob. **2.** small hard seed of a cereal plant. **3.** *Informal*. trite or sentimental art. **4.** painful growth on the foot. —*v.t.*

5. pickle in brine. —**corn'starch'',** *n*.

côr'nē·à, *n*. outer coating of the eyeball.

côr'nêr, *n*. **1.** angular junction. **2.** intersection of two streets. **3.** monopoly of a commodity or stock. —*v.t.* **4.** trap in a corner. **5.** get a monopoly on.

côr'nêr·stōne'', *n*. stone at the corner of a building with its date, etc.

côr'nĕt', *n*. trumpetlike musical instrument.

côr'nĭce, *n*. major horizontal molding on or at the top of a wall.

côr''nŭ·cō'pĭ·à, *n*. hornlike container with fruits, flowers, etc. spilling from it.

côr'ŏl·lār''ÿ, *n., pl.* **-ies.** statement deduced from one already proven.

côr'ò·nār''ÿ, *adj., n., pl.* **-ies.** *adj*. **1.** pertaining to the arteries supplying the heart. —*n*. **2.** coronary thrombosis.

côr''ò·nā'tion, *n*. installation of a monarch.

côr'ò·nêr, *n*. official who investigates suspicious deaths.

côr''ò·nĕt, *n*. crown of a noble.

côr'pö·ral, *adj*. **1.** bodily. —*n*. **2.** lowest noncommissioned military officer.

côr'pó·ràte, *adj*. pertaining to organizations.

côr'pò·ra''tion, *n*. **1.** business organization existing as an entity apart from its members. **2.** municipal government.

côr·pō'rē·àl, *adj*. physical.

côrps (kor), *n., pl.* **corps** (korz). military branch.

côrpse, *n*. dead body.

côr'pū·lĕnce, *n*. fatness. —**cor'pu·lent,** *adj*.

côr·pŭs·cle, *n*. blood or lymph cell.

côr·răl', *n., v.t.,* **-ralled, -ralling.** *n*. **1.** enclosure for cattle, horses, etc. —*v.t.* **2.** enclose in a corral.

cór·rĕct', *adj*. **1.** accurate. **2.** according to rules. —*v.t.* **3.** make correct. **4.** punish. —**cor·rect'ly,** *adv*. —**cor·rect'ness,** *n*. —**cor·rec'tion,** *n*. —**cor·rec'tive,** *adj*.

côr're·lāte'', *v.,* **-lated, -lating.** *v.t.* **1.** put into a mutual relationship. —*v.i.* **2.** have a mutual relationship. —**cor''re·la'tion,** *n*. —**cor·rel'a·tive,** *adj*.

côr're·spŏnd'', *v.i.* **1.** write or exchange letters, news, etc. **2.** match. —**cor''re·spond'ence,** *n*. —**cor''re·spond'ent,** *n*.

côr'rĭ·dör, *n*. narrow passageway.

cór·rŏb'ó·rāte'', *v.t.*, -rated, -rating. support or confirm with evidence, etc. —cor·rob''o·ra'tion, *n*. —cor·rob'o·ra·tive, *adj*.

cór·rōde', *v.*, -roded, -roding. *v.t.*, *v.i.* decay, esp. by chemical action. —cor·ro'sion, *n*. —cor·ro'sive, *adj.*, *n*.

côr'rŭ·gāte'', *v.*, -gated, -gating. *v.t.*, *v.i.* bend into parallel ridges and furrows. —cor''ru·ga'tion, *n*.

cór·rŭpt', *adj*. 1. impure. 2. depraved. —*v.t.* 3. make corrupt. —*v.i.* 4. become corrupt. —cor·rupt'ly, *adv*. —cor·rupt'i·ble, *adj*. —cor·rup'tion, *n*.

côr·säge', *n*. small bouquet for a party dress.

côr'sĕt, *n*. garment for shaping the torso.

côr'tĕge', *n*. ceremonial procession. Also, cor·tège'.

côr'ŭs·cāte'', *v.i.*, -cated, -cating. glitter. —cor''us·ca'tion, *n*.

cŏs·mĕt'ĭc, *n*. 1. preparation applied to the body to improve its appearance. —*adj*. 2. improving outer appearance.

cŏs'mĭc, *adj*. pertaining to the cosmos.

cŏs'mŏ·nau̅t'', *n*. astronaut.

cŏs''mŏ·pŏl'ĭ·tán, *n*. 1. Also, cos·mop'o·lite'', person regarding the entire world as his home. —*adj*. 2. characteristic of such persons.

cŏs'mŏs, *n*. the entire universe.

cŏst, *v.t.*, cost, costing, *n*. *v.t* 1. require or exact as specified. —*n*. 2. something given up in exchange. 3. loss; grief.

cŏst'lў, *adj.*, -lier, -liest. costing much.

cŏs'tūme, *n.*, *v.t.*, -tumed, -tuming. *n*. 1. dress, esp. of a special or unusual kind. —*v.t.* 2. supply with such dress.

cŏt, *n*. narrow folding bed.

cō'té·riē, *n*. small, exclusive group of friends.

cŏt'tàge, *n*. small house. —cot'tag·er, *n*.

cŏt'têr pĭn'', split fastener passed through the things to be attached, then bent open.

cŏt'tòn, *n*. fiber from a plant of the mallow family. —cot'ton·y, *adj*. —cot'ton·seed, *n*.

cŏt'tòn·mou̅th'', water moccasin.

cŏt'tòn·tāil'', *n*. white-tailed American rabbit.

cŏt'tòn·wōod'', *n*. poplar with hairy seeds.

cou̅ch, *n*. 1. bedlike article of furniture. —*v.t.* 2. put into words.

cou̅'gàr, *n*. tawny American wildcat.

cou̅gh, *n*. 1. loud expulsion of breath from the lungs, as to clear the throat. —*v.i.* 2. emit a cough. —*v.t.* 3. expel with a cough.

cou̅n'cĭl, *n*. body of legislators, advisors, etc. —coun'cil·man, coun'cil·or, coun'cil·lor, *n*.

cou̅n'śel, *v.t.*, -seled, -seling. *n*. *v.t.* 1. advise. —*n*. 2. legal representative. 3. advice. —coun'se·lor, coun'sel·lor, *n*.

cou̅nt, *v.t.* 1. note one by one to get a total. 2. include in a total or group. 3. consider as being. —*v.i.* 4. count numbers or items. 5. be important. 6. depend. —*n*. 7. act or instance of counting. 8. total. 9. legal accusation. 10. continental European nobleman equal to an earl.

cou̅nt'dŏwn'', *n*. count of seconds in reverse order before an action.

cou̅n'té·nànce, *n.*, *v.t.*, -nanced, -nancing. *n*. 1. face, esp. with regard to expression. 2. approval. —*v.t.* 3. approve.

cou̅nt'êr, *n*. 1. person or thing that counts. 2. tablelike surface for serving, displaying goods, etc. 3. token used in games.

cou̅n'têr, *v.i.* 1. act in retaliation. —*v.t.* 2. oppose. —*adj*. 3. opposed. —*adv*. 4. in opposition. —coun''ter·act', *v.t.* —coun'ter·at·tack'', *v.t.*, *v.i.*, *n*. —coun''ter·bal''ance, *v.t.*, *n*. —coun''ter·clock'wise, *adj.*, *adv*. —coun''ter·rev''o·lu'tion, *n*. —coun''ter·rev''o·lu'tion·ar''y, *adj.*, *n*. —coun'ter·weight'', *n.*, *v.t.*

cou̅n'têr·feĭt'', *v.t.* 1. imitate closely, esp. money. 2. pretend. —*adj*. 3. having been counterfeited. —*n*. 4. something counterfeit. —coun'ter·feit''er, *n*.

cou̅n'têr·mănd'', *v.t.* cancel with a contrary order.

cou̅n'têr·pârt'', *n*. 1. similar person or thing. 2. duplicate.

cou̅n'têr·poĭnt'', *n*. *Music*. interaction of melodies.

cou̅n'têr·sĭgn'', *n*. 1. reply to a password establishing identity. 2. secret sign. **3.** confirming signature. —*v.t.* **4.** sign as a confirmation.

coun′ter·sink″, *v.t.,* **-sunk, -sinking. 1.** drive or set flush with or below a surface. **2.** cut to receive the head of a countersunk part.

count′ess, *n.* wife of a count or earl.

count′less, *adj.* innumerable.

coun′try, *n., pl.* **-tries. 1.** rural area. **2.** land of which one is a citizen. **3.** region. **—coun′try·man,** *n.*

coun′try·side″, *n.* rural terrain.

coun′ty, *n.* **1.** political division of a U.S. state. **2.** political division of a European country.

coup (kōō), *n., pl.* **coups** (kōōz). bold, adroit, successful act.

coup de grace (kōō″de grahs′), something putting an end to a miserable existence.

coupé (kōō pā′), *n.* two-door hard-top car.

cou′ple, *n., v.,* **-pled, -pling.** *n.* pair. —*v.t., v.i.* **2.** join one to another. **—coup′ling,** *n.*

coup′let, *n.* pair of verses that rhyme.

cou′pon, *n.* valuable certificate to be cut or detached from a bond, advertisement, etc.

cour′age, *n.* bravery or fortitude. **—cou·ra′geous,** *adj.*

cou′ri·er, *n.* messenger.

course, *n., v.i.,* **coursed, coursing.** *n.* **1.** path or direction of a moving thing. **2.** natural progress or outcome. **3.** way of acting. **4.** phase of a meal. **5.** program of instruction in one subject. **6.** layer of stones, shingles, etc. in a building. —*v.i.* **7.** run or race.

court, *n.* **1.** Also, **court′yard,** area surrounded by buildings. **2.** agency for trying civil or criminal cases. **3.** group immediately attached to a sovereign. **4.** act of wooing. **5.** place to play ball games. —*v.t.* **6.** woo. **7.** ingratiate oneself with. **8.** seek to obtain. —*v.i.* **9.** engage in courtship. **—court′house″,** *n.* **—court′room″,** *n.*

cour′te·ous, *adj.* polite.

cour′te·san, *n.* prostitute.

cour′te·sy, *n., pl.* **-sies.** politeness.

cour′ti·er, *n.* member of a royal court.

court′ly, *adj.,* **-lier, -liest.** worthy of a royal court, esp. in manner.

court′-mâr″tial, *n., pl.* **courts-martial,** *v.t.,* **-tialed, -tialing.** *n.* **1.** military court or trial. —*v.t.* **2.** try before such a court.

court′ship″, *n.* wooing.

cous′in, *n.* offspring of an uncle or aunt.

cove, *n.* small inlet or bay; small valley.

cov′e·nant, *n.* agreement.

cov′er, *v.t.* **1.** put a lid, shelter, etc. over. **2.** conceal. **3.** protect or shield. **4.** clothe. **5.** hold at bay with a gun, etc. **6.** investigate or watch. —*n.* **7.** something that covers. **8.** means of concealing actions, identity, etc. **—cov′er·age,** *n.* **—cov′er·ing,** *n.*

cov′er·let, *n.* bedspread.

cov′ert, *adj.* concealed. **—cov′ert·ly,** *adv.*

cov′er-up″, *n.* plot to conceal guilt or guilty actions.

cov′et, *v.t.* desire enviously. **—cov′et·ous,** *adj.*

cov′ey, *n., pl.* **-ies.** flock of quail or partridge.

cow, *n.* **1.** four-footed milk-giving bovine animal. **2.** female elephant, whale, etc. —*v.t.* **3.** intimidate. **—cow′hide″,** *n.*

cow′ard, *n.* person without courage. **—cow′ard·ly,** *adj., adv.* **—cow′ard·ice,** *n.*

cow′boy″, *n.* ranch worker. Also, **cow′hand″.**

cow′er, *v.i.* cringe.

cowl, *n.* hood or hooded cloak.

co′work″er, *n.* fellow worker.

cox·swain (kok′sàn), *n.* steerer of a boat.

coy, *adj.* affectedly shy.

coy·ō′te, *n.* small North American wolf.

co′zy, *adj.,* **-zier, -ziest.** snug and comfortable. **—coz′i·ly,** *adv.* **—coz′i·ness,** *n.*

crab, *n.* four-legged crustacean.

crab ap′ple, *n.* small, sour apple.

crabbed, *n.* **1.** Also, **crab′by,** ill-tempered. **2.** hard to read.

crab″grass′, *n.* grass regarded as a weed.

crack, *v.i., v.t.* **1.** break across abruptly. —*n.* **2.** act or instance of cracking. **3.** narrow break or opening.

crack′er, *n.* **1.** crisp wafer. **2.** firecracker.

crack′le, *v.i.,* **-led, -ling,** *n.* **1.** make rapid snapping sounds in bending. —*n.* **2.** irregular cracked pattern.

crăck′pŏt″, *n. Informal.* person with delusions.

cra′dle, *n., v.t.,* **-dled, -dling.** *n.* **1.** rocking, high-sided bed for a baby. **2.** concave support, as for a boat. —*v.t.* **3.** place or rock in a cradle. **4.** support in or as in a cradle.

crăft, *n., pl.* **crafts** (for 1 and 2), **craft** (for 3). **1.** cunning. **2.** skilled trade. **3.** vehicle for movement through water or air.

crăfts′măn, *n.* **1.** skilled handworker. **2.** skilled, conscientious worker of any kind. —**crafts′man·ship″**, *n.*

crăft′ÿ, *adj.,* **-ier, -iest.** cunning. —**craft′i·ly**, *adv.*

crăg, *n.* abruptly rising rock formation. —**crag′gy**, *adj.*

crăm, *v.,* **crammed, cramming.** *v.t.* **1.** pack tightly or excessively. —*v.i.* **2.** *Informal.* study in a hasty, superficial way.

crămp, *n.* **1.** painful muscular contraction. **2.** Often, **cramps,** abdominal spasm. —*v.t.* **3.** afflict with cramp. **4.** hamper or confine.

crăn′bĕr″rÿ, *n., pl.* **-ries.** sour red berry from an evergreen.

crāne, *n., v.t.,* **craned, craning.** *n.* **1.** long-legged, long-billed water bird. **2.** hoisting machine. —*v.t.* **3.** stretch and bend, as the neck.

crā′nĭ·ŭm, *n., pl.* **-niums, -nia. 1.** bone covering the brain. **2.** skull. —**cra′ni·al**, *adj.*

crănk, *n.* **1.** rotating device incorporating a lever. **2.** *Informal.* person with an ill temper or delusion. —*v.t.* **3.** move with a crank. —**crank′case″**, *n.* —**crank′shaft″**, *n.*

crănk′ÿ, *adj.,* **-ier, -iest.** ill-tempered. —**crank′i·ly**, *adv.*

crăn′nÿ, *n., pl.* **-nies.** crevice.

crăps, *n.* dice game. —**crap′shoot″er**, *n.*

crăsh, *n.* **1.** destructive collision, fall, etc. **2.** noise of this. **3.** business failure. **4.** coarse linen. —*v.i.* **5.** suffer a crash. —*v.t.* **6.** cause to have or produce a crash. **7.** batter one's way through.

crăss, *adj.* stupid and coarse.

crāte, *n., v.t.,* **crated, crating.** *n.* **1.** wooden shipping case. —*v.t.* **2.** pack in a crate.

crā′têr, *n.* pit in the ground made by volcanic eruption, meteors, bombs, etc.

crà·văt′, *n.* necktie.

crāve, *v.t.,* **craved, craving.** desire or request eagerly. —**crav′ing**, *n.*

crā′vĕn, *n.* **1.** coward. —*adj.* **2.** cowardly.

crăw, *n.* **1.** sac in a bird's gullet. **2.** stomach.

crawl, *v.i.* **1.** move slowly with the body horizontal. **2.** move slowly. **3.** feel as if crawled on. —*n.* **4.** crawling movement. **5.** swimming stroke.

crăy′fish″, *n.* small lobsterlike crustacean. Also, **craw′fish″**.

crăy′ŏn, *n.* stick of pigmented material for making lines or tones.

crāze, *v.,* **crazed, crazing,** *n., v.t.* **1.** make insane. **2.** cause to crack in random patterns. —*v.i.* **3.** become crazed. —*n.* **4.** fad.

crā′zÿ, *adj.,* **-zier, -ziest. 1.** insane. **2.** rickety. —**cra′zi·ly**, *adv.*

crēak, *v.t.* **1.** make a squeak or groan from bending or rubbing. —*n.* **2.** sound from such a cause. —**creak′y**, *adj.*

crēam, *n.* **1.** richer part of milk. **2.** substance with a creamlike or salvelike consistency. **3.** yellowish white. **4.** finest part or element. —*v.t.* **5.** make with cream. **6.** beat to a creamlike consistency. —**cream′y**, *adj.*

crēam′êr, *n.* cream pitcher.

crēam′êr·ÿ, *n., pl.* **-ies.** place for processing or selling dairy products.

crēase, *n., v.t.,* **creased, creasing.** *n.* **1.** ridge made by pressing. **2.** furrow. —*v.t.* **3.** make a crease or creases in.

crē·āte′, *v.t.* **-ated, -ating. 1.** bring into existence. **2.** bring about. —**cre·a′tion**, *n.*

crē·ā′tĭve, *adj.* **1.** pertaining to creation. **2.** of an original mind; inventive. —**cre″a·tiv′i·ty**, *n.*

crē·ā′tör, *n.* **1.** person who creates. **2.** **the Creator,** God.

crē′dĕnce, *n.* belief, as in the truth of a statement.

crē·dĕn′tiǎls, *n.* documentation proving authority, identity, etc.

crĕd′ĭ·ble, *adj.* able to be believed. —**cred″i·bil′i·ty**, *n.*

crĕd′ĭt, *n.* **1.** deference of payment. **2.** money paid or owed to one. **3.** praise or good reputation. **4.** source of this. **5.**

acknowledgment for participation. **6.** unit of academic accomplishment. —*v.t.* **7.** believe. **8.** give a credit or credits to.

crĕd′it·a·ble, *adj.* deserving of credit.

crĕd′i·tör, *n.* person to whom a debt is owed.

crē′dō, *n., pl.* **-dos.** creed.

crĕd′u·loŭs, *adj.* too ready to believe things. —**cre·du′li·ty,** *n.*

crēed, *n.* formally stated belief.

crēek, *n.* small stream.

crēep, *v.i.,* **crept, creeping. 1.** crawl. **2.** move stealthily. **3.** grow along the ground.

crē′māte″, *v.t.,* **-mated, -mating.** burn a body, etc. to ashes. —**cre·ma′tion,** *n.* —**cre′ma·to″ry, cre″ma·to′ri·um,** *n.*

Crē′ole, *n.* descendant of the original settlers of Louisiana.

crē′o·sōte″, *n.* wood preservative distilled from wood or coal tar.

crēpe, *n.* **1.** thin, crinkled cloth. **2.** rolled, filled pancake. Also, **crêpe.**

crè·scĕn′dō, *adj., n., pl.* **-dos.** *adj., adv.* **1.** increasing in loudness. —*n.* **2.** increase in loudness.

crĕs′cĕnt, *n.* shape like that of a new moon.

crĕst, *n.* **1.** uppermost edge or feature. **2.** feature surmounting a heraldic escutcheon.

crĕst′fäl″lèn, *adj.* abashed.

crē′tĭn, *n.* mentally deficient person resulting from a thyroid condition.

crē′tönne, *n.* heavy, printed upholstery or curtain material.

crè·vässe′, *n.* crevice, esp. in a glacier.

crĕv′īce, *n.* deep, narrow gap.

crēw, *n.* labor force, esp. on a ship. —**crew′man,** *n.*

crĭb, *n., v.t.,* **cribbed, cribbing.** *n.* **1.** small child's bed with high slatted sides. **2.** receptacle for corn, animal fodder, etc. **3.** stall for cattle. **4.** *Informal.* aid to cheating in school. —*v.t.* **5.** confine as in a crib. **6.** *Informal.* copy dishonestly.

crĭb′båge, *n.* card game.

crĭck, *n.* cramp in the neck or back.

crĭck′ët, *n.* **1.** grasshopperlike insect. **2.** game played with wide bats, esp. in England.

crī′êr, *n.* maker of vocal announcements.

crīme, *n.* violation of the law.

crĭm′ĭn·ål, *adj.* **1.** pertaining to or guilty of crime. —*n.* **2.** committer of crimes.

crĭm″ĭn·ŏl′o·gỹ, *n.* study of crime. —**crim″in·ol′o·gist,** *n.*

crĭmp, *n., v.t.* pleat.

crĭm′sòn, *n.* deep red.

crĭnge, *v.i.,* **cringed, cringing. 1.** crouch or draw back out of fear. **2.** behave servilely.

crĭn′kle, *v.* **-kled, -kling,** *v.t., v.i.* **1.** wrinkle. **2.** rustle, as crisp paper. —**crin′kly,** *adj.*

crĭp′ple, *v.t.,* **-pled, -pling,** *n., v.t.* **1.** deprive of the use of arms or legs. **2.** render ineffective. —*n.* **3.** crippled person.

crī′sĭs, *n., pl.* **-ses.** point that determines a good or bad outcome.

crĭsp, *n.* **1.** brittle. **2.** clear; fresh. **3.** briskly abrupt in manner.

crĭss′crŏss″, *n.* **1.** pattern of crossed lines. —*adj., adv.* **2.** in this pattern. —*v.t.* **3.** mark with this pattern. —*v.i.* **4.** move in or bear this pattern.

crī·tēr′Ĭ·òn, *n., pl.* **-ions, ia.** basis for judgment.

crĭt′ĭc, *n.* person who evaluates good and bad qualities.

crĭt′Ĭ·căl, *adj.* **1.** pertaining to critics. **2.** pertaining to crises. **3.** fault-finding. —**crit′i·cal·ly,** *adv.*

crĭt′Ĭ·cīze′, *v.t.,* **-cized, -cizing. 1.** evaluate. **2.** find fault with. —**crit′i·cism,** *n.*

crī·tĭque′, *n.* evaluation by a critic.

crōak, *v.i.* **1.** make a deep froglike noise. —*n.* **2.** croaking sound.

cro·chet (krō shā′), *v.t.,* **-cheted, -cheting.** make with a hooked needle and thread.

crŏck, *n.* earthenware vessel. —**crock′er·y,** *n. Informal.* nonsense.

crŏc′o·dīle″, *n.* large tropical river reptile.

crō′cŭs, *n., pl.* **-cuses.** early-blooming flower of the iris family.

crōne, *n.* shriveled old woman.

crō′nỹ, *n., pl.* **-nies.** close friend.

crŏŏk, *n., v.,* **crooked, crooking.** *n.* **1.** hooked staff. **2.** curve. **3.** *Informal.* thief. —*v.i., v.t.,* **4.** bend.

crŏŏk′ĕd, *adj.* **1.** full of bends. **2.** dishonest.

croon, *v.i., v.t.* sing or hum in low, sweet sounds. —**croon'er,** *n.*

crop, *n., v.t.,* **cropped, cropping.** *n.* **1.** yield at a harvest. **2.** whip. **3.** craw of a bird. —*v.t.* **4.** cut short.

cro·quet (krō kā'), *n.* lawn game with balls driven by mallets.

cro·quette', *n.* deep-fried piece of ground meat, etc.

cross, *n.* **1.** upright with a side-to-side beam used in Roman crucifixions. **2.** this form as a symbol of Christianity. **3.** modification of this symbolizing Christian saints, sects, etc. **4.** source of trouble or unhappiness. **5.** mixture of breeds. —*v.t.* **6.** go across. **7.** thwart. **8.** mix with another breed. —*adj.* **9.** ill-tempered. —**cross'road'',** *n.* —**cross' roads'',** *n. sing.* —**cross'wise'', cross' ways'',** *adv.* —**cross'ly,** *adv.*

cross'bow'', *n.* weapon with a short bow mounted on a guide for a type of arrow.

cross''-ex·am·ine, *v.t. Law.* examine after examination by an opposing attorney. Also, **cross''-ques'tion.** —**cross''-ex·am'i·na''tion.** *n.*

cross'-eyed'', *adj.* with eyes not properly aligned.

cross-ref'êr·ence, *n.* reference to another part of a book. **cross'-re·fer',** *v.i., v.t.*

crotch, *n.* **1.** place where a tree limb branches from a larger one. **2.** place where the legs meet.

crotch'et, *n.* eccentric whim or attitude. —**crotch'et·y,** *adj.*

crouch, *v.i., n.* stoop or squat.

croup, *n.* inflammation of respiratory passages.

crow, *v.i.,* **crowed,** or (for 1) **crew, crowed, crowing,** *n. v.i.* **1.** cry like a rooster. **2.** boast or exult. —*n.* **3.** crowing sound. **4.** shiny dark bird.

crow'bâr'', *n.* heavy metal lever.

crowd, *n.* **1.** large, random group. —*v.t.* **2.** fill with a crowd. **3.** force into a restricted space. —*v.i.* **4.** push one's way. **5.** gather in a crowd.

crown, *n.* **1.** symbol of sovereignty. **2.** royalty as the head of state. **3.** upper part. —*v.t.* **4.** give a crown to. **5.** reward or fulfill.

cru'cial, *adj.* **1.** decisive. **2.** trying. —**cru'cial·ly,** *adv.*

cru'ci·ble, *n.* melting pot.

cru'ci·fix'', *n.* image of the Christian cross.

cru'ci·fy'', *v.t.,* **-fied, fying. 1.** nail to a cross as punishment. **2.** ruin the reputation, happiness, etc. of. —**cru''ci·fix' ion,** *n.*

crude, *adj.* **1.** unrefined or unfinished. **2.** boorish. —**crude'ly,** *adv.* —**crud'i· ty, crude'ness,** *n.*

cru'el, *adj.* **1.** causing suffering. **2.** desiring to cause suffering. —**cruel'ly,** *adv.* —**cru·el·ty,** *n.*

cru'et, *n.* small bottle for oil, vinegar, etc.

cruise, *v.,* **cruised, cruising,** *n. v.i.* **1.** travel slowly, as for recreation or inspection. **2.** move at normal speed, as a ship. —*v.t.* **3.** cruise in or over. —*n.* **4.** act or instance of cruising.

cruis'êr, *n.* large, lightly armored warship.

crul'ler, *n.* piece of twisted deep-fried dough.

crumb, *n.* small fragment, esp. from dough.

crum'ble, *v.,* **-bled, -bling.** *v.t., v.i.* break or drop in pieces.

crum'ple, *v.,* **-pled, -pling,** *v.i., v.t.* collapse into wrinkles.

crunch, *v.t.* **1.** crush, chew, grind, etc. with a brittle sound. —*v.i.* **2.** emit such a sound.

cru·sade', *n., v.i.,* **-saded, -sading.** *n.* **1.** Christian campaign to recover the tomb of Christ from the Muslims. **2.** idealistic campaign. —*v.i.* **3.** engage in a crusade. —**cru·sad'er,** *n.*

crush, *v.t.* **1.** break or squeeze with pressure. **2.** reduce to helplessness or despair through an attack. —*v.i.* **3.** become crushed. —*n.* **4.** crowd. **5.** *Informal.* infatuation. —**crush'er,** *n.*

crust, *n.* **1.** hardened outer surface. —*v.t.* **2.** cover with a crust. —**crust'y,** *adj.*

crus·ta'cean, *n.* sea animal with jointed feet and a hard outer shell.

crutch, *n.* prop for a lame person.

crux, *n., pl.* **cruxes, cruces.** decisive feature or aspect.

cry, *v.,* **cried, crying,** *n., pl.* **cries.** *v.i.* **1.** weep loudly. **2.** utter a call. **3.** ask for something loudly. —*v.t.* **4.** announce in a shout. —*n.* **5.** act or instance of crying.

crypt, *n*. underground church vault, esp. for burial.

cryp'tic, *adj*. defying interpretation.

cryp'to·gram'', *n*. code message.

cryp·tog'ra·phy, *n*. encoding and decoding of messages, etc. —**cryp·tog'ra·pher**, *n*.

crys'tal, *n*. **1**. clear quartz. **2**. geometrically formed fused mineral, sugar, etc. **3**. brilliant glass or glassware. **4**. window of a watch dial. —**crys'tal·line**, *adj*. —**crys'ta·lize''**, *v.t.*, *v.i.*

cub, *n*. young animal.

cub'by·hole'', *n*. small enclosure.

cube, *n.*, *v.t.*, **cubed, cubing**. *n*. **1**. solid with six square sides. **2**. *Math*. third power of a number. —*v.t.* **3**. divide into cubes. **4**. *Math*. multiply to the third power. —**cu'bic**, *adj*. —**cu'bic·al**, *adj*.

cu'bi·cle, *n*. small alcove.

cu'bit, *n*. measure of about 18 inches.

cuck'old, *n*. **1**. husband of an unfaithful wife. —*v.t.* **2**. make a cuckold of. —**cuck'old·ry**, *n*.

cuck'oo'', *n*. **1**. bird with a two-note call. —*adj*. **2**. *Informal*. crazy.

cu'cum''ber, *n*. long, green fruit used in salads or as pickles.

cud, *n*. food chewed by cows, etc. after regurgitation.

cud'dle, *v.*, **-dled, -dling**. *v.t.* **1**. hold and caress. —*v.i.* **2**. lie or curl up snugly.

cudg'el, *n.*, *v.t.*, **-eled, -eling**. *n*. **1**. short club. —*v.t.* **2**. beat with a cudgel.

cue, *n.*, *v.t.*, **cued, cuing** or **cueing**. *n*. **1**. signal for speech or action. **2**. stick used in billiards or pool. —*v.t.* **3**. give a cue to.

cuff, *n*. **1**. feature terminating a sleeve or trouser leg. **2**. slap. —*v.t.* **3**. slap.

cui·sine'', *n*. manner of cooking.

cul'-de·sac'', *n*. blind street with a turning circle at the end.

cu·li·nar''y, *adj*. pertaining to cooking.

cull, *v.t.* select.

cul'mi·nate'', *v.i.*, **-nated, -nating**. reach a final development. —**cul''mi·na'tion**, *n*.

cul'pa·ble, *adj*. at fault. —**cul''pa·bil'i·ty**, *n*.

cul'prit, *n*. **1**. accused person. **2**. guilty person.

cult, *n*. **1**. religious sect. **2**. religious practice or devotion. —**cult'ist**, *n*.

cul'ti·vate, *v.t.*, **-vated, -vating**. **1**. work on to grow crops. **2**. develop, as personal qualities. **3**. seek to make a friend or associate. —**cul'ti·va''tor**, *n*.

cul''ti·va'tion, *n*. **1**. development of culture, manners, etc. **2**. act or instance of cultivating.

cul'ture, *n*. **1**. familiarity with the arts, etc. **2**. society, esp. with regard to its art or technology. **3**. development through special care. —**cul'tur·al**, *adj*.

cul'vert, *n*. drain under an embankment.

cum'ber·some, *adj*. heavy; burdensome.

cu'mu·la''tive, *adj*. increasing from additions.

cu'mu·lus, *n.*, *pl*. **-li**. dense cloud with domelike upper parts.

cun'ning, *adj*. **1**. crafty; sly. **2**. clever; skillful. —*n*. **3**. craftiness; slyness. **4**. skill.

cup, *n.*, *v.t.*, **cupped, cupping**, *n*. **1**. small bowl-like drinking utensil. **2**. contents of a cup. —*v.t.* **3**. form into a cuplike shape.

cup'board, *n*. storage cabinet, esp. for dishes or food.

cup'cake'', *n*. small cup-shaped cake.

Cu'pid, *n*. mythological god of love, represented as a naked boy with a bow and arrow.

cu·pid'i·ty, *n*. greed; avarice.

cu'po·la, *n*. windowed structure on top of a roof.

cur, *n*. mongrel dog.

cu'rate, *n*. clergyman with a parish. —**cu'ra·cy**, *n*.

cu·ra'tor, *n*. custodian or director of a museum department.

curb, *n*. **1**. Also, **curb'ing**, edge of a sidewalk. **2**. wall at the top of a well. **3**. border or framework. **4**. something that restrains. —*v.t.* **5**. check or restrain.

curd, *n*. coagulated milk substance, used esp. to make cheese.

cur'dle, *v.*, **-dled, dling**. *v.t.*, *v.i.* form into curds.

cure, *n*. **1**. method of remedial treatment, esp. for disease. **2**. recovery from disease. —*v.t.* **3**. restore to health; heal. **4**. preserve, as food.

cur'few, *n*. ban on being out late.

cu'ri·o, *n*. small beautiful or rare object.

cu'ri·ous, *adj*. **1**. inquisitive. **2**. odd.

—**cu·ri·ous·ly,** *adv.* —**cu"ri·os'i·ty,** *n.*

cûrl, *v.t., v.i.* **1.** form into spiral shapes; coil. —*v.i.* **2.** become curved, spiraled or undulated. **3.** move in a curving direction. —*n.* **4.** something with a curved or twisted form. —**curl'y,** *adj.*

cûr'lēw, *n., pl.* **-lews** or **-lew.** shore bird with a downcurved beak.

cûrl'ĭ·cūe", *n.* fancifully curved ornamental figure.

cûr'rănt, *n.* **1.** small seedless raisin. **2.** acid edible berry of a wild shrub.

cûr'rĕn·cÿ, *n.* **1.** money. **2.** general acceptance or use.

cûr'rĕnt, *adj.* **1.** happening in the present. **2.** practiced or accepted. —*n.* **3.** continuous movement of a fluid. **4.** flow of electricity. —**cur'rent·ly,** *adv.*

cŭr·rĭc'ū·lŭm, *n., pl.* **-lums, -la.** program of studies. —**cur·ric'u·lar,** *adj.*

cûr'rÿ, *n., pl.* **-ries,** *v.t.,* **-ried, -rying.** *n.* **1.** spicy condiment. **2.** food made with this. —*v.t.* **3.** brush, as a horse. **4.** make with curry.

cûrse, *n., v.t.,* **cursed** or **curst, cursing.** *n.* **1.** prayer, etc. invoking harm to another. **2.** blasphemy, etc. **3.** source of constant trouble. —*v.t.* **4.** make the object of a curse. —**curs'ed,** *adj.*

cûr'sör, *n.* indicator on a computer monitor showing where the next input will appear.

cûr'sò·rÿ, *adj.* hasty or superficial.

cûrt, *adj.* rude; abrupt. —**curt'ly,** *adv.*

cûr·tāil', *v.t.* cut short. —**cur·tail'ment,** *n.*

cûr'taĭn, *n.* cloth hanging before a window, theater stage, etc.

cûrt'sÿ, *n., pl.* **-sies,** *v.i.,* **-sied, sying.** *n.* **1.** woman's bow in which the knees are bent. —*v.i.* **2.** make such a bow. Also, **curt'sey.**

cûr'và·tûre, *n.* **1.** curve. **2.** degree of curving. **3.** abnormal curve, as of the spine.

cûrve, *n., v.,* **curved, curving.** *n.* **1.** continuous line continually changing direction. **2.** anything formed along such a line. —*v.t., v.i.* **3.** bend along a curve.

cŭsh'iȯn, *n.* **1.** soft pad for support. —*v.t.* **2.** preserve from a shock, as from impact.

cŭsp, *n.* pointed projection.

cŭs'pĭd, *n.* single pointed tooth; canine tooth.

cŭs'pĭ·dôr", *n.* spittoon.

cŭs'tȧrd, *n.* sweet milk and egg mixture that sets after cooking.

cŭs'tò·dÿ, *n., pl.* **-dies. 1.** guardianship; care. **2.** legal restraint; imprisonment. —**cus·to'di·an,** *n.* —**cus·to'di·al,** *adj.*

cŭs'tȯm, *n.* **1.** habitual practice or manner of thinking. **2. customs,** revenue on foreign goods. —*adj.* **3.** made to personal order. —**cus'tom·ar''y,** *adj.* —**cus"tom·ar'i·ly,** *adv.*

cŭs'tò·mêr, *n.* buyer; purchaser.

cŭt, *v.,* **cut, cutting.** *v.t.* **1.** divide or penetrate with something sharp. **2.** form with sharp tools. **3.** terminate abruptly. **4.** *Informal.* **a.** shun ostentatiously. **b.** be absent from. —*v.i.* **5.** become cut. **6.** swerve. —*n.* **7.** wound from cutting. **8.** act or instance of cutting. **9.** wounding or snubbing remark. **10.** illustration for printing.

cū·tā'nē·oŭs, *adj.* pertaining to the skin.

cūte, *adj.,* **-ter, -test, 1.** attractive; pretty. **2.** clever; shrewd.

cū'tĭ·cle, *n.* outer layer of skin.

cŭt'lȧss, *n.* short, heavy-edged sword.

cŭt'lêr·ÿ, *n.* cutting tools, esp. for food.

cŭt'lĕt, *n.* slice or patty food for frying or broiling.

cŭt'têr, *n.* **1.** person or implement for cutting. **2.** ship's boat with oars. **3.** Coast Guard ship.

cÿ'à·nĭde", *n.* potassium- or sodium-based poisonous substance.

cÿ"bêr·nĕt'ĭcs, *n.* study of human control systems and functions and of mechanical systems that can be used to replace them. —**cy"ber·net'ic,** *adj.*

cÿ'clà·māte", *n.* artificial sweetening agent.

cÿ'cle, *n., v.i.,* **-cled, -cling.** *n.* **1.** repeated series. **2.** repeated period of time. **3.** two-wheeled vehicle. —*v.i.* **4.** ride a cycle. —**cy'clic, cy'cli·cal,** *adj.* —**cy'clist,** *n.*

cÿ'clōne, *n.* storm with rotating winds.

cÿ'clò·pē'dĭȧ, *n.* encyclopedia. Also, **cy"clo·pae'di·a.**

cÿ'clò·trȯn", *n.* machine for giving acceleration to charged particles by electric and magnetic forces.

cÿl'ĭn·dêr, *n.* **1.** solid generated by a rectangle turned on its centerline. **2.** ex-

pansion chamber in an engine. —cy·
lin′dri·cal, *adj.*

cym′bal, *n.* one of a pair of concave brass
or bronze plates struck together to produce a sound.

cyn′ic, *n.* person who sees all actions as
selfishly motivated. —cyn′i·cal, *adj.*
—cyn·i·cism (sin′ə siz′′əm), *n.*

cy′no·sure′′, *n.* center of attraction.

cy′press, *n.* scaly-leaved evergreen tree.

cyst, *n.* abnormal sac or growth, usually
filled with fluid.

czar (zar), *n.* Slavic emperor. Also, *fem.*,
cza·ri′na.

D

D, d, *n.* 1. fourth letter of the English alphabet. 2. fourth-best grade.

dab, *v.*, dabbed, dabbing, *n.* *v.t.* 1.
touch or apply lightly. —*n.* 2. small
moist lump.

dab′ble, *v.i.*, -bled, -bling. 1. play in
water. 2. be superficially active.
—dab′bler, *n.*

daft, *adj.* 1. insane. 2. silly.

dag′ger, *n.* short-pointed weapon.

dahl′ia, *n.* showy perennial-flowering
plant.

dai′ly, *adj.*, *n.*, *pl.* -lies. *adj.* 1. happening each day. —*n.* 2. daily periodical.

dain′ty, *adj.*, -tier, -tiest, *n.*, *pl.* -ties.
adj. 1. delicate; fine. —*n.* 2. delicacy.
—dain′ti·ly, *adv.* —dain′ti·ness, *n.*

dair′y, *n.*, *pl.* -ies. place where milk and
milk products are processed. —dair′y·
man, *n.*

da′is, *n.*, *pl.* -ises. raised platform.

dai′sy, *n.*, *pl.* -sies. flower with a yellow
diskshaped center and white petals.

dale, *n.* valley.

dal′ly, *v.i.*, -lied, -lying. 1. play in a loving way. 2. delay; waste time. —dal′li·
ance, *n.*

dam, *n.*, *v.t.*, dammed, damming. *n.* 1.
barrier to hold back water. 2. female
parent, esp. of quadrupeds. —*v.t.* 3.
obstruct, as with a dam.

dam′age, *n.*, *v.t.*, -aged, -aging. *n.* 1.
injury. 2. damages, compensation for

injury. —*v.t.* 3. injure; harm. —dam′
age·a·ble, *adj.*

dam′ask, *n.* 1. fabric woven in patterns.
—*adj.* 2. pink.

damn, *v.t.* condemn. —dam′na·ble,
adj. —dam·na′tion, *n.*

damp, *adj.* 1. moist. —*n.* 2. moisture.
—*v.t.* 3. make moist. 4. deaden, as a
shock. —damp′ness, *n.*

damp′en, *v.t.* 1. make damp. 2. deaden
or depress, as the spirits. —*v.i.* 3. become damp.

damp′er, *n.* 1. something that deadens or
depresses. 2. valve in a flue to regulate
draft.

dam′sel, *n.* *Archaic.* girl.

dance, *v.*, danced, dancing, *n.* *v.i.* 1.
move one's body and feet in rhythm,
esp. to music. —*v.t.* 2. execute as a
dance. 3. cause to dance. —*n.* 4. social
gathering for dancing. —danc′′er, *n.*

dan′de·li′′on, *n.* weedy plant with yellow flowers.

dan′druff, *n.* scales that form on the
scalp and fall off.

dan′dy, *n.* *pl.*, -dies, *adj.*, -dier, -diest.
n. 1. man overly particular about his appearance. —*adj.* 2. *Informal.* very
good.

dan′ger, *n.* exposure to harm; risk.
—dan′ger·ous, *adj.*

dan′gle, -gled, -gling. *v.i.*, *v.t.* hang
loosely.

dank, *adj.* unpleasantly moist.

dap′per, *adj.* 1. neat. 2. small and active.

dap′ple, *adj.*, *n.*, *v.*, -pled, -pling. *adj.*
1. Also, dap′pled, spotted. —*n.* 2.
spot or marking. —*v.t.* 3. mark with
spots.

dare, *v.*, dared, daring. *n.* *v.i.* 1. have
the necessary courage or audacity.
—*v.t.*, *n.* 2. challenge. —dar′ing, *adj.*,
n.

dark, *adj.* 1. having little or no light. 2.
tending in color toward black. 3.
gloomy. 4. ignorant. —*n.* 5. absence of
light. —dark′en, *v.t.*, *v.i.* —dark′
ness, *n.*

dar′ling, *n.* 1. person dear to another.
—*adj.* 2. very dear; cherished.

darn, *v.t.* mend by weaving rows of
stitches.

dart, *n.* 1. small pointed missile usually
thrown by hand. 2. sudden motion.

—*v.t.*, *v.i.* **3.** move suddenly and swiftly.

dăsh, *v.t.* **1.** hurl violently. **2.** smash. **3.** frustrate. —*v.i.* **4.** rush; sprint. —*n.* **5.** small amount shaken from a bottle, etc. **6.** short race. **7.** punctuation mark (—) indicating a break.

dăsh'bôard'', *n.* instrument panel.

dăsh'ĭng, *adj.* **1.** lively. **2.** showy; stylish. —**dash'ing·ly**, *adv.*

dăs'tȧrd, *n.* coward; sneak. —**das'tard·ly**, *adj.*

dā''tȧ, *n. pl.* **1.** facts; figures. **2.** (computers) information stored in a memory.

dā''tȧ·bāse, *n.* (computers) a structured file facilitating data access and manipulation.

dāte, *n.*, *v.*, **dated, dating.** *n.* **1.** particular time. **2.** day of the month. **3.** appointment. **4.** sweet, fleshy fruit of a palm tree. —*v.t.* **5.** give a date to. —*v.i.* **6.** belong to a specific time.

dāt'ĕd, *adj.* **1.** antiquated. **2.** showing a date.

daub, *v.t.* **1.** cover or smear with a soft, muddy substance. —*v.t.*, *v.i.* **2.** paint clumsily. —*n.* **3.** something daubed. —**daub'er**, *n.*

daugh'têr, *n.* female child. —**daugh'ter·ly**, *adj.*

daugh'têr-ĭn-law'', *n. pl.*, **daughters-in-law.** son's wife.

daunt, *v.t.* frighten; dishearten. —**daunt'less**, *adj.*

dăv'ĕn·pôrt'', *n.* large couch.

daw'dle, *v.i.*, **-dled, -dling.** waste time. —**daw'dler**, *n.*

dawn, *v.i.* **1.** begin to grow light in the morning. —*n.* **2.** break of day.

dāy, *n.* **1.** period between sunrise and sunset. **2.** period of earth's rotation on its axis. **3.** era; period of time.

dāy'drēam'', *n.* **1.** period of pleasant, dreamy thought. —*v.t.* **2.** have daydreams.

dāy'līght'', *n.* **1.** light of day. **2.** openness.

dāy'tīme'', *n.* period between sunrise and sunset.

dāze, *v.t.*, **dazed, dazing,** *n.*, *v.t.* **1.** stun; bewilder. —*n.* **2.** stunned condition.

dăz'zle, *v.t.*, **-zled, -zling. 1.** overwhelm with intense light. **2.** impress with brilliance.

dēa'cŏn, *n.* **1.** cleric just below a priest in rank. **2.** lay church officer. —**dea'con·ry**, *n.*

dĕad, *adj.* **1.** no longer alive. **2.** without life. **3.** obsolete. **4.** accurate; unerring. —*adj.*, *adv.* **5.** straight. —*n.* **6.** the **dead**, persons no longer living. **dead'en**, *v.t.*

dĕad'līne'', *n.* latest time by which something must be completed.

dĕad'lŏck'', *n.* **1.** frustrated standstill. —*v.t.*, *v.i.* **2.** bring or come to a deadlock.

dĕad'lȳ, *adj.* **-lier, -liest. 1.** likely to cause death. **2.** typical of death. —**dead'li·ness**, *n.*

dĕaf, *adj.* incapable of hearing. —**deaf'ness**, *n.* —**deaf'en**, *v.t.*

dēal, *v.*, **dealt, dealing,** *n. v.t.* **1.** portion out. **2.** administer, as a blow. —*v.i.* **3.** do or have business. **4.** portion out cards, etc. —*n.* **5.** business transaction or agreement. —**deal'er**, *n.*

dēan, *n.* **1.** college official who supervises students or faculty. **2.** presiding cleric in a cathedral.

dēar, *adj.* **1.** beloved. **2.** expensive. —*n.* **3.** beloved person. —**dear'ly**, *adv.*

dĕarth, *n.* scarcity; lack.

dĕath, *n.* **1.** act of dying. **2.** state of being dead. —**death'less**, *adj.* —**death'like''**, *adj.* —**death'ly**, *adj.*, *adv.*

dė·bă'cle, *n.* ruinous collapse.

dė·bâr', *v.t.*, **-barred, -barring.** exclude; prohibit.

dė·bāse', *v.t.*, **-based, -basing.** lower in value. —**de·base'ment**, *n.*

dė·bāte', *v.* **-bated, -bating.** *n. v.t.* **1.** discuss; argue. **2.** consider. —*v.i.* **3.** take part in discussion. —*n.* **4.** discussion of opposing views. —**de·bat'a·ble**, *adj.* —**de·bat'er**, *n.*

dė·bauch'', *v.t.* **1.** corrupt; seduce. —*n.* **2.** seduction. —**de·bauch'er·y**, *n.*

dė·bĭl'ĭ·tāte, *v.t.*, **-tated, -tating.** weaken. —**de·bil''i·ta'tion**, *n.*

dė·bĭl'ĭ·tȳ, *n.*, *pl.* **-ties.** weakness.

dĕb'ĭt, *n.* **1.** recorded debt. —*v.t.* **2.** charge with a debt.

dĕb''ȯ·nâir', *adj.* **1.** courteous; pleasantly mannered. **2.** carefree.

dė·brĭs (dė brē), *n.* rubbish; remains.

dĕbt, *n.* **1.** something owed. **2.** condition of owing. —**debt'or**, *n.*

de·but (dā byoo'), *n*. **1**. first public appearance. **2**. formal introduction into society.

dĕb'ū·tânte'', *n*. girl making a society debut.

dĕc'āde, *n*. ten-year period.

dĕc'à·dénce, *n*. decay; deterioration. —**dec'a·dent**, *adj., n*.

dĕc''à·hē'dròn, *n., pl*. **-drons, -dra**. tensided solid.

dē'căl, *n*. transfer of a picture or design from paper to glass, wood, etc. Also, **de·cal''co·ma'ni·a**.

Dĕc'à·lŏgue'', *n*. Ten Commandments. Also, **Dec'a·log''**.

de·càmp', *v.i.* **1**. break camp. **2**. depart suddenly.

de·cănt', *v.t.* pour gently so as not to disturb sediment.

de·cănt'êr, *n*. ornamental bottle, esp. for wine.

de·căp'ĭ·tāte'', *v.t.*, -tated, -tating. behead. —**de·cap''i·ta'tion**, *n*.

de·căth'lŏn, *n*. contest consisting of ten track and field events.

de·cāy', *v.i., v.t.* **1**. deteriorate; rot. —*n*. **2**. deterioration.

de·cēase', *n., v.i.* -ceased, -ceasing. *n*. **1**. death. —*v.i.* **2**. die. —**de·ceased'**, *adj., n*.

de·cēit', *n*. lying; fraud. —**de·ceit'ful**, *adj*.

de·cēive', *v.t.* -ceived, -ceiving. mislead.

Dè·cěm'bêr, *n*. twelfth and final month.

dē'cènt, *adj*. **1**. appropriate. **2**. not offensive to modesty. **3**. respectable. **4**. adequate. —**de'cent·ly**, *adv*. —**de'cen·cy**, *n*.

dē·cěn'trȧl·īze'', *v.t.*, -ized, -ising. free from dependency on a central authority, source, etc. —**de·cen''tral·i·za'tion**, *n*.

de·cěp'tion, *n*. **1**. act or instance of deceiving. **2**. fraud. —**de·cep'tive**, *adj*.

de·cīde', *v.*, -cided, -ciding. *v.t.* **1**. reach a decision regarding. —*v.i.* **2**. make a judgment or choice.

de·cīd'ĕd, *adj*. **1**. clear-cut. **2**. determined. —**de·cid'ed·ly**, *adv*.

de·cīd'ū·oŭs, *adj*. shedding leaves at a particular season, as a tree or shrub.

dĕc'ĭ·mȧl, *adj*. **1**. based on the number ten. **2**. pertaining to fractions whose denominators are ten or some power of ten. —*n*. **3**. decimal fraction.

dĕc'ĭ·māte'', *v.t.*, -mated, -mating. destroy a sizable number of.

dè·cī'phêr, *v.t.* determine the meaning of.

dè·cī'sion, *n*. **1**. choice or judgment. **2**. emphasis; firmness.

dè·cī'sĭve, *adj*. **1**. determining an outcome or conclusion. **2**. emphatic; firm. —**de·ci'sive·ly**, *adv*. —**de·ci'sive·ness**, *n*.

dĕck, *n*. **1**. floor of a ship, bridge, etc. **2**. pack of playing cards. —*v.t.* **3**. adorn.

de·clāim', *v.i., v.t.*, speak or utter rhetorically. —**de''clam·a'tion**, *n*. —**de·clam'a·to''ry**, *adj*.

de·clāre', *v.t.* -clared, -claring. **1**. make known. **2**. say emphatically. —**de·clar'a·tive, de·clar'a·to''ry**, *adj*. —**dec''la·ra'tion**, *n*.

de·clĕn'sion, *n*. **1**. grammatical inflection of nouns, pronouns, or adjectives. **2**. decline.

de·clīne', *v.*, -clined, -clining, *n. v.t., v.i.* **1**. bend or slope downward. **2**. deteriorate. **3**. refuse. —*v.i.* **4**. give grammatical inflections. —*n*. **5**. deterioration. **6**. downward slope.

dé·clĭv'ĭ·tў, *n., pl*. -ties. downward slope.

dē·cōde', *v.t.* -coded, -coding. decipher from code.

dē''còm·pōse', *v.*, -posed, -posing. *v.t., v.i.* **1**. break up into parts. **2**. decay. —**de''com·po·si'tion**, *n*.

dē·côr', *n*. style of decoration.

dĕc'ò·rāte'', *v.t.*, -rated, -rating. **1**. adorn. **2**. give a medal to. —**dec'o·ra·tive**, *adj*. —**dec'o·ra''tor**, *n*. —**dec''o·ra'tion**, *n*.

dĕc'ò·roŭs, *adj*. proper.

dè·cô'rŭm, *n*. propriety.

dē·cŏy', *n*. **1**. artificial bird used as a lure in hunting. **2**. lure. —*v.t.* **3**. lure into a trap.

de·crēase', *v.*, -creased, -creasing, *n. v.t., v.i.* **1**. gradually lessen. —*n*. **2**. lessening.

de·crēe', *n., v.*, -creed, -creeing. *n*. **1**. edict. —*v.t.* **2**. ordain by decree.

de·crĕp'ĭt, *adj*. worn by old age or long use. —**de·crep'i·tude''**, *n*.

de·crў', *v.t.*, -cried, -crying. denounce. —**de·cri'al**, *n*.

dĕd'ĭ·cāte'', *v.t.*, -cated, -cating. **1**. set

apart; devote. **2.** inscribe. **—ded″i·ca′ tion,** *n.*

dè·dūce′, *v.t.,* **-duced, -ducing.** infer; derive. **—de·duc′i·ble,** *adj.*

dè·dŭct′, *v.t.* subtract; take away. **—de· duct′i·ble,** *adj.*

dè·dŭc′tion, *n.* **1.** act or result of reasoning from the general to the specific. **2.** amount deducted. **—de·duc′tive,** *adj.*

dēed, *n.* **1.** something that is done; an act. **2.** legal conveyance esp. of land. **—***v.t.* **3.** transfer by deed.

dēem, *v.t., v.i.* believe; adjudge.

dēep, *adj.* **1.** extending far downward or inward. **2.** difficult to understand. **3.** profound; serious. **4.** dark and rich, esp. a color. **5.** low in pitch. **—***n.* **6.** deep place. **—***adv.* **7.** far down. **—deep′en,** *v.t., v.i.* **—deep′ly,** *adv.*

dēer, *n., pl.* **deer, deers.** ruminant animal, the male of which have antlers or horns.

dè·fāce′, *v.t.,* **-faced, -facing.** mar; disfigure. **—de·face′ment,** *n.*

dè·făc′tō, actually existing but not lawfully authorized.

dè·fāme′, *v.t.* **-famed, -faming.** attack the reputation of; slander. **—def″am·a′tion,** *n.* **—de·fam′a·to″ry,** *adj.*

dè·fault′, *n.* **1.** failure, esp. to pay a debt. **—***v.t., v.i.* **2.** fail, esp. to pay, when required.

dè·fēat, *v.t.* **1.** overthrow; conquer. **—***n.* **2.** act or instance of defeating.

dè·fēat′ĭst, *n.* person who accepts defeat. **-de·feat′ism,** *n.*

dē′fè·cāte″, *v.i.,* **-cated, -cating.** *v.i.* excrete waste from the bowels. **—def″e·ca′tion,** *n.*

dē′fĕct, *n.* **1.** imperfection; fault. **—***v.i.* (dē fekt′) **2.** desert a cause, esp. to join another. **—de·fec′tive,** *adj.* **—de·fec′tion,** *n.* **—de·fec′tor,** *n.*

dè·fĕnd′, *v.t.* **1.** protect; guard against attack. **2.** support with one's words. **—de·fend′er,** *n.*

dè·fĕnd′ant, *n. Law.* accused person.

dè·fĕnse′, *n.* **1.** protection against attack. **2.** justification. **3.** *Law.* reply to a charge. **—de′fense·less,** *adj.* **—de· fen′si·ble,** *adj.*

dè·fĕn′sĭve, *adj.* **1.** pertaining to defense. **2.** anxious to justify oneself. **—***n.* **3.** situation of a defender.

dè·fêr′, *v.,* **-ferred, -ferring.** *v.t., v.i.* **1.**

postpone. **—***v.i.* **2.** yield politely. **—de· fer′ment,** *n.* **—def′er·ence,** *n.* **—de″ fer·en′tial,** *adj.*

dè·fī′ance, *n.* open disregard of or bold resistance to authority. **—de·fi′ant,** *adj.*

dè·fī′cièn·cÿ, *n., pl.* **-cies.** lack; inadequate amount. **—de·fi′cient,** *adj.*

dĕf′ī·cĭt, *n.* deficiency, esp. of assets.

dè·fīle′, *v.,* **-filed, -filing.** *v.t.* **1.** desecrate. **2.** make filthy. **—***v.i.* **3.** march in file. **—***n.* **4.** narrow passage. **—de·file′ ment,** *n.*

dè·fīne′, *v.t.,* **-fined, -fining. 1.** state the meaning of. **2.** determine. **—def″i·ni′ tion,** *n.* **—de·fin′a·ble,** *adj.*

dĕf′ī·nĭte, *adj.* **1.** exact. **2.** within precise limits. **—def′i·nite·ly,** *adv.*

dè·fĭn′ĭ·tĭve, *adj.* **1.** conclusive. **2.** defining.

dè·flāte, *v.,* **-flated, -flating.** *v.t., v.i.* **1.** collapse by releasing air. **2.** increase in purchasing power. **—de·fla′tion,** *n.* **—de·fla′tion·ar″y,** *adj.*

dè·flĕct′, *v.t., v.i.* turn from a course; swerve. **—de·flec′tion,** *n.*

dè·fôrm′, *v.t.* **1.** mar the form of. **2.** make ugly. **—de″for·ma′tion,** *n.* **—de· form′i·ty,** *n.*

dè·fraud′, *v.t.* cheat; take rights or property of by fraud.

dè·frāy′, *v.t.* pay, as expenses.

dè·frŏst′, *v.t., v.i.* free or be freed of ice.

dĕft, *adj.* skillful. **—deft′ly,** *adv.* **—deft′ ness,** *n.*

dè·fŭnct′, *adj.* no longer alive or in existence.

dè·fÿ′, *v.t.,* **-fied, -fying. 1.** openly resist. **2.** challenge.

dè·gĕn′êr·àte, *adj., n., v.,* **-ated, -ating.** *adj.* **1.** deteriorated. **2.** depraved. *n.* **3.** depraved person. **—***v.i.* (de gen″er ate′) **4.** deteriorate. **—de·gen″er·a′ tion,** *n.* **—de·gen′er·a·cy,** *n.* **—de· gen′er·a·tive,** *adj.*

dè·grāde′, *v.t.,* **-graded, -grading.** reduce in quality or rank. **—de″gra·da′ tion,** *n.*

dè·grēe′, *n.* **1.** stage or point, as in a process. **2.** extent or intensity. **3.** title conferred by a college. **4.** unit of temperature. **5.** 360th of a circle.

dē·hū′màn·īze″, *v.t.,* **-ized, -izing.** deny human qualities to.

dē·hÿ′drāte, *v.,* **-drated, -drating.** *v.t.*

v.i. remove or lose water. —**de''hy·dra'tion,** *n.*

dē'ĭ·fy'', *v.t.,* **-fied, -fying.** make a god of. —**de''i·fi·ca'tion,** *n.*

deign, *v.t., v.i.* condescend.

dē'ĭsm, *n.* belief that a god created the world but has had no control over it. —**de'ist,** *n.*

dē'ĭ·tў, *n., pl.* **-ties.** god or goddess

dè·jĕct', *v.t.* dishearten. —**de·jec'tion,** *n.*

dè·lāy', *v.t.* **1.** postpone. **2.** hinder; make late. —*v.i.* **3.** linger; procrastinate. —*n.* **4.** act or instance of delaying.

dè·lĕc'tà·ble, *adj.* delightful; delicious. —**de''lec·ta'tion,** *n.*

dĕl'è·gàte, *n., v.t.,* **-gated, -gating.** *n.* **1.** representative. —*v.t.* (del' ə gāt) **2.** send as a representative. **3.** entrust to another, as authority. —**del''e·ga'tion,** *n.*

dè·lēte', *v.t.,* **-leted, -leting.** remove from a text. —**de·le'tion,** *n.*

dĕl''è·tē'rĭ·oŭs, *adj.* injurious to health;

dè·lĭb'êr·āte, *v.,* **-ated, -ating,** *adj. v.t., v.i.* **1.** ponder. —*adj.* **2.** intentional. **3.** unhurried. —**de·lib'er·ate·ly,** *adv.* —**de·lib''er·a'tion,** *n.* —**de·lib'er·a·tive,** *adj.* —**de·lib'er·a''tor,** *n.*

dĕl'ĭ·cà·cў, *n., pl.* **-cies.** **1.** fineness of quality. **2.** choice food.

dĕl'ĭ·càte, *adj.* **1.** fine in quality or texture. **2.** easily damaged. **3.** considerate; tactful. **4.** functioning precisely. —**del'i·cate·ly,** *adv.*

dĕl''ĭ·cà·tĕs'sèn, *n.* store selling food specialties.

dè·lĭ'cioŭs, *adj.* **1.** pleasing to taste. **2.** delectable. —**de·li'cious·ly,** *adv.*

dè·līght', *v.t., v.i.* **1.** give great pleasure. —*n.* **2.** joy or great pleasure. —**de·light'ed,** *adj.* —**de·light'ful,** *adj.*

dè·lĭn'ē·āte'', *v.t.,* **-ated, -ating.** trace the outline of. —**de·lin''e·a'tion,** *n.*

dè·lĭn'quènt, *adj.* **1.** neglectful of duty or law. **2.** late, as a debt. —*n.* **3.** delinquent person. —**de·lin'quen·cy,** *n.*

dè·līr'ĭ·ŭm, *n.* temporary excited mental disorder. —**de·lir'i·ous,** *adj.*

dè·lĭv'êr, *v.t.* **1.** set free or save. **2.** hand over. **3.** assist at the birth of. **4.** present to an audience. **5.** distribute. —**de·liv'er·ance,** *n.* —**de·liv'er·y,** *n.*

dĕl·phĭn'ĭ·ŭm, *n.* tall blue garden flower.

dĕl'tà, *n.* deposit of soil formed at a divided river mouth.

dè·lūde', *v.t.,* **-luded, -luding.** mislead.

dèl·ūge, *n., v.t.,* **-uged, -uging.** *n.* **1.** flood. **2.** heavy rainfall. —*v.t.* **3.** flood. **4.** overwhelm.

dè·lū'sion, *n.* false conception, esp. one persistent and opposed to reason. —**de·lu'sive,** *adj.*

dè·lŭxe', *adj.* of specially fine quality.

dĕlve, *v.i.,* **delved, delving.** dig.

dĕm'à·gŏgue'', *n.* unscrupulous player on popular emotion. Also, **dem'a·gog''.** —**dem'a·gog''y, dem'a·gogu''er·y,** *n.*

dè·mănd', *v.t.* **1.** ask for boldly; claim as a right. **2.** require. —*v.i.* **3.** make a demand. —*n.* **4.** act or instance of demanding. **5.** thing demanded. —**de·mand'ing,** *adj.*

dè·mēan', *v.t.* **1.** debase; humble. **2.** behave; conduct.

dè·mēan'ör, *n.* behavior or conduct.

dè·mĕnt'ĕd, *adj.* mentally deranged.

dè·mĕr'ĭt, *n.* **1.** fault. **2.** mark against a person for a fault.

dĕm'ĭ·gŏd, *n.* **1.** mythological being who is divine and human. **2.** godlike human.

dē·mĭl'ĭ·tàr·īze'', *v.t.,* **-ized, -izing.** free from military control. **de·mil''i·tar·i·za'tion,** *n.*

dè·mīse', *n., v.t.,* **-mised, -mising.** *n.* **1.** death. —*v.t.* **2.** transfer by lease.

dē·mō'bĭ·līze'', *v.t.,* **-lized, -lizing.** free from military service; disband. —**de·mo''bi·li·za'tion,** *n.*

dè·mŏc'rà·cў, *n.* **1.** government by the people. **2.** country with such government. **3.** social equality. —**dem'o·crat'',** *n.* —**dem''o·crat'ic,** *adj.* —**de·moc'ra·tize'',** *v.t.*

Dĕ'mó·crăt, *n.* member of the Democratic party.

dè·mŏl'ĭsh, *v.t.* destroy. —**dem''o·li'tion,** *n.*

dē'mŏn, *n.* **1.** evil spirit; devil. **2.** person regarded as evil. —**de·mon'ic, de·mo'ni·ac'', de''mo·ni'a·cal,** *adj.*

dĕm'ŏn·strāte'', *v.* **-strated, -strating.** *v.t.* **1.** prove in detail. **2.** explain by example. **3.** reveal. —*v.i.* **4.** call public attention to one's attitude. —**dem''on·stra'tion,** *n.* —**dem'on·stra''tor,** *n.* —**de·mon'stra·ble,** *adj.*

dè·mŏn'strà·tĭve, *adj.* **1.** self-expressive. **2.** illustrative or explanatory. **3.** conclusive.

dè·môr′ål·īze″, v.t., -ized, -izing. lower the morale of. **—de·mor″al·i·za′tion,** n.

dè·mōte′, v.t., -moted, -moting. lower in rank. **—de·mo′tion,** n.

dè·mûr′, v.i., -murred, -murring, n. v.i. **1.** object. **—**n. **2.** objection.

dè·mūre′, adj. modest; coy. **—de·mure′ly,** adv.

dĕn, n. **1.** cave of a wild animal. **2.** vile place. **3.** small, private room for a man.

dè·nī′ål, n. **1.** refusal of consent. **2.** contradiction. **3.** refusal to believe.

dĕn′ĭ·grāte″, v.t., -grated, -grating. blacken or malign the character of. **—den″i·gra′tion,** n.

dĕn′ĭm, n. heavy twill cotton cloth.

dĕn′ĭ·zĕn, n. inhabitant.

dè′nŏm′ĭ·nāte″, v.t., -nated, -nating. name.

dè·nŏm″ĭ·nā′tion, n. **1.** name. **2.** act of naming. **3.** religious sect. **—de·nom″i·na′tion·al,** adj.

dè·nŏm′ĭ·nā″tôr, n. Math. term below the line in a fraction; divisor.

dè·nōte′, v.t., -noted, -noting. indicate; mean. **—de″no·ta′tion,** n.

de·noue·ment (dā noo mäh′), n. Literature. resolution of a conflict.

dè·nŏunce′, v.t., -nounced, -nouncing. **1.** accuse openly. **2.** inform against. **—de·nounce′ment,** n.

dĕnse, adj. **1.** thick. **2.** stupid. **—dense′ly,** adv. **—dense′ness,** n. **—den′si·ty,** n.

dĕnt, n. **1.** hollow area made by a blow. **—**v.t., v.i. **2.** make or receive a dent.

dĕn′tål, adj. pertaining to teeth or dentistry.

dĕn′tĭ·frīce, n. preparation used in brushing the teeth.

dĕn′tĭst, n. doctor specializing in teeth and gums. **—den′tist·ry,** n.

dĕn′tûre, n. set of false teeth.

dè·nūde′, v.t., -nuded, -nuding. strip. **—den″u·da′tion,** n.

dè·nŭn″cĭ·ā′tion, n. **1.** condemnation. **2.** accusation.

dè·nȳ′, v.t., -nied, -nying. **1.** reject as untrue. **2.** refuse to give or allow. **3.** refuse something to.

dè·ō′dòr·ånt, n. **1.** preparation for de-

stroying odors. **—**adj. **2.** destroying odors.

dè·pärt′, v.i. **1.** leave; go away. **2.** die. **—de·par′ture,** n.

dè·pärt′mènt, n. **1.** part or section. **2.** field of activity. **—de·part″men′tal,** adj.

dè·pĕnd′, v.i. **1.** look outside oneself for support, help, etc. **2.** be according to conditions. **—de·pend′a·ble,** adj. **—de·pend′a·bly,** adv. **—de·pend″a·bil′i·ty,** n. **—de·pend′ent,** adj., n. **—de·pend′ence, de·pend′en·cy,** n.

dè·pĭct′, v.t. **1.** portray; delineate. **2.** describe. **—de·pic′tion,** n.

dè·plēte′, v.t., -pleted, -pleting. exhaust or reduce in amount. **—de·ple′tion,** n.

dè·plōre′, v.t., -plored, -ploring. regret strongly. **—de·plor′a·ble,** adj.

dē·pŏp′ū·lāte″, v.t., -lated, -lating. remove the population of. **—de·pop″u·la′tion,** n.

dè·pôrt′, v.t. expel from a country. **—de″por·ta′tion,** n.

dè·pôrt′mènt, n. conduct or behavior.

dè·pōse′, v.t., -posed, -posing. **1.** remove from office or power. **2.** testify. **—dep″o·si′tion,** n.

dè·pŏs′ĭt, v.t. **1.** put in a bank, etc. **2.** give in partial payment. **3.** drop or cause to settle. **—**n. **4.** something deposited. **—de·pos′i·tor,** n.

dē′pōt, n. **1.** bus or railroad station. **2.** storage place for military supplies.

dè·prāve′, v.t. -praved, -praving. corrupt. **—de·prav′i·ty,** n.

dĕp′rè·cāte″, v.t., -cated, -cating. **1.** express disapproval of. **2.** belittle. **—dep″re·ca′tion,** n. **—dep′re·ca·to″ry,** adj.

dē·prē′cĭ·āte″, v., -ated, -ating. v.t., v.i. **1.** lessen in value or seeming importance. **—**v.t. **2.** belittle. **—de·pre′ci·a′tion,** n.

dĕp″rè·dā′tion, n. robbery.

dè·prĕss′, v.t. **1.** deject; sadden. **2.** push down. **3.** weaken. **—de·pressed′,** adj. **—de·press′ant,** n.

dè·prĕs′sion, n. **1.** act of depressing or being depressed. **2.** depressed state. **3.** period when business and employment decline. **—de·pres′sive,** adj.

dè·prīve′, v.t., -prived, -priving. withhold from. **—de″pri·va′tion,** n.

dĕpth, n. **1.** distance downward or inward. **2.** quality of being deep. **3.** intensity or profundity. **4.** profundity. **5.** depths, deepest part.

dĕp″u·tā′tion, *n.* delegation.

dĕp′u·tў, *n., pl.* **-ties.** person appointed to act as a substitute for another.

de·rāil′, *v.t., v.i.* run off the rails. —**de·rail′ment,** *n.*

de·rānge′, *v.t.,* **-ranged, -ranging. 1.** disturb the arrangement of. **2.** make insane. —**de·range′ment,** *n.*

dĕr′bў, *n.* stiff hat with a round crown.

dĕr′é·lĭct″, *adj.* **1.** abandoned by its owner. **2.** negligent. —*n.* **3.** something abandoned, esp. a ship. **4.** destitute person.

dĕr″é·lĭc′tion, *n.* **1.** negligence of a duty. **2.** forsakenness.

de·rīde′, *v.t.,* **-rided, -riding.** mock. —**de·ri′sion,** *n.* —**de·ri′sive,** *adj.*

de·rīve′, *v.* **-rived, -riving.** *v.t.* **1.** obtain from a source. **2.** trace to or from a source. **3.** deduce; infer. —*v.i.* **4.** originate or be derived. —**der″i·va′tion,** *n.* —**de·riv′a·tive,** *adj., n.*

dĕr′ó·gāte″, *v.,* **-gated, -gating.** *v.t., v.i.,* detract. —**der″o·ga′tion,** *n.* —**de·rog′a·to″ry,** *adj.*

dĕr′rĭck, *n.* **1.** crane for lifting and moving heavy objects. **2.** tall framework over an oil well.

dĕs′cănt, *n.* **1.** melody. —*v.i.* (des·cant′) **2.** sing. **3.** discourse.

de·scĕnd′, *v.t.* **1.** move down, along or through. —*v.i.* **2.** move downward. **3.** slope downward. **4.** make a sudden attack, etc. **5.** be derived from specified ancestors. —**des·cent′,** *n.* —**de·scen′dant,** *n.*

de·scrībe′, *v.t.,* **-scribed, -scribing. 1.** give a conception or account of. **2.** trace by movement. —**de·scrib′a·ble,** *adj.* —**de·scrip′tion,** *n.* —**de·scrip′tive,** *adj.*

de·scrȳ′, *v.t.,* **-scried, -scrying.** perceive.

dĕs′é·crāte″, *v.t.,* **-crated, -crating.** profane. —**des″e·cra′tion,** *n.*

de·sĕg′ré·gāte″, *v.,* **-gated, -gating.** *v.t., v.i.* eliminate racial segregation in. —**de·seg″re·ga′tion,** *n.*

de·sĕrt′, *v.t.* **1.** abandon. **2.** abscond from permanently, as duty. —*n.* **3.** Often, **deserts,** something deserved. **4.** (des′ert) wasteland, esp. a sandy one. —*adj.*

5. desolate; barren. —**de·sert′er,** *n.* —**de·ser′tion,** *n.*

de·sĕrve′, *v.,* **-served, -serving.** *v.t.* **1.** have as a rightful outcome or reward. —*v.i.* **2.** be worthy. —**de·serv′ing,** *adj., n.*

dĕs′ĭc·cāte″, *v.,* **-cated, -cating.** *v.t., v.i.* dry completely. —**des″ic·ca′tion,** *n.*

de·sīgn′, *v.t.* **1.** plan the form and making of. **2.** contrive. **3.** intend. —*n.* **4.** plan or pattern. **5.** designing of artistic objects. **6.** scheme or intention.

dĕs′ĭg·nāte″, *v.t.,* **-nated, -nating. 1.** specify; indicate. **2.** name. **3.** appoint. —**des″ig·na′tion,** *n.*

de·sīgn″ér, *n.* **1.** one who designs. —*adj.* **2.** of or pertaining to clothing, etc. styled by a designer, as *designer jeans.*

de·sīgn′ĭng, *adj.* scheming.

de·sīre′, *v.* **-sired, -siring,** *n. v.t.* **1.** long for. **2.** request. —*v.i.* **3.** have a desire. —*n.* **4.** craving. **5.** request. **6.** lust. **7.** thing desired. —**de·sir′a·ble,** *adj.* —**de·sir′a·bly,** *adv.* —**de·sir″a·bil′i·ty,** *n.* —**de·sir′ous,** *adj.*

de·sīst′, *v.i.* stop; cease.

dĕsk, *n.* table with drawers used for writing.

dĕs′ó·lāte, *adj., v.* **-lated, -lating.** *adj.* **1.** barren. **2.** lonely. **3.** uninhabited. —*v.t.* (des′o·late″) **4.** make barren. —**des″o·la′tion,** *n.*

de·spāir′, *v.i.* **1.** lose hope. —*n.* **2.** hopelessness.

dĕs″pêr·â′dō, *n., pl.* **-does, -dos.** reckless criminal.

dĕs′pêr·ate, *adj.* **1.** reckless due to despair. **2.** having an urgent need. **3.** very serious. **4.** extreme or drastic. —**des″per·a′tion,** *n.*

dĕs′pĭ·ca·ble, *adj.* contemptible. —**des′pi·ca·bly,** *adv.*

de·spīse′, *v.t.,* **-spised, -spising.** scorn; loathe.

de·spīte′, *prep.* in spite of.

de·spoĭl′, *v.t.* rob; pillage.

de·spŏnd′, *v.i.* lose hope or courage. —**de·spond′en·cy, de·spond′ence,** *n.* —**de·spond′ent,** *adj.*

dĕs′pŏt, *n.* tyrant or absolute ruler. —**des·pot′ic,** *adj.* —**des′pot·ism,** *n.*

des·sêrt′, *n.* sweet course ending a meal.

dĕs″tĭ·nā′tion, *n.* place to be reached.

dĕs'tĭne, *v.t.,* **-tined, -tining. 1.** intend. **2.** predetermine.

dĕs'tĭn·ÿ, *n., pl.* **-nies. 1.** predetermined course of events. **2.** rate.

dĕs'tĭ·tūte'', *adj.* **1.** deprived. **2.** without means of existence. —**des''ti·tu'tion,** *n.*

dĕ·strōÿ', *n.* **1.** damage so as to eliminate. **2.** kill.

dĕ·strōÿ'êr, *n.* **1.** light, fast warship. **2.** person or thing that destroys.

dĕ·strŭc'tion, *n.* **1.** act or instance of destroying. **2.** agency by which one is destroyed. —**de·struct'i·ble,** *adj.* —**de·struc'tive,** *adj.*

dĕs'ŭl·tô''rÿ, *adj.* **1.** random. **2.** disconnected. —**des''ul·to'ri·ly,** *adv.*

dĕ·tăch', *v.t.* separate; disconnect. —**de·tach'a·ble,** *adj.*

dĕ·tăched', *adj.* **1.** separate; not connected. **2.** disinterested.

dĕ·tăch'mĕnt, *n.* **1.** state of being detached. **2.** military unit on a special mission.

dĕ·tāil', *n.* **1.** subordinate part or feature. **2.** soldiers for a specific duty. —*v.t.* **3.** make, plan, or relate the details of. **4.** assign to a duty.

dĕ·tāin', *v.t.* **1.** keep from going on; delay. **2.** keep in custody. —**de·ten'tion,** *n.*

dĕ·tĕct', *v.t.* discover. —**de·tec'tion,** *n.* —**de·tec'tor,** *n.* —**de·tect'a·ble, de·tect'i·ble,** *adj.*

dĕ·tĕc'tĭve, *n.* investigator seeking private or hidden information.

de·tente (dā tahnt'), *n.* lessening of tension, esp. internationally.

dĕ·têr', *v.t.,* **-terred, -terring.** discourage or prevent. —**de·ter'ment,** *n.* —**de·ter'rent,** *n.*

dĕ·têr'gĕnt, *adj.* **1.** cleansing. —*n.* **2.** preparation used for cleaning.

dĕ·tĕ''rĭ·ó·rāte'', *v.,* **-rated, -rating.** *v.t., v.i.* worsen. —**de·te''ri·o·ra'tion,** *n.*

dĕ·têr''mĭ·nā·tion, *n.* **1.** act or instance of determining. **2.** firmness of resolve. **3.** firm intention.

dĕ·têr'mĭne, *v.,* **-mined, -mining.** *v.t.* **1.** settle. **2.** ascertain. **3.** direct; impel. **4.** set limits to. —*v.i.* **5.** decide. —**de·ter'mi·na·ble,** *adj.* —**de·ter'mi·nate,** *adj.*

dĕ·têr'mĭned, *adj.* showing determination.

dĕ·tĕst', *v.t.* hate. —**de·test'a·ble,** *adj.* —**de·test'a·bly,** *adv.* —**de''tes·ta'tion,** *n.*

dĕ·thrōne', *v.t.,* **-throned, -throning.** remove from sovereign power.

dĕt'ó·nāte'', *v.,* **-nated, -nating.** *v.t., v.i.* explode. —**det''o·na'tion,** *n.* —**det''o·na'tor,** *n.*

dē'toûr, *n.* **1.** roundabout course. —*v.t., vi.* **2.** go or route on a detour.

dĕ·trăct', *v.t.* **1.** take away. —*v.i.* **2.** take a desirable quality. —**de·trac'tion,** *n.*

dĕt'rĭ·mĕnt, *n.* **1.** injury or loss. **2.** something that causes injury or loss. —**det''ri·men'tal,** *adj.*

dē·văl'ŭ·āte'', *v.t.,* **-ated, -ating.** lessen in value. Also, **de·val'ue.** —**de·val''u·a'tion,** *n.*

dĕv'ás·tāte'', *v.t.,* **-tated, -tating.** destroy everywhere. —**dev''as·ta'tion,** *n.*

dĕ·vĕl'óp, *v.t.* **1.** bring to maturity or completeness. **2.** elaborate. **3.** fall ill with. **4.** *Photography.* bring out the picture on. —*v.i.* **5.** be developed. —**de·vel'op·ment,** *n.* —**de·vel''op'men'tal,** *adj.*

dē'vĭ·āte'', *v.i.,* **-ated, -ating.** *adj., n. v.i.* **1.** turn aside; digress. —*adj.* (dē'vi ate) **2.** deviant. —*n.* **3.** deviant person. **4.** sexual pervert. —**de''vi·a'tion,** *n.*

dĕ·vīce', *n.* **1.** tool, etc. **2.** plan. **3.** symbol or representation.

dĕv'ĭl, *n., v.t.,* **-iled** or **-illed, -iling** or **-illing.** *n.* **1.** fiend of hell. **2. the Devil,** Satan. **3.** malicious or formidable person. —*v.t.* **4.** torment. —**dev'il·ish,** *adj.* —**dev'il·ry, dev'il·try,** *n.*

dē'vĭ·oŭs, *adj.* **1.** indirect; circuitous. **2.** shifty; not straightforward. —**de'vi·ous·ly,** *adv.*

dĕ·vīse', *v.t.,* **-vised, -vising.** *n. v.t.* **1.** contrive. **2.** bequeath. —*n.* **3.** bequest. —**de·vis'er,** *n.*

dĕ·vŏid', *adj.* empty of something specified.

dĕ·vŏlve', *v.,* **-volved, -volving.** *v.i., v.t.* pass to another, as a duty.

dĕ·vōte', *v.t.,* **-voted, -voting.** dedicate. —**de·vot'ed,** *adj.*

dĕ''vó·tēe', *n.* admirer or enthusiast.

dĕ·vō'tion, *n.* **1.** dedication. **2.** devout act, esp. a prayer. —**de·vo'tion·al,** *adj.*

dè·voŭr', *v.t.* **1.** eat hungrily. **2.** consume or take in greedily.

dè·voŭt', *adj.* pious; very religious.

dēw, *n.* moisture condensed at ground level. —dew'drop", *n.* —dew'y, *adj.*

dĕx'têr·oŭs, *adj.* skillful; cunning. Also, dex'trous. —dex·ter'i·ty, *n.*

dĕx'trōse, *n.* type of sugar found in plants and animals.

dī''á·bē'tės, *n.* disease characterized by the body's inability to use sugar properly. —di''a·be'tic, *adj., n.*

dī''á·bŏl'ĭc, *adj.* devilish. Also, di''a·bol'i·cal.

dī'á·dĕm", *n.* crown.

dī''ăg·nōse", *v.t.*, -nosed, -nosing. **1.** make a diagnosis of. **2.** establish by diagnosis.

dī''ăg·nō'sĭs, *n., pl.* -ses. determination of the nature of an illness or situation. —di''ag·nos'tic, *adj.*

dī·ăg'ó·nàl, *adj.* **1.** connecting two nonadjacent angles. **2.** oblique. —*n.* **3.** something that is diagonal.

dī'á·grăm", *n., v.t.*, -gramed, -graming. *n.* **1.** chart or plan that explains something simply. —*v.t.* **2.** make a diagram of. —di''a·gram·mat'ic, *adj.*

dī'·àl, *n., v.t.*, -aled or -aling. *n.* **1.** disk or strip with a calibrated edge, as on a clock or gauge. **2.** disk turned to get radio frequencies, make telephone calls, etc. —*v.t.* **3.** obtain or reach by turning a dial.

dī'á·lĕct", *n.* variety of a language peculiar to a region or class. —di''a·lec'tal, *adj.*

dī'á·lŏgue", *n.* conversation between two or more people. Also, di'a·log".

dī'ăm'e·têr, *n.* **1.** straight line passing through the center of a circle. **2.** length of such a line. —di''a·met'ri·cal, *adj.*

dī'a·mónd, *n.* **1.** hard, transparent crystallization of carbon. **2.** parallelogram. **3. diamonds,** suit of playing cards. **4.** baseball field.

dīa'pêr, *n.* **1.** piece of absorbent material that forms a baby's undercloth. —*v.t.* **2.** put a diaper on.

dī·à·phrăgm (dī'ə fram"), *n.* **1.** muscular wall, esp. between the chest and abdomen. **2.** vibrating disk in a microphone etc. **3.** contraceptive device for women.

dī''àr·rhē'à, *n.* intestinal disorder characterized by too frequent and too loose bowel movements.

dī'á·rỹ, *n.* daily record of experiences. —di'a·rist, *n.*

dī·ăs'tò·lē, *n.* normal rhythmic expansion of the heart. —di''a·stol'ic, *adj.*

dī'á·trībe", *n.* bitter denunciation.

dīce, *n. pl., sing.* die, *v.*, diced, dicing. *n.* **1.** small cubes commonly marked on each side with one to six spots, used in games. —*v.i.* **2.** play with dice. —*v.t.* **3.** cut into small cubes.

dī'chŏt'ò·mỹ, *n.* division into two parts.

dĭck' êr, *v.i.* bargain.

dĭc'tāte", *v.*, -tated, -tating. *v.t., v.i.* **1.** speak for preservation in writing. **2.** impose on others, as terms. —dic·ta'tion, *n.*

dĭc'tā·tör, *n.* de facto absolute ruler. —dic'ta·tor·ship", *n.* —dic''ta·to'ri·al, *adj.*

dĭc'tion, *n.* **1.** choice of words. **2.** enunciation.

dĭc'tion·ār''ỹ, *n., pl.* -ies. book explaining the meanings, etc. of alphabetically listed words.

dĭc'tŭm, *n.* authoritative statement; pronouncement.

dī·dăc'tĭc, *adj.* intended for instruction. —di·dac'ti·cism, *n.*

dīe, *v.i.*, died, dying. *n. v.i.* **1.** cease to live. **2.** lose vigor or strength. —*n.* **3.** shaping device.

dī·êr'e·sĭs, *n., pl.* -ses. mark placed over a vowel to show that it is pronounced separately.

diē'sèl, *n.* internal-combustion engine in which fuel is ignited by air compression. Also, **diesel engine.**

dī'ĕt, *n.* **1.** food normally eaten. **2.** selection of food for purposes of health. **3.** legislature. —*v.i.* **4.** be on a diet. —di'e·tar''y, *adj.* —di''e·ti'tian, di''e·ti'cian, *n.* —di''e·tet'ic, *adj.*

dĭf'fêr, *v.i.* **1.** be different. **2.** disagree.

dĭf'fêr·ènce, *n.* **1.** unlikeness. **2.** disagreement. **3.** amount after subtraction. —dif'fer·ent, *adj.* —dif'fer·ent·ly, *adv.*

dĭf''fêr·ĕn'tiàl, *adj.* **1.** pertaining to difference. —*n.* **2.** difference. **3.** Also, **differential gear,** gear turning axles at individual speeds.

dĭf''fêr·ĕn'ti·āte", *v.*, -ated, -ating. *v.t.* **1.** make unlike. **2.** distinguish between or from another. —*v.i.* **3.** make a distinction.

dif′fi·cŭlt, *adj.* **1.** hard to do or understand. **2.** hard to deal with or satisfy. —**dif′fi·cul′′ty,** *n.*

dif′′fi·dĕnt, *adj.* shy; self-conscious. —**dif′fi·dence,** *n.*

dif·frăc′tion, *n.* breaking of light, sound, etc. into separate components.

dif·fuse, *v.* -fused, -fusing, *adj. v.t., v.i.* (dif fyo͞oz′) **1.** disseminate; spread. —*adj.* (dif fyo͞os′) **2.** not concentrated. **3.** wordy. —**dif·fu′sion,** *n.*

dĭg, *v.,* dug, digging, *n. v.t.* **1.** cut into or turn over. **2.** form by digging. **3.** discover or remove by or as if by digging. —*v.i.* **4.** break up earth, etc. by digging. —*n.* **5.** act or instance of digging. **6.** taunting remark.

di·gĕst′, *v.t.* **1.** transform food in the body so it is absorbable. **2.** absorb mentally. —*n.* (di′gest). **3.** abridged and systematic collection of information; summary. —**di·gest′i·ble,** *adj.* —**di·ges′tion,** *n.* —**di·ges′tive,** *adj.*

dĭg′ĭt, *n.* **1.** finger or toe. **2.** any Arabic figure: 0 to 9. —**dig′it·al,** *adj.*

dĭg′ĭ·tăl, *adj.* represented by numerals.

dĭg′′ĭ·tăl′ĭs, *n.* dried leaves of a plant, used as a heart stimulant.

dĭg′ni·fīed′′, *adj.* showing dignity; stately.

dĭg′ni·fȳ′′, *v.t.,* -fied, -fying. honor; give dignity to.

dĭg′ni·tār′′ÿ, *n., pl.* -ies. eminent person, esp. because of rank.

dī·grĕss′, *v.i.* wander away from the main subject or purpose. —**di·gres′sion,** *n.* —**di·gres′sive,** *adj.*

dīke, *n.* dam made to prevent flooding.

dĭ·lăp′ĭ·dāt′′ĕd, *adj.* ruined; broken down. —**di·lap′′i·da′tion,** *n.*

dī·lāte′, *v.,* -lated, -lating. *v.t., v.i.* **1.** widen; expand. **2.** speak at length. —**di·la′tion, dil′′a·ta′tion,** *n.*

dĭl′ạ·tô′′rÿ, *adj.* delaying.

dĭ·lĕm′mȧ, *n.* predicament requiring a puzzling choice between two alternatives.

dĭl′′ĕt·tănte′, *n., pl.* -tantes, -tanti. amateur; superficial artist, thinker, etc.

dĭl′′ĭ·gĕnt, *adj.* hard-working. —**dil′i·gence,** *n.*

dĭll, *n.* plant with aromatic leaves and seeds used for flavoring.

dĭ·lūte′, *v.t.,* -luted, -luting. water down; thin out. —**di·lu′tion,** *n.*

dĭm, *adj.,* dimmer, dimmest, *v.,* dimmed, dimming. *adj.* **1.** not bright; indistinct. **2.** not clearly seeing or understanding. —*v.t., v.i.* **3.** make or grow dim. —**dim′ly,** *adv.*

dīme, *n.* ten-cent coin.

dĭ·mĕn′sion, *n.* **1.** length, breadth, or height. **2.** coordinate used in locating something in space and/or time. —**dimen′sion·al,** *adj.*

dĭ·mĭn′ĭsh, *v.t., v.i.* lessen in size or importance. —**dim′′i·nu′tion,** *n.*

dĭ·mĭn′ū·tĭve, *adj.* **1.** very small. —*n.* **2.** suffix or variant modifying a word to indicate smallness.

dĭm′ĭ·tÿ, *n.* thin woven cloth.

dĭm′ple, *n., v.,* -pled, -pling. *n.* **1.** small, natural hollow, esp. on the cheek or chin. —*v.t., v.i.* **2.** form dimples.

dĭn, *n., v.t.,* dinned, dinning. *n.* **1.** confused or continuous noise. —*v.t.* **2.** repeat insistently.

dīne, *v.,* dined, dining. *v.i.* **1.** eat dinner. —*v.t.* **2.** provide dinner for.

dī′nêr, *n.* **1.** person eating. **2.** railroad dining car. **3.** restaurant resembling such a car.

dĭn·ghÿ, *n.* small boat belonging to a larger boat.

dĭn·gÿ, *adj.,* -gier, -giest. dark; grimy. —**din′gi·ness,** *n.*

dĭn′nêr, *n.* main meal of the day.

dī′nò·sâur′′, *n.* large reptile of prehistoric times.

dĭnt, *n.* **1.** exertion. **2.** dent.

dī′ó·cése, *n.* district under a bishop. —**di·oc′e·san,** *adj., n.*

dĭp, *v.,* dipped, dipping, *n. v.t.* **1.** lower briefly and raise. **2.** remove with a scoop. —*v.i.* **3.** be dipped. **4.** plunge abruptly. —*n.* **5.** short swim or bath. **6.** abrupt plunge or slope.

diph·thong (dif′thong, dip′thong), *n.* sound containing two vowels.

dĭ·plō′mȧ, *n.* certificate conferring a degree.

dĭ·plô′măt′′, *n.* **1.** official representing a state. **2.** person of tact. —**di·plo′macy,** *n.* —**dip′′lo·mat′ic,** *adj.*

dĭp′pêr, *n.* **1.** ladle. **2.** Dipper, either of two constellations in the shape of a dipper.

dĭp′′sò·mā′nĭ·à, *n.* irresistible craving for alcohol. **—dip′′so·ma′ni·ac′′**, *n.*

dīre, *adj.*, **direr**, **direst**. **1.** Also, **dire′ful**, dreadful. **2.** urgent.

dĭ·rĕct′, *adj.* **1.** straight. **2.** straightforward. **3.** unbroken; continuous. **4.** faithful to an original. **—v.t. 5.** guide. **6.** supervise or command. **7.** address. **—di·rect′ly**, *adv.* **—di·rect′ness**, *n.* **—di·rec′tor**, *n.*

dĭ·rĕc′tion, *n.* **1.** line toward a place, point of the compass, etc. **2.** instruction. **3.** act, instance, or responsibility of directing. **—di·rec′tion·al**, *adj.*

dĭ·rĕc′tive, *n.* general order.

dĭ·rĕc′to·rў, *n.*, *pl.* **-ries.** book with names, addresses, etc.

dîrge, *n.* funeral song.

dĭr′ĭ·gĭ·ble, *n.* maneuverable airship.

dîrk, *n.* dagger.

dîrt, *n.* **1.** any unclean substance; filth. **2.** soil.

dîrt′ў, *adj.*, **-ier**, **-iest**, *v.*, **-ied**, **-ying.** *adj.* **1.** not clean; soiled. **2.** indecent. **—v.t.**, *v.i.* **3.** make or become dirty. **—dirt′i·ness**, *n.* **—dirt′i·ly**, *adv.*

dĭs·ā′ble, *v.t.*, **-bled**, **-bling.** make incapable or unfit. **—dis′′a·bil′i·ty**, *n.*

dĭs′′à·būse′, *v.t.*, **-bused**, **-busing.** rid of false ideas; set right.

dĭs′′àd·văn′tàge, *n.* **1.** unfavorable circumstance. **2.** injury or detriment. **—dis′′ad·van′taged**, *adj.* **—dis·ad′′van·ta′geous**, *adj.*

dĭs′′àf·fĕct′, *v.t.* make unfriendly; antagonize. **—dis′′af·fec′tion**, *n.*

dĭs′′à·grēe′, *v.i.* **-greed**, **-greeing. 1.** fail to agree. **2.** quarrel. **—dis′′a·gree′ment**, *n.*

dĭs′′à·grēe′à·ble, *adj.* not agreeable; unpleasant. **—dis′′a·gree′a·bly**, *adv.*

dĭs′′àp·pēar′, *v.i.* **1.** vanish. **2.** cease to exist. **—dis′′ap·pear′ance**, *n.*

dĭs′′àp·poĭnt′, *v.t.* thwart the expectations or hopes of. **—dis′′ap·point′ment**, *n.*

dĭs′′àp·prove′, *v.*, **-proved**, **-proving.** *v.t.*, *v.i.* not to approve. **—dis′′ap·prov′al**, *n.*

dĭs·ârm′, *v.t.* **1.** take away or deprive of weapons. **2.** make friendly. **—v.i. 3.** reduce armed forces. **—dis·ar′ma·ment**, *n.*

dĭs′′àr·rānge′, *v.t.*, **-ranged**, **-ranging.** put in disorder. **—dis′′ar·range′ment**, *n.*

dĭs′′àr·rāy, *v.t.* **1.** throw into disorder. **—n. 2.** disorder; confusion.

dĭs·ăs′têr, *n.* cause of much damage. **—dis·as′trous**, *adj.*

dĭs′′à·vŏw′, *v.t.* disclaim knowledge of or responsibility for. **—dis′′a·vow′al**, *n.*

dĭs·bănd′, *v.t.*, *v.i.* break up, as an organization. **—dis·band′ment**, *n.*

dĭs·bâr′, *v.t.*, **-barred**, **-barring.** expel from the legal profession. **—dis·bar′ment**, *n.*

dĭs·bè′′liēve′, *v.*, **-lieved**, **-lieving.** *v.t.*, *v.i.* refuse to believe. **—dis′′be·lief′**, *n.*

dĭs·bûrse′, *v.t.*, **-bursed**, **-bursing. 1.** pay out. **2.** scatter. **—dis·burse′ment**, *n.*

dĭsc, *n.* disk.

dĭs·cârd′, *v.t.* **1.** throw away. **—n.** (dis′card) **2.** state of being thrown away. **3.** something thrown away.

dĭs·cêrn′, *v.t.* perceive; recognize; distinguish. **—dis·cern′i·ble**, *adj.* **—dis·cern′ment**, *n.* **—dis·cern′ing**, *adj.*

dĭs·chârge′, *v.*, **-charged**, **-charging.** *n.* *v.t.* **1.** emit. **2.** shoot or fire. **3.** unload. **4.** perform. **5.** release or dismiss from service. **—v.i. 6.** release a load, etc. **—n.** (dis′charge) **7.** act, instance, or means of discharging. **8.** something discharged.

dĭs·cī′ple, *n.* follower of a teacher or teaching.

dĭs′cĭ·plīne, *n.*, *v.*, **-plined**, **-plining.** *n.* **1.** training that develops self-control. **2.** punishment. **3.** set or system of rules and regulations. **4.** branch of learning. **—v.t. 5.** train. **6.** punish. **—dis′ci·pli·na′′ry**, *adj.* **—dis′ci·pli·nar′′i·an**, *n.*

dĭs·clāim′, *v.t.* disown.

dĭs·clāim′êr, *n.* disavowal or renunciation.

dĭs·clōse′, *v.t.*, **-closed**, **-closing.** reveal or uncover. **—dis·clo′sure**, *n.*

dĭs′cō, *n.* **1.** discotheque; a club featuring dancing to rock music. **2.** a style of dance music with a pronounced beat.

dĭs·cól′ôr, *v.t.*, *v.i.* fade or stain. **—dis·col′′or·a′tion**, *n.*

dĭs·cóm′fĭt, *v.t.* frustrate the plans of; disconcert. **—dis·com′fi·ture**, *n.*

dĭs·cóm′fört, *n.* lack of comfort.

dĭs''cón·cért', *v.t.* upset; disarrange; perturb.

dĭs''cón·nĕct', *v.t.* finish the connection of; separate. —dis''con·nec'tion, *n.*

dĭs·cŏn'sȯ·làte, *adj.* unhappy; dejected.

dĭs''cón·tĕnt', *adj.* 1. Also, dis''content'ed, dissatisfied with something; not content. —*n.* 2. dissatisfaction; lack of content.

dĭs''cón·tĭn'ūe, *v.*, -ued, -uing. *v.t.*, *v.i.* stop. —dis''con·tin'u·ance, dis''con·tin''u·a'tion, *n.*

dĭs'côrd, *n.* 1. lack of harmony. 2. disagreement. —dis·cord'ance, *n.* —dis·cord'ant, *adj.*

dĭs·cȯ'thĕque, *n.* place where people dance to recorded music.

dĭs'cŏunt, *n.* 1. reduction in price. —*v.t.* 2. deduct from a bill. 3. advance with deduction or interest. 4. sell at less than the regular price. 5. disregard. —dis'count'a·ble, *adj.*

dĭs·coûr'áge, *v.t.*, -aged, -aging. hamper or stop with predictions of failure, disapproval, etc. —dis·cour'age·ment, *n.*

dĭs'côurse, *n.*, *v.i.*, -coursed, -coursing. *n.* 1. conversation. 2. essay or lecture. —*v.i.* 3. converse.

dĭs·coûr'tė·sȳ, *n.*, *pl.* -sies. lack of courtesy; rudeness. —dis·cour'te·ous, *adj.*

dĭs·cóv'êr, *v.t.* perceive for the first time. —dis·cov'er·er, *n.* —dis·cov'er·y, *n.* —dis·cov'er·a·ble, *adj.*

dĭs·crĕd'ĭt, *v.t.* 1. cast doubt on. 2. injure the reputation of. —*n.* 3. state of being discredited.

dĭs·crēet', *adj.* prudent. —dis·creet'ly, *adv.*

dĭs·crĕp'án·cȳ, *n.* inconsistency.

dĭs·crēte', *adj.* separate; distinct.

dĭs·crē'tion, *n.* 1. prudence. 2. freedom of choice in actions. —dis·cre'tion·ary'', *adj.*

dĭs·crĭm'ĭ·nāte'', *v.i.*, -nated, -nating, *adj. v.i.* 1. make careful distinctions. 2. show unjust favor or disfavor. —*adj.* (dis crim'i nate) 3. making careful distinctions. —dis·crim''i·na'tion, *n.* —dis·crim'i·nat''ing, *adj.* —dis·crim'i·na·to''ry, *adj.*

dĭs·cûr'sĭve, *adj.* rambling; wandering from topic to topic.

dĭs·cŭss', *v.t.* talk or write about. —dis·cus'sion, *n.*

dĭs·dāin', *v.t.* 1. scorn; despise. —*n.* 2. scorn. —dis·dain'ful, *adj.*

dĭs·ēase', *n.*, *v.t.*, -eased, -easing. *n.* 1. ailment; sickness. —*v.t.* 2. affect with sickness.

dĭs''ĕm·bârk', *v.i.* leave a ship or aircraft. —dis''em·bar·ka'tion, dis''em·bark'ment, *n.*

dĭs''ĕm·bŏd'ȳ, *v.t.*, -ied, -ying. free from the body. —dis''em·bod'i·ment, *n.*

dĭs''ĕn·chănt', *v.t.* destroy the enthusiasm of. —dis''en·chant'ment, *n.*

dĭs''ĕn·gāge', *v.*, -gaged, -gaging. *v.t.*, *v.i.* disconnect. —dis''en·gage'ment, *n.*

dĭs·fā'vör, *n.* 1. disapproval. —*v.t.* 2. treat with disfavor.

dĭs·fĭg'ûre, *v.t.*, -ured, -uring. mar. —dis·fig'ure·ment, *n.*

dĭs·frăn'chīse, *v.t.*, -chised, -chising. deprive of a right or privilege, esp. voting. Also, dis''en·fran'chise.

dĭs·gôrge', *v.*, -gorged, -gorging. *v.t.*, *v.i.* pour out.

dĭs·grāce', *n.*, *v.t.*, -graced, -gracing. *n.* 1. state or cause of shame. —*v.t.* 2. bring shame upon. —dis·grace'ful, *adj.*

dĭs·grŭn'tle, *v.t.*, -tled, -tling. make discontent or sulky.

dĭs·guīse', *v.t.*, -guised, -guising, *n. v.t.* 1. render temporarily unrecognizable. 2. misrepresent. —*n.* 3. something that disguises. —dis·guise'ment, *n.*

dĭs·gŭst', *v.t.* 1. offend the good taste or senses of. —*n.* 2. sickening dislike.

dĭsh, *n.* 1. shallow container for food. 2. food that is served.

dĭs·heârt'ĕn, *v.t.* discourage.

dĭ·shĕv'ĕl, *v.t.*, -eled, -eling. cause disarray in.

dĭs·hŏn'ĕst, *adj.* not honest. —dis·hon'est·ly, *adv.* —dis·hon'es·ty, *n.*

dĭs·hŏn'ör, *n.* 1. lack of respect; disgrace. —*v.t.* 2. disgrace. —dis·hon'or·a·ble, *adj.*

dĭs''ĭl·lū'sion, *v.t.* free from illusion. —dis''il·lu'sion·ment, *n.*

dĭs''ĭn·clīne', *v.t.*, -clined, -clining. make unwilling or averse. —dis·in''cli·na'tion, *n.*

dĭs''ĭn·fĕct', *v.t.* rid of infection. —dis''in·fect'ant, *n.*, *adj.*

dĭs''ĭn·hĕr'ĭt, *v.t.* deprive of inheritance.

dĭs·ĭn'tĕ·grāte'', *v.*, **-grated, -grating.** *v.t., v.i.* separate. —*v.t., v.i.* separate into elements. —**dĭs·ĭn''tĕ·grā'tion**, *n.*

dĭs·ĭn'tĕr·ĕst, *n.* indifference.

dĭs·ĭn'tĕr·ĕst·ĕd, *n.* **1.** impartial. **2.** indifferent.

dĭs·jŏĭnt'ĕd, *adj.* **1.** separated at the joints. **2.** incoherent.

dĭsk, *n.* **1.** thin, flat, round object. **2.** phonograph record.

dĭsk·ĕtte', *n.* (computers) a 5¼-inch magnetic disk or a 3½-inch disk used for data storage.

dĭs·līke', *v.t.*, **-liked, -liking**, *n. v.t.* **1.** regard with aversion or distaste. —*n.* **2.** aversion; distaste.

dĭs·lō·cāte'', *v.t.*, **-cated, -cating.** put out of the proper or customary place. —**dis''lo·ca'tion**, *n.*

dĭs·lŏdge', *v.t.*, —**lodged, -lodging.** force from a place. —**dis·lodg'ment**, *n.*

dĭs·lŏȳ'ȧl, *adj.* not loyal; unfaithful. —**dis·loy'al·ty**, *n.*

dĭs'mȧl, *adj.* **1.** gloomy; dreary. **2.** causing dreariness or misery.

dĭs·măn'tle, *v.t.*, **-tled, -tling. 1.** deprive or strip of equipment. **2.** take apart.

dĭs·māy', *v.t.* **1.** dishearten. —*n.* **2.** disheartenment.

dĭs·mĕm'bȇr, *v.t.* deprive of limbs. —**dis·mem'ber·ment**, *n.*

dĭs·mĭss', *v.t.* **1.** direct or allow to leave. **2.** discharge from employment. **3.** put out of consideration. —**dis·mis'sal**, *n.*

dĭs·mŏŭnt', *v.i.* **1.** alight from a horse, bicycle, etc. —*v.t.* **2.** take from a mounting. **3.** dismantle.

dĭs''ō·bē'dĭ·ȩnt, *adj.* not obedient. —**dis''o·be'di·ence**, *n.* —**dis''o·bey'**, *v.t.*

dĭs·ȏr'dȇr, *n.* **1.** confusion. **2.** ailment. **3.** riot. —*v.t.* **4.** create disorder in. —**dis·or'der·ly**, *adj.*

dĭs·ȏr'gȧn·īze'', *v.t.*, **-ized, -izing.** throw into confusion. —**dis·or''gan·i·za'tion**, *n.*

dĭs·ŏwn', *v.t.* repudiate.

dĭs·pär'ȧge, *v.t.*, **-aged, -aging.** belittle. —**dis·par'age·ment**, *n.*

dĭs'pȧ·rȧte, *adj.* distinct in kind. —**dis·par'i·ty**, *n.*

dĭs·pặs'sion·ȧte, *adj.* impartial. —**dis·pas'sion·ate·ly**, *adv.*

dĭs·pătch', *v.t.* **1.** send off. **2.** kill. **3.** transact quickly. —*n.* **4.** sending-off. **5.** killing. **6.** promptness. **7.** message. —**dis·patch'er**, *n.*

dĭs·pĕl', *v.t.*, **-pelled, -pelling.** scatter; drive off.

dĭs·pĕn'sȧ·rȳ, *n.*, *pl.* **-ries.** place where medical aid is given.

dĭs''pĕn·sā'tion, *n.* **1.** act or instance of dispensing. **2.** something dispensed. **3.** release from obligation. **4.** divine ordering of events.

dĭs·pĕnse', *v.*, **-pensed, -pensing.** *v.t.* **1.** distribute. **2.** prepare and give out as medicine. —*v.i.* **3. dispense with, a.** forgo **b.** get rid of. —**dis·pen'sa·ble**, *adj.*

dĭs·pȇrse', *v.*, **-persed, -persing.** *v.t., v.i.* scatter. —**dis·per'sal, dis·per'sion**, *n.*

dĭs·plāce', *v.t.*, **-placed, -placing. 1.** put out of place. **2.** take the place of. —**dis·place'ment**, *n.*

dĭs'plāy, *v.t.*, *n.* exhibit.

dĭs·plēase', *v.t.*, **-pleased, -pleasing.** offend. —**dis·pleas'ure**, *n.*

dĭs·pōse', *v.*, **-posed, -posing.** *v.t.* **1.** arrange. **2.** incline or make willing. —*v.i.* **3.** rid oneself. —**dis·pos'a·ble**, *adj.* —**dis·pos'al**, *n.*

dĭs''pō·sĭ'tion, *n.* **1.** temperament. **2.** tendency. **3.** arrangement. **4.** settlement. **5.** disposal.

dĭs''pŏs·sĕss', *v.t.* deprive of possession. —**dis''pos·ses'sion**, *n.*

dĭs''prȯ·pȏr'tion, *n.* lack of proportion. —**dis''pro·por'tion·ate**, *adj.*

dĭs·prōve', *v.t.*, **-proved, -proving.** prove false. —**dis·proof'**, *n.*

dĭs·pūte', *v.*, **-puted, -puting.** *n. v.i., v.t.* **1.** argue. —*v.t.* **2.** express doubt regarding. **3.** oppose or fight. —*n.* **4.** act or instance of disputing. **5.** state of being disputed. —**dis·pu'tant**, *n.*, *adj.* —**dis·put'a·ble**, *adj.* —**dis''pu·ta'tion**, *n.* —**dis''pu·ta'tious**, *adj.*

dĭs·quăl'ĭ·fȳ'', *v.t.*, **-fied, -fying.** make or declare unqualified. —**dis·qual''i·fi·ca'tion**, *n.*

dĭs·quī'ȩt, *v.t.* **1.** disturb; make uneasy. —*n.* **2.** Also, **dis·qui'e·tude**, restlessness.

dĭs''quĭ·sĭ'tion, *n.* formal discourse.

dĭs''rė·gârd', *v.t.* **1.** ignore. **2.** treat with little or no respect. —*n.* **3.** neglect. **4.** lack of respect.

dĭs''rė·pāir', *n.* impaired condition.

dĭs''rė·pūte', *n.* bad reputation. —**dis·rep'u·ta·ble**, *adj.*

dĭs''rė·spĕct', *n.* lack of respect. —**dis''re·spect'ful**, *adj.*

dĭs·rōbe', *v.*, **-robed, -robing.** *v.t.*, *v.i.* undress.

dĭs·rŭpt', *v.t.*, *v.i.* **1.** break up. **2.** disturb. —**dis·rup'tion**, *n.* —**dis·rup'tive**, *adj.*

dĭs·săt'ĭs·fȳ, *v.t.*, **-fied, -fying.** fail to satisfy; displease. —**dis·sat''is·fac'tion**, *n.*

dĭs·sĕct', *v.t.* **1.** cut apart. **2.** examine closely. —**dis·sec'tion**, *n.*

dĭs·sĕm'ble, *v.*, **-bled, -bling.** *v.t.*, *v.i.* disguise. —**dis·sem'blance**, *n.* —**dis·sem'bler**, *n.*

dĭs·sĕm'ĭ·nāte'', *v.t.*, **-nated, -nating.** distribute widely. —**dis·sem''i·na'tion**, *n.*

dĭs·sĕn'sion, *n.* disagreement or quarreling.

dĭs·sĕnt', *v.i.* **1.** disagree. —*n.* **2.** disagreement. —**dis·sent'er**, *n.*

dĭs''sêr·tā'tion, *n.* formal essay; thesis.

dĭs·sĭm'ĭ·lår, *adj.* not similar. —**dis·sim''i·lar'i·ty**, *n.*

dĭs·sĭm'ŭ·lāte'', *v.*, **-lated, -lating.** *v.t.*, *v.i.* dissemble. —**dis·sim''u·la'tion**, *n.*

dĭs'sĭ·pāte'', *v.*, **-pated, -pating.** *v.t.* **1.** scatter. **2.** squander. —*v.i.* **3.** live in extravagance or vice. —**dis''si·pa'tion**, *n.*

dĭs'sĭ·pāt''ĕd, *adj.* living in extravagance or vice.

dĭs·sō'cĭ·āte'', *v.t.*, **-ated, -ating.** break the connection between.

dĭs'sȯ·lūte'', *adj.* dissipated. —**dis'so·lute''ly**, *adv.* —**dis''so·lu'tion**, *n.*

dĭs·sŏlve', *v.*, **-solved, -solving.** *v.t.*, *v.i.* **1.** melt; combine with a liquid. **2.** terminate. **3.** destroy. —**dis''so·lu·tion**, *n.*

dĭs'sȯ·nȧnce, *n.* musical discord. —**dis'so·nant**, *adj.*

dĭs·suāde', *v.t.*, **-suaded, -suading.** deter by persuasion. —**dis·sua'sion**, *n.*

dĭs'tȧnce, *n.* **1.** interval of space or time. **2.** remoteness. **3.** reserve; aloofness. —**dis'tant**, *adj.*

dĭs·tāste', *n.* dislike. —**dis·taste'ful**, *adj.*

dĭs·tĕm'pêr, *n.* infectious disease of dogs.

dĭs·tĕnd', *v.t.*, *v.i.* expand. —**dis·ten'tion**, *n.*

dĭs·tĭll', *v.t.* **1.** make or purify by evaporation and condensation. —*v.t.* **2.** become distilled. —**dis·till'er**, *n.* —**dis·till'er·y**, *n.* —**dis''til·la'tion**, *n.*

dĭs·tĭnct', *adj.* **1.** individual. **2.** clearly noticeable or understandable. —**dis·tinct'ly**, *adv.*

dĭs·tĭnc'tion, *n.* **1.** act or instance of distinguishing. **2.** difference. **3.** eminence. **4.** something that gives or betokens eminence.

dĭs·tĭnc'tive, *adj.* characteristic.

dĭs·tĭn'guĭsh, *v.t.* **1.** characterize as individual. **2.** perceive. **3.** make eminent or excellent. —**dis·tin'guish·a·ble**, *adj.* —**dis·tin'guished**, *adj.*

dĭs·tôrt', *v.t.* **1.** alter from a normal shape. **2.** corrupt the true meaning of. —**dis·tor'tion**, *n.*

dĭs·trăct', *v.t.* **1.** prevent from concentrating. **2.** bewilder. —**dis·trac'tion**, *n.*

dĭs·trăct'ĕd, *adj.* frantic. Also, **dis·traught'**.

dĭs·trĕss', *n.* **1.** pain or need. **2.** source of this. **3.** danger. —*v.t.* **4.** cause distress in.

dĭs·trĭb'ūte, *v.t.*, **-uted, -uting.** **1.** give out in portions. **2.** disperse. —**dis''tri·bu'tion**, *n.* —**dis·trib'u·tor**, *n.*

dĭs'trĭct, *n.* distinct geographical area.

dĭs·trŭst', *n.* **1.** lack of trust. —*v.t.* **2.** place no trust in. —**dis·trust'ful**, *adj.*

dĭs·tûrb', *v.t.* **1.** end the quiet state of. **2.** upset or trouble. **3.** interrupt. —**dis·turb'ance**, *n.*

dĭs·ūse', *n.* absence of use.

dĭtch, *n.* channel dug in the ground.

dĭt'tō, *n.*, *pl.* **-tos. 1.** the same as before. **2.** Also, **ditto mark**, a mark, ", used to indicate that the word or line above is repeated.

dĭt'tȳ, *n.*, *pl.* **-ties.** simple tune.

dī·ûr'nȧl, *adj.* **1.** daily. **2.** pertaining to the day.

dī·văn', *n.* long, low couch.

dīve, *v.i.*, **dived** or **dove, dived, diving**, *n.* *v.i.* **1.** fall intentionally. **2.** descend below the water. **3.** lose altitude quickly.

—n. 4. act, instance, or form of diving. —div′er, n.

di·vêrge′, v.i., -verged, -verging. 1. part in two or more directions. 2. become of unlike opinion, etc. —di·ver′gent, adj. —di·ver′gence, n.

di′vêrs, adj. Archaic. various.

di·vêrse′, adj. 1. different. 2. various. —di·verse′ly, adv. —di·vers′i·ty, n.

di·vêr″si·fy″, v.t., -fied, -fying. vary. —di·ver″si·fi·ca′tion, n.

di·vêrt′, v.t. 1. turn aside from a path or course. 2. entertain; amuse. —di·ver′sion, n.

di·vest′, v.t. 1. deprive or strip. 2. rid.

di·vīde′, v., -vided, -viding. v.t. 1. separate into parts or classes. 2. prevent from uniting. —v.i. 3. separate. —n. 4. line separating two drainage areas. —di·vid′er, n.

div′i·dend″, n. 1. number to be divided. 2. sum allotted to a stockholder.

di·vīne′, adj., v.t., -vined, -vining. adj. 1. godly or godlike. 2. religious. —v.t. 3. prophesy. 4. perceive intuitively. —div″i·na′tion, n.

di·vĭn′i·tў, n., pl. -ties. 1. deity. 2. theology.

di·vĭs′i·ble, adj. able to be divided, esp. evenly.

di·vī′sión, n. 1. act or instance of dividing. 2. element or component. 3. Math. process of determining the ratio of one number to another. 4. military unit.

di·vī′sĭve, adj. causing disunity.

di·vī′sŏr, n. Math. number used to divide another.

di·vôrce′, n., v.t., -vorced, -vorcing. n. 1. legal dissolution of a marriage. 2. conceptual separation. —v.t. 3. separate oneself from by a divorce. 4. separate by a divorce. 5. separate conceptually. —di·vorce′ment, n.

di·vôr″cee′, n. divorced woman.

di·vŭlge′, v.t., -vulged, -vulging. reveal. —di·vulg′ence, n.

Dĭx′iē, n. southern part of the U.S.

dĭz′zў, adj., -zier, -ziest. 1. unsteady. 2. causing unsteadiness, as a height.

do, v., did, done, doing. v.t. 1. be at work upon or occupied with. 2. complete. 3. cause. —v.i. 4. act. 5. succeed in or accomplish something. 6. suffice. 7. happen.

dŏc′īle, adj. readily disciplined. —do·cil′i·ty, n.

dŏck, n. 1. place for ships between voyages. 2. pier or wharf. 3. fleshy part of an animal's tail. —v.t. 4. put into a dock. 5. deduct from the wages of. —v.i. 6. enter a dock.

dŏck′ĕt, n. 1. list of agenda, esp. of a court. —v.t. 2. put on a docket.

dŏc′tŏr, n. 1. person who practices medicine, etc. 2. person with a high academic degree. —v.t. 3. Informal. heal or fix. —doc′tor·al, adj. —doc·tor·ate, n.

dŏc″tri·nāire,′ adj. rigidly adhering to or following doctrine.

dŏc′trĭne, n. body of teaching, esp. in religion or politics. —doc′trin·al, adj.

dŏc′ū·mėnt, n. 1. writing, etc. used as a proof. —v.t. 2. prove or support with documents. —doc″u·men·ta′tion, n.

dŏc″ū·mėn′ta·rў, adj., n., pl. -ries. adj. 1. pertaining to documents. 2. serving as a record of events. —n. 3. film, etc. serving as a record of events.

dŏdge, v., dodged, dodging, n. v.t. 1. avoid by moving quickly. 2. evade by a trick. —v.i. 3. dodge something. —n. 4. act or instance of dodging. 5. trick.

dōe, n. female of certain animals, as deer or rabbits.

dŏff, v.t. Archaic. remove, as a hat.

dŏg, n., v.t., dogged, dogging. n. 1. four-legged domestic animal. —v.t. 2. track; follow.

dŏg′gėd, adj. stubborn in difficulty.

dŏg′gêr·ėl, n. simple verse.

dŏg·mà, n. doctrine, esp. in religion, regarded as unquestionable.

dŏg·măt′ĭc, adj. 1. pertaining to or published as dogma. 2. offering personal opinions as dogma. —dog′ma·tism, n.

dŏg′wŏŏd″, n. tree with white or pink blossoms.

dŏi′lў, n., pl. -lies. small mat, often of lace.

dŏl′drŭms, n. pl. 1. equatorial region with little wind. 2. period of depression or inactivity.

dōle, n., v.t., doled, doling. n. 1. money, food, etc. given to the unemployed. —v.t. 2. portion out sparingly.

dōle′fŭl, adj. sad.

dŏll, n. toy shaped like a baby or other human being.

dŏl′lår, *n*. currency unit of the U.S., Canada, etc.

dō′lór·oŭs, *adj*. sorrowful or painful.

dŏl′phĭn, *n*. aquatic mammal.

dōlt, *n*. oaf. —dolt′ish, *adj*.

dō·māin′, *n*. **1.** territory of a ruler. **2.** area of influence or power.

dōme, *n*. structure like an upcurved segment of a sphere.

dó·mĕs′tĭc, *adj*. **1.** pertaining to the home. **2.** belonging to or originating in one's own country. **3.** tamed. —do″mes·ti′ci·ty, *n*.

dó·mĕs′tĭ·cāte″, *v.t.*, -cated, -cating. adapt to domestic conditions. —do″mes″ti·ca′tion, *n*.

dŏm′ĭ·cīle″, *n.*, *v.t.*, -ciled, -ciling. *n.* **1.** residence. —*v.t.* **2.** house.

dŏm′ĭ·nànt, *adj*. prevailing. —dom′i·nance, *n*.

dŏm′ĭ·nāte″, *v.t.*, -nated, -nating. **1.** master. **2.** be most conspicuous in. —dom″i·na′tion, *n*.

dŏm″ĭ·nēer′, *v.t.*, *v.i.* tyrannize.

dó·mĭn′ión, *n*. **1.** sovereign power. **2.** territory reigned over or ruled by a sovereign.

dŏm′ĭ·nō, *n.*, *pl*. -noes. **1.** small plaque marked with spots. **2.** dominoes, a game played with these plaques. **3.** mask.

dŏn, *n.*, *v.t.*, donned, donning. *n.* **1.** title of respect for a Spanish gentleman. —*v.t.* **2.** *Archaic*. put on, as clothes.

dō′nāte, *v.*, -nated, -nating. *v.t.*, *v.i.* give, esp. in charity or friendship. —do·na′tion, *n*. —do′nor, *n*.

dŏn′kēy, *n.*, *pl*. -keys. domesticated ass.

dōo′dle, *v.i.*, -dled, -dling, *n. v.i.* **1.** scribble or draw absentmindedly. —*n.* **2.** product of doodling.

dōom, *n*. **1.** death or annihilation. **2.** fate. —*v.t.* **3.** predestine or sentence to death, damnation, etc.

dôor, *n*. **1.** movable partition for barring access. **2.** Also, door′way″, entrance. **3. out of doors,** outdoors.

dōpe, *n.*, *v.t.*, doped, doping. *n.* **1.** *Informal*. **a.** habit-forming drug. **b.** fool. **c.** information. **2.** thick liquid used for industrial purposes. —*v.t.* **3.** *Informal*. drug.

dôr′mànt, *adj*. **1.** asleep or at rest. **2.** not active. —dor′man·cy, *n*.

dôr′mêr, *n*. window structure in a roof.

dôr′mĭ·tô″rȳ, *n.*, *pl*. -ries. place for residents of an institution to sleep.

dō′rȳ, *n.*, *pl*. -ries. flat-bottomed rowboat used for fishing, etc.

dōse, *n.*, *v.t.*, dosed, dosing. *n.* **1.** amount of medicine taken at one time. —*v.t.* **2.** give medicine to. —dos′age, *n*.

dos·si·er (dos″sē ā′), *n*. file of documents on one subject.

dŏt, *n.*, *v.t.*, dotted, dotting. *n.* **1.** tiny round mark. —*v.t.* **2.** mark or make with dots.

dōte, *v.i.*, doted, doting. **1.** show excessive fondness. **2.** be senile. —dot′ing, *adj*. —dot′age, *n*.

doŭ′ble, *adj.*, *adv.*, *n.*, *v.*, -bled, -bling. *adj.* **1.** twice as much. **2.** intended for two. **3.** having two aspects. —*adv.* **4.** twice. —*n.* **5.** duplicate. —*v.t.* **6.** fold over. **7.** make twice as much or as many of. —*v.i.* **8.** fold in two. **9.** reverse one's direction. —doub′ly, *adv*.

doŭ″ble-crŏss′, *v.t. Informal*. cheat or betray.

doŭbt, *v.t.* **1.** be unsure or skeptical of. —*n.* **2.** uncertainty or distrust. **3.** something unsettled or uncertain. —doubt′ful, *adj.* —doubt′less, *adv*.

dōugh, *n*. pastry mixture of flour and water for baking. —dough′y, *adj*.

dōugh′nŭt″, *n*. deep-fried ring-shaped cake.

dōur, *adj*. gloomily severe.

dōuse, *v.t.*, doused, dousing. plunge into or drench with liquid.

dóve, *n*. cooing pigeonlike bird.

dóve′tāil″, *n*. **1.** interlocking carpentry joint. —*v.t.* **2.** join with dovetails.

dōw′à·gêr, *n*. widow endowed with a title or property.

dōw′dȳ, *adj.*, -dier, -diest. plainly or untidily dressed, made up, etc.

dōw′èl, *n.*, *v.t.*, -eled, -eling. *n.* **1.** round length of wood, used as a fastening between two joined pieces. —*v.t.* **2.** fasten with dowels.

dŏwn, *adv.*, *adj.* **1.** to or at a lower place. **2.** to or in a lower condition, amount, etc. **3.** in writing. **4.** in advance. **5.** out of operation. —*adv.* **6.** to a later period. **7.** dejected. **8.** completed. —*prep.* **9.** descending along, through, etc. **10.** soft feathers or hair. —*v.t.* **11.** put down. —down′stairs′, *adv.*, *adj.*, *n.* —down′

ward, down'wards, *adv.* —**down'y**, *adj.*

down'fäll'', *n.* **1.** fall, as of snow. **2.** fall, as from power or eminence.

down'gräde'', *v.t.*, **-graded, -grading,** *adv., adj., n. v.t.* **1.** demote. —*adv., adj.* **2.** downward. —*n.* **3.** downward slope.

down''heârt'éd, *adj.* discouraged. —**down'heart'ed·ly**, *adv.*

down'hïll'', *adv., adj.* downward.

down'pôur'', *n.* heavy rainstorm.

down'rïght'', *adj.* **1.** utter. —*adv.* **2.** utterly.

down'stäirs'', *adv.* to or at a lower level.

down''-tò-êarth', *adj.* realistic.

down'town', *adv., adj.* toward or in the business district of a town.

down'trŏd''dèn, *adj.* oppressed.

dow'rÿ, *n., pl.* **-ries.** property bestowed on a bride by her family.

dŏx·ŏl'ò·gÿ, *n., pl.* **-gies.** hymn of praise.

dōze, *v.i.*, **dozed, dozing,** *n. v.i.* **1.** sleep lightly. —*n.* **2.** light sleep.

dŏz'èn, *n., pl.* **-ens** or (after a number) **-en.** group of twelve. —**doz'enth**, *adj.*

drăb, *n., adj.*, **drabber, drabbest.** *n.* **1.** yellow-brown. —*adj.* **2.** dreary. —**drab'ly**, *adv.* —**drab'ness**, *n.*

drăft, *n.* **1.** act or amount of drawing. **2.** swallowing or inhalation. **3.** current of air. **4.** tentative version of writing. **5.** order to pay. **6.** selection for conscription. —*v.t.* **7.** make a draft of. **8.** conscript. —**draft'ee**, *n.* —**draft'y**, *adj.*

drăfts'măn, *n.* person who makes working drawings or sketches.

drăg, *v.*, **dragged, dragging.** *v.t.* **1.** pull with effort. **2.** search with a dragnet. —*v.t.* **3.** move slowly or with effort. —*n.* **4.** act or instance of dragging. **5.** *Informal.* something or someone dreary or obstructive.

drăg'nĕt'', *n.* **1.** net for fishing up submerged objects. **2.** methodical police search.

drăg'òn, *n.* mythical large reptile.

drăg'òn·flÿ'', *n.* large, stiff-winged insect.

drāin, *n.* **1.** channel for carrying away liquids. **2.** steady depletion. —*v.t.* **3.** remove through a channel. **4.** deplete steadily. —*v.i.* **5.** be drained. —**drain'age**, *n.*

drăm, *n.* **1.** eighth part of an apothecary's ounce or fluid ounce. **2.** small drink.

drä'mà, *n.* **1.** play. **2.** theater as an art. **3.** sensational event. **4.** emotionalism. —**dram'a·tist**, *n.* —**dram'a·tize''**, *v.t.* —**dra·mat'ic**, *adj.*

drāpe, *n., v.*, **draped, draping.** *n.* **1.** cloth hanging or curtain. —*v.t., v.i.* **2.** hang loosely or in folds. —**drap'er·y**, *n.*

drăs'tĭc, *adj.* severe or extreme.

drăught, *n., v.t., adj.* draft.

draw, *v.*, **drew, drawn, drawing.** *n. v.t.* **1.** pull, attract, or take in. **2.** elicit or provoke. **3.** receive. **4.** sketch with a pencil, pen, etc. **5.** *Nautical.* need a depth of. —*v.i.* **6.** exert a pulling force. **7.** move. **8.** pass smoke, etc. readily. **9.** make demands. **10.** lessen in size. —*n.* **11.** act or instance of drawing. **12.** even final score. —**draw'ing**, *n.*

draw'băck'', *n.* lessening of advantage.

draw'brĭdge'', *n.* bridge that can be lifted or pulled.

draw·er, *n.* **1.** person or thing that draws. (drôr) **2.** sliding compartment in a piece of furniture. **3. drawers.** underpants.

drawl, *n.* **1.** slow speech. —*v.t., v.i.* **2.** speak in a drawl.

drawn, *adj.* haggard.

drāy, *n.* heavy freight wagon.

drĕad, *n.* **1.** fearful anticipation. **2.** awe. —*adj.* **3.** awesome. —*v.t.* **4.** anticipate fearfully.

drĕad'fŭl, *adj.* **1.** very bad. **2.** inspiring dread.

drēam, *n., v.*, **dreamed** or **dreamt, dreaming.** *n.* **1.** succession of images appearing in sleep or reverie. **2.** vision of something possible or desirable. —*v.t.* **3.** imagine in a dream. —*v.i.* **4.** have a dream. **dream'er**, *n.* —**dream' less**, *adj.* **dream'like''**, *adj.* —**dream' y**, *adj.*

drēar'ÿ, *adj.*, **-ier, -iest.** causing sadness or boredom.

drĕdge, *v.*, **dredged, dredging**, *n. v.t.* **1.** dig, esp. under water. **2.** coat with flour. —*n.* **3.** digging device.

drĕgs, *n., pl.* sediment, as of wine.

drĕnch, *v.t.* soak with falling liquid.

drĕss, *v.t.* **1.** put clothing on. **2.** prepare or finish. —*v.i.* **3.** put on clothing. **4.**

wear formal clothing. —*n.* **5.** clothing. **6.** skirt. —**dress'mak''er,** *n.*

drĕs'sêr, *n.* **1.** person who dresses. **2.** chest of drawers with a mirror.

drĕs'sĭng, *n.* **1.** material applied to wounds, bruises, etc. **2.** sauce for salad. **3.** stuffing for fowl.

drĭb'ble, *v.,* **-bled, -bling,** *n. v.t.* **1.** let drip untidily. —*n.* **2.** act or instance of dribbling.

drī'ér, *n.* thing or substance for drying.

drĭft, *v.i.* **1.** be carried by a current. **2.** move or live aimlessly or passively. —*n.* **3.** drifting motion. **4.** force or gist, as of an argument. **5.** pile of wind-driven snow.

drĭft'wŏŏd'', *n.* wood weathered and driven ashore by the sea.

drĭll, *n.* **1.** boring tool. **2.** system of exercises. **3.** seed-planting machine. **4.** coarse fabric. —*v.t.* **5.** bore with a drill. **6.** train or exercise with a drill.

drī'lў, *adv.* in a dry manner.

drĭnk, *n., v.,* **drank, drunk, drinking.** *n.* **1.** liquid for swallowing. **2.** alcoholic liquor. —*v.t.* **3.** swallow as a drink. —*v.i.* **4.** swallow liquid. **5.** take alcoholic liquor. —**drink'er,** *n.*

drĭp, *v.,* **dripped, dripping,** *n. v.i.* **1.** fall in drops. —*v.t.* **2.** let liquid fall in drops. **3.** let fall in drops. —*n.* **4.** act, instance, or sound of dripping.

drīve, *v.,* **drove, driven, driving,** *n. v.t.* **1.** force along. **2.** compel. **3.** control, as a vehicle. **4.** transport in a road vehicle. —*v.i.* **5.** operate a road vehicle. **6.** advance forcefully. —*n.* **7.** forceful campaign. **8.** energy. **9.** motivation. **10.** pleasure trip in an automobile. **11.** road for pleasure driving. —**driv'er,** *n.* —**drive'way,** *n.* —**drive'-in'',** *adj., n.*

drĭv'él, *n., v.i.,* **-eled, -eling.** *n.* **1.** stupid, nonsensical utterance. —*v.i.* **2.** write or talk drivel.

drĭz'zle, *n., v.,* **-zled, -zling.** *n.* **1.** fine rain. —*v.i., v.t.* **2.** rain in fine drops.

drŏll, *adj.* **1.** oddly amusing. —*n.* **2.** oddly amusing person. —**drol'ly,** *adv.* —**droll'ness, drol'ler·y,** *n.*

drŏm'é·dār''ў, *n., pl.* **-ies.** single-humped camel.

drōne, *n., v.i.,* **droned, droning.** *n.* **1.** low hum. **2.** nonworking male bee. **3.** idler. —*v.i.* **4.** emit a drone.

drōōl, *v.i.* **1.** drip saliva. —*n.* **2.** saliva that drips.

drōōp, *v.i.* **1.** hang loosely. **2.** lose energy or hope. —*n.* **3.** act or instance of drooping. —**droop'y,** *adj.*

drŏp, *v.t.,* **dropped, dropping,** *n. v.t.* **1.** allow to fall. **2.** abandon. **3.** put down. —*v.i.* **4.** fall. —*n.* **5.** globule of liquid that falls or is about to fall. **6.** descent. **7.** small drink. —**drop'per,** *n.*

drŏp'sў, *n.* edema.

drŏss, *n.* **1.** waste on top of molten metal. **2.** waste matter.

drŏŭght, *n.* long dry spell. Also, **drouth.**

drōve, *n.* group of driven cattle. —**drov'er,** *n.*

drŏwn, *v.t., v.i.* **1.** suffocate in water. —*v.t.* **2.** flood.

drŏwse, *v.i.,* **drowsed, drowsing,** *n. v.i.* **1.** be close to sleep. —*n.* **2.** sleepy state. —**drows'y,** *adj.*

drŭb, *v.t.,* **drubbed, drubbing.** beat. —**drub'bing,** *n.*

drŭdge, *v.i.,* **drudged, drudging,** *n. v.i.* **1.** do dull, hard work. —*n.* **2.** a person who drudges. —**drudg'er·y,** *n.*

drŭg, *n., v.t.,* **drugged, drugging.** *n.* **1.** medicinal substance. **2.** narcotic, hallucinogen, etc. —*v.t.* **3.** stupefy with a drug. —**drug'gist,** *n.* —**drug'store'',** *n.*

drŭm, *n., v.,* **drummed, drumming.** *n.* **1.** percussion musical instrument. **2.** eardrum. **3.** cylindrical object. —*v.i.* **4.** beat rhythmically. —*v.t.* **5.** play on a drum. —**drum'mer,** *n.* —**drum'stick'',** *n.*

drŭnk, *adj.* **1.** overcome by alcohol. —*n.* **2.** *Informal.* **a.** drunken person. **b.** alcoholic.

drŭnk'ârd, *n.* alcoholic.

drŭnk'ėn, *adj.* drunk.

drў, *adj.,* **drier, driest,** *v.,* **dried, drying.** *adj.* **1.** free of moisture. **2.** thirsty. **3.** not sweet. **4.** not emotional or expressive. —*v.t.* **5.** free of moisture. —*v.i.* **6.** become dry. —**dry'ly,** *adv.* —**dry'ness,** *n.*

drў'-clēan'', *v.t.* clean with chemicals rather than water. —**dry cleaner,** *n.*

drў gŏŏds, cloth or things made of cloth.

dū'ăl, *adj.* **1.** pertaining to two. **2.** two-fold. —**du·al'i·ty,** *n.*

dŭb, *v.t.*, **dubbed, dubbing. 1.** make a knight of. **2.** give a name to.

dū′bĭ·oŭs, *adj.* doubtful.

dū′càl, *adj.* pertaining to dukes.

dŭch′ĕss, *n.* woman equal in rank to a duke.

dŭch′ÿ, *n.*, *pl.* **-ies.** area ruled by a duke or duchess.

dŭck, *n.* **1.** flat-billed waterfowl. **2.** canvaslike cloth. —*v.i.* **3.** stoop or crouch to avoid a blow. —*v.t.*, *v.i.* **4.** plunge into water briefly. —**duck′ling**, *n.*

dŭct, *n.* passage for fluids. —**duct′less**, *adj.*

dŭc′tĭle, *adj.* able to be stretched. —**duc·til′i·ty**, *n.*

dūde, *n. Informal.* **1.** fancy dresser. **2.** man from the city.

dūe, *adj.* **1.** owed. **2.** proper. **3.** adequate. **4.** expected to arrive. —*adv.* **5.** directly. —*n.* **6.** something due.

dū′ĕl, *n.*, *v.*, **-eled, -eling.** *n.* **1** formal mortal combat between two persons. —*v.t.*, *v.i.* **2.** fight in a duel. —**du′elist, duel′er.**

dū·ĕt′, *n.* **1.** musical composition for two. **2.** pair of musicians.

dūke, *n.* nobleman next in rank to a prince. —**duke′dom**, *n.*

dŭll, *adj.* **1.** not vivid. **2.** not interesting. **3.** not intelligent. **4.** not sharp. —*v.t.*, *v.i.* **5.** make or become dull. —**dul′ly**, *adv.* —**dull′ness, dul′ness**, *n.*

dū′lÿ, *adv.* in a due manner.

dŭmb, *adj.* **1.** unable to speak or make sound. **2.** silent. **3.** *Informal.* stupid.

dŭmb′bĕll′′, *n.* weight for exercising the arms.

dŭmb′fŏund′′, *v.t.* render speechless with astonishment. Also, **dum′found′′**.

dŭmb′′wāit′êr, *n.* **1.** hoist for food. **2.** small serving table.

dŭm′mÿ, *n.*, *pl.* **-ies**, *adj.* **1.** lifesized object in human form. **2.** imitation or mockup. —*adj.* **3.** serving as an imitation.

dŭmp, *v.t.* **1.** throw down or away and abandon. **2.** unload in a heap. —*n.* **3.** place for refuse. **4.** military storage place.

dŭmp′lĭng, *n.* rounded piece of baked dough, sometimes with a fruit filling.

dŭmp′stêr, *n.* a large, metal bin for holding garbage until pick-up.

dŭmp′ÿ, *adj.*, **-ier, -iest.** squat.

dŭn, *n.*, *v.t.*, **dunned, dunning.** *n.* **1.** dull gray-brown. —*v.t.* **2.** attempt to recover a debt from.

dŭnce, *n.* poor learner.

dūne, *n.* mound of wind-driven sand.

dŭng, *n.* manure. —**dung′heap′′, dung′hill**, *n.*

dŭn′′gà·rēes′, *n.*, *pl.* blue cotton work pants or overalls.

dŭn′geòn, *n.* dark prison, as in a castle.

dŭnk, *v.t.* dip into a drink.

dū′ō, *n.*, *pl.* **-os.** duet.

dūpe, *v.t.*, **duped, duping.** *n.* *v.t.* **1.** cheat. —*n.* **2.** person who is cheated. —**dup′er**, *n.*

dū′plĕx, *adj.* **1.** double. —*n.* **2.** two-floored apartment. **3.** two-family house.

dū·plĭ·cāte′′, *v.t.*, **-cated, -cating**, *adj.*, *n.* *v.t.* **1.** imitate exactly. —*n.* (dū′plicate) **2.** exact imitation. —*adj.* **3.** serving as a duplicate. —**du′′pli·ca′tion**, *n.* —**du′pli·ca′′tor**, *n.*

dū·plĭc′ĭ·tÿ, *n.*, *pl.* **-ties.** deceit.

dū′rà·ble, *adj.* long-lasting; sturdy. —**du′ra·bly**, *adv.* —**dura·bil′i·ty**, *n.*

dû·rā′tiòn, *n.* period of existence.

dû·rĕss′, *n.* coercion.

dûr′ĭng, *prep.* in or throughout the period of.

dŭsk, *n.* **1.** darker part of twilight. **2.** gloom. —**dusk′y**, *adj.*

dŭst, *n.* **1.** powder, esp. of earth. **2.** disintegrated human remains. —*v.t.* **3.** remove dust from. **4.** put powder on. —*v.i.* **5.** remove dust from furniture, etc. —**dust′y**, *adj.*

dū′tē·oŭs, *adj.* dutiful.

dū′tĭ·à·ble, *adj.* subject to customs duty.

dū′tĭ·fŭl, *adj.* faithful to duty. —**du′ti·ful·ly**, *adv.*

dū′tÿ, *n.*, *pl.* **-ties. 1.** moral requirement. **2.** requirement by authority. **3.** action, conduct, etc. required by morality or authority. **4.** tax on an import.

dwärf, *n.*, *pl.* **dwarfs, dwarves.** *v.t.* **1.** abnormally small living thing. —*v.t.* **2.** make abnormally small. **3.** make seem small.

dwĕll, *v.i.*, **dwelled** or **dwelt, dwelling. 1.** have one's habitation. **2.** linger, as in speech or thought. —**dwel′ler**, *n.* —**dwel′ling**, *n.*

dwĭn′dle, *v.i.*, **-dled, -dling.** diminish.

dȳe, *n., v.t.,* dyed, dying. *n.* **1.** stain for cloth, etc. —*v.t.* **2.** stain with dye. —dy'er, *n.* —dye'stuff, *n.*

dȳ·năm'ĭc, *adj.* **1.** pertaining to motion. **2.** vigorous, as a person. —dy·nam'i·cal·ly, *adv.* —dy'na·mism, *n.*

dȳ'nà·mō'', *n., pl.* -mos. electrical generator.

dȳ'nàs·tȳ, *n., pl.* -ties. succession of rulers in one family. —dy·nas'tic, *adj.*

dȳs'ėn·tĕr''ȳ, *n.* intestinal inflammation.

dȳs·pĕp'sĭ·à, *n.* indigestion. —dys·pep'tic, *adj., n.*

E

E, e, *n.* **1.** fifth letter of the English alphabet. **2.** fifth-best grade.

ēach, *adj.* **1.** every one individually. —*adv.* **2.** apiece.

ēa'gêr, *adj.* full of desire. —ea'ger·ly, *adv.* —ea'ger·ness, *n.*

ēa'gle, *n.* large bird of prey.

ēar, *n.* **1.** part of the body for hearing. **2.** grain-bearing part of a plant. —ear'drum'', *n.* —ear'muffs'', *n., pl.*

êarl, *n.* British nobleman equal to a count. —earl'dom, *n.*

êar'lȳ, *adj., adv.,* -lier, -liest. **1.** before the expected time. **2.** in good time. **3.** toward the beginning.

ēar'mârk'', *v.t.* note for the future.

êarn, *v.t.* work or deserve to acquire. —earn'ings, *n., pl.*

êar'nėst, *adj.* **1.** sincere; serious. —*n.* **2.** pledge. —ear'nest·ly, *adv.*

ēar'rĭng'', *n.* ornament hung from an ear lobe.

ēar'shŏt'', *n.* hearing distance.

êarth, *n.* **1.** this planet. **2.** ground level. **3.** regions below ground level. **4.** soil. —earth'en, *adj.* —earth'en·ware'', *n.* —earth'ly, *adj.* —earth'quake'', *n.*

êarth'lȳ, *adj.* pertaining to this world.

êarth'wörm'', *n.* worm living in soil.

êarth'ȳ, *adj.,* -ier, -iest. matter-of-fact.

ēase, *n., v.t.,* eased, easing. *n.* **1.** freedom from toil, pain, etc. —*v.t.* **2.** make easy.

ēa'sėl, *n.* stand for a painting, etc.

ēast, *n.* **1.** direction to the right of north. **2.** eastern area. —*adj., adv.* **3.** toward, in, or from the east. —east'er·ly, *adj.* —east'ern, *adj.* —east'ern·er, *n.* —east'ward, *adv., adj.* —east'wards, *adv.*

Ēast'êr, *n.* celebration of the resurrection of Christ.

ēas'ȳ, *adj.,* -ier, -iest. **1.** not difficult. **2.** free of pain, etc. —eas'i·ly, *adv.* —eas'i·ness, *n.*

ēat, *v.t.,* ate, eaten, eating. **1.** consume as food. **2.** dissolve, erode, etc.

ēaves, *n., pl.* projecting edge of a roof.

ēaves'drŏp'', *v.i.,* -dropped, -dropping. overhear conversation, esp. intentionally.

ĕbb, *n.* **1.** going out of a tide. **2.** decline or lessening. —*v.i.* **3.** go out, as the tide. **4.** decline or lessen.

ĕb'ò·nȳ, *n.* **1.** hard, dark wood. **2.** very deep brown or black.

ė·bŭl'lïent, *adj.* **1.** exuberant. **2.** bubbling. —e·bul'lience, *n.*

ėc·cĕn'trĭc, *adj.* **1.** peculiar in manner. **2.** off center. —*n.* **3.** eccentric person. **4.** eccentric machine part. —ec''cen·tric'i·ty, *n.*

ėc·clē''sĭ·ăs'tĭc, *adj.* **1.** Also, ec·cle''si·as'ti·cal. pertaining to churches. —*n.* **2.** clergyman.

ech·e·lon (ĕsh'é·lŏn''), *n.* **1.** formation of troops, etc., each line being to the right or left of that preceding it. **2.** level of responsibility.

ĕch'ō, *n., pl.* -oes, *v.t.,* -oed, -oing. *n.* **1.** reflected sound. —*v.t.* **2.** reflect as an echo.

ė·clâir', *n.* custard-filled pastry.

ė·clĕc'tĭc, *adj.* using those thought best, regardless of source.

ė·clipse', *n., v.t.,* -clipsed, -clipsing. *n.* **1.** obscuring of the sun or moon. —*v.t.* **2.** obscure.

ė·clĭp'tĭc, *n.* apparent annual path of the sun.

ē·cŏl'ò·gȳ, *n., pl.* -gies. **1.** study of the relation of living things to their environment. **2.** system permitting living things to exist. —e'co·log'i·cal, *adj.* —e·col'o·gist, *n.*

ē''cò·nŏm'ĭ·càl, *adj.* thrifty.

ē''cò·nŏm'ĭcs, *n.* **1.** *sing.* study of wealth. **2.** *pl* resources and demands

on wealth. —e''co·nom'ic, *adj*. —e·
con'o·mist, *n*.

e·cŏn'ŏ·mў, *n*., *pl*. -mies. **1**. thrift. **2**.
system of producing and dividing
wealth. —e·con'o·mize'', *v.i.*

ĕc'stă·sў, *n*., *pl*. -sies. state of overwhelming emotion. —ec·stat'ic, *adj*.,
n.

ĕc''ū·mĕn'ĭ·cȧl, *adj*. **1**. universal. **2**.
promoting universal accord, esp. in religion.

ĕc'zė·mȧ, *n*. scaly skin disease.

ĕd'dў, *n*., *pl*. -dies, *v.i.*, -died, -dying.
n. **1**. turbulence of water or wind. —*v.i.*
2. move in a circular current.

ĕdge, *n*., *v*., edged, edging. *n*. **1**. outer
limit. **2**. sharp intersection. —*v.t*. **3**.
border. —*v.i*. **4**. side. —edge'wise'',
edge'ways'', *adv*. —edg'ing, *n*.

ĕd'ĭ·ble, *adj*. suitable for eating. —ed''i·
bil'i·ty, *n*.

ē'dĭct, *n*. decree.

ĕd'ĭ·fĭce, *n*. building.

ĕd'ĭ·fȳ'', *v.t.*, -fied, -fying. educate or
improve the mind of. —ed''i·fi·ca'
tion, *n*.

ĕd'ĭt, *v.t*. prepare for publication or presentation. —ed'i·tor, *n*. —ed''i·tor'
ial, *n*., *adj*.

e·dĭ''tion, *n*. printing of a book.

ĕd''ĭ·tôr'ĭ·ȧl, *n*. **1**. periodical's com-
mentary on public issues. —*adj*. **2**. pertaining to editing.

ĕd'ŭ·cāte'', *v.t.* -cated, -cating. develop
the mind, knowledge or skill of. —ed''
u·ca'tion, *n*. —ed''u·ca'tion·al, *adj*.
—ed'u·ca''tor, *n*.

ēel, *n*. long, snakelike fish.

ēe'rlē, *adj*., -rier, -riest. weird; uncanny.

ėf·fāce', *v.t.*, -faced, -facing. eliminate
all trace of. —ef·face'ment, *n*.

ėf·fĕct', *n*. **1**. result. **2**. influence. **3**. effects, personal property. —*v.t*. **4**.
cause. —ef·fect'ive, *adj*. —ef·fec'tu·
al, *adj*.

ėf·fĕm'ĭ·nȧte, *adj*. having feminine
qualities. —ef·fem'i·na·cy, *n*.

ĕf''fêr·vĕsce', *v.i.*, -vesced, -vescing.
bubble. —ef''fer·ves'cent, *adj*. —ef''
fer·ves'cence, *n*.

ĕf·fēte', *adj*. decadent.

ĕf''fĭ·cā'cioŭs, *adj*. producing the desired result. —ef'fi·ca·cy, *n*.

ėf·fĭ'cĭent, *adj*. efficacious without

waste. —ef·fi'cient·ly, *adv*. —ef·fi'
cien·cy, *n*.

ĕf'fĭ·gў, *n*., *pl*. -gies. copy or image, esp.
in three dimensions.

ĕf'fôrt, *n*. **1**. expenditure of strength,
thought, etc. **2**. attempt.

ĕf·frŏnt'êr·ў, *n*., *pl*. -ies. impudence.

ėf·fū'sion, *n*. outpouring of enthusiasm.
—ef·fu'sive, *adj*.

ė·gǎl'ĭ·târ''ĭ·ȧn, *adj*. believing that all
people should be equal.

ĕgg'hĕad'', *n*. *Informal*. intellectual.

ĕgg'plǎnt'', *n*. purple-skinned vegetable.

ē'gō, *n*. self. —e''go·cen'tric, *adj*., *n*.

ē'gō·ĭsm, *n*. selfishness. —e'go·ist, *n*.
—e''go·is'tic, e''go·is'ti·cal, *adj*.

ē'gō·tĭsm, *n*. self-conceit; vanity. —e'
go·tist'', *n*. —e''go·tis'tic, e''go·tis'
ti·cal, *adj*.

ė·grē'gioŭs, *adj*. conspicuous in a bad
way.

eight (āt), *n*. seven plus one. —eighth,
adj.

eight·ēen', *n*. seventeen plus one.

eight'ў, *n*. eight times ten. —eight'i·
eth, *adj*.

ei·ther (ēth̀er, ī'th̀er), *adj*. **1**. one or the
other but not both. **2**. each. —*pron*. **3**.
one or the other. *conj*. **4**. (used to emphasize choice). —*adj*. **5**. as well.

ė·jĕct', *v.t*. hurl or force out. —e·jec'
tion, *n*.

ēke, *v.t.*, eked, eking. eke out, gain with
difficulty.

ē·lǎb·ȯ·rȧte, *adj*., *v.t.*, -rated, -rating.
adj. **1**. having many parts or aspects.
—*v.t*. (ē lab'ō rāte') **2**. plan in detail.
—e·lab''o·ra'tion, *n*.

ė·lǎpse', *v.i.*, -lapsed, -lapsing. pass, as
time.

ė·lǎs'tĭc, *adj*. able to recover from
stretching or bending. —*n*. elastic material or object. —e·las''tic'i·ty, *n*.

ė·lāte', *v.t.*, -lated, -lating. raise in spirits. —e·la'tion, *n*.

ĕl'bōw, *n*. joint halfway up the arm.
—*v.t.*, *v.i.* push with the elbows.

ĕl'dêr, *adj*. **1**. senior. —*n*. **2**. senior. **3**.
shrub with red or purple berries. —eld'
est, *adj*. —eld'er·ly, *adj*.

ė·lĕct', *v.t*. **1**. choose, esp. by a vote.
—*adj*. **2**. chosen. **3**. elected to but not
yet in public office. —e·lec'tion, *n*.

—e·lec′tor, *n*. —e·lec′tor·al, *adj*.
—e·lec′tor·ate, *n*. —e·lec′tive, *adj*.

e·lec″tric′i·tў, *n*. **1**. property of motion in certain particles composing matter. **2**. current created by such motion. —e· lec′tric, e·lec′tri·cal, *adj*. —e·lec′ tri·fy″, *v.t*.

e·lec′trŏ·cūte″, *v.t*., -cuted, -cuting. injure or kill with electricity. —e·lec″ tro·cu′tion, *n*.

e·lec′trōde, *n*. object conducting electricity into or out of a battery, etc.

e·lec·trŏl′ў·sĭs, *n*. decomposition of a material by the passage of electricity. —e·lec″tro·lyt′ic, *adj*.

e·lec″trō·măg′nėt, *n*. magnet operating through an electric current. —e·lec″ tro·mag·net′ic, *adj*.

e·lec′trŏn, *n*. negatively charged particle of an atom.

e·lec″trŏn′ĭcs, *n*., *sing*. study of the action of electrons and its application to technology. —e·lec″tron′ic, *adj*.

ĕl′e·gȧnt, *adj*. tasteful and dignified. —el′e·gance, *n*.

ĕl′e·gў, *n*., *pl*. -gies. poem of lament, esp. for the dead. —el″e·gi′ac, el″e· gi′a·cal, *adj*.

ĕl′e·mėnt, *n*. **1**. major or basic component. **2**. natural environment. **3**. elements, natural forces, esp. of weather. —el″e·men′tal, *adj*.

ĕl″e·mĕn′tȧ·rў, *n*. fundamental; rudimentary.

ĕl′e·phȧnt, *n*. large four-legged animal with a long prehensile nose.

ĕl·e·vāte′, *v.t*., -vated, -vating. **1**. raise to a greater height. **2**. raise in rank, spirits, etc.

ĕl″e·vā′tion, *n*. **1**. height. **2**. drawing of one side of a building, etc., in its true dimensions.

ĕl′e·vā″tör, *n*. **1**. cabinet or platform for raising or lowering persons or goods. **2**. storage place for grain.

e·lĕv′ėn, *n*. ten plus one.

ĕlf, *n*., *pl*. elves. small fairy. —ĕlf′in, elf′ish, *adj*.

e·lĭc′ĭt, *v.t*. draw forth, as a reaction or comment.

ĕl′ĭ·gĭ·ble, *adj*. suitable for choice. —el″i·gi·bil′i·ty, *n*.

e·lĭm′ĭ·nāte″, *v.t*., -nated, -nating. get rid of. —e·lim″i·na′tion, *n*.

e·līte, *n*. choice element. —e·lit′ism, *n*.

e·lĭx′îr, *n*. medicine in a solution of alcohol.

ĕlk, *n*., *pl*. elks, elk. large mooselike deer.

el·lĭpse′, *n*. oval symmetrical about two axes. —el·lip′ti·cal, *adj*.

ĕlm, *n*. tall deciduous tree.

ĕl″ō·cū′tion, *n*. public speaking.

e·lŏn′gāte″, *v.t*., *v.i*., -gated, -gating. lengthen. —e″lon·ga′tion, *n*.

e·lōpe″, *v.i*., -loped, -loping. flee, esp. in order to marry. —e·lope′ment, *n*.

ĕ″lȯ·quėnt, *adj*. convincing in speech. —e′lo·quence, *n*.

ĕlse, *adj*. **1**. other. **2**. more. —*adv*. **3**. otherwise.

ĕlse′whĕre″, *adv*. somewhere else.

e·lū′cĭ·dāte″, *v.t*., -dated, -dating. clarify; explain. —e·lu″ci·da′tion, *n*.

e·lūde′, *v.t*., -luded, -luding. escape or evade. —e·lu′sive, *adv*.

e·mā′cĭ·āte″, *v.t*., -ated, -ating. make abnormally thin. —e·ma″ci·a′tion, *n*.

ĕm″ȧ·nāte″, *v.i*., -nated, -nating. come forth; issue. —em″a·na′tion, *n*.

e·măn′cĭ·pāte″, *v.t*., -pated, -pating. free, as from bondage. —e·man″ci· pa′tion, *n*. —e·man′ci·pa″tor, *n*.

e·măs′cū·lāte″, *v.t*., -lated, -lating. castrate.

ĕm·bȧlm′, *v.t*. preserve against decay after death.

ĕm·bănk′, *v.t*. support, strengthen, etc., with piled earth, etc. —em·bank′ ment, *n*.

ĕm·bâr′gō, *n*., *pl*. -goes, *n*. ban on shipping or commerce.

ĕm·bârk′, *v.i*. **1**. set forth, esp. on a ship. —*v.t*., *v.i*. **2**. board, esp. a ship. —em″ bar·ka′tion, *n*.

ĕm·băr′rȧss, *v.t*. **1**. make ashamed or self-conscious. **2**. put at a loss for money. —em·bar′rass·ment, *n*.

ĕm′bȧs·sў, *n*., *pl*. -sies. permanent mission to a foreign government.

ĕm·bĕd′, *v.t*., -bedded, -bedding. sink and fix firmly.

ĕm·bĕl′lĭsh, *n*. decorate. —em·bel′lish· ment, *n*.

ĕm′bêr, *n*. red-hot piece of fuel.

ĕm·bĕz′zle, *v.t*., -zled, -zling. steal from an employer, client, etc. —em·bez′ zler, *n*. —em·bez′zle·ment, *n*.

ĕm·bĭt′têr, *v.t*. make bitter.

ĕm'blĕm, *n.* symbolic design. —em''blem·at'ic, *adj.*

ĕm·bŏd'ў, *v.t.*, -died, -dying. 1. realize in bodily form. 2. incorporate. —em·bod'i·ment, *n.*

ĕm·bŏss', *v.t.* mark with raised designs or lettering.

ĕm'brāce', *v.*, -braced, -bracing, *n. v.t.* 1. put the arms around. 2. accept readily. —*v.i.* 3. embrace each other. —*n.* 4. act or instance of embracing.

ĕm·brōi'dêr, *v.t.* decorate with applied colored yarns. —em·broi'der·y, *n.*

ĕm'brў·ō'', *n., pl.* -oes. animal or plant in the first stage of development. —em''bry·on'ic, *adj.*

ĕ·mĕnd', *v.t.* correct; edit. —e''men·da'tion, *n.*

ĕm'êr·ăld, *n.* vivid green gem.

ĕ·mêrge', *v.i.*, -merged, -merging. appear into notice. —e·mer'gence, *n.*

ĕ·mêr'gĕn·cў, *n., pl.* -cies. mishap demanding prompt action.

ĕ·mĕt'ĭc, *adj.* 1. causing vomiting. —*n.* 2. emetic substance.

ĕm'ĭ·grāte'', *v.i.*, -grated, -grating. leave one's country to settle elsewhere. —em''i·gra'tion, *n.* —em''i·grant, *n., adj.*

ĕm'ĭ·nĕnt, *adj.* high in standing or rank. —em'i·nence, *n.* —em'i·nent·ly, *adv.*

ĕm'ĭs·sār'ў, *n., pl.* -ies. person sent on a mission.

ĕ·mĭt', *v.t.*, -mitted, -mitting. send out or forth; discharge. —e·mis'sion, *n.*

ĕ·mō'tion, *n.* 1. natural feelings and reactions. 2. specific feeling or reaction. —e·mo'tion·al, *adj.*

ĕm'pêr·ör, *n.* ruler of an empire.

ĕm'phà·sĭs, *n., pl.* -ses. force or stress. —em·phat'ic, *adj.* —em'pha·size'', *v.t.*

ĕm'pīre, *n.* number of countries or regions under one monarch.

ĕm·pĭr'ĭ·càl, *adj.* derived from experience.

ĕm·plŏў', *v.t.* 1. hire or use. —*n.* 2. hire. —em·ploy'er, *n.* —em·ploy'ee, *n.* —em·ploy'ment, *n.*

ĕm·pô'rĭ·ŭm, *n., pl.* -ums, -a. store with varied merchandise.

ĕm·pōw'êr, *v.t.* give official power to.

em'press, *n.* woman married to or with the rank of an emperor.

ĕmp'tў, *adj.*, -tier, -tiest, *v.*, -tied, -tying. *adj.* 1. lacking contents. —*v.t.* 2. make empty. —*v.i.* 3. become empty. —emp'ti·ness, *n.*

ĕm'ū·lāte'', *v.t.*, -lated, -lating. imitate, esp. in excellence. —em''u·la'tion, *n.* —em'u·lous, *adj.*

ĕ·mŭl'sion, *n.* mixture of two liquids made possible by addition of a third. —e·mul'si·fy'', *v.t., v.i.*

ĕn·ā'ble, *v.t.*, -bled, -bling. make able.

ĕn·ăct', *v.t.* 1. make into law. 2. represent in a play. —en·act'ment, *n.*

ĕn·ăm'ĕl, *n., v.t.*, -eled or -elled, -eling or -elling. *n.* 1. glassy, fused coating. 2. hard, glossy paint. 3. exterior material of teeth. —*v.t.* 4. cover with enamel.

ĕn·ăm'ōred, *adj.* full of love.

ĕn·cămp', *v.i., v.t.* camp. —en·camp'ment, *n.*

ĕn·cāse', *v.t.*, -cased, -casing. enclose.

ĕn·chănt', *v.t.* 1. charm. 2. put a magic spell on. —en·chant'ment, *n.*

ĕn·cĭr'cle, *v.t.*, -cled, -cling. surround.

ĕn·clōse', *v.t.*, -closed, -closing. 1. surround. 2. put into a container, envelope, etc. —en·clo'sure, *n.*

ĕn·cŏm'pàss, *v.t.* 1. surround. 2. include.

en·core (ahn'kōr), *interj.* 1. again: request to a musician. —*n.* 2. repetition of a musical performance.

ĕn·cōūn'têr, *v.t.* 1. happen to meet. 2. meet in combat. —*n.* 3. act or instance of encountering.

ĕn·coŭr'àge, *v.t.*, -aged, -aging. give courage or resolution to. —en·cour'age·ment, *n.*

ĕn·crōach', *v.i.* trespass. —en·croach'ment, *n.*

ĕn·cŭm'bêr, *v.t.* burden or hinder. —en·cum'brance, *n.*

ĕn·cў''clō·pē'dĭ·à, *n.* reference work dealing at length with all areas of knowledge. Also, en·cy''clo·pae'di·a. —en·cy''clo·pe'dic, *adj.*

ĕnd, *n.* 1. far or final part. 2. result. 3. purpose. —*v.t.* 4. put an end to. —*v.i.* 5. come to an end. —end'less, *adj.*

ĕn·dăn'gêr, *v.t.* put in danger.

ĕn·dēar', *v.t.* make dear. —en·dear'ing, *adj.* —en·dear'ment, *n.*

ĕn·dĕav'ör, *v.t., v.i.* attempt.

ĕnd'ĭng, *n.* conclusion.

ĕnd'mōst'', *adj.* farthest.

ĕn·dôrse', *v.t.*, -dorsed, -dorsing. 1.

write on the back of, esp. a signature. 2. approve. —en·dors′er, *n.* —en·dorse′ment, *n.*

en·dow′, *v.t.* 1. provide with personal resources or qualities. 2. give money for. —en·dow′ment, *n.*

en·dure′, *v.,* -dured, -during. *v.t.* 1. tolerate. 2. suffer. —*v.i.* 3. survive. —en·dur′able, *adj.* —en·dur′ance, *n.*

en′e·my, *n., pl.* -mies. 1. person who wishes one harm. 2. hostile nation or military force.

en′er·gy, *n., pl.* -gies. 1. force able to produce motion, heat, light, etc. 2. vigor. —en′′er·get′ic, *adj.*

en′er·vate′′, *v.t.,* -vated, -vating. deprive of vitality. —en′′er·va′tion, *n.*

en·fee′ble, *v.t.,* -bled, -bling. make feeble.

en·fold′, *v.t.* wrap.

en·force′, *v.t.,* -forced, -forcing. administer forcefully, as a law. —en·force′ment, *n.*

en·gage′, *v.t.,* -gaged, -gaging. 1. commit. 2. commit to marriage. 3. hire. 4. hold or connect with. 5. meet and fight. —en·gage′ment, *n.*

en·gag′ing, *adj.* charming. —en·gag′ing·ly, *adv.*

en·gen·der, *v.t.* bring into being.

en′gine, *n.* 1. machine producing mechanical force, esp. by means of heat energy. 2. locomotive.

en′′gi·neer′, *n.* 1. person who designs systems or structures applying static or dynamic forces or various sources of energy. 2. skilled operator of machines, etc. —en′′gi·neer′ing, *n.*

en·grave′, *v.t.,* -graved, -graving. form designs or letters with shallow cuts on wood, steel, etc. —en·grav′er, *n.* —en·grav′ing, *n.*

en·gross′, *v.t.* capture the attention of.

en·gulf′, *v.t.* swallow up; submerge.

en·hance′, *v.t.,* -hanced, -hancing. increase or improve.

e·nig′ma, *n., pl.* -mas. puzzle. —e′′nig·mat′ic, *adj.*

en·join′, *v.t.* forbid.

en·joy′, *v.t.* 1. get pleasure from. 2. have the benefit of. —en·joy′a·ble, *adj.* —en·joy′ment, *n.*

en·large′, *v.,* -larged, -larging. *v.t.* 1. make larger. —*v.i.* 2. become larger. —en·large′ment, *n.*

en·light′en, *v.t.* free of ignorance or wrong attitudes. —en·light′en·ment, *n.*

en·list′, *v.t., v.i.* enroll. —en·list′ment, *n.*

en·liv′en, *v.t.* make lively.

en′mi·ty, *n., pl.* -ties. hostility.

en·nui′ (ahn wē′), *n.* boredom.

e·nor′mi·ty, *n., pl.* -ties. 1. wickedness. 2. outrage.

e·nor′mous, *adj.* beyond normal size or extent. —e·nor′mous·ly, *adv.*

e·nough′, *n., adj., adv. n.* 1. as much as is wanted; sufficiency. —*adj.* 2. adequate; sufficient. —*adv.* 3. sufficiently.

en·quire′, *v.t., v.i.,* -quired, -quiring. inquire. —en·quir′y, *n.*

en·rage′, *v.t.,* -raged, -raging. put in a rage.

en·rich′, *v.t.* make rich or richer. —en·rich′ment, *n.*

en·roll′, *v.t.* name on a list or record. —en·roll′ment, *n.*

en route, on the way.

en·sconce′, *v.t.* put in a snug or secure place.

en·sem′ble (ón sóm′būl), *n.* related group.

en·shrine′, *v.t.,* -shrined, -shrining. put in or as if in a shrine.

en′sign, *n.* 1. flag, as on a ship. 2. lowest commissioned naval officer.

en·slave′, *v.t.,* -slaved, -slaving. make a slave of. —en·slave′ment, *n.*

en·sue′, *v.i.,* -sued, -suing. follow, esp. as a consequence.

en·sure′, *v.t.,* -sured, -suring. make sure.

en·tail′, *v.t.* necessitate.

en·tan′gle, *v.t.,* -gled, -gling. trap or impede. —en·tan′gle·ment, *n.*

en′ter, *v.t.* 1. go into. 2. have enrolled in or admitted to something. 3. list or record.

en′′ter·prise′′, *n.* 1. project with some risk. 2. willingness to undertake such projects. —en′ter·pris′′ing, *adj.*

en′′ter·tain′, *v.t.* 1. have as a guest. 2. amuse. 3. consider. —en′′ter·tain′er, *n.* —en′′ter·tain′ment, *n.*

en·thu′si·asm, *n.* intense approval, or favor. —en·thu′si·ast, *n.* —en·thu′′si·as′tic, *adj.*

en·tice′, *v.t.,* -ticed, -ticing. tempt, esp. deceitfully. —en·tice′ment, *n.*

en·tire′, *adj.* complete. —en·tire′ly, *adv.* —en·tire′ty, *n.*

en·ti′tle, *v.t.*, -tled, -tling. give a right or claim.

en′ti·ty, *n.*, *pl.* -ties. one that exists.

en″to·mŏl′o·gy̆, *n.* study of insects. —en″to·mol′o·gist, *n.*

en·tou·rage (ahn″too̅ rahzh′), *n.* followers of an important person.

en′trails, *n. pl.* internal organs, esp. viscera.

en′trance, *n.*, *v.t.*, -tranced, -trancing. *n.* 1. way of entering. 2. right to enter. 3. act of entering. —*v.t.* (en trans′). 4. fill with wonder.

en·trăp′, *v.t.* catch, as if in a trap. —en·trap′ment, *n.*

en·trēat′, *v.t.*, *v.i.* ask earnestly. en·treat′y, *n.*

en·tree (ahn trā′), *n.* main dinner course.

en·trĕnch′, *v.t.* secure the position of.

en″tre·pre·neûr′, *n.* undertaker of business ventures.

en·trŭst′, *v.t.* 1. give to someone in trust. 2. trust with something.

en′try, *n.*, *pl.* -tries. 1. entrance. 2. something noted. 3. competitor.

e·nū′mer·āte″, *v.t.*, -ated, -ating. 1. cite one by one. 2. count. —e·nu″mer·a′tion, *n.*

e·nŭn′ci·āte″, *v.*, -ated, -ating. *v.t.*, *v.i.* speak distinctly. —e·nun″ci·a′tion, *n.*

en·vĕl′op, *v.i.* wrap up.

en′ve·lōpe″, *n.* 1. paper cover for letters, papers, etc. 2. outer covering.

en·vī′ron·mĕnt, *n.* 1. surroundings. 2. conditions. —en·vi″ron′men′tal, *adj.*

en·vī′rons, *n.*, *pl.* surrounding area.

en·vĭs′age, *v.t.*, -aged, -aging. visualize; contemplate

en·vi′sion, *v.t.* contemplate as likely.

en′voy̆, *n.* diplomatic representative.

en′vy̆, *n.*, *v.t.*, -vied, -vying. *n.* 1. resentment over another's good luck. —*v.t.* 2. feel envy toward. —en′vi·a·ble, *adj.* —en′vi·ous, *adj.*

ē′on, *n.* very long period.

e·phĕm′êr·ăl, *n.* short-lived.

ĕp′ĭc, *adj.* 1. heroic. —*n.* 2. long poem about heroism.

ĕp′ĭ·cūre″, *n.* person with refined tastes, esp. for food and drink. —ep″i·cu·re′an, *adj.*, *n.*

ĕp″ĭ·dĕm′ĭc, *adj.* 1. spreading through a community. —*n.* 2. epidemic disease.

ĕp″ĭ·dêr′mĭs, *n.* outer layer of skin. —ep″i·der′mal, ep″i·der′mic, *adj.*

ĕp′ĭ·grăm″, *n.* short witty observation. —ep″i·gram·mat′ic, *adj.*

ĕp′ĭ·lĕp″sy̆, *n.* nervous disease with convulsions and unconsciousness. —ep″i·lep·tic, *adj.*, *n.*

ĕp′i·lŏgue″, *n.* final statement of a play, etc.

E·pĭph′à·ny̆, *n.* revelation of Jesus as the Christ, celebrated January 6.

e·pĭs′co·pàl, *adj.* pertaining to or governed by a bishop.

ĕp′ĭ·sōde″, *n.* occurrence. —ep″i·sod′ic, *adj.*

e·pĭs′tle, *n.* letter; written message.

ĕp′ĭ·tăph″, *n.* inscription on a tomb.

ĕp′ĭ·thĕt″, *n.* characterizing name.

e·pĭt′o·mē″, *n.*, *pl.* -mes. 1. summary. 2. ideal example. —e·pit′o·mize″, *v.t.*

ĕp′och, *n.* distinct historical or geological period. —ep′och·al, *adj.*

ĕq′uà·ble, *adj.* emotionally steady.

ē′qual, *adj.*, *n.*, *v.t.*, -qualed, -qualing. *adj.* 1. of the same amount, rank, etc. 2. competent; adequate. —*n.* 3. equal person or thing. —*v.t.* 4. be equal to. —e·qual′i·ty, *n.* —e·qual·ize″, *v.t.*

ē″quá·nĭm′ĭ·ty̆, *n.* calm.

e·quāte′, *v.t.*, -quated, -quating. regard as equal. —e·qua′tion, *n.*

e·quā′tör, *n.* imaginary line bisecting the earth. —e″qua·to′ri·al, *adj.*

ē″quĭ·dĭs′tant, *adj.* equally far.

ē″quĭ·lăt′êr·àl, *adj.* with equal sides.

ē″quĭ·lĭb′rĭ·ŭm, *n.* balance.

ē′quĭ·nŏx″, *n.* time of equal day and night periods, marking the beginning of spring or autumn. —e″qui·noc′ti·al, *adj.*

e·quĭp′, *v.t.*, -quipped, -quipping. furnish with what is necessary. —equip′ment, *n.*

ē′quĭ·tà·ble, *adj.* just; fair. —e′qui·ta·bly, *adv.*

ē′quĭ·ty̆, *n.* 1. fairness. 2. value of something in excess of money owed for it.

e·quĭv′·à·lènt, *adj.*, *n.* equal. —e·quiv′a·lence, *n.*

e·quĭv′o·càl, *adj.* of doubtful meaning or nature.

e·quĭv′o·cāte, *v.i.*, -cated, -cating.

speak equivocally. —e·quiv''o·ca'
tion, n.

ĕr'a̤, n. distinctive historical period.

e·răd'ĭ·cāte'', v.t., -cated, -cating.
eliminate by destroying. —e·rad''i·ca'
tion, n.

e·rāse', v.t., -rased, -rasing. obliterate.
—e·ras'er, n. —e·ra'sure, n.

e·rĕct', adj. 1. upright. —v.t. 2. build.
—e·rec'tion, n.

ĕr'mĭne, n. weasel with white winter fur.

e·rōde', v., -roded, -roding. v.t., v.i.
wash away or out. —e·ro'sion, n.

e·rŏt'ĭc, adj. pertaining to or arousing
sexual desire. —e·rot'i·cism, n.

ĕrr, v.i. be in error.

ĕr'ra̤nd, n. journey for some purpose.

êr'ra̤nt, adj. wandering.

ĕr·răt'ĭc, adj. unreliable.

ĕr·rât'ŭm, n., pl. -a. printing or writing
error.

ĕr·rō'nē·oŭs, adj. in error.

ĕr'rôr, n. mistaken belief or action.

êrst'whĭle'', adj. former.

ĕr'ū·dīte'', adj. informed; scholarly.
—er''u·di'tion, n.

e·rŭpt', v.i. break forth. —e·rup'tion,
n.

ĕs'ca̤·lāte'', v.i., -lated, -lating. 1. rise
on an escalator. 2. increase rapidly, as
in intensity.

ĕs'ca̤·lā''tŏr, n. endless moving stair.

ĕs'ca̤·pāde'', n. reckless adventure.

es·cāpe', v., -caped, -caping, n. v.t., v.i.
1. flee. —v.t. 2. evade the notice of.
—n. 3. act or instance of escaping.

es·cāp'ĭsm, n. tendency to attempt to escape reality. —es·cap'ist, n., adj.

ĕs·chēw', v.t. shun; do without.

ĕs·côrt', v.t. 1. take charge of and accompany. —n. 2. person or thing that es-
corts.

ĕs'crōw, n. Law. state of property that is
temporarily held in trust for another.

es·cŭtch'eo̤n, n. symbolic shield holding
a coat of arms.

ĕs''ō·tĕr'ĭc, adj. reserved for an understanding few.

ĕs·pĕ'cia̤l, adj. special. —es·pe'cial·ly,
adv.

ĕs'pĭ·o̤·näge'', n. practice of spying.

es·pōuse', v.t., -poused, -pousing. 1.
marry. 2. devote oneself to. —es'pous'
al, n.

es·prit de corps (es prē'de kor'), morale
of an organization.

es·pȳ', v.t., -pied, -pying. discern.

ĕs'sāy, n. 1. writing on some theme.
—v.t. (es sāy') 2. attempt. —es'say·ist,
n.

ĕs'sence, n. 1. basic nature. 2. concentrated substance.

ĕs·sĕn'tial, adj. 1. indispensable. —n.
2. something indispensable. —es·sen'
tial·ly, adv.

ĕs·tăb'lĭsh, v.t. 1. bring into being. 2.
prove. —es·tab'lish·ment, n.

es·tāte', n. 1. personal property. 2.
grounds belonging to a house.

es·tēem', n. 1. evaluation. —v.t. 2. deem.
—es'tim·a·ble, adj.

ĕs'thēte'', n. aesthete.

ĕs·thĕt'ĭcs, n. aesthetics.

ĕs'ti·ma̤te, n., v.t., -mated, -mating. n.
1. rough calculation or appraisal. —v.t.
(es'ti māte'') 2. make an estimate of.
—esti·ma'tion, n.

es·trānge', v.t., -tranged, -tranging.
lose the affection of.

ĕs'tū·ârȳ, n., pl. -ies. tidal river mouth.

ĕt cĕtêra̤, and other persons or things.
Abbreviated etc.

ĕtch, v.t. make or mark by the corrosion
of acid. —etch'ing, n.

e·têr'na̤l, adj. lasting or valid forever.
—e·ter'nal·ly, adv. —e·ter'ni·ty, n.

ē'thêr, n. 1. upper part of the atmosphere. 2. volatile, flammable anes-
thetic or solvent.

e·thē'rē·a̤l, adj. 1. delicate. 2. un-
earthly.

ĕth'ĭcs, n. 1. study of right and wrong in
actions. 2. pl. a. Also, eth'ic, personal
standards of right and wrong action. b.
standards of conduct adopted by professionals. —eth'i·cal, adj.

ĕth'nĭc, adj. 1. pertaining to distinct nations or tribes. —n. 2. member of a minority national group. —eth·nic'i·ty,
n.

ĕt'ĭ·quĕtte, n. code of acceptable conduct.

ĕ''tȳ·mŏl'o̤·gȳ, n. study of word origins.

Eū'cha̤·rĭst, n. 1. Holy Communion. 2.
bread and wine used at Holy Communion. —Eu'cha·ris'tic, adj.

Eū·clĭd'ē·a̤n, adj. pertaining to traditional geometry. Also, Eu·clid'i·an.

eū·gĕn'ĭcs, n. attempt to improve hu-

manity by controlled mating. —eu·
gen'ic, adj.

eū'lo·ġy. n., pl. -gies. praise in speech or
writing. —eu''lo·gize', v.t.

eū'nŭch, n. castrated man.

eū'phe·mĭsm, n. expression substituted
for a less agreeable one. —euphe·mis'
tic, adj.

eū·phō'nĭ·oŭs, adj. pleasant-sounding.
—eu'pho·ny, n.

eū·phô'rĭ·à, n. sensation of well-being.
—eu·phor'ic, adj.

eū·rē'kà, interj. I have found it!

eū''thà·nā'sĭ·à, n. killing to prevent or
end suffering.

è·văc'ū·āte'', v.t., -ated, -ating. 1.
empty. 2. send to a place of security.
—e·vac''u·a'tion, n. —e·vac''u·ee',
n.

è·vāde', v.t., -vaded, -vading. avoid or
escape from. —e·va'sion, n. —e·va'
sive, adj.

è·văl'ū·āte'', v.t., -ated, -ating. estimate the worth of. —e·val''u·a'tion,
n.

ē''văn·ġĕl'ĭ·cál, adj. 1. pertaining to
the New Testament. 2. emphasizing salvation through Jesus.

ē·văn'ġĕl·ĭst, n. 1. author of a Gospel. 2.
itinerant preacher. —e·van'gel·ism, n.

è·văp'ó·rāte'', v.t., v.i., -rated, -rating.
turn into vapor. —e·vap''o·ra'tion, n.

ēve, n. time just before.

ē'vĕn, adj. 1. level or smooth. 2. unvarying. 3. equal. 4. divisible by two. 5.
with nothing owed. —adv. 6. although
improbable. 7. yet; still. —v.t. 8. make
even. —e'ven·ness, n.

ēve'nĭng, n. time between afternoon and
night.

è·vĕnt', n. something that happens. —e·
vent'ful, adj.

è·vĕn'tū·ál, adj. at some future time.
—e·ven'tu·al·ly, adv.

è·vĕn''tū·ál'ĭ·tÿ, n., pl. -ties. possible
occurrence.

ĕv'êr, adv. at any time.

ĕv'êr·grēen'', adj. 1. with green leaves
all the year round. —n. 2. evergreen
tree or plant.

ĕv''êr·lăst'ĭng, adj. eternal or lifelong.

ĕv'êr·ÿ, adj. 1. each individual. 2. any
possible. —ev'er·y·one'', pron. —ev'
er·y·thing'', n.

ĕv'êr·ÿ·bŏd''ÿ, n. every person.

ĕv'êr·ÿ·whêre'', adv. at or to every
place.

è·vĭct', v.t. drive out, as from rented
lodgings. —e·vic'tion, n.

ĕv'ĭ·dĕnce, n., v.t., -denced, -dencing.
n. 1. matter supporting an argument.
—v.t. 2. make evident.

ĕv'ĭ·dĕnt, adj. obvious. —ev'i·dent·ly,
adv.

ē'vĭl, adj. 1. wrong or wicked. 2. injurious. —e'vil·ly, adv.

è·vĭnce', v.t., -vinced, -vincing. make
obvious.

è·vōke', v.t., -voked, -voking. call forth.
—e·voc'a·tive, adj. —ev''o·ca'tion,
n.

è·vŏlve', v., -volved, -volving. v.t., v.i.
develop gradually. —ev''o·lu'tion, n.

ĕx·ăc'êr·bāte, v.t., -bated, -bating. ag-
gravate.

ĕx·ăct', adj. 1. accurate. 2. precise.
—v.t. 3. extort or demand. —ex·act'ly,
n. —ex·act'ing, adj. —ex·ac'tion, n.

ĕx·ăġ'ġêr·āte'', v.t., -ated, -ating. over-
state the importance of. —ex·ag''ger·
a'tion, n.

ĕx·ălt', v.t. 1. raise in status. 2. praise.
—ex''al·ta'tion, n.

ĕx·ăm'ĭne, v.t., -ined, -ining. 1. inspect. 2. test for knowledge. —ex·am''
i·na'tion, n. —ex·am'in·er, n.

ĕx·ăm'ple, n. 1. sample. 2. illustrative
instance.

ĕx·ăs'pêr·āte'', v.t., -ated, -ating. anger
or annoy seriously. —ex·as''per·a'
tion, n.

ĕx'cá·vāte'', v.t., -vated, -vating. dig, as
in or from earth. —ex''ca·va'tion, n.

ĕx·cēed', v.t. 1. be in excess of. 2. surpass.

ĕx·cēed'ĭng·lÿ, adv. extremely.

ĕx·cĕl', v., -celled, -celling. v.t., v.i. surpass.

ĕx'cĕl·lĕnt, adj. among the finest of its
kind. —ex'cel·lent·ly, adv. —ex·cel-
lence, n.

ĕx·cĕpt', prep. 1. Also, ex·cept''ing,
aside from. —v.t. 2. exclude or disregard. —ex·cep'tion, n.

ĕx·cĕp'tion·a·ble, adj. objectionable.

ĕx·cĕp'tion·ál, adj. highly unusual.
—ex·cep'tion·al·ly, adv.

ĕx'cêrpt, n. quotation, esp. printed.

ĕx·cĕss', n. 1. lack of self-restraint or

moderation. **2.** surplus. —*adj.* **3.** surplus. —**ex·ces'sive,** *adj.*

ex·change', *v.t.,* **-changed, -changing,** *n. v.t.* **1.** give in return for something else. —*n.* **2.** act or instance of exchanging.

ex·cise, *n., v.t.,* **-cised, -cising.** *n.* **1.** tax on merchandise. —*v.t.* **2.** cut out. —**ex·ci'sion,** *n.*

ex·cite', *v.t.,* **-cited, -citing. 1.** stimulate. **2.** rouse emotionally. —**ex·cit'a·ble,** *adj.* —**ex·cite'ment,** *n.* —**ex·cit'ed·ly,** *adv.* —**ex·cit'ing,** *adj.*

ex·claim', *v.i., v.t.* shout or speak loudly and emotionally. —**ex''cla·ma'tion,** *n.*

ex·clude', *v.t.,* **-cluded, -cluding.** leave or keep out. —**ex·clu'sion,** *n.* —**ex·clu'sive,** *adj.*

ex·cô'rï·āte'', *v.t.,* **-ated, -ating.** denounce bitterly. —**ex·co''ri·a'tion,** *n.*

ex'crė·mėnt, *n.* excreted matter.

ex·crēs'cence, *n.* abnormal outgrowth.

ex·crēte', *v.t.,* **-creted, -creting.** eliminate as waste from the body. —**ex·cre'tion,** *n.* —**ex'cre·to''ry,** *adj.*

ex·crü'cï·āt''ïng, *adj.* racking.

ex'cŭl·pāte'', *v.t.,* **-pated, -pating.** prove guiltless. —**ex''cul·pa'tion,** *n.*

ex·cûr'sion, *n.* short pleasure journey. —**ex·cur'sion·ist,** *n.*

ex·cūse', *v.t.,* **cused, -cusing,** *n. v.t.* **1.** remove or mitigate the blame of or for. **2.** forgive. **3.** permit to leave. —*n.* **4.** something that excuses. —**ex·cus'a·ble,** *adj.* —**ex·cus'a·bly,** *adv.*

ex'ė·crāte'', *v.t.,* **-crated, -crating. 1.** denounce. **2.** detest. —**ex'e·cra·ble,** *adj.*

ex'ė·cūte'', *v.t.,* **-cuted, -cuting. 1.** perform. **2.** kill after condemnation. —**ex''e·cu'tion,** *n.* —**ex''e·cu'tion·er,** *n.*

ex·ĕc'ū·tĭve, *adj.* **1.** concerned with administration of laws, policies, etc. —*n.* **2.** person in an executive capacity.

ex·ĕc'ū·tör, *n.* person who administers a will. Also, *fem.,* **ex·ec'u·trix.**

ex·ĕm'plâ·rÿ, *adj.* serving as a good example.

ex·ĕm'plĭ·fÿ'', *v.t.,* **-fied, -fying.** be an example of. —**ex·em''pli·fi·ca'tion,** *n.*

ex·ĕmpt', *v.t., adj.* free from an obligation. —**ex·emp'tion,** *n.*

ex'êr·cīse'', *n., v.,* **-cised, -cising.** *n.* **1.** activity developing skill, knowledge, strength, etc. **2.** performance. **3.** exercises, ceremony. —*v.t.* **4.** cause to do exercises. **5.** put into effect.

ex·êrt', *v.t.* put into action. —**ex·er'tion,** *n.*

ex·hāle', *v.,* **-haled, -haling.** *v.t., v.i.* breathe out. —**ex''ha·la'tion,** *n.*

ex·haust', *v.t.* **1.** empty; deplete. **2.** tire thoroughly. —*n.* **3.** waste gas, etc. from machinery. —**ex·haus'tion,** *n.*

ex·haus'tive, *adj.* omitting nothing.

ex·hĭb'ĭt, *v.t., n.* display. —**ex''hi·bi'tion,** *n.* —**ex·hib'i·tor,** *n.*

ex''hĭ·bĭ'tion·ism, *n.* ostentation; self-display. —**ex''hi·bi'tion·ist,** *n.*

ex·hĭl'à·rāte'', *v.t.,* **-rated, -rating. 1.** fill with delight. **2.** stimulate. —**ex·hil''a·ra'tion,** *n.*

ex·hôrt', *v.t.* urge strongly. —**ex''hor·ta'tion,** *n.*

ex·hūme', *v.t.,* **-humed, -huming.** dig up after burial. —**ex''hu·ma'tion,** *n.*

ex'ĭ·gėn·cÿ, *n., pl.* **-cies.** urgency. —**ex'i·gent,** *adj.*

ex'īle, *v.t.,* **-iled, -iling.** *n. v.t.* **1.** banish from a country. —*n.* **2.** state of banishment. **3.** exiled person.

ex·ĭst', *v.i.* **1.** have being. **2.** be alive. —**ex·ist'ence,** *n.* —**ex·ist'ent,** *adj.*

ex'ĭt, *n.* **1.** departure. **2.** means of departure.

ex ôf·fĭ'cĭ·o, by virtue of his or her office.

ex·ŏn'êr·āte'', *v.t.,* **-ated, -ating.** declare guiltless. —**ex·on''er·a'tion,** *n.*

ex·ôr'bĭ·tànt, *adj.* beyond reason or moderation. —**ex·or'bi·tance,** *n.*

ex'ôr·cīze'', *v.t.,* **-cized, -cizing.** expel with incantations. —**ex'or·cism,** *n.*

ex·ŏt'ĭc, *adj.* markedly foreign.

ex·pănd', *v.t., v.i.* widen. —**ex·pan'sion,** *n.* —**ex·pan'sive,** *adj.*

ex·pănse', *n.* broad, unbroken area.

ex·pā'tĭ·āte'', *v.i.,* **ated, -ating.** talk or write at length.

ex·pā'trĭ·āte, *n.* person living outside his country.

ex·pĕct', *v.t.* **1.** regard as going to happen. **2.** regard as obligatory. —**ex''pec·ta'tion, ex·pect'an·cy,** *n.* —**ex·pec'tant,** *adj.*

ex·pĕc'tô·rāte'', *v.t., v.i.* **-rated, -rating.** spit.

ex·pe'di·ent, *adj*. **1.** useful on a given occasion. **2.** determined by self-interest alone. —*n*. **3.** something expedient. —ex·pe'di·en·cy, *n*.

ĕx'pe·dīte'', *v.t.*, -dited, -diting. **1.** make faster or easier. **2.** do quickly.

ĕx''pe·dĭ'tion, *n*. journey for exploration or invasion. —ex''pe·di'tion·ar'' y, *adj*.

ĕx''pe·dĭ'tious, *adj*. prompt.

ex·pĕl', *v.t.*, -pelled, -pelling. **1.** oust. **2.** emit.

ex·pĕnd', *v.t.* **1.** spend. **2.** use up. —ex·pend'i·ture, *n*.

ex·pĕnd'a·ble, *adj*. able or intended to be sacrificed, as in war.

ex·pĕnse', *n*. **1.** act or instance of spending. **2.** cost.

ex·pĕn'sĭve, *adj*. high in price.

ex·pĕr'ĭ·ence, *n., v.t.*, -enced, -encing. *n*. **1.** something lived through. **2.** knowledge from life, work, etc. —*v.t.* **3.** have experience of.

ex·pĕr'ĭ·ment, *n*. **1.** test establishing facts. —*v.i.* **2.** engage in experiments. —ex·per''i·men·ta'tion, *n*. —ex·per''i·men'tal, *adj*.

ĕx'pêrt, *n*. **1.** person with specialized knowledge or skill. —*adj*. **2.** pertaining to such persons. —ex'pert·ly, *adv*. —ex''per·tise', ex'pert·ness, *n*.

ĕx'pĭ·āte'', *v.t.*, -ated, -ating. atone for. —ex''pi·a'tion, *n*. —ex'pi·a·to''ry, *adj*.

ex·pīre', *v.i.*, -pired, -piring. **1.** die. **2.** cease to be in effect. **3.** breathe out. —ex''pi·ra'tion, *n*.

ex·plāin', *v.t.* **1.** make understandable or meaningful. **2.** account for. —ex''pla·na'tion, *n*. —ex·plan'a·to''ry, *adj*.

ĕx'ple·tĭve, *n*. exclamation.

ĕx'plĭ·ca·ble, *adj*. able to be explained.

ex·plĭc'ĭt, *adj*. **1.** clear. **2.** outspoken.

ex·plōde', *v.*, -ploded, -ploding. *v.i.* **1.** burst from internal pressure. —ex·plo'sive, *adj., n*. —ex·plo'sion, *n*.

ĕx'ploĭt, *n*. **1.** daring deed. —*v.t.* (ex ploit') **2.** take advantage of. —ex''ploi·ta'tion, *n*. —ex·ploit'a·tive, *adj*.

ex·plōre', *v.*, -plored, -ploring. *v.t., v.i.* investigate thoroughly. —ex·plor'er, *n*. —ex''plo·ra'tion, *n*. —ex·plor'a·to''ry, *adj*.

ĕx·pō'nent, *n*. **1.** expounder of a principle. **2.** *Math.* number indicating how many times a quantity is to be multiplied by itself.

ex·pôrt', *v.t.* **1.** ship out of the country. —*n*. (eks'port) **2.** something exported.

ex·pōse', *v.t.*, -posed, -posing. **1.** reveal. **2.** make vulnerable. —ex·pos'ure, *n*.

ĕx''pō·sĭ'tion, *n*. **1.** event presenting manufactures, processes, etc. to the public. **2.** explanation.

ĕx pōst fāctō, retroactive; retroactively.

ēx·pŏs'tū·lāte'', *v.i.*, -lated, -lating. argue in objection. —ex·pos''tu·la'tion, *n*.

ex·pŏūnd', *v.t.* state or explain.

ex·prĕss', *v.t.* **1.** communicate adequately. **2.** squeeze. —*adj*. **3.** precise; definite. —*n*. **4.** vehicle on a fast, direct schedule. **5.** agency for sending things. —ex·press'ive, *adj*.

ex·prĕs'sion, *n*. **1.** means of expressing. **2.** facial attitude. **3.** revelation of feeling.

ex·prō'prĭ·āte'', *v.t.*, -ated, -ating. seize for public use.

ex·pŭl'sion, *n*. act or instance of being expelled.

ex·pŭnge', *v.t.*, -punged, -punging. erase.

ĕx'pûr·gāte'', *v.t.*, -gated, -gating. censor.

ĕx'quĭ·sīte, *adj*. of extreme refinement.

ex·tant', *adj*. alive; present.

ex·tĕm''pō·rā'nē·oŭs, *adj*. without prior preparation.

ex·tĕnd', *v.t.* **1.** stretch or expand. **2.** offer. —*v.i.* **3.** be extended. —ex·ten'sion, *n*.

ex·tĕn'sĭve, *adj*. large in extent or scope.

ĕx·tĕnt', *n*. amount or degree of extending.

ex·tĕn'ū·āte'', *v.t.*, -ated, -ating. prompt leniency for.

ex·tē'rĭ·ör, *adj*. **1.** outer or outward. —*n*. **2.** outside.

ex·têr'mĭ·nāte'', *v.t.*, -nated, -nating. destroy wholly. —ex·ter''mi·na'tion, *n*. —ex·ter'mi·na''tor, *n*.

ex·têr'nal, *adj*. exterior; outward.

ex·tĭnct', *adj*. no longer in existence.

ex·tĭnc'tion, *n*. dying-out or destruction.

ex·tĭn'guĭsh, *v.t.* put out of existence, as a flame.

ĕx'tĭr·pāte'', *v.t.*, -pated, -pating. uproot; exterminate.

ex·tōl′, *v.t.*, -tolled, -tolling. praise highly.

ex·tôrt′, *v.t.* obtain by threats or force. —ex·tor′tion, *n.* —ex·tor′tion·ist, *n.* —ex·tor′tion·ate, *adj.*

ex′trȧ, *adj.* additional.

ex·tract′, *v.t.* 1. draw out. —*n.* (ek′strakt) 2. something extracted. —ex·trac′tion, *n.*

ex′trȧ·dīte″, *v.t.*, -dited, -diting. surrender for prosecution to a foreign country. —ex′tra·di″tion, *n.*

ex·trā′nē·oŭs, *adj.* 1. from outside. 2. irrelevant.

ex·traôr′dĭ·nār″ÿ, *adj.* 1. remarkable. 2. out of the ordinary.

ex·trăv′ȧ·gȧnt, *adj.* beyond economy, reason, etc. —ex·trav′a·gance, *n.*

ex·trēme′, *adj.* 1. farthest. 2. ultimate. 3. immoderate. —*n.* 4. farthest point, position, etc. —ex·treme′ly, *adv.*

ex·trĕm′ĭ·tÿ, *n., pl.* -ties. *n.* 1. something extreme. 2. end. 3. extremities, hands and feet.

ex′trĭ·cāte″, *v.t.*, -cated, -cating. free.

ex′trō·vêrt″, *n.* person oriented toward the outside world. —ex″tro·ver′sion, *n.*

ex·ū′bêr·ȧnt, *adj.* full of health and spirits. —ex·u′ber·ance, *n.*

ex·ūde′, *v.*, -uded, -uding. *v.t., v.i.* 1. pass through the pores. 2. seem to radiate. —ex·u·da′tion, *n.*

ex·ŭlt′, *v.i.* rejoice. —ex″ul·ta′tion, *n.*

eȳe, *n.* 1. organ of sight. 2. eyelike opening. 3. visual sensitivity. —eye′brow″, *n.* —eye′ball″, *n.* —eye′lid″, *n.* —eye′sight″, *n.*

eȳe′lăsh″, *n.* row of stiff hairs over the eye.

eȳe′sôre″, *n.* unpleasant sight.

F

F, f., *n.* 1. sixth letter of the English alphabet. 2. failing grade.

fā′ble, *n.* 1. moralizing story. 2. legend.

făb′rĭc, *n.* cloth.

făb′rĭ·cāte, *v.t.*, -cated, -cating. 1. assemble. 2. invent for deception. —fab″ri·ca′tion, *n.*

făb′ū·loŭs, *adj.* wonderful.

fȧ·cäde (fa sahd′), *n.* 1. decorative building front. 2. false appearance. Also, fȧ·çade′.

fāce, *n., v.*, faced, facing. *n.* 1. front of the human head. 2. main surface. 3. outer appearance. —*v.t.* 4. confront. —*v.i.* 5. look or be turned toward. —fa′cial, *adj.*

făc′ĕt, *n.* 1. plane surface of a gem, etc. 2. aspect.

fȧ·cē′tioŭs, *adj.* joking; impish; frivolous.

făc′ile, *adj.* revealing no effort.

fȧ·cĭl′ĭ·tāte″, *v.t.*, -tated, -tating. make easy.

fȧ·cĭl′ĭ·tÿ, *n., pl.* -ties. 1. ease. 2. skill. 3. facilities, equipment, staff, etc.

făc·sĭm′ĭ·lē, *n.* copy; reproduction.

făct, *n.* objective truth. —fac′tu·al, *adj.*

făc′tion, *n.* group promoting its own interests. —fac′tion·al, *adj.*

făc′tör, *n.* 1. influential thing. 2. quantity multiplied by another.

făc′tö·rÿ, *n., pl.* -ries. place of manufacture.

făc·tō′tŭm, *n.* person who does odd jobs.

făc′ŭl·tÿ, *n., pl.* -ties. 1. aptitude or ability. 2. teaching staff.

făd, *n.* brief fashion or whim.

fāde, *v.*, faded, fading. *v.i.* 1. lose color or freshness. 2. disappear slowly.

făg, *v.t.*, fagged, fagging. tire.

Fähr′ĕn·heīt″, *adj.* pertaining to a temperature scale with the freezing point of water at 32 degrees and the boiling point at 212 degrees.

fāil, *v.t.* 1. attempt without success. 2. not to do. 3. disappoint. —*v.i.* 4. have no success. 5. die away. —fail′ing, *n.* —fail′ure, *n.*

fāint, *adj.* 1. weak. —*n.* 2. temporary loss of consciousness. —*v.i.* 3. go into a faint. —faint′ly, *adv.* —faint′ness, *n.*

fāir, *adj.* 1. honest; just. 2. beautiful or handsome. 3. light. 4. mediocre. 5. sunny. 6. gathering for sales or display. —fair′ly *adv.*

fāir′ÿ, *n., pl.* -ies. creature with magic powers.

fāith, *n.* 1. belief; confidence. 2. loyalty. 3. religion. —faith′ful, *adj.* —faith′less, *adj.*

fāke, *adj., n., v.t.*, faked, faking. *adj.* 1.

false. —*n*. **2.** something false. —*v.t.* **3.** give a false appearance of. —**fak′er,** *n*.

făl′cŏn, *n*. small hawk.

făll, *v.i.,* **fell, fallen, falling,** *n. v.i.* **1.** descend without support. —*n*. **2.** act or instance of falling. **3.** autumn.

făl′là·cў, *n., pl.* **-cies.** instance of false reasoning. —**fal·la′cious,** *adj*.

făl′lĭ·ble, *adj*. capable of mistakes. —**fal′′li·bil′i·ty,** *n*.

făl′lōw, *adj*. unplanted.

fălse, *adj., falser,* **falsest. 1.** not true. **2.** untruthful or unfaithful. —**false′ly,** *adv.* —**false′hood′′,** *n*. —**fal′si·fy′′,** *v.t.* —**fal′si·ty,** *n*.

făl·sĕt′tō, *n., pl.* **-tos.** artificially high voice.

făl′têr, *v.i.* act, speak, etc. hesitantly or unsteadily.

fāme, *n*. widespread reputation. —**fa′mous, famed,** *adj*.

fà·mĭl′iàr, *adj*. **1.** well known. **2.** well acquainted. —**fa·mil′iar·ly,** *adv.* —**fa·mil′′i·ar′i·ty,** *n*. —**fa·mil′iar·ize′′,** *v.t.*

făm′ĭ·lў, *n., pl.* **-lies. 1.** group of relatives. **2.** group of related things. —**fa·mil′ial,** *adj*.

făm′ĭne, *n*. severe food shortage.

făm′ĭsh, *v.t.* starve.

făn, *n., v.t.,* **fanned, fanning.** *n*. **1.** device for moving air. **2.** *Informal.* devotee. —*v.t.* **3.** cool or move with a fan.

fà·năt′ĭc, *n*. irrational enthusiast or hater. —**fa·nat′i·cal,** *adj.* —**fa·nat′i·cism,** *n*.

făn′cĭ·êr, *n*. breeder of animals or plants.

făn′cў, *adj.,* **-cier, -ciest,** *n., v.t.,* **-cied, -cying.** *adj*. **1.** elaborate. —*n*. **2.** imagination. **3.** liking. —*v.t.* **4.** take a liking to. —**fan′ci·ful,** *adj.* —**fan′ci·ly,** *adv*.

făn′fāre′, *n*. **1.** introductory call of trumpets, etc. **2.** publicity.

făng, *n*. long, pointed tooth.

făn·tăs′tĭc, *adj*. odd and extravagant.

făn′tà·sў, *n., pl.* **-sies. 1.** imagination. **2.** something imagined.

fär, *adj., adv.,* **farther, farthest.** at or to a great distance.

fârce, *n*. ridiculous comedy. —**far′ci·cal,** *adj*.

fāre, *n., v.i.,* **fared, faring.** *n*. **1.** money paid to travel. **2.** food. —*v.i.* **3.** prosper or succeed.

fāre·wĕll′, *interj., n., adj*. good-bye.

fâr′-fĕtched′, *adj*. implausible.

fârm, *n*. **1.** place for raising plants or animals. —*v.t.* **2.** cultivate. —**farm′er,** *n*. —**farm′hand′′,** *n*. —**farm′house′′,** *n*. —**farm′yard′′,** *n*.

fâr′-ŏff′, *adj*. remote.

fâr′-rēach′ing, *adj*. with extensive effects.

fâr′sīght′′ĕd, *adj*. **1.** provident. **2.** seeing distant objects better than close ones.

făs′cĭ·nāte′′, *v.t.,* **-nated, -nating.** hold the entire attention of. —**fas′′ci·na′tion,** *n*.

Făs′cĭsm, *n*. authoritarian, militaristic system of government. —**Fas′cist,** *n., adj.* —**Fas·cis′tic,** *adj*.

făsh′iŏn, *n*. **1.** manner of acting. **2.** prevailing style. —*v.t.* **2.** make. —**fash′ion·a·ble,** *adj*.

făst, *adj*. **1.** speedy. **2.** firm; fixed. —*adv.* **3.** firmly. —*v.i.* **4.** abstain from food or drink. *n.* **5.** act or instance of fasting.

făst′ĕn, *v.t.* attach; make secure. —**fas′ten·er,** *n*. —**fast′en·ing,** *n*.

făs·tĭd′i·oŭs, *adj*. not readily pleased. —**fas·tid′i·ous·ly,** *adv*.

făt, *adj., fatter,* **fattest,** *n. adj*. **1.** having much fat. —*n*. **2.** greasy material. —**fat′ness,** *n*. —**fat′ty,** *adj*.

fā′tàl, *adj*. causing death or destruction. —**fa′tal·ly,** *adv*.

fā′tàl·ĭsm, *n*. **1.** belief in fate. **2.** resignation. —**fa′tal·ist,** *n*. —**fa′′tal·is′tic,** *adj.* —**fa′′tal·is·ti·cal·ly,** *adv*.

fà·tăl′ĭ·tў, *n., pl.* **-ties. 1.** deadliness. **2.** death by accident.

fāte, *n*. **1.** power determining events. **2.** death.

fä′thêr, *n*. **1.** male parent. **2.** founder or originator. **3.** Christian priest. —**fa′ther·hood′′,** *n*. —**fa′ther·ly,** *adj*.

fä′thêr-ĭn-lāw′, *n., pl.* **fathers-in-law.** father of a spouse.

făth′ŏm, *n*. **1.** *Nautical.* unit of 6 linear feet. —*v.t.* **2.** probe to understand.

fà·tïgue′, *n., v.t.,* **-tigued, -tiguing.** *n*. **1.** weariness. **2.** **fatigues,** military work clothes. —*v.t.* **3.** tire thoroughly.

făt′tĕn, *v.t.* **1.** make fat. —*v.i.* **2.** become fat.

făt′tў, *adj*. containing fat.

făt′ū·oŭs, *adj*. foolishly self-satisfied. —**fa·tu′i·tў,** *n*.

105 fete

fau'cet, *n.* valve for running water; tap.

fault, *n.* defect. —fault'y, *adj.*

fau'na, *n. pl.* animals.

faux pas (fō'pah'), *n., pl.* faux pas. social mistake.

fa'vör, *n.* 1. act of kindness. 2. approval. —*v.t.* 3. do a favor for. 4. treat as a favorite. 5. advocate or support. —fa'vor·a·ble, *adj.* —fa'vor·ite, *adj., n.*

fa'vör·ĭt·ĭsm, *n.* preferential treatment for favorites.

fawn, *v.i.* 1. show servility. —*n.* 2. young deer.

faze, *v.t.*, fazed, fazing. daunt.

fear, *n.* 1. desire to escape danger. 2. awe. —*v.t.* 3. have fear of. 4. believe with regret. —fear'ful, *adj.* —fear'less, *adj.*

fea'sĭ·ble, *adj.* able to be done; practical. —fea''si·bil'i·ty, *n.*

feast, *n.* 1. religious festival. 2. lavish meal. —*v.i.* 3. have a feast.

feat, *n.* act of skill or daring.

feath'êr, *n.* part of a bird's covering. —feath'er·y, *adj.*

fea'tûre, *n., v.t.*, -tured, turing. *n.* 1. distinct aspect. 2. features, face. —*v.t.* 4. present as a feature.

Fĕb'rū·âr''ÿ, *n.* second month.

fe'cēs, *n., pl.* solid excrement. —fe'cal, *adj.*

fĕck'lĕss, *adj.* 1. ineffectual. 2. irresponsible.

fe'cŭnd, *adj.* fertile. —fe·cun'di·ty, *n.*

fĕd'êr·àl, *adj.* 1. composed of federated states. 2. pertaining to a federation.

fĕd''êr·ā'tion, *n.* union of states or organizations under a central government or authority.

fee, *n.* charge for services.

fee'ble, *adj.*, -bler, -blest. without energy or force. —fee'bly, *adv.* —fee'ble·ness, *n.*

feed, *v.*, fed, feeding, *n., v.t.*, 1. nourish with food. —*v.i.* 2. eat. —*n.* 3. animal food.

feed'băck'', *n.* 1. noise caused by a microphone picking up its own amplified signal. 2. reactions to an idea or course of action.

feel, *v.*, felt, feeling. *n. v.t.* 1. sense by touch. 2. be aware of. 3. believe. —*v.i.* 4. be sensed as specified. —*n.* 5. feeling; sensation. —feel'ing, *n.*

feign (fān), *v.t.* pretend.

feint (fānt), *n.* 1. false attack made as a diversion. —*v.i.* 2. make a feint.

fè·lĭc'ĭ·tāte'', *v.t.*, -tated, -tating. congratulate. —fe·lic''i·ta'tion, *n.*

fè·lĭc'ĭ·toŭs, *adj.* appropriate. —fe·lic'i·tous·ly, *adv.*

fè·lĭc'ĭ·tÿ, *n., pl.* -ties. happiness.

fē'līne, *adj.* pertaining to the cat family.

fĕll, *v.t.* cause to fall.

fĕl'lōw, *n.* 1. man. 2. companion. —fel'low·ship'', *n.*

fĕl'ŏn, *n.* committer of a major crime. —fel'on·y, *n.* —fe·lo'ni·ous, *adj.*

fĕlt, *n.* fabric of compacted wool, etc.

fē'māle, *adj.* 1. pertaining to the sex bearing offspring. —*n.* 2. someone or something female.

fĕm'ĭ·nĭne, *adj.* characteristic of girls and women. —fem''i·nin'i·ty, *n.*

fĕnce, *n., v.*, fenced, fencing. *n.* 1. light barrier. —*v.i.* 2. fight with thrusting swords.

fĕnd, *v.t.* drive or ward.

fĕnd'êr, *n.* cover for a wheel on a vehicle.

fêr·mĕnt', *v.t.* 1. break down, as through bacterial action. —*v.i.* 2. be broken down, as an organic substance. —*n.* (fer'ment) 3. anticipatory excitement. —fer''men·ta'tion, *n.*

fêrn, *n.* fronded plant reproduced by spores.

fè·rō'cioŭs, *adj.* savage. —fe·ro'cious·ly, *adv.* —fe·roc'i·ty, *n.*

fĕr'rĕt, *n.* 1. weasellike animal. —*v.i.* 2. hunt; search.

fĕr'roŭs, *adj.* pertaining to iron. Also, fer'ric.

fĕr'rÿ, *n., pl.* -ries, *v.t.*, -ried, -rying. *n.* 1. Also, fer'ry·boat'', boat on a shuttle service. 2. service running such a boat. —*v.t.* 3. transport by or as by a ferry.

fêr'tĭle, *adj.* yielding offspring, crops, etc. —fer·til'i·ty, *n.* —fer'til·ize'', *v.t.*

fêr'vĕnt, *adj.* passionate. Also, fer'vid. —fer'vent·ly, *adv.* —fer'ven·cy, fer'vor, *n.*

fĕs'tĭ·vàl, *n.* occasion of celebration or merrymaking. —fes'tive, *adj.* —fes·tiv'i·ty, *n.*

fĕs·tōōn', *n.* 1. decorative hanging suspended between two supports. —*v.t.* 2. drape.

fĕtch, *v.t.* 1. get. 2. summon.

fete (fāt), *n., v.t.*, feted, feting. *n.* 1. fes-

fetid

106

tive entertainment. —*v.t.* **2.** honor with a fete. Also, **fête.**

fet′id, *adj.* evil-smelling.

fet′ish, *n.* subject of obsessive concern.

fet′ter, *n., v.t.* shackle or chain.

fet′tle, *n.* **in fine fettle,** in excellent state.

fe′tus, *n., pl.* **-tuses,** unborn young in its later state. —**fe′tal,** *adj.*

feud, *n.* murderous rivalry between families.

feu′dal·ism, *n.* system of serfs and overlords. —**feu′dal,** *adj.*

fe′ver, *n.* excess of body temperature. —**fe′ver·ish,** *adj.*

fe′ver blis′ter, *n.* a cold sore.

few, *adj., pron., n.* some but not many.

fi·an·cé (fē″ahn sā′), *n.* man engaged to be married. Also, *fem.,* **fi″an·cée′.**

fi·as′co, *n., pl.* **-coes, -cos.** ridiculous failure.

fi′at, *n.* decree.

fi′ber, *n.* long thin piece of material. Also, **fi′bre.**

fick′le, *adj.* capricious and untrustworthy.

fic′tion, *n.* **1.** not factually true. **2.** novels, etc. —**fic′tion·al,** *adj.*

fic·ti′tious, *adj.* not factually true.

fid′dle, *n., v.i.,* **-dled, -dling.** *n.* **1.** violin. —*v.i.* **2.** play a fiddle. **3.** fumble. —**fid′dler,** *n.*

fi·del′i·ty, *n.* faithfulness.

fid′get, *v.i.* move or fumble nervously. —*n.* **2.** nervous state. —**fid′get·y,** *adj.*

fi·du′ci·ar′y, *adj., n., pl.* **-ies.** *adj.* **1.** pertaining to a trust. —*n.* **2.** trustee.

field, *n.* **1.** area of open land. **2.** area of work or knowledge.

fiend, *n.* **1.** evil spirit. **2.** vicious person. —**fiend′ish,** *adj.*

fierce, *adj.,* **fiercer, fiercest. 1.** savage. **2.** violent. —**fierce′ly,** *adv.*

fier′y, *adj.,* **-ier, -iest. 1.** covered or filled with fire. **2.** passionate.

fi·es′ta, *n.* festival in a Spanish-speaking region.

fife, *n.* small flute.

fif·teen′, *n.* ten plus five. —**fif′teenth′,** *adj.*

fifth, *adj.* **1.** following the fourth. —*n.* **2.** fifth thing, person, or part.

fif′ty, *n., adj.* five times ten. —**fif′ti·eth,** *adj.*

fig, *n.* small sweet tree fruit.

fight, *n., v.,* **fought, fighting.** *n.* **1.** dispute or competition with violence. **2.** angry argument. —*v.t.* **3.** make a fight against. —*v.i.* **4.** engage in a fight.

fig′ment, *n.* something merely imaginary.

fig′u·ra·tive, *adj.* using or forming a figure of speech.

fig′ure, *n., v.t.,* **-ured, -uring.** *n.* **1.** shape. **2.** numeral. **3.** sum. —*v.t., v.i.* **4.** calculate.

figure of speech, word or idiom not to be taken literally or in the usual way.

fil′a·ment, *n.* narrow thread or wire.

fil′bert, *n.* hazelnut.

filch, *v.t.* steal.

file, *n., v.t.,* **-filed, -filing.** *n.* **1.** group of documents. **2.** tool for rubbing. **3.** front-to-rear row. —*v.t.* **4.** preserve in a file. **5.** rub with a file.

fil′i·al, *adj.* pertaining to or appropriate in a son or daughter.

fil′i·bus″ter, *n.* meaningless speech hindering legislation.

fil′i·gree″, *n.* lace-like gold or silver wirework.

fill, *v.t.* **1.** cause to be completely occupied. **2.** satisfy the requirements of. —*v.i.* **3.** become full. —*n.* **4.** enough to fill.

fil·let (fil ā′), *n.* boneless lean cut of meat or fish.

fil′lip, *n.* stimulus.

film, *n.* **1.** thin coating. **2.** strip or sheet for registering photographic images. —*v.t.* **3.** make a motion picture or photograph of.

fil′ter, *n.* **1.** something screening out unwanted things. —*v.t., v.i.* **2.** pass through a filter. —*v.t.* **3.** exclude with a filter.

filth, *n.* foul matter. —**filth′y,** *adj.*

fin, *n.* bladelike extension.

fi′nal, *adj.* at the end. —**fi′nal·ly,** *adv.* —**fi·nal′i·ty,** *n.*

fi·na′le, *n.* concluding feature.

fi′nal·ist, *n.* competitor in a final contest.

fi·nance (fi năns′, fī′năns), *n., v.t.,* **-nanced, -nancing.** *n.* **1.** management of money. **2. finances,** resources of money. —*v.t.* **3.** lend or obtain money for. —**fi·nan′cial,** *adj.* —**fi″nan·cier′,** *n.*

find, *v.t.,* **found, finding,** *n. v.t.* **1.** come

upon by chance. **2.** succeed in a search for. —*n.* **3.** valuable discovery. —**find'er**, *n.* —**find'ing**, *n.*

fīne, *adj.*, **finer**, **finest**, *n.*, *v.t.*, **fined**, **fining**. *adj.* **1.** in tiny pieces. **2.** excellent. —*n.* **3.** money penalty. —*v.t.* **4.** impose a fine on. —**fine'ly**, *adv.* —**fine'ness**, *n.*

fīn'êr·ỹ, *n.* fine costume.

fĭ'nĕsse', *n.* skill, esp. in human relations.

fīne'-tūne', *v.* to make minor adjustments.

fĭn'gêr, *n.* extension of the hand.

fĭn'ĭck·ỹ, *adj.* too particular or demanding. Also, **fin'i·cal**, **fin'ick·ing**.

fĭ'nĭs, *n.*, *pl.* **-nises**. end; finish.

fĭn'ĭsh, *v.t.* **1.** bring to an end. **2.** give a desired surface to. —*v.i.* **3.** end an activity.

fī'nīte, *adj.* not endless.

fîr, *n.* cone-bearing evergreen tree.

fīre, *n.*, *v.* **fired**, **firing**. *n.* **1.** burning. **2.** deep feeling. **3.** discharge of guns. —*v.t.* **4.** set fire to. **5.** discharge, as of a gun. —**fire'proof''**, *adj.*

fīre'ârm'', *n.* weapon operated by explosives.

fīre'crăck''êr, *n.* a firework.

fīre'măn, *n.* **1.** person who extinguishes fires. **2.** person who tends fires.

fīre'trăp'', *n.* building dangerous in fires.

fīre'wörks'', *n.*, *pl.* explosive and burning devices used in celebrations.

fîrm, *adj.* **1.** unyielding. **2.** steady. —*n.* **3.** business organization. —**firm'ly**, *adv.* **firm'ness**, *n.*

fîr'må·mênt, *n.* heavens.

fîrst, *adj.*, *adv.* **1.** at the very front or beginning. **2.** before all others. —*n.* **3.** first person or thing.

fîrst'-hănd', *adj.*, *adv.* without intermediaries.

fĭs'căl, *adj.* pertaining to income and expense; financial.

fĭsh, *n.*, *pl.* **fish**, *v.i.* **1.** cold-blooded water animal, breathing with gills. —*v.i.* **2.** attempt to catch fish. —**fish'er·man**, *n.*

fĭs'sion, *n.* splitting; cleaving. —**fis'sion·a·ble**, *adj.*

fĭs'sûre, *n.* crack.

fĭst, *n.* ball of the hand and fingers for striking.

fĭt, *v.*, **fitted**, **fitting**, *adj.*, **fitter**, **fittest**, *n.* *v.i.* **1.** be suitable, esp. in size. —*v.t.* **2.** be suitable for. **3.** cause to be suitable. —*adj.* **4.** suitable. **5.** healthy. —*n.* **6.** manner of fitting. **7.** bodily seizure.

fĭt'fŭl, *adj.* intermittent; spasmodic. —**fit'ful·ly**, *adv.* —**fit'ful·ness**, *n.*

fĭt'tĭng, *adj.* suitable.

fīve, *adj.*, *n.* four plus one.

fĭx, *v.t.*, **fixed**, **fixing**. **1.** repair or adjust. **2.** prepare. **3.** establish firmly. —**fix'i·ty**, *n.*

fĭx·ā'tion, *n.* psychological obsession.

fĭx'tûre, *n.* attached piece of equipment.

fĭzz, *v.i.*, **fizzed**, **fizzing**, *n. v.i.* **1.** emit a buzzing bubbling sound. —*n.* **2.** such a sound.

fĭz'zle, *v.i.*, **-zled**, **-zling**, *n. v.i.* **1.** fail. —*n.* **2.** failure.

flăb'bỹ, *adj.*, **-bier**, **-biest**. fat, soft, and weak.

flăc'cĭd, *adj.* flabby.

flăg, *n.*, *v.*, **flagged**, **flagging**. *n.* **1.** emblem-bearing cloth. **2.** Also, **flag'stone''**, flat paving stone. —*v.t.* **3.** signal with a flag.

flā'grant, *adj.* outrageously evident. —**fla'grant·ly**, *adv.* —**fla'gran·cy**, *n.*

flāil, *n.* **1.** hand-held threshing device. —*v.t.* **2.** beat or move in a flaillike manner.

flāir, *n.* shrewd perceptiveness or talent.

flāke, *n.*, *v.*, **flaked**, **flaking**. *n.* **1.** thin piece. —*v.i.* **2.** fall off in flakes.

flăm·boy'ànt, *adj.* brashly ostentatious. —**flam·boy'ance**, *n.*

flāme, *n.*, *v.*, **flamed**, **flaming**. *n.* burning gas. —*v.i.* **2.** be burned with flames.

flå·mĭn'gō, *n.*, *pl.* **-gos**. pink tropical wading bird.

flăm'må·ble, *adj.* burnable.

flănge, *n.* perpendicular edge.

flănk, *n.* **1.** side. —*v.t.* **2.** be beside. **3.** attack or get around the flank of.

flăn'nĕl, *n.* loosely woven wool or cotton.

flăp, *n.*, *v.*, **-flapped**, **flapping**. *n.* **1.** hinged panel. **2.** sound of flapping. —*v.t.*, *v.i.* **3.** move to and fro.

flāre, *v.i.*, **flared**, **flaring**, *n. v.i.* **1.** blaze. **2.** curve outward. —*n.* **3.** torchlike signal.

flăsh, *n.* **1.** momentary bright light. **2.**

moment. —*v.i.* **3.** emit a flash. —*v.t.* **4.** cause to flash.

flăsh'līght'', *n.* hand-held battery-operated light.

flăsh'ÿ, *adj.*, **-ier, -iest.** showy. —**flash'i·ness**, *n.*

flăsk, *n.* bottle, often flat.

flăt, *adj.*, **flatter, flattest,** *n. adj.* **1.** without rises or hollows. **2.** absolute. **3.** featureless. **4.** *Music.* slightly low in pitch. —*n.* **5.** apartment. **6.** something flat. —**flat'ly**, *adv.* —**flat'ten**, *v.t., v.i.*

flăt'têr, *v.t.* compliment, as in order to wheedle. —**flat'ter·y**, *n.*

flaŭnt, *v.t.* display proudly.

flā'vòr, *n.* **1.** taste. **2.** Also, **fla'vor·ing**, something giving a certain taste. —*v.t.* **3.** add a flavor to.

flăw, *n.* shortcoming; fault. —**flaw'less**, *adj.*

flăx, *n.* threadlike plant fiber for linen.

flēa, *n.* bloodsucking. wingless jumping insect.

flĕck, *n.* spot or flake.

flĕdg'lĭng, *n.* beginner at a profession, etc.

flēe, *v.*, **fled, fleeing.** *v.t., v.i.* escape; run.

flēece, *n.* **1.** covering of a sheep, etc. —*v.t.* **2.** cheat. —**fleec'y**, *adj.*

flēet, *n.* **1.** ships under one command. —*adj.* **2.** swift.

flēet'ĭng, *adj.* passing quickly.

flĕsh, *n.* **1.** muscle tissue. **2.** soft part of a plant. **3.** animal meat. —**flesh'y**, *adj.*

flĕx, *v.t., v.i.* bend. —**flex'i·ble**, *adj.*

flĕx'tīme, flex'i·time, *n.* system in which work hours are flexible.

flĭck, *n.* **1.** quick, light motion. —*v.t.* **2.** throw, etc. with such a motion.

flĭck'êr, *v.i.* have a wavering light or appearance.

flī'êr, *n.* **1.** aviator. **2.** advertising paper.

flīght, *n.* **1.** act or instance of flying or fleeing. **2.** stair between floors.

flīght'ÿ, *adj.*, **-ier, -iest.** overly emotional or whimsical. —**flight'i·ness**, *n.*

flĭm'sÿ, *adj.*, **-ier, -iest.** readily torn or broken. —**flim'si·ly**, *adv.*

flĭnch, *v.i.* hold back or retreat, as from a blow.

flĭng, *v.t.*, **flung, flinging**, *n. v.t.* **1.** hurl. —*n.* **2.** act or instance of flinging. **3.** brief indulgence.

flĭnt, *n.* spark-producing gray siliceous rock. —**flint'y**, *adj.*

flĭp, *v.t.*, **flipped, flipping**, *n. v.t.* **1.** toss jerkily. —*n.* **2.** act or instance of flipping.

flĭp'pànt, *adj.* cheerfully disrespectful. —**flip'pan·cy**, *n.*

flĭp'pêr, *n.* flat limb for paddling.

flĭrt, *v.i.* **1.** make mild erotic advances. **2.** consider something unseriously. —**flir·ta'tion**, *n.* —**flir·ta'tious**, *adj.*

flĭt, *v.i.*, **flitted, flitting.** move quickly and lightly.

flōat, *v.i.* **1.** be carried on water, etc. —*n.* **2.** something that floats.

flŏck, *n.* **1.** group of sheep, etc. —*v.i.* **2.** join in a flock.

flŏg, *v.t.*, **flogged, flogging.** whip.

flood, *n.* **1.** overflow, as of a river. —*v.t., v.i.* **2.** fill to excess.

flood'līght'', *n.* lamp casting a directed light.

flŏor, *n.* **1.** supporting interior surface. **2.** bottom surface. **3.** right to speak. —*v.t.* **4.** supply with a floor. —**floor'ing**, *n.*

flŏor ĕx'êr·cīse', *n.* tumbling maneuvers performed on a mat in a competitive gymnastics event.

flŏp, *v.*, **flopped, flopping**, *n. v.t., v.i.* **1.** overturn heavily. —*v.i.* **2.** move clumsily. **3.** *Informal.* fail. —*n.* **4.** act or instance of flopping.

flō'rà, *n. pl.* plants.

flō'ràl, *adj.* pertaining to flowers.

flôr'ĭd, *adj.* **1.** ruddy. **2.** gaudy.

flō'rĭst, *n.* flower merchant.

flŏss, *n.* soft down or twisted thread. —**flos'sy**, *adj.*

flō·tĭl'là, *n.* small fleet.

floŭnce, *v.i.*, **flounced, flouncing**, *n. v.i.* **1.** move quickly and jerkily. —*n.* **2.** act or instance of flouncing.

floŭn'dêr, *n.* **1.** edible flat fish. —*v.i.* **2.** struggle.

floŭr, *n.* powdered grain, etc.

floŭr'ĭsh, *v.i.* **1.** thrive. —*v.t.* **2.** wave.

flōw, *v.i.* **1.** move steadily, as a liquid. —*n.* **2.** act or instance of flowing.

flōw'êr, *n.* **1.** petaled seed-producing part of a plant; blossom. —*v.i.* **2.** produce blossoms. —**flow'er·y**, *adj.*

flū, *n.* influenza.

flŭc'tū·āte'', *v.i.*, **-ated, -ating.** change

rate or quantity irregularly. —**fluc"tu·a'tion,** *n.*

flūe, *n.* passage for smoke, etc.

flū'ĕnt, *adj.* speaking or writing readily. —**flu'en·cy,** *n.*

flŭff, *n.* soft fibrous material. —**fluf'fy,** *adj.*

flū'ĭd, *adj.* **1.** flowing. —*n.* **2.** liquid or gas.

flūke, *n.* **1.** barb. **2.** stroke of luck.

flūme, *n.* chute carrying water.

flŭnk, *v.t., v.i. Informal.* fail at school.

flûr'rў, *n., pl.* **-ries.** brief spells of activity, weather, etc.

flŭsh, *v.t.* **1.** wash out. **2.** frighten from cover. —*v.i.* **3.** be flushed. **4.** blush. —*n.* **5.** act or instance of flushing. —*adj.* **6.** even. **7.** wealthy.

flŭs'têr, *v.t.* confuse.

flūte, *n.* **1.** high-pitched wind instrument. **2.** Also **flut'ing,** longitudinal concavity. —**flut'ist,** *n.*

flŭt'têr, *v.t., v.i.* **1.** oscillate rapidly. —*n.* **2.** excited state. —**flut'ter·y,** *adj.*

flŭx, *n.* **1.** fluid state. **2.** substance aiding metal fusion.

flȳ, *v.,* **flew, flown, flying,** *n., pl.* **flies.** *v.i.* **1.** move in the air. **2.** go quickly. —*v.t.* **3.** cause to move in the air. **4.** flee from. —*n.* **5.** two-winged insect.

flȳing cŏlŏrs, great success.

flȳ'whēel", *n.* heavy wheel regulating a machine by inertia.

fōam, *n.* **1.** fine bubbles. —*v.i.* **2.** emit or break into foam. —**foam'y,** *adj.*

fō'cūs, *n., pl.* **-cuses, -ci,** *v.,* **-cused, -cusing.** *n.* **1.** point of concentration. **2.** state of sharpness or clarity. —*v.t.* **3.** bring into focus.

fŏd'dêr, *n.* food for horses, cows, etc.

fōe, *n.* enemy.

foe'tūs, *n.* fetus.

fŏg, *n., v.,* **fogged, fogging.** *n.* **1.** water vapor obscuring vision. —*v.t., v.i.* **2.** obscure with fog. —**fog'gy,** *adj.*

fō'gȳ, *n., pl.* **-gies.** reactionary. Also, **fo'gey.**

foi'ble, *n.* weakness.

foĭl, *v.t.* **1.** frustrate. —*n.* **2.** thin metal sheeting. **3.** pointed sword. **4.** contrasting feature.

fōist, *v.t.* get accepted by trickery.

fōld, *v.t., v.i.* **1.** double over. **2.** wrap. —*n.* **3.** folded place.

fōld'êr, *n.* **1.** bent sheet for holding papers. **2.** folded, unbound pamphlet.

fōl'ĭ·age, *n.* leaves.

fōlk, *n.* **1.** folks, **a.** people. **b.** relatives. —*adj.* **2.** pertaining to ethnic groups. —**folk'lore",** *n.*

fōlk'sȳ, *adj.,* **-sier, -siest.** *Informal.* characteristic of ordinary people.

fŏl'lōw, *v.t.* **1.** go after or along. **2.** happen after. **3.** conform to. **4.** learn from or understand. —*v.i.* **5.** go or happen after. **6.** be logically deductible.

fŏl'lōw·êr, *n.* disciple or adherent.

fŏl'lōw·ĭng, *adj.* **1.** happening afterwards. —*prep.* **2.** after. —*n.* **3.** group of followers.

fŏl'lȳ, *n., pl.* **-lies.** mad or foolish thing or disposition.

fō·mĕnt', *v.t.* incite, as trouble.

fŏnd, *adj.* full of affection. —**fond'ly,** *adv.* —**fond'ness,** *n.*

fŏn'dle, *v.t.,* **-dled, -dling.** handle fondly.

fŏnt, *n.* baptismal basin.

fōod, *n.* material that nourishes. —**food'stuff",** *n.*

fōol, *n.* **1.** person of bad judgment. —*v.t.* **2.** deceive. —*v.i.* **3.** act like a fool. —**fool'ish,** *adj.*

fōol'hârd"ȳ, *adj.,* **-dier, -diest.** unwisely audacious.

fōol'prōof", *adj.* proof against failure.

fōot, *n.* **1.** extremity of a leg. **2.** lowermost feature; bottom; pedestal. **3.** unit of 12 inches. —**foot'hold",** *n.* —**foot'step",** *n.*

fōot'băll", *n.* **1.** game with a kicked ball. **2.** ball used.

fōot'ĭng, *n.* **1.** support for a foot. **2.** basis.

fōot'prĭnt, *n.* **1.** mark left by a foot. **2.** area required for an office machine.

fŏp, *n.* foolish or vain person. —**fop'pish,** *adj.*

fôr, *prep.* **1.** in favor of. **2.** in place of. **3.** in order to reach, etc. **4.** to be used, etc. by. **5.** during. **6.** obtaining in exchange. **7.** considering the nature of. —*conj.* **8.** because.

fôr'age, *v.i.,* **-aged, -aging,** search, as for food.

fôr'āy, *n.* plundering expedition.

fôr·bear', *v.,* **-bore, -borne, -bearing.** *v.t.* **1.** refrain. —*v.i.* **2.** control oneself. —**for·bear'ance,** *n.*

fôr·bĭd′, *v.t.*, -bade or -bad, -bidden, -bidding. **1.** give an order against. **2.** prevent.

fôr·bĭd′dĭng, *adj.* formidable or unapproachable.

fôrce, *n.*, *v.t.*, forced, forcing. *n.* **1.** agency influencing events. **2.** power. **3.** compulsion. **4.** organization or group. —*v.t.* **5.** compel. —force′ful, *adj.* —for′ci·ble, *adj.*

fôrd, *n.* **1.** wadeable part of a stream. —*v.t.* **2.** wade across.

fôre, *adj.*, *adv.* **1.** forward. —*n.* **2.** front.

fôre′ârm, *n.* **1.** arm between the elbow and wrist. —*v.t.* (fore arm′) **2.** arm in advance.

fôre′beār″, *n.* ancestor.

fôre·bōd′ĭng, *n.* premonition.

fôre′căst″, *v.t.*, -cast or -casted, -casting, *n.* *v.t.* **1.** predict. —*n.* **2.** prediction.

fôre·căs·tle (fōk′səl), *n.* upper forward part of a ship.

fôre·clōse′, *v.t.*, -closed, -closing. deprive a mortgagor of the right of redeeming. —fore·clos′ure, *n.*

fôre′fä″thêr, *n.* ancestor.

fôre′fĭn″gêr, *n.* finger nearest the thumb.

fôre′frŏnt″, *n.* extreme forward position.

fôre·găth′êr, *v.i.* come together.

fôre·gō″ĭng, *adj.* preceding.

fôre·gŏne′, *adj.* **1.** determined in advance. **2.** previous.

fôre′grŏund″, *n.* area nearest the viewer.

fôre′hĕad, *n.* front of the head between the eyebrows and hair.

fôr′eĭgn, *adj.* **1.** belonging to an area outside the country. **2.** not belonging where found. —for′eign·er, *n.*

fôre′măn, *n.* supervising worker.

fôre′mōst″, *adj.*, *adv.* first.

fôre′nōon″, *n.* morning after sunrise.

fó·rĕn′sĭc, *adj.* pertaining to legal proceedings or public debate.

fôre″ôr·dāin′, *v.t.*, predestine. —fore·or″di·na′tion, *n.*

fôre′rŭn″nêr, *n.* predecessor.

fôre·sēe′, *v.t.*, -saw, -seen, -seeing. anticipate. —fore·see′a·ble, *adj.* —fore′sight″, *n.*

fôre·shăd′ōw, *v.t.* hint in advance.

fôr′ĕst, *n.* area of trees. —for″es·ta′tion, *n.* —for′est·ry, *n.*

fôre·ställ′, *v.t.* prevent by early action.

fôre·tĕll′, *v.t.*, -told, -telling. predict.

fôre′thŏught″, *n.* planning, etc. in advance.

fôr·ĕv′êr, *adj.* **1.** eternally. **2.** ceaselessly.

fôre·wärn′, *v.t.* warn beforehand.

fôre′wôrd″, *n.* book introduction.

fôr′feĭt, *v.t.* **1.** have taken away because of a misdeed, etc. —*n.* **2.** something forfeited. —*adj.* **3.** forfeited. —for′fei·ture, *n.*

fôrge, *n.*, *v.*, forged, forging. *n.* **1.** place for hammering hot metal. —*v.t.* **2.** shape or assemble by hammering. **3.** counterfeit. —*v.i.* **4.** move against obstacles. —forg′er, *n.* —forg′er·y, *n.*

fôr·gĕt′, *v.t.*, -got, -gotten, -getting. **1.** lose the memory of. **2.** ignore. —for·get′ful, *adj.*

fôr·gĭve′, *v.t.*, -gave, -given, -giving. regard without ill will despite an offense. —for·giv′a·ble, *adj.* —for·giv′ing·ly, *adv.*

fôr·gō′, *v.t.*, -went, -gone, -going. do without.

fôrk, *n.* **1.** pronged lifting instrument. **2.** division into two branches from one. —*v.i.* **3.** divide into two branches.

fôr·lôrn′, *adj.* forsaken. —for·lorn′ly, *adv.*

fôrm, *n.* **1.** outline or contour. **2.** basic organizing principle. **3.** information blank. —*v.t.* **4.** give form to. **5.** develop. —for·ma′tion, *n.* —form′a·tive, *adj.*

fôr′măl, *adj.* **1.** emphasizing rules or customs. **2.** explicit. **3.** correct in manner. —for′mal·ly, *adv.* —for·mal′i·ty, *n.*

fôr′măt, *n.* basic design or plan.

fôr′mêr, *adj.* **1.** past. **2.** being the first of two mentioned. —for′mer·ly, *adv.*

fôr′mĭ·dà·ble, *adj.* **1.** awe-inspiring. **2.** difficult.

fôr′mū·là, *n.*, *pl.* -las, lae. **1.** rule to be followed. **2.** words to be uttered. **3.** ingredients to be used. —for·mu·late″, *v.t.*

fôr′nĭ·cāte″, *v.i.*, -cated, -cating. have illicit sexual intercourse. —for″ni·ca′tion, *n.* —for′ni·ca″tor, *n.*

fôr·sāke', *v.t.*, **-sook, -saken, -saking.** 1. desert. 2. give up.

fôrt, *n.* 1. strongly fortified place. 2. army post.

fôr'te (fôr'tā), *adj.*, *adv. Music.* loud; loudly.

fôrte, *n.* special ability.

fôrth, *adv.* 1. forward. 2. outward.

fôrth'cŏm''ĭng, *adj.* soon to appear.

fôrth'rīght'', *adj.* frank.

fôrth''wĭth', *adj.* without delay.

fôr'tĭ·fȳ'', *v.t.*, **-fied, -fying.** 1. make resistant to attack. 2. strengthen. **—for''ti·fi·ca'tion**, *n.*

fôr·tĭs'sĭ·mō'', *adj.*, *adv. Music.* with extreme loudness.

fôr'tĭ·tūde'', *n.* persistent courage.

fôrt'nīght'', *n.* two-week period. **—fort'night''ly**, *adj.*, *adv.*

fôr'trĕss, *n.* large fort.

fôr·tū'ĭ·toŭs, *adj.* happening by chance.

fôr'tù·nàte, *adj.* lucky. **—for'tu·nate·ly**, *adv.*

fôr'tūne, *n.* 1. luck. 2. riches.

fôr'tȳ, *adj.*, *n.* four times ten. **—for'ti·eth**, *adj.*

fô'rŭm, *n.* place for or occasion of public discussion.

fôr'wàrd, *adv.* 1. Also, **for'wards**, to the front. **—*adj.*** 2. at the front. 3. presumptuous.

fŏs'sĭl, *n.* hardened or petrified plant or animal. **—fos'sil·ize''**, *v.t.*

fŏs'têr, *v.t.* 1. raise, as young. 2. promote. **—*adj.*** 3. in a family relationship of adoption rather than blood.

foŭl, *adj.* 1. dirty. 2. disgusting. 3. unethical. **—*v.t.*** 4. make foul. 5. obstruct or tangle. **—*n.*** 6. illicit act. **—foul'ly**, *adv.* **—foul'ness**, *n.*

foŭnd, *v.t.* establish.

foŭnd'êr, *v.i.* 1. sink. 2. break down. **—*n.*** 3. person who founds.

foŭnd'lĭng, *n.* child abandoned by unknown parents.

foŭn'drȳ, *n.*, *pl.* **-dries.** place for casting metal.

foŭn'taĭn, *n.* source of flowing water.

fôur, *adj.*, *n.* three plus one. **—fourth**, *adj.*, *n.*

fôur·tēen', *adj.*, *n.* ten plus four.

foŭl, *n.*, *pl.* **fowl.** 1. any bird. 2. domestic bird eaten as food.

fŏx, *n.* 1. small canine predatory animal. **—*v.t.*** 2. cheat; trick.

fŏx'ȳ, *adj.* cunning.

fŏy'êr, *n.* lobby, esp. of a theater.

frā'càs, *n.* brawl.

frăc'tion, *n.* portion. **—frac'tion·al**, *adj.*

frăc'tioŭs, *adj.* rebellious.

frăc'tûre, *n.*, *v.t.*, *v.i.*, **-tured, -turing.** break.

frăg'īle, *adj.* readily broken. **—fra·gil'i·ty**, *n.*

frăg'mĕnt, *n.* 1. broken or torn-away piece. **—*v.t.*, *v.i.*** 2. break into pieces. **—frag'men·tar'y**, *adj.*

frā'grànt, *adj.* sweet-smelling. **—fra'grance**, *n.*

fraĭl, *adj.* 1. fragile. 2. weak, physically or morally. **—frail'ty**, *n.*

frāme, *n.*, *v.t.*, **framed, framing.** *n.* 1. open structure. 2. border. **—*v.t.*** 3. make a frame for. 4. put into words or concepts. **—frame'work''**, *n.*

frănc, *n.* currency unit in French-speaking countries.

frăn'chīse, *n.* 1. right to vote. 2. right to do business.

frănk, *adj.* 1. not deceitful or evasive. **—*n.*** 2. right to mail without postage. **—frank'ly**, *adv.* **—frank'ness**, *n.*

frănk'fûrt·êr, *n.* wiener.

frăn'tĭc, *adj.* wild with emotion. **—fran'ti·cal·ly**, *adv.*

frà·têr'nàl, *adj.* brotherly.

frà·têr'nĭ·tȳ, *n.*, *pl.* **-ties.** male social organization.

frăt'êr·nīze'', *v.i.*, **-ized, -izing.** be in friendly association.

fraŭd, *n.* 1. deceit for gain. 2. impostor. **—fraud'u·lent**, *adj.* **—fraud'u·lent·ly**, *adv.* **—fraud'u·lence**, *n.*

fraŭght, *adj.* filled, as with some quality.

frāy, *v.t.*, *v.i.* 1. wear thin. **—*n.*** 2. fight.

frăz'zle, *v.t.*, *v.i.*, **-zled, -zling.** *n. Informal.* fatigue.

frēak, *n.* oddity, esp. of nature.

frĕck'le, *n.* brownish skin spot.

frēe, *adj.*, **freer, freest**, *adv.*, *v.t.*, **freed, freeing.** *adj.* 1. not bound or controlled. 2. without charge. 3. without obstructions. **—*adv.*** 4. without charge. **—*v.t.*** 5. make free. **—free'ly**, *adv.* **—free'dom**, *n.*

frēe'hănd'', *adj.*, *adv.* without rulers, compasses, etc.

frēe'lănce'', *n.*, *v.i.*, **-lanced.** *n.* 1. person paid by the assignment. —*v.i.* **2.** work as a freelancer.

free'think''er, *n.* person without standard religious beliefs.

freeze, *v.,* **froze, frozen, freezing,** *n.* *v.t., v.i.* **1.** harden from cold. —*v.i.* **2.** suspend all visible motion. —*n.* **3.** suspension of change.

freight (frāt), *n.* **1.** merchandise, etc. in transit. —*v.t.* **2.** load with freight.

freight'er, *n.* freight ship.

French horn, coiled wind instrument with a flaring bell.

frè·nèt'ic, *adj.* frantic.

frĕn'zÿ, *n., pl.* **-zies.** wild excitement. —**fren'zied,** *adj.*

frē'quèn·cÿ, *n., pl.* **-cies.** number of occurrences in a given period.

frē'quènt, *adj.* **1.** occurring often. —*v.t.* **2.** be often present at. —**fre'quent·ly,** *adv.*

fresh, *adj.* **1.** in good, new condition. **2.** rested and energetic. **3.** inexperienced. —**fresh'ly,** *adv.* —**fresh'ness,** *n.* —**fresh'en,** *v.t., v.i.*

fresh'et, *n.* flooded stream.

fresh'man, *n.* person in his first year, esp. in school or Congress.

fret, *v.,* **fretted, fretting,** *n. v.i.* **1.** be anxious. —*v.t.* **2.** fray or gnaw. —*n.* **3.** state of anxiety. **4.** repeated geometrical design. —**fret'ful,** *adj.* —**fret'work'',** *n.*

Freud'i·àn, *adj.* **1.** pertaining to the theories of Sigmund Freud. —*n.* **2.** follower of Freud.

frī'à·ble, *adj.* readily crumbled.

frī'àr, *n.* monk.

fric'às·see'', *n., v.t.,* **-seed, -seeing.** *n.* **1.** cut and stewed meat. —*v.t.* **2.** make a fricassee of.

fric'tion, *n.* **1.** rubbing. **2.** resistance to sliding. **3.** conflict; antagonism. —**fric'tion·al,** *adj.*

Frī'dāy, *n.* sixth day.

friĕnd, *n.* **1.** person who likes or is helpful to one. **2.** supporter or sympathizer. —**friend'less,** *adj.* —**friend'ly,** *adj.* —**friend'ship,** *n.*

frieze, *n.* horizontal decorative band.

frig'àte, *n.* **1.** sailing warship with one gun deck. **2.** medium-sized modern warship.

fright, *n.* sudden fear. —**fright'en,** *v.t.* —**fright'ful,** *adj.*

frig'id, *adj.* **1.** cold. **2.** sexually unresponsive. —**fri·gid'i·ty,** *n.*

frill, *n.* **1.** minor ornament. **2.** something unnecessary. —**fril'ly,** *adj.*

fringe, *n., v.t.,* **fringed, fringing.** *n.* **1.** border. **2.** edging or parallel loose strands. —*v.t.* **3.** supply or constitute a fringe for.

frisk, *v.i.* **1.** gambol; frolic. —**frisk'y,** *adj.*

frit'ter, *v.t.* **1.** waste gradually. —*n.* **2.** fried cake.

friv'o·loŭs, *adj.* without proper seriousness. —**friv'o·lous·ly,** *adv.* —**fri·vol'i·ty,** *n.*

frō, *adv.* **to and fro,** away and back again.

frŏck, *n.* robe; dress.

frŏg, *n.* leaping amphibian.

frŏl'ĭc, *v.i.,* **-icked, -icking,** *n. v.i.* **1.** romp. **2.** make merry. —*n.* **3.** occasion of frolicking. —**frol'ick·er,** *n.* —**frol'ic·some,** *adj.*

frŏm, *prep.* **1.** beginning or originating at. **2.** with no opportunity or use of. **3.** as unlike. **4.** because of.

frŏnd, *n.* branchlike leaf.

frŏnt, *n.* **1.** foremost part or surface. **2.** vertical side. **3.** pretense; mask. **4.** forward battle area. —*v.i.* **5.** face. —**front'age,** *n.* —**front'al,** *adj.*

frŏn·tiēr', *n.* outer limit. —**fron''tiers'man,** *n.*

frŏn'tĭs·piēce'', *n.* illustration beginning a book.

frŏst, *n.* **1.** frozen vapor. **2.** freezing temperature. —*v.t.* **3.** cover with frost. **4.** cover with frosting. —**frost'y,** *adj.*

frŏst'bīte'', *n.* injury to the body from freezing.

frŏst'ĭng, *n.* sweetened coating for a cake; icing.

frŏth, *n., v.i.* foam. —**froth'y,** *adj.*

frō'wàrd, *adj.* willful.

frown, *n.* **1.** expression of displeasure. —*v.i.* **2.** assume such an expression. **3.** look with disapproval.

frū'gàl, *adj.* **1.** thrifty. **2.** meager. —**fru'gal·ly,** *adv.* —**fru·gal'i·ty,** *n.*

frūit, *n.* **1.** juicy, seedbearing growth. **2.** reward of endeavor. —**fruit'ful,** *adj.* —**fru·i'tion,** *n.* —**fruit'less,** *adj.*

frŭmp, *n.* dowdy woman. —**frump'ish, frump'y,** *adj.*

frŭs'trāte'', *v.t.,* **-trated, -trating.** prevent from succeeding. —**frus·tra'tion,** *n*.

frŭs'tŭm, *n*. lower part of a severed cone.

frȳ, *v.t*. cook in grease, over direct heat. —**fry'er,** *n*.

fūch·siȧ (fyōō'shə), *n*. shrub with pink-to-purple flowers.

fŭd'dle, *v.t., -dled, -dling*. stupefy, as with liquor.

fŭdge, *n*. **1.** soft candy made of butter, milk, sugar and flavoring. —*v.i*. **2.** cheat.

fū'ėl, *n., v., -eled* or *-elled, -eling* or *-elling*. *n*. **1.** substance for burning. —*v.t*. **2.** supply with fuel. —*v.i*. **3.** take on fuel.

fū'gĭ·tĭve, *n*. **1.** person who flees. —*adj*. **2.** fleeing. **3.** transitory.

fŭl'crŭm, *n*. support for a lever.

fŭl''fĭll', *v.t., -filled, -filling*. **1.** satisfy. **2.** accomplish. —**ful·fill'ment, ful·fil' ment,** *n*.

fŭll, *adj*. **1.** completely occupied. **2.** complete. **3.** broad or ample. —*adv*. **4.** completely. **5.** directly. —**ful'ly,** *adv*. —**full'ness, ful'ness,** *n*.

fŭll'-scāle', *adj*. unreduced.

fŭl'sȯme, *adj*. annoyingly excessive.

fŭm'ble, *v., -bled, -bling, n. v.i*. **1.** grope. —*v.t*. **2.** handle clumsily. —*n*. **3.** act or instance of fumbling.

fūme, *n., v., fumed, fuming. n*. **1.** odor, smoke, etc. —*v.t*. **2.** treat with fumes. —*v.i*. **3.** show petulance. **4.** give off fumes.

fūm'ĭ·gāte'', *v.t., -gated, -gating*. expose to fumes, as to kill vermin. —**fum''i·ga'tion,** *n*.

fŭn, *n*. **1.** enjoyment. **2.** source of enjoyment.

fŭnc'tion, *n*. **1.** purpose. **2.** ceremony. —*v.i*. **3.** operate; work. —**func'tion·al,** *adj*.

fŭnc'tion·ār''ȳ, *n., pl. -ries*. official.

fŭnd, *n*. **1.** money for a purpose. **2. funds,** ready money. —*v.t*. **3.** supply money.

fŭn''dȧ·mĕn'tȧl, *adj*. **1.** basic; essential. —*n*. **2.** something fundamental. —**fun''da·men'tal·ly,** *adv*.

fŭn''dȧ·mĕn'tȧl·ĭsm, *n*. literal belief in a sacred text. Also, **Fun''da·men'tal· ism.** —**fun''da·men'tal·ist,** *n., adj*.

fū'nêr·ȧl, *n*. ceremony of farewell to the dead.

fū·ne'rē·ȧl, *adj*. mournful; solemn.

fŭn'gŭs, *n., pl. -gi* or *-guses*. spore-reproduced plant without chlorophyll. —**fun'gous,** *adj*.

fŭn'nėl, *n*. **1.** tapered channel used to help pouring. **2.** smokestack.

fŭn'nȳ, *adj., -nier, -niest,* **1.** comical. **2.** peculiar.

fûr, *n*. thick animal hair with its hide. —**fur'ry,** *adj*.

fū'rĭ·oŭs, *adj*. **1.** wildly angry. **2.** wild. —**fu'ri·ous·ly,** *adv*.

fûrl, *v.t*. bundle up.

fûr'lŏng, *n*. eighth of a mile.

fûr'lōugh, *n*. **1.** military leave of absence. —*v.t*. **2.** grant a furlough to.

fûr'nȧce, *n*. heating chamber.

fûr'nĭsh, *v.t*. **1.** supply. **2.** put furniture in.

fûr'nĭsh·ĭngs, *n. pl*. **1.** furniture and decorative objects. **2.** minor clothing, etc.

fûr'nĭ·tûre, *n*. tables, chairs, etc.

fū'rôr, *n*. frenzied excitement.

fûr'rĭ·ėr, *n*. dealer in furs.

fûr'rōw, *n*. **1.** groove or wrinkle. —*v.t*. **2.** make furrows in.

fûr'thêr, *adv*. **1.** to a greater distance or extent. **2.** in addition. —*adj*. **3.** additional. **4.** farther. —*v.t*. **5.** promote. —**fur'ther·ance,** *n*.

fûr'thêr·môre'', *adv*. in addition.

fûr'thėst, *adj*. **1.** most distant. —*adv*. **2.** to the greatest distance or extent.

fûr'tĭve, *adj*. sneaking. —**fur'tive·ly,** *adv*.

fū'rȳ, *n., pl. -ries*. **1.** extreme rage. **2.** violence.

fūse, *n., v.t., fused, fusing. n*. **1.** Also, **fuze,** detonating device. **2.** device of fusible metal for preventing electrical overloads. —*v.t., v.i*. **3.** melt. —**fu'si· ble,** *adj*. —**fu'sion,** *n*.

fū'sĭl·lāde'', *n*. discharge of massed guns.

fŭss, *n*. **1.** unreasonable show of concern. —*v.i*. **2.** make a fuss. —**fus'sy,** *adj*.

fū'tĭle, *adj*. vain; useless. —**fu·til'i·ty,** *n*.

fū'tûre, *n*. **1.** time to come. **2.** what will happen. **3.** promise of success.

fŭzz, *n*. fine hair or fibers. —**fuz'zy,** *adj*.

G

G, g, *n.* seventh letter of the English alphabet.

găb, *v.i.*, gabbed, gabbing, *n.* chatter.

găb′ble, *v.*, -bled, -bling, *v.i.*, *v.t.*, *n.* babble.

gā′ble, *n.* wall area perpendicular to a roof ridge.

gădg′ĕt, *n.* mechanical contrivance. —gadg′et·ry, *n.*

găff, *n.* **1.** spar for the head of a fore-and-aft sail. **2.** hook for landing fish.

găffe, *n.* social blunder.

găg, *n.*, *v.*, gagged, gagging. *n.* **1.** device to prevent speech by stopping the mouth. **2.** joke. —*v.t.* **3.** silence with a gag. —*v.i.* **4.** retch.

gāi′e·tў, *n.*, *pl.* -ties. **1.** quality of being gay. **2.** merrymaking.

gāi′lў, *adv.* in a gay manner.

gāin, *v.t.* **1.** acquire. **2.** reach. —*v.i.* **3.** profit. —*n.* **4.** profit. —gain′ful, *adj.*

gāin″sāy′, *v.t.*, -said, -saying. **1.** deny. **2.** contract.

gāit, *n.* manner of walking or running.

gā′là, *adj.* **1.** festive. —*n.* **2.** celebration.

gā′lăx·ў, *n.*, *pl.* -ies. vast cluster of stars. —ga·lac′tic, *adj.*

gāle, *n.* high wind.

gäll, *n.* **1.** liquid secreted by the liver. **2.** *Informal.* impudence.

găl′lànt, *adj.* **1.** brave; high-spirited. **2.** polite to women. —gal′lant·ry, *n.*

găl′lêr·ў, *n.*, *pl.* -ies. **1.** covered passage. **2.** uppermost theater balcony. **3.** place for the display of art.

găl′lēy, *n.*, *pl.* -leys. **1.** rowed ship. **2.** ship's kitchen.

găl′lòn, *n.* liquid measure of 4 quarts or 128 fluid ounces.

găl′lòp, *n.* **1.** fastest gait of a horse. —*v.i.* **2.** move at a gallop.

găl′lōws, *n.*, *pl.* -lowses, -lows. frame for hanging condemned persons.

gäll′stōne″, *n.* stony mass in the gall bladder.

gà·lōre′, *adv.* in abundance.

gà·lŏsh′, *n.* rubber or rubberized boot.

găl·văn′ĭc, *adj.* pertaining to electric currents, esp. from batteries.

găl′và·nīze″, *v.t.*, -nized, -nizing. **1.** apply electricity to. **2.** plate with zinc. **3.** stimulate.

găm′bĭt, *n.* opening in chess involving a sacrifice.

găm′ble, *v.*, -bled, -bling, *n.* *v.i.* **1.** stake money on the outcome of a game, race, etc. —*v.t.* **2.** stake by gambling. —*n.* **3.** risky undertaking. —gam′bler, *n.*

găm′bòl, *v.i.*, -boled or -bolled, -boling or -bolling, *n.* romp.

gāme, *n.*, *adj.*, gamed, gaming. *n.* **1.** contest decided by skill or chance. **2.** hunted animals or birds. —*adj.* **3.** *Informal.* willing to meet a challenge.

gāme′cŏck″, *n.* rooster used in cockfights.

găm′ŭt, *n.* **1.** musical scale. **2.** complete range.

găn′dêr, *n.* male goose.

găng, *n.* group of workers, criminals, etc. acting or associating together.

găn′glĭng, *adj.* awkwardly tall. Also, gan′gly.

găn′glĭ·òn, *n.*, *pl.* -a, -ons. mass of nerve cells.

găn′grēne, *n.* decay of body tissue deprived of blood. —gan′gre·nous, *adj.*

găng′stêr, *n.* member of a criminal gang.

găng′wāy″, *n.* **1.** entrance to a ship. —*interj.* **2.** clear the way!

găp, *n.* opening; hiatus.

gāpe, *v.i.*, gaped, gaping. **1.** open the mouth wide. **2.** stare with stupefied astonishment. **3.** open wide.

gà·räge′, *n.* place for keeping automobiles.

gârb, *n.* clothing.

gâr′bàge, *n.* food refuse, etc.

gâr′ble, *v.t.*, -bled, -bling. confuse.

gâr′dèn, *n.* **1.** area for growing plants. —*v.i.* **2.** work in a garden. —gar′den·er, *n.*

gâr·dē′nĭ·à, *n.* white fragrant flower.

gâr·găn′tū·àn, *adj.* gigantic.

gâr′gle, *v.i.*, -gled, -gling. rinse the throat with liquid and air bubbles.

gâr′goÿle, *n.* grotesque, carved waterspout.

gâr′ĭsh, *adj.* vulgarly showy.

gâr′lànd, *n.* wreath.

gâr′lĭc, *n.* strong-flavored material from a plant bulb.

gâr′mènt, *n.* article of clothing.

gâr′nèt, *n.* deep-red gemstone.

gâr′nĭsh, *v.t.* **1.** decorate. —*n.* **2.** decoration.

gâr″nĭsh·ēe′, *v.t.*, -eed, -eeing. *Law.* attach (money or property) to settle a bad debt.

gâr′rĕt, *n.* attic.

găr′rĭ·sŏn, *n.* **1.** resident body of troops. —*v.t.* **2.** station as a defensive force.

gâr·rŏte′, *n.*, *v.t.*, **-roted, -roting.** *n.* **1.** device for strangling. —*v.t.* **2.** kill with a garrote.

gâr′rŭ·loŭs, *adj.* talkative. —**gar·ru′li·ty**, *n.*

gâr′tēr, *n.* band for holding up a stocking.

găs, *n.*, *v.t.*, **gassed, gassing.** *n.* **1.** expansive fluid. **2.** *Informal.* gasoline. —*v.t.* **3.** injure or kill with a gas. —**gas′e·ous**, *adj.* —**gas′sy**, *adj.*

găsh, *n.* **1.** long, deep cut. —*v.t.* **2.** make a gash in.

găs′kĕt, *n.* seal against leakage.

găs′ŏ·hŏl, *n.* a mixture of gasoline and alcohol.

găs′ŏ·līne″, *n.* engine fuel derived from petroleum.

găsp, *v.i.* **1.** sudden, short breath. —*n.* **2.** act or instance of gasping.

găs′trĭc, *adj.* pertaining to the stomach.

găs·trŏn′ŏ·mỹ, *n.* cooking as an art. —**gas″tro·nom′ic, gas″tro·nom′i·cal**, *adj.*

gāte, *n.* **1.** open-air door. **2.** Also **gate′way″**, structure holding such a door.

găth′ĕr, *v.t.* **1.** bring together. **2.** infer. —*v.i.* **3.** come together. **4.** increase. —**gath′er·ing**, *n.*

gauche (gōsh), *adj.* socially awkward.

gaŭd′ỹ, *adj.*, **-ier, -iest.** bright and showy. —**gaud′i·ly**, *adv.*

gāuge, *n.*, *v.t.*, **gauged, gauging.** *n.* **1.** measuring instrument. **2.** standard measure. —*v.t.* **3.** measure. **4.** estimate the amount of. Also, **gage.**

gāunt, *adj.* lean; bony.

gāunt′lĕt, *n.* **1.** glove with a flaring cuff. **2.** hazardous passage.

gāuze, *n.* loosely woven cloth. —**gauz′y**, *adj.*

găv′ĕl, *n.* hammerlike noisemaker.

gāwk, *v.i.* stare stupidly.

gāwk′ỹ, *adj.*, **-ier, -iest.** ungainly.

gāy, *adj.* **1.** cheerful. —*n.*, *adj.* **2.** homosexual. —**gay″e·ty, gai″e·ty**, *n.* —**gay″ly**, *adv.*

gāze, *v.i.*, **gazed, gazing.** look steadily.

gȧ·zĕtte′, *n.* published official record.

găz″ĕt·tēer′, *n.* geographical reference work.

gēar, *n.* **1.** Also, **gear′wheel″**, toothed machine wheel. **2.** mechanical assembly. **3.** equipment. —*v.t.* **4.** furnish with gears or a gear.

gee (jē), *interj.* exclamation of surprise.

gĕl′ȧ·tĭn, *n.* jellylike substance from bones or various vegetable substance. Also, **gel′a·tine.** —**ge·lat′i·nous**, *adj.*

gĕld, *v.t.*, **gelded, gelding.** castrate.

gĕl′ĭd, *adj.* icy.

gĕm, *n.* jewel. Also, **gem′stone″.**

gĕn′dêr, *n.* classification into masculine, feminine, and neuter.

gēne, *n.* entity by which hereditary characteristics are transmitted.

gē″nē·ăl′ŏ·gỹ, *n.*, *pl.* **-gies.** study of ancestry. —**ge″ne·a·log′i·cal**, *adj.* —**ge″ne·al′o·gist**, *n.*

gĕn′êr·ăl, *adj.* **1.** pertaining to a whole group. **2.** unspecific. **3.** common. —*n.* **4.** military officer ranking above a colonel. —**gen′er·al·ly**, *adv.*

gĕn′êr·ăl′ĭ·tỹ, *n.*, *pl.* **-ties.** statement supposed to be generally true.

gĕn′êr·ăl·īze″, *v.i.*, **-ized, -izing.** infer or speak in generalities. —**gen″er·al·i·za′tion**, *n.*

gĕn′êr·āte″, *v.t.*, **-ated, -ating.** bring into being. —**gen′er·a·tive**, *adj.*

gĕn′êr·ā′tion, *n.* **1.** group of persons of about the same age. **2.** period of about 30 years. **3.** production, esp. of electricity.

gĕn′êr·ā′tör, *n.* machine for producing electricity.

gė·nêr′ĭc, *adj.* pertaining to a group. —**ge·ner′i·cal·ly**, *adv.*

gĕn′êr·oŭs, *adj.* **1.** giving freely. **2.** ample. —**gen′er·ous·ly**, *adv.* —**gen″er·os′i·ty**, *n.*

gė·nĕt′ĭcs, *n.* study of heredity. —**ge·net′i·cal·ly**, *adv.* —**ge·net′ic**, *adj.* —**ge·net′i·cist**, *n.*

gē′nĭ·ăl, *adj.* warmly outgoing. —**ge″ni·al′i·ty**, *n.*

gĕn′ĭ·tăls, *n.*, *pl.* sexual organs. Also, **gen″i·ta′li·a.** —**gen′i·tal**, *adj.*

gēn′iŭs, *n.* **1.** presiding spirit. **2.** great mental power. **3.** person with such powers.

gĕn′ŏ·cīde″, *n.* willful killing of a whole race or nation

gĕn·tēel', *adj.* overrefined. —gen·til'ity, *n.*

gĕn'tīle, *n.* 1. non-Jew. —*adj.* 2. non-Jewish.

gĕn'tle, *adj.* mild in manner or effect. —gen'tly, *adv.*

gĕn'tlè·màn, *n.* 1. Also, *fem.,* gen'tle·wom''an, man of the upper class. 2. well-mannered man.

gĕn'trў, *n.* persons of the upper class.

gĕn'ŭ·flĕct'', *v.i.* bend the knee in homage. —gen''u·flec'tion, *n.*

gĕn'ū·ĭne, *adj.* 1. true; real. 2. sincere. —gen'u·ine·ly, *adv.* —gen'u·ine·ness, *n.*

gē'nŭs, *n., pl.* genera, genuses. 1. type. 2. *Biology.* distinctive group of plant or animal species.

gē·ŏg'rȧ·phў, *n., pl.* -phies. 1. study of the earth or its features. 2. terrain. —ge''o·graph'i·cal, ge''o·graph'ic, *adj.* —ge·og'ra·pher, *n.*

gē·ŏl'ȯ·gў, *n.* study of the earth's crust. —ge''o·log'ic, ge''o·log'i·cal, *adj.*

gē·ŏm'é·trў, *n., pl.* -tries. study of points, lines, planes, and solids. —ge''o·met'ric, ge''o·met'ri·cal, *adj.*

gē''ō·phўs'ĭcs, *n.* study of the effects of climate, etc. on the earth.

gĕr''ĭ·ăt'rĭcs, *n.* branch of medicine dealing with old age. —ger''i·at'ric, *adj.*

gêrm, *n.* 1. disease-causing organism. 2. origin.

gêr·māne', *adj.* relevant.

gêr'mĭ·cīde'', *n.* destroyer of germs. —ger''mi·ci'dal, *adj.*

gêr'mĭ·nāte'', *v.,* -nated, -nating. *v.i., v.t.* sprout. —ger''mi·na'tion, *n.*

gĕr'rў·măn''dêr, *v.t.* manipulate election districts so as to favor one side.

gĕs'tāte, *v.t.,* -tated, -tating. bear in the uterus. —ges·ta'tion, *n.*

gés·tĭc'ū·lāte'', *v.i.,* -lated, -lating. make gestures. —ges·tic·u·la'tion, *n.*

gĕs'tûre, *v.i.,* -tured, -turing, *n. v.i.* 1. move the hands, arms, etc. as a signal. —*n.* 2. act or instance of gesturing. 3. act intended to impress others.

gĕt, *v.,* got, gotten, getting. *v.t.* 1. take or receive. 2. cause to be or do. —*v.i.* 3. become. 4. go or arrive.

geў'sêr, *n.* natural eruption of water or steam.

ghăst'lў, *adj.,* -lier, -liest. 1. horrible. 2. ghostlike. —ghast'li·ness, *n.*

ghêr'kĭn, *n.* small pickle.

ghĕt'tō, *n., pl.* -tos, -toes. neighborhood populated by particular minority ethnic group.

ghōst, *n.* spirit from the dead. —ghost'ly, *adj.*

ghoūl, *n.* 1. robber of the dead. 2. person morbidly fascinated by disasters. —ghoul'ish, *adj.*

GI, *n., pl.* GI's, GIs, *adj. n.* enlisted man. —*adj.* 2. government issue.

gī'ȧnt, *n.* 1. greatly oversized creature or thing. —*adj.* 2. gigantic. Also, *fem.,* gi'ant·ess.

gĭb'bêr, *v.i.* make incoherent utterances. —gib'ber·ish, *n.*

gībe, *v.i.,* gibed, gibing, *n.* jeer.

gĭb·lĕt, *n.* internal organ of fowl.

gĭd'dў, *adj.,* -dier, -diest. 1. dizzy. 2. frivolous.

gĭft, *n.* 1. something given. 2. natural ability.

gĭft'ĕd, *adj.* intelligent or talented.

gī·găn'tĭc, *adj.* huge.

gĭg'gle, *v.i.,* -gled, -gling, *n. v.i.* 1. laugh in a quick, high-pitched way. —*n.* 2. act or instance of giggling.

gĭld, *v.t.,* gilded or gilt, gilding. cover with gold leaf. —gilt, *adj.*

gĭll, *n.* 1. (jil) quarter of a pint; 4 fluid ounces. 2. (gill) breathing apparatus of a fish, etc.

gĭm'lĕt, *n.* small boring tool.

gĭm'mĭck, *n. Informal.* gadget.

gĭn, *n., v.t.,* ginned, ginning. *n.* 1. distilled grain liquor. 2. cotton seed remover. —*v.t.* 3. process with a cotton gin.

gĭn'gêr, *n.* tropical spice. —gin'ger·y, *adj.*

gĭn'gêr·lў, *adj.* 1. cautious. —*adv.* 2. cautiously.

gĭng'hàm, *n.* checked or striped cotton.

gĭ·răffe', *n.* long-necked, long-legged African animal.

gîrd, *v.t.,* -girded or girt, girding. surround, as with a belt.

gîrd'êr, *n.* major structural beam.

gîr'dle, *n., v.t.,* -dled, -dling. *n.* 1. woman's undergarment. 2. belt. —*v.t.* 3. encircle.

gîrl, *n.* young female. —girl'hood'', *n.* —girl'ish, *adj.*

gîrth, n. circumference.

gĭst, n. basic meaning or content.

gĭve, v., gave, given, giving, n. v.t. **1.** transfer. **2.** make a present of. **3.** supply or afford. **4.** concede. —v.i. **5.** yield, as to force. —n. **6.** compressibility. —**giv'er,** n.

gĭv'ĕn, adj. **1.** specified. **2.** granted. **3.** habituated.

glā'cĭăl, adj. icy.

glā'cĭêr, n. broad, moving mass of ice.

glăd, adj., gladder, gladdest. **1.** happy. **2.** quite willing. —**glad'ly,** adv. —**glad'ness,** n. —**glad'den,** v.t., v.i.

glāde, n. open space in a forest.

glăd'ĭ·ā''tŏr, n. swordsman in ancient Roman contests.

glăd''ĭ·ō'lŭs, n., pl. -luses, -li. flower with spikes of funnel-shaped blossoms. Also, **glad''i·o'la.**

glăm'ŏr, n. mysterious charm. Also, **glam'our.** —**glam'or·ous,** adj. —**glam'or·ize,** v.t.

glănce, v.t., glanced, glancing, n. v.i. **1.** look briefly. **2.** ricochet. —n. **3.** act or instance of glancing.

glănd, n. bodily organ that extracts and processes elements in the blood. —**glan'du·lar,** adj.

glāre, n., v.i., glared, glaring. n. **1.** dazzling brightness. **2.** furious look. —v.i. **3.** cast a glare.

glăr'ĭng, adj. **1.** dazzlingly bright. **2.** ostentatious; loud. **3.** flagrant.

glăss, n. **1.** substance of fused silicates. **2.** object of this substance. **3.** object with a lens or lenses. **4.** glasses, lenses in a frame, used to aid vision. —**glass'ful,** n. —**glas'sy,** adj.

glāze, v.t., glazed, glazing, n. v.t. **1.** fill with glass, as a window. **2.** put a glassy coating on. —v.i. **3.** become glassy. —n. **4.** glassy coating.

glā'zĭêr, n. person who glazes windows.

glēam, n. **1.** beam of light. —v.i. **2.** emit a gleam.

glēan, adj. gather.

glēe, n. joy. —**glee'ful,** adj.

glĕn, n. isolated, small valley.

glĭb, adj., glibber, glibbest. unconvincingly ready with explanations. —**glib'ly,** adv. —**glib'ness,** n.

glīde, v., glided, gliding, n. v.i., v.t. **1.** slider. —n. **2.** act or instance of gliding.

glīd'êr, n. unpowered aircraft.

glĭm'mêr, n., v.i. gleam.

glĭmpse, v.t., -glimpsed, glimpsing, n. v.t. **1.** see briefly or in part. —n. **2.** act or instance of glimpsing.

glĭnt, v.i., n. gleam or glitter.

glĭs'tĕn, v.i. reflect with a dull shine.

glĭtch, n. (computers) a problem or error in a program.

glĭt'têr, v.i. **1.** shine or reflect brightly. —n. **2.** act or instance of glittering.

glōam'ĭng, n. evening twilight.

glōat, v.i. experience proud or malicious pleasure.

glōbe, n. **1.** the earth. **2.** model of the earth. **3.** spherical object. —**glob'al,** adj.

glŏb'ūle, n. tiny ball or drop. —**glob'u·lar,** adj.

gloōm, n. **1.** darkness. **2.** sadness or dreariness. —**gloom'y,** adj.

glô'rĭ·fy'', v.t., -fied, -fying. **1.** give glory to. **2.** exaggerate the importance or worth of. —**glo''ri·fi·ca'tion,** n.

glô'rÿ, n., pl. -ries, v.i., -ried, -rying. n. **1.** high honor. **2.** splendor or splendid feature. —v.i. **3.** take pride. —**glo'ri·ous,** adj.

glŏss, n. **1.** sheen. **2.** explanation. —**glos'sy,** adj.

glŏs'să·rÿ, n., pl. -ries. list of terms with definitions.

glŏve n. garment for the hand.

glōw, v.i. **1.** give off soft light or color. —n. **2.** act or instance of glowing.

glŏw'êr, v.i. stare threateningly.

glu'cōse, n. sugar in fruit and honey.

glūe, n., v.t., glued, gluing. n. **1.** adhesive substance. —v.t. **2.** fasten with glue.

glŭm, adj., glummer, glummest. gloomy; moody. —**glum'ly,** adv.

glŭt, v., glutted, glutting, n., v.i. **1.** eat to excess. —v.t. **2.** satiate. **3.** oversupply. —n. **4.** act or instance of glutting.

glu'tĭ·noŭs, adj. sticky.

glŭt'tŏn, n. person who overeats. —**glut'ton·ous,** adj. —**glut'ton·y,** n.

glÿ'cêr·ĭn, n. liquid derived from fats and oils. Also, **gly'cer·ine.**

gnârled, adj. twisted or knotted, like a tree trunk.

gnăsh, v.t. grind together, as the teeth, with anger or frustration.

gnăt, n. small, stinging insect.

gnăw, v.t., v.i. bite away gradually.

gnōme, *n.* dwarf who guards treasure. —**gnom'ish,** *adj.*

gō, *v.i.,* **went, going,** *n., pl.* **goes.** *v.i.* **1.** leave. **2.** operate. **3.** belong. **4.** become.

gōad, *n., v.t.* prod.

gōal, *n.* **1.** object to be reached or attained. **2.** *Sports.* area to be defended.

gōat, *n.* horned, cud-chewing mammal.

gōat·ēe', *n.* small, pointed beard.

gŏb'ble, *v.,* **-bled, -bling,** *n. v.t.* **1.** eat greedily. —*v.i.* **2.** make turkeylike sounds. —*n.* **3.** sound of a turkey.

gŏb'ble·dy·gook'', *n. Informal.* jargon.

gō'-bè·twēen'', *n.* arranger of bargains between others.

gŏb'lĕt, *n.* stemmed, deep-bowled drinking vessel.

gŏb'lĭn, *n.* evil supernatural being.

gŏd, *n.* **1.** one of the supreme beings. **2. God,** the Supreme Being. Also, *fem.,* **god'dess. —god'hood'',** *n.* **—god'less,** *adj.*

gŏd'chīld'', *n.* child sponsored in religion by a godparent.

gŏd'hĕad'', *n.* **1.** godhood. **2. the Godhead,** God.

gŏd'lў, *adj.,* **-lier, -liest.** devout. **—god'li·ness,** *n.*

gŏd'pår''ĕnt, *n.* sponsor of a godchild. Also, *masc.,* **god'fa''ther,** *fem.,* **god' mother.**

gŏd'sĕnd'', *n.* piece of good luck.

gŏg'gle, *v.i.,* **-gled, -gling,** *n. v.i.* **1.** stare with eyes bulging. —*n.* **2. goggles,** protective glasses.

gō'ĭng, *adj.* **1.** current. **2.** operative. —*n.* **3.** departure. **4.** conditions.

goī'tĕr, *n.* enlargement of the thyroid gland. Also, **goi'tre.**

gōld, *n.* soft, yellow, precious metallic element. **—gold'en,** *adj.*

gōld'ĕn·rŏd'', *n.* plant with tiny yellow flowers.

gōldĕn rūle, do unto others as you would have others do unto you.

gōld'fĭsh'', *n.* small yellow-orange fish.

gŏlf, *n.* outdoor game played with balls knocked from ground level with clubs. **—golf'er,** *n.*

gō'năd, *n.* animal reproductive organ.

gŏn'dō·là, *n.* **1.** one-oared Venetian boat. **2.** low-sided railroad freight car. **3.** airship cabin. **—gon''do·lier',** *n.*

gŏng, *n.* thin brass disk beaten to produce sound.

gŏn''ŏr·rhē'à, *n.* a venereal disease.

gŏŏd, *adj.,* **better, best,** *n. adj.* **1.** right; proper. **2.** kind. **3.** beneficial. —*n.* **5.** good purpose or result. **6. goods,** valuable objects or material.

gŏŏd''-bȳe', *interj.* **1.** (departing salutation). —*n.* **2.** saying of good-bye. Also, **good''-by'.**

Gŏŏd Frīdāy, Friday before Easter.

gŏŏd'lў, *adj.,* **-lier, -liest. 1.** considerable in amount. **2.** good. **3.** good-looking.

gŏŏf, *Informal. n.* **1.** blunderer. **2.** blunder. **—goof'y,** *adj.*

gŏŏse, *n., pl.* **geese.** web-footed ducklike bird.

gō'phêr, *n.* **1.** burrowing rodent. **2.** prairie squirrel.

gōre, *n., v.t.,* **gored, goring.** *n.* **1.** blood. **2.** triangular segment. —*v.t.* **3.** pierce, as with a horn. **—gor'y,** *adj.*

gōrge, *n., v.,* **gorged, gorging.** *n.* **1.** narrow canyon. **2.** gullet. —*v.t.* **3.** glut. —*v.i.* **4.** eat greedily.

gōr'geoŭs, *adj.* dazzlingly attractive.

gò·rĭl'là, *n.* powerful manlike African ape.

Gŏs'pĕl, *n.* **1.** teachings of Jesus and the Apostles.

gŏs'sà·mêr, *adj.* **1.** light and frail. —*n.* **2.** cobweb.

gŏs'sĭp, *n.* **1.** rumors and conjectures about others. **2.** person who originates or spreads these. —*v.i.* **3.** engage in gossip. **—gos'sip·y,** *adj.*

gouge, *n., v.t.,* **gouged, gouging.** *n.* **1.** chisel for cutting grooves. —*v.t.* **2.** cut out with a scooping motion.

gou'lăsh, *n.* stew seasoned with paprika.

gôurd, *n.* decorative fruit of the squash or melon family.

gour'mănd, *n.* heavy eater and drinker.

gour·met (gŏŏr mā'), *n.* connoisseur of food and drink.

gŏut, *n.* illness causing pain in the joints. **—gout'y,** *adj.*

gŏv'êrn, *v.t.* **1.** have authority over. **2.** guide. **3.** determine.

gŏv'êrn·mĕnt, *n.* **1.** system for running a country. **2.** group in political control. **—gov''ern·men'tal,** *adj.*

gŏv'êr·nŏr, *n.* **1.** supreme local official. **2.** device for controlling machinery speed. **—gov'er·nor·ship,** *n.*

gŏwn, *n.* long outer garment.

grăb, *v.t.*, *v.i.*, **grabbed, grabbing**, *n.* snatch.

grāce, *n.*, *v.t.*, **graced, gracing**, *n.* **1.** beauty of form, movement or manner. **2.** kindness or favor. **3.** prayer before a meal. —*v.t.* **4.** add grace to, as by being present. —**grace'ful**, *adj.* —**grace'less**, *adj.*

grā'cioŭs, *adj.* **1.** charming in manner. **2.** kind. **3.** discriminatingly luxurious.

grăck'le, *n.* crowlike blackbird.

grá·dā'tion, *n.* succession of increasing or decreasing amounts, etc.

grāde, *n.*, *v.t.*, **graded, grading**. *n.* **1.** step in a progressive series. **2.** Also, **gra'di·ent**, slope. —*v.t.* **3.** assign a grade to. **4.** give a level to, as a road.

grăd'ū·ȧl, *adj.* in small amounts. —**grad'u·al·ly**, *adv.*

grăd'ū·āte'', *v.*, **-ated, -ating**, *n.*, *adj.* *v.t.* **1.** leave after satisfying academic requirements. **2.** certify as having satisfied requirements. **3.** divide into grades. —*n.* (grad'yōŏ et) **4.** person who has graduated. —*adj.* **5.** postbaccalaureate. —**grad''u·a'tion**, *n.*

grăf·fī·tō, *n.*, *pl.* **-ti.** writing or drawing by a passer-by.

grăft, *n.* **1.** transplant of organic material. **2.** dishonest use of public funds. —*v.t.* **3.** transplant. **4.** obtain by graft.

grāin, *n.* **1.** hard seed, as of wheat. **2.** hard particle. **3.** pattern of fiber, as in wood.

grăm, *n.* metric unit of weight, about ¹/₂₈ of an ounce. Also, **gramme**.

grăm'màr, *n.* forms and arrangement of words. —**gram·mat'i·cal**, *adj.*

grăn'à·rỹ, *n.*, *pl.* **-ries.** place for storing grain.

grănd, *adj.* **1.** impressive. **2.** illustrious. —**grand'ly**, *adv.* —**gran'deur**, *n.*

grănd'chīld'', *n.* child of a son or daughter. Also, *masc.*, **grand'son''**, *fem.*, **grand'daugh''ter**.

grăn·dĭl'o·quėnt, *adj.* pretentious in speech. —**gran·dil'o·quence**, *n.*

grăn'dĭ·ōse'', *adj.* **1.** full of grandeur. **2.** pompous.

grănd'păr''ėnt, *n.* parent of a parent. Also, *masc.*, **grand'fa''ther**, *fem.*, **grand'moth''er**.

grănd'stănd'', *n.* stand for spectators at sporting events.

grăn'īte, *n.* grainy igneous rock.

grănt, *v.t.* **1.** give. **2.** admit. —*n.* **3.** something granted.

grăn'ū·lāte'', *v.t.*, **-lated, -lating.** form as or in granules.

grăn'ūle, *n.* small particle. —**gran'u·lar**, *adj.*

grāpe, *n.* small juicy fruit.

grāpe'frūit'', *n.* large, sharp-tasting citrus fruit.

grăph, *n.* two-dimensional visual representation of interrelated data.

grăph'ĭc, *adj.* **1.** pertaining to two-dimensional visual art. **2.** vividly realistic.

grăph'īte, *n.* soft carbon used as a writing material or lubricant.

grăp'ple, *v.*, **-pled, -pling.** *v.i.* **1.** wrestle; struggle. —*v.t.* **2.** grasp and hold.

grăsp, *v.t.* **1.** take hold of with the hand; clutch. **2.** comprehend. —*v.i.* **3.** make clutching motions. —*n.* **4.** act or instance of grasping. **5.** ability to grasp.

grăsp'ĭng, *adj.* avaricious.

grăss, *n.* **1.** narrow-leafed green plant with seedlike fruit. —**gras'sy**, *adj.*

grăss'hŏp''pêr, *n.* jumping, plant-eating insect.

grāte, *v.*, **grated, grating**, *n.* *v.t.* **1.** scrape into particles. **2.** grind. —*v.i.* **3.** grind or rasp. **4.** be irritating. —*n.* **5.** Also, **grat'ing**, framework of metal, etc. bars. —**grat'er**, *n.*

grāte'fŭl, *adj.* **1.** appreciative of favors. **2.** welcome.

grăt'ĭ·fÿ'', *adj.* **-fied, -fying.** be pleasing to. —**grat''i·fi·ca'tion**, *n.*

grā'tĭs, *adj.* free of charge.

grăt'ĭ·tūde'', *n.* appreciation for favors.

grá·tū'ĭ·toŭs, *adj.* **1.** gratis. **2.** uncalled-for.

grá·tū'ĭ·tỹ, *n.*, *pl.* **-ties.** gift, esp. a tip.

grāve, *adj.* **1.** solemn. **2.** important; serious. —*n.* **2.** place of burial.

grăv'ėl, *n.* mixture of stone fragments. —**grav'el·ly**, *adj.*

grăv'ĭ·tāte'', *v.i.*, **-tated, -tating. 1.** move by gravity. **2.** move or tend naturally. —**grav''i·ta'tion**, *n.* —**grav''i·ta'tion·al**, *adj.*

grăv'ĭ·tỹ, *n.* **1.** seriousness. **2.** pull toward the center of the earth.

grā'vỹ, *n.*, *pl.* **-ies.** meat juice, or a sauce from this.

grāy, *adj.* **1.** mixed black and white. **2.** dreary.

gr̄ay măttêr, 1. brain tissue. 2. *Informal.* intelligence.

grāze, *v.*, grazed, grazing. *v.t. v.i.* 1. scrape in passing. —*v.i.* 2. feed on grasses.

grēase, *n., v.t.*, greased, greasing. *n.* (grēs). 1. thick, fatty or oily substance. —*v.t.* (grēz) 2. coat or lubricate with grease. —greas′y, *adj.*

grēat, *adj.* 1. large. 2. eminent. —great′ly, *adv.*

grēed, *n.* excessive passion for money, food, etc. —greed′y, *adj.*

grēen, *n.* 1. color of leaves and plants. 2. greens, leafy vegetables. —*adj.* 3. of the color green. 4. unripened or unprocessed.

grēen′er·ÿ, *n.* plant life.

grēen′house″, *n.* glazed building for growing plants.

grēet, *v.t.* 1. acknowledge meeting. 2. receive in a specified way. —greet′ing, *n.*

grē·gār′ĭ·oŭs, *adj.* associating with others of one's kind.

grē·nāde″, *n.* small hand bomb.

grĕn′à·dĭne″, *n.* pomegranate syrup.

grey, *adj.* gray.

grey′hound″, *n.* fast, slender hound.

grĭd, *n.* system of crisscrossed elements.

grĭd′dle, *n.* pan for cooking pancakes, etc.

grĭd′īron″, *n.* 1. broiling frame. 2. football field.

grĭd′lŏck, *n.* severe, urban traffic jam.

grĭef, *n.* 1. great unhappiness. 2. ruin; failure.

grĭev′ànce, *n.* 1. cause for complaint. 2. complaint.

grĭeve, *v.*, grieved, grieving. *v.i.* 1. suffer grief. —*v.t.* 2. cause grief to.

grĭev′oŭs, *adj.* 1. seriously injurious. 2. being in grief.

grĭll, *n.* 1. gridiron. 2. broiled dish. —*v.t.* 3. broil. 4. *Informal.* question severely.

grĭlle, *n.* open screen; grating. —grille′work″, *n.*

grĭm, *adj.*, grimmer, grimmest. 1. harsh. 2. menacing. —grim′ly, *adv.*

grĭ′màce, *n., v.i.*, -maced, -macing. *n.* 1. smirk, esp. of displeasure. —*v.i.* 2. give such a smirk.

grĭme, *n.* clinging dirt. —grim′y *adj.*

grĭn, *n. v.i.*, grinned, grinning. *n.* 1. broad, toothy smile. —*v.i.* 2. give such a smile.

grīnd, *v.t.*, ground, grinding. 1. wear down with pressure or friction. 2. turn the crank of. —grind′er, *n.*

grĭp, *v.t.*, gripped, gripping, *n. v.t.* 1. grasp firmly. —*n.* 2. firm grasp. 3. handle. 4. small piece of luggage.

grīpe, *v.*, griped, griping, *n. v.t.* 1. produce pain in the bowels. —*v.i.* 2. *Informal.* complain. —*n.* 3. pain in the bowels. 4. *Informal.* complaint.

grĭs′lÿ, *adj.*, -lier, -liest. horrible.

grĭst, *n.* grain for grinding. —grist′mill″, *n.*

grĭs′tle, *n.* cartilage. —gris′tly, *adv.*

grĭt, *n., v.t.*, gritted, gritting. *n.* 1. rough, hard particles. 2. fortitude. —*v.t.* 3. grind together, as the teeth. —grit′ty, *adj.*

grĭts, *n. pl.* coarsely ground grain.

grĭz′zlĕd, *adj.* with gray hair.

grĭz′zlÿ, *adj.* -zlier, -zliest, *n. adj.* 1. grayish. —*n.* 2. Also, grizzly bear, large, ferocious American bear.

grōan, *n.* 1. deep utterance, as of pain. —*v.i.* 2. give such an utterance.

grō′cêr, *n.* food merchant. —gro′cer·y, *n.*

grŏg′gÿ, *adj.* -gier, -giest. befuddled.

grōĭn, *n.* junction of the abdomen and thighs.

grŏm′mĕt, *n.* eyelet.

grōōm, *n.* 1. man at his wedding. 2. tender of horses. —*v.t.* 3. comb, etc. to make tidy.

grōōve, *n., v.t.*, grooved, grooving. *n.* 1. long, shallow depression. —*v.t.* 2. make a groove in.

grōpe, *v.i.*, groped, groping. feel for something blindly.

grōss, *adj.* 1. coarse. 2. flagrant. 3. before deductions. —*n.* 4. *pl.* gross, quantity of 144.

grō·tĕsque′, *adj.* fantastically distorted.

grŏt′tō, *n., pl.* -tos, -toes. cave.

grŏuch, *v.i.* 1. sulk, —*n.* 2. sulky mood. 3. person who sulks. —grouch′y, *adj.*

grōund, *n.* 1. solid surface of the earth. 2. earth. 3. grounds, a. basis. b. land of an estate or institution. c. dregs of coffee, etc. —*v.t.* 4. instruct in rudiments.

grōund′hŏg″, *n.* woodchuck.

grōund′lĕss, *adj.* without reason.

grŏūnd'wŏrk'', *n*. basic or preparatory work.

groūp, *n*. **1.** number of persons or things considered together. *v.t.*, *v.i.* **2.** form into a group or groups.

groŭse, *n*., *pl*. **grouse**, *v.i.*, **groused**, **grousing**. *n*. **1.** plump game bird. —*v.i.* **2.** complain.

grŏve, *n*. cluster of trees.

gróv'ĕl, *v.i.*, **-eled**, **-eling**. **1.** crouch low or crawl. **2.** behave servilely.

grōw, *v.*, **grew**, **grown**, **growing**. *v.i.* **1.** become. **2.** develop. —*v.t.* **3.** cause to live, as plants. —**grow''er**, *n*. —**growth**, *n*.

grŏwl, *n*. **1.** low, rumbling vocal noise. —*v.i.* **2.** make such a noise.

grōwn'-ŭp', *adj.*, *n*. adult.

grŭb, *v.*, **grubbed**, **grubbing**, *n*. *v.i.*, *v.t.* **1.** dig. —*n*. **2.** beetle larva. **3.** drudge. **4.** *Informal*. food.

grŭb'bў, *adj*. **-bier**, **-biest**. nastily dirty.

grŭdge, *n.*, *v.t.*, **grudged**, **grudging**. *n*. **1.** long-held resentment. —*v.t.* **2.** begrudge. —**grudg'ing·ly**, *adv*.

grū'ĕl·ing, *adj.* exhausting; very tiring.

grūe'sŏme, *adj.* horrifying or loathsome.

grŭff, *adj.* curt.

grŭm'ble, *v.i.* **-bled**, **-bling**. complain in a suppressed manner.

grŭm'pў, *adj.* **-pier**, **-piest**. surly.

grŭnt, *n*. **1.** throaty sound caused by exertion, etc. —*v.i.* **2.** utter such a sound.

guăr''ăn·tēe', *n.*, *v.t.*, **-teed**, **-teeing**. *n*. **1.** firm assurance. **2.** promise to make good if necessary. —*v.t.* **3.** assure with a guarantee. Also, **guar'an·ty**. —**guar'an·tor''**.

guârd, *v.t.*, *v.i.* **1.** watch, esp. in order to protect or confine. —*n*. **2.** person or group that guards. **3.** protection. **4.** protective device.

guârd'ĕd, *adj.* cautious.

guârd'ĭ·ȧn, *n*. **1.** person who guards. **2.** person responsible for a minor or incompetent. —**guard'ian·ship''**, *n*.

gū''bĕr·nȧ·tô'rĭ·ȧl, *adj.* pertaining to governors.

guĕr·rĭl'lȧ, *n*. irregular soldier using surprise tactics.

guĕss, *v.t.* **1.** form an opinion about without knowing. —*n*. **2.** act or instance of guessing. —**guess'work''**, *n*.

guĕst, *n*. **1.** enjoyer of hospitality. **2.** customer of a hotel, etc.

gŭf·fäw', *n*. **1.** raucous laugh. —*v.i.* **2.** emit such a laugh.

guīde, *v.t.*, **guided**, **guiding**, *n*. *v.t.* **1.** tell how to proceed. —*n*. **2.** person or thing that guides. —**guid'ance**, *n*.

guīle, *n*. unscrupulous cunning.

guĭlt, *n*. **1.** responsibility for a wrong action. **2.** shame. —**guilt'y**, *adj*.

guĭn'ēa pĭg, **1.** small, fat rodent. **2.** subject of an experiment.

guīse, *n*. semblance; false face.

guĭ·târ', *n*. six-stringed plucked instrument. —**gui·tar'ist**, *n*.

gŭlch, *n*. deep narrow ravine.

gŭlf, *n*. **1.** ocean area partly surrounded by land. **2.** wide deep void.

gŭll, *n*. light-colored soaring water bird.

gŭl'lĕt, *n*. throat.

gŭl'lĭ·ble, *adj.* credulous. —**gul''li·bil'i·ty**, *n*.

gŭl'lў, *n.*, *pl*. **-lies**. narrow ravine.

gŭlp, *v.t.*, *v.i.* **1.** swallow hastily. —*n*. **2.** act or instance of gulping.

gŭm, *n.*, *v.t.*, **gummed**, **gumming**. *n*. **1.** sticky, semisolid substance. **2.** area of flesh surrounding teeth. —*v.t.* **3.** stick with gum.

gŭmp'tion, *n*. **1.** enterprise. **2.** common sense.

gŭn, *n.*, *v.*, **gunned**, **gunning**. *n*. **1.** weapon shooting a missile by means of an explosive charge. —*v.t.*, *v.i.* **2.** hunt with a gun. —**gun'ner·y**, *n*.

gŭnk, *n*. *Informal*. viscous substance.

gŭn'nў, *n*. coarse cloth of jute or hemp.

gŭn'pōw''dêr, *n*. explosive used in guns.

gun·wale (gun'l), *n*. upper edge of a ship's side.

gûr'gle, *v.i.*, **-gled**, **-gling**, *n*. *v.i.* **1.** emit a bubbling sound in flowing. —*n*. **2.** such a sound.

gū'rū, *n*. Hindu spiritual teacher.

gŭsh, *v.i.* **1.** flow out abundantly. **2.** express oneself effusively. —*n*. **3.** act or instance of gushing. —**gush'y**, *adj*.

gŭs'sĕt, *n*. triangular reinforcement.

gŭst, *n*. **1.** strong puff of air. **2.** sudden outburst. —**gust'y**, *adj*.

gŭs'tȧ·tô''rў, *adj.* pertaining to the sense of taste.

gŭs'tō, *n*. great enjoyment or vigor.

gŭt, *n.*, *v.t.*, **gutted**, **gutting**. *n* **1.** intes-

tine. **2. guts,** *Informal.* courage. —*v.t.*
3. destroy the inside of.

gŭt'têr, *n.* **1.** channel for rain water. **2.**
realm of sordidness. —*v.t.* **3.** splutter
before being extinguished, as a candle.

gŭt'tŭr·ȧl, *adj.* pertaining to or produced in the throat.

guÿ, *n.* **1.** *Informal.* male person. **2.** Also,
guy'wire", steadying wire.

gŭz'zle, *v.i., v.t.,* **-zled, -zling.** drink
greedily.

gȳm·nā'sĭ·ŭm, *n., pl.* **-ums, -a.** place
for physical exercise. Also, *Informal.*
gym.

gȳm·nǎs'tĭcs, *n. pl.* physical exercises.
—**gym'nast,** *n.* —**gym·nas'tic,** *adj.*

gȳ"nė·cŏl'ȯ·gȳ, *n.* branch of medicine
concerned with women's diseases.
—**gy"ne·col'o·gist,** *n.*

gȳp, *n., v.t.,* **gypped, gypping.** *Informal.* swindle.

gȳp'sŭm, *n.* sulfate of calcium, used to
make plaster of Paris.

gȳ·rāte', *v.i.,* **-rated, -rating.** whirl.
—**gy·ra'tion** *n.*

gȳ'rȯ·scōpe", *n.* object maintaining its
position by the inertia of a rapidly turned wheel. —**gy"ro·scop'ic,** *adj.*

H

H, h, *n.* eighth letter of the English alphabet.

hăb'ĭt, *n.* **1.** custom, esp. one hard to depart from. **2.** distinctive costume.
—**ha·bit'u·al,** *adj.* —**ha·bit'u·ate",**
v.t.

hăb'ĭt·ȧ·ble, *adj.* able to be lived in.

hăb'ĭ·tăt", *n.* usual area of habitation.

hăb"ĭ·tā'tion, *n.* home.

hăck, *v.i., v.t.* **1.** chop roughly. —*v.i.* **2.**
cough hoarsely. —*n.* **3.** artistic drudge.

hăck"êr, *n.* a computer enthusiast.

hăck'saw", *n.* frame-mounted metal-
cutting saw.

hăd'dȯck, *n., pl.* **-dock, -docks.** Atlantic codlike fish.

Hā'dēs, *n.* hell. Also, **ha'des.**

hăft, *n.* knife or ax handle.

hăg, *n.* ugly old woman.

hăg'gȧrd, *adj.* weary-looking.

hăg'gle, *v.i.,* **-gled, -gling.** dispute over a
price.

hāil, *v.t.* **1.** greet loudly. **2.** shout to. **3.**
welcome as desirable. **4.** shower heav-
ily. —*n.* **5.** frozen rain in small balls.
—**hail'stone",** *n.*

hāir, *n.* **1.** slender growth from the skin.
2. these growths collectively. —**hair'y,**
adj. —**hair'i·ness,** *n.*

hāir'rāis"ĭng, *adj.* terrifying.

hāir'splĭt"tĭng, *n.* making of trivial distinctions.

hăl'cÿ"ȯn, *adj.* idyllic.

hāle, *adj., v.t.,* **haled, haling.** *adj.* **1.** full
of health and vigor. —*v.t.* **2.** summon
forcibly.

hălf, *n., pl.* **halves,** *adj., adv. n.* **1.** one of
two equal divisions. —*adj.* **2.** being a
half. —*adv.* **3.** as far as a half.

hălf'-brēed", *n.* child of parents from
different races.

hălf-heârt'ėd, *adj.* without enthusiasm
or determination. —**half'-heart'ed·ly,**
adv.

hălf'wāy', *adj., adv.* **1.** at or to a mid-
point. **2.** to a partial extent.

hălf'wĭt", *n.* person of subnormal intelligence. —**half'wit'ted,** *adj.*

hăl'ĭ·bŭt, *n., pl.* **-but, -buts.** northern
saltwater flatfish.

hăl"ĭ·tō'sĭs, *n.* bad breath.

hăll, *n.* **1.** large room, as for meetings. **2.**
Also, **hall'way",** corridor or vestibule.

hăl"lė·lū'jȧh, *interj.* praise the Lord!
Also, **hal"le·lu'iah.**

hăl'lōw, *v.t.* sanctify.

Hăl"lōw·ēen', *n.* eve of All Saints' Day,
celebrated October 31. Also, **Hal"low·
e'en'.**

hăl·lū"cĭ·nā'tion, *n.* deluded percep-
tions of a nonexistent sight, sound, etc.
—**hal·lu'ci·nate",** *v.i.* —**hal·lu'ci·na·
to"ry,** *adj.*

hā'lō, *n., pl.* **-los, -loes.** ring of light, as
around the portrayed head of a holy per-
son.

hălt, *v.t., v.i., n.* stop.

hăl'têr, *n.* line for securing an animal.

hălve, *v.t.,* **halved, halving. 1.** divide
into halves. **2.** reduce by half.

hăm, *n.* upper part of a hog's hind leg.

hăm'bûr"gêr, *n.* sandwich of ground
beef in a bun. Also, **ham'burg.**

hăm'lėt, *n.* small village.

hăm'mêr, *n.* **1.** device for beating or

driving with blows. —*v.t.*, *v.i.* **2.** strike with repeated blows.

hăm'mŏck, *n.* flexible bed suspended at the ends.

hăm'pêr, *v.t.*, **1.** encumber. —*n.* **2.** covered basket.

hănd, *n.* **1.** extremity of the arm. **2.** active part. **3.** hired worker. **4.** handwriting. **5.** side or direction. —*v.t.* **6.** give with the hand. —**hand'ful**, *n.*

hănd'băll'', *n.* game with a thrown rubber ball.

hănd'bōōk'', *n.* manual.

hănd'clăsp'', *n.* handshake.

hănd'gŭn'', *n.* pistol.

hănd'ĭ·căp, *n.*, *v.t.*, **-capped, -capping.** *n.* **1.** hindrance. —*v.t.* **2.** hinder. **3.** disability.

hănd'ĭ·wörk'', *n.* **1.** work done by hand. **2.** work done personally.

hănd'kêr·chĭef'', *n.* small wiping cloth.

hăn'dle, *n.*, *v.t.*, **-dled, -dling.** *n.* **1.** something to be grasped. —*v.t.* **2.** grasp, as in order to wield. **3.** manage or dominate. **4.** sell.

hănd'ōut'', *n.* **1.** charitable gift. **2.** news release.

hănd'-pĭck', *v.t.* **1.** pick by hand. **2.** choose carefully and individually.

hănd'shāke'', *n.* friendly gripping and shaking of another's hand.

hănd'sŏme'', *adj.* **1.** good-looking. **2.** generous.

hănds'-ŏn', *adj.* practical; making actual use of, as *hands-on training.*

hănd'wrīt''ĭng, *n.* freehand writing. —**hand'writ''ten**, *adj.*

hănd'ÿ, *adj.*, **-ier, -iest.** convenient. —**hand'i·ly**, *adv.* —**hand'i·ness**, *n.*

hănd'ÿ·măn, *n.* man who does odd jobs.

hăng, *v.*, **hung** or (for 2) **hanged, hanging.** *n.* *v.t.* **1.** hold up from above. **2.** kill by suspending from a rope around the neck. —*v.i.* **3.** be hung or hanged. —**hang'man**, *n.*

hăng'ȧr, *n.* aircraft shelter.

hăng'dŏg'', *adj.* abject.

hăn'kêr, *v.i.* yearn.

Hä'nŭ·kȧ'', *n. Judiasm.* festival of the rededication of the Temple at Jerusalem. Also, **Ha'nuk'kah''.**

hăp''hăz'ȧrd, *adj.* **1.** random. —*adv.* **2.** by chance.

hăp'lĕss, *adj.* unlucky.

hăp'pĕn, *v.i.* come about by chance. —**hap'pen·ing**, *n.*

hăp'pÿ, *adj.*, **-pier, -piest. 1.** feeling pleased. **2.** fortunate. —**hap'pi·ly**, *adv.* —**hap'pi·ness**, *n.*

hȧ·răngue', *n.*, *v.t.*, **-rangued, -ranguing.** *n.* **1.** long vehement speech. —*v.t.* **2.** deliver a harangue to.

hȧ·răss', *v.t.* trouble persistently. —**harass'ment**, *n.*

hâr'bĭn·gêr, *n.* forerunner.

hâr'bör, *n.* **1.** sheltered place for shipping. —*v.t.* **2.** shelter.

hârd, *adj.* **1.** unyielding. **2.** difficult. —*adv.* **3.** energetically. —**hard'en**, *v.t.*, *v.i.*

hârd'-heârt'ĕd, *adj.* callous.

hârd'lÿ, *adv.* barely; scarcely.

hârd'shĭp, *n.* something hard to endure.

hârd'wāre, *n.* **1.** tools, fasteners, etc. **2.** (computers) equipment, as microchips, disk drives, printers, etc.

hâr'dÿ, *adj.* **-dier, -diest.** *n.* **1.** of much endurance. **2.** vigorous. —**har'di·ly**, *adv.*

hāre, *n.* rabbitlike mammal.

hā'rĕm, *n.* **1.** women's quarters of a Muslim house. **2.** its inhabitants.

hârk, *v.i.* listen.

hârk'ĕn, *v.i.* hearken.

hâr'lŏt, *n.* prostitute.

hârm, *n.* **1.** injury. —*v.t.* **2.** injure. —**harm'ful**, *adj.* —**harm'ful·ly**, *adv.* —**harm'less**, *adj.* —**harm'less·ly**, *adv.*

hâr·mŏn'ĭ·cȧ, *n.* mouth organ.

hâr'mŏ·nÿ, *n.* **1.** pleasant combination. **2.** agreement; accord. —**har·mo'ni·ous**, *adj.* —**har'mo·nize''**, *v.t.*, *v.i.*

hâr'nĕss, *n.* **1.** straps, etc. on an animal that pulls or carries. —*v.t.* **2.** put a harness on. **3.** control the energy of.

hârp, *n.* **1.** large plucked stringed instrument. —*v.i.* **2.** speak tediously. —**harp'ist**, *n.*

hâr·pōōn, *n.* **1.** spear for whales, etc. —*v.t.* **2.** spear with a harpoon.

hăr'rōw, *n.* **1.** device for breaking and leveling plowed ground. —*v.t.* **2.** work on with a harrow. **3.** cause anxiety to.

hăr'rÿ, *v.t.*, **-ried, -rying.** harass.

hârsh, *adj.* **1.** unpleasantly rough. **2.** severe. —**harsh'ly**, *adv.* —**harsh'ness**, *n.*

hâr'vĕst, *n.* **1.** occasion of gathering

crops. **2.** crop gathered. —*v.t.* **3.** gather as a harvest. —**har′vest·er,** *n.*

hăsh, *v.t.* **1.** chop finely for cooking. —*n.* **2.** chopped mixture of meat and vegetables.

hăsp, *n.* bolted fastening fitted over a shackle.

hăs′sle, *n., v.i.,* **-sled, -sling.** *Informal.* squabble.

hăs′sock, *n.* cushionlike seat.

hāste, *n.* speed, esp. when excessive. —**hast′y,** *adj.* —**hast′i·ly,** *adv.*

hās′těn, *v.t., v.i.* hurry.

hăt, *n.* head garment, esp. a formal one.

hătch, *v.t.* **1.** bring forth from eggs. —*v.i.* **2.** open to release young. —*n.* **3.** Also, **hatch′way″,** opening serving as a door or window.

hătch′ět, *n.* short-handled chopping tool.

hāte, *v.t.,* **hated, hating,** *n. v.t.* **1.** dislike violently. *n.* **2.** Also, **hat′red,** feeling of hating.

hāte′fŭl, *adj.* to be hated.

haugh′tỹ, *adj.* **-tier, -tiest.** arrogant. —**haugh′ti·ness,** *n.* —**haugh′ti·ly,** *adv.*

haul, *v.t., v.i.* **1.** pull. —*n.* **2.** act or instance of hauling.

haunch, *n.* area from upper thigh to buttock.

haunt, *v.t.* **1.** be often present at. —*n.* **2.** favorite place or resort.

hăve, *v.t.,* **had, having. 1.** own or possess. **2.** acquire. **3.** experience or engage in. **4.** cause. **5.** be obliged.

hā′věn, *n.* place of shelter.

hăv′ŏc, *n.* vast destruction.

hăwk, *n.* **1.** bird of prey. —*v.t.* **2.** peddle.

haw′sěr, *n.* mooring or towing rope.

hāy, *n.* grass, etc. dried as fodder.

hāy fēvěr, allergy to pollen.

hāy′wīre″, *adv. Informal.* awry.

hăz′ărd, *n., v.t.* risk. —**haz′ard·ous,** *adj.*

hāze, *n., v.t.,* **hazed, hazing.** *n.* **1.** light mist or vapor. —*v.t.* **2.** harass or humiliate, as in an initiation. —**haz′y,** *adj.* —**haz′i·ly,** *adv.*

hăz′ěl, *n.* tree of the birch family. —**haz′-el·nut″,** *n.*

hē, *pron., pl.* **they,** *n., pl.* **they. pron. 1.** the male person or animal mentioned. —*n.* **2.** often used when gender is not known.

hěad, *n.* **1.** part of the body for thinking, eating, seeing, etc. **2.** director. **3.** uppermost or working feature. —*adj.* **4.** at or against the head. —*v.t.* **5.** direct. —*v.i.* **6.** direct oneself. —**head′ache″,** *n.*

hěad′ĭng, *n.* title or subtitle.

hěad′līne″, *n.* title of a newspaper article.

hěad′lŏng″, *adv., adj.* **1.** with the head first. **2.** at reckless speed.

hěad′-ŏn″, *adj., adv.* with the front end or ends foremost.

hěad′quâr″těrs, *n. pl.* main center of command.

hěad′strŏng″, *adj.* willful and impulsive.

hěad′wāy″, *n.* forward motion.

hěad′ỹ, *adj.,* **-ier, -iest.** intoxicating.

hēal, *v.t.* **1.** return to health. **2.** make whole again.

hěalth, *n.* **1.** well-being. **2.** condition of the body or mind. —**health′fŭl,** *adj.* —**health′y,** *adj.*

hēap, *n.* **1.** loose pile. —*v.t.* **2.** pile up.

hēar, *v.,* **heard, hearing.** *v.t.* **1.** perceive through the ears. **2.** understand from others. **3.** listen to. —**hear′ing,** *n.*

heark′ěn, *v.i.* listen carefully.

hēar′sāy″, *n.* rumor.

hêarse, *n.* funeral car.

hêart, *n.* **1.** organ that pumps blood. **2.** compassion or sensitivity. **3.** courage. **4.** enthusiasm. **5.** center. **6.** essence. —**heart′less,** *adj.*

hêart′brēak″, *n.* great sorrow. —**heart′bro″ken,** *adj.*

hêart′ěn, *v.t.* encourage.

hêart′fĕlt″, *adj.* deeply sincere.

hêarth, *n.* floor of a fireplace, furnace.

hêart′ỹ, *adj.,* **-ier, -iest.** enthusiastic. —**heart′i·ly,** *adv.* —**heart′i·ness,** *n.*

hēat, *n.* **1.** warmth. **2.** strong feeling. —*v.t., v.i.* **3.** warm. —**heat′er,** *n.*

hēa′thěn, *n., pl.* **-thens, -then,** *adj. n.* **1.** person not Christian, Jewish, or Muslim. —*adj.* **2.** pertaining to such persons.

hēave, *v.,* **heaved** or **hove, heaving,** *n. v.t.* **1.** lift, or lift and throw, with effort. —*v.i.* **2.** rise and fall in rhythm. —*n.* **3.** act or instance of heaving.

hěav′ěn, *n.* **1.** heavens; sky. **2. Heaven,** dwelling of God, the angels, and the blessed. —**heav′en·ly,** *adj.*

hĕav'ў, *adj.*, **-ier, -iest. 1.** with much weight. **2.** with much difficulty. —**heav'i·ly**, *adv.*

hĕav'ў-hănd'ĕd, *adj.* **1.** clumsy. **2.** tyrannical.

hĕck'le, *v.t.*, **-led, -ling.** harass verbally.

hĕc'tăre, *n.* area of 10,000 square meters.

hĕc'tĭc, *adj.* **1.** feverish. **2.** hasty and confused.

hĕdge, *n.*, *v.*, **hedged, hedging.** *n.* **1.** barrier of close-growing shrubs. —*v.t.* **2.** partition off with a hedge. —*v.i.* **3.** refuse to commit oneself.

hĕdge'hŏg'', *n.* American porcupine.

hē'dŏn·ĭsm, *n.* doctrine that pleasure is the highest good. —**he'don·ist**, *n.* —**he''do·nis'tic**, *adj.*

hēed, *v.t.* **1.** pay attention to. —*n.* **2.** attention. —**heed'ful**, *adj.* —**heed'less**, *adj.*

hēel, *n.* **1.** rear of the foot. **2.** something similar in form or location. —*v.i.*, *v.t.* **3.** lean; list. **4.** a contemptible person.

hĕft, *v.t.* pick up in order to weigh.

hĕft'ў, *adj.*, **-ier, -iest. 1.** heavy. **2.** large.

hĕif'ȇr, *n.* young cow.

hēight, *n.* **1.** dimension from bottom to top. **2.** raised area. **3.** highest point.

hēight'ĕn, *v.t.* **1.** make higher. —*v.i.* **2.** increase.

hei'noŭs, *adj.* outrageously wicked.

hĕir, *n.* person who inherits. Also, *fem.*, **heir'ess.**

hĕir'lōōm'', *n.* family possession.

hĕl'ĭ·cŏp''tȇr, *n.* aircraft flying by means of a propellerlike rotor.

hē'lĭ·ŭm, *n.* light gaseous chemical element.

hē'lĭx, *n.*, *pl.* **-lixes, -lices.** rising curve. —**hel'i·cal**, *adj.*

hĕll, *n.* Also **Hell,** place of confinement for those not redeemed. —**hel'lish**, *adj.*

hĕl·lō', *interj.* exclamation of greeting.

hĕlm, *n.* means of steering a ship. —**helms'man**, *n.*

hĕl'mĕt, *n.* protective head covering.

hĕlp, *v.t.* **1.** assist. **2.** rescue. **3.** prevent or mitigate. —*v.i.* **4.** be useful. —*n.* **5.** assistance. **6.** rescue. —**help'ful**, *adj.*

hĕlp'ĭng, *n.* portion of food.

hĕlp'lĕss, *adj.* unable to act. —**help'less·ly**, *adv.* —**help'less·ness**, *n.*

hĕlp'māte'', *n.* helpful companion. Also, **help'meet''.**

hĕm, *n.*, *v.t.*, **hemmed, hemming.** *n.* **1.** edge formed on a cloth. —*v.t.* **2.** make a hem on.

hĕm'ĭ·sphēre'', *n.* **1.** half a sphere. **2.** half of the earth. —**hem''i·spher'i·cal**, *adj.*

hĕm'lŏck'', *n.* **1.** pinelike evergreen. **2.** poisonous plant related to parsley.

hĕm'ŏr·rhăge, *n.* massive loss of blood.

hĕmp, *n.* Asiatic plant used for rope and hashish.

hĕn, *n.* female bird, esp. a chicken.

hĕnce, *adv.* **1.** away. **2.** from this time. **3.** therefore.

hĕnce'fôrth'', *adv.* from now on.

hĕnch'màn, *n.* assistant villain.

hȇr, *pron.* **1.** objective of *she.* —*adj.* **2.** pertaining to a female previously mentioned.

hĕr'ăld, *n.* **1.** officer who announces. **2.** signifier of what is to come. —*v.t.* **3.** signify in advance.

hĕr'ăld·rў, *n.* study of coats of arms, etc. —**he·ral'dic**, *adj.*

hȇrb (ȇrb), *n.* annual, biennial, or perennial seed plant used in cookery or medicine. —**her·ba'cious**, *adj.* —**herb'age**, *n.* —**herb'al**, *adj.*

hȇr''cū·lē'àn, *adj.* with immense effort.

hȇrd, *n.* **1.** group of cows, sheep, etc. **2.** person who tends such a group. —*v.i.*, *v.t.* **3.** gather or move as a herd.

hēre, *adv.* **1.** in or to this place. **2.** now.

hēre·ăf'tȇr, *adv.* **1.** after this. —*n.* **2.** next world.

hēre'bў, *adv.* by this means.

hė·rĕd'ĭ·tār''ў, *adj.* so by inheritance or heredity.

hēre·ĭn', *adv.* in this.

hēre·ŏf', *adv.* of or concerning this.

hĕr'ė·sў, *n.*, *pl.* **-sies.** contradiction of a dogma. —**her'e·tic**, *n.* —**he·ret'i·cal**, *adj.*

hēre'to·fôre'', *adv.* until now.

hēre·wĭth', *adv.* **1.** with this. **2.** by this means.

hĕr'ĭt·àge, *n.* traditions, etc. from predecessors.

hȇr·mĕt'ĭc, *adj.* airtight. Also, **her·met'i·cal.** —**her·met'i·cal·ly**, *adv.*

hȇr'mĭt, *n.* person willingly living alone. —**her'mit·age**, *n.*

hȇr'nĭ·à, *n.* abdominal rupture.

hē′rō, *n., pl.* **-roes. 1.** person of courage and accomplishment. **2.** protagonist. Also, *fem.,* **he′ro·ine. —he·ro′ic,** *adj.* **—he′ro·ism,** *n.*

hĕ′rō·ĭn, *n.* morphine-based narcotic.

hĕr′ŏn, *n.* wading bird.

hĕr′pēs, *n.* a viral infection causing sores.

hĕr′rĭng, *n.* North Atlantic fish.

hêrs, *pron.* something belonging or pertaining to *her*.

hêr·sĕlf′, *pron.* **1.** intensive and reflexive of *she*. **2.** her true self.

hêrtz, *n. Physics*. one cycle per second.

hĕs′ĭ·tāte′, *v.i.,* **-tated, -tating. 1.** be unresolved. **2.** pause briefly. **3.** be reluctant. **—hes″i·ta′tion,** *n.* **—hes′i·tant,** *adj.*

hĕt′êr·ò·dŏx″, *adj.* unorthodox. **—het′er·o·dox″y,** *n.*

hĕt″êr·ò·gē′nē·oŭs, *adj.* **1.** dissimilar. **2.** of dissimilar components. **—het″er·o·ge·ne′i·ty,** *n.*

hĕt″êr·ò·sĕx′ù·ȧl, *adj.* **1.** attracted solely to the opposite sex. **—n. 2.** heterosexual person. **—het″er·o·sex″u·al′i·ty,** *n.*

hēw, *v.t.,* **hewed, hewed** or **hewn, hewing.** chop.

hĕx, *v.t.* **1.** put an evil spell on. **—n. 2.** evil spell.

hĕx′a·gŏn″, *n.* six-sided plane figure. **—hex·ag′o·nal,** *adj.*

hī·ā′tŭs, *n., pl.* **-tuses, -tus.** interruption.

hī′bêr·nāte″, *v.i.,* **-nated, -nating.** be dormant through winter. **—hi″ber·na′tion,** *n.*

hĭc′cŭp, *n., v.i.,* **-cuped, -cuping. n. 1.** sharp sound due to involuntary contraction of the diaphragm. **—v.i. 2.** emit such a sound. Also, **hic′cough.**

hĭck′ò·rў, *n., pl.* **-ries.** tree of the walnut family.

hīde, *v.,* **hid, hidden, hiding, n. v.t. 1.** keep from being seen. **—v.i. 2.** conceal oneself. **—n. 3.** animal skin.

hĭd′ē·oŭs, *adj.* horribly ugly.

hī′ėr·âr″chў, *n., pl.* **-ies.** organization of higher officials.

hī″ėr·ò·glўph′ĭc, *n.* picture representing a word or sound.

hīgh, *adj.* **1.** being or reaching far up. **2.** of a specified height. **3.** superior. **4.** notably large in amount. **—adv. 5.** in or to a high place or situation. **—high′ly,** *adv.*

hīgh′-flōwn″, *adj.* pretentious, as speech.

hīgh′-hănd′ĕd, *adj.* overbearing. **—high′-hand′ed·ly,** *adv.* **—high′-hand′ed·ness,** *n.*

hīgh′lȧnd, *n.* hilly or mountainous region.

hīgh′līght″, *n.* **1.** brilliant reflection. **2.** salient fact. **—v.t. 3.** emphasize.

hīgh′nĕss, *n.* **1.** height. **2. Highness**, title of respect for royalty.

hīgh′rīse′, *n.* multistoried building. Also, **high′rise″.**

hīgh′-strŭng′, *adj.* nervous.

hīgh′wāy″, *n.* major road.

hī′jăck″, *v.t. Informal.* take in transit by robbery. **—hi′jack″er,** *n.*

hīke, *v.i.,* **hiked, hiking, n. v.i. 1.** go for a long walk. **—n. 2.** long walk.

hĭ·lār′ĭ·oŭs, *adj.* **1.** merry. **2.** very funny. **—hi·lar′i·ty,** *n.*

hĭll, *n.* distinctive area of rising ground. **—hill′y,** *adj.*

hĭll′ŏck, *n.* small hill.

hĭlt, *n.* handle of a sword, etc.

hĭm, *pron.* objective of *he*.

hĭm·sĕlf′, *pron.* **1.** intensive or reflexive of *him*. **2.** his true self.

hīnd, *adj.,* **hinder, hindmost** or **hindermost**. *adj.* behind.

hĭn′dêr, *v.t.* **1.** stop or slow down. **—adj. 2.** rear. **—hin′drance,** *n.*

hĭnd′sĭght″, *n.* belated perception.

hĭnge, *n., v.i.,* **hinged, hinging. n. 1.** support allowing the supported part to turn. **—v.i. 2.** depend.

hĭnt, *n.* **1.** something that allows an inference to be made. **—v.t. 2.** imply. **—v.i. 3.** make a hint.

hĭp, *n.* area around the upper leg joints.

hĭp′pie, *n., pl.* **-pies.** *Informal.* person alienated from conventional society.

hĭp″pò·pŏt′a·mŭs, *n., pl.* **-muses, -mi.** large river-loving African mammal.

hīre, *v.t.,* **hired, hiring, n. v.t. 1.** employ or use for wages or a fee. **—n. 2.** amount paid in hiring.

hīre′lĭng, *n.* unscrupulous mercenary.

hîr′sūte, *adj.* hairy.

hĭs, *pron.* **1.** something belonging or pertaining to him. **—adj. 2.** pertaining to him.

hĭss, *n.* **1.** prolonged s-like sound. **—v.i.**

2. emit a hiss. —*v.t.* 3. hiss at to show disapproval.

hĭs′tŏ·rў, *n.*, *pl.* **-ries.** 1. study of the past. 2. account of the past. 3. known or recorded past. 4. determining forces as inferred from past events. —**his·to′ri·an**, *n.* —**his·tor′ic, his·tor′i·cal,** *adj.*

hĭt, *v.*, **hit, hitting,** *n. v.t.* 1. come against or send something against with force. —*v.i.* 2. come by chance. 3. strike a blow. —*n.* 4. accurate discharge of a missile. 5. successful song, etc.

hĭtch, *v.t.* 1. tie or harness. —*n.* 2. simple knot. 3. obstacle or drawback.

hĭtch′hīke′′, *v.i.* **-hiked, -hiking.** solicit a free automobile ride.

hĭth′êr, *adv.* 1. to this place. —*adj.* 2. nearer.

hĭth′êr·to′′, *adv.* until now.

hīve, *n.* 1. beehive. 2. **hives,** itchy skin condition.

hôard, *n.* 1. precious hidden accumulation. —*v.t.* 2. accumulate and secrete.

hôarse, *adj.* emitting or having a harsh, grating sound.

hôar′ў, *adj.* **-ier, -iest.** 1. gray-haired from age. 2. very old.

hōax, *n.* 1. fraud. —*v.t.* 2. perpetrate a hoax on.

hŏb′ble, *v.*, **-bled, -bling.** *v.i.* 1. limp. —*v.t.* 2. hamper.

hŏb′bў, *n.*, *pl.* **-bies.** spare-time activity. —**hob′by·ist**, *n.*

hŏb′nŏb′′, *v.i.*, **-nobbed, -nobbing.** be on social terms.

hō′bō, *n.*, *pl.* **-bos, -boes.** 1. migrant worker. 2. transient.

hŏck′ēy, *n.* game played on ice with long, clublike sticks and a puck.

hō′cŭs-pō′cŭs, *n.* 1. meaningless jargon. 2. trickery.

hŏd, *n.* 1. trough for bricks or mortar. 2. coal scuttle.

hŏdge′pŏdge′′, *n.* random mixture.

hōe, *n.*, *v.t.*, **hoed, hoeing.** *n.* 1. long-handled tool for loosening earth. —*v.t.* 2. dig with a hoe.

hŏg, *n.* 1. pig raised for meat. 2. *Informal.* greedy person.

hŏgs′hĕad′′, *n.* 1. large cask. 2. measure of 63 liquid gallons.

hoī′pŏl·loī′, the common people.

hoīst, *v.t.* 1. lift, as by a crane. —*n.* 2. hoisting device.

hōld, *v.*, **held, holding,** *n. v.t.* 1. have in the hand. 2. keep from moving or changing. 3. embrace. 4. contain. 5. possess. 6. carry on. 7. consider. —*v.i.* 8. remain firm or fixed. —*n.* 9. act or instance of holding. 10. means of holding. 11. cargo space. —**hold′er**, *n.* —**hold′ing**, *n.*

hōle, *n.* opening, esp. a deep one.

hŏl′ĭ·dāy′′, *n.* 1. day specially celebrated. 2. day of no work.

hŏl′ĭ·nĕss, *n.* 1. quality of being holy. 2. **Holiness,** title of respect for a pope.

hŏl′lŏw, *adj.* 1. empty inside. 2. worthless; vain. 3. booming. —*v.t.* 4. make hollow.

hŏl′lў, *n.*, *pl.* **-ies.** evergreen shrub with red berries.

hŏl′lў·hŏck′′, *n.* tall plant with showy flowers.

hō′lŏ·caūst′′, *n.* widely destructive fire.

hŏl′stêr, *n.* pistol holder.

hō′lў, *adj.*, **-lier, -liest.** 1. dedicated to religion. 2. spiritually pure.

Hōlў Cŏmmūnìòn, *n.* Christian ritual of bread and wine.

Hōlў Spĭrĭt, *n.* spirit of God. Also, **Holy Ghost.**

hŏm′àge, *n.* reverent respect.

hōme, *n.* 1. place of residence. 2. one's own place. —*adv.* 3. to one's home. 4. into the proper place. —**home′land′′**, *n.* —**home′ward**, *adv.*

hōme′lў, *adj.*, **-lier, -liest.** 1. commonplace. 2. not handsome or beautiful.

hōme′sĭck′′, *adj.* sad at being away from home.

hōme′wörk, *n.* schoolwork done at home.

hōme′ў, *adj.*, **-ier, -iest.** cozy.

hŏm′ĭ·cīde′′, *n.* killing of one person by another. —**hom′′i·cid′al**, *adj.*

hŏm′ĭ·lў, *n.*, *pl.* **-lies.** sermon or moral lecture.

hō′′mŏ·gē′nē·oŭs, *adj.* of uniform composition or content. —**ho·mo′′ge·ne′i·ty**, *n.*

hò·mŏg′è·nīze′′, *v.t.*, **-nized, -nizing.** make homogeneous.

hŏm′ò·nўm, *n.* word like another in pronunciation but not in other ways.

Hō′mō sā′pĭ·èns′′, man.

hō′′mō·sĕx′ū·àl, *adj.* 1. sexually attracted to one's own sex. —*n.* 2. homosexual person. —**ho′′mo·sex′′u·al′i·ty**, *n.*

hōne, *v.t.,* **honed, hone.** bring to a fine, sharp edge.

hŏn′ĕst, *adj.* **1.** without desire to steal, lie, etc. **2.** genuine. **3.** frank. —**hon′est·ly,** *adv.* —**hon′es·ty,** *n.*

hŏn′ēy, *n., pl.* **-neys.** syrup made by bees from flowers.

hŏn′ēy·cōmb′′, *n.,* **1.** structure with hexagonal cells made by bees to store honey. **2.** openwork geometrical pattern.

hŏn′ēy·dēw′′ melon, *n.* sweet, green melon.

hŏn′ēy·mōon′′, *n.* vacation of newlyweds. —**hon′ey·moon′′er,** *n.*

hŏn′ēy·sŭck′′le, *n.* climbing plant with small, sweet blossoms.

hŏn′ör, *n.* **1.** high respect. **2.** good reputation. **3.** integrity. **4.** chastity. **5.** conferred distinction. —*v.t.* **6.** hold in honor. **7.** confer distinction or praise on. **8.** accept as valid. —**hon′or·a·ble,** *adj.* —**hon′or·ar′′y,** *adj.*

hŏn′′ör·ĭf′ĭc, *adj.* conferring honor.

hŏod, *n.* **1.** cloth covering for the head and nape. **2.** engine cover of an automobile, etc.

hŏod′lŭm, *n.* violent criminal.

hŏod′wĭnk′′, *v.t.* cheat.

hŏof, *n., pl.* **hoofs, hooves.** hard foot covering of a horse, etc.

hŏok, *n.* **1.** curved object for hanging or attaching things. —*v.t.* **2.** attach with a hook. —*v.i.* **3.** curve as a hook does.

hŏop, *n.* circular band.

hŏot, *n.* **1.** loud, shrill sound. —*v.i.* **2.** utter a hoot. —*v.t.* **3.** show scorn for by hooting.

hŏp, *v.i.,* **hopped, hopping,** *n. vi.* **1.** jump on one foot or with both feet together. —*n.* **2.** act or instance of hopping.

hōpe, *n., v.,* **hoped, hoping.** *n.* **1.** belief that something good may happen. **2.** source or cause of such a belief. —*v.t., v.i.* **3.** entertain hopes. —**hope′ful,** *adj., n.* —**hope′less,** adj.

hŏp′pêr, *n.* funnel-like chute.

hôrde, *n., v.i.,* **horded, hording,** *n.* **1.** swarm; multitude. —*v.i.* **2.** gather in a horde.

hŏ·rī′zŏn, *n.* apparent edge of a scene.

hō′′rī·zŏn′tal, *adj.* running across, like a featureless horizon. —**ho′′ri·zon′tal·ly,** *adv.*

hôr′mōne′′, *n.* substance influencing one part of the body but made in another. —**hor·mo′nal,** *adj.*

hôrn, *n.* **1.** hard, pointed protuberance from an animal head. **2.** substance of this. **3.** pointed projection. **4.** wind instrument. —**horn′y,** *adj.*

hôr′nĕt, *n.* yellow and black wasp.

hôr′ŏ·scōpe′′, *n.* chart of zodiacal signs.

hôr·rĕn′dŏŭs, *adj.* horrible.

hôr′rĭ·ble, *adj.* **1.** causing horror. **2.** *Informal.* very bad. —**hor′ri·bly,** *adv.*

hôr′rĭd, *adj.* **1.** causing horror. **2.** very unpleasant.

hôr′rĭ·fȳ′′, *v.t.,* **-fied, -fying.** fill with horror.

hôr′rör, *n.* strong fear and disgust.

hors de com·bat (ôr′′dĕ kŏm bä′), out of action.

hors d′oeuvre (ôr dêrv′), *n., pl.* **hors d′oeuvres,** appetizer.

hôrse, *n.* **1.** four-footed grass eating animal. **2.** supporting frame. —**horse′back′′,** *adv., n.* —**horse′man, horse′wom′′an,** *n.*

hôrse chĕstnŭt, large-leaved flowering tree.

hôrse′lăugh′′, *n.* loud, open laugh.

hôrse′plāy′′, *n.* rough play.

hôrse′pŏw′′êr, *n.* unit of power equalling 33,000 foot-pounds/minute or 746 watts.

hôrse′răd′′ĭsh, *n.* plant with a pungent root used as a relish.

hôrse′shoe′′, *n.* iron reinforcement for a hoof in the form of an open loop.

hôr′tĭ·cŭl′′tûre, *n.* gardening. —**hor′′ti·cul′tur·al,** *adj.* —**hor′′ti·cul′tur·ist,** *n.*

hō·săn′nà, *interj.* exclamation of praise to God.

hōse, *n., pl.* (for 1) **hoses,** (for 2) **hose. 1.** flexible tube for water, etc. **2.** long stocking.

hō′siêr·ÿ, *n.* stockings.

hŏs′pĭce, *n.* facility for terminally ill persons.

hŏs′pĭ·tà·ble, *adj.* readily offering hospitality.

hŏs′pĭ·tàl, *n.* place for healing. —**hos′pi·tal·ize′′,** *v.t.*

hŏs′′pĭ·tăl′ĭ·tÿ, *n.* generosity and friendship toward visitors.

hōst, *n.* **1.** Also, *fem.,* **hos′tess,** person who entertains guests. **2.** organism supporting parasites. **3.** multitude. **4.** wafer eaten in Holy Communion.

hŏs'tăge, *n.* prisoner kept to enforce demands.

hŏs'tĕl, *n.* institution providing lodgings.

hŏs'tĭle, *adj.* in a state of enmity. —hos·til'i·ty, *n.*

hŏt, *adj.,* **hotter, hottest. 1.** very warm. **2.** very spicy. **3.** intense, as in emotion. —hot'ly, *adv.*

hŏt'bĕd'', *n.* **1.** miniature greenhouse. **2.** prolific source.

hŏt'-blŏod'ĕd, *adj.* impetuous.

hō·tĕl', *n.* place renting rooms and often serving food.

hŏt'-hĕad'ĕd, *adj.* quick-tempered. —hot'head'', *n.*

hŏt rŏd, standard automobile with a supercharged engine. —hot rod'der.

hŏund, *n.* **1.** hunting dog. —v.t. **2.** persecute.

hŏur, *n.* twenty-fourth of a day. —hour'ly, *adv., adj.*

house, *n., pl.* **houses,** *v.t.,* **housed, housing.** *n.* (hŏws). **1.** building to live in. **2.** family. **3.** business firm. **4.** legislative body. —v.t. (hŏwz) **5.** provide lodgings or shelter for.

hŏuse'flȳ'', *n.* ordinary fly.

hŏuse'hŏld'', *n.* inhabitants of a house.

hŏuse'hŏld''êr, *n.* **1.** head of a household. **2.** owner of a house.

hŏuse'kēep''êr, *n.* person responsible for keeping a house in order.

hŏuse'wīfe'', *n.* wife who runs a home.

hŏus·ĭng, *n.* **1.** complex of dwellings. **2.** provision of dwellings.

hŏv'êr, *v.i.* **1.** remain poised in the air. **2.** linger near by. **3.** waver.

hŏw, *adv.* **1.** in what way. **2.** in what state. **3.** for what reason. **4.** to what extent.

hŏw·ĕv'êr, *adv.* **1.** regardless of how. —conj. **2.** nevertheless.

hŏw'ĭtz·êr, *n.* short-barreled, high-trajectory cannon.

hŏwl, *v.i.* **1.** raise a loud, animal-like cry. **2.** laugh uproariously. **3.** complain bitterly. —n. **4.** act or instance of howling.

hŭb, *n.* center of a wheel.

hŭb'bŭb, *n.* confusion; disorder.

hŭck'le·bĕr''rȳ, *n., pl.* -ries. dark blue shrub berry.

hŭck'stêr, *n.* peddler.

hŭd'dle, *n., v.,* -dled, -dling. *n.* **1.** close,

irregular group. —v.t., v.i. **2.** gather in a huddle.

hūe, *n.* **1.** color. **2.** tint.

hŭff, *n.* mood of silent resentment. —huf'fy, *adj.*

hŭg, *v.,* **hugged, hugging,** *n. v.t., v.i.* **1.** embrace. —v.t. **2.** keep close to. —n. **3.** embrace.

hūge, *adj.* very large. —huge'ness, *n.* —huge'ly, *adv.*

hŭlk, *n.* hull of a ship deprived of masts, etc.

hŭlk'ĭng, *adj.* large and bulky.

hŭll, *n.* **1.** shell of a seed, etc. **2.** body of a ship. —v.t. **3.** remove the hulls from.

hŭl'là·bà·lōo'', *n.* clamor.

hŭm, *v.,* **hummed, humming,** *n. v.i.* **1.** make an inarticulate sound between closed lips. —v.t. **2.** render by humming. —n. **3.** low, continuous murmur.

hū'măn, *adj.* **1.** being a man, woman, or child. **2.** characteristic of man. —hu'man·ly, *adv.* —hu'man·kind'', *n.*

hū·māne', *adj.* **1.** merciful. **2.** civilizing.

hū'măn·ĭsm, *n.* intellectual movement centered around man. —hu'man·ist, *n.* —hu''man·is'tic, *adj.*

hū·măn''ĭ·tār'ĭ·àn, *n.* **1.** philanthropist. —adj. **2.** philanthropic. —human''i·tar'i·an·ism, *n.*

hū·măn''ĭ·tȳ, *n.* **1.** human beings collectively. **2.** quality of being humane.

hŭm'ble, *adj.,* -bler, -blest, *v.t.,* -bled, -bling. *adj.* **1.** unpretentious; unconceited. **2.** low in rank. —v.t. **3.** make humble. —hum'bly, *adv.*

hŭm'drŭm'', *adj.* drearily ordinary.

hū'mĭd, *adj.* moist. —hu·mid'i·fy'', *v.t.* —hu·mid'i·ty, *n.*

hū·mĭl'ĭ·āte'', *v.t.,* -ated, -ating. cause to feel shame. —hu·mil''i·a'tion, *n.*

hū·mĭl'ĭ·tȳ, *n.* humble quality.

hŭm'mĭng·bĭrd'', *n.* tiny bird with fast-moving wings.

hū'mör, *n.* **1.** mood. **2.** comical quality. **3.** bodily fluid. —hu'mor·ist, *n.* —hu'mor·ous, *adj.*

hŭmp, *n.* high lump on a back of a camel.

hū'mŭs, *n.* soil with decayed leaf matter, etc.

hŭnch, *n.* **1.** *Informal.* intuitive feeling. **2.** hump.

hŭnch'băck'', *n.* person with a hump on the back. Also, **hump'back''.**

hŭn'drėd, *adj., n.* ten times ten. —**hun'dredth,** *adj.*

hŭn'drėd·weight", *n. U.S.* 100 pounds.

hŭn'gêr, *n.* **1.** desire to eat. **2.** deprivation of food. **3.** strong desire. —*v.i.* **4.** be hungry. —**hun'gry,** *adj.* —**hun'gri·ly,** *adv.*

hŭnk, *n. Informal.* large piece.

hŭnt, *v.t.* **1.** pursue to kill or harass. —*v.i.* **2.** hunt game. **3.** search. —*n.* **4.** act or instance of hunting. —**hunt'er, hunts'man,** *fem.* **hunt'ress,** *n.*

hûr'dle, *n., v.t.,* -dled, -dling. *n.* **1.** barrier to be leapt. —*v.t.* **2.** leap over.

hûrl, *n.* throw with force.

hûr'lў-bûr'lў, *n., pl.*-lies. turmoil.

hûr·räh', *interj., n.* shout of approval. Also **hur·ray'.**

hûr'rĭ·cāne", *n.* tropical cyclone.

hûr'rў, *v.,* -ried, -rying, *v.i.* **1.** move or act quickly. —*v.t.* **2.** cause to hurry. —*n.* **3.** reason for hurrying. **4.** eagerness to hurry. —**hur'ried·ly,** *adv.*

hûrt, *v.,* hurt, hurting, *v.t.* **1.** damage; injure. **2.** feeling of pain. —*v.i.* **3.** cause pain. **4.** do harm. —*n.* **5.** damage; injury. —**hurt'ful,** *adj.*

hûr'tle, *v.i.,* -tled, -tling. move at high speed.

hŭs'bånd, *n.* **1.** woman's spouse. —*v.t.* **2.** manage economically.

hŭs'bånd·rў, *n.* **1.** farming. **2.** management.

hŭsh, *n., v.t.* silence.

hŭsk, *n.* **1.** outer covering. —*v.t.* **2.** remove the husk from.

hŭs'kў, *adj.* **1.** hoarse. **2.** robust.

hŭs'tle, *v.,* -tled, -tling, *n. v.t.* **1.** jostle. **2.** force roughly. —*v.i.* **3.** move or act energetically. —*n.* **4.** act or instance of hustling. **5.** *Informal.* enterprise.

hŭt, *n.* small, crude dwelling.

hŭtch, *n.* **1.** cupboard. **2.** coop for rabbits, etc.

hy'a·cĭnth", *n.* bell-shaped flower of the lily family.

hy'brĭd, *n.* **1.** offspring or product of mixed species or varieties. —**hy'brid·ize",** *v.t.*

hy·drăn'gē·å, *n.* shrub with clusters of white, blue, or pink flowers.

hy'drånt, *n.* valved pipe from a water main.

hy·drau'lĭc, *adj.* **1.** operated by liquid pressure. —*n.* **2. hydraulics,** study of the mechanical properties of liquids. —**hy·drau'li·cal·ly,** *adv.*

hy"drô·câr'bon, *n.* compound of hydrogen and carbon.

hy"drô·ė·lĕc'trĭc, *adj.* pertaining to electricity produced by water power.

hy'drô·gėn, *n.* flammable gaseous element.

hy"drô·phō'bĭ·a, *n.* rabies.

hy'drô·plāne", *n.* **1.** seaplane. **2.** motorboat with hydrofoils or a planing hull.

hy"drô·pŏn'ĭcs, *n.* growing of plants in liquids.

hy·ē'nå, *n.* wolflike African or Asian animal.

hy'giēne, *n.* **1.** system of health preservation. **2.** cleanliness. —**hy"gi·en'ic,** *adj.* —**hy"gi·en'i·cal·ly,** *adv.*

hўmn, *n.* poem or song of praise, as to God. —**hymn'book",** **hym'nal,** *n.*

hype, *n.* exaggerated publicity.

hy·pêr'bo·lē", *n.* exaggeration for the rhetorical effect. —**hy"per·bol'ic,** *adj.*

hy"pêr·crĭt'ĭ·cål, *adj.* over-critical.

hy"pêr·sĕn'sĭ·tĭve, *adj.* too sensitive.

hy"pêr·tĕn'sion, *n.* excessive blood pressure.

hy'phėn, *n.* dash, -, used to join words or syllables. —**hy'phen·ate",** *v.t.* —**hy"phen·a'tion,** *n.*

hўp·nō'sĭs, *n., pl.* -ses. sleeplike, obedient condition induced by suggestion from another. —**hyp·not'ic,** *adj.* —**hyp'no·tism,** *n.* —**hyp'no·tist,** *n.* —**hyp'no·tize",** *v.t.*

hy"po·chŏn'drĭ·å, *n.* fear of imaginary illness. —**hy"po·chon'dri·ac",** *n., adj.*

hy·pŏc'rĭ·sў, *n., pl.* -sies. false pretension to virtue, affection, etc. —**hy'po·crite,** *n.* —**hy"po·crit'i·cal,** *adj.*

hy"po·dêr'mĭc, *adj.* **1.** under the skin. —*n.* **2.** hypodermic injection or injecting device. —**hy"po·der'mi·cal·ly,** *adv.*

hy·pŏt'e·nūse", *n.* side of a right triangle opposite the right angle.

hy·pŏth'e·sĭs, *n., pl.* -ses. unproved theory. —**hy"po·thet'i·cal,** *adj.*

hўs·tē'rĭ·å, *n.* **1.** pathologically excitable condition. **2.** Also, **hys·ter'ics,** outbreak of uncontrolled emotion. —**hys·ter'i·cal,** *adj.*

I

I, i, *n.* **1.** ninth letter of the English alphabet. —*pron.* **2. I** (first person singular as a subject).

ĭbĭd., in the same place: used in scholarly notes.

īce, *n., v.,* **iced, icing.** *n.* **1.** water frozen solid. **2.** frozen dessert. —*v.t.* **3.** put ice over or around. **4.** put icing over. —*v.i.* **5.** freeze or form ice. —**ice′box′′,** *n.* —**ice′skate′′,** *n.* —**ic′y,** *adj.*

īce′bĕrg′′, *n.* floating fragment from a polar icecap.

īce′căp′′, *n.* polar mass of ice.

ĭch′′thў·ŏl′ò·gў, *n.* study of fish. —**ich′′thy·ol′o·gist,** *n.*

ī′cĭ·cle, *n.* conical hanging mass of frozen water.

ic′ĭng, *n.* sweet cover for a cake.

ī′cŏn, *n.* religious image, esp. in an Eastern Orthodox church.

ī·cŏn·ó·clăst′′, *n.* destroyer of long-held values. —**i·con′′o·clas′tic,** *adj.*

ī·dē′à, *n.* image in the mind; conception.

ī·dē′ál, *adj.* **1.** perfect. **2.** imaginary. —*n.* **3.** something perfect. —**i·de′al·ly,** *adv.* —**i·de′al·ize′′,** *v.t.*

ī·dē′ál·ĭsm, *n.* conformity to or belief in ideals. —**i·de′al·ist,** *n.* —**i′′de·al·is′tic,** *adj.*

ī·dĕn′tĭ·cál, *adj.* exactly alike or the same. —**i·den′ti·cal·ly,** *adv.*

ī·dĕn′tĭ·fy′′, *v.t.,* **-fied, -fying. 1.** establish the identity of. **2.** associate with another person or thing. —**i·den′′ti·fi·ca′tion,** *n.*

ī·dĕn′tĭ·tў, *n., pl.* **-ties. 1.** state of being identical. **2.** individuality.

ī′′dē·ŏl′ò·gў, *n., pl.* **-gies.** political or social doctrine. —**i′′de·o·log′i·cal,** *adj.*

ĭd′ĭ·ŏm, *n.* **1.** dialect. **2.** combination of words with a nonliteral meaning. —**id′′i·o·mat′ic,** *adj.*

ĭd′′ĭ·ò·sўn′crá·sў, *n., pl.* **-sies.** personal trait.

ĭd′′ĭ·ŏt, *n.* feeble-minded person. —**id′′i·ot′ic,** *adj.* —**id′i·o·cy,** *n.*

ī′dle, *adj.,* **idler, idlest,** *v.i.,* **idled, idling.** *adj.* **1.** not at work or in use. **2.** lazy. **3.** frivolous. —*v.i.* **4.** be idle. —**id′ly,** *adv.* —**id′ler,** *n.*

ī′dŏl, *n.* **1.** statue of a god. **2.** idealized person. —**i′dol·ize′′,** *v.t.*

ī·dŏl′á·trў, *n., pl.* **-tries.** worship of idols. —**i·dol′a·ter,** *n.* —**i·dol′a·trous,** *adj.*

ī′dўll, *n.* **1.** poem of pastoral life. **2.** beautiful episode. Also, **i′dyl.** —**i·dyl′ic,** *adj.*

ī.ē., that is.

ĭf, *conj.* **1.** on condition that. **2.** supposing that. **3.** whether.

ĭg′lōō, *n., pl.* **-loos.** domed Eskimo snow house.

ĭg′nē·oŭs, *adj.* resulting from intense heat.

ĭg·nīte′, *v.,* **-nited, -niting.** *v.t.,* **1.** set on or catch fire. —*v.i.* **2.** catch fire. —**ig·ni′tion,** *n.*

ĭg·nō′ble, *adj.* base; mean.

ĭg′nó·mĭn′′ў, *n.* shame. —**ig′′no·min′i·ous,** *adj.*

ĭg′′nó·rā′mŭs, *n., pl.* **-muses.** ignorant person.

ĭg′nó·ránt, *adj.* **1.** uneducated. **2.** unaware. —**ig′no·rance,** *n.* —**ig′no·rant·ly,** *adv.*

ĭg·nōre′, *v.t.,* **-nored, -noring.** take no heed of.

ĭll, *adj.,* **worse,** (for 1) **worst,** *adv.,* **worse, worst,** *n. adj.* **1.** bad. **2.** sick. —*adv.* **3.** badly. **4.** scarcely. —*n.* **5.** harm.

ĭll′·ad·vīsed′, *adj.* showing bad judgment.

ĭl·lē′gál, *adj.* unlawful. —**il·le′gal·ly,** *adv.* —**il′′le·gal′i·ty,** *n.*

ĭl·lĕg′ĭ·ble, *adj.* unable to be read. —**il·leg′′i·bil′i·ty,** *n.*

ĭl′′lè·gĭt′ĭ·máte, *adj.* **1.** not legitimate. **2.** born out of wedlock. —**il′′le·git′i·ma·cy,** *n.*

ĭl·lĭc′ĭt, *adj.* not allowed. —**il·lic′it·ly,** *adv.*

ĭl·lĭt′ĕr·áte, *adj.* **1.** unable to read. —*n.* **2.** illiterate person. —**il·lit′er·a·cy,** *n.*

ĭll′nĕss, *n.* sickness.

ĭl·lŏg′ĭ·cál, *adj.* opposed to logic.

ĭl·lū′mĭ·nāte′′, *v.t.,* **-nated, -nating. 1.** Also, **il·lu′mine,** light up. **2.** elucidate. **3.** decorate with gold and color. —**il·lu′′mi·na′tion,** *n.*

ĭll-ūse′, *v.t.,* **-used, -using.** abuse. —**ill′use′, ill′-us′age,** *n.*

ĭl·lū′sion, *n.* **1.** deceptive impression. **2.**

false conception. —il·lu'sive, —il·lu' so·ry, adj.

il'lŭs·trāte", v.t., -trated, -trating. 1. explain with examples. 2. add pictures to, as a narrative. —il"lus·tra'tion, n. —il'lus·tra"tor, n. —il·lus'tra·tive, adj.

il·lŭs'trĭ·oŭs, adj. distinguished; famous.

ĭll wĭll, hostility.

ĭm'āge, n. 1. picture. 2. popular conception. —im'age·ry, n.

ĭ·mǎg'ĭne, v.t., -ined, -ining. 1. create in the mind. 2. suppose to exist. 3. believe wrongly to exist. —i·mag'in·a· ble, adj. —i·mag'in·a·bly, adv. —i· mag'in·a"ry, adj. —i·mag"i·na' tion, n. —i·mag'i·na·tive, adj.

ĭm·bǎl'ance, n. lack of balance.

ĭm'bē·cĭle, n. idiot. —im"be·cil'ic, adj. —im'be·cil'i·ty, n.

ĭm·bībe', v., -bibed, -bibing. v.t., v.i. drink.

im·bro·gli·o (ĭm brōl'yō), n., pl. -os. confused situation.

ĭm·būe', v.t., -bued, -buing. permeate.

ĭm'ĭ·tāte", v.t., -tated, -tating. have the same characteristics as. —im"i·ta' tion, n. —im'i·ta"tor, n. —im'i·ta" tive, adj.

ĭm·mǎc'ū·late, adj. without dirt or sin. —im·mac'u·late·ly, adv.

ĭm'må·nent, adj. inherent. —im'ma· nent·ly, adv. —im'ma·nence, n.

ĭm"må·tē'rĭ·ál, adj. 1. irrelevant. 2. not composed of matter.

ĭm'må·tûre, n. with an undeveloped character. —im"ma·tu'ri·ty, n.

ĭm·mĕas'ûr·å·ble, adj. not to be measured. —im·meas'ur·a·bly, adv.

ĭm·mē'dĭ·āte, adj. 1. unseparated by anything else. 2. direct. —im·me'di·a· cy, n. —im·me'di·ate·ly, adv.

ĭm"mē·mō'rĭ·ál, adj. from before memory.

ĭm·mĕnse', adj. huge. —im·men'si·ty, n. —im·mense'ly, adv.

ĭm·mêrse', v.t., -mersed, -mersing. bury completely, as in a liquid. —im· mer'sion, n.

ĭm'mĭ·grāte", v.i., -grated, -grating. enter a country to settle. —im'mi· grant, n., adj. —im"mi·gra'tion, n.

ĭm'mĭ·nent, adj. soon to happen. —im' mi·nence, im'mi·nen·cy, n.

ĭm·mō'bĭle, adj. fixed in place. —im" mo·bil'i·ty, n. —im·mo'bi·lize", v.t.

ĭm·mŏd'e·råte, adj. lacking moderation. —im·mod'e·rate·ly, adv.

ĭm·mŏd'ĕst, adj. lacking modesty. —im· mod'es·ty, n.

ĭm'mō·lāte", v.t., -lated, -lating. kill as a sacrifice. —im"mo·la'tion, n.

ĭm·môr'ál, adj. not moral. —im"mo· ral'i·ty, n.

ĭm·môr'tål, adj. 1. never to die. 2. never to be forgotten. —n. 3. immortal being. —im"mor·tal'i·ty, n. —im·mor'tal· ize", v.t.

ĭm·mov'å·ble, adj. fixed in place.

ĭm·mūne', adj. proof against disease, etc. —im·mun'i·ty, n. —im'mu·nize" , v.t. —im"mu·ni·za'tion, n.

ĭm·mū'tå·ble, adj. unchangeable. —im· mu"ta·bil'i·ty, n.

ĭmp, n. small demon. —imp'ish, adj.

ĭm'păct, n. 1. violent shock. —v.t. (im pact') 2. force against something else.

ĭm·pāir', v.t. put out of order. —im·pair' ment, n.

ĭm·pāle', v.t., -paled, -paling. pierce and support with a sharpened pole, etc.

ĭm·pǎl'på·ble, adj. 1. imperceptible to the touch. 2. subtle.

ĭm·pǎn'ĕl, v.t., -eled, -eling. enroll for or as a jury.

ĭm·pârt', v.t. reveal, as news.

ĭm·pâr'tial, adj. unbiased. —im·par' tial·ly, adv. —im·par"ti·al'i·ty, n.

ĭm·pǎs'så·ble, adj. impossible to pass along or over.

ĭm'pǎsse, n. deadlock.

ĭm·pǎs'sioned, adj. passionate.

ĭm·pǎs'sĭve, adj. revealing no emotion. —im"pas·siv'i·ty, n.

ĭm·pā'tiĕnt, adj. without patience. —im·pa'tience, n.

ĭm·pēach', n. try for wrongdoing in office. —im·peach'ment, n.

ĭm·pĕc'cà·ble, adj. flawless.

ĭm"pē·cū'nĭ·oŭs, adj. penniless.

ĭm·pēde', v.t., -peded, -peding. hinder. —im·ped'ance, im·ped'i·ment, n.

ĭm·pĕd"ĭ·mĕn'tå, n. pl. things to be carried along.

ĭm·pĕl', v.t., -pelled, -pelling. 1. drive forward. 2. urge.

ĭm·pĕnd', v.i. be about to happen.

ĭm·pĕn'e·trå·ble, adj. impossible to penetrate.

ĭm·pĕn'ĭ·tĕnt, *adj*. not repentant.

ĭm·pĕr'a·tĭve, *adj*. 1. vitally necessary. 2. pertaining to command.

ĭm·pêr·cĕp'tĭ·ble, *adj*. impossible or difficult to perceive. —im''per·cep'ti·bly, *adv*.

ĭm·pêr'fĕct, *adj*. 1. flawed; deficient. 2. pertaining to uncompleted or continuing action. —im·per'fect·ly, *adv*. —im''per·fec'tion, *n*.

ĭm·pē'rĭ·al, *adj*. pertaining to empires or emperors.

ĭm·pē'rĭ·al·ĭsm, *n*. policy of creating or holding an empire. —im·pe'ri·al·ist, *n*., *adj*. —im·pe''ri·al·is'tic, *adj*.

ĭm·pĕr'ĭl, *v.t.*, -iled, -iling. endanger.

ĭm·pē'rĭ·oŭs, *adj*. imposing one's will on others. —im·pe'ri·ous·ly, *adv*.

ĭm·pĕr'ĭsh·a·ble, *adj*. not perishable.

ĭm·pêr'ma·nĕnt, *adj*. not permanent.

ĭm·pêr'mē·a·ble, *adj*. impossible to seep through.

ĭm·pêr'sŏn·al, *adj*. pertaining to no individuals —im·per'son·al·ly, *adv*.

ĭm·pêr'sŏn·āte'', *v.t.*, -ated, -ating. pretend to be, as in acting. —im·per''son·a'tion, *n*. —im·per'son·a''tor, *n*.

ĭm·pêr'tĭ·nĕnt, *adj*. insolent. —im·per'ti·nence, *n*.

ĭm''pêr·tûrb'a·ble, *adj*. impossible to disturb visibly. —im''per·turb'a·bly, *adv*.

ĭm·pêr'vĭ·oŭs, *adj*. impenetrable, esp. by moisture.

ĭm·pĕt'ū·oŭs, *adj*. hasty; rash. —im·pet''u·os'i·ty, *n*.

ĭm'pe·tŭs, *n*. 1. force in motion. 2. motivation.

ĭm·pī'e·tÿ, *n*. disrespect, esp. for God. —im'pi·ous, *adj*.

ĭm·pĭnge', *v.i.*, -pinged, -pinging. encroach. —im·pinge'ment, *n*.

ĭm·plăc'a·ble, *adj*. impossible to appease. —im·plac'a·bly, *adv*.

ĭm·plănt', *v.t.* fix or plant firmly.

ĭm·plaŭs'ĭ·ble, *adj*. not plausible.

ĭm'ple·mĕnt, *n*. 1. piece of equipment. —*v.t.* 2. put in effect. —im''ple·men·ta'tion, *n*.

ĭm'plĭ·cāte'', *v.t.*, -cated, -cating. reveal as party to a crime.

ĭm''plĭ·cā'tion, *n*. act or instance of implying or implicating.

ĭm·plĭc'ĭt, *adj*. 1. implied. 2. absolute, as trust. —im·plic'it·ly, *adv*.

ĭm·plōre', *v.t.*, -plored, -ploring. plead earnestly with or for. —im·plor'ing·ly, *adv*.

ĭm·plȳ', *v.t.*, -plied, -plying. suggest as existing or being so.

ĭm''po·līte', *adj*. rude.

ĭm·pŏl'ĭ·tĭc, *adj*. unwise as giving offense.

ĭm·pŏn'dêr·a·ble, *adj*. 1. immeasurable. —*n*. 2. something imponderable.

ĭm·pôrt', *v.t.* 1. bring into a country, esp. for sale. 2. signify. —*n*. (im'port). 3. something imported. 4. significance. —im·port'er, *n*. —im''por·ta'tion, *n*.

ĭm·pôrt'ant, *adj*. 1. of great significance. 2. of great power. —im·por'tance, *n*.

ĭm''pôr·tūne', *v.t.*, -tuned, -tuning. urge insistently. —im''por·tun'i·ty, *n*. —im·por'tu·nate, *adj*.

ĭm·pōse', *v.*, -posed, -posing. *v.t.* 1. force to accept. —*v.i.* 2. take advantage. —im''po·si'tion, *n*.

ĭm·pōs'ĭng, *adj*. impressive. —im·pos'ing·ly, *adv*.

ĭm·pŏs'sĭ·ble, *adj*. 1. not possible. 2. totally unsuitable or disagreeable. —im·pos''si·bil'i·ty, *n*.

ĭm'pŏst, *n*. tax on imports.

ĭm·pŏs'tör, *n*. person pretending to an identity, competence, etc. he does not have. —im·pos'ture, *n*.

ĭm'po·tĕnt, *adj*. 1. helpless. 2. without strength. 3. incapable of sexual intercourse. —im'po·tence, im'po·ten·cy, *n*.

ĭm·poŭnd', *v.t.* 1. seize and hold legally. 2. dam.

ĭm·pŏv'êr·ĭsh, *v.t.* make poor. —im·pov'er·ish·ment, *n*.

ĭm·prăc'tĭ·ca·ble, *adj*. impossible to do.

ĭm·prăc'tĭ·cal, *adj*. not practical.

ĭm''pre·cā'tion, *n*. curse.

ĭm''pre·cīse', *n*. not precise; vague. —im''pre·ci'sion, *n*.

ĭm·prĕg'na·ble, *adj*. proof against attack.

ĭm·prĕg'nāte'', *v.t.*, -nated, -nating. 1. saturate. 2. make pregnant. —im''preg·na'tion, *n*.

ĭm·prĕss', *v.t.* 1. command respectful attention. **2.** print. **3.** force into military service.

ĭm·prĕs′sion, *n.* **1.** mental effect. **2.** vague idea. **3.** pressed mark.

ĭm·prĕs′sion·a·ble, *adj.* easily influenced.

ĭm·prĕs′sĭve, *adj.* commanding respect. —**im·pres′sive·ly,** *adv.*

ĭm·prĭnt′, *v.t.* **1.** affix or print as a mark. —*n.* (im′print). **2.** imprinted mark. **3.** effect.

ĭm·prĭs′ŏn, *v.t.* confine in prison. —**im·pris′on·ment,** *n.*

ĭm·prŏb′a·ble, *adj.* unlikely. —**im·prob′a·bil′i·ty,** *n.*

ĭm·prŏmp′tū, *adj., adv.* without preparation.

ĭm·prŏp′êr, *adj.* not proper. —**im′pro·pri′e·ty,** *n.*

ĭm·prove′, *v.,* -**proved,** -**proving.** make or become better. —**im·prove′ment,** *n.*

ĭm·prŏv′ĭ·dĕnt, *adj.* not thrifty. —**im·prov′i·dence,** *n.*

ĭm′prŏ·vīse′′, *v.,* -**vised,** -**vising.** *v.t.* **1.** create at short notice or with what is available. —*v.i.* **2.** perform extemporaneously. —**im·prov′′i·sa′tion,** *n.*

ĭm·prūd′ĕnt, *adj.* not prudent. —**im·prud′ence,** *n.*

ĭm·pūgn′, *v.t.* oppose as false.

ĭm′pŭlse, *n.* **1.** surge of force. **2.** sudden decision to act. —**im·pul′sive,** *adj.*

ĭm·pū′nĭ·tў, *n.* freedom from punishment.

ĭm·pūre′, *adj.* **1.** adulterated. **2.** immoral. —**im·pur′i·ty,** *n.*

ĭm·pūte′, *v.t.,* -**puted,** -**puting.** attribute. —**im′′pu·ta′tion** *n.*

ĭn, *prep.* **1.** surrounded or contained by. **2.** during. **3.** into. **4.** subjected to. —*adv.* **5.** to the inside.

ĭn-, prefix meaning "not" or "lack of." **inaccurate, inadequate, inapplicable, inappropriate, inarticulate, incertitude, inclement, incoherent, incompetent, incongruous, inconsequential, inconsistent, inconspicuous, incontinent, incredible, incredulous, incurable, indecent, indecision, indefinite, indelicate, indigestible, indiscreet, indispensable, indistinct, indivisible, inedible, ineligible, inequitable, inexact, infallible, infertile, informal, infrequent, inhu-**

mane, inhumanity, inoffensive, insane, insatiable, insecure, insincere, insufficient, intemperate, intolerable, intransitive, invisible, involuntary, invulnerable.

ĭn äb·sĕn′tĭ·à, in his, her, or their absence.

ĭn′′ăd·vêrt′ĕnt, *adj.* **1.** unobservant. **2.** due to unawareness or oversight. —**in′′ad·vert′ent·ly,** *adv.* —**in′′ad·vert′ence,** *n.*

ĭn·āl′ĭ·ĕn·a·ble, *adj.* not to be taken away.

ĭn·āne′, *adj.* pointless; silly. —**in·an′i·ty,** *n.*

ĭn′′ăs·mŭch′ăs 1. considering that. **2.** to the extent that.

ĭn·ău′gù·rāte′′, *v.t.,* -**rated,** -**rating.** begin formally in a term of office, service, etc. —**in·aug′′u·ra′tion,** *n.* —**in·aug′u·ral,** *adj., n.*

ĭn′bôard′′, *adj., adv.* within a ship or aircraft.

ĭn′bôrn′′, *adj.* present at birth; innate.

ĭn′brĕd′, *adj.* **1.** inborn. **2.** resulting from inbreeding.

ĭn′brēed′, *v.,* -**bred,** -**breeding.** *v.t., v.i.* breed from closely related stocks.

ĭn′′căn·dĕs′cent, *adj.* glowing from heat. —**in′′can·des′cence,** *n.*

ĭn′′căn·tā′tion, *n.* formula producing a magic spell.

ĭn′′ca·păc′ĭ·tāte′′, *v.t.,* -**tated,** -**tating.** make unable or incompetent. —**in′′ca·pac′i·ty,** *n.*

ĭn·câr′cêr·āte′′, *v.t.,* -**ated,** -**ating.** imprison.

ĭn·câr′nàte, *adj., v.t.,* -**nated,** -**nating.** *adj.* **1.** in fleshly, mortal form. —*v.t.* (in kahr′nāt) **2.** create in incarnate form. —**in′′car·na′tion,** *n.*

ĭn′′cĕn·dĭ·âr′′ў, *adj., n.,* pl. -**ies.** *adj.* **1.** causing fires. —*n.* **2.** incendiary bomb. **3.** deliberate setter of fires.

ĭn′cĕnse, *n., v.t.,* -**censed,** -**censing.** *n.* **1.** gum or resin giving off perfumed smoke. —*v.t.* (in cense′) **2.** enrage.

ĭn·cĕn′tĭve, *n.* motive.

ĭn·cĕp′tion, *n.* beginning.

ĭn·cĕs′sànt, *adj.* never ceasing. —**in·ces′sant·ly,** *adv.*

ĭn′cĕst, *n.* sexual relations between very close relatives. —**in·ces′tu·ous,** *adj.*

ĭnch, *n.* **1.** twelfth part of a foot, as in linear measure. —*v.i.*, *v.t.* **2.** move very slowly.

in·cho·ate (in kō it), *adj.* new and formless.

in′ci·dence, *n.* frequency of occurrence.

in′ci·dent, *n.* **1.** something that happens. **2.** minor fight, etc. —*adj.* **3.** probably consequent.

in′′ci·den′tal, *adj.* **1.** happening in connection with something important. —*n.* **2.** something incidental. **3.** miscellaneous item.

in′′ci·den′tal·ly, *adv.* **1.** while we are on the subject. **2.** in an incidental manner.

in·cin′er·āte′′, *v.*, **-ated, -ating.** *v.t.*, *v.i.* burn to ashes. —**in·cin′er·at′′or**, *n.*

in·cip′i·ent, *adj.* beginning to develop. —**in·cip′i·ence**, *n.*

in·cīse′, *v.t.*, **-cised, -cising.** cut into. —**in·ci′sion**, *n.*

in·cīs′īve, *adj.* penetrating in perception.

in·cīs′ör, *n.* human front tooth.

in·cīte′, *v.t.*, **-cited, -citing.** urged to act. —**in·cite′ment**, *n.*

in·clīne′, *v.*, **-clined, -clining,** *v.i.* **1.** slope or slant. **2.** have a tendency or liking. —*v.t.* **3.** cause to incline. —*n.* (in′ cline) **4.** slope. —**in·cli·na′tion**, *n.*

in·clōse′, *v.t.*, **-closed, -closing.** enclose.

in·clūde′, *v.t.*, **-cluded, -cluding.** have or consider among other things. —**in· clu′sion**, *n.*

in·clū′sive, *adj.* **1.** including the limiting items mentioned. **2.** considering everything.

in·cŏg·nī′tō, *adj.* under an assumed name.

in′cŏme′′, *n.* money received.

in′′cŏm·mū′′nī·cā′dō, *adj.* without being allowed to communicate.

in·cŏm′pár·à·ble, *adj.* not to be compared to others, esp. as an equal. —**in· com′par·a·bly**, *adv.*

in·côr′pō·rāte′′, *v.*, **-rated, -rating.** *v.t.*, *v.i.* **1.** form into a corporation. —*v.t.* **2.** embody. —**in·cor′′po·ra′ tion**, *n.*

in·côr′ri·gi·ble, *adj.* incapable of correction.

in·crēase′, *v.*, **-creased, -creasing,** *n.* *v.t.* **1.** add to. —*v.i.* **2.** become larger or more numerous. —*n.* (in′crease) **3.**

act, instance or amount of increasing. —**in·creas′ing·ly**, *adv.*

in′crē·mènt, *n.* increase.

in·crĭm′i·nāte′′, *v.t.*, **-nating, -nating. 1.** accuse of crime. **2.** subject to such accusation.

in·crŭst′, *v.t.* cover thickly. —**in′′crus· ta′tion**, *n.*

in′cū·bāte′′, *v.t.*, **-bated, -bating. 1.** hatch. **2.** encourage the development of. —**in′′cu·ba′tion**, *n.* —**in′cu·ba′′tor**, *n.*

in′cù·bùs, *n.* **1.** annoying burden. **2.** evil spirit.

in·cŭl′cāte, *v.t.*, **-cated, -cating.** impress on the mind.

in·cùl′pāte, *v.t.*, **-pated, -pating.** incriminate.

in·cŭm′bènt, *adj.* **1.** obligatory. **2.** in office. —*n.* **3.** present office holder. —**in· cum′ben·cy**, *n.*

in·cûr′, *v.t.*, **-curred, -curring.** bring on oneself.

in·cûr′sion, *n.* invasion.

in·dĕbt′èd, *adj.* owing a debt of money or gratitude. —**in·debt′ed·ness**, *n.*

in·dēed′, *adv.* **1.** truly. —*interj.* **2.** exclamation of surprise.

in′′dè·făt′ī·gà·ble, *adj.* tireless.

in·dĕf′ī·nīte·lỹ, *adj.* **1.** in an indefinite way. **2.** with no known termination.

in·dĕl′ī·ble, *adj.* impossible to erase.

in·dĕm′nĭ·fÿ′′, *v.t.*, **-fied, -fying.** compensate for. —**in·dem′ni·ty**, *n.*

in·dĕnt′, *v.t.* **1.** notch. **2.** begin to the right of the normal margin. —**in·den′ tion, in′′den·ta′tion**, *n.*

in·dĕn′tûre, *n.*, *v.t.*, **-tured, -turing.** *n.* **1.** contract, esp. for work. —*v.t.* **2.** bind with an indenture.

in′′dē·pĕn′dènt, *adj.* free of or needing no outside control. —**in′′de·pen′dent· ly**, *adv.* —**in′′de·pen′dence**, *n.*

in′dĕx, *n.*, *pl.* **-dexes, -dices,** *v.t.* *n.* **1.** orderly list of subjects. **2.** something that indicates. **3.** forefinger. —*v.t.* **4.** make an index for.

in·dī′cāte′′, *v.t.*, **-cated, -cating. 1.** call attention to. **2.** imply. —**in′′di·ca′ tion**, *n.* —**in·dic′a·tive**, *adj.* —**in′di· ca′′tor**, *n.*

in·dict′ (in dīt′), *v.t.* charge formally with crime. —**in·dict′ment**, *n.*

in·dĭf′fèr·ènt, *adj.* **1.** not caring. **2.** mediocre. **3.** neutral. —in·dif′fer·ence, *n.*

ĭn·dĭg′ĕn·oŭs, *adj.* native.

ĭn′dĭ·gĕnt, *adj.* needy. —in′di·gence, *n.*

ĭn·dĭ·gĕs′tion, *n.* difficulty in digesting food; discomfort caused by this.

ĭn·dĭg′nănt, *adj.* righteously angry. —in·dig′nant·ly, *adv.* —in′′dig·na′tion, *n.*

ĭn·dĭg′nĭ·tў, *n., pl.* -ties. offense to dignity.

ĭn′dĭ·gō′′, *n.* deep blue dye.

ĭn′′dĭs·pōsed′, *adj.* **1.** disinclined. **2.** slightly ill. —in·dis′′po·si′tion, *n.*

ĭn′′dĭ·vĭd′ū·ăl, *adj.* **1.** separate or distinct. **2.** pertaining to one person or thing. *n.* **3.** single or unique person or thing. —in′′di·vid′u·al·ly, *adv.* —in′′di·vid′′u·al′i·ty, *n.*

ĭn′′dĭ·vĭd′ū·ăl·ĭsm, *n.* use of personal judgment alone. —in′′di·vid′u·al·ist, *n.*

ĭn·dŏc′trĭ·nāte′, *v.t.,* -nated, -nating. instill doctrine into. —in·doc′′tri·na′tion, *n.*

ĭn′dò·lĕnt, *adj.* making little effort. —in′do·lence, *n.*

ĭn·dŏm′ĭ·tà·ble, *adj.* impossible to defeat or dishearten.

ĭn′dôor′′, *adj.* for use, etc. inside.

ĭn′dôors′, *adv.* within a building.

ĭn·dū′bĭ·tà·ble, *adj.* impossible to doubt. —in·du′bi·ta·bly, *adv.*

ĭn·dūce′, *v.t.,* -duced, -ducing. **1.** persuade. **2.** cause. **3.** infer. —in·duce′ment, *n.*

ĭn·dŭct′, *v.t.* enter formally, as in a military organization. —in·duc·tee′, *n.*

ĭn·dŭc′tion, *n.* **1.** act or instance of inducing or inducting. **2.** reasoning from the particular to the general. —in·duc′tive, *adj.*

ĭn·dŭlge′, *v.,* -dulged, -dulging. satisfy.

ĭn·dŭl′gence, *n.* **1.** act or instance of indulging. **2.** indulgent manner.

ĭn·dŭl′gĕnt, *adj.* leniently kind.

ĭn′dŭs·trў, *n., pl.* -tries. **1.** manufacture and commerce. **2.** type of manufacture or commerce. **3.** diligent work. —in·dus′tri·al, *adj.* —in·dus′tri·al·ist, *n.* —in·dus′tri·al·ize′′, *v.t.* —in·dus′tri·ous, *adj.*

ĭn·ē′brĭ·āte′′, *v.t.,* -ated, -ating, *n. v.t.* **1.** make drunk. —*n.* (in e′bri·ate) **2.** drunkard. —in·e′′bri·a′tion, *n.*

ĭn·ĕf′fà·ble, *adj.* indescribable in words.

in′′e·luc′ta·ble, *adj.* inescapable.

ĭn·ĕpt′, *adj.* **1.** unsuitable. **2.** foolish or awkward. —in·ept′i·tude′′, in·ept′ness, *n.*

ĭn·êrt′, *adj.* **1.** powerless to move. **2.** without active properties. —in·er′tia, *n.* —in·er′tial, *adj.*

ĭn·ĕv′ĭ·tà·ble, *adj.* impossible to avoid. —in·ev′i·ta·bly, *adv.* —in·ev′′i·ta·bil′i·ty, *n.*

ĭn·ĕx′ö·rà·ble, *adj.* **1.** impossible to persuade. **2.** impossible to halt or change. —in·ex′o·ra·bly, *adv.*

ĭn·ĕx′plĭ·cà·ble, *adj.* impossible to explain.

ĭn ĕx·trē′mĭs, at the point of death.

ĭn′fà·moŭs, *adj.* of evil reputation.

ĭn′fà·mў, *n., pl.* -mies. infamous state or act.

ĭn′fànt, *n.* very young child. —in′fan·cy, *n.* —in′fan·tile′′, adj.

ĭn′fàn·trў, *n., pl.* -tries. corps of foot soldiers. —in′fan·try·man, *n.*

ĭn·făt′ū·āte′′, *v.t.,* -ated, -ating. make foolish with love. —in·fat′′u·a′tion, *n.*

ĭn·fĕct′, *v.t.* **1.** afflict with germs or a virus. **2.** influence with one's feelings. —in·fec′tion, *n.* —in·fec′tious, *adj.*

ĭn·fêr′, *v.t.,* -ferred, -ferring. conclude from evidence. —in′fer·ence, *n.* —in′′fer·en′tial, *adj.*

ĭn·fē′rĭ·ōr, *adj.* **1.** of lesser worth. **2.** inadequate. **3.** of lesser rank. —*n.* **4.** inferior person. —in·fe′′ri·or′i·ty, *n.*

ĭn·fêr′năl, *adj.* hellish.

ĭn·fêr′nō, *n.* hell, esp. as a fiery place.

ĭn·fĕst′, *v.t.* penetrate harmfully in large numbers. —in′′fes·ta′tion, *n.*

ĭn′fĭ·dĕl, *n.* unbeliever.

ĭn′fīght′′ĭng, *n.* combat at close range.

ĭn′fĭl·trāte′′, *v.t.,* -trated, -trating. penetrate in many places. —in′′fil·tra′tion, *n.*

ĭn′fĭ·nĭte, *adj.* without bounds or end. —in′fin·ite·ly, *adv.* —in·fin′i·tude′′, *n.* —in·fin′i·ty, *n.*

ĭn′′fĭn·ĭ·tĕs′ĭ·màl, *adj.* extremely small.

ĭn·fĭn′ĭ·tĭve, *n.* form of a verb without person, number, or tense.

ĭn·fîrm′, *adj.* not in good health. —in·firm′i·ty, *n.*

in·fîr'má·rȳ, n., pl. -ries. place for treating the sick.

in·flāme', v.t., -flamed, -flaming. 1. cause to become red, sore, swollen, etc. 2. rouse to anger, etc. —in''flam·ma'tion, n. —in·flam'ma·to''ry, adj.

in·flăm'má·ble, adj. 1. readily burned. 2. readily aroused to anger, etc.

in·flāte', v., -flated, -flating. v.t. 1. cause inflation in or to. —v.i. 2. be filled with air or gas. —in·flat'a·ble, adv.

in·flā'tion, n. 1. filling with air or gas. 2. fall in the value of money. —in·fla'tion·ar''y, adj.

in·flĕct', v.t. vary in tone, form, etc. —in·flec'tion, n. —in·flec'tion·al, adj.

in·flĭct', v.t. harm or punish someone with. —in·flic'tion, n.

in·flū·ence, n., v.t., -enced, -encing. n. 1. ability to determine events or decisions. 2. person or thing that influences. —v.t. 3. use influence on.

in''flū·ĕn'tial, adj. having much influence.

in''flū·ĕn'zá, n. contagious virus infection.

in·flŭx'', n. inward flow.

in·fôrm', v.t. give knowledge to. —in·form'ant, in·form'er, n. —in''for·ma'tion, n. —in·form'a·tive, adj.

in·fôrmed', adj. 1. in possession of essential facts. 2. learned; erudite.

in·frăc'tion, n. violation, as of a law.

in''frá·rĕd', adj. pertaining to invisible rays beyond the red end of the spectrum.

in·frĭnge', v., -fringed, -fringing. v.t. 1. violate —v.i. 2. encroach. —in·fringe'ment, n.

in·fū'rĭ·āte'', v.t., -ated, -ating. make furious.

in·fūse', v.t., -fused, -fusing. 1. instill. 2. steep. —in''fu'sion, n.

in·gēn'ioŭs, adj. clever. —in·gen'ious·ly, adv. —in''gen·u'i·ty, n.

in·gĕn'ū·oŭs, adj. 1. naive. 2. candid. —in·gen'u·ous·ness, n.

in·gĕst', v.t. eat. —in·ges'tion, n.

in·gŏt, n. cast piece of metal.

in·grāined', adj. deeply imbedded.

in'grāte, n. ungrateful person.

in·grā''tĭ·āte'', v.t., -ated, -ating. to gain favor of another. —in·gra''ti·a'tion, n.

in·grē'dĭ·ĕnt, n. component.

in'grĕss, n. entry.

in'grōwn'', adj. grown into the flesh.

in·hăb'ĭt, v.t. live in. —in·hab'it·ant, n.

in·hāle', v.t., v.i., -haled, -haling. breathe in. —in''ha'la'tion, n.

in·hēre', v.i., -hered, -hering. be naturally part of something. —in·her'ent, adj.

in·hĕr'ĭt, v.t. be an heir to. —in·her'i·tance, n.

in·hĭb'ĭt, v.t. check; restrain. —in''hi·bi'tion, n.

in·hū'mán, adj. emotionally cold; callous. —in''hu·man'i·ty, n.

in·ĭm'ĭ·cál, adj. hostile.

in·ĭq'uĭ·tȳ, n., pl. -ties. wickedness or wicked act. —in·iq'ui·tous, adj.

in·ĭ'tial, adj., n., v.t., -tialed, -tialing. adj. 1. beginning. —n. 2. beginning letter of a word. —v.t. 3. mark with initials. —in·i'tial·ly, adv.

in·ĭ'tĭ·āte'', v.t., -ated, -ating. 1. begin. 2. acquaint with basics. 3. accept as a member with ceremony. —in·i''ti·a'tion, n.

in·ĭ'tĭ·á·tĭve, n. 1. readiness to initiate actions. 2. personal decision to act.

in·jĕct', v.t. force beneath the skin. —in·jec'tion, n.

in·jŭnc'tion, n. order, as from a court.

in'jûre, v.t., -jured, -juring. harm. —in''ju'ri·ous, adj. —in'ju·ry, n.

ĭnk, n. 1. pigmented liquid for printing, writing, or drawing. —v.t. 2. apply ink to. —ink'y, adj.

ĭnk'lĭng, n. vague perception.

in'lánd'', adj., adv. 1. away from the shore, etc. —n. 2. inland region.

in'-lăw'', n. relative by marriage.

in'lāy'', v.t., -laid, -laying, n. v.t. 1. set into another piece. —n. 2. something inlaid.

in'lĕt, n. small extension of a body of water.

in'māte'', n. person under confinement.

ĭnn, n. small hotel or restaurant.

in'nāte'', adj. present from birth. —in·nate'ly, adv.

ĭn'nêr, adj. farther inside. —in'ner·most'', adj.

in'nĭng, n. turn at bat.

ĭn'nŏ·cĕnt, *adj.* **1.** free of guilt. **2.** unsophisticated. —*n.* **3.** innocent person. —in'no·cent·ly, *adv.* —in'no·cence, *n.*

ĭn·nŏc'ū·oŭs, *adj.* harmless.

ĭn''nŏ·vā'tion, *n.* new discovery or development. —in'no·vat''or, *n.* —in'no·vat''ive, *adj.*

ĭn''nū·ĕn'dō, *n., pl.* -does, -dos. sly implication.

ĭn·nū'mêr·à·ble, *adj.* too many to count.

ĭn·ŏc'ū·lāte'', *v.t.*, -lated, -lating. immunize with an injection. —in·oc''u·la'tion, *n.*

ĭn·ôr'dĭ·nāte, *adj.* excessive. —in·or'di·nate·ly, *adv.*

ĭn'pŭt, *n.* **1.** something supplied. **2.** (computers) data entered into a computer.

ĭn'quĕst'', *n.* coroner's investigation.

ĭn·quīre', *v.i.*, -quired, -quiring. **1.** ask. **2.** investigate. —in'quir·y, *n.*

ĭn·quĭs'ĭ·tīve, *adj.* desiring to know many things.

ĭn'rōad'', *n.* encroachment.

ĭn·scrībe', *v.t.*, -scribed, -scribing. write or letter. —in·scrip'tion, *n.*

ĭn·scrū'tà·ble, *adj.* hard to understand. —in·scru'ta·bly, *adv.*

ĭn'sĕct, *n.* six-legged invertebrate.

ĭn·sĕc'tĭ·cīde'', *n.* insect-killing preparation.

ĭn·sĕm'ĭ·nāte'', *v.t.*, -nated, -nating. inject semen into. —in·sem''i·na'tion, *n.*

ĭn·sĕn'sāte, *adj.* insensitive.

ĭn·sĕn'sĭ·ble, *adj.* **1.** unconscious. **2.** impossible to sense. —in·sen''si·bil'i·ty, *n.*

ĭn·sêrt', *v.t.* **1.** place into something. —*n.* (in'sert) **2.** something inserted. —in·ser'tion, *n.*

ĭn'sīde', *adv., prep.* **1.** within. —*adj.* **2.** inner. —*n.* **3.** inner part. —in·sid'er, *n.*

ĭn·sĭd'ĭ·oŭs, *adj.* slyly dangerous.

ĭn'sīght'', *n.* deep understanding.

ĭn·sĭg'nĭ·à, *n., pl.* distinguishing badges, etc.

ĭn·sĭn'ū·āte'', *v.t.*, -ated, -ating. **1.** imply slyly. **2.** introduce imperceptibly. —in·sin''u·a'tion, *n.*

ĭn·sĭp'ĭd, *adj.* flavorless; dull. —in''si·pid'i·ty, *n.*

ĭn·sĭst', *v.t.* make repeated demands or assertions. —in·sis'tent, *adj.* —in·sis'tence, *n.*

ĭn'sō·fâr', *adv.* to such an extent.

ĭn'sŏ·lĕnt, *adj.* disrespectful. —in'so·lence, *n.*

ĭn·sŏm'nĭ·à, *n.* inability to sleep. —in·som''ni·ac'', *n.*

ĭn·spĕct', *v.t.* examine carefully. —in·spec'tion, *n.* —in·spec'tor, *n.*

ĭn·spīre', *v.*, -spired, -spiring. *v.t., v.i.* **1.** breathe in. —*v.t.* **2.** stimulate to mental activity. **3.** arouse in someone. —in''spi·ra'tor, *n.* —in''spi·ra'tion·al, *adj.*

ĭn·stăll', *v.t.* -stalled, -stalling. put in place. —in''stal·la'tion, *n.*

ĭn·stăll'mĕnt, *n.* item in a series.

ĭn'stàncè, *n., v.t.*, -stanced, -stancing. *n.* **1.** example. **2.** occasion. —*v.t.* **3.** cite.

ĭn'stànt, *n.* **1.** moment. —*adj.* **2.** happening or ready quickly. **3.** imminent. —in''stan·ta'ne·ous, *adj.* —in'stant'ly, *adv.*

ĭn·stĕad', *adv.* in the place.

ĭn'stĭ·gāte'', *v.t.*, -gated, -gating. urge, as to action. —in''sti·ga'tion, *n.* —in'sti·ga''tor.

ĭn·stĭll', *v.t.*, -stilled, -stilling. implant. Also, in·stil'.

ĭn'stĭnct, *n.* inborn prompting or reaction. —in·stinc'tive, *adj.* —in·stinc'tu·al, *adj.*

ĭn'stĭ·tūte'', *n., v.t.*, -tuted, -tuting. *n.* **1.** professional organization or school. —*v.t.* **2.** establish. **3.** start.

ĭn''stĭ·tū'tion, *n.* **1.** act or instance of instituting. **2.** institute. **3.** established law or custom. —in'sti·tu'tion·al, *adj.*

ĭn·strŭct', *v.t.*, **1.** inform or advise. **2.** command. —in·struc'tion, *n.* —in·struc'tive, *adj.* —in·struc'tor, *n.*

ĭn'strŭ·mĕnt, *n.* **1.** tool, etc. **2.** means. **3.** measuring device. **4.** musical device. **5.** legal document.

ĭn''strŭ·mĕn'tàl, *adj.* **1.** pertaining to music by instruments. **2.** useful. —in''stru·men'tal·ist, *n.* —in''stru·men'tal'i·ty, *n.*

ĭn'sŭ·làr, *adj.* **1.** pertaining to islands. **2.** narrow-minded; parochial.

ĭn'sŭ·lāte'', *v.t.*, -lated, -lating. isolate, esp. from heat, sound, or electricity. —in''su·la'tion, *n.* —in'su·la''tor, *n.*

ĭn′sŭ·lĭn, *n.* hormone secreted by the pancreas.

ĭn·sŭlt′, *v.t.* **1.** treat so as to hurt the feelings. —*n.* (ĭn′sŭlt) **2.** epithet, etc. that insults. —**ĭn·sŭlt′ing,** *adj.*

ĭn·su′per·a·ble, *adj.* impossible to overcome.

ĭn″sŭp·pôrt′à·ble, *adj.* **1.** intolerable. **2.** impossible to prove.

ĭn·sūre′, *v.t.,* **-sured, -suring. 1.** guarantee against loss with money. **2.** make sure. —**ĭn·sur′ance,** *n.*

ĭn·sûr′gėnt, *n., adj.* revolutionary. —**ĭn·sur′gence,** *n.*

ĭn″sŭr·rĕc′tion, *n.* revolution.

ĭn·tăct′, *adj.* undamaged.

ĭn′tāke″, *n.* **1.** amount received, absorbed, etc. **2.** opening for receiving air, etc.

ĭn·tăn′gĭ·ble, *adj.* **1.** non-material. **2.** non-monetary. **3.** indefinable.

ĭn′tė·gêr, *n.* whole number.

ĭn′tė·grȧl, *adj.* **1.** forming an essential part. **2.** complete.

ĭn′tė·grāte″, *v.t.,* **-grated, -grating. 1.** make complete. **2.** bring together into a whole. **3.** end racial segregation in or among. —**ĭn″te·gra′tion,** *n.*

ĭn·tĕg′rĭ·tỹ, *n.* **1.** intactness. **2.** firmness of character, honesty, etc.

ĭn·tĕg′ų·mėnt, *n.* covering, e.g. skin.

ĭn′tĕl·lĕct, *n.* ability to comprehend or reason. —**ĭn″tel·lec′tu·al,** *adj., n.*

ĭn·tĕl′lĭ·gėnce, *n.* **1.** ability to comprehend, reason, and think creatively. **2.** news. —**ĭn·tel′li·gent,** *adj.*

ĭn·tĕl″lĭ·gĕnt′sĭ·à, *n. pl.* intellectuals as a group.

ĭn·tĕl′lĭ·gĭ·ble, *adj.* able to be understood.

ĭn·tĕnd′, *v.t.* have as a purpose.

ĭn·tĕnd′ėd, *n.* fiancé or fiancée.

ĭn·tĕnse′, *adj.* **1.** very strong. **2.** with much emotion. —**ĭn·ten′si·ty,** *n.* —**ĭn·ten′si·fy,** *v.t., v.i.*

ĭn·tĕn′sĭve, *adj.* **1.** thorough. **2.** *Grammar.* giving emphasis.

ĭn·tĕnt′, *adj.* **1.** earnest. **2.** firmly intending. —*n.* **3.** purpose. —**ĭn·tent′ly,** *adv.*

ĭn·tĕn′tion, *n.* purpose. —**ĭn·ten′tion·al,** *adj.*

ĭn·tĕr′, *v.t.,* **-terred, -terring.** bury.

ĭn″têr·cēde′, *v.i.,* **-ceded, -ceding.** mediate. —**ĭn″ter·ces′sion,** *n.*

ĭn″têr·cĕpt′, *v.t.* halt or attack along the way. —**ĭn″ter·cep′tion,** *n.*

ĭn″têr·chānge′, *v.,* **-changed, -changing,** *n. v.i., v.t.* **1.** exchange. **2.** alternate. —*n.* (ĭn′ter change″) **3.** access to an express highway. —**ĭn″ter·change′a·ble,** *adj.*

ĭn″têr·cŏn·nĕct′, *v.i.* connect with one another. —**ĭn″ter·con·nec′tion,** *n.*

ĭn′têr·côurse″, *n.* **1.** communication. **2.** copulation.

ĭn″têr·dė·pĕn′dėnt, *adj.* dependent on one another. —**ĭn″ter·de·pen′dence,** *n.*

ĭn″têr·dĭct′, *v.t.* **1.** prohibit. —*n.* (ĭn′ter dict″) **2.** prohibition. —**ĭn″ter·dic′tion,** *n.*

ĭn″têr·dĭs′cĭ·plĭ·när″ỹ, *adj.* involving varied disciplines.

ĭn′tėr·ĕst, *n.* **1.** willing attention. **2.** share in a business. **3.** profit on a loan. —*v.t.* **4.** obtain willing attention from.

ĭn″têr·fēre′, *v.i.,* **-fered, -fering. 1.** meddle. **2.** intervene. —**ĭn′ter·fer′ence,** *n.*

ĭn′têr·ĭm, *n.* intervening time.

ĭn·tē′rĭ·ör, *n.* **1.** inside. **2.** room. —*adj.* **3.** inside. **4.** personal.

ĭn″têr·jĕct′, *v.t.* insert as an interruption or addition.

ĭn″têr·jĕc′tion, *n.* **1.** exclamation. **2.** act or instance of interjecting.

ĭn″têr·lāce″, *v.i.* be entwined or woven together.

ĭn′têr·lärd″, *v.t.* scatter throughout.

ĭn′têr·lŏck″, *v.i.* be connected or act together.

ĭn′têr·lŏp″êr, *n.* person who interferes.

ĭn′têr·lūde″, *n.* episode, musical piece, etc. between major events.

ĭn″têr·mär′rỹ, *v.i.,* **-ried, -rying. 1.** become associated by marriage. **2.** marry a close relation. —**ĭn″ter·mar′riage,** *n.*

ĭn″têr·mē′dĭ·ār″ỹ, *adj., n., pl.* **-ies.** *adj.* **1.** coming between. —*n.* **2.** go-between.

ĭn″têr·mē′dĭ·ȧte, *adj.* coming between.

ĭn·têr′mėnt, *n.* burial.

ĭn·têr′mĭn·à·ble, *adj.* seemingly endless. —**ĭn·ter′min·a·bly,** *adv.*

ĭn″têr·mĭn′gle, *v.i.,* **-gled, -gling.** be blended.

ĭn''têr·mĭs'sion, *n*. pause, as between acts of a play.

ĭn''têr·mĭt'tĕnt, *adj*. occurring at intervals. —in''ter·mit'tent·ly, *adv*.

ĭn'têrn, *n*. 1. Also, in'terne. assistant resident doctor. —*v.t.* (in tern') 2. detain and confine. —in'tern'ment, *n*.

ĭn·têr'nǎl, *adj*. 1. interior. 2. non-foreign. —in·ter'nal·ly, *adv*.

ĭn''têr·nǎ'tion·ǎl, *adj*. 1. among nations. 2. regardless of nation.

ĭn''têr·nĕ'cĭne, *adj*. deadly to both sides.

ĭn'têr·nĭst, *n*. doctor using non-surgical treatment.

ĭn'têr·plāy'', *n*. mutual influence.

ĭn·têr'pò·lāte'', *v.t.*, -lated, -lating. alter with new material. —in·ter''po·la'tion, *n*.

ĭn'têr·pōse'', *v.t.*, -posed, -posing. place between or among. —in''ter·po·si'tion, *n*.

ĭn·têr'prĕt, *v.t* 1. clarify. 2. understand. 3. translate. —in·ter'pret·er, *n*. —in·ter''pre·ta'tion, *n*. —in·ter'pre·tive, *adj*.

ĭn'têr·rǎ'cĭǎl, *adj*. among races.

ĭn'têr·rè·lāte'', *v.t.*, -lated, -lating. relate one to the other. —in''ter·re·la'tion, *n*.

ĭn·têr'rò·gāte'', *v.t.*, -gated, -gating. question. —in·ter''ro·ga'tion, *n*. —in·ter'ro·ga'tor, *n*. —in·ter·rog'a·tive, in''ter·rog'a·to·ry, *adv*.

ĭn''têr·rŭpt', *v.t.*, 1. halt with an action, remark, etc. 2. break the uniformity of. —in''ter·rup'tion, *n*.

ĭn''têr·sĕct', *v.t.*, *v.i.* cross. —in''ter·sec'tion, *n*.

ĭn'têr·spêrse'', *v.t.*, -spersed, -spersing. 1. scatter. 2. vary with scattered things.

ĭn'têr·stāte'', *adj*., *adv*. from state to state.

ĭn·têr'stĭce, *n*. gap.

ĭn''têr·ûr'bȧn, *adj*. from city to city.

ĭn'têr·vȧl, *n*. intervening period or space.

ĭn''têr·vēne', *v.i.*, -vened, -vening. 1. come or occur between. 2. mediate. —in''ter·ven'tion, *n*.

ĭn''têr·view'', *n*. 1. person-to-person meeting. —*v.t.* 2 question at an interview. —in'ter·view''er, *n*. —in''ter·view''ee', *n*.

ĭn·tĕs'tāte'', *adj*. without having made a will.

ĭn·tĕs'tĭne, *n*. either of two organs for converting food. Also, in·tes'tines. —in·tes'tin·al, *adj*.

ĭn'ti·mȧte, *adj*., *n*., *v.t.*, -mated, -mating. *adj*. 1. emotionally close. 2. personal. 3. thorough. —*n*. 4. intimate friend. —*v.t.* (in''ti māte') 5. hint. —in'ti·mate·ly, *adv*. —in'ti·ma·cy, *n*. —in''ti·ma'tion, *n*.

ĭn·tĭm'ĭ·dāte'', *v.t.*, -dated, -dating. command through fear. —in·tim''i·da'tion, *n*.

ĭn'to, *prep*. 1. to the interior or depths of. 2. up against. 3. to some material, number of parts, etc.

ĭn·tōne', *v.t.*, -toned, -toning. 1. utter in a songlike tone. 2. utter with a controlled or varied pitch. —in''to·na'tion, *n*.

ĭn tō'tō, as a whole.

ĭn·tŏx'ĭ·cāte'', *v.t.*, -cated, -cating. make drunk. —in·tox''i·ca'tion, *n*. —in·tox'i·cant, *n*.

ĭn·trăc'tȧ·ble, *adj*. unruly.

ĭn''trȧ·mū'rȧl, *adj*. within an institution.

ĭn·trăn'sĭ·gĕnt, *adj*. uncompromising. —in·tran'si·gence, *n*.

ĭn''trȧ·vē'noŭs, *adj*. into a vein from outside the body.

ĭn·trĕp'ĭd, *adj*. fearless. —in''tre·pid'i·ty, *n*.

ĭn'tri·cȧte, *adj*. complicated; complex. —in'tri·cate·ly, *adv*. —in'tri·ca·cy, *n*.

ĭn·trīgue', *v.*, -trigued, -triguing. *v.i.* 1. plot in stealth. —*v.t.* 2. make curious. —*n*. 3. stealthy plot or plotting.

ĭn·trĭn'sĭc, *adj*. essential; inherent. —in·trin'si·cal·ly, *adv*.

ĭn''trò·dūce', *v.t.*, -duced, -ducing. 1. present for the first time. 2. bring into use. 3. insert. —in''tro·duc'tion, *n*. —in''tro·duc'to·ry, *adj*.

ĭn''trò·spĕc'tion, *n*. self-examination. —in''tro·spec'tive, *adj*.

ĭn'trò·vêrt'', *n*. withdrawn person. —in''tro·ver'sion, *n*.

ĭn·trūde', *v.*, -truded, -truding. *v.i.* 1. come as an interruption or surprise. —*v.t.* 2. force upon others. —in·trud'er, *n*. —in·tru'sion, *n*. —in·tru'sive, *adj*.

ĭn''tū·ĭ'tion, *n*. non-logical insight. —in·tu'i·tive, *adj*.

ĭn'ŭn·dāte'', *v.t.*, -dated, -dating. flood. —in''un·da'tion, *n*.

ĭn·ūre', *v.t.*, -ured, -uring. to harden oneself to something disagreeable; accustom.

ĭn·vāde', *v.t.*, -vaded, -vading. enter with force. —in·vad'er, *n*. —in·va'sion, *n*.

ĭn·văl·ĭd, *n*. **1.** sick person. —*adj*. (in val'id). **2.** not valid. —in·val'i·date'', *v.t.*

ĭn·văl'ū·à·ble, *adj*. valuable beyond reckoning.

ĭn·věc'tĭve, *n*. verbal attack.

in·veigh' (ĭn·vā'), *v.i.* make a verbal attack.

ĭn·vēi'gle, *v.t.*, -gled, -gling. trick into an action.

ĭn·věnt', *v.t.* discover, as a product or process. —in·ven'tion, *n*. —in·ven'tive, *adj*. —in·ven'tor, *n*.

ĭn'věn·tô''rў, *n.*, *pl.* -ries. *v.t.*, -ried, -rying. *n*. **1.** precise list. **2.** stock of goods. —*v.t.* **3.** make an inventory of.

ĭn·vêrse', *adj*. **1.** oppose in kind. —*n*. **2.** something inverse. —in·verse'ly, *adv*.

ĭn·vêrt', *v.t.* **1.** turn upside down. **2.** reverse in order or position. —in·ver'sion, *n*.

ĭn·vêr'tè·brate, *adj*. **1.** having no backbone. —*n*. **2.** invertebrate animal.

ĭn·věst', *v.t.* **1.** put into something in the hope of profit. **2.** give authority or office to. —*v.i.* **3.** invest money. —in·vest'or, *n*. —in·vest'ment, *n*. —in·vest'i·ture'', *n*.

ĭn·věs'tĭ·gāte'', *v.t.*, -gated, -gating. examine or explore. —in·ves'ti·ga''tor, *n*. —in·ves''ti·ga'tion, *n*.

ĭn·vět'êr·àte, *adj*. habitual. —in·vet'er·a·cy, *n*.

ĭn·vĭd'ĭ·oŭs, *adj*. causing ill will.

ĭn·vĭg'ör·āte'', *v.t.*, -ated, -ating. make vigorous. —in·vig''or·a'tion, *n*.

ĭn·vĭnc'ĭ·ble, *adj*. impossible to conquer. —in·vinc''i·bil'i·ty, *n*.

ĭn·vī'ól·à·ble, *adj*. not to be violated. —in·vi''ol·a·bil'i·ty, *n*.

ĭn·vī'ó·làte, *adj*. unviolated.

ĭn·vīte', *v.t.*, -vited, -viting. **1.** ask to be present. **2.** give a pretext for. —in''vi·ta'tion, *n*.

ĭn·vīt'ĭng, *adj*. enticing.

ĭn''vò·cā'tion, *n*. prayerlike speech.

ĭn'vǒīce, *n*. list of goods supplied.

ĭn·vǒke', *v.t.*, -voked, -voking. **1.** call upon, as a god. **2.** cite as a justification.

ĭn''vó·lū'tion, *n*. intricacy. —in'vo·lut''ed, *adj*.

ĭn·vǒlve', *v.t.*, -volved, -volving. **1.** include as relevant. **2.** affect or trouble. **3.** occupy. **4.** complicate. —in·volve'ment, *n*.

ĭn'wàrd, *adj*. **1.** inside. **2.** toward the inside. **3.** mental. —*adv*. **4.** Also, in'wards, towards the inside. —in'ward'ly, *adv*.

ī'ó·dīne'', *n*. nonmetallic chemical element. —i'o·dize'', *v.t.*

ī'ón, *n*. electrically charged atom or group of atoms.

ī·ō'tà, *n*. minute quantity.

ĭp'sō fǎc'tō, by the very fact.

IQ, intelligence quotient (measure of intelligence). Also **I.Q.**

ĭr-, prefix meaning "not" or "lack of." **irrational, irreconcilable, irredeemable, irregular, irrelevant, irreligious, irremediable, irreparable, irreplaceable, irresponsible, irreverent, irreversible, irrevocable.**

ĭ·răs'cĭ·ble, *adj*. easily angered.

īre, *n*. wrath. —i·rate', *adj*.

ĭr''ĭ·děs'cĕnt, *adj*. with a play of rainbow-like colors. —ir''i·des'cence, *n*.

ī'rĭs, *n.*, *pl.* **irises.** *n*. **1.** pigmented part surrounding the eye pupil. **2.** plant with sword-shaped leaves.

îrk, *v.t.* annoy. —irk'some, *adj*.

ī'ron, *n*. **1.** metallic element attracting magnets. **2.** device made of iron. **3.** irons, shackles. —*v.t.* **4.** smooth with an iron.

Iron Curtain, *n*. former barrier to travel, information, etc. around the communist countries.

ī'ró·nў, *n.*, *pl.* -nies. figure of speech conveying meaning through words of opposite meaning. —i·ron'i·cal, i·ron'ic, *adj*.

ĭr·rā'dĭ·āte'', *v.t.*, -ated, -ating. expose to rays.

ĭr''rè·gârd'lèss, *adj., adv*. regardless.

ĭr''rè·sĭst'ĭ·ble, *adj*. **1.** impossible to resist. **2.** overwhelmingly tempting.

ĭr'rĭ·gāte'', *v.t.*, -gated, -gating. introduce water to, to raise crops. **—ir″ri·ga′tion,** *n.*

ir′ri·ta·ble, *adj.* readily irritated. **—ir′ri·ta·bly,** *adv.* **—ir″ri·ta·bil′i·ty,** *n.*

ir′ri·tāte″, *v.t.,* **-tated, -tating. 1.** annoy. **2.** make sore. **—ir″ri·ta′tion,** *n.* **—ir′ri·tant,** *adj., n.*

ir·rŭpt′, *v.i.* **1.** burst forth; expand. **—ir·rup′tion,** *n.*

ī′sĭn·glăss″, *n.* **1.** gelatin from fish bladders. **2.** mica.

Is′lâm, *n.* religion of Muhammad.

īs·lánd (ī′lənd), *n.* **1.** body of land surrounded by water. **2.** isolated platform, etc.

īs·lĕt (ī′lət), *n.* small island.

ī′sò·lāte″, *v.t.,* **-lated, -lating.** keep apart. **—i″so·la′tion,** *n.*

ī″sò·lā′tion·ĭst, *n.* believer in no alliances with other countries. **—i″so·la′tion·ism,** *n.*

ī″sò·mĕt′rĭc, *adj.* **1.** with all dimensions represented to the same scale. **2.** pertaining to isometrics. **—n. 3.** isometrics, type of muscular exercise.

ī·sŏs′cèl·ēs″, *adj.* pertaining to triangles with two equal sides.

ī′sò·tōpe″, *n.* form of an element coinciding in atomic number but not in atomic weight with another.

ĭs′sūe, *v.,* **-sued, -suing,** *v.t.* **1.** give out. **2.** publish. **—v.i. 3.** emerge. **—n. 4.** something that issues. **5.** periodical of one date. **6.** thing in dispute. **7.** offspring. **8.** result. **—is′su·ance,** *n.*

ĭsth′mŭs, *n., pl.* **-muses.** narrow neck of connecting land between bodies of water.

ĭt, *pron., pl.* **they 1.** thing referred to. **2.** (subject of various impersonal verbs).

ĭ·tăl′ĭc, *adj.* **1.** pertaining to letters printed thus: *Italics.* **—n. 2.** italics, italic letters. **—i·tal′i·cize″,** *v.t.*

ĭtch, *v.i.* **1.** feel a mild irritation tempting one to scratch. **2.** desire restlessly. **—n. 3.** act or instance of itching. **—itch′y,** *adj.*

ī′tèm, *n.* **1.** listed thing. **2.** piece of news. **—i′tem′ize″,** *v.t.* **—i″tem·i·za′tion,** *n.*

ĭt′ẽr·āte″, *v.t.,* **-ated, -ating.** repeat. **—it″er·a′tion,** *n.*

ī·tĭn′ẽr·ànt, *adj.* **1.** traveling; migratory. **—n. 2.** itinerant person.

ī·tĭn′ẽr·ār″ÿ, *n., pl.* **-ies.** plan of travel.

ĭts, *pron.* belonging or pertaining to it.

ĭt's, *pron.* contraction of *it is.*

ĭt·sĕlf′, *pron.* **1.** (intensive or reflexive of *it*). **2.** its true self.

ī′vö·rÿ, *n.* creamy-white substance of tusks.

ī′vÿ, *n., pl.* **ivies.** climbing evergreen vine. **—i′vied,** *adj.*

J

J, j, *n.* tenth letter of the English alphabet.

jăb, *v.,* **jabbed, jabbing.** *v.t., v.i., n.* poke.

jăb′bẽr, *n.* **1.** fast, incoherent talk. **—v.i. 2.** talk in a jabber.

jăck, *n.* **1.** lifting machine. **2.** playing card; knave. **3.** flag at a ship's stern. **4.** point of connection; place where something is plugged in. **—v.t. 5.** to raise something with a jack.

jăck′ál, *n.* wild African and Asian dog.

jăck′ăss″, *n.* **1.** male donkey. **2.** fool.

jăck′ét, *n.* **1.** short coat. **2.** covering.

jăck′knīfe″, *n., v.i.,* **-knifed, -knifing.** *n.* **1.** folding knife. **2.** type of swimmer's dive. **—v.i. 3.** fold accidentally at a joint.

jăck′pŏt″, *n.* accumulated stakes that are won.

jăck′răb″bĭt, *n.* large North American hare.

jāde, *n., v.t.,* **jaded, jading.** *n.* **1.** ornamental stone, usually green. **—v.t. 2.** satiate.

jăg, *n.* **1.** sharp point. **2.** *Informal.* orgy.

jăg′gèd, *adj.* with a rough, sharp edge or surface.

jăg′uâr, *n.* large cat of Latin America and the U.S. Southwest.

jāil, *n.* **1.** prison for short confinements. **—v.t. 2.** put in jail. **—jail′er, jail′or,** *n.*

jà·lŏp′ÿ, *n., pl.* **-ies.** old, ill-kept car.

jăl′ou·sie, *n.* louvered blind.

jăm, *v.,* **jammed, jamming,** *n. v.t., v.i.* **1.** crowd. **2** stick tight. **—n. 3.** act or instance of jamming. **4.** fruit boiled with sugar. **5.** *Informal.* adverse situation.

jămb, *n.* upright of a doorway or window.

jăm″bȯ·rēe′, *n. Informal.* noisy celebration.

jăm′păcked′, *adj.* crowded to capacity.

jăn′gle, *v.* -gled, -gling. *v.i.* **1.** jingle harshly. —*v.t.* **2.** irritate, as the nerves.

jăn′ĭ·tör, *n.* person who takes care of a building.

Jăn′ū·ăr″ÿ, *n.* first month.

jâr, *n., v.*, jarred, jarring. *n.* **1.** cylindrical container. **2.** jolt. —*v.t.* **3.** jolt. —*v.i.* **4.** clash. **5.** have an irritating effect.

jâr′gȯn, *n.* abstruse technical language.

jăs′mĭne, *n.* fragrant-flowered plant.

jăs′pêr, *n.* opaque, colored quartz.

jaūn′dĭce, *n., v.t.*, -diced, -dicing. *n.* **1.** disease characterized by yellowing due to bile in the blood. —*v.t.* **2.** predispose against.

jaūnt, *n.* **1.** pleasure excursion. —*v.i.* **2.** go on a jaunt.

jaūn′tÿ, *adj.*, -tier, -tiest. cheerful. —**jaun′ti·ly**, *adv.*

jăv′ė·lĭn, *n.* throwing spear.

jăw, *n.* **1.** bony framing member of the mouth. **2.** gripping part of a vise, etc.

jāy, *n.* **1.** crowlike bird. **2.** bluejay.

jāy′wälk″, *v.i.* cross a street heedlessly. —**jay′walk″er**, *n.*

jăzz, *n.* syncopated, rhythmic modern music.

jĕal′oŭs, *adj.* **1.** feeling jealousy. **2.** watchful.

jēans, *n., pl.* trousers of strong cloth.

jēep, *n.* rugged, military-style car.

jēer, *v.i.* **1.** make scornful utterances. —*n.* **2.** such an utterance.

Jė·hō′vȧh, *n.* God.

jė·jūne′, *adj.* **1.** unfulfilling. **2.** childish.

jĕll, *v.i.* **1.** harden, as gelatin. **2.** come to fulfillment.

jĕl′lÿ, *n., pl.* -lies, *v.t.* -lied, -lying. *n.* **1.** gelatinous food. —*v.t.* **2.** make into jelly.

jĕo′pȧrd·īze″, *v.t.*, -ized, -izing. put in danger. —**jeo′pard·y**, *n.*

jĕr″ė·mī′ȧd, *n.* tale of lamentation or anger.

jêrk, *n.* **1.** sharp pull. —*v.t.* **2.** pull sharply. —*v.i.* **3.** twitch. —**jerk′y**, *adj.*

jĕr′rÿ-buĭlt, *adj.* cheaply and flimsily built.

jêr′sēy, *n., pl.* -sies. closefitting knitted shirt.

jĕst, *n.* joke.

jĕt, *n., v.i.* jetted, jetting. *n.* **1.** forced stream. **2.** jet-propelled airplane. **3.** coal-like mineral used in jewelry. —*v.i.* **4.** emerge in a jet. **5.** travel by jet.

jĕt prȯpŭlsion, propulsion by the reactive thrust of a jet. —**jet′pro·pelled′**, *adj.*

jĕt′sȧm, *n.* material thrown overboard.

jĕt′tĭ·sȯn, *v.t.* throw away or overboard.

jĕt′tÿ, *n., pl.* -ties. pier or wall into the water.

jēw′ėl, *n.* precious stone. —**jew′el·er, jew′el·ler**, *n.* —**jew′el·ry**, *n.*

jĭb, *n.* triangular sail at the bow.

jĭbe, *v.i.*, jibed, jibing, *n.* gibe.

jĭf′fÿ, *n., pl.* -fies. *Informal.* short period.

jĭg, *n., v.i.*, jigged, jigging. *n.* **1.** fast dance. **2.** tool guide. **3.** fishing device. —*v.i.* **4.** dance a jig.

jĭg′gêr, *n.* one-and-a-half ounce glass.

jĭg′gle, *v.*, -gled, -gling, *n. v.i., v.t.* **1.** move in rapid jerks. —*n.* **2.** act or instance of jiggling.

jĭg′sȧw″, *n.* narrow-bladed saw.

jĭlt, *v.t.* reject.

jĭn′gle, *v.*, -gled, -gling, *n. v.i., v.t.* **1.** ring lightly and rapidly. —*n.* **2.** act or instance of jingling. **3.** simple verse.

jĭnx, *n.* **1.** bringer of ill-luck. —*v.t.* **2.** bring ill-luck to.

jĭt′têrs, *n. Informal.* nervousness. —**jit′ter·y**, *adj.*

jŏb, *n., v.t.*, jobbed, jobbing, *n.* **1.** task. **2.** occupation. **3.** duty. —*v.t., v.i.* **4.** buy in quantity for resale to dealers. —**job′less**, *adj.* —**job′ber**, *n.*

jŏck′ēy, *n., pl.* -eys, *v.i.*, -eyed, -eying. *n.* **1.** rider of race horses. —*v.i.* **2.** maneuver for advantage.

jō·cōse′, *adj.* playful. Also, **joc′und.** —**jo·cos′i·ty**, *n.*

jŏc′ū·lȧr, *adj.* joking; playful.

jŏg, *v.*, jogged, jogging, *n. v.t.* **1.** nudge. —*v.i.* **2.** run steadily. —*n.* **3.** act or instance of jogging. **4.** abrupt change of direction.

joĭn, *v.t.* **1.** put together. **2.** become a member of. —*v.i.* **3.** come or act together.

joĭn′êr, *n.* **1.** woodworker. **2.** *Informal.* person who likes to join groups. —**join′er·y**, *n.*

joĭnt, *n.* **1.** connection. —*adj.* **2.** shared.

3. sharing with others. —*v.t.* **4.** assemble with joints. —**joint′ly,** *adv.*

joist, *n.* floor beam.

joke, *n., v.i.,* **joked, joking,** *n.* **1.** laugh-provoking story or remark. **2.** playful act. —*v.i.* **3.** make a joke.

jŏl′lў, *adj.,* **-lier, -liest,** *v.t.,* **-lied, -lying.** *adj.* **1.** full of high spirits. —*v.t.* **2.** *Informal.* **a.** cajole. **b.** tease. —**jol′li·ly,** *adv.* —**jol′lity,** *n.*

jŏlt, *v.t.* **1.** shake or bump. —*v.i.* **2.** move bumpily. —*n.* **3.** act or instance of jolting.

jŏsh, *v.t.* banter.

jŏs′tle, *v.,* **-tled, -tling.** *v.t., v.i.* shove, as in a crowd.

jŏt, *n., v.t.,* **jotted, jotting.** *n.* **1.** minimal amount. —*v.t.* **2.** make a note of.

joūnce, *v.i.,* **jounced, jouncing.** jolt and bounce. —**jounc′y,** *adj.*

joûr′nàl, *n.* **1.** periodical. **2.** diary. **3.** section of an axle in a bearing.

joûr′nàl·ĭsm, *n.* work for a periodical. —**jour′nal·ist,** *n.* —**jour″nal·is′tic,** *adj.*

joûr′nēy, *n., pl.* **-neys,** *v.i.,* **-neyed, -neying.** *n.* **1.** long trip. —*v.i.* **2.** go on a journey.

joûr′nēy·màn, *n.* skilled worker.

jō′vĭ·àl, *adj.* merry. —**jo″vi·al′i·ty,** *n.*

jōwl, *n.* lower cheek.

jŏў, *n.* **1.** intense happiness. **2.** source of this. —**joy′ful, joy′ous,** *adj.*

jŏў′stĭck, *n.* (computers) grippable device for data manipulation, used mostly for graphics and games.

jū′bĭ·lànt, *adj.* rejoicing. —**ju″bi·la′tion,** *n.*

jū′bĭ·lēe″, *n.* **1.** major anniversary. **2.** time of rejoicing.

Jū′dà·ĭsm, *n.* Jewish religion. —**Ju·da′ic,** *adj.*

jŭdge, *n., v.t.,* **judged, judging.** *n.* **1.** preside over a trial, contest, etc. **2.** qualified evaluator. —*v.t.* **3.** evaluate. —**judg′ment,** *n.* —**judge′ship″,** *n.*

jū·dĭ′cìàl, *adj.* **1.** pertaining to judges or courts. **2.** impartial.

jū·dĭ′cĭ·ār″ў, *adj., n., pl.* **-ies.** *adj.* **1.** judicial. —*n.* **2.** judges.

jū·dĭ′cĭoŭs, *adj.* with sound judgment. —**ju·di′cious·ly,** *adv.*

jū′dō, *n.* Japanese system of wrestling.

jŭg, *n.* broad vessel with a narrow neck.

jŭg′gêr·naŭt″, *n.* crushing force.

jŭg′gle, *v.,* **-gled, -gling.** *v.t.* toss, balance with skill. —*v.i.* **2.** perform such activities for a living. —**jug′gler,** *n.*

jŭg′ū·làr, *adj.* **1.** pertaining to the neck. —*n.* **2.** neck vein.

jūice, *n., v.t.,* **juiced, juicing.** *n.* **1.** liquid from a fruit, etc. —*v.t.* **2.** extract juice from. —**juic′y,** *adj.*

jū·jĭt′sū, *n.* Japanese system of wrestling. Also, **ju·jut′su.**

jūke′bŏx″, *n.* coin-operated record player.

Jū·lў′, *n.* seventh month.

jŭm′ble, *v.t.,* **-bled, -bling,** *n. v.t.* **1.** mix in disorder. —*n.* **2.** disorderly mixture.

jŭm′bō, *adj.* very large.

jŭmp, *v.i.* **1.** leave the ground with a muscular effort. **2.** move abruptly. —*v.t.* **3.** jump over. —*n.* **4.** act or instance of jumping.

jŭmp′êr, *n.* sleeveless dress.

jŭm′pў, *adj.* **-pier, -piest.** very nervous.

jŭnc′tion, *n.* place of joining.

jŭnc′tûre, *n.* **1.** junction. **2.** moment. **3.** crisis.

Jūne, *n.* sixth month.

jŭn′gle, *n.* densely grown tropical area.

jūn′iŏr, *adj.* **1.** being the son of a father with the same name. **2.** lesser in rank, size, etc. —*n.* **3.** junior person. **4.** third-year student.

jū′nĭ·pêr, *n.* evergreen with berry-like cones.

jŭnk, *n.* **1.** rejected or worthless material. **2.** Chinese sailing boat. —*v.t.* **3.** scrap.

jŭnk′ĕt, *n.* **1.** curdled milk dish. **2.** excursion. —*v.i.* **3.** go on a junket.

jŭnk′iē, *n. Informal.* narcotics addict. Also, **junk′y.**

jun·ta (hoŏn tà), *n.* military in power after a coup d'etat.

jû″rĭs·dĭc′tion, *n.* **1.** administration of justice. **2.** area of authority. —**ju″ris·dic′tion·al,** *adj.*

jû″rĭs·prū′dénce, *n.* philosophy of law.

jû′rĭst, *n.* expert in law.

jû′rў, *n., pl.* **-ries.** group deciding the outcome of a trial, hearing, or contest. —**ju′ry·man, ju′ror,** *n.*

jŭst, *adj.* **1.** fair. **2.** righteous. **3.** accurate. —*adv.* **4.** exactly. **5.** only. **6.** by a short margin. —**just′ly,** *adv.* —**just′ness,** *n.*

jŭs'tĭce, n. 1. fairness. 2. righteousness. 3. administration of law. 4. judge.

jŭs'tĭ·fy'', v.t., -fied, -fying. give valid reasons for. —jus''ti·fi'a·ble, adj. —jus''ti·fi·ca'tion, n.

jŭt, v.i., jutted, jutting. project.

jūte, n. coarse plant fiber.

jū'vĕn·ĭle, adj. 1. pertaining to children. 2. childish. —n. 3. child.

jŭx'tà·pōse'', v.t., -posed, -posing. place close or in contrast. —jux''ta·po·si'tion, n.

K

K, k, n. eleventh letter of the English alphabet.

kaī'sēr, n. Germanic emperor.

kāle, n. type of cabbage. Also, kail.

kà·leī'dó·scōpe'', n. device creating symmetrical patterns for viewing. —ka·lei''do·scop'ic, adj.

kăn''gà·roō', n. leaping Australian marsupial.

kà·pŭt', adj. destroyed or out of order.

kăr'àt, n. twenty-fourth part pure gold.

kà·râ'tē, n. Japanese technique of fighting with hands and feet.

kâr'mà, n. one's acts as a determinant of one's fate.

kā'tÿ·dĭd'', n. shrill, green insect.

kaÿ'ăk, n. Eskimo canoe.

kēel, n. central structural member of a ship.

kēen, adj. 1. sharp. 2. eager. 3. shrewd.

kēep, v., kept, keeping. n. v.t. 1. retain. 2. look after. 3. protect or support. 4. be observant of. —v.i. 5. be preserved. 6. abstain. 7. remain or continue. —n. 8. support; custody.

kēep'ĭng, 1. care; custody. 2. conformity.

kēep'sāke'', n. souvenir.

kĕg, n. small barrel.

kĕn, n. range of awareness or knowledge.

kĕn'nèl, n., v.t., -neled, -neling. n. doghouse. —v.t. 2. put in a kennel.

kêr'chĭef, n. cloth for covering the head.

kêr'nèl, n. 1. seed. 2. inner nut.

kĕr'ò·sēne'', n. petroleum derivative.

kĕtch'ŭp, n. sauce, often made with tomatoes.

kĕt'tle, n. pot for boiling water.

kĕt'tle-drŭm'', n. large, potlike drum.

kēy, n., adj., v.t., keyed, keying. n. 1. metal instrument operating a lock. 2. device on a piano, etc. pressed to produce a tone. 3. thing that explains. 4. system of musical tones. —adj. 5. decisive. —v.t. 6. Music. put into a key. —key'hole'', n.

kēy'bôard, n. (computers). 1. device resembling a typewriter keyboard used for data input. —v. 2. to input data with a keyboard.

kēy'nōte'', n. 1. lowest note of a scale. 2. basic theme.

kēy'stōne'', n. top stone of an arch.

khă'kĭ, n., pl. -kis. 1. dull yellowish brown. 2. khakis, clothing made of cloth this color.

kĭb'bitz, v.t. give unwanted advice.

kĭb·bŭtz'', n., pl. -butzim. Israeli collective settlement.

kĭck, v.t., v.i. 1. strike with the foot. —v.i. 2. recoil. 3. Informal. complain. —n. 4. act or instance of kicking. 5. Informal. a. grievance. b. thrill.

kĭck'băck'', n. Informal. rebate, usually illicit.

kĭd, n., v., kidded, kidding. n. 1. young goat. 2. Informal. child. —v.t. 3. Informal. tease. —v.i. 4. Informal. joke.

kĭd'năp'', v.t., -napped or -naped, -napping or -naping. abduct and hold prisoner. —kid'nap''er, n.

kĭd'nēy, n. 1. organ that forms urine. 2. sort or kind.

kĭll, v.t. 1. cause to die. 2. end abruptly. —n. 3. act or instance of killing. 4. game killed. —kill'er, n.

kĭln (kil, kiln), n. furnace for processing materials.

kĭ'lō, n., pl. -los. 1. kilogram. 2. kilometer.

kĭ'lò·grăm'', n. one thousand grams or 2.2046 pounds.

kĭ'lò·hêrtz'', n. one thousand hertz. Also, ki'lo·cy''cle.

kĭ'lò·mē''tèr, n. one thousand meters or 3,281 feet.

kĭ'lò·wätt'', n. one thousand watts.

kĭlt, n. knee-length Scottish skirt for men.

kĭl'têr, n. Informal. good condition.

kĭ·mō′nó, *n., pl.* -nos. *n.* full-length Japanese dress.

kĭn, *n.* relatives.

kĭnd, *n.* 1. sort. —*adj.* 2. benevolent; compassionate. —kind′ness, *n.*

kĭn′dêr·gâr′′tén, *n.* pre-elementary school.

kĭn′dle, *v.*, -dled, -dling. *v.t.* 1. set on fire. 2. arouse. —*v.i.* 3. be kindled. —kind′ling, *n.*

kĭnd′lӯ, *adj.* 1. kind. —*adv.* 2. in a kind way. 3. graciously; favorably. —kind′li·ness, *n.*

kĭn′drĕd, *n., pl.* 1. relatives. —*adj.* 2. of the same kind.

kĭ·nĕt′ĭc, *adj.* pertaining to motion.

kĭn′fōlk′′, *n., pl.* relatives. Also, kin′folks′′.

kĭng, *n.* 1. male national ruler. 2. playing card. —king′ly, *adj.*

kĭng′dóm, *n.* 1. state ruled by a king. 2. major category.

kĭng′fĭsh′′êr, *n.* diving bird that eats fish.

kĭng′-sīze′′, *adj. Informal.* extra-large.

kĭnk, *n.* short loop or coil. —kink′y, *adj.*

kĭn′shĭp′′, *n.* family relationship.

kĭ′ŏsk, *n.* small open shelter.

kĭp′pêr, *n.* salted, smoked herring.

kĭss, *n.* 1. touching with the lips as a sign of affection, etc. —*v.t.* 2. give a kiss to. —*v.i.* 3. exchange kisses.

kĭtch′ĕn, *n.* place for preparing meals.

kīte, *n.* flying toy on a string.

kĭth ănd kĭn, friends and relatives.

kĭtsch, *n.* vulgar, affected art. —kitsch′y, *adj.*

kĭt′tĕn, *n.* young cat. —kit′ten·ish, *adj.*

kĭt′tӯ, *n., pl.* -ties. *n. Informal.* 1. cat. 2. accumulated stakes.

kĭ′wĭ, *n.* 1. any flightless bird of genus Apteryx. *n.* 2. fuzzy fruit of Asian climbing plant, the Chinese gooseberry.

klĕp′′tó·mā′nĭ·á, *n.* compulsion to steal. —klep′′to·ma′ni·ac, *n.*

knăck, *n.* talent.

knăp′săck′′, *n.* sack worn on the back.

knāve, *n.* 1. *Archaic.* deceitful person. 2. playing card; jack. —knav′ish, *adj.* —knav′er·y, *n.*

knēad, *v.t.* press and work with the fingers.

knēe, *n.* joint of the leg.

knēel, *v.i.*, knelt or kneeled, kneeling. be upright on the knees.

knĕll, *n.* slow tolling of a bell.

knĭck′êrs, *n. pl.* trousers ending at the knees. Also knick′er·bock′′ers.

knĭck′knăck′′, *n.* small decorative object.

knīfe, *n., pl.* knives, *v.t.*, knifed, knifing. *n.* 1. small cutting tool. —*v.t.* 2. stab with a knife.

knīght, *n.* 1. possessor of an honorable rank, formerly military. 2. chesspiece. —*v.t.* 3. declare to be a knight. —knight′hood, *n.* —knight′ly, *adj.*

knīght′′-êr′ránt, *n., pl.* knights-errant. knight seeking adventure.

knĭsh (kė nish′), *n.* filled, baked dish of thin dough.

knĭt, *v.*, knitted or knit, knitting. *v.t.* 1. assemble from yarn with two needles. 2. draw together in wrinkles, as the brows. —*v.i.* 3. join again after a fracture.

knŏb, *n.* rounded projection or handle. —knob′by, *adj.*

knŏck, *v.t.* 1. hit, as with the fist. 2. *Informal.* disparage. —*v.i.* 3. strike blows. —*n.* 4. act or instance of knocking. 5. adverse happening. —knock′er, *n.*

knŏck′ōut′′, *n.* victory in boxing, esp. by knocking an opponent unconscious.

knŏll, *n.* small, round hill.

knŏt, *n., v.t.*, knotted, knotting. *n.* 1. fastening of intertwined cord. 2. small cluster. 3. hard lump in wood. 4. one nautical mile per hour. —*v.t.* 5. make into a knot. —knot′ty, *adj.*

knōw, *v.t.*, knew, known, knowing. 1. have full evidence. 2. be fully informed or skilled. 3. have as an acquaintance. 4. recognize. —know′ing·ly, *adv.*

knōw-hōw′′, *n.* technical ability.

knōw′ĭng, *n.* 1. ability to know. —*adj.* 2. shrewd.

knōw′-ĭt-ăll′′, *n.* pretender to omniscience.

knŏwl′ĕdge, *n.* 1. state of knowing. 2. what is known.

knŏwl′ĕdge·a·ble, *adj.* well-informed.

knŭck′le, *n.* central finger joint.

Kȯ·răn′, *n.* Muslim holy scriptures.

kō′shêr, *adj. Judaism.* fit to eat under religious law.

kŏw´tŏw´, v.t. show servility or deference.

kū´dōs, n. Informal. praise; fame.

kŭm´quăt´´, n. small, tart citrus fruit.

L

L, l, n. twelfth letter of the English alphabet.

lā´běl, n., v.t., -beled, -beling. n. 1. attached paper with information. —v.t. 2. designate with a label.

lā´bǐ·ǎl, adj. pertaining to lips.

lā´bör, n. 1. hard work. 2. workers collectively. 3. process of giving birth. —v.i. 4. work hard. —la´bor·er, n.

lăb´o·rà·tô´´rÿ, n., pl. -ries. place for scientific research.

là·bô´rī·oŭs, adj. difficult; tedious.

lăb´ÿ·rǐnth´´, n. 1. maze. 2. intricate problem. —lab´´y·rin´thine, adj.

lāce, n., v.t., laced, lacing. n. 1. binding string, as on a shoe. 2. openwork cloth. —v.t. 3. fasten or furnish with a lace. —lace´work´´, n.

lăc´êr·āte´´, v.t., -ated, -ating. tear jaggedly. —lac´´er·a´tion, n.

lăch´rÿ·mōse´´, adj. tearful.

lăck, n. 1. absence or shortage. —v.t. 2. be without. —v.i. 3. be deficient.

lăck´´ă·dāi´sǐ·cal, adj. without spirit or drive.

lăck´lŭs´´têr, adj. dull.

là·cŏn´ǐc, adj. short-spoken; terse. —la·con´i·cal·ly, adv.

lăc´quêr, n. 1. transparent varnish-like coating. —v.t. 2. coat with lacquer.

là·crŏsse´, n. game with netlike racquets.

là·cū´nà, n., pl. -nas, -nae. gap.

lāc´ÿ, adj., -ier, -iest. open and intricate.

lăd, n. boy.

lăd´dêr, n. steep set of steps.

lā´děn, adj. burdened; loaded.

lād´ǐng, n. freight.

lā´dle, n., v.t., -dled, -dling. n. 1. long-handled bowl for dipping. —v.t. 2. dip with a ladle.

lā´dÿ, n., -dies. 1. respectable woman. 2. title of certain British women. —la´dy·like´, adj. —la´dy·ship´´, n.

lā´dÿ·bŭg´´, n. small, spotted red beetle. Also, la´dy·bird´´.

lăg, v.i., lagged, lagging, n. v.i. 1. fall behind. —n. 2. act or instance of lagging. —lag´gard, n., adj.

lä´gêr, n. type of beer.

là·gōōn´, n. enclosed body of water near a larger one.

lāid´´băck´´, adj. relaxed; serene.

lāir, n. den, as of an animal.

lais´´sez faire´ (lä´´zā·fâr´), noninterference, esp. in economic activity.

lā´ǐ·tÿ, n., pl. -ties. laymen collectively.

lāke, n. inland body of water.

lâ´mà, n. Tibetan Buddhist monk. —la´ma·ser´´y, n.

lămb, n. young sheep.

lăm·bāste´, v.t., -basted, -basting. Informal. punish with blows or words.

lăm´běnt, adj. gently glowing. —lam´ben·cy, n.

lāme, adj., v.t., lamed, laming. adj. 1. unable to walk properly. 2. ineffectual. —v.t. 3. make lame. —lame´ly, adv.

là·měnt´, v.t., v.i. 1. mourn. —n. 2. speech, poem, or song of mourning. —la´´men·ta´tion, n. —lam·en´ta·ble, adj.

lăm´ǐ·nāte´´, v.t., -nated, -nating. 1. build up in layers. 2. cover with a layer of material. —lam´´i·na´tion, n.

lămp, n. device for emitting rays of light, etc. —lamp´post´´, n.

lămp´blăck´´, n. pigment of fine soot.

lăm·pōōn´, n. 1. satirical writing. —v.t. 2. satirize in a lampoon.

là·naī´, n. Hawaiian open-air living area.

lănce, n., v.t., lanced, lancing. n. 1. spear carried by a horseman. —v.t. 2. prick, as to discharge pus.

lănd, n. 1. earth's surface above water. 2. nation; country. 3. real estate. —v.t. 4. bring to shore or earth. 5. secure; obtain. —v.i. 6. come to shore or earth. 7. fall.

lănd´ěd, adj. land-owning.

lănd´făll´´, n. 1. land sighted from a ship. 2. sighting of such land.

lănd´ǐng, n. 1. act of coming to shore or earth. 2. place to land. 3. unstepped area on a stair.

lănd´lŏcked´´, adj. with little or no access to the sea.

lănd´lôrd´´, n. 1. man from whom one

rents. **2.** innkeeper. Also, *fem.*, **land'la"dy.**

lănd'mârk", *n.* visible aid to finding one's way.

lănd'măss", *n.* major land area.

lănd'scāpe", *n.*, *v.t.*, **-scaped, -scaping.** *n.* **1.** large visible area of land. —*v.t.* **2.** create a landscape from.

lănd'slīde", *n.* fall of earth down a slope.

lāne, *n.* **1.** path or narrow road. **2.** path of highway travel.

lăn'guȧge, *n.* system of communication.

lăn'guĭd, *adj.* without energy. —**lan'guid·ly,** *adv.*

lăn'guĭsh, *v.i.* **1.** long wistfully. **2.** weaken.

lăn'gŭor, *n.* lack of vitality. —**lan'guor·ous,** *adj.*

lănk, *adj.* **1.** lean. **2.** long and straight, as hair.

lăn'kў, *adj.* **-ier, -iest.** awkwardly tall and lean.

lăn'o·lĭn, *n.* oil from wool used in ointments and cosmetics.

lăn'têrn, *n.* **1.** transparent lamp casing. **2.** cupola.

lăp, *n.*, *v.*, **lapped, lapping.** *n.* **1.** area between waist and knees when seated. **2.** overlap. **3.** once around a racetrack. —*v.t.* **4.** wrap. **5.** overlap. —*v.i.* **6.** drink by licking. **7.** splash gently. —**lap'dog".**

là·pĕl', *n.* continuation of a coat collar folded back.

lăp'ĭ·dār"ў, *n.*, *pl.* **-ies,** *adj.* *n.* **1.** worker in gems. —*adj.* **2.** fine; meticulous.

lăpse, *v.i.*, **lapsed, lapsing,** *n.* *v.i.* **1.** go passively. **2.** elapse. **3.** become void. —*n.* **4.** act or instance of lapsing. **5.** minor error.

lâr'ce·nў, *n.*, *pl.* **-nies.** theft. —**lar'ce·nous,** *adj.*

lârd, *n.* rendered animal fat.

lârd'êr, *n.* place for storing food.

lârge, *adj.*, *adv.*, **larger, largest,** *n.* *adj.* **1.** big. **2.** large-scale. —*adv.* **3.** in a large way. —*n.* **4. at large,** unconfined. —**large'ly,** *adv.*

lâr'gĕss', *n.* **1.** generous gift. **2.** generosity. Also, **lar·gesse'.**

lâr'gō, *adj.*, *adv. Music.* slow.

lăr'ĭ·ȧt, *n.* tether or lasso.

lârk, *n.* **1.** songbird. **2.** frolic. —*v.i.* **3.** frolic.

lâr·vȧ, *n.*, *pl.* **-vae.** early form of an animal. —**lar'val,** *adj.*

lăr"ўn·gī'tis, *n.* inflammation of the larynx.

lâr'ўnx, *n.*, *pl.* **-ynxes, -ynges.** container of the vocal cords.

lás·cĭv'ĭ·oŭs, *adj.* lustful.

lā'sêr, *n.* device for amplifying and concentrating light waves.

lăsh, *v.t.* **1.** tie. **2.** whip. —*v.i.* **3.** strike. —*n.* **4.** whip. **5.** blow from a whip. **6.** eyelash.

lăss, *Dialect.* young woman.

lăs'sĭ·tūde", *n.* lack of vigor.

lăs'sō, *n.*, *pl.* **-sos, -soes,** *v.t.*, **-soed, -soing.** *n.* **1.** rope for capturing cattle, etc. —*v.t.* **2.** capture with a lasso.

lăst, *adj.*, *adv.* **1.** after all others. —*n.* **2.** last one. —*v.i.* **3.** remain. —*v.t.* **4.** be enough for. —**last'ly,** *adv.*

lătch, *n.* **1.** device to hold a door, etc. shut. —*v.t.* **2.** fasten with a latch.

lāte, *adj.*, *adv.*, **later** or (for adj.) **latter, latest** or **last.** *adj.*, *adv.* **1.** after the right time. **2.** near the end. **3.** in recent times. —*adj.* **4.** recently alive.

lāte'lў, *adv.* recently.

lā'tĕnt, *n.* unmanifested or undeveloped. —**la'ten·cy,** *n.*

lă'têr·ȧl, *adj.* pertaining to a side. —**la'ter·al·ly,** *adv.*

lăth, *n.*, *pl.* **laths. 1.** wood strip for holding plaster. **2.** any material for this.

lāthe, *n.* machine for cutting a rotating object.

lăth'êr, *n.* **1.** foam. —*v.t.* **2.** cover with foam.

lăt'ĭ·tūde", *n.* **1.** north-south measurement. **2.** scope.

lá·trĭne', *n.* military bathroom.

lăt'têr, *adj.* **1.** more recently mentioned. **2.** more recent. —**lat'ter·ly,** *adv.*

lăt'tĭce, *n.* screen of crisscrossed strips. —**lat'tice·work",** *n.*

laŭd, *v.t.* praise. —**laud'a·ble,** *adj.* —**laud'a·to"ry,** *adj.*

laŭ'dȧn·ŭm, *n.* opium-alcohol solution.

lăugh, *n.* **1.** rhythmic sound indicating amusement, scorn, etc. —*v.i.* **2.** make such a sound. —**laugh'a·ble,** *adj.* —**laugh'ter,** *n.*

laŭnch, *v.t.* **1.** send from land. **2.** put into effect, use, etc. —*n.* **3.** open boat.

laūn′dêr, *v.t.* wash, as clothes. **—laun′der·er,** *fem.,* **laun′dress,** *n.*

laūn′drў, *n., pl.* **-dries.** place for laundering. **—laun′dry·man,** *n.*

lâu′rĕl, *n.* **1.** shrub with glossy leaves. **2. laurels,** honors.

lâ′vå, *n.* molten volcanic rock.

lăv′å·tô′′rŷ, *n., pl.* **-ries.** washing place.

lăv′ĕn·dêr, *n.* **1.** pale purple. **2.** European mint with pale purple flowers.

lăv′ĭsh, *adj.* **1.** very ample. **2.** generous. **—v.t. 3.** give generously. **—lav′ish·ly,** *adv.* **—lav′ish·ness,** *n.*

lâw, *n.* **1.** rule established by government. **2.** legal profession. **3.** police. **4.** rule of natural phenomena. **—law′-a·bid′′ing,** *adj.* **—law′break′′er,** *n. adj.* **—law′giv′′er,** *n.* **—law′less,** *adj.* **—law′mak′′er,** *n.* **—law′suit′′,** *n.*

lâwn, *n.* **1.** expanse of grass. **2.** sheer cotton or linen.

lâw′yêr, *n.* professional legal adviser and representative.

lăx, *adj.* negligent. **—lax′i·ty,** *n.*

lăx′å·tĭve, *adj.* **1.** easing constipation. **—n. 2.** laxative medicine.

lāy, *v.t.,* **laid, laying,** *n., adj. v.t.* **1.** set down gently. **2.** set in place. **3.** place, as emphasis or a claim. **—n. 4.** situation. **5.** ballad. **—adj. 6.** not professional or clerical. **—lay′man,** *n.*

lāy′êr, *n.* level or thickness of material.

lāy′ŏff′′, *n.* dismissal due to lack of work.

lā′zў, *adj.,* **-zier, -ziest.** unwilling to work. **—la′zi·ly,** *adv.* **—la′zi·ness,** *n.*

lēach, *v.t., v.i.,* dissolve with a filtering liquid.

lead (lēd for 1 to 6; lĕd for 7), *v.,* **led, leading,** *n. v.t.* **1.** direct or guide. **2.** be ahead of. **3.** conduct. **—v.i. 4.** tend or result. **—n. 5.** leading role or place. **6.** guidance. **7.** heavy metallic chemical element. **—lead·er,** *n.* **—lead′er·ship′′,** *n.* **—lead·en,** *adj.*

lēaf, *n., pl.* **leaves,** *v.i. n.* **1.** flat thin termination of a plant stem. **2.** thin sheet. **—v.i. 3.** turn over pages. **—leaf′y,** *adj.*

lēaf′lĕt, *n.* small printed sheet.

lēague, *n., v.,* **leaguing.** *n.* **1.** alliance. **2.** unit of about 3 miles. **—v.t., v.i. 3.** form into a league.

lēak, *n.* **1.** accidental release or admission. **—v.i. 2.** have or pass through a

leak. **—v.t. 3.** pass through a leak. **—leak′age,** *n.* **—leak′y,** *adj.*

lēan, *v.,* **leaned** or **leant, leaning,** *adj. v.t., v.i.* **1.** stand against something supporting the upper end. **—v.i. 2.** bend; incline. **3.** be predisposed. **4.** rely. **—adj. 5.** with little fat.

lēap, *v.,* **leaped** or **leapt, leaping,** *n.* jump.

lēap yēar, year with 29 days in February.

lêarn, *v.,* **learned** or **learnt, learning.** *v.t.* **1.** come to know or know how. **—v.i. 2.** get information. **—learn′er,** *n.* **—learn′ing,** *n.* **—learn′ed,** *adj.*

lēase, *n., v.t.,* **leased, leasing.** *n.* **1.** rental contract. **—v.t. 2.** rent by lease.

lēash, *n.* tether, as for a dog.

lēast, *adj.* **1.** smallest in size, importance, etc. **—adv. 2.** to the smallest extent.

lĕath′êr, *n.* tanned hide.

lēave, *v.,* **left, leaving,** *n. v.i.* **1.** go away. **—v.t. 2.** go away from. **3.** abandon. **4.** to cause to remain behind one. **5.** bequeath. **—n. 6.** departure. **7.** permission. **—leave′tak′′ing,** *n.*

lĕav′ĕn, *n.* **1.** substance making dough rise **—v.t. 2.** cause to rise.

lĕav′ĭngs, *n. pl.* leftovers.

lĕch′êr, *n.* lustful person. **—lech′er·ous,** *adj.* **—lech′er·y,** *n.*

lĕc′tûre, *n., v.,* **-tured, -turing.** *n.* **1.** informative speech. **—v.t. 2.** give a lecture to. **—v.i. 3.** give a lecture.

lĕdge, *n.* narrow shelf or platform.

lĕd′gêr, *n.* accountant's book.

lēe, *adj.* **1.** away from the wind. **—n. 2.** lee side, etc. **3. lees,** dregs.

lēech, *n.* blood-sucking worm.

lēek, *n.* onionlike vegetable.

lēer, *n.* **1.** sly, malicious or lustful look. **—v.i. 2.** give a leer.

lēe′wāy′′, *n.* **1.** *Informal.* scope for action. **2.** *Nautical.* leeward drift.

lĕft, *n.* **1.** west when facing north. **2.** liberal or socialistic position. **—adv. 3.** toward the left. **4.** at or in the left. **—left′ist,** *n., adj.* **—left′-hand′,** *adj.*

lĕft′ō′′vêr, *n.* remnant for later use.

lĕft wĭng, political left. **—left′-wing′′,** *adj.* **—left′-wing′er,** *n.*

lĕg, *n.* **1.** supporting and walking limb. **2.** vertical support.

lĕg′å·cў, *n., pl.* **-cies.** something left to posterity.

lē'gȧl, *adj.* **1.** permitted by law. **2.** pertaining to law. —le'gal·ly, *adv.* —le·gal'i·ty, *n.* —le'gal·ize'', *v.t.*

lĕg'ȧte, *n.* papal envoy.

lĕg''ȧ·tēe', *n.* recipient of a legacy.

le·gā'tion, *n.* office of a diplomat.

le·gä'tō, *adj. Music.* smooth and even.

lĕg'end, *n.* **1.** folk tale. **2.** inscription. —leg'end·ar''y, *adj.*

lĕg''ēr·de·māin', *n.* cunning of the hand.

lĕg'gĭng, *n.* outer leg covering.

lĕg'i·ble, *adj.* possible to read. —leg''i·bil'i·ty, *n.*

lē'giȯn, *n.* large band, esp. of soldiers. —le'gion·ar''y, *adj., n.* —le''gion·naire', *n.*

lĕg'ĭs·lāte'', *v.,* -lated, -lating. *v.t.* **1.** determine by law. —*v.i.* **2.** enact laws. —leg''is·la'tion, *n.* —leg''is·la'tive, *adj.* —leg''is·la''tor, *n.*

lĕg'ĭs·lā''tūre, *n.* lawmaking body.

le·gĭt'ĭ·mȧte, *adj.* **1.** right; proper. **2.** of married parents. —le·git'i·ma·cy, *n.* —le·git'i·mize'', *v.t.*

lĕg'ūme, *n.* vegetable with seed pods. —le·gu'mi·nous, *adj.*

lei (lā), *n., pl.* leis. Hawaiian flower garland.

lēi'sûre, *n.* **1.** time for rest or recreation. **2. at one's leisure,** when convenient.

lēi'sûre·lȳ, *adj., adv.* without haste or hurry.

lĕm'ȯn, *n.* yellow citrus fruit. —lem''on·ade', *n.*

lĕnd, *v.t.,* lent, lending. **1.** give for later return. **2.** impart.

lĕngth, *n.* **1.** end-to-end extent. **2.** piece measured by length. —length'en, *v.t., v.i* —length'wise'', length'ways'', *adj., adv.* —length'y, *adj.*

lē'nĭ·ent, *adj.* not strict or harsh. —le'ni·en·cy, le'ni·ence, *n.*

lĕns, *n., pl.* lenses. transparent object concentrating or dispersing rays of light.

Lĕnt, *n.* Christian time of penance from Ash Wednesday to Easter. —Lent'en, *adj.*

lĕn'tĭl, *n.* small legume seed used as food.

lē'ȯ·nīne, *adj.* lion-like.

lĕop'ȧrd, *n.* spotted cat of the panther family.

lĕp'er, *n.* person with leprosy.

lĕp'rē·chäun'', *n.* Irish fairy.

lĕp'rȯ·sȳ, *n.* deforming chronic disease. —lep'rous, *adj.*

lĕs'bĭ·ȧn, *n.* **1.** homosexual woman. —*adj.* **2.** pertaining to such women. —les'bi·an·ism, *n.*

lē·sion, *n.* bodily injury resulting in impairment of function.

lĕss, *adj.* **1.** smaller or fewer. —*adv.* **2.** to a smaller extent. —*prep.* **3.** minus. —les'sen, *v.t., v.i.*

lĕs·sēe', *n.* tenant on a lease.

lĕs'sêr, *adj.* smaller; less important.

lĕs'sȯn, *n.* something learned at one time.

lĕs'sör, *n.* landlord on a lease.

lĕst, *conj.* for fear that.

lĕt, *v.t.,* let, letting, *n. v.t.* **1.** allow. **2.** rent. **3.** allow to issue. —*n.* **4.** obstacle.

lĕt'down'', *n.* **1.** disappointment. **2.** slackening.

lē'thȧl, *adj.* deadly.

lĕth'ȧr·gȳ, *n., pl.* -gies. sluggishness. —le·thar'gic, *adj.*

lĕt'têr, *n.* **1.** alphabetic character. **2.** message in an envelope. **3.** literal meaning. **4. letters,** literature. —*v.t.* **5.** write letter by letter. —let'ter·ing, *n.*

lĕt'têred, *adj.* educated.

lĕt'tŭce, *n.* green, leafy vegetable.

leū·kē'mĭ·ȧ, *n.* blood disease.

lĕv'ēe, *n.* embankment against rising water.

lĕv'ĕl, *n., v.t.,* -eled, -eling. *n.* **1.** point or plane between top and bottom. **2.** device for finding horizontals or verticals. **3.** point on a scale of values. —*adj.* **4.** flat. **5.** horizontal. **6.** even. —*v.t.* **7.** make level.

lĕv'ĕl-hĕad'ĕd, *adj.* of calm, sound judgment.

lĕv'êr, *n.* pivoted raising device lifted at one end. —lev'er·age, *n.*

le·vī'ȧ·thȧn, *n.* sea monster.

lĕv''ĭ·tā'tion, *n.* raising or rising without physical support.

lĕv'ĭ·tȳ, *n.* mirth, often unseemly.

lĕv'ȳ, *v.t.,* -ied, -ying, *n., pl.* -ies. *v.t.* **1.** impose for payment. **2.** enlist. —*n.* **3.** something levied.

lewd, *adj.* obscene. —lewd'ly, *adv.* —lewd'ness, *n.*

lĕx'ĭ·cȯn, *n.* dictionary.

lī''ȧ·bĭl'ĭ·tȳ, *n., pl.* -ties. **1.** loss or payment of money. **2.** state of being liable. **3.** disadvantage.

li′a·ble, *adj.* **1.** responsible. **2.** subject to something. **3.** likely.

li′ai·sŏn″, *n.* **1.** connection, as for communication. **2.** love affair.

li′ar, *n.* teller of lies.

li·ba′tion, *n.* outpouring of liquid.

li′bel, *n., v.t.,* **-beled, -beling.** *n.* **1.** defamation in writing or print. —*v.t.* **2.** defame by this means. —**li′bel·ous, li′bel·lous,** *adj.*

lib′er·al, *adj.* **1.** generous. **2.** not literal. **3.** favoring more civil liberty. —*n.* **4.** person favoring more civil liberty. —**lib″er·al′i·ty,** *n.* —**lib′er·al·ism,** *n.* —**lib′er·al·ize″,** *v.t.*

lib′er·āte″, *v.t.,* **-ated, -ating.** free. —**lib″er·a′tion,** *n.* —**lib′er·a″tor,** *n.*

lib″er·tār′i·an, *n.* believer in personal liberties.

lib′er·tïne″, *n.* licentious person.

lib′er·tÿ, *n., pl.* **-ties. 1.** freedom. **2.** privilege. **3. liberties,** impertinences.

li·bi′dō, *n.* **1.** sexual urge. **2.** psychic energy.

li′brār″ÿ, *n., pl.* **-ies. 1.** collection of books. **2.** place for books. —**li·brar′i·an,** *n.*

li·brĕt′tō, *n., pl.* **-tos, -ti.** text of an opera, etc. —**li·bret′tist,** *n.*

li′cĕnse, *n., v.t.,* **-censed, -censing.** *n.* **1.** privilege of doing. **2.** abuse of liberty. —*v.t.* **3.** grant a license to. —**li″cen·see′,** *n.* —**li·cen′tious,** *adj.*

li′chĕn, *n.* mosslike growth.

lĭc′ĭt, *adj.* permitted.

lĭck, *v.t.* **1.** rub with the tongue. **2.** *Informal.* **a.** defeat. **b.** beat. —*v.i.* **3.** lap. —*n.* **4.** act or instance of licking.

lĭc′o·rĭce, *n.* European root used for flavoring.

lĭd, *n.* cover.

līe, *v.i.,* **lay** (for 1, 2) or **lied** (for 3), **lain** (for 1, 2), **lying,** *n. v.i.* **1.** rest on something horizontal. **2.** be situated. **3.** make statements intended to deceive. —*n.* **4.** situation. **5.** lying statement.

lief, *adv. Archaic.* willingly.

liĕn, *n.* legal claim on property.

lieū, *n.* **in lieu of,** in place of.

lieū·tĕn′ant, *n.* commissioned military or naval officer below a captain or lieu-

tenant commander. —**lieu·ten′an·cy,** *n.*

līfe, *n., pl.* **lives. 1.** period of existence. **2.** living things collectively. **3.** human experience. **4.** way of living. **5.** animation. **6.** biography. —**life′less,** *adj.* —**life′long″,** *adj.* —**life′time″,** *n.*

līfe′bōat″, *n.* emergency boat.

līfe′guârd″, *n.* one employed to protect swimmers, esp. from drowning, etc.

līfe′līke″, *adj.* resembling a living being.

līfe′-sīze″, *adj.* as large as the living model. Also, **life′-sized″.**

līft, *v.t.* **1.** raise. —*v.t.* **2.** attempt to raise something. **3.** rise. —*n.* **4.** act or instance of lifting. **5.** hoist.

lĭg′a·mĕnt, *n.* body connective tissue.

lĭg′a·tûre, *n.* tie.

līght, *n., adj., v.,* **lighted** or **lit, lighting.** *n.* **1.** visible radiant energy. **2.** lamp. **3.** flame. **4.** truth. **5.** public awareness. —*adj.* **6.** not dark or serious. **7.** not heavy. **8.** not serious. —*v.t.* **9.** set fire to. **10.** cause to give off light. **11.** show in light. —*v.i.* **12.** be lighted. **13.** alight. **14.** happen; venture. —**light′en,** *v.t., v.i.* —**light′weight″,** *adj.*

līght′êr, *n.* **1.** lighting device. **2.** freight barge.

līght′-hĕad′ĕd, *adj.* dizzy.

līght′-heârt′ĕd, *adj.* cheerful.

līght′hŏuse″, *n.* tower with a navigational beacon.

līght′nĭng, *n.* flash of electricity in the sky.

līght′-yēar′, *n.* distance light travels in a year, about 6 trillion miles.

lĭg′nīte, *n.* soft brown coal.

līke, *prep., adj., n., v.t.,* **liked, liking.** *prep.* **1.** similar or similarly to. **2.** characteristic or suggestive of. **3.** inclined to. —*adj.* **4.** similar. —*n.* **5.** similar person or thing. **6.** preference. —*v.t.* **7.** be pleased with. **8.** wish. —**like′a·ble, lik′a·ble,** *adj.* —**like′ness,** *n.*

līke′lÿ, *adj.,* **-lier, -liest,** *adv. adj.* **1.** probable. **2.** suitable. —*adv.* **3.** probably.

līk′ĕn, *v.t.* compare.

līke′wīse″, *adv.* similarly, also.

li′lac, *n.* pale purple flower.

lĭlt, *n.* light, bouncy rhythm.

lĭl′ÿ, *n., pl.* **-ies.** flower with trumpet-shaped blossoms.

lī′mȧ bēan, broad, pale green bean.

limb, *n.* **1.** large tree branch. **2.** arm or leg.

lim′bêr, *adj.* **1.** flexible. —*v.t.* **2.** make limber. —*v.i.* **3.** become limber.

lim′bō, *n.* **1.** abode of the unbaptized, innocent dead. **2.** oblivion.

līme, *n., v.t.,* limed, liming. *n.* **1.** calcium oxide. **2.** tart green citrus fruit. —*v.t.* **3.** treat with lime. —lime′ade′, *n.*

līme′līght″, *n.* state of much publicity.

lim′êr·ick, *n.* amusing five-lined verse.

līme′stōne″, *n.* stone containing much calcium carbonate.

lim′it, *n.* **1.** edge or boundary. **2.** permissible extent. —*v.t.* **3.** set a limit to. —lim″i·ta′tion, *n.* —lim′it·ed, *adj.* —lim′it·less, *adj.*

lim′ou·sïne″, *n.* long, chauffeured automobile.

limp, *v.i.* **1.** walk lamely. —*n.* **2.** lame gait. —*adj.* **3.** not rigid or firm.

lim′pid, *adj.* perfectly clear. —lim·pid′i·ty, *n.*

lin′dèn, *n.* tree with heart-shaped leaves.

līne, *n., v.,* lined, lining. *n.* **1.** long, narrow mark. **2.** row. **3.** boundary. **4.** course. **5.** transit system. **6.** rope, pipe, etc. **7.** occupation. —*v.t.* **8.** put a lining in. **9.** mark with lines. —*v.i.* **10.** assemble in a line.

lin′ē·àge, *n.* ancestry.

lin′ē·ȧl, *adj.* **1.** pertaining to direct ancestry. **2.** linear.

lin′ē·ȧ·mènts, *n. pl.* features of the face.

lin′ē·ȧr, *adj.* pertaining to lines or length.

lin′èn, *n.* **1.** cloth made of flax. **2.** linens, bedsheets, etc.

lin′êr, *n.* **1.** ship or airplane on scheduled service. **2.** something that lines.

līne′ŭp″, *n.* arrangement or muster in a row.

lin′gêr, *v.i.* remain; stay.

lin·ger·ie (län″zè rā′), *n.* women's underwear.

lin′gō, *n., pl.* -goes. *Informal.* strange language.

lin′guist, *n.* **1.** speaker of many languages. **2.** student of languages. —lin·guis′tics, *n.* —lin·guis′tic, *adj.*

lin′i·mènt, *n.* soothing liquid for external use.

lin′īng, *n.* material applied to an interior.

link, *n.* **1.** unit of a chain or series. **2.** connection. —*v.t., v.i.* **3.** connect. —link′age, *n.*

links, *n. pl.* golf course.

li·nō′lē·ŭm, *n.* smooth sheeting for floors.

lin′sēed″, *n.* flax seed.

lint, *n.* fibrous waste.

lin′tel, *n.* beam over a doorway, etc.

lī′ŏn, *n.* **1.** large catlike animal of Africa and southwest Asia. **2.** celebrity. Also, *fem.,* li′on·ess.

lī′on·īze″, *v.t.,* -ized, -izing. treat as a celebrity.

lip, *n.* **1.** feature at top and bottom of the mouth. **2.** surface for pouring.

lip′stick″, *n.* coloring for the lips.

liq′ue·fȳ″, *v.,* -fied, -fying. *v.t., v.i.* change to liquid. —liq″ue·fac′tion, *n.*

li′queûr, *n.* sweet strong alcoholic drink.

liq′uid, *n.* **1.** fluid incapable of indefinite expansion. —*adj.* **2.** in the form of a liquid. **3.** readily turned into cash. —li·quid′i·ty, *n.*

liq′ui·dāte″, *v.t.,* -dated, -dating. **1.** terminate, as a business. **2.** convert into cash. **3.** kill. —liq″ui·da′tion, *n.*

liq′uör, *n.* alcoholic liquid.

līsle (līl), *n.* fine cotton.

lisp, *n.* **1.** mispronunciation of *s* and *z.* —*v.i.* **2.** make such mispronunciations.

lis′sòme, *adj.* agile and supple.

list, *n.* **1.** series of related items. **2.** tilt, as of a ship. —*v.t.* **3.** put on a list. —*v.i.* **4.** tilt.

lis′tèn, *v.i.* **1.** hear attentively. **2.** pay heed. —lis′ten·er, *n.*

list′less, *adj.* indifferent from fatigue, etc. —list′less·ly, *adv.* —list′less·ness, *n.*

lit′ȧ·nÿ, *n., pl.* -nies. uttered prayer with responses.

lī′têr, *n.* metric unit equal to 1.0567 liquid quarts or 0.908 dry quart. Also, li′tre.

lit′êr·ȧl, *adj.* according to the exact wording. —lit′er·al·ly, *adv.*

lit′êr·ār″ÿ, *adj.* pertaining to literature.

lit′êr·āte, *adj.* **1.** able to read. **2.** well-read. —lit′er·a·cy, *n.*

lit″′è·rä′tī, *n. pl.* well-read persons.

lit′êr·à·tūre, *n.* fiction, poetry, etc. of lasting value.

līthe, *adj.* supple.

lĭth′o·grăph″, *n*. print from a flat surface with special ink. —**lith″o·graph′ic**, *adj*. —li·thog′ra·phy, *n*. —li·thog′ra·pher, *n*.

lĭt′ĭ·gāte″, *v*., -gated, -gating. *v.t., v.i.* contest in a lawsuit. —lit″i·ga′tion, *n*. —lit′i·gant, lit′i·ga″tor, *n*.

lĭt′têr, *n*. **1.** trash. **2.** newly-born animals. **3.** animal bedding. **4.** frame for carrying a person. —*v.t.* **5.** scatter carelessly.

lĭt′tle, *adj*. littler or less or lesser, littlest or least, *adv*., less, least, *n. adj*. **1.** small. **2.** petty. —*adv*. **3.** not much. —*n*. **4.** short while. **5.** small amount.

lĭt′ûr·gy̆, *n., pl.* -gies. ritual of worship. —li·tur′gi·cal, *adj*.

lĭv′a·ble, *adj*. pleasant to inhabit. Also, **live′a·ble**.

līve′li·hŏŏd″, *n*. means of sustenance.

līve (liv for 1-5; līv for 6-8). *v.i.* **1.** be alive. **2.** dwell. **3.** spend one's life. **4.** depend for existence. —*v.t.* **5.** experience or spend. —*adj*. **6.** alive. **7.** vital. **8.** electrically charged.

līve′ly̆, *adj., -lier, -liest, adv. adj*. **1.** full of vitality. —*adv*. **2.** in a lively way. —live′li·ness, *n*.

līv′ĕn, *v.t.* **1.** make lively. —*v.i.* **2.** become lively.

lĭv′êr, *n*. organ secreting bile.

lĭv′êr·wûrst″, *n*. sausage made with ground liver.

līve′stŏck″, *n*. cattle, sheep, etc.

lĭv′ĭd, *adj*. **1.** discolored, as flesh. **2.** enraged.

lĭv′ĭng, *adj*. **1.** alive. **2.** pertaining to being alive. —*n*. **3.** livelihood.

lĭz′ârd, *n*. scaly, four-legged reptile.

llä′mà, *n*. South American beast of burden.

lōad, *n*. **1.** something carried. —*v.t.* **2.** put a load on or in. **3.** supply in large amounts. **4.** make ready for firing. —*v.i.* **5.** take on a load.

lōaf, *n., pl.* loaves, *v.i., n*. **1.** regularly shaped piece of bread. —*v.i.* **2.** be idle. —loaf′er, *n*.

lōam, *n*. rich soil. —loam′y, *adj*.

lōan, *n*. **1.** act or instance of lending. **2.** something lent. —*v.t., v.i.* **3.** lend.

lōath, *adj*. reluctant.

lōathe, *v.t.*, loathed, loathing. dislike intensely. —loath′some, *adj*.

lŏb, *v.t.*, lobbed, lobbing. hurl with a high curve.

lŏb′by̆, *n., pl.* -bies. *v.i.*, -bied, -bying. *n*. **1.** entrance room. **2.** group seeking favorable legislation. —*v.i.* **3.** seek favorable legislation. —lob′by·ist, *n*.

lōbe, *n*. rounded projection. —lo′bar, lo′bate, *n*.

lŏb′stêr, *n*. sea crustacean with pincers.

lō′càl, *adj*. **1.** pertaining or limited to a place. **2.** making most or all stops. —*n*. **3.** local train or bus. **4.** local branch of a labor union. —lo′cal·ly, *adv*.

lō·căle′, *n*. scene of an event.

lō·căl′ĭ·ty̆, *n., pl.* -ties. **1.** location. **2.** district.

lō′càl·īze″, *v.t.*, -ized, -izing. trace or confine to one place. —lo″cal·i·za′tion, *n*.

lō′cāte, *v.t.*, -cated, -cating. establish the place of. —lo·ca′tion, *n*.

lŏck, *n*. **1.** device for securing doors, etc. **2.** canal chamber between levels. **3.** firing mechanism. **4.** curl of hair. —*v.t.* **5.** fasten with a lock. **6.** shut in or out. —*v.i.* **7.** be jammed. —lock′smith″, *n*.

lŏck′êr, *n*. compartment that can be locked.

lŏck′ĕt, *n*. round case worn as a pendant to a necklace.

lŏck′jăw″, *n*. form of tetanus.

lŏck′ōut″, *n*. exclusion of workers from a workplace.

lō′cō, *adj. Informal*. crazy.

lō″co·mō′tion, *n*. movement from place to place.

lō″co·mō′tĭve, *n*. **1.** railroad traction engine. —*adj*. **2.** pertaining to locomotion.

lō′cŭst, *n*. **1.** crop-eating insect. **2.** flowering tree.

lō·cū′tion, *n*. spoken expression.

lōde, *n*. deposit of metallic ore.

lōde′stōne″, *n*. magnetic iron ore.

lŏdge, *n., v.*, lodged, lodging. *n*. **1.** forest house. **2.** fraternity chapter. —*v.t.* **3.** house. **4.** push into a fixed position. —*v.i.* **5.** become fixed. **6.** dwell.

lŏdg′ĭng, *n*. **1.** temporary home. **2.** lodgings, rented rooms.

lŏft, *n*. open upper floor.

lŏft′y̆, *adj., -ier, -iest*. very high. —loft′i·ly, *adv*.

lŏg, *n., v.t.*, logged, logging. *n*. **1.** cut

tree trunk or limb. **2.** record of events. —*v.t.* **3.** take logs from. **4.** record in a log.

lo′gan·ber″rў, *n.* hybrid of blackberry and red raspberry.

lŏg′a·rĭthm, *n. Math.* power of one number if multiplied to equal another. —**log″a·rith′mic,** *adj.*

lōge, *n.* theater mezzanine.

lŏg′gêr·hĕad″, *n.* **at loggerheads,** in sharp dispute.

lŏg′ĭc, *n.* **1.** correct reasoning. **2.** predictable sequence. —**log′i·cal,** *adj.* —**log′i·cal·ly,** *adv.* —**lo·gi′cian,** *n.*

lo·gĭs′tĭcs, *n.* science of military housing, supply, etc. —**lo·gis′tic, lo·gis′ti·cal,** *adj.*

lō″gō, *n.* symbol or trademark of an enterprise.

lō′gў, *adj.* **-gier, -giest.** sluggish.

loĭn, *n.* **1.** Also, **loins,** lower human back. **2.** front hindquarter as a cut of meat.

loĭ′têr, *n.* linger in one place. —**loi′ter·er,** *n.*

lŏll, *v.i.* **1.** remain idle. **2.** hang loosely.

lŏl′li·pop″, *n.* candy on a stick for sucking.

lōne, *adj.* single; solitary.

lōne′lў, *adj.* **-lier, -liest. 1.** sad because alone. **2.** isolated. Also, **lone′some.** —**lone′li·ness,** *n.*

lŏng, *adj., adv.,* **longer, longest,** *v.i. adj.* **1.** of great distance between ends. **2.** in length. **3.** occupying much time. —*adv.* **4.** for a long time. **5.** from start to finish. **6.** at a long time. —*v.i.* **7.** wish passionately. —**long′ing,** *n., adj.*

lŏn·gĕv′i·tў, *n.* long life.

lŏng′hănd″, *n.* ordinary handwriting.

lŏn′gi·tūde″, *n.* east-west measurement.

lŏn″gi·tū′di·nal, *adj.* pertaining to length or longitude.

lŏng′shōre″măn, *n.* loader and unloader of ships.

lŏng′-stănd′ing, *adj.* long-continued.

lŏng′-sŭf′fêr·ing, *adj.* patient.

lŏng tòn, ton of 2,240 pounds.

lŏŏk, *v.i.* **1.** direct one's gaze. **2.** search. **3.** appear to be. —*v.t.* **4.** stare at. —*n.* **5.** act or instance of looking. **6.** appearance. —*interj.* **7.** pay heed!

lŏŏk′ŏut″, *n.* **1.** vigilance. **2.** spy or sentinel. **3.** place for observing.

lŏŏm, *n.* **1.** weaving frame. —*v.i.* **2.** appear indistinctly as huge.

lŏŏn, *n.* diving bird.

lŏŏn′ў, *adj.,* **-ier, -iest.** *Informal.* crazy.

lŏŏp, *n.* **1.** closed curve of rope, etc. —*v.t.* **2.** make into a loop. —*v.i.* **3.** form a loop.

lŏŏp′hōle″, *n.* **1.** slit for shooting. **2.** means of evasion.

lŏŏse, *adj.,* **looser, loosest,** *v.t.,* **loosed, loosing.** *adj.* **1.** not tight. **2.** not confined. **3.** not strict or precise. **4.** immoral. —*v.t.* **5.** make loose. —**loose′ly,** *adv.* —**loos′en,** *v.t., v.i.*

lŏŏt, *n.* **1.** things stolen. —*v.t.* **2.** steal the contents of.

lŏp, *v.t.,* **lopped, lopping.** chop.

lŏp′sīd″ĕd, *adj.* out of balance.

lō·quā′cioŭs, *adj.* talkative. —**lo·quac′i·ty,** *n.*

lôrd, *n.* **1.** landed noble. **2. the Lord,** a. God. b. Christ. —**lord′ly,** *adj., adv.* —**lord′ship″,** *n.*

lôre, *n.* traditional learning.

lose, *v.,* **lost, losing.** *v.t.* **1.** fail to keep. **2.** misplace. **3.** fail to win. —*v.i.* **4.** have a loss. —**los′er,** *n.* —**lost,** *adj.*

lŏss, *n.* **1.** act or instance of losing. **2.** something lost.

lŏt, *n.* **1.** chance. **2.** personal fate. **3.** area of ground. **4.** Also, **lots.** *Informal.* many or much.

lō′tion, *n.* skin preparation.

lŏt′têr·ў, *n., pl.* **-ies.** choice by chance, esp. of a winner.

lō′tŭs, *n.* **1.** tropical waterlily. **2.** legendary plant causing forgetfulness.

loŭd, *adj.* **1.** with much noise. **2.** *Informal.* flashy. —*adv.* **3.** loudly. —**loud′ly,** *adv.* —**loud′ness,** *n.*

lŏŭnge, *v.i.,* **lounged, lounging,** *n. v.i.* **1.** be idle or relaxed. —*n.* **2.** couch. **3.** place for lounging.

loŭse, *n., pl.* **lice.** parasitic insect.

loŭs′ў, *adj.,* **-ier, -iest.** *Informal.* bad.

loŭt, *n.* stupid, offensive person. —**lout′ish,** *adj.*

loŭ′vêr, *n.* opening screened with inclined slats.

lŏve, *n., v.t.,* **loved, loving.** *n.* **1.** powerful attraction to another. **2.** warm concern. **3.** loved person. —*v.t.* **4.** feel love for. —**lov′a·ble, love′a·ble,** *adj.* —**love′less,** *adj.* —**lov′er,** *n.* —**lov′ing,** *adj.* —**lov′ing·ly,** *adv.*

lŏve'lôrn'', *adj.* pining with love.

lŏve'lÿ, *adj.*, -lier, -liest. beautiful.

lōw, *adj.* **1.** of less than average height. **2.** of less than average quantity, etc. **3.** depressed. **4.** vulgar. **5.** meanly wicked. —*adv.* **6.** in a low way. —*n.* **7.** something low. —*v.i.* **8.** moo.

lōw'brōw'', *n.*, *adj.* non-intellectual.

lōw'êr, *adj.* **1.** more low. —*v.t.* **2.** cause to be low or lower. —*v.i.* **3.** become low or lower. **4.** (lō̄'ēr) frown.

lōw'lÿ, *adj.*, -lier, -liest. humble.

lŏy'ȧl, *adj.* faithful. —loy'al·ly, *adv.* —loy'al·ty, *n.*

lŏz'enge, *n.* cough drop, etc..

lu·au', *n.* (lō̄'ow) Hawaiian feast.

lŭb'bêr, *n.* clumsy person. —lub'ber·ly, *adj.*

lū'brĭ·cāte'', *v.t.*, -cated, -cating. **1.** make slippery. **2.** cause the wearing parts of to slide easily. —lu''bri·ca'tion, *n.* —lu'bri·cant, *n.*

lū·cĭd, *adj.* **1.** clear, as to understand. **2.** mentally competent. —lu'cid·ly, *adv.* —lu·cid'i·ty, *n.*

lŭck, *n.* **1.** chance. **2.** favorable chance. —luck'less, *adj.*

lŭck'ÿ, *adj.*, -ier, -iest. having or marked by good luck. —luck'i·ly, *adv.*

lūc'rȧ·tĭve, *adj.* profitable.

lū'crê, *n.* riches.

lū'dĭ·croŭs, *adj.* laughable.

lŭg, *v.t.*, lugged, lugging, *n.* *v.t.* **1.** haul with effort. —*n.* **2.** projection for lifting, etc.

lŭg'gȧge, *n.* baggage.

lū·gū'brĭ·oŭs, *adj.* foolishly mournful.

lūke'wȧrm'', *adj.* **1.** slightly warm. **2.** unenthusiastic.

lŭll, *v.t.*, *v.i.*, *n.* calm.

lŭll'a·bÿ'', *n.*, *pl.* -bies. soothing song for children.

lŭm·bā'gō, *n.* pain in the lower back.

lŭm'bȧr, *adj.* pertaining to the loins.

lŭm'bêr, *n.* **1.** building wood. —*v.i.* **2.** move ponderously. —lum'ber·man, *n.*

lŭm'bêr·jăck'', *n.* feller of trees.

lū'mĭ·nȧr''ÿ, *n.*, *pl.* -ies. **1.** light source. **2.** brilliant person.

lū'mĭ·něs'cėnce, *n.* light without heat. —lu''min·nes'cent, *adj.*

lū'mĭ·noŭs, *adj.* light-giving. —lu''mi·nos'i·ty, *n.*

lŭmp, *n.* **1.** shapeless mass. **2.** swelling. —*adj.* **3.** collective. —*v.t.* **4.** assemble or treat in a lump. **5.** tolerate despite oneself. —*v.i.* **6.** form in lumps. —lump'y, *adj.*

lū'nȧr, *adj.* pertaining to the moon.

lū'nȧ·tĭc, *n.* **1.** insane person. —*adj.* **2.** insane. —lu'na·cy, *n.*

lŭnch, *n.* **1.** midday meal. —*v.i.* **2.** eat lunch.

lŭnch'eón, *n.* formal lunch.

lŭng, *n.* breathing organ.

lŭnge, *n.*, *v.*, lunged, lunging. *n.* **1.** sudden move forward. —*v.t.*, *v.i.* **2.** move with a lunge.

lûrch, *n.* **1.** sudden sideways movement. **2. leave in the lurch,** desert in time of need. —*v.i.* **3.** make a lurch.

lūre, *v.t.*, lured, luring, *n.* *v.t.* **1.** entice —*n.* **2.** enticement; bait.

lūr'ĭd, *adj.* **1.** glowing through haze. **2.** violently sensational.

lûrk, *v.i.* be in hiding.

lŭs'cioŭs, *adj.* appealing to the senses.

lŭsh, *adj.* **1.** rich; abundant. —*n.* **2.** *Informal.* alcoholic.

lŭst, *n.* **1.** strong appetite. **2.** strong sexual appetite. —*v.i.* **3.** feel lust. —lust'ful, *adj.*

lŭs'têr, *n.* **1.** sheen. **2.** brightness. —lus'trous, *adj.*

lŭst'ÿ, *adj.*, -ier, -iest. vigorous. —lust'i·ly, *adv.*

lŭx·ū'rĭ·ȧnt, *adj.* lavishly growing. -lux·u'ri·ance, *n.*

lŭx·ū'rĭ·āte'', *v.i.*, -ated, -ating. live luxuriously.

lŭx'ū·rÿ, *n.*, *pl.* -ries. **1.** great comfort or pleasure. **2.** something superfluous. —lux·u'ri·ous, *adj.*

lÿ·cē'ùm, *n.* institute for lectures.

lÿe, *n.* strong alkaline substance.

lÿ'ĭng-ĭn', *n.* confinement in childbirth.

lýmph, *n.* clear, watery body liquid. —lym·phat'ic, *adj.*

lÿnch, *v.t.* kill as a mob.

lÿnx, *n.*, *pl.* lynxes, lynx. wildcat of the northern hemisphere.

lÿr'ĭc, *adj.* **1.** pertaining to emotion expressed in poetry. —*n.* **2.** lyric poem. **3.** Usually **lyrics,** words to music. —lyr'i·cal, *adj.* —lyr'i·cist, *n.*

M

M, m, *n.* thirteenth letter of the English alphabet.

măch·i·nā·tion, *n.* plot, scheme.

má·chīne′, *n., v.t.,* **-chined, -chining.** *n.* **1.** device for doing work. **2.** political organization. —*v.t.* **3.** shape by machine. —**ma·chin′er·y,** *n.*

má·chĭn′ĭst, *n.* worker with machine-operated tools.

mâ·chĭs′mō, *n.* assertion of masculinity.

măck′êr·el, *n., pl.* **-el, -els.** North Atlantic fish.

măck′ĭ·nāw″, *n.* heavy jacketlike coat.

măck′ĭn·tŏsh″, *n.* rubberized cloth coat.

mac′ra·me″ (măk′rė·mā″), *n.* lace or string tied in patterns.

măc′rō·bī·ŏt′ĭcs, *n.* art of lengthening life. —**mac″ro·bi·ot′ic,** *adj.*

măc′rō·cŏsm, *n.* **1.** universe. **2.** complex of microcosms.

măd, *adj.,* **madder, maddest. 1.** insane. **2.** infatuated. **3.** angry. —**mad′ly,** *adv.* —**mad′ness,** *n.* —**mad′den,** *v.t.* —**mad′house,** *n.* —**mad′man″,** **mad′wom″an,** *n.*

măd′ám, *n.* **1.** polite form of address to a woman. **2.** woman running a brothel.

mád′āme, *n., pl.* **mesdames.** *French.* madam or Mrs.

măd′căp″, *adj.* **1.** reckless. —*n.* **2.** reckless person.

mă″dé·môi·sĕlle′, *n., pl.* **mesdemoiselles.** *French.* Miss.

Má·dŏn′ná, *n.* Virgin Mary.

măd′rĭ·gàl, *n.* **1.** a part song for several voices sung a capella. **2.** a short lyric poem.

mãel′strōm, *n.* whirlpool.

măg′á·zĭne, *n.* **1.** periodical with covers. **2.** storage chamber, esp. for ammunition.

má·gĕn′tà, *n.* purplish red.

măg′gŏt, *n.* wormlike larva. —**mag′got·y,** *adj.*

măg′ĭc, *n.* **1.** use of supernatural methods. **2.** illusions using sleight of hand. —*adj.* **3.** existing or operated by magic. —**mag′i·cal,** *adj.* —**ma·gi′cian,** *n.*

măg″ĭs·tĕ′rĭ·àl, *adj.* authoritative.

măg′ĭs·trāte, *n.* minor judge. —**mag′is·tra·cy,** *n.*

măg·năn′ĭ·moŭs, *adj.* above pettiness. —**mag·nan′i·mous·ly,** *adv.* —**mag″na·nim′i·ty,** *n.*

măg′nāte, *n.* man of wealth or power.

măg·nē′sĭŭm, *n.* light metallic element.

măg′nĕt, *n.* object attracting ferrous metal. —**mag·net′ic,** *adj.* —**mag′net·ism,** *n.* —**mag′net′ize″,** *v.t.*

măg·nē′tō, *n., pl.* **-toes.** generator with permanent magnets.

măg·nĭf′ĭ·cĕnt, *adj.* splendid in form, accomplishments, etc. —**mag·nif′i·cence,** *n.* —**mag·nif′i·cent·ly,** *adv.*

măg′nĭ·fy″, *v.t.,* **-fied, -fying.** increase the apparent or real size of. —**mag″ni·fi·ca′tion,** *n.* —**mag′ni·fi″er,** *n.*

măg′nĭ·tūde″, *n.* size.

măg·nō′lĭ·à, *n.* flowering tree.

măg′pīe″, *n.* black-and-white bird.

mâ″hà·râ′jàh, *n.* major Indian ruler. Also, **ma″ha·ra′ja,** *fem.,* **ma″ha·ra′ni, ma″ha·ra′nee.**

mà·hŏg′á·nÿ, *n.* reddish-brown tropical wood.

māid, *n.* **1.** Also, **maid′ser″vant,** woman servant. **2.** *Archaic.* young woman.

māid′ĕn, *n.* **1.** *Archaic.* young woman. —*adj.* **2.** very first. —**maid′en·hood″,** *n.* —**maid′en·ly,** *adj.*

māid′ĕn·hĕad″, *n.* hymen.

māil, *n.* **1.** material shipped by post offices. **2.** flexible armor. —*v.t.* **3.** give to a post office for shipping. —**mail′box″,** *n.* —**mail′man″,** *n.*

māil′grăm, *n.* message teletyped between post offices and finally delivered by mail.

māim, *v.t.* mutilate.

māin, *adj.* **1.** principal. —*n.* **2.** major utility line. **3.** *Archaic.* sea. —**main′ly,** *adv.* —**main′spring″,** *n.*

māin′frāme, *n., adj.* (computers) large-scale, high-speed computing system.

māin′lănd″, *n.* continental land, as opposed to islands.

māin′stāy″, *n.* main support.

māin′strēam″, *n.* main way of thinking, acting, etc.

māin·tāin′, *v.t.* **1.** keep in good order. **2.** house, feed, etc. **3.** assert persistently. —**main′ten·ance,** *n.*

mâi·tre d′ho·tel (mē′trä dô tĕl′), *n.* headwaiter. Also, *Informal.* **mai·tre d′** (māt′êr dē′).

măj′ĕs·tў, n., pl. -ies. 1. Majesty, title of respect for a sovereign. 2. grandeur. —ma·jes′tic, adj.

mā′jŏr, adj. 1. greater. 2. Music. in a scale a half tone above the minor. —v.i. 3. Education. specialize. —n. 4. army officer. 5. specialty in school.

má·jôr′ĭ·tў, n., pl. -ties. 1. greater number. 2. legal adulthood.

māke, v.t., made, making. 1. cause to be or occur. 2. force. 3. constitute. 4. earn. 5. interpret.

māke′-bè·liēve′′, n. 1. pretense to oneself. —adj. 2. imaginary.

māke′shĭft′′, adj. improvised; temporary.

māke′ŭp′′, n. 1. constitution; contents. 2. cosmetics, etc.

măl′′ăd·jŭst′ĕd, adj. badly adjusted, esp. to life. —mal′′ad·just′ment, n.

măl′′á·drŏĭt′, adj. clumsy.

măl′á·dў, n., pl. -dies. illness.

má·lāise′, n. uneasiness.

măl′′á·prŏp′ĭsm, n. ludicrous misuse of a word.

má·lār′ĭ·á, n. mosquito-transmitted disease. —ma·lar′i·al, adj.

măl′cōn·tĕnt′′, n. person discontented, esp. with society.

māle, adj. 1. of the sex that inseminates. —n. 2. male being.

măl′′ê·dĭc′tion, n. curse.

măl′é·făc′′tör, n. doer of evil.

má·lĕv′o·lĕnt, adj. wishing harm. —ma·lev′o·lence, n.

măl·fēa′sánce, n. wrongdoing in office.

măl′′fôr·mā′tion, n. bad formation, esp. of a body part. —mal·formed′, adj.

măl′′ĭce, n. ill will. —ma·li′cious, adj.

má·līgn′, adj. 1. intending or doing harm. —v.t. 2. slander.

má·lĭg′nánt, adj. harmful or dangerous. —ma·lig′nan·cy, n.

má·lĭn′gêr, v.i. pretend sickness or weakness.

mäll, n. 1. tree-lined walk or lawn. 2. shopping area.

măl′lärd, n. wild duck.

măl′lē·á·ble, adj. readily shaped by hammering. —mal′′le·a·bil′i·ty, n.

măl′lĕt, n. short, heavy hammer.

măl′′nū·trī′tion, n. inadequate nutrition. —mal·nour′ished, adj.

măl·ō′dör·oŭs, adj. bad-smelling.

măl·prăc′tĭce, n. improper professional practice.

mält, n. soaked and dried grain.

măl′trēat′′, v.t. treat badly. —mal·treat′ment, n.

mäm′′bō, n. dance of Latin American origin.

mäm′má, n. mother. Also, ma′ma.

măm′măl, n. 1. animal giving milk. —adj. 2. being such an animal. —mam·mal′i·an, adj., n.

măm′má·rў, adj. pertaining to breasts.

Măm′mòn, n. riches or their pursuit, personified.

măm′mŏth, adj. 1. very large. —n. 2. extinct, long-tusked elephant.

măn, n., pl. men, v.t., manned, manning. 1. human being. 2. adult male human. 3. humanity. —v.t. 4. furnish with persons.

măn′á·cles, n. pl. shackles.

măn′áge, v., -aged, -aging. v.t. 1. supervise. 2. control. —v.i. 3. contrive to succeed. —man′age·a·ble, adj. —man′age·ment, n. —man′ag·er, n. —man′′a·ge′ri·al, adj.

má·ñá′ná, adv. Spanish. tomorrow; some time later.

măn′dá·rĭn, n. imperial Chinese official.

măn′dāte, n. command.

măn′dá·tô′′rў, adj. required.

măn′′dĭ·ble, n. lower jaw bone.

măn′dò·lĭn, n. plucked musical instrument.

măn′drĕl, n. support for work being shaped. Also, man′dril.

māne, n. long hair on an animal's neck.

má·neū′vêr, n. 1. military exercise. 2. controlled movement. —v.t., v.i. 3. move under control.

măn′fŭl, adj. courageous.

măn′gá·nēse′′, n. grayish chemical element.

mānge, n. animal skin disease. —man′gy, adj.

măn′gêr, n. feeding trough.

măn′gle, v.t., -gled, -gling, n. v.t. 1. crush out of shape. —n. 2. ironing machine.

măn′gō, n., pl. -goes. fruit-bearing tropical tree.

măn′grōve, n. tropical tree.

măn′hăn′dle, v.t., -dled, -dling. handle roughly.

măn'hōle'', *n.* small access hole.

măn'hŏŏd'', *n.* **1.** virility. **2.** majority.

mā'nĭ·à, *n.* **1.** violent insanity. **2.** excitement.

mā'nĭ·ăc'', *n.* violently insane person. —ma·ni'a·cal, *adj.*

măn'ĭc, *adj.* displaying unstable, frenzied behavior.

măn'ĭ·cūre, *n.* care of the hands. —man'i·cur''ist, *n.*

măn'ĭ·fĕst'', *v.t.* **1.** make apparent. —*adj.* **2.** obvious. —*n.* **3.** list of cargo or passengers.

măn''ĭ·fĕs'tō, *n., pl.* -toes. public declaration.

măn'ĭ·fōld'', *adj.* in many forms.

măn'ĭ·kĭn, *n.* professional model. Also, man'ne·quin.

măn·ĭl''à, *n.* strong, light brown paper.

mà·nĭp'ū·lāte'', *v.t.*, -lated, -lating. handle cunningly. —ma·nip'u·la''tor, *n.*

măn'kīnd', *n.* humanity.

măn'lỹ, *adj.* -lier, -liest. virile; brave. —man'li·ness, *n.*

măn·nà, *n.* miraculous food.

măn'nêr, *n.* **1.** way of doing. **2.** sort. **3.** manners, personal conduct.

măn'nêr·ĭsm, *n.* personal pecularity.

măn'nêr·lỹ, *adj.* well-mannered.

măn'nĭsh, *adj.* man-like.

mà·noeū'vrê, *n., v.*, -vred, -vring. *n., v.t., v.i.* maneuver.

măn'-ŏf-wâr', *n.* warship.

măn'ör, *n.* large estate. —ma·no'ri·al, *adj.*

măn'pŏw''êr, *n.* available labor force.

măn'sârd, *n.* hip roof with two pitches.

mănse, *n.* home of a clergyman.

măn'sion, *n.* impressive house.

măn'slaŭgh''têr, *n.* unintentional homicide.

măn'tĕl, *n.* fireplace surround. Also, man'tel·piece''.

man·tĭl'la, *n.* lace shawl.

măn'tle, *n., v.t.*, -tled, -tling. cloak.

măn'ū·àl, *adj.* **1.** pertaining to or operated by hands. —*n.* **2.** handbook. —man'u·al·ly, *adv.*

măn''ū·făc'tūre, *v.t.*, -tured, -turing. *n. v.t.* **1.** make industrially. —*n.* **2.** act or instance of manufacturing. —man''u·fac'tur·er, *n.*

mà·nūre', *n., v.t.*, -nured, -nuring. *n.* **1.** animal feces. —*v.t.* **2.** spread with manure as fertilizer.

măn'ū·scrĭpt, *n.* **1.** unprinted writing. —*adj.* **2.** written or typed.

măn'ỹ, *adj.* **more, most.** in a large number.

măp, *n., v.t.*, **mapped, mapping.** *n.* **1.** measured representation of an area of land, etc. —*v.t.* **2.** measure for a map. **3.** plan.

mā'ple, *n.* broad-leafed deciduous tree.

mâr, *v.t.*, **marred, marring.** make imperfect.

măr'à·thŏn'', *n.* **1.** foot race of 26 miles, 385 yards. **2.** endurance contest.

mà·raŭd'êr, *n.* raider and plunderer.

mâr'ble, *n.* **1.** hard, fine-grained limestone. **2.** colored glass ball. **3.** marbles, game played with such balls.

mârch, *v.i.* **1.** walk with measured steps to a cadence. —*v.t.* **2.** cause to march. —*n.* **3.** marching walk or journey. **4.** piece of music accompanying such a walk. **5.** **March,** third month.

mâr'chiòn·ĕss, *n.* wife of a marquess, or woman equal to one in rank.

mâre, *n.* female horse.

mâr'gà·rīne, butter-like vegetable oil compound.

mâr'gĭn, *n.* **1.** border or border area. **2.** difference in amounts. —mar'gin·al, *adj.*

măr'ĭ·gōld'', *n.* orange-flowered plant.

mă''rĭ·juä'nà, *n.* dried hemp leaves and blossoms, sometimes smoked. Also, ma''ri·hua'na.

mà·rĭm'bà, *n.* xylophone with tubelike resonators.

mà·rĭ'nà, *n.* yacht landing.

mă''rĭ·nāde', *n.* pickling solution.

măr'ĭ·nāte'', *v.t.*, -nated, -nating. steep in a marinade.

mà·rīne', *adj.* **1.** pertaining to the sea. —*n.* **2.** soldier performing sea duty.

măr'ĭ·nêr, *n.* sailor.

măr''ĭ·ò·nĕtte', *n.* puppet hung from strings.

măr'ĭ·tàl, *adj.* pertaining to marriage. —mar'i·tal·ly, *adv.*

măr'ĭ·tīme'', *adj.* pertaining to shipping.

mâr'jò·ràm, *n.* fragrant herb.

mârk, *n.* **1.** something visible on a surface. **2.** target. —*v.t.* **3.** make a mark on. **4.** indicate. **5.** note. **6.** review and grade. —**mark′er**, *n*. —**mark′ing**, *n*.

mârked, *adj*. noticeable; emphatic. —**mark′ed·ly**, *adv*.

mârk′ĕt, *n*. **1**. place for selling. —*v.t*. **2**. offer for sale. —*v.i*. **3**. shop. —**mark′et·a·ble**, *adj*.

mârks′măn, *n*. shooter at targets. —**marks′man·ship′′**, *n*.

mâr′lĭn, *n*., *pl*. -**lins**, -**lin**. large deep-sea fish.

mâr′mà·lāde′′, *n*. fruit preserve.

mà·rōōn′, *v.t*. **1**. abandon on a deserted island. —*n*. **2**. dark brownish red.

mâr·quēe′, *n*. open projecting shelter.

mâr′quĕss, *n*. nobleman superior to an earl or count. Also, **mar′quis**, *fem*., **mar·quise′**.

măr′rōw, *n*. inner bone tissue.

măr′rў, *v*., -**ried**, -**rying**. *v.t*. **1**. take as spouse. **2**. unite as spouses. —*v.i*. **3**. be married. —**mar′riage**, *n*. —**mar′riage·a·ble**, *adj*.

mârsh, *n*. swamp. —**marsh′y**, *adj*.

mâr′shàl, *n*., *v.t*., -**shaled**, -**shaling**. *n*. **1**. sheriff-like U.S. officer. —*v.t*. **2**. put in order. **3**. guide; escort.

mârsh′măl′′lōw, *n*. sweet, spongy confection.

mâr·sū′pĭ·àl, *n*. animal carrying its young in a pouch.

mârt, *n*. salesplace.

mâr′tĕn, *n*. soft-furred weasel-like animal.

mâr′tiàl, *adj*. pertaining to war or the military.

mâr′tĭn, *n*. bird of the swallow family.

mâr′′tĭ·nĕt′, *n*. rigid disciplinarian.

mâr·tĭ′nĭ, *n*. cocktail of gin or vodka and dry vermouth.

mâr′tўr, *n*. **1**. person who dies or suffers for beliefs. —*v.t*. **2**. kill as a martyr. —**mar′tyr·dom**, *n*.

mâr′vĕl, *n*., *v.i*., -**veled**, -**veling**. wonder. —**mar′vel·ous**, *adj*.

măs·că′rà, *n*. cosmetic for darkening eyelashes.

măs′cŏt, *n*. **1**. thing kept for luck. **2**. group pet.

măs′cū·līne, *adj*. pertaining to or characteristic of males. —**mas′′cu·lin′i·ty**, *n*.

măsh, *v.t*. **1**. crush to pulp. —*n*. **2**. pulped and watered grain.

măsk, *n*. **1**. face covering. **2**. concealment. —*v.t*. **3**. cover with a mask.

măs′och·ĭsm, *n*. abnormal pleasure obtained from suffering pain. —**mas′och·ist**, *n*. —**mas′′och·is′tic**, *adj*.

mā′sŏn, *n*. **1**. builder with stones, bricks, etc. **2**. Mason, Freemason. —**Ma·son′ic**, *adj*. —**ma′son·ry**, *n*.

măs′′quêr·āde′′, *n*., *v.i*., -**aded**, -**ading**. *n*. **1**. ball of masked and costumed persons. **2**. something falsified. —*v.i*. **3**. appear falsely.

măs′sà·crê, *n*., *v.t*., -**cred**, -**cring**. *n*. **1**. killing of many. —*v.t*. **2**. kill in a massacre.

màs·säge′, *n*., *v.t*., -**saged**, -**saging**. *n*. **1**. manipulation of muscles, as to stimulate circulation. —*v.t*. **2**. give a massage to. —**mas·seur′**, *fem*., **mas·seuse′**, *n*.

măs′sĭve, *adj*. in large mass.

măst, *n*. tall spar used as a support.

măs′têr, *n*. **1**. person in control. **2**. accomplished craftsman. —*adj*. **3**. principal; controlling. —*v.t*. **4**. make submissive. **5**. become expert in. —**mas′ter·y**, *n*.

măs′têr·fŭl, *adj*. imposing one's will.

măs′têr·lў, *adj*. accomplished.

măs′têr·piēce′′, *n*. **1**. greatest accomplishment. **2**. proof of masterly skill. Also, **mas′ter·work′′**.

măstêr sergĕant, army sergeant of high rank.

măs′tĭ·cāte′′, *v.t*., -**cated**, -**cating**. chew.

măs′tĭff, *n*. large, strong-jawed dog.

măs′tò·dŏn, *n*. extinct elephantlike animal.

măs′tûr·bāte′′, *v.t*., -**bated**, -**bating**. manipulate one's genitals.

măt, *n*., *v.t*., **matted**, **matting**, *adj*. *n*. **1**. thick, flat, flexible object. **2**. tangled mass. —*v.t*. **3**. cover with mats. **4**. make into a mat. —*adj*. **5**. without gloss.

măt′à·dôr′′, *n*. bullfighter who kills.

mătch, *n*. **1**. fire-making friction device. **2**. equal or counterpart. **3**. marriage. **4**. game. —*v.t*. **5**. compare. **6**. equal. —*v.i*. **7**. be a match or matches. —**match·mak′′er**, *n*.

mătch′lĕss, *adj*. incomparable.

māte, *n*., *v*., **mated**, **mating**. *n*. **1**. spouse. **2**. companion. **3**. co-worker. **4**.

one of a pair. **5.** ship's officer. —*v.t.*, *v.i.* **6.** join as mates.

ma·tē′rĭ·ȧl, *n.* **1.** that which an object is made of. —*adj.* **2.** composed of material. **3.** non-spiritual. **4.** relevant.

ma·tē′rĭ·ȧl·ĭsm, *n.* **1.** doctrine that all is matter. **2.** concern with wealth, goods, etc. —**ma·te′ri·al·ist,** *n.*, *adj.* —**ma·te″ri·al·is′tic,** *adj.*

ma·tē″rĭ·ĕl′, *n.* military supplies.

ma·têr′nȧl, *adj.* **1.** pertaining to mothers. **2.** motherlike. —**ma·ter′ni·ty,** *n.*

māth″ė·măt′ĭcs, *n.* study of the relations of quantities or forms. Also, *Informal,* math. —**math″e·mat′i·cal,** *adj.* —**math″e·ma·ti′cian,** *n.*

măt″ĭ·nee′, *n.* afternoon performance.

măt′ĭns, *n.* morning prayer service.

mā′trĭ·ârch″, *n.* woman acting as master or ruler. —**ma″tri·ar′chal,** *adj.* —**ma′tri·ar′chy,** *n.*

ma·trĭc′ū·lāte″, *v.,* -lated, -lating. *v.i., v.t.* enroll as a student.

măt′rĭ·mō″nŷ, *n., pl.* -nies. marriage. —**mat″ri·mo′ni·al,** *adj.*

mā′trĭx, *n.* environment in which one comes to be.

mā′trŏn, *n.* **1.** mature woman. **2.** woman supervisor or guard. —**ma′tron·ly,** *adj.*

mătte, *n.* not glossy; flat.

măt′têr, *n.* **1.** solid, liquid, or gas. **2.** affair. **3.** importance. —*v.i.* **4.** be important.

măt′tŏck, *n.* digging tool.

măt′trĕss, *n.* pad for a bed.

ma·tūre′, *adj., v.,* -tured, -turing. *adj.* **1.** fully ripe or grown. **2.** due for payment. —*v.t.* **3.** make mature. —*v.i.* **4.** become mature. —**mat″u·ri′tion,** *n.* —**ma·tu′ri·ty,** *n.*

măt′zŏ, *n., pl.* -zos, -zot, -zoth. unleavened wafer.

maŭd′lĭn, *adj.* foolishly sentimental.

maŭl, *v.t.* handle or beat severely.

mäu″sō·lė′ŭm, *n., pl.* -leums, -lea. large and magnificient tomb.

mäuve, *n.* light bluish purple.

măv′êr·ĭck, *n.* nonconformist.

maw, *n.* mouth and throat.

mäwk′ĭsh, *adj.* weakly sentimental.

măx′ĭm, *n.* rule of conduct.

măx′ĭ·mŭm, *n., pl.* -mums, -ma, *adj. n.* **1.** greatest amount. —*adj.* **2.** Also, **max′i·mal,** greatest.

māy, *v.t.* **1.** am, are, or is permitted to. **2.** will possibly. **3.** can. —*n.* **4. May,** fifth month.

māy′bē, *adv.* possibly.

māy′dāy, *n.* distress call used by aircraft and ships.

māy′hĕm″, *n.* criminal maiming.

māy′ŏn·nāise″, *n.* salad dressing made with egg yolks.

māy′ŏr, *n.* chief city official. —**may′or·al·ty,** *n.*

māze, *n.* intricate system of corridors, lines, etc.

ma·zûr′kȧ, *n.* fast Polish dance.

mĕad′ōw, *n.* area of grassy land.

mēa′gêr, *adj.* scanty; inadequate. Also, **mea′gre.** —**mea′ger·ly,** *adv.* —**mea′ger·ness,** *n.*

mēal, *n.* **1.** food at one sitting. **2.** coarsely ground grain. —**meal′y,** *adj.*

mēal′ȳ-mōuthed″, *adj,* not frank.

mēan, *v.t.,* meant, meaning, *adj., n. v.t.* **1.** intend. **2.** wish to say. **3.** signify. —*adj.* **4.** ill-tempered. **5.** shabby. **6.** average. —*n.* **7.** part between extremes. **8.** means, **a.** something serving a purpose. **b.** personal resources. —**mean′ly,** *adv.* —**mean′ness,** *n.*

mē·ăn′dêr, *v.i.* wander aimlessly.

mēan′ĭng, *n.* **1.** intended message. —*adj.* **2.** intended as expressive. —**mean′ing·ful,** *adj.* —**mean′ing·less,** *adj.*

mēan′tīme″, *n.* **1.** time in between. —*adv.* **2.** during the meantime. **3.** at the same time. Also, **mean′while″.**

mēa′slės, *n.* virus disease producing a rash.

mēas′lȳ, *adj.,* -lier, -liest. *Informal.* contemptibly small.

mēas′ūre, *v.,* -ured, -uring, *n. v.t.* **1.** find the size or amount of. —*v.i.* **2.** amount to. —*n.* **3.** measurement. **4.** means of measuring. **5.** course of action. —**meas′ur·a·ble,** *adj.* —**meas′ure·less,** *adj.* —**meas′ure·ment,** *n.*

mēas′ūred, *adj.* deliberate.

mēat, *n.* **1.** animal flesh. **2.** edible part of a nut. **3.** essential part. —**meat′y,** *adj.*

mė·chăn′ĭc, *n.* **1.** worker with machinery. **2. mechanics,** study of the action of forces.

mė·chăn′ĭ·cȧl, *adj.* **1.** working by machinery. **2.** unthinkingly automatic.

mĕch′ȧ·nĭsm, *n.* piece of machinery.

mĕch'á·nīze'', *v.t.*, **-nized, -nizing.** equip with machinery.

mĕd'ál, *n.* metal disk indicating distinction, religious affiliation, etc.

mè·dăl'liớn, *n.* round design.

mĕd'ál·lĭst, *n.* winner of a medal.

mĕd'dle, *v.i.*, **-dled, -dling.** interfere mischievously. **—med'dler**, *n.* **—med'dle·some**, *adj.*

mē'dĭ·àn, *n.* **1.** *Math.* central in a series of numbers. **—adj. 2.** *Math.* pertaining to a median. **3.** middle.

mē'dĭ·āte'', *v.*, **-ated, -ating.** v.i. **1.** act as an intermediary. **—v.t. 2.** resolve as an intermediary. **—me'di·a''tor**, *n.*

mĕd'ĭ·cál, *adj.* pertaining to medicine.

mĕd'ĭ·cāte'', *v.t.*, **-cated, -cating. 1.** treat with medicine. **2.** put medicine in. **—med''i·ca'tion**, *n.*

mè·dĭc'ĭ·nál, *adj.* serving as medicine.

mĕd'ĭ·cīne, *n.* **1.** science of healing. **2.** healing substance.

mē''di·ē'vál, *adj.* pertaining to the Middle Ages.

mē''dĭ'ō'crê, *adj.* of indifferent value. **—me''di·oc'ri·ty**, *n.*

mĕd'ĭ·tāte'', *v.i.*, **-tated, -tating.** think deeply. **—med''i·ta'tion**, *n.* **—med''i·ta'tive**, *adj.*

mē'dĭ·ŭm, *n.*, *pl.* **-ums, -a**, *adj. n.* **1.** something in the middle. **2.** means. **3.** *pl.*, **media,** means of communication. **4.** *pl.*, **mediums,** communicators with the dead. **—adj. 5.** intermediate.

mĕd'lēy, *n.*, *pl.* **-leys.** mixture of tunes.

mēek, *adj.* mild; submissive. **—meek'ly**, *adv.* **—meek'ness**, *n.*

mēer'schaŭm, *n.* white, claylike mineral.

mēet, *v.*, **met, meeting**, *n.*, *adj. v.t.* **1.** come into contact with. **2.** be introduced to. **—v.i. 3.** be mutually met. **—n. 4.** sports meeting. **—adj. 5.** *Archaic.* suitable. **—meet'ing**, *n.*

mĕg'á·hêrtz'', *n.*, *pl.* **-hertz.** one million hertz.

mĕg''á·lō·mā'nĭ·á, *n.* delusions of or appetite for grandeur.

mĕg'á·lŏp''ò·lĭs, *n.* huge urban area.

mĕg'á·phōne'', *n.* horn magnifying the voice.

mĕg'á·tón'', *n.* explosive force equal to one million tons of TNT.

mĕl''án·chŏ'li·á, *n.* pathological melancholy.

mĕl'án·chŏl''ÿ, *n.* **1.** sadness. **—adj. 2.** sad.

mê'lee, *n.* confused combat.

mĕl·lĭ'flṵ·oŭs, *n.* smooth and sweet-sounding. Also, **mel·lif'flu·ent.**

mĕl'lōw, *adj.* **1.** rich-flavored. **2.** gentle. **—v.t. 3.** make mellow. **—v.i. 4.** become mellow.

mè·lō'dĭ·oŭs, *adj.* tuneful.

mĕl'ò·drä''má, *n.* drama of suspense and extravagant emotion. **—mel''o·dra·mat'ic**, *adj.* **—mel''o·dra·mat'ics**, *n.*, *pl.*

mĕl'ó·dÿ, *n.*, *pl.* **-dies.** tune. **—me·lod'ic**, *adj.*

mĕl'ȯn, *n.* large, juicy fruit.

mĕlt, *v.*, **melted, melted** or **molten, melting.** *v.t.*, *v.i.* liquefy by applying heat.

mĕm'bêr, *n.* **1.** person in an organization. **2.** component part. **—mem'ber·ship''**, *n.*

mĕm'brāne, *n.* thin organic tissue.

mè·mĕn'tō, *n.*, *pl.* **-tos, -toes.** souvenir.

mĕm'ȯirs, *n.*, *pl.* written personal recollections.

mĕm'ȯ·rà·ble, *adj.* compelling remembrance. **—mem'o·ra·bly**, *adv.*

mĕm''ȯ·răn'dŭm, *n.*, *pl.* **-dums, -da.** note of something to be remembered. Also, *Informal*, **mem'o.**

mè·mô'rĭ·ál, *adj.* **1.** in remembrance. **—n. 2.** something made or done in remembrance.

Mèmôrĭäl Dāy, legal holiday in May, in memory of dead servicemen.

mĕm'ȯ·rīze'', *v.t.*, **-rized, -rizing.** act so as to remember. **—mem''o·ri·za'tion**, *n.*

mĕm'ȯ·rÿ, *n.*, *pl.* **-ries. 1.** ability to recall past experience. **2.** something remembered. **3.** thing of the past. **4.** (computers) electronic data storage through circuitry or a recording medium.

mĕn'áce, *n.*, *v.t.*, **-aced, -acing.** *n.* **1.** visible threat. **—v.t. 2.** threaten. **—men'ac·ing·ly**, *adv.*

mè·năg'êr·iē, *n.* collection of captive wild animals.

mĕnd, *v.t.* **1.** repair. **—v.i. 2.** improve in condition. **—n. 3.** mended place.

mĕn·dā'cioŭs, *adj.* lying. **—men·dac'i·ty**, *n.*

měn′dĭ·cánt, *adj*. **1.** begging. —*n*. **2.** mendicant person.

mē′nĭ·ál, *adj*. **1.** servile. —*n*. **2.** menial person.

měn′o·pause′′, *n*. permanent end of menstruation.

mén·ō′ráh, *n*. *Judiasm*. branched candlestick.

měn′sēs, *n*. *pl*. periodic discharge of blood from the uterus.

měn′strū·āte′′, *v.i.*, -ated, -ating. experience menses. —men′stru·al, *adj*. —men′′stru·a′tion, *n*.

měn′′sŭ·rā′tion, *n*. measurement.

měn′tál, *adj*. pertaining to the mind. —men′tal·ly, *adv*.

měn·tăl′ĭ·tў, *n.*, *pl*. -ties. mental power.

měn′thŏl, *n*. alcohol from oil of peppermint. —men′tho·lat′′ed, *adj*.

měn′tion, *n*. **1.** brief allusion. —*v.t.* **2.** make a mention of.

měn′tôr, *n*. teacher or advisor.

měn′ū, *n*. list of dishes offered.

mē·ōw′, *n*. sound of a cat.

mêr′cán·tĭle, *adj*. pertaining to trade.

mêr′cè·nār′′ў, *adj.*, *n.*, *pl*. -ies. *adj*. **1.** devoted to money-making. **2.** done for pay. —*n*. **3.** hired soldier.

mêr′cêr·īze′′, *v.t.*, -ized, -izing. impart gloss and strength to, chemically.

mêr′chán·dīse′′, *n.*, *v.t.*, **-dised**, -dising. *n*. **1.** goods for sale. —*v.t.* **2.** Also, **mer′chan·dize′′**, promote the sale of.

mêr′chánt, *n*. seller of goods.

mêrchánt márïne, commercial ships of a country.

mêr·cū′rĭ·ál, *adj*. quick to change, esp. in emotion.

mêr·cū′rў, *n*. heavy metallic chemical element.

mêr′cў, *n.*, *pl*. -cies. **1.** kindness toward the helpless. **2.** lucky thing. —mer′ci·ful, *adj*. —mer′ci·less, *adj*.

mēre, *adj*. no more than. —mere′ly, *adv*.

mêr′′è·trĭ′cioŭs, *adj*. showy and specious.

mêrge, *v.*, merged, merging. *v.t.*, *v.i.* combine.

mêrg′êr, *n*. unification of business organizations.

mé·rĭd′ĭ·án, *n*. north-south line.

me·ringue′ (mé·răng′), *n*. stiff-beaten egg white.

mêr′ĭt, *n*. **1.** worth. **2.** merits, aspects right or wrong. —*v.t.* **3.** deserve. —mer′′i·to′ri·ous, *adj*.

mêr′māid′′, *n*. legendary sea creature, half-woman, half-fish. Also, *masc.*, mer′man′′.

mêr′rў, *adj.*, -rier, -riest. cheerful. —mer′ri·ly, *adv*. —mer′ri·ment, *n*.

mêr′rў-gō-rŏund′′, *n*. rotating structure giving a pleasure ride.

mêr′rў·māk′′ĭng, *n*. festivity. —mer′ry·mak′′er, *n*.

mē′sá, *n*. high, steep-sided plateau.

měsh, *n*. **1.** open space in a net. **2.** netlike material. **3.** engagement of gears. *v.t.*, *v.i.* **4.** entangle. —*v.i.* **5.** become engaged.

měs′mêr·īze′′, *v.t.*, -ized, -izing. hypnotize. —mes′mer·ism, *n*. —mes′mer·ist, *n*.

měs·quïte, *n*. southwestern U.S. tree.

měss, *n*. **1.** disorder or disorderly scene. **2.** difficult situation. **3.** military meal. —*v.t.* **4.** make untidy. **5.** do badly. —*v.i.* **6.** eat mess. —mes′sy, *adj*. —mes′si·ly, *adv*. —mes′si·ness, *n*.

měs′sàge, *n*. **1.** communication. **2.** idea, etc. to communicate.

měs′sén·gêr, *n*. carrier of messages.

Mès·sī′·áh, *n*. deliverer of mankind.

měs′tï·zō, *n.*, *pl*. -zos, -zoes. Hispano-Indian.

mé·tăb′ó·lĭsm, *n*. breakdown of an organism's nourishment into protoplasm, energy, and waste. —met′′a·bol′ic, *adj*.

mět′ál, *n*. iron, gold, brass, etc. —me·tal′lic, *adj*.

mět′ál·lûr′′gў, *n*. separation and refining of metals. —met′′al·lur′gi·cal, *adj*. —met′al·lur′′gist, *n*.

mět′′à·môr′phò·sĭs, *n*. transformation. —met′′a·mor′phic, *adj*. —met′′a·mor′phose, *v.t.*, *v.i.*

mět′á·phôr′′, *n*. use of an analogous idea. —met′′a·phor′i·cal, *adj*.

mět′′à·phўs′ĭcs, *n*. study of the nature of being and reality. —met′′a·phys′i·cal, *adj*. —met′′a·phy·si′cian, *n*.

mèt′′ěm·psў′chō′sĭs, *n.*, *pl*. -ses. transfer of souls from body to body.

mē′tē·ör, *n*. meteoroid in the earth's atmosphere.

mē′′tē·ör′ĭc, *adj*. temporarily brilliant.

mē′′tē·ör·īte′′, *n*. meteoroid surviving a fall to earth.

mē′tē·ör·oĬd″, *n.* solid body traveling through outer space.

mē″tē·ör·ŏl′o·gў, *n.* study of climate and weather. **—me″te·or·o·log′i·cal,** *adj.* **—me″te·or·ol′o·gist,** *n.*

mē′têr, *n.* **1.** unit of 100 centimeters or 39.37 inches. **2.** rhythmic pattern. **3.** measuring device for fluids, etc. **—**v.t. **4.** measure with a meter.

mĕth′ŏd, *n.* process or system of doing.

mè·thŏd′ĭ·cȧl, *adj.* orderly; deliberate. **—me·thod′i·cal·ly,** *adv.*

mĕth″ŏd·ŏl′o·gў, *n., pl.* **-gies.** system of methods.

mè·tĭc′ū·loŭs, *adj.* attentive to details.

mĕt′rĭc, *adj.* **1.** pertaining to the metric system. **2.** metrical. **—met′ri·cal·ly,** *adv.*

mĕt′rĭ·cȧl, *adj.* **1.** pertaining to poetic meter. **2.** pertaining to measurement.

mĕt′rĭ·cīze″, *v.t.,* **-cized, -cizing.** express in the metric system.

mĕtrĭc sўstèm, decimal system of measurement based on the meter, gram, and liter.

mĕt′rȯ·nōme″, *n.* time-beating machine.

mè·trŏp′ȯ·lĭs, *n.* **1.** principal or major city. **2.** city and surrounding built-up area. **—met″ro·pol′i·tan,** *adj.*

mĕt′tle, *n.* spirit; courage. **—met′tle·some,** *adj.*

mĕz′zà·nĭne″, *n.* balcony-like floor.

mĕz′zō·sȯ·prä′nō, *n., pl.* **-nos, -ni.** singer with a range between soprano and contralto.

mĭ·ăs′mà, *n.* marsh vapor.

mī′cà, *n.* crystallized transparent laminated mineral.

mī′crōbe, *n.* microorganism, esp. harmful.

mī′crō chĭp, *n.* small wafer of silicon, etc., containing electronic circuits.

mĭc″rō·cȯm·pū′têr, *n.* a complete computing system of compact size, sometimes portable.

mī′crȯ·cŏsm, *n.* little world.

mī′crȯ·fīche″, *n.* card on microfilm images.

mī′crȯ·fĭlm″, *n.* **1.** film with images at greatly reduced size. **—**v.t. **2.** record on microfilm.

mī·crŏm′ė·têr, *n.* instrument for fine measurements.

mī″crō·ör′gȧn·ĭsm, *n.* organism visible only through a microscope.

mī′crȯ·phōne″, *n.* instrument transforming sound into electrical impulses.

mī′crȯ·scōpe″, *n.* instrument for very high magnification. **—mi″cro·scop′ic,** *adj.*

mĭc′rȯ·wāve, *n.* electromagnetic radiation of extremely high frequency.

mĭd′āir′, *n.* area away from the ground.

mĭd′dāy″, *n.* noon.

mĭd′dle, *n.* **1.** place with ends equally far away. **—**adj. **2.** intermediate.

mĭd′dle-āged′, *adj.* neither young nor old.

mĭd′dle·mȧn″, *n.* intermediary between producer and consumer.

mĭd′dlĭng, *adj.* **1.** intermediate. **—**adv. **2.** *Informal.* moderately.

mĭd′lȧnd, *n.* middle region.

mĭd′nīght″, *n.* twelve o'clock at night.

mĭd′pōĭnt″, *n.* center point.

mĭd′rĭff, *n.* middle part of the torso.

mĭd′shĭp″man, *n.* naval cadet.

mĭdst, *n.* middle part.

mĭd′wāy″, *n.* **1.** thoroughfare of sideshows. **—**adj., adv. **2.** halfway.

mĭd′wīfe″, *n.* deliverer of babies. **—mid′wife″ry,** *n.*

mĭd′yēar″, *n.* middle of the year.

miēn, *n.* manner; bearing.

mĭff, *v.t.* offend.

mĭght, *n.* **1.** strength. **—**v. **2.** (past tense of *may*). **3.** will possibly. **—might′y,** *adj.* **—might′i·ly,** *adv.*

mī′grāine, *n.* intense headache.

mī′grāte, *v.i.,* **-grated, -grating.** move in a group. **—mi·gra′tion,** *n.* **—mi′grant,** *adj., n.* **—mi′gra·to″ry,** *adj.*

mĭld, *adj.* not severe or harsh. **—mild′ly,** *adv.* **—mild′ness,** *n.*

mĭl′dew″, *n.* fungus of damp cloth, etc.

mīle, *n.* unit equal to 5,280 feet on land, 6,076 feet on water.

mīle′àge, *n.* **1.** rate per mile. **2.** number of miles per unit.

mĭ·lieū′, *n.* social or working environment.

mĭl′i·tȧnt, *adj.* **1.** fighting for a cause. **—**n. **2.** militant person. **—mil′i·tan·cy,** *n.*

mĭl′i·tȧr·ĭsm, *n.* emphasis on military affairs. **—mil′i·tar·ist,** *n.* **—mil″i·ta·ris′tic,** *adj.*

mĭl′i·tăr·īze″, *v.t.*, -ized, -izing. invest or equip with military force.

mĭl′ĭ·tăr″y̆, *adj.* **1.** pertaining to armed forces. —*n.* **2. the military,** armed forces.

mĭl′i·tāte″, *v.i.*, -tated, -tating. be an influence.

mi·lĭ′tiȧ, *n.* emergency citizen army. —**mi·li′tia·man**, *n.*

mĭlk, *n.* **1.** white fluid secreted by female mammals for nourishing their young. —*v.t.* **2.** get milk from. —**milk′maid″**, *n.* —**milk′man″**, *n.* —**milk′y̆**, *adj.*

mĭlk′shāke″, *n.* shaken drink of milk, ice cream, and flavoring.

mĭll, *n.* **1.** place for processing or manufacturing; factory. **2.** tenth of a cent. —*v.t.* **3.** process in a mill. —*v.i.* **4.** move about confusedly. —**mill′er**, *n.*

mĭl·lĕn′i·ŭm, *n., pl.* -ums, -a. **1.** period of a thousand years. **2.** time of perfection.

mĭl′lĭ·grăm″, *n.* thousandth of a gram.

mĭl′lĭ·mē″têr, *n.* thousandth of a meter.

mĭl′lĭ·nêr, *n.* dealer in women's hats. —**mil′lin·er·y̆**, *n.*

mĭl′liȯn, *n.* a thousand thousand. —**mil′lionth**, *adj.*

mĭl″liȯn·āire′, *n.* owner of at least a million dollars.

mĭll′stōne″, *n.* stone for grinding flour.

mīme, *n., v.t.*, mimed, miming. *n.* **1.** acting without words. —*v.t.* **2.** imitate in mime. —**mi·met′ic**, *adj.*

mĭm′ĭc, *n., v.t.*, -icked, -icking. *n.* **1.** person who imitates mannerisms of others. —*v.t.* **2.** imitate as a mimic. —**mim′ic·ry̆**, *n.*

mĭ·mō′sȧ, *n.* flowering plant of warm regions.

mĭn″ȧ·rĕt′, *Islam.* tower for summoning to prayer.

mĭnce, *v.*, minced, mincing. *v.t.* **1.** chop finely. **2.** mitigate the meaning of. —*v.i.* **3.** be affectedly dainty. —**minc′ing**, *adj.*

mĭnce′mēat″, *n.* finely chopped fruit mixture, with or without meat.

mīnd, *n.* **1.** that which thinks. **2.** personality. **3.** sanity. —*v.t.* **4.** heed. **5.** be troubled or annoyed by.

mīnd′fŭl, *adj.* heedful.

mīnd′lĕss, *adj.* **1.** heedless. **2.** stupid.

mīne, *pron., n., v.*, mined, mining. *pron.* **1.** my own. —*n.* **2.** excavation for coal or minerals. **3.** buried or floated bomb. —*v.t.* **4.** dig for a mine. **5.** put mines in. —*v.i.* **6.** work a mine. —**min′er**, *n.*

mĭn′êr·ȧl, *n.* **1.** something neither vegetable nor animal. **2.** inorganic earth material.

mĭn″êr·äl′ȯ·gy̆, *n.* study of minerals. —**min″er·al·og′i·cal**, *adj.* —**min″er·al·o·gist**, *n.*

mĭn′gle, *v.*, -gled, -gling. *v.t., v.i.* mix together.

mĭn′ĭ·ȧ·tūre″, *n.* **1.** small copy. **2.** small painting. —*adj.* **3.** smaller than standard. —**min′i·a·tur·ize″**, *v.t.*

mī″nĭ·cȯm·pū′têr, *n.* a computing system that is larger than a microcomputer but smaller than a mainframe computer.

mĭn′ĭm, *n.* **1.** *Pharmacy.* liquid measure equalling a drop. **2.** *Music.* half note.

mĭn′ĭ·mīze″, *v.t.*, -mized, -mizing. **1.** reduce to a minimum. **2.** treat as of minimum importance.

mĭn′ĭ·mŭm, *n., pl.* -mums, -ma, *adj. n.* **1.** least amount. —*adj.* **2.** Also, **min′i·mal,** least.

mĭn′iȯn, *n.* minor official.

mĭn′ĭs·têr, *n.* **1.** clergyman. **2.** diplomat. **3.** cabinet member. —*v.i.* **4.** give help. —**min″is·te′ri·al**, *adj.* —**min″is·tra′tion**, *n.* —**min′is·trant**, *n., adj.*

mĭn′ĭs·try̆, *n., pl.* -tries. **1.** profession of a minister. **2.** government department. **3.** act of ministering.

mĭnk, *n.* weasel-like mammal.

mĭn′nōw, *n.* tiny fresh-water fish.

mī′nȯr, *adj.* **1.** lesser in size or importance. **2.** *Music.* in a scale a half tone below the major. —*n.* **3.** person not of age.

mī·nȯr′ĭ·ty̆, *n., pl.* -ities. **1.** lesser part. **2.** social group too small to have control. **3.** state of being a minor.

mĭn′strĕl, *n.* **1.** medieval strolling singer. **2.** blackface singer.

mĭnt, *n.* **1.** place for coining money. **2.** plant with aromatic leaves. —*adj.* **3.** absolutely fresh. —*v.t.* **4.** coin.

mĭn′ü·ĕnd″, *n. Math.* number subtracted from.

mĭn′ü·ĕt, *n.* slow dance.

mī′nŭs, *prep.* **1.** from which is subtracted. **2.** without.

mī·nŭs′cūle, *adj.* tiny.

mĭn'ŭte, *n.* **1.** one sixtieth of an hour. **2.** one sixtieth of a degree of arc. **3. minutes,** record of a meeting. —*adj.* (mī nyōōt') **4.** tiny. **5.** precise.

mĭn'ŭte·măn'', *n.* volunteer soldier of the American Revolution.

mĭ·nū'tï·åe, *n. pl.* minor details.

mĭr'å·cle, *n.* supernatural event. —**mi·rac'u·lous,** *adj.*

mĭ·râge', *n.* optical illusion caused by the atmosphere.

mīre, *n., v.t.,* **mired, miring.** *n.* **1.** sticky mud. —*v.t.* **2.** stick fast, as with mud. —**mir'y,** *adj.*

mĭr'rör, *n.* **1.** reflecting object. —*v.t.* **2.** reflect.

mîrth, *n.* gaiety. —**mirth'ful,** *adj.* —**mirth'less,** *adj.*

mĭs- prefix meaning "wrong" or "wrongly." **misapply, misbehave, miscalculate, misconceive, misconduct, misconstrue, miscount, misdeed, misdirect, misdoing, misgovern, misguide, mishandle, misinform, misinterpret, misjudge, mismanage, mismatch, misprint, mispronounce, misquote, misread, misrule, misshapen, misspell, misspend, misstate, mistime, mistreat, misunderstand.**

mĭs''åd·vĕn'tûre, *n.* bad luck.

mĭs'ăn·thrōpe'', *n.* hater of mankind. Also, **mis·an'thro·pist.** —**mis''an·throp'ic,** *adj.* —**mis·an'thro·py,** *n.*

mĭs·ăp''pré·hĕnd', *v.t.* understand wrongly. —**mis·ap''pre·hen'sion,** *n.*

mĭs''åp·prō'pri·āte'', *v.t.,* **-ated, -ating.** take and use wrongly.

mĭs''bé·gŏt'tĕn, *adj.* begotten wrongly; illegitimate.

mĭs·căr'rÿ, *v.t.,* **-ried, -rying. 1.** give birth to a fetus that cannot live. **2.** go wrong. —**mis·car'riage,** *n.*

mĭs·cĕ''gé·nā'tion, *n.* interbreeding of races.

mĭs''cĕl·lā'nē·oŭs, *adj.* various. —**mis'cel·la·ny,** *n.*

mĭs·chănce', *n.* bad luck.

mĭs'chĭef, *n.* **1.** damage. **2.** malice. **3.** gentle malice. —**mis'chie·vous,** *adj.*

mĭs''còn·strŭc'tion, *n.* wrong interpretation.

mĭs''crē·ånt, *n.* villain.

mĭs''dè·mēa'nör, *n.* offense less serious than a felony.

mī'sêr, *n.* morbid saver of money. —**mi'ser·ly,** *adj.*

mĭs'êr·å·ble, *adj.* **1.** very unhappy. **2.** causing misery. **3.** contemptibly meager or poor. —**mis'er·a·bly,** *adv.*

mĭs'êr·ÿ, *n., pl.* **-ies. 1.** suffering. **2.** source of suffering.

mĭs·fīre', *v.i.,* **-fired, -firing. 1.** fail to fire. **2.** fail to be effective.

mĭs·fĭt', *n., v.i.,* **-fitted, -fitting.** *n.* **1.** person unhappy in society. —*v.t., v.i.* **2.** fit badly.

mĭs·fôr'tŭne, *n.* **1.** bad luck. **2.** piece of bad luck.

mĭs·gĭv'ĭng, *n.* apprehension; doubt.

mĭs'hăp, *n.* unfortunate incident.

mĭs·lāy, *v.t.,* **-laid, -laying.** put somewhere later forgotten.

mĭs·lēad', *v.t.,* **-led, -leading. 1.** advise or urge wrongly. **2.** deceive.

mĭs·nō'mêr, *n.* wrong name.

mĭ·sŏg'y·nÿ, *n.* hatred of women. —**mi·sog'y·nist,** *n.*

mĭs·plāce', *v.t.,* **-placed, -placing. 1.** mislay. **2.** put in a wrong place.

mĭs·prī'sion, *n.* deviation from duty.

mĭs''rĕp·rè·sĕnt', *v.t.* give a wrong idea of. —**mis''rep·re·sen'ta'tion,** *n.*

mĭss, *v.t., n., pl.* **misses.** *v.t.* **1.** fail to hit, seize, meet, etc. **2.** be lonely without. —*n.* **3.** act or instance of missing. **4. Miss,** title for an unmarried woman.

mĭs'sàl, *n.* book of prayers for Mass.

mĭs'sīle, *n.* something thrown or shot to hit a target.

mĭs'sĭng, *adj.* lost or absent.

mĭs'sion, *n.* **1.** commanded or requested journey. **2.** group of missionaries. **3.** group sent to a place. **4.** duty or purpose.

mĭs'sion·ār''ÿ, *n., pl.* **-ies.** person sent to make religious conversions.

mĭs'sīve, *n.* written message.

mĭs·stĕp', *n.* **1.** wrong step. **2.** wrong act.

mĭst, *n.* **1.** thin fog. —*v.t.* **2.** fog. —*v.i.* **3.** become misty. —**mist'y,** *adj.*

mĭs·tāke', *n., v.t.,* **-took, -taken, -taking.** *n.* **1.** wrong act or opinion. —*v.t.* **2.** understand wrongly. —**mis·tak'a·ble,** *adj.*

mĭs'tlè·tōe'', *n.* semi-parasitic evergreen.

mĭs'trĕss, *n.* **1.** female master. **2.** unmarried female sexual partner.

mĭs·trī'ál, *n.* trial invalidated for technical reasons.

mĭs·trŭst', *v.t.* **1.** have no trust in. —*n.* **2.** lack of trust. —**mis·trust'ful**, *adj.*

mis·use, *v.t.* -used, -using, *n.*, *v.t.* (mis yōōz') **1.** use wrongly. **2.** mistreat. —*n.* (mis yōōs') **3.** wrong use or treatment.

mīte, *n.* **1.** tiny arachnid. **2.** tiny sum of money.

mī'tēr, *n.* **1.** bishop's headpiece. **2.** diagonal joint. —*v.t.* **3.** join in a miter.

mĭt'ĭ·gāte'', *v.*, -gated, -gating. *v.t.*, *v.i.* lessen in severity. —**mit''i·ga'tion**, *n.*

mĭtt, *n.* padded glove.

mĭt'tĕn, *n.* glove with only the thumb separate.

mĭx, *v.*, **mixed, mixing**, *n.* *v.t.* **1.** assemble and make uniform. **2.** have together. —*v.i.* **3.** be on social terms. —*n.* **4.** mixture. —**mix'ture**, *n.*

mĭxed, *adj.* **1.** blended. **2.** imperfect or impure.

mĭx'ŭp'', *n.* confusion.

mne·mon'ic (nĭ·mŏn'ĭk), *adj.* helping memory.

mōan, *n.* **1.** low, sad sound. —*v.i.* **2.** make such a sound.

mōat, *n.* defensive, water-filled ditch.

mŏb, *n.*, *v.t.*, **mobbed, mobbing**. *n.* **1.** disorderly or hostile crowd. —*v.t.* **2.** attack in a mob.

mō'bĭle, *adj.* movable. —**mo·bil'i·ty**, *n.*

mō'bĭ·līze'', *v.*, -lized, -lIzing. *v.t.*, *v.i.* make ready for war.

mŏc'cá·sĭn, *n.* soft heelless slipper.

mō'chà, *n.* **1.** type of coffee. —*adj.* **2.** coffee-flavored.

mŏck, *n.* **1.** ridicule. **2.** imitate; mimic. —*adj.* **3.** imitation. —**mock'er·y**, *n.*

mŏck'ĭng·bîrd'', *n.* bird imitating calls of other birds.

mŏck'ŭp'', *n.* full-scale model.

mōde, *n.* **1.** manner of doing. **2.** fashion. —**mod'ish**, *adj.*

mŏd'ĕl, *n.* **1.** small-scale three-dimensional copy. **2.** something to imitate. **3.** poser for pictures. —*adj.* **4.** exemplary. —*v.t.* **5.** copy in three dimensions. **6.** mold as in making a model. **7.** make as a copy.

mō'dĕm, *n.* (computers) device for linking computers via telephone lines.

mod·er·ate, *adj.*, *n.*, *v.*, -ated, -ating. *adj.* (mod'ər ət). **1.** avoiding extremes. —*n.* **2.** moderate person. —*v.t.* (mod'ər āt) **3.** make moderate. **4.** preside over. —*v.i.* **5.** become moderate. —**mod'er·ate·ly**, *adv.* —**mod'er·a''tor**, *n.*

mŏd'ĕrn, *adj.* **1.** pertaining to the present. **2.** reflecting advanced taste, thought, technology, etc. —*n.* **3.** modern person. —**mo·dern'i·ty**, *n.* —**mod'ern·ize''**, *v.t.*, *v.i.*

mŏd'ĕrn·ĭsm, *n.* advocacy of something deemed modern.

mŏd''ĕrn·ĭs'tĭc, *adj.* self-consciously modern in style.

mŏd'ĕst, *adj.* **1.** disliking praise, publicity, etc. **2.** avoiding self-exposure. **3.** not outstanding. —**mod'est·ly**, *adv.* —**mod·es'ty**, *n.*

mŏd'ĭ·cŭm, *n.* small amount.

mŏd'ĭ·fȳ'', *v.*, -fied, -fying. *v.t.*, *v.i.* **1.** alter in nature. —*v.t.* **2.** limit slightly. —**mod''i·fi·ca'tion**, *n.* —**mod'i·fi''er**, *n.*

mŏd'ŭ·lāte'', *v.t.*, -lated, -lating. vary or adjust. —**mod''u·la'tion**, *n.*

mŏd'ūle, *n.* **1.** unit of measurement. **2.** part scaled to the dimensions of such a unit.

mō'hāir, *n.* fabric of Angora goat hair.

Mō·hăm'méd·àn, *n.*, *adj.* Muslim. —**Mo·ham'med·an·ism**, *n.*

moīst, *adj.* slightly wet. —**moist'en**, *v.t.*, *v.i.* —**mois'ture**, *n.*

mō'làr, *n.* grinding tooth.

mò·lăs'sès, *n.* syrup from sugar refining.

mōld, *n.* **1.** device for forming a casting. **2.** model. **3.** destructive fungus. —*v.t.* **4.** model. **5.** cast in a mold. —*v.i.* **6.** become moldy. —**mold'y**, *adj.*

mōld'êr, *v.i.* crumble to dust.

mōld'ĭng, *n.* shaped strip or band.

mōle, *n.* **1.** spot on the skin. **2.** burrowing animal. **3.** breakwater. —**mole'hill''**, *n.* —**mole'skin''**, *n.*

mŏl'e·cūle'', *n.* smallest characteristic particle of an element or compound. —**mo·lec'u·lar**, *adj.*

mò·lĕst', *v.t.* trouble or interfere with. —**mo''les·ta'tion**, *n.*

mŏl'lĭ·fȳ'', *v.t.*, -fied, -fying. **1.** appease. **2.** mitigate.

mŏl'lŭsk, *n.* soft-bodied invertebrate, often in a shell. Also, **mol'lusc.**

mōlt, *v.i.* shed hair, feathers, etc. for replacement.

mōl'tĕn, *adj.* melted.

mō'mĕnt, *n.* **1.** very brief period. **2.**

present time. **3.** importance. **—mo′men·tar″y,** *adj.* **—mo″men·tar′i·ly,** *adv.*

mō·měn′toŭs, *adj.* of great importance.

mō·měn′tŭm, *n., pl.* **-tums, -ta.** force of a moving object.

mŏm′mÿ, *n., pl.* **-mies.** mother: child's word.

mŏn′ârch, *n.* king, queen, etc. **—mon′arch·y,** *n.* **—mo·nar′chi·cal,** *adj.*

mŏn′ârch·ĭst, *n.* person in favor of a monarchy. **—mon′ar·chism″,** *n.*

mŏn′às·tĕr″ÿ, *n., pl.* **-ies.** *n.* home of monks or nuns.

mò·nǎs′tĭc, *adj.* pertaining to monks or nuns. Also, **mo·nas′ti·cal,** *adj.*

mòn·äu′ràl, *adj.* reproducing sound on one channel.

Mòn′dāy, *n.* second day.

mòn′ēy, *n., pl.* **-eys, -ies.** paper or metal accepted everywhere in payment of debts. **—mon′eyed,** *adj.* **—mon′e·tar″y,** *adj.*

mŏn′grĕl, *adj.* **1.** of mixed breed. **—**n. **2.** animal with mixed bloodlines.

mŏn′ĭ·tör, *n.* **1.** device for checking or supervising. **—**v.t. **2.** check or supervise.

mònk, *n.* member of a religious order.

mòn′kēy, *n., pl.* **-keys. 1.** primate other than a human or ape. **2.** small, long-tailed primate.

mŏn′ò·chrōme″, *n.* color with shading varied but not hue.

mŏn′ò·cle, *n.* corrective lens for one eye.

mò·nŏg′à·mÿ, *n.* marriage to one spouse at a time. **—mo·nog′a·mous,** *n.*

mŏn′ò·gräph″, *n.* scholarly work on one subject.

mŏn′ò·lĭth″, *n.* object made from one stone. **—mon″o·lith′ic,** *adj.*

mŏn′ò·lōgue″, *n.* uninterrupted speech of one person. Also, **mon′o·log″.** **—mon′o·log″ist,** *n.*

mŏn″ò·mā′nĭ·à, *n.* obsession with one thing. **—mon″o·ma′ni·ac″,** *n.*

mò·nŏp′ò·lÿ, *n., pl.* **-lies.** exclusive use, control, or possession. **—mo·nop′o·list,** *n.* **—mo·nop″o·lis′tic,** *adj.* **—mo·nop′o·lize″,** *v.t.*

mŏn′ò·rāil″, *n.* one-rail railway.

mŏn′ò·sÿl″là·ble, *n.* one-syllable word. **—mon″o·syl·lab′ic,** *adj.*

mŏn″ò·thē′ĭsm, *n.* belief in one god.

—mon″o·the′ist, *n.* **—mon″o·the·is′tic,** *adj.*

mŏn′ò·tōne″, *n.* sound with unvarying pitch.

mò·nŏt′ò·noŭs, *adj.* tediously unvaried. **—mo·not′o·ny,** *n.*

mon·sieur (mė syūr′), *n., pl.* **messieurs.** *French.* **1.** gentleman. **2. Monsieur. a.** Sir. **b.** Mister.

Mon·si·gnor (mŏn sēn′yər), *n., pl.* **-gnors, -gnori.** high-ranking Roman Catholic priest.

mŏn·sōōn′, *n.* season of wind and rain in south Asia.

mŏn′stĕr, *n.* **1.** frightening legendary creature. **2.** grotesque or disgusting person. **—mon′strous,** *adj.* **—mon·stros′i·ty,** *n.*

mon·tage (mahn tahzh′), *n.* composite photograph, etc.

mònth, *n.* one of the twelve divisions of the year. **—month′ly,** *adj., adv., n.*

mŏn′ū·mėnt, *n.* **1.** something built or put up in remembrance. **2.** formal. impressive construction. **—mon″u·men′tal,** *adj.*

mōō, *n., v.i.,* **mooed, mooing.** *n.* **1.** sound of a cow. **—**v.i. **2.** make this sound.

mōōch, *Informal. v.i.* **1.** beg; cadge. **—**v.t. **2.** obtain by begging.

mōōd, *n.* state of mind.

mōōd′ÿ, *adj.,* **-ier, -iest. 1.** gloomy. **2.** changing mood quickly. **—mood′i·ly,** *adv.* **—mood′i·ness,** *n.*

mōōn, *n.* **1.** satellite of the earth. **2.** lighted portion of this satellite as seen from the earth. **—**v.i. **3.** be abstracted or sentimental. **—moon′beam″,** *n.* **—moon′light″,** *n.* **—moon′lit″,** *adj.* **—moon′scape″,** *n.*

mōōn′līght″ĭng, *n.* holding of a second job.

mōōn′shīne″, *n.* **1.** illicit whiskey. **2.** moonlight. **—moon′shin″er,** *n.*

mōōn′shŏt″, *n.* start of a trip to the moon.

mōōn′strŭck″, *adj.* **1.** crazy. **2.** dreamy.

mōōn′wälk″, *n.* walk on the moon.

môor, *v.t.* tie or anchor.

môor′ĭngs, *n. pl.* **1.** tackle for mooring. **2.** place to moor.

mōōse, *n., pl.* **moose.** large animal of the deer family.

mōōt, *adj*. **1**. hypothetical. **2**. open to question.

mŏp, *n.*, *v.t.*, **mopped, mopping**. *n*. **1**. long-handled device for washing or dusting. —*v.t*. **2**. clean with a mop.

mōpe, *v.i.*, **moped, moping**. brood. —mop′ey, mop′y, *adj*.

mò·rāine′, *n*. mass of rock, etc. left by a glacier.

môr′ȧl, *adj*. **1**. pertaining to morality. **2**. in accord with morality. **3**. pertaining to morale. —*n*. **4**. lesson of an experience. **5**. **morals**, moral principles. —mor′al·ist, *n*. —mo·ral′i·ty, *n*.

mò·rāle′, *n*. confidence in oneself, a situation, etc.

môr′′ȧl·ĭs′tĭc, *adj*. **1**. pertaining to morals. **2**. overconcerned with morals.

môr′ȧl·īze′′, *v.i.*, **-ized, -izing**. discuss morality.

mò·răss′, *n*. swamp.

môr′′ȧ·tô′rĭ·ŭm, *n.*, *pl*. **-ums, -a**. authorized delay.

môr′bĭd, *adj*. **1**. pertaining to disease. **2**. mentally unhealthy. —mor·bid′i·ty, *n*. —mor′bid·ly, *adv*.

môr′dȧnt, *adj*. biting. —mor′dan·cy, *n*.

môre, *adj*. **1**. greater in number, amount, etc. **2**. additional. —*adv*. **3**. additionally. —*n*. **4**. greater number, amount, etc. **5**. something additional.

môre·ō′vêr, *adj*. besides.

mô′rēs, *n. pl*. prevailing social customs.

môrgue, *n*. place for keeping the unidentified dead.

môr′ĭ·bŭnd, *adj*. about to die.

môrn′ĭng, *n*. early part of the day.

môrnĭng glôrȳ, vine with trumpet-shaped flowers.

mò·rŏc′cō, *n*. goat leather.

mô′rŏn, *n*. feeble-minded person. —mo·ron′ic, *adj*.

mó·rōse′, *adj*. downhearted or surly. —mo·rose′ly, *adv*. —mo·rose′ness, *n*.

môr′phĭne, *n*. analgesic opiate.

môrse, *n*. code of dots and dashes. Also, **Morse**.

môr′sėl, *n*. small portion of food.

môr′tȧl, *adj*. **1**. having eventually to die. **2**. human. **3**. fatal. **4**. threatening the soul. —*n*. **5**. human being. —mor′tal·ly, *adv*. —mor·tal′i·ty, *n*.

môr′tȧr, *n*. **1**. adhesive for masonry. **2**. bowl for grinding. **3**. short cannon.

môr′tȧr·bôard′′, *n*. academic cap.

môrt′gȧge, *n.*, *v.t.*, **-gaged, -gaging**. *n*. **1**. pledge of property as security for a loan. —*v.t*. **2**. pledge in this way. —mort′′ga·gee′, *n*. —mort′ga·gor, *n*.

môr·tĭ′cĭȧn, *n*. undertaker.

môr′tĭ·fȳ′′, *v.t.*, **-fied, -fying**. **1**. humiliate. **2**. suppress with austerities. —mor′′ti·fi·ca′tion, *n*.

môr′tĭse, *n.*, *v.t*. **-tised, -tising**. *n*. **1**. socket forming part of a joint. —*v.t*. **2**. join with a mortise.

môr′tū·ār′′ȳ, *adj.*, *n.*, *pl*. **-ies**. *adj*. **1**. pertaining to death or funerals. —*n*. **2**. place for receiving the dead.

mō·sā′ĭc, *n*. picture of inlaid pieces.

mō′sēy, *v.i. Informal*. amble.

Mŏs′lĕm, *n*. Muslim.

mŏsque, *n*. Muslim house of prayer.

mòs·quī′tō, *n.*, *pl*. **-toes, -tos**. small blood-sucking insect.

mŏss, *n*. green, velvety plant. —mos′sy, *adj*.

mōst, *adj*. **1**. greatest in number, amount, etc. **2**. in the majority. —*adv*. **3**. to the greatest extent. —*n*. **4**. greatest number, extent, etc.

mōst′lȳ, *adv*. in most cases.

mō·tĕl′, *n*. hotel for motorists.

mŏth, *n.*, *pl*. **moths**. nocturnal flying insect.

mŏth′bȧll′′, *n*. ball of moth repellent.

mŏth′êr, *n*. **1**. female parent. —*v.t*. **2**. act as a mother to. —moth′er·hood′′, *n*. —moth′er·less, *adj*. —moth′er·ly, *adj*.

mŏth′êr-ĭn-lȧw′′, *n.*, *pl*. **mothers-in-law**. mother of a spouse.

mŏth′êr-ŏf-pêarl′, *n*. inner shell of the pearl oyster.

mō′tĭf′, *n*. basic theme or subject.

mō′tion, *n*. **1**. movement. **2**. formal proposal. —*v.i*. **3**. gesture. —*v.t*. **4**. direct with a gesture. —mo′tion·less, *n*.

mōtion pĭctûre, series of photographs projected at high speed.

mō′tĭ·vāte′′, *v.t.*, **-vated, -vating**. give desire or incentive. —mo′′ti·va′tion, *n*.

mō′tĭve, *n*. **1**. desire for action. **2**. motif. —*adj*. **3**. pertaining to motion.

mŏt′lēy, *adj*. of many colors or kinds.

mō′tör, *n*. **1**. machine providing motive force. —*adj*. **2**. causing motion. —mo′tor·bike′′, *n*. —mo′tor·boat′′, *n*. —mo′tor·car′′, *n*. —mo′tor·ize′′, *v.t*.

mō′tŏr·cāde′′, *n*. procession of automobiles.

mō′tŏr·cȳ′′cle, *n*. two-wheeled motorized vehicle.

mō′tŏr·ĭst, *n*. automobile driver.

mō′tŏr·măn, *n*. driver of a streetcar.

mŏt′tle, *v.t.*, **-tled, -tling.** mark with spots, etc.

mŏt′tō, *n*., *pl*. **-toes, -tos.** formal statement of aims or ideals.

mōuld, *n.*, *v.t.* mold.

mōund, *n.*, *v.t.* heap.

mōunt, *v.t.* **1.** climb onto or up. **2.** set in place. —*v.i.* **3.** climb. —*n.* **4.** steed. **5.** setting or support. —**mount′ing**, *n.*

mōun′taĭn, *n.* very high feature of the earth. —**moun′tain·ous**, *adj*.

mōun′′tăin·ēer′, *n.* **1.** mountain dweller. **2.** mountain climber. —**moun′′tain·eer′ing**, *n.*

mōun′tè·bănk′′, *n.* charlatan.

môurn, *v.t.*, *v.i.* lament. —**mourn′ful**, *adj*. —**mourn′ing**, *n.*

mōuse, *n.*, *pl*. **mice. 1.** small, timid rodent. **2.** (computers) compact device for convenient data manipulation on a monitor.

mōus·tăche′, *n.* mustache.

mōus′ÿ, *adj.*, **-ier, -iest.** mouselike, esp. in timidity.

mōuth, *n.* **1.** orifice for eating and breathing. **2.** opening of a river, etc. —**mouth′ful**, *n.*

mōuth′piēce′′, *n.* **1.** part of a horn, etc. blown through. **2.** spokesman or apologist.

move (mōōv), *v.*, **moved, moving**, *n. v.t.* **1.** change the place of. **2.** inspire or motivate. **3.** propose formally. —*v.i.* **4.** change place. **5.** change residence or workplace. **6.** become in motion. —*n.* **7.** act or instance of moving. **8.** purposeful action. —**mov′a·ble, move′a·ble**, *adj*.

move′mĕnt (mōōv′mĕnt), *n.* **1.** motion. **2.** action in a cause. **3.** assembly of clockwork. **4.** division of a musical composition.

mov′iē (moo′vē), *n.* motion picture. Also, **moving picture.**

mōw, *v.t.*, **mowed, mowed** or **mown, mowing. 1.** cut down, as grass. **2.** cut down the plants on.

Mr. (mis′tĕr), title for a man. Also, **Mis′ter.**

Mrs. (mis′iz), title for a married woman.

Ms. (miz, em′es′), *n.* title for a woman disregarding marital status.

mŭch, *adj.*, *adv.*, *n. adj.* **1.** in great quantity. —*adv.* **2.** to a great extent. **3.** about. —*n.* **4.** something considerable. **5.** a great amount.

mū′cĭ·làge, *n.* liquid glue.

mŭck, *n.* sticky filth. —**muck′y**, *adj*.

mŭck′rāk′′ĭng, *n.* searching for scandalous information. —**muck′rak′′er**, *n.*

mū′coŭs, *adj.* **1.** having mucus. **2.** slimy.

mū′cŭs, *n.* slimy body secretion, esp. from the nose.

mŭd, *n.* sticky earth. —**mud′dy**, *adj.*, *v.t.*

mŭd′dle, *v.t.*, **-dled, -dling**, *n. v.t.* **1.** bungle or confuse. —*n.* **2.** act or instance of muddling. —**mud′dle·head′ed**, *adj*.

mŭd′slĭng′′ĭng, *n.* defamation, esp. of a political opponent. —**mud′sling′′er**, *n.*

mū·ĕz′zĭn, *n.* Muslim caller to prayer.

mŭff, *n.* **1.** cylinder made esp. of fur for keeping the hands warm. —*v.t.* **2.** bungle.

mŭf′fĭn, *n.* small round bread or cake.

mŭf′fle, *v.t.*, **-fled, -fling. 1.** wrap closely. **2.** deaden, as sound.

mŭf′flêr, *n.* **1.** heavy scarf. **2.** sound deadener.

mŭf′tĭ, *n.* dress other than a uniform.

mŭg, *n.*, *v.t.*, **mugged, mugging.** *n.* **1.** cylindrical cup. —*v.t.* **2.** attack from behind, esp. in order to rob.

mŭg′gÿ, *adj.*, **-gier, -giest.** hot and humid.

Mu·hăm′mà·dàn, *n.*, *adj.* Muslim.

mŭl′bĕr′′rÿ, *n.*, *pl*. **-ries.** tree with purplish-red fruit.

mŭlch, *n.* plant matter spread to keep the ground from freezing.

mŭlct, *v.t.* **1.** fine. **2.** obtain by fraud.

mūle, *n.* **1.** offspring of a donkey and a mare. **2.** heelless slipper. —**mu·le·teer′**, *n.*

mūl′ĭsh, *adj.* stubborn.

mŭll, *v.t.* **1.** to warm and spice, as wine. —*v.i.* **2.** *Informal.* ponder.

mŭl′′tĭ·făr′ĭ·oŭs, *adj.* with many components.

mŭl′′tĭ·mĭl′′liòn·āire′, *n.* one who has many millions of dollars.

mŭl′tĭ·ple, *adj.* **1.** in a large number. —*n.* **2.** number evenly divisible by another.

mŭl′′tĭ·plĭ′cănd′, *n. Math.* number to be multiplied.

mŭl′′tĭ·plĭc′ĭ·tў, *n.* large number or variety.

mŭl′tĭ·plȳ′′, *v.,* -plied, -plying. *v.t.* **1.** repeat a specified number of times for a final sum. —*v.i.* **2.** increase in size or number. —**mul′ti·pli′′er,** *n.* —**mul′′ti·pli·ca′tion,** *n.*

mŭl′tĭ·stāge′′, *adj.* in many stages.

mŭl′tĭ·tūde′′, *n.* large number. —**mul′′ti·tu·di·nous,** *adj.*

mŭm, *adj.* **1.** unspeaking. **2.** short for chrysanthemum.

mŭm′ble, *v.i.,* -bled, -bling, *n. v.i.* **1.** say something quietly and indistinctly. —*n.* **2.** mumbling speech or remark.

mŭm′bō jŭm′bō, pretentious or meaningless ceremony.

mŭm′mêr, *n.* wearer of a mask or costume. —**mum′mer·y,** *n.*

mŭm′mў, *n., pl.* -mies. preserved dead body. —**mum′mi·fy′′,** *v.t., v.i.*

mŭmps, *n.* communicable disease characterized by swollen glands.

mŭnch, *v.t., v.i.* chew crunchingly.

mŭn·dāne′, *adj.* **1.** worldly. **2.** commonplace.

mū·nĭc′ĭ·pảl, *adj.* pertaining to city government.

mū·nĭc′′ĭ·pảl′ĭ·tў, *n., pl.* -ties. incorporated community.

mū·nĭf′ĭ·cênt, *adj.* lavish; generous. —**mu·nif′i·cence,** *n.*

mū·nĭ′tions, *n. pl.* military supplies, esp. guns and ammunition.

mū′rȧl, *n.* wall painting. —**mu′ral·ist,** *n.*

mûr′dêr, *n.* **1.** willful unlawful killing. —*v.t.* **2.** commit murder against. —**mur′der·er,** *fem.,* **mur′der·ess,** *n.* —**mur′der·ous,** *adj.*

mûrk, *n.* gloom; darkness. —**murk′y,** *adj.*

mûr′mûr, *n.* **1.** low, indistinct speech or sound. —*v.i.* **2.** make a murmur.

mŭs′′cȧ·tĕl′, *n.* sweet wine.

mŭs′cle, *n.* body tissue which contracts to cause movement. —**mus′cu·lar,** *adj.* —**mus′cu·la·ture,** *n.*

mūse, *v.i.* **1.** be meditative. —*n.* **2.** Muse, goddess presiding over an art.

mū·sē′ŭm, *n.* public institution for displaying things of interest.

mŭsh, *n.* **1.** porridge of boiled meat. **2.** *Informal.* foolish sentiment. —**mush′y,** *adj.*

mŭsh′rōōm′′, *n.* **1.** edible fungus. —*v.i.* **2.** grow rapidly.

mū′sĭc, *n.* art of composing series of tones, etc. —**mu·si′cian,** *n.* —**mu′′si·col′o·gy,** *n.*

mū′sĭ·cȧl, *adj.* **1.** pertaining to music. **2.** sweet-sounding. —*n.* **3.** Also, **musical comedy,** play with frequent musical numbers.

mū′′sĭ·cȧle′, *n.* party with music.

mŭsk, *n.* animal secretion used in perfumes. —**musk′y,** *adj.*

mŭs′kĕt, *n.* antique smooth-bored gun. —**mus′′ket·eer′,** *n.*

mŭsk′mĕl′ȯn, *n.* type of sweet melon.

Mŭs′lĭm, *n.* **1.** follower of the teachings of Muhammad. —*adj.* **2.** pertaining to Islam or the Muslims.

mŭs′lĭn, *n.* cotton cloth.

mŭss, *n.* **1.** disorderly state. —*v.t.* **2.** put in a muss. —**mus′sy,** *adj.*

mŭs′sĕl, *n.* type of bivalve.

mŭst, *v.* **1.** have or has to. **2.** compelled to do as stated.

mŭs·tȧche′, *n.* hair on the upper lip.

mŭs′tăng, *n.* wild horse of the Southwest.

mŭs′tȧrd, *n.* condiment made from ground yellow seeds.

mŭs′têr, *v.t.* **1.** summon; rally. **2.** enlist or discharge from military service. —*n.* **3.** gathering, as for inspection.

mŭs′tў, *adj.,* -ier, -iest. moldy in smell or taste.

mū′tȧ·ble, *adj.* changeable. —**mu′′ta·bil′i·ty,** *n.*

mū·tā′tion, *n.* **1.** living things with characteristics not inherited; sport. **2.** change. —**mu′tate,** *v.i., v.t.* —**mu′tant,** *adj., n.*

mūte, *adj., n., v.t.,* **muted, muting.** *adj.* **1.** unable to speak. **2.** not speaking. —*n.* **3.** mute person. —*v.t.* **4.** soften the effect of. —**mute′ly,** *adv.* —**mute′ness,** *n.*

mū′tĭ·lāte′′, *v.t.,* -lated, -lating. injure severely and conspicuously. —**mu′′ti·la′tion,** *n.*

mū′tĭ·nў, *n., pl.* -nies, *v.i.,* -nied, -nying. revolt against superiors.

—mu''ti·neer', *n*. —mu'ti·nous, *adj*.

mŭt'têr, *v.i.* **1.** speak in a low, indistinct voice. —*n*. **2.** muttering voice.

mŭt'tŏn, *n*. sheep meat.

mū'tū·ȧl, *adj*. affecting one another. —mu'tu·al·ly, *adj*.

mŭz'zle, *n*., *v.t.*, -zled, -zling. *n*. **1.** nose and jaws of an animal. **2.** device to prevent biting. **3.** end of a gun facing the target. —*v.t.* **4.** put a muzzle on. **5.** keep from talking.

mȳ, *pron*. pertaining or belonging to me.

mȳ·ō'pï·ȧ, *n*. nearsightedness. —my·op'ic, *adj*.

mȳr'ï·ȧd, *adj*. **1.** very many. —*n*. **2.** great number.

mȳr'mĭ·dŏn, *n*. follower.

mȳrrh, *n*. fragrant resin.

mȳr'tle, *n*. flowering evergreen shrub.

mȳ·sĕlf', *pron*., *pl*. ourselves. **1.** (intensive and reflexive of *me*). **2.** my true self.

mȳs'têr·ÿ, *n*., *pl*. -ies. **1.** something not readily explained. **2.** secrecy. **3.** story based on the solution of a criminal case. —mys·te'ri·ous, *adj*.

mȳs'tĭc, *adj*. **1.** pertaining to secret rites and teachings. **2.** Also, mys'ti·cal, of spiritual significance. —*n*. **3.** person having deep spiritual experiences. —mys'ti·cism, *n*.

mȳs'tĭ·fȳ'', *v.t.*, -fied, -fying. puzzle. —mys''ti·fi·ca'tion, *n*.

mȳs·tĭque, *n*. air of mysticism surrounding a person, profession, etc.

mȳth, *n*. **1.** religious legend. **2.** false belief. —myth'i·cal, *adj*. —my·thol'o·gy, *n*. —myth''o·log'i·cal, *adj*. —my·thol'o·gist, *n*.

N

N, n, *n*. fourteenth letter of the English alphabet.

nȧb, *v.t.*, nabbed, nabbing. *Informal*. seize.

nā'dĭr, *n*. lowest point.

nȧg, *v.t.*, nagged, nagging, *n. v.t* **1.** pester. —*n*. **2.** poor horse.

nāil, *n*. **1.** pointed, driven fastening. **2.**

horny growth on fingers or toes. —*v.t*. **3.** fasten with nails.

na·ive (nah ēv'), *adj*. simple; unsophisticated. —na·ive·té', *n*.

nā'kėd, *adj*. **1.** unclothed; unconcealed. **2.** unassisted by lenses.

nȧm'bÿ-pȧm'bÿ, *adj*. insipid; characterless.

nāme, *n*., *v.t.*, named, naming. *n*. **1.** word or words by which a person or thing is recognized. **2.** reputation. **3.** insulting epithet. —*v.t.* **4.** give a name to. **5.** appoint. —name'less, *adj*.

nāme'lÿ, *adv*. that is to say.

nāme'sāke'', *n*. person or thing having the same name as another.

nȧp, *n*., *v.i.*, napped, napping. *n*. **1.** brief sleep. **2.** fuzzy surface. —*v.i.* **3.** have a brief sleep.

nāpe, *n*. back of the neck.

nȧph'thȧ, *n*. inflammable fluid.

nȧp'kĭn, *n*. cloth covering the lap at meals.

nâr'cĭs·sĭsm, *n*. love of oneself. —nar'cis·sist, *n*. —nar''cis·sis'tic, *adj*.

nâr·cĭs'sŭs, *n*. flowering bulb plant.

nâr·cō'sĭs, *n*. unconsciousness from a narcotic.

nâr·cŏt'ĭc, *n*. **1.** pain-relieving drug, often addictive. —*adj*. **2.** pertaining to narcotics.

nȧr'rāte, *v.t.*, -rated, -rating. tell the story of. —nar'ra·tor, *n*.

nȧr'rȧ·tĭve, *adj*. **1.** story-telling. —*n*. **2.** story; account.

nȧr'rōw, *n*. **1.** not wide. **2.** not ample. **3.** illiberal. —*v.t.* **4.** make narrow. —*v.i* **5.** become narrow.

nȧr'rōw-mīnd'ėd, *adj*. lacking a broad, liberal outlook.

nâr'whâl, *n*. small, tusked whale.

nȧr'ÿ, *adj*. *Dialect*. not any.

nā'sȧl, *adj*. spoken through the nose.

nȧs'cėnt, *adj*. coming into being.

nȧs·tûr'tïŭm, *n*. pungent-smelling flowering herb.

nȧs'tÿ, *adj*., -tier, -tiest. **1.** revolting as from filth. **2.** unpleasant.

nā'tȧl, *adj*. pertaining to birth.

nā'tion, *n*. **1.** group with common ancestral and traditional associations. **2.** politically independent state. —na'tion·al, *adj*. —na'tion·wide'', *adj*., *adv*.

nā'tion·ȧl·ĭsm, *n*. assertion of the rights, cultural values, etc. of a nation. —na'

tion·al·ist, *n. adj.* **—na''tion·al·is'
tic,** *adj.*

nă'tion·àl·īze'', *v.t.,* **-ized, -izing.** put
under government ownership. **—na''
tion·al·i·za'tion,** *n.*

nā'tĭve, *adj.* **1.** born in or characteristic
of a certain place. **2.** inborn. **—***n.* **3.** native person.

nā·tĭv'ĭ·tў, *n., pl.* **-ties. 1.** birth. **2.** the
Nativity, birth of Jesus.

nătˈtў, *adj.,* **-tier, -tiest.** neat and stylish.

nătˈuˑràl, *adj.* **1.** pertaining to nature. **2.**
inborn. **3.** unaffected; easy. **4.** to be expected. **5.** *Music.* not sharped or flat-
ted.

nătˈuˑràlˑĭst, *n.* student of nature.

nătˈuˑràlˑīze'', *v.t.,* **-ized, -izing.** admit
to citizenship.

nătˈuˑràlˑlў, *adv.* **1.** by nature. **2.** of
course. **3.** in a natural way.

nā'tûre, *n.* **1.** everything not man-made.
2. essential quality or composition.

năught, *n.* **1.** nothing. **2.** zero.

nāughˈtў, *adj.,* **-tier, -tiest.** ill-behaved.
—naughˈtiˑly, *adv.*

nău'sē·à, *n.* sickness at the stomach.
—nauˈse·ate'', *v.t.* **—nauˈse·ous,** *adj.*

nău'tĭˑcàl, *adj.* pertaining to ships and
navigation.

nău'tĭˑlŭs, *n.* mollusk with a spiral shell.

nā'vàl, *adj.* **1.** pertaining to navies. **2.**
pertaining to ships.

nā'vèl, *n.* mark where the umbilical cord
was attached.

năv'ĭˑgà·ble, *adj.* able to be sailed over.

năv'ĭˑgāte'', *v.,* **-gated, -gating.** *v.t.* **1.**
cross or pass through in a ship or air-
craft. **2.** determine the position and
course of. **—***v.i.* **3.** direct a ship or aircraft. **—nav'iˑga''tor,** *n.*

nā'vў, *n., pl.* **-ies.** seagoing fighting
force.

nāy, *n.* vote of no.

nēap tĭde, lowest of high tides.

nēar, *adj.* **1.** short in distance. **2.** closely
related. **—***adv.* **3.** at a short distance.
—*prep.* **4.** close to. **—***v.t.* **5.** approach.

nēar'bў', *adj., adv.* near.

nēar'lў, *adv.* almost.

nēar'sīght'ĕd, *adj.* seeing distant objects poorly.

nēat, *adj.* **1.** free of dirt and clutter. **2.**
finely done.

nĕb'ū·là, *n., pl.* **-lae, -las.** cloudlike
cluster of stars, etc. **—neb'uˑlar,** *adj.*

nĕb'ū·loŭs, *adj.* vague.

nĕc'ĕs·sâr''ў, *adj.* **1.** not to be dispensed
with. **2.** inevitable. **—nec''es·sar'iˑly,**
adv.

nè·cĕs'sĭˑtāte'', *v.t.,* **-tated, -tating.** require.

nè·cĕs'sĭˑtoŭs, *adj.* needy.

nè·cĕs'sĭˑtў, *n., pl.* **-ties. 1.** state of needing. **2.** something needed.

nĕck, *n.* **1.** part of the body which supports the head. **2.** narrow feature.
—neck'wear'', *n.*

nĕck'êr·chĭef, *n.* broad covering for the
neck.

nĕck'làce, *n.* ornamental chain, string of
beads, etc. worn around the neck.

nĕck'tĭe'', *n.* decorative band of cloth
tied around the neck.

nè·crŏl'ó·gў, *n., pl.* **-gies.** list of the
dead.

nĕc'ró·măn''cў, *n.* **1.** divination by
communication with the dead. **2.** sor-
cery. **—nec'ro·man''cer,** *n.*

nĕc'tàr, *n.* **1.** drink of the classical gods.
2. sweetish liquid of flowers.

nĕc''tàr·ĭne', *n.* small, smooth peach.

nēe, *adj.* born as: said of the maiden
name of a married woman. Also, **née.**

nēed, *v.t.* **1.** be obligated to have or do.
—*n.* **2.** state of needing. **3.** thing
needed. **4.** poverty or trouble. **—need'
ful,** *adj.* **—need·less,** *adj.*

nēe'dle, *n., v.t.,* **-dled, -dling.** *n.* **1.**
sharp object used for passing thread
through cloth. **2.** any of various sharp
or pointed objects. **—***v.t.* **3.** *Informal.*
goad; annoy. **—nee'dle·work'',** *n.*

nēe'dle·poĭnt'', *n.* **1.** embroidery on
canvas. **2.** lace made on a paper pattern.

nēeds, *adv.* of necessity.

nēed'ў, *adj.,* **-ier, -iest.** in need. **—need'
i·ness,** *n.*

nĕ'er'-do-wĕll'', *n.* shiftless person.

nè·fâr'ĭ·oŭs, *adj.* wicked.

nè·gāte', *v.t.,* **-gated, -gating. 1.** deny. **2.**
render ineffective.

nĕg'àˑtĭve, *adj.* **1.** saying or meaning no.
2. opposite to positive. **3.** less than
zero. **—***n.* **4.** negative statement or attitude. **5.** photographic film, etc. that re-
verses light and shade. **—neg'a·tive·ly,**
adv.

nĕgˑlĕct', *v.t.* **1.** deny proper care to. **2.**

disregard. —*n*. **3**. state of being neglected. **4**. state of neglecting. —**neg·lect'ful**, *adj*.

neg·li·gee (něg''lē zhā'), *n*. loosely fitting woman's gown.

něg'li·gėnt, *adj*. neglecting responsibilities. —**neg'li·gence**, *n*.

něg'li·gi·ble, *adj*. too unimportant to matter.

ne·gō'ti·a·ble, *adj*. **1**. transferable. **2**. capable of being dealt with.

ne·gō'ti·āte'', *v*., **-ated, -ating.** *v.i.* **1**. bargain. —*v.t*. **2**. establish by bargaining. **3**. succeed in passing through or across. —**ne·go'ti·a''tor**, *n*.

Nē'grō, *n., pl.* **-groes**. dark-skinned person of African origin. —**Neg'roid**, *adj*.

neigh (nā), *n*. **1**. sound of a horse. —*v.i.* **2**. emit such a sound.

neigh'bŏr (nā'ber), *n*. **1**. person living near by. **2**. fellow human. —*v.i.* **3**. be situated near by. —**neigh'bor·ing**, *adj*. —**neigh'bor·ly**, *adj*.

neigh'bŏr·hōŏd'', *n*. **1**. area within a town. **2**. approximate area or range.

nēither, *adj., pron., conj*. not either.

něm'e·sĭs, *n., pl.* **-ses. 1**. just fate or vengeance. **2**. bringer of this.

Nē''o·lĭth'ĭc, *adj*. pertaining to the later Stone Age.

nē·ŏl'ō·gĭsm, *n*. newly invented word or expression.

nē'ŏn, *n*. gaseous element used in lighting tubes.

nē'o·phȳte'', *n*. beginner.

něph'ew, *n*. son of a brother, sister, brother-in-law, or sister-in-law.

něp'o·tĭsm, *n*. favoritism toward relatives in giving employment.

nêrve, *n*. **1**. fiber carrying signals through the body. **2**. courage. **3**. insolent boldness. **4**. **nerves**, nervousness.

nêrve'lėss, *adj*. **1**. without strength. **2**. not nervous.

nêrve'-răck''ĭng, *adj*. emotionally upsetting. Also, **nerve'wrack''ing**.

nêrv'oŭs, *adj*. **1**. full of apprehension or restlessness. **2**. pertaining to nerves.

nêrv'ȳ, *adj*. **-ier, -iest**. *Informal*. impudent.

něst, *n*. **1**. place for bearing and sheltering young. —*v.i.* **2**. settle in a nest.

n'est-ce pas? (něs päh'), *French*. isn't it so?

něs'tle, *v.i.*, **-tled, -tling**. settle down.

nět, *n., adj., v.t.*, **netted, netting**. *n*. **1**. open cloth for capturing or supporting. **2**. amount after deductions. —*adj*. **3**. after deductions. —*v.t.* **4**. capture, as in a net.

nĕth'êr, *adj*. lower. —**neth'er·most''**, *adj*.

nět'tle, *n., v.t.*, **-tled, -tling**. *n*. **1**. prickly weed. —*v.t.* **2**. irritate; annoy.

nět'wôrk'', *n*. **1**. net-like arrangement. **2**. system of isolated entities working in coordination.

neū'răl, *adj*. pertaining to nerves.

neū·răl'giȧ, *n*. pain along a nerve.

neū''rȧs·thē'nĭ·ȧ, *n*. neurosis with lassitude, anxiety, etc. —**neu''ras·the'nic**, *adj., n*.

neū·rī'tĭs, *n*. inflammation of a nerve.

neū·rŏl'o·gȳ, *n*. study of nerves. —**neu''ro·log'i·cal**, *adj*. —**neu·rol'o·gist**, *n*.

neū·rō'sĭs, *n., pl.* **-ses**. compulsive mental disorder. —**neu·rot'ic**, *adj., n*.

neū'têr, *adj*. **1**. without sex. **2**. without gender. —*v.t.* **3**. remove the sex organs of.

neū'trȧl, *adj*. **1**. taking no sides. **2**. having no pronounced character. —*n*. **3**. neutral person or country. —**neu'tral·ism**, *n*. —**neu·tral'i·ty**, *n*. —**neu'tra·lize**, *v.t*.

neū'trŏn, *n*. uncharged atomic particle.

něv'êr, *adv*. at no time.

něv''êr·môre', *adv*. never again.

něvêr-něvêr lănd, purely imaginary place.

něv''êr·thė·lėss', *adv*. despite this.

new, *adj*. **1**. never existing before. **2**. unfamiliar. **3**. fresh. **4**. additional. —**new'born'**, *adj*. —**new'com''er**, *n*.

něw'el, *n*. support for a winding stair.

news, *n. sing*. **1**. information of public interest, esp. as published. **2**. recent information. —**news'boy''**, *n*. —**news'deal''er**, *n*. —**news'let''ter**, *n*. —**news'man''**, *n*. —**news'pa''per**, *n*. —**news'stand''**, *n*. —**news'wor''thy**, *adj*.

news'căst'', *n*. broadcast of news.

newt, *n*. amphibious salamander.

next, *adj*. **1**. directly alongside another. —*adv*. **2**. directly afterward.

next'-dôor', *adj*. in the next building.

nĭb, *n*. **1**. bird's beak. **2**. pen point.

nĭb'ble, *v.*, **-bled, -bling**, *n. v.t., v.i.* **1**. eat with small bites. —*n*. **2**. small bite.

nīce, *adj.*, **nicer, nicest. 1.** agreeable. **2.** delicate; subtle.

nī'ce·tỹ, *n., pl.* **-ties. 1.** precision. **2.** fine detail or distinction.

nīche, *n.* recessed area in a wall, as for a statue.

nĭck, *n.* **1.** small notch. —*v.t.* **2.** cut such a notch.

nĭck'ĕl, *n.* **1.** white metallic element. **2.** five-cent piece.

nĭck''ĕl·ō'dē·ŏn, *n.* coin-operated automatic piano.

nĭck'nāme'', *n., v.t.,* **-named, -naming.** *n.* **1.** informal name. —*v.t.* **2.** give a nickname to.

nĭc'ŏ·tīne'', *n.* poisonous extract from tobacco leaves.

nièce, *n.* daughter of a brother, sister, brother-in-law, or sister-in-law.

nĭf'tỹ, *adj.,* **-tier, -tiest.** *Informal.* smart; handsome.

nĭg'gàrd·lỹ, *adj.* stingy.

nĭgh, *adj., adv. Archaic.* near.

nĭght, *n.* period when the sun is absent. —**night'clothes''**, *n. pl.* —**night' dress''**, *n.* —**night'fall''**, *n.* —**night' gown''**, *n.* —**night'ly**, *adv., adj.* —**night'time''**, *n.* —**night'wear''**, *n.*

nĭght'căp'', *n.* **1.** cap for sleeping in. **2.** *Informal.* drink just before bed.

nĭght'māre'', *n.* bad dream. —**night' mar''ish**, *adj.*

nĭght'shāde'', *n.* plants related to potatoes, tomatoes, etc., some being poisonous.

nī'hĭl·ĭsm, *n.* rejection of all social institutions. —**ni'hil·ist**, *n.* —**ni''hil·is' tic**, *adj.*

nĭm'ble, *adj.,* **-bler, -blest.** quick and deft.

nĭm'bŭs, *n., pl.* **-bi, -buses.** halo.

nĭn'cŏm·pōōp'', *n.* fool.

nīne, *n.* eight plus one. —**ninth**, *adj.*

nīne·tēen', *n.* ten plus nine. —**nine' teenth'**, *adj.*

nīne'tỹ, *adj., n.* nine times ten. —**nine' ti·eth**, *adj.*

nĭp, *v.t.,* **nipped, nipping**, *n. v.t.* **1.** bite or pinch lightly. **2.** freeze injuriously. —*n.* **3.** act or instance of nipping. **4.** sharp chill. **5.** tiny drink. —**nip'per**, *n.* —**nip'pers**, *n.*

nĭp'ple, *n.* **1.** small projection from the breast from which milk is sucked. **2.** anything resembling this.

nĭr·vâ'nà, *n. Buddhism.* loss of self in ultimate bliss.

nĭt'-pĭck''ĭng, *n.* quibbling. —**nit'- pick''er**, *n.*

nī'trŏ·gĕn, *n.* gaseous element. —**ni· trog'e·nous**, *adj.*

nī''trŏ·glỹc'êr·ĭn, *n.* explosive oil used in dynamite.

nĭt'tỹ-grĭt'tỹ, *n. Informal.* fundamentals.

nĭt'wĭt'', *n.* stupid person.

nĭx, *adv. Informal.* no.

nō, *adv., adj., n., pl.* **noes.** *adv.* **1.** it is not so. **2.** I will not. **3.** do not. **4.** not at all. —*adj.* **5.** not any. —*n.* **6.** vote of no.

nō'ble, *adj.,* **-bler, -blest.** *adj.* **1.** of high and titled rank. **2.** having or revealing a fine character. **3.** of high quality. —*n.* **4.** person of noble rank. —**no'bly**, *adv.* —**no·bil'i·ty**, *n.* —**no'ble·man**, *n.*

nō'bŏd·ỹ, *pron., n., pl.* **-ies.** *pron.* **1.** no person. —*n.* **2.** unimportant person.

nŏc·tûr'nàl, *adj.* pertaining to night.

nŏc'tûrne, *n.* musical composition to be heard at night.

nŏd, *v.i.,* **nodded, nodding**, *n. v.i.* **1.** give a quick forward motion of the head, esp. meaning affirmation. —*n.* **2.** act or instance of nodding.

nōde, *n.* **1.** swelling. **2.** focal point. —**nod'al**, *adj.*

nŏg'gĭn, *n.* **1.** small cup. **2.** a person's head.

nŏise, *n.* loud sound. —**noise'less**, *adj.* —**nois'y**, *adj.* —**nois'i·ly**, *adv.*

nŏī'sŏme, *adj.* smelly.

nō'măd, *n.* wanderer. —**no·mad'ic**, *adj.*

nŏm dė plūme, author's assumed name.

nō'mĕn·clā''tûre, *n.* system of names, terms, or symbols.

nŏm'ĭn·àl, *adj.* **1.** in name only. **2.** trifling in amount.

nŏm'ĭ·nāte'', *v.t.,* **-nated, -nating. 1.** appoint. **2.** propose for election. —**nom''i·nee'**, *n.*

nŏm'ĭ·nà·tĭve, *n. Grammar.* case of a verb subject.

nŏn-, prefix meaning "not." **nonalcoholic, nonassignable, nonattendance, nonbeliever, nonbreakable, nonburnable, noncombatant, noncombustible, noncommunicable, noncompetitive, noncompliance, nonconducting, nonconductor, non-**

conforming, nonconformist, nonconformity, nondeductible, nonessential, nonexclusive, nonexempt, nonexistence, nonexistent, nonfactual, nonfiction, nonflammable, nonhazardous, nonhereditary, nonhuman, noninclusive, noninterference, nonintervention, nonintoxicating, nonirritating, nonliterary, nonmilitary, nonobjective, nonobligatory, nonobservance, nonpartisan, nonpayment, nonperishable, nonpolitical, nonproductive, nonprofessional, nonracial, nonreciprocal, nonreligious, nonresident, nonresidential, nonresistant, nonreturnable, nonscientific, nonseasonal, nonsectarian, nonsmoker, nonspiritual, nonstandard, nonstop, nonstructural, nonsupport, nontaxable, nontoxic, nontransferable, nonuser, nonviolent, nonvoter, nonvoting.

nŏn'ȧge, *n*. minority; non-adulthood.

nŏn''ȧ·gė·nār'ĭ·ȧn, *n*. person in his or her nineties.

nŏnce, *n*. time being.

nŏn''chȧ·länt', *adj*. casual in manner. —non''cha·lance', *n*.

nŏn''cŏm·mĭs'sioned ŏffĭcêr, military or naval officer with no commission, e.g. a sergeant or petty officer.

nŏn''cŏm·mĭt'tȧl, *adj*. not committing oneself.

nŏn' cŏm'pós mĕn'tĭs, of unsound mind.

nŏn''dė·scrĭpt', *adj*. not to be described precisely.

nóne, *pron*. 1. not one or any. —*n*. 2. not any amount. —*adv*. 3. by no means.

nŏn·ĕn'tĭ·tỹ, *n*., *pl*. -ties. very unimportant person or thing.

nóne''thė·lĕss', *adv*. nevertheless.

nŏn'plŭs', *v.t.*, -plused, -plusing. baffle into inaction.

nŏn·prŏf'ĭt, *adj*. not established for profit.

nŏn'sĕnse, *n*. meaningless talk or action. —non·sen'si·cal, *adj*.

nŏn·sė'quĭ·tûr, illogical continuation of something previously said.

noo'dle, *n*. strip of dough.

nook, *n*. semi-enclosed place.

noon, *n*. twelve o'clock in the daytime.

nō one, nobody.

noose, *n*. loop made with a knot.

nôr, *conj*. and not; and yet not.

nôrm, *n*. something generally expected.

nôr'mȧl, *adj*. 1. conforming to a norm. 2. average. —nor·mal'i·ty, *n*. —nor'mal·ize'', *v.t.*

nôrm'ȧ·tĭve, *adj*. establishing a norm.

nôrth, *n*. 1. direction of the north pole. 2. region lying northward. —*adv*. 3. toward or in the north. —north'ern, *adj*. —north'ern·er, *n*. —north'er·ly, *adj*. —north'ward, *adj.*, *adv*. —north'wards, *adv*.

nôrth''ēast', *n*. 1. direction halfway between north and east. 2. region lying northeastward. —*adj.*, *adv*. 3. toward or in the northeast. —north''east'ern, *adj*. —north''east·ern·er, *n*.

nôrth''wĕst', *n*. 1. direction halfway between north and west. 2. region lying northwestward. —*adj.*, *adv*. 3. toward or in the northwest. —north''west'ern, *adj*. —north''west'ern·er, *n*.

nōse, *n.*, *v.*, nosed, nosing. *n*. 1. part of the head with nostrils. 2. noselike features. —*v.t.* 3. nuzzle. —*v.i.* 4. sniff. 5. advance. —nose'bleed'', *n*.

nōse dīve, *n*. headlong plunge. —nose'dive'', *v.i.*

nōse'gāy'', *n*. small bouquet.

nŏs·tăl'giȧ, *n*. sentiment over the bygone or remote. —nos·tal'gic, *adj*.

nŏs'trĭl, *n*. one of the openings in the nose for breathing.

nŏs'trŭm, proprietary medicine.

nŏs'ỹ, *adj.*, -ier, -iest. *Informal*. inquisitive. Also, nos'ey.

nŏt, *adv*. in no way.

nō'tȧ·ble, *adj*. remarkable.

nō'tȧ·rỹ, *n.*, *pl*. -ries. official who certifies documents. Also, **notary public.** —no'ta·rize'', *v.t.*

nō·tā'tion, *n*. 1. symbol or system of symbols. 2. brief note.

nŏtch, *n*. 1. shallow knife cut. —*v.t.* 2. make such cuts in.

nōte, *n.*, *v.t.*, noted, noting. *n*. 1. short message. 2. reminder of something. 3. sound. 4. notice. 5. distinction. 6. feeling; air. —*v.t.* 7. observe. 8. make a note of. —note'book'', *n*. —note'wor''thy, *adj*.

nōt'ėd, *adj*. well-known.

nŏth'ĭng, *n*. 1. not any thing. 2. something non-existent. 3. something insignificant. —*adv.* **4.** in no way. —**noth'ing·ness,** *n.*

no'tice, *v.t.,* **-ticed, -ticing,** *n. v.t.* **1.** be aware of. —*n.* **2.** awareness. **3.** announcement or warning. —**no'tice·a·ble,** *adj.*

no'ti·fy'', *v.t.,* **-fied, -fying.** give notice to.

no'tion, *n.* **1.** idea. **2.** vague opinion. **3.** whim. **4. notions,** minor but useful merchandise. —**no'tion·al,** *adj.*

no·to'ri·ous, *adj.* unfavorably well-known. —**no''to·ri'e·ty,** *n.*

not''with·stand'ing, *adv.* **1.** nevertheless. —*prep.* **2.** in spite of. —*conj.* **3.** although.

nou'gat, *n.* soft candy with nuts.

noun, *n.* name of a person, place, or thing.

nour'ish, *v.t.* feed. —**nour'ish·ment,** *n.*

nou'veau riche (nū'vō rēsh), *n. French.* person recently acquiring large sums of money.

nov'el, *adj.* **1.** new; unprecedented. —*n.* **2.** long written story. —**nov'el·ty,** *n.* —**nov''el·ette',** *n.* —**nov'el·ist,** *n.*

No·vem'ber, *n.* eleventh month.

nov'ice, *n.* **1.** monk or nun in a religious house who has not yet taken the vow. **2.** beginner. —**no·vi'ti·ate,** *n.*

now, *adj.* **1.** at present. **2.** at some past or future moment. **3.** as matters are. —*conj.* **4.** inasmuch. —*n.* **5.** present moment.

now'a·days'', *adv.* at present.

no'where'', *adv.* not in any place.

nox'ious, *adj.* harmful.

noz'zle, *n.* pouring end of a pipe, etc.

nth, *adj.* concluding an unspecified number or amount.

nu'ance, *n.* slight variation in meaning, etc.

nu'bile, *adj.* mature enough to take a spouse.

nu'cle·ar, *adj.* **1.** forming a nucleus. **2.** pertaining to atomic nuclei.

nu'cle·us, *n., pl.* **-clei, -cleuses. 1.** core. **2.** center of growth or development. **3.** center of an atom.

nude, *adj.* **1.** naked. —*n.* **2.** state of nakedness. —**nu'di·ty,** *n.*

nudge, *v.t.,* **nudged, nudging,** *n. v.t.* **1.** jab with the elbow. **2.** hint to sharply. —*n.* **3.** act or instance of nudging.

nud'ism, *n.* practice of nudity. —**nud'ist,** *n., adj.*

nu'ga·tô''ry, *adj.* **1.** worthless. **2.** invalid.

nug'get, *n.* lump of natural gold.

nui'sance, *n.* source of annoyance.

null, *adj.* **null and void,** invalid; without force.

nul'li·fy'', *v.t.,* **-fied, -fying.** invalidate.

numb, *adj.* **1.** without feeling. —*v.t.* **2.** make numb.

num'ber, *n.* **1.** expression of quantity or order. **2.** quantity or order. **3.** item on a program of entertainment. —*v.t.* **4.** establish the number of. **5.** include in a group. —**num'ber·less,** *adj.*

numb'skull'', *n. Informal.* stupid person. Also, **num'skull''.**

nu'mer·al, *n.* symbol for a number.

nu'mer·a''tor, *n.* expression of the number of parts in a fraction.

nu·mer'i·cal, *adj.* pertaining to or expressed in numbers.

nu''mer·ol'o·gy, *n.* study of occult meanings in numbers.

nu'mer·ous, *adj.* in large numbers.

nu''mis·mat'ics, *n.* study of money and medals. —**nu·mis'ma·tist,** *n.*

nun, *n.* female member of a religious order. —**nun'ner·y,** *n.*

nup'tial, *adj.* **1.** pertaining to marriage. —*n.* **2. nuptials,** wedding.

nurse, *n., v.t.,* **nursed, nursing.** *n.* **1.** attendant of the sick. **2.** attendant of children. —*v.t.* **3.** suckle. **4.** tend in illness. **5.** conserve or foster.

nurse'maid'', *n.* children's nurse.

nurs'er·y, *n., pl.* **-ies. 1.** day room for children. **2.** place for the care of children. **3.** place for raising plants. —**nurs'er·y·man,** *n.*

nur'ture, *v.t.,* **-tured, -turing,** *n. v.t.* **1.** nourish. **2.** raise, as a child. —*n.* **3.** food. **4.** upbringing.

nut, *n.* **1.** dry seed in a woody husk. **2.** threaded block used with a bolt. **3.** *Informal.* insane person. —*adj.* **4. nuts,** *Informal.* crazy. —*interj.* **5. nuts,** bah! —**nut'crack''er,** *n.* —**nut'meat'',** *n.* —**nut'shell'',** *n.* —**nut'ty,** *adj.*

nut'meg'', *n.* East Indian spice.

nu'tri·ent, *adj.* **1.** nourishing. —*n.* **2.** Also, **nu'tri·ment,** nourishment.

nu·tri'tion, *n.* **1.** assimilation of food. **2.**

food. —nu·tri'tion·al, *adj*. —nu'tri·
tive, *adv*. —nu·tri'tious, *adj*.

nŭz'zle, *v*., -zled, -zling. *v.t*., *v.i*. rub
with the nose.

nȳ'lŏn, *n*. synthetic material.

nȳmph, *n*. classical nature goddess.

nȳm''phō·mā'nĭ·à, *n*. uncontrollable
sexual desire in women. —nym''pho·
ma'ni·ac'', *n*., *adj*.

O

Ō, o, *n*. fifteenth letter of the English alphabet.

ōaf, *n*. clumsy person. —oaf'ish, *adj*.

ōak, *n*. acorn-bearing hardwood tree.
—oak'en, *adj*.

ōar, *n*. bladed lever for rowing. —oars'
man, *n*. —oar'lock'', *n*.

ō·ā'sĭs, *n*., *pl*. -ses. **1**. place in the desert
with water. **2**. refuge.

ōat, *n*. cereal grass. —oat'meal', *n*.

ōath, *n*., *pl*. oaths. **1**. vow in the name of
a god. **2**. blasphemous remark.

ŏb·dū'ràte, *adj*. stubborn. —ob'du·ra·
cy, *n*.

ō·bēi'sànce, *n*. bow.

ŏb'è·lĭsk, *n*. tapered monument.

ō·bēse', *adj*. very fat. —o·bes'i·ty, *n*.

ō·bey', *v.i*. **1**. do as told. —*v.t*. **2**. perform
as told. **3**. perform the orders of. —o·
be'di·ent, *adj*. —o·be'di·ence, *n*.

ŏb'fŭs·cāte'', *v.t*., -cated, -cating. obscure or confuse.

ō·bĭt'ū·ār''ȳ, *n*., *pl*. -ies. death notice.

ŏb'jĕct, *n*. **1**. something tangible. **2**.
something acted toward or aimed for. **3**.
matter for consideration. —*v.i*. (ob
jekt') **4**. protest. —ob·jec'tion, *n*.
—ob·jec'tion·a·ble, *adj*. —ob·jec'
tion·a·bly, *adv*. —ob·jec'tor, *n*.

ŏb·jĕc'tĭve, *adj*. **1**. in the world outside
the mind. **2**. concerned with reality,
rather than thought or emotion. —ob''
jec·tiv'i·ty, *n*.

ŏb'jūr·gāte'', *v.t*., -gated, -gating. rebuke. —ob·jur'ga·to''ry, *adj*.

ŏb'lĭ·gāte'', *v.t*., -gated, -gating. bind
with a duty. —ob·lig'a·to''ry, *adj*.

ò·blīge', *v.t*., -bliged, -bliging. **1**. force.
2. put in one's debt.

ò·blīg'ĭng, *adj*. ready to do favors. —o·
blig'ing·ly, *adv*.

ŏb·līque', *adj*. **1**. slanting. **2**. indirect.
—ob·liq'ui·ty, ob·lique'ness, *n*.

ŏb·lĭt'êr·āte'', *v.t*., -ated, -ating. efface.

ŏb·lĭv'ĭ·òn, *n*. **1**. forgetfulness. **2**. unre-
membered past. —ob·liv'i·ous, *adj*.

ŏb'lŏng, *adj*. **1**. longer than broad. —*n*.
2. oblong figure, esp. a rectangle.

ŏb'lò·quȳ, *n*., *pl*. -quies. **1**. censure. **2**.
infamy.

ŏb·nŏx'ioŭs, *adj*. offensive.

ō'bōe, *n*. low-pitched musical reed instrument. —o'bo·ist, *n*.

ŏb·scēne', *adj*. offensive to decency.
—ob·scen'i·ty, *n*.

ŏb·scûre', *adj*., *v.t*., -scured, -scuring.
adj. **1**. indefinite. **2**. dark. **3**. little-
known. —*v.t*. **4**. make obscure. —ob·
scur'i·ty, *n*. —ob''scu·ra'tion, *n*.

ŏb'sè·quies, *n*. *pl*. funeral ceremonies.

ŏb·sē'quì·oŭs, *adj*. fawningly servile.

ŏb·sêrv'à·tô''rȳ, *n*., *pl*. -ries. place for
observing heavenly bodies.

ŏb·sêrve', *v.t*., -served, -serving. **1**.
study with the eye. **2**. notice. **3**. remark.
4. obey or respect. —ob·serv'ance, *n*.
—ob·serv'ant, *adj*. —ob''ser·va'
tion, *n*. —ob·serv'er, *n*.

ŏb·sĕss', *v.t*. preoccupy constantly. —ob·
ses'sive, *adj*. —ob''ses'sion, *n*.

ŏb''sò·lĕs'cènt, *adj*. going out of date.
—ob''so·les'cence, *n*. —ob·so·lesce',
v.i.

ŏb''sò·lēte', *adj*. out of date.

ŏb'stà·cle, *n*. something hindering advance.

ŏb·stĕt'rĭcs, *n*. branch of medicine for
pregnancy and childbirth. —ob·stet'
ric, ob·stet'ri·cal, *adj*. —ob''ste·tri'
cian, *n*.

ŏb'stĭ·nàte, *adj*. stubborn. —ob'sti·na·
cy, *n*.

ŏb·strĕp'êr·oŭs, *adj*. rowdy.

ŏb·strŭct', *v.t*. **1**. hinder; thwart. **2**.
block. —ob·struc'tion, *n*. —ob·struc'
tion·ism, *n*. —ob·struc'tion·ist, *n*.,
adj. —ob·struc'tive, *adj*.

ŏb·tāin', *v.t*. **1**. get. —*v.i*. **2**. be in effect.
—ob·tain'ment, *n*.

ŏb·trūde', *v*., -truded, -truding. *v.t*. **1**.
force on others. —*v.i*. **2**. obtrude oneself. —ob·tru'sion, *n*. —ob·tru'sive,
adj.

ŏb·tūse', *adj.* **1.** blunt, as an angle. **2.** slow to understand.

ŏb·vêrse', *adj.* **1.** toward an observer. **2.** being a counterpart. —*n.* **3.** counterpart.

ŏb'vĭ·āte'', *v.t.* -ated, -ating. avoid by alternatives.

ŏb'vĭ·oŭs, *adj.* perceived or understood without effort.

oc·cā'sion, *n.* **1.** specific time or event. **2.** opportunity. **3.** reason; pretext. —*v.t.* **4.** bring about.

oc·cā'sion·ȧl, *adj.* occurring now and then.

Ŏc'cĭ·dĕnt, *n.* Europe and the Americas. —Oc''ci·den'tal, *adj.*

oc·cŭlt', *adj.* **1.** hidden from ordinary persons. **2.** mystical. —oc·cult'ism, *n.*

ŏc''cū·pā'tion, *n.* **1.** type of work. **2.** act or instance of occupying.

ŏc'cū·py'', *v.t.,* -pied, -pying. **1.** be in. **2.** be engaged in or concerned with. **3.** take possession of, as by capture. —oc'cu·pan·cy, *n.* —oc'cu·pant, *n.*

oc·cûr', *v.i.,* -curred, -curring. **1.** happen. **2.** come to mind. —oc·cur'rence, *n.*

ō'cêan, *n.* vast body of salt water. —o·ce·an'ic, *adj.*

ō''cêan·ŏg'rȧ·phў, *n.* study of the ocean.

ō'cê·lŏt'', *n.* American wildcat.

ō'chêr, *n.* yellow or reddish-brown clay used as pigment. Also, o'chre.

o'clŏck', *adv.* by the clock.

ŏc'tȧ·gŏn, *n.* eight-sided plane figure. —oc·tag'o·nal, *adj.*

ŏc''tȧ·hē'drŏn, *n.* eight-sided solid.

ŏc'tȧve, *n.* **1.** *Music.* group including eight full tones. **2.** *Poetry.* unit of eight lines.

ŏc·tĕt', *n.* group of eight musicians. Also, oc·tette'.

Ŏc·tō'bêr, *n.* tenth month.

ŏc''tȯ·gė·nār'ĭ·ȧn, *n.* person in his or her eighties.

ŏc'tȯ·pŭs, *n., pl.* -puses, -pi. soft mollusk with eight arms.

ŏc'ū·lȧr, *adj.* pertaining to the eyes.

ŏc'ū·list, *n.* ophthalmologist.

ŏdd, *adj.* **1.** not evenly divisible by two. **2.** peculiar. **3.** occasional. **4.** remaining. —*n.* **5.** odds, factors for or against. —odd'i·ty, *n.*

ŏdds ănd ĕnds, miscellaneous things.

ōde, *n.* poem of praise.

ō'dĭ·oŭs, *adj.* hateful.

ō'dĭ·ŭm, *n.* hatred or disgrace.

ō'dȯr, *n.* smell. —o'dor·ous, *adj.* —o'dor·less, *adj.*

ō''dȯr·ĭf'êr·oŭs, *adj.* giving off an odor.

ȯf, *prep.* **1.** coming from or produced by. **2.** belonging to. **3.** owning. **4.** regarding. **5.** specified as.

ȯff, *prep.* **1.** away or up from. **2.** with sustenance from. —*adv.* **3.** away or up. **4.** so as not to work or be in effect. —*adj.* **5.** not working or in effect. **6.** on one's way. **7.** not right.

ȯf'fȧl, *n.* garbage.

ȯff'-cȯl'ȯr, *adj.* risqué.

ȯf·fĕnd', *v.i.* **1.** commit an offense. —*v.t.* **2.** annoy or wound. **3.** displease.

ȯf·fĕnse', *adj.* **1.** unlawful act. **2.** resentment or hurt. **3.** cause of this. **4.** attack. Also, of·fence'.

ȯf·fĕn'sĭve, *adj.* **1.** tending to offend. **2.** attacking. —*n.* **3.** attacker's status.

ȯf'fêr, *v.t.* **1.** present, as for acceptance or consideration. **2.** shown signs of. —*v.i.* **3.** present itself. —*n.* **4.** act or instance of offering. —of'fer·ing, *n.*

ȯff'hănd', *adv.* **1.** unprepared. —*adj.* **2.** Also, off'hand'ed, casual.

ȯf'fĭce, *n.* **1.** position of authority. **2.** Often offices, work done for another. **3.** place for commercial or government work.

ȯf'fĭ·cêr, *n.* **1.** holder of a position of authority. **2.** policeman.

ȯf·fĭ'cĭȧl, *adj.* **1.** pertaining to or coming from supreme authority. —*n.* **2.** person in public office. —of·fi'cial·dom, *n.*

ȯf·fĭ'cĭ·āte'', *v.i.,* -ated, -ating. perform official or ceremonial duties.

ȯf·fĭ'cĭoŭs, *adj.* giving unwanted help or orders.

ȯf'fĭng, *n.* distance.

ȯff'-lĭm'ĭts, *adj.* Military. not to be entered.

ȯff'-līne', *n.* not connected to a network or system.

ȯff'-rōad', *adj.* designed to be used in rough terrain, as in *off-road vehicle*.

ȯff'sĕt'', *v.t.,* -set, -setting. compensate for.

ȯff'shōot'', *n.* thing derived from a major source.

ŏff'shōre', *adj.*, *adv.* away from the shore.

ôff'sprĭng'', *n.*, *pl.* -spring, -springs. young of a human or animal.

ôff'-whīte', *n.* white tinted with grey or yellow.

ôf'tĕn, *adv.* many times.

ō'grê, *n.* man-eating giant. Also, *fem.*, **o'gress. —o'gre·ish**, *adj.*

ōh, *interj.* exclamation of surprise, etc.

ōhm, *n. Electricity.* unit of resistance.

ō·hō', *interj.* (exclamation of surprise or triumph).

ŏil, *n.* **1.** any of various combustible liquids. **2.** paint with an oil vehicle. —*v.t.* **3.** lubricate with oil. —**oil'y**, *adj.* —**oil' i·ness**, *n.*

ŏil'clŏth'', *n.* cloth treated to be waterproof.

ŏint'mĕnt, *n.* fatty salve.

O.K. or **ōkāy**, *interj.*, *adj.*, *adv.*, *v.t.*, **O.K.'d, O.K.'ing.** *interj.*, *adj.*, *adv.* **1.** all right. —*v.t.* **2.** approve.

ō'krà, *n.* plant with edible pods.

ōld, *adj.*, **older** or **elder, oldest** or **eldest. 1.** long in existence. **2.** experienced. **3.** longer in existence than another. **4.** former.

ōld'-făsh'iŏned, *adj.* **1.** obsolete. **2.** favoring older manners, etc. —*n.* **3.** whiskey cocktail.

ōld māid, mature, virginal woman.

ōld schōol, *n.* conservatives collectively. —**old'-school'**, *adj.*

ōld'-tīm'êr, *n. Informal.* **1.** old man. **2.** long-time incumbent.

Ōld Wörld, Europe, Asia, and Africa. —**Old'-World', old'-world'**, *adj.*

ō''lē·ō·mâr'gà·rĭne, *n.* margarine. Also, **o''le·o·mar'ga·rin.**

ŏl·făc'tò·rȳ, *adj.* pertaining to smell.

ŏl'ĭ·gârch''ȳ, *n.*, *pl.* -ies. government by a few. —**ol''i·garch'ic**, *adj.* —**oli·garch**, *n.*

ŏl'ĭve, *n.* fruit of a Mediterranean tree.

ŏm·bŭds'màn, *n.*, *pl.* -men. investigator of citizen's complaints.

ŏm'elĕt, *n.* fried pancake of beaten eggs. Also, **om'elette.**

ō'mĕn, *n.* sign of the future.

ŏm'ĭ·noŭs, *adj.* threatening.

ō·mĭt', *v.t.*, **-mitted, -mitting. 1.** leave out. **2.** forget; neglect. —**o·mis'sion**, *n.*

ŏm'nĭ·bŭs, *n.* **1.** bus. **2.** complete anthology.

ŏm·nĭp'ò·tĕnt, *adj.* all-powerful. —**om· nip'o·tence**, *n.*

ŏm''nĭ·prĕs'ĕnt, *adj.* present everywhere at once. —**om''ni·pres'ence**, *n.*

ŏm·nĭs'ciĕnt, *adj.* knowing everything. —**om·nis'cience**, *n.*

ŏm·nĭv'ò·roŭs, *adj.* consuming anything.

ŏn, *prep.* **1.** supported by. **2.** down against. **3.** regarding. **4.** with the help or sustenance of. **5.** at the time of. **6.** engaged in. **7.** being part of. —*adv.* **8.** onto oneself or something else. **9.** further; forward. **10.** into operation. —*adj.* **11.** in operation or effect.

once (wuns), *adv.* **1.** one time. **2.** formerly. **3.** at any time. —*conj.* **4.** when.

ŏn'cŏm''ĭng, *adj.* approaching.

one (wun), *n.* **1.** lowest whole cardinal number. **2.** person. —*adj.* **3.** being one in number. **4.** identical. **5.** united. —*pron.* **6.** one person or thing.

ŏn'êr·oŭs, *adj.* burdensome.

one·sĕlf', *pron.* **1.** person's own self. **2.** person's true self. Also, **one's self.**

one'-sīd'ĕd, *adj.* **1.** involving only one side. **2.** with all advantages on one side. **3.** prejudiced.

ŏn'gō''ĭng, *adj.* in progress.

ŏn'iŏn, *n.* edible bulb of the lily family.

ŏn'-līne', *n.* connected to a network or system.

ŏn'lōok''êr, *n.* spectator.

ōn'lȳ, *adj.* **1.** single; sole. —*adv.* **2.** solely. **3.** at last, however. **4.** as lately as.

on·o·mat·o·poe·ia (ahn''ə mat''ə pē'ə), *n.* coining of a word imitating a sound.

ŏn'sĕt'', *n.* attack.

ŏn'slaught'', *n.* vigorous attack.

ŏn'to, *prep.* into a position on.

ō'nŭs, *n.* **1.** burden. **2.** blame.

ŏn'wàrd, *adv.* **1.** Also, **on'wards, forward. —*adj.* **2.** forward.

ŏn'ȳx, *n.* striped agate.

ōō'dles, *n. pl. Informal.* vast amounts.

ōōze, *v.* **oozed, oozing,** *n. v.i.* **1.** flow slowly. —*v.t.* **2.** emit slowly. —*n.* **3.** slime. —**ooz'y**, *adj.*

ō'pàl, *n.* gem of multicolored silica. —**o''pal·es'cent**, *adj.*

ō·pāque', *adj.* **1.** passing no light. **2.** obscure. —**o'paque'ness, o·pac'i·ty**, *n.*

ō′pĕn, *adj.* **1.** able to be entered, seen through, etc. **2.** with the inside revealed. **3.** available or accessible. **4.** candid. —*v.t.* **5.** make open. —*v.i.* **6.** become open. —*v.t., v.i.* **7.** start. —*n.* **8.** open or unconcealed place or state.

ō′pĕn-āir′, *adj.* outdoor.

ō′pĕn-ĕnd′ĕd, *adj.* unrestricted.

ō′pĕn-hănd′ĕd, *adj.* generous.

ō′pĕn-ĭng, *n.* **1.** perforation. **2.** beginning. **3.** opportunity.

ŏp′ĕr·à, *n.* musical drama. —op′′er·at′ ic, *adj.*

ŏp′ĕr·à·ble, *adj.* **1.** treatable by surgery. **2.** able to be operated.

ŏp′ĕr·āte′′, *v.*, -ated, -ating. *v.t.* **1.** cause to function. **2.** control; manage. —*v.i.* **3.** function; act. **4.** perform surgery. —op′′er·a′tion, *n.* —op′′er·a′ tion·al, *adj.* —op′er·a′′tor, *n.*

ŏp′ĕr·à·tĭve, *adj.* **1.** pertaining to operations. **2.** able to operate. —*n.* **3.** detective.

ŏp′ĕr·ā′′tör, *n.* **1.** person who operates something, as telephone equipment. **2.** *Informal.* person living by his wits.

ŏp′′ĕr·ĕt′tà, *n.* light opera.

ŏphth′′ăl·mŏl′ō·gy̆, *n.* branch of medicine concerning the eye. —ophth′′al mo·log′i·cal, *adj.* —ophth′′al·mol′o· gist, *n.*

ō′pĭ·āte, *n.* opium-based drug.

ò·pĭn′ion, *n.* **1.** personal belief. **2.** personal evaluation.

ò·pĭn′ion·āt′′ĕd, *adj.* stubborn in one's opinions.

ō′pĭ·ŭm, *n.* drug derived from poppies.

ò·pŏs′sŭm, *n.* small tree-dwelling marsupial.

òp·pō′nĕnt, *n.* adversary.

ŏp′′pör·tūne′, *adj.* occurring when useful.

ŏp′′pör·tūn′ĭsm, *n.* unprincipled advantage-taking.

ŏp′′pör·tūn′ĭ·ty̆, *n.*, *pl.* -ties. favorable occasion.

òp·pōse′, *v.t.*, -posed, -posing. **1.** resist; fight. **2.** be in contrast with. —op′′po· si′tion, *n.*

ŏp′pò·sĭte, *adj.* **1.** in the other direction from somewhere between. **2.** totally different in nature. —*n.* **3.** something opposite.

òp·prĕss′, *v.t.* **1.** bully or exploit. **2.** worry or make uncomfortable. —op·

pres′sion, *n.* —op·pres′sor, *n.* —op· pres′sive, *adj.*

òp·prō′brĭ·ŭm, *n.* scorn; shame. —op· pro′bri·ous, *adj.*

ŏpt, *v.i.* make a choice.

ŏp′tĭc, *adj.* pertaining to sight.

ŏp′tĭ·căl, *adj.* **1.** visual. **2.** pertaining to optics.

ŏp′tĭ′cian, *n.* dealer in aids to eyesight.

ŏp′tĭcs, *n.* study of light and vision.

ōp′tĭ·mĭsm, *n.* readiness to see or predict the best. —op′ti·mist, *n.* —op′′ti· mis′tic, *adj.*

ŏp′tĭ·mŭm, *adj.* **1.** best, esp. in amount, etc. —*n.* **2.** optimum amount, etc.

ŏp′tion, *n.* **1.** choice. **2.** right to buy or not to buy something. —op′tion·al, *adj.*

ŏp·tŏm′è·trÿ, *n.* profession of testing and prescribing for eye conditions. —op· tom′e·trist, *n.*

ŏp′ū·lĕnt, *adj.* **1.** rich. **2.** lavish. —op′u· lence, *n.*

ō′pŭs, *n.*, *pl.* -pera, -puses. work of an artist, musician, etc., esp. when numbered.

ôr, *conj.* **1.** (indicating alternatives). **2.** (indicating synonyms).

ôr′à·cle, *n.* **1.** medium for consulting a god. **2.** great authority. —o·rac′u·lar, *adj.*

ô′răl, *adj.* **1.** pertaining to the mouth. **2.** spoken.

ôr′ange, *n.* **1.** mixture of red and yellow. **2.** fruit of this color. —or′ange·ade′, *n.*

ò·răng′ū·tăn′′, *n.* manlike ape of Indonesia. Also, o·rang′u·tang′′.

ô·rā′tion, *n.* formal speech. —o·rate′, *v.i.* —o′ra·tor, *n.*

ôr′′à·tô′′rĭ·ō′′, *n.*, *pl.* -os. play sung but not acted.

ôr′à·tô′′rÿ, *n.*, *pl.* -ies. **1.** public speaking. **2.** small chapel. —or′′a·tor′i·cal, *adj.*

ôrb, *n.* **1.** heavenly body. **2.** spherical object.

ôr′bĭt, *n.* **1.** path of a heavenly body. —*v.i.* **2.** be in orbit. —or′bit·al, *adj.*

ôr′chàrd, *n.* grove of fruit trees.

ôr′chès·trà, *n.* **1.** large, varied musical group. **2.** main floor in an auditorium. —or·ches′tral, *adj.*

ôr′chès·trāte′′, *v.t.*, -trated, -trating. arrange for orchestra.

ôr′chĭd, *n*. tropical flowering plant.

ôr·dāin′, *v.t.* **1.** decree; establish. **2.** grant the office of clergyman to. —or·′dain′ment, or′′di·na′tion, *n*.

ôr·dēal′, *n*. severe trial.

ôr′dêr, *n*. **1.** proper or meaningful condition. **2.** command. **3.** request to purchase. **4.** religious group. —*v.t.* **5.** make an order for. **6.** put in order.

ôr′dêr·lȳ, *adj., n., pl.* -lies. *adj.* **1.** in order. **2.** quiet in behavior. —*n*. **3.** attendant.

ôr′dĭ·nâl, *adj.* **1.** pertaining to a meaningful series. —*n*. **2.** ordinal number.

ôr′dĭ·nânce, *n*. law.

ôr′dĭ·nār′′ȳ, *adj.* **1.** usual, customary. —*n*. **2.** customary experience.

ôrd′nânce, *n*. military weapons.

ôre, *n*. metal-bearing mineral.

ô·rĕg′à·nō, *n*. fragrant-leafed plant.

ôr′gàn, *n*. **1.** body part performing a specific function. **2.** keyboard, wind, or electronic instrument. **3.** institutional periodical. —or′gan·ist, *n*.

ôr·găn′ĭc, *adj.* **1.** pertaining to or suggesting organisms. **2.** pertaining to bodily organs. **3.** containing carbon.

ôr′gàn·ĭsm, *n*. living thing.

ôr′gàn·īze′′, *v.*, -ized, -izing. *v.t., v.i.* **1.** join in a coordinated group. —*v.t.* **2.** coordinate the functioning of. **3.** arrange for. **4.** cause to join a group. —or′′gan·i·za′tion, *n*. —or′′gan·i·za′tion·al, *adj.*

ôr′găsm, *n*. climax of a sex act.

or·gy (or′jē), *n., pl.* -gies. wild revelry.

ô′rī·ênt, *v.i.* **1.** establish one's location or course. —*v.t.* **2.** establish the location or course of. **3.** initiate in fundamentals. **4.** face in a certain direction. —*n*. **5.** the Orient, Asia. —o′′ri·en·ta′tion, *n*. —O′′ri·en′tal, *adj., n*.

ôr′ī·fīce, *n*. opening.

ôr′ĭ·gĭn, *n*. **1.** commencement. **2.** source.

o·rĭg′ĭ·nâl, *adj.* **1.** earliest. **2.** copied to make others. **3.** never before seen. **4.** creative. —*n*. **5.** authentic. —o·rig′′i·nal′i·ty, *n*. —o·rig′i·nate′′, *v.t., v.i.* —o·rig′i·na′′tor, *n*.

ô′rī·ole′′, *n*. black and orange bird.

or·na·ment, *n*. (or′nə ment) **1.** decoration. —*v.t.* (or′nə ment′′) **2.** decorate. —or′′na·men′tal, *adj.* —or′′na·men·ta′tion, *n*.

ôr·nāte′, *adj.* greatly ornamented.

ôr′nêr·ȳ, *adj. Dialect.* mean or stubborn. —or′ner·i·ness, *n*.

ôr′′nĭ·thŏl′ó·gȳ, *n*. study of birds. —or′′ni·thol′o·gist, *n*. —or′′ni·tho·log′i·cal, *adj.*

ô′rò·tŭnd′′, *adj.* with resonant, often pompous, speech.

ôr′phàn, *n*. **1.** child of dead parents. —*v.t.* **2.** kill the parents of.

ôr′phàn·àge, *n*. home for orphans.

ôr′′thò·dŏn′tĭcs, *n*. branch of dentistry that corrects irregular teeth. —or′′tho·don′tist, *n*.

ôr′thò·dŏx′′, *adj.* **1.** conforming to standard doctrine. **2.** Orthodox, pertaining to an east European or Near Eastern church. —or′tho·dox′′y, *n*.

ôr·thŏg′rà·phȳ, *n., pl.* -phies. spelling. —or′′tho·graph′ic, *adj.*

ôr′′thò·pē′dĭcs, *n*. surgery of bones and joints. —or′′tho·pe′dic, *adj.* —or′′tho·pe′dist, *n*.

ŏs′cĭl·lāte′′, *v.* -lated, -lating. *v.t., v.i.* swing back and forth.

ŏs′cū·lāte′′, *v.*, -lated, -lating. *v.i., v.t.* kiss.

ŏs·mō′sĭs, *n*. passage of fluids through membranes. —os·mot′ic, *adj.*

ŏs′sē·oŭs, *adj.* bony.

ŏs′sĭ·fȳ′′, *v.*, -fied, -fying. *v.t., v.i.* **1.** turn to bone. **2.** turn inadaptable, as a custom.

ŏs·tĕn′sĭ·ble, *adj.* seeming.

ŏs′′tĕn·tā′tion, *n*. great and deliberate display. —os′′ten·ta′tious, *adj.*

ŏs′′tē·ŏp′à·thȳ, *n*. school of medicine emphasizing bones and muscles. —os′′te·o·path′ic, *adj.* —os′te·o·path′′, *n*.

ŏs′trà·cīze′′, *v.t.*, -cized, -cizing. expel; exclude. —os′tra·cism, *n*.

ŏs′trĭch, *n*. running, flightless bird of Africa and the Near East.

óth′êr, *adj.* **1.** not yet mentioned. **2.** additional; remaining. —*pron.* **3.** other one. —*adv.* **4.** otherwise.

óth′êr·wīse′′, *adv.* **1.** in a different way. **2.** in other respects. **3.** under other conditions.

ō′tĭ·ōse′, *adj.* idle; useless.

ŏt′têr, *n*. furred swimming mammal.

ŏt′tò·màn, *n*. upholstered footstool.

oŭch, *interj.* exclamation of pain.

oŭght, *aux. v.* **1.** am, is, or are obligated. **2.** will very probably.

ouï, *adv. French*. yes.

ounce, *n*. **1**. sixteenth of an avoirdupois pound or twelfth of a troy pound. **2**. thirty-second of a liquid quart.

our, *adj*. pertaining to us.

ours, *pron*. our own.

our·selves', *pron*. **1**. (intensive or reflexive of *we*). **2**. our true selves.

oust, *v.t.* expel.

oust'êr, *n*. act or instance of ousting.

out, *adv*. **1**. away from inside. **2**. away from existence, action, etc. **3**. away from a group. **4**. away from consciousness. —*adj*. **5**. away from one's usual place. **6**. out of existence, action, etc. **7**. inaccurate. **8**. unconsciousness. **9**. out of, with no supply of. —*n*. **10**. *Informal*. means of evasion.

out'-ănd-out', *adj*. utter.

out'bôard'', *adj., adv*. outside the hull of a boat.

out'break'', *n*. sudden manifestation.

out'build''ing, *n*. separate, subsidiary building.

out'bûrst'', *n*. vigorous outbreak.

out'căst'', *adj*. **1**. rejected by all. —*n*. **2**. outcast person.

out'còme'', *n*. result.

out'cròp'', *n*. rock rising above the soil.

out'crȳ'', *n., pl*. **-cries**. strong protest.

out''dāt'ėd, *adj*. obsolete.

out''dĭs'tánce, *v.t.*, **-tanced, -tancing**. get ahead of in a race or pursuit.

out''do', *v.t.*, **-did, -done, -doing**. act more effectively than.

out'dôor'', *adj*. pertaining to the outdoors.

out'dôors', *adv*. **1**. away from the insides of buildings. —*n*. **2**. nature.

out'êr, *adj*. further out. —**out'er·most''**, *adj*.

out'fĭt'', *n., v.t.*, **-fitted, -fitting**. *n*. **1**. equipment. **2**. ensemble of clothes. —*v.t.* **3**. supply with an outfit.

out''fŏx', *v.t.* outwit.

out''gō''ĭng, *adj*. **1**. departing. **2**. affable.

out'grōw'', *v.t.*, **-grew, -grown, -growing**. become too large or mature for.

out'growth'', *n*. **1**. something that grows out. **2**. development; consequence.

out'guĕss'', *v.t.* guess better than.

out'ĭng, *n*. pleasure trip.

out'lănd''ĭsh, *adj*. strange.

out'lăst'', *v.t.* last longer than.

out'lăw'', *n*. **1**. criminal. —*v.t.* **2**. forbid by law.

out'lāy'', *n*. expenditure.

out'lĕt'', *n*. **1**. means of emergence. **2**. sales market.

out'līne'', *n., v.t.*, **-lined, -lining**. *n*. **1**. outer edge; silhouette. **2**. summary of essentials. —*v.t.* **3**. make an outline of.

out''lǐve', *v.t.*, **-lived, -living**. live longer than.

out'lŏŏk'', *n*. **1**. view. **2**. viewing place. **3**. prospect.

out'lȳ''ĭng, *adj*. situated at a distance.

out·mŏd'ėd, *adj*. no longer in use.

out''nŭm'bêr, *v.t.* be more than.

out'-ŏf-dāte', *adj*. obsolete.

out'-ŏf-thė-wāy', *adj*. not often encountered.

out'pā''tiėnt, *n*. non-resident hospital patient.

out'pŏst'', *n*. remote fort, settlement, etc.

out'pŭt, *n*. **1**. production. **2**. (computers) data sent from a computer after processing.

out'rāge, *n., v.t.*, **-raged, -raging**. *n*. **1**. indignation. **2**. act causing indignation. —*v.t.* **3**. make indignant. —**out·ra'geous**, *adj*.

out'rĭg''gêr, *n*. **1**. floating spar giving a narrow boat stability. **2**. boat with such a spar.

out'rīght'', *adj*. **1**. pure and unambiguous. —*adv*. **2**. entirely. **3**. candidly.

out'sĕt'', *n*. beginning.

out'sīde', *n*. **1**. exterior. —*adj*. **2**. pertaining to an exterior. **3**. extreme. **4**. remotely possible. —*adv*. **5**. to the exterior. —*prep*. **6**. away from the interior of.

out''sīd'êr, *n*. non-member.

out'sīze'', *adj*. over normal size.

out'skîrts'', *n. pl*. border areas.

out''smärt', *v.t.* be more cunning than.

out''spō'kėn, *adj*. frank.

out''sprĕad', *adj*. extended.

out''stănd'ĭng, *adj*. **1**. prominent. **2**. unpaid.

out''strĕtch', *v.t.* extend.

out''strĭp', *v.t.*, **-stripped, -stripping**. **1**. go faster than. **2**. surpass.

out'wàrd, *adj*. **1**. outer; exterior. —*adv*. **2**. Also, **out'wards**, toward the outside.

o͞ut''weigh', *v.t.* **1.** matter more than. **2.** be heavier than.

o͞ut''wĭt', *v.t.*, **-witted, -witting.** outsmart.

ō'vāl, *n.* **1.** racetrack in an oval shape. —*adj.* **2.** shaped like an egg.

ō'vȧ·rÿ, *n., pl.* **-ries.** female reproductive gland. —**o'var'i·an,** *adj.*

ō·vā'tion, *n.* act of enthusiastic applause.

ȯv'ĕn, *n.* heating chamber.

ō'vêr, *prep.* **1.** above or on. **2.** to or on the far side of. **3.** superior to. **4.** more than. **5.** concerning. —*adj.* **6.** above. **7.** across. **8.** more. **9.** again. **10.** upside down. **11.** to a new attitude or belief. **12.** to completion. —*adj.* **13.** upper. **14.** finished.

ō'vêr-, prefix indicating "to excess." **overabundant, overactive, overanxious, overburden, overcautious, overcharge, overconfident, overcrowd, overdo, overdose, overeat, overemphasize, overestimate, overexert, overexpose, overheat, overindulge, overload, overmuch, overpopulate, overprice, overproduce, overreact, overripe, oversexed, overspend, overstock, overstrict, oversupply, overwork.**

ō'vêr·äll'', *adj., adv.* **1.** end-to-end. —*adj.* **2.** total. —*n.* **3. overalls,** protective covering for other clothes.

ō''vêr·āwe', *v.t.*, **-awed, -awing.** subdue with awe.

ō''vêr·beār'ĭng, *adj.* domineering.

ō'vêr·bôard'', *adv.* into the water from a vessel.

ō'vêr·căst'', *adj.* cloudy, as the sky.

ō'vêr·cōat'', *n.* heavy outer coat.

ō''vêr·cȯme', *v.t.*, **-came, -come, -coming.** get the better of.

ō'vêr·dōse', *v.* to ingest, with harmful effect, too much of a drug.

ō''vêr·draw͞', *v.t.*, **-draw, -drawn, -drawing.** draw on in excess of one's balance. —**o'ver·draft'',** *n.*

ō'vêr·dūe', *adj.* past the time when due.

ō''vêr·ĕs'tĭ·māte'', *v.t.*, **-mated, -mating.** esteem too highly or as too much. —**o''ver·es'ti·mate, o''ver·es''ti·ma'tion,** *n.*

o·ver·flow, *v.t.* (o''vȯr flō') **1.** spill over the rim of. —*v.i.* **2.** be filled beyond capacity. —*n.* (o'vȯr flō'') **3.** act or instance of overflowing. **4.** amount that overflows.

ō''vêr·grōw', *v.t.* **-grew, -grown, -growing.** cover with growth.

ō''vêr·hånd'', *adv., adj.* with the hand raised.

ō''vêr·haūl', *v.t.* **1.** inspect thoroughly. **2.** repair. —*n.* **3.** act or instance of overhauling.

ō''vêr·hĕad'', *adj., adv.* **1.** above one's head. —*n.* **2.** continuing business costs.

ō''vêr·hēar', *v.t.*, **-heard, -hearing.** hear without being spoken to.

ō''vêr·jōyed', *adj.* filled with joy.

ō'vêr·lånd'', *adj., adv.* across the land.

ō·vêr·lăp, *v.*, **-lapped, -lapping,** *n. v.t.* (ō''vȯr lap') **1.** extend within the edge of. —*v.i.* **2.** extend within each other's edges. —*n.* (ō'vȯr lap'') **3.** act or instance of overlapping.

ō''vêr·lāy', *v.t.*, **-laid, -laying.** cover or lay over.

ō''vêr·lo͞ok', *v.t.* **1.** omit by mistake. **2.** look out over.

ō'vêr·lÿ, *adv.* excessively.

ō''vêr·nīght', *adv.* **1.** during the night. —*adj.* (ō'vȯr nīt'') **2.** from beginning to end of one night. **3.** for one night.

ō'vêr·păss'', *n.* roadway passing over another, etc.

ō''vêr·pȯw'êr, *v.t.* reduce to helplessness.

ō''vêr·rāte', *v.t.*, **-rated, -rating.** rate too highly.

ō''vêr·rēach', *v.t.* reach beyond.

ō''vêr·rīde', *v.t.*, **-rode, -ridden, -riding.** prevail against or nullify.

ō''vêr·rūle', *v.t.*, **-ruled, -ruling.** nullify with superior authority.

ō''vêr·rŭn', *v.t.*, **-ran, -run, -running. 1.** overflow. **2.** infest.

ō'vêr·sēas', *adv., adj.* **1.** beyond the sea. —*adj.* Also, **o''ver·sea''. 2.** foreign.

ō''vêr·sēe', *v.t.* **-saw, -seen, -seeing.** supervise.

ō''vêr·shoe'', *n.* waterproof shoe covering.

ō''vêr·sīght'', *n.* mistaken omission.

ō''vêr·sĭm'plĭ·fÿ'', *v.t.*, **-fied, -fying.** distort by simplification.

ō''vêr·sīze'', *adj.* **1.** too large. **2.** larger than usual. Also, **o'ver·sized''.**

ō''vêr·slēep', *v.i.* **-slept, -sleeping.** sleep too long.

ō''vêr·stāte', *v.t.*, -stated, -stating. exaggerate.

ō''vêr·stĕp', *v.t.*, -stepped, -stepping.
exceed.

ō''vêr·stŭff', *v.t.* **1.** upholster with stuffing all over. **2.** stuff to excess.

ō·vêrt', *adj.* **1.** unhidden. **2.** open and deliberate.

ō''vêr·tāke', *v.t.*, -took, -taken,
-taking. catch up with.

ō''vêr-the·cŏun''têr, *adj.* (drugs) available without a prescription.

ō·vêr·thrōw, *v.t.*, -threw, -thrown,
-throwing, *n. v.t.* (ō''vər thrō') **1.**
cause to fall over. **2.** banish from power.
—*n.* (ō'vər thrō''). **3.** act or instance of
overthrowing.

ō'vêr·tīme'', *adj., adv.* **1.** beyond regular hours. —*n.* **2.** time beyond regular
hours. **3.** overtime pay.

ō'vêr·tōne'', *n.* **1.** tone modifying a pure
tone. **2.** subtle implication.

ō'vêr·tûre'', *n.* **1.** musical composition
beginning an opera, etc. **2.** friendly advance.

ō''vêr·tûrn', *v.t., v.i.* upset.

ō''vêr·wēen'ing, *adj.* arrogant.

ō'vêr·weight', *adj.* too heavy.

ō'vêr·whĕlm'', *v.t.* render powerless.

ō'vêr·wrôught'', *adj.* very nervous.

ō'vŏid, *adj.* egg-shaped.

ō'vŭm, *n., pl.* -va. female germ cell.

ōwe, *v.t.* owed, owing. **1.** be obligated to
give or pay. **2.** be obligated to. **3.** have
someone to thank for.

ōwl, *n.* nocturnal bird of prey.

ōwn, *v.t.* **1.** be the rightful possessor of.
—*v.t., v.i.* **2.** admit or confess. —*adj.* **3.**
personally or individually possessed.
—own'er·ship, *n.*

ŏx, *n., pl.* oxen. domesticated bovine.

ŏx'īde, *n.* compound containing oxygen.

ŏx'y·gĕn, *n.* gaseous element needed for
breathing and burning.

ŏx·ȳ·môr'ŏn, *n.* figure of speech in
which two ideas of opposite meaning
are combined to form an expressive
phrase.

ōys'têr, *n.* edible mollusk.

ō'zōne, *n.* a form of oxygen created by
electric spark.

P

P, p, *n.* sixteenth letter of the English alphabet.

păb'ū·lŭm. *n.* soft food, esp. for babies.

pāce, *n., v.,* paced, pacing. *n.* **1.** rate of
movement, esp. in walking or running.
2. linear measure roughly equivalent to
a footstep. **3.** an individual step. —*v.t.*
4. establish the pace for, esp. in a race.
5. measure by pacing off. —*v.i.* **6.** take
slow, measured steps.

pāce'māk''êr, *n.* artificial device to regulate the heartbeat.

păch'y·dêrm, *n.* thick-skinned mammal, e.g. an elephant.

pá·cĭf'ĭc, *adj.* **1.** peaceful; calm. **2.**
peace-making; conciliatory.

păc'ĭ·fĭsm, *n.* opposition to violence and
war. —pac'i·fist, *n.* —pac''i·fis'tic,
adj.

păc'i·fȳ'', *v.t.*, -fied, -fying. **1.** quiet or
calm. **2.** appease. —pac'i·fi·ca'tion,
n. —pac'i·fi''er, *n.*

păck, *n.* **1.** bundle or package. **2.** group
of people, animals, or things. **3.** complete set of. —*v.t.* **4.** make into a bundle.
5. fill, as with things for a journey. **6.**
cram. **7.** carry, as a gun.

păck'âge, *n., v.t.*, -aged, -aging. *n.* **1.**
bundle; parcel. **2.** container. —*v.t.* **3.**
enclose or wrap in a package.

păck'ĕt, *n.* **1.** small package or bundle.
2. passenger boat on a regular schedule.

păct, *n.* agreement; treaty.

păd, *n., v.t.*, padded, padding. *n.* **1.** soft
cushion. **2.** tablet of writing paper. **3.**
cushioned part of an animal foot. —*v.t.*
4. furnish with pads. **5.** lengthen or fal-
sify with extraneous matter.

păd'dle, *n., v.*, -dled, -dling. *n.* **1.**
oarlike implement, esp. for a canoe. **2.**
Ping-Pong racket. —*v.t.* **3.** move with
paddles. **4.** spank. —*v.i.* **5.** move in water using the hands.

păd'dŏck, *n.* enclosed area for horses.

păd'lŏck, *n.* **1.** portable lock with a
shackle. —*v.t.* **2.** fasten with a padlock.

paē'an, *n.* song of praise, joy, or thanksgiving.

pā'gàn, *n.* **1.** heathen; —*adj.* **2.** heathen:
barbaric. —pa'gan·ism, *n.*

pāge, *n., v.t.* paged, paging. *n.* **1.** single
side of a leaf, as in a book. **2.** young ser-

vant. —*v.t.* **3.** number the pages of. **4.** hail by naming loudly.

păg'ėant, *n.* elaborate spectacle. —**pag'eant·ry,** *n.*

păg'ẽr, *n.* electronic device for remote alerting and communication with a person.

pà·gō'då, *n.* tall Oriental building, usually a Buddhist temple.

pāil, *n.* bucket.

pāin, *n.* **1.** physical or mental suffering. **2.** effort; struggle. **3.** punishment. —*v.t.* **4.** hurt; distress. —**pain'ful,** *adj.* —**pain'less,** *adj.*

pāins'tāk''ĭng, *adj.* careful.

pāint, *n.* **1.** pigmented liquid used to coat surfaces. —*v.i.* **2.** engage in the art of painting. —*v.t.* **3.** cover with paint. —**paint'er,** *n.* —**paint'ing,** *n.*

pāir, *n.*, *pl.* **pairs, pair,** *v. n.* **1.** set of two, esp. when matching. —*v.t.* **2.** arrange in pairs. —*v.i.* **3.** **pair off,** separate in couples.

pāis'lēy, *n.* soft fabric with colorful, intricate design.

pà·jä'mås, *n. pl.* loose, two-piece sleeping clothes.

păl, *n. Informal.* friend or acquaintance.

păl'áce, *n.* official residence of a sovereign, etc. —**pa·la'tial,** *adj.*

păl'át·à·ble, *adj.* tasty.

păl'áte, *n.* roof of the mouth. —**pal'a·tal,** *adj.*

pà·lăv'êr, *n.* long parley.

pāle, *adj.*, **paler, palest,** *v.*, **paled, paling,** *n. adj.* **1.** lacking intensity of color; whitish. **2.** lacking vividness. —*v.i.* **3.** become pale. —*n.* **4.** stake. **5.** limits; bounds. **6.** enclosed area.

pā''lē·ō·lĭth'ĭc, *adj.* pertaining to the earlier part of the Stone Age.

păl'étte, *n.* board on which a painter spreads colors.

păl'ĭd, *adj.* pale, drawn. —**pal'lor,** *n.*

pāl'ĭng, *n.* board or picket.

păl'ĭ·sāde'', *n.* **1.** high fence of palings. **2.** line of high cliffs.

pāll'beār''êr, *n.* person who attends or carries the coffin at a funeral.

păl'lėt, *n.* **1.** straw mattress. **2.** platform used to support freight.

păl'lĭ·āte'', *v.t.* **1.** ease without curing. **2.** mitigate with excuses. —**pal'li·a'' tive,** *adj.*

päll, *n.* **1.** cloth draped over a coffin.

—*v.i.* **2.** become tiresome or distasteful.

pälm, *n.* **1.** soft inner surface of the hand. **2.** tall unbranched tropical tree or shrub topped with large leaves. —*v.i.* **3.** conceal in the hand.

pälm'ĭs·trỷ, *n.* fortune-telling from the lines of a person's palm.

păl''ȯ·mĭ'nō, *n.*, *pl.* **-nos.** *n.* light tan horse.

păl'pà·ble, *adj.* **1.** tangible. **2.** obvious, clear. —**pal'pa·bly,** *adv.*

păl'pĭ·tāte'', *v.i.*, **-tated, -tating.** pulsate with unnatural rapidity. —**pal''pi·ta'tion,** *n.*

păl'sỷ, *n.*, *pl.* **-sies,** *v.t.*, **-sied, -sying.** *n.* **1.** paralysis. **2.** condition characterized by tremors. —*v.t.* **3.** paralyze.

păl'trỷ, *adj.*, **-trier, -triest.** *adj.* trifling, trivial.

păm'pêr, *v.t.* treat with excessive indulgence; coddle.

păm'phlėt, *n.* unbound booklet with a paper cover.

păn, *n.*, *v.*, **panned, panning.** *n.* **1.** broad, shallow metal container. —*v.t.* **2.** separate from sand by washing. **3.** *Informal.* criticize severely, in a review. **4.** to rotate, esp. a camera.

păn''à·cē'à, *n.* cure-all.

păn'cāke'', *n.* flat batter cake fried on both sides.

păn'crē·ás, *n.* gland that secretes digestive fluid. —**pan''cre·at'ic,** *adj.*

păn'då, *n.* bearlike, black and white Asiatic mammal.

păn''dė·mō'nĭ·ŭm, *n.* wild uproar, chaos.

păn'dêr, *n.* **1.** pimp. —*v.i.* **2.** cater to another's passions or weaknesses. —**pan' der·er,** *n.*

pāne, *n.* sheet of glass, esp. for doors and windows.

păn''ė·gỷr'ĭc, *n.* eulogy.

păn'ėl, *n.* **1.** list of persons called for a special task, e.g. jury duty. **2.** wood filling for a wall or door. **3.** mounting for controls or instruments. —**pan'el·ing,** *n.* —**pan'el·ist,** *n.*

păng, *n.* sudden feeling of distress or guilt.

păn'hăn''dle, *v.i.* **-dled, -dling.** *Informal.* beg for money on the street. —**pan'han''dler,** *n.*

păn'ĭc, *n.* **1.** sudden, overpowering fear.

—*v.i.* **2.** be affected by panic. —**pan'ick·y,** *adj.* —**pan'ic-strick''en,** *adj.*

păn'ȯ·plȳ, *n.,* *pl.* **-plies.** *n.* **1.** impressive array. **2.** suit of armor.

păn''ȯ·răm'ȧ, *n.* **1.** wide view of a large area. **2.** continuously changing scene or unfolding of events. —**pan''o·ram'ic,** *adj.*

păn'sȳ, *n.* colorful outdoor flower related to the violet.

pănt, *v.i.* **1.** breathe hard and quickly, as after exercise. **2.** long or yearn for.

păn'thē''ĭsm, *n.* doctrine that equates God with nature and natural forces.

păn'thêr, *n.* large wild cat, e.g. leopard, cougar, puma.

păn'tȯ·mīme'', *n.,* *v.t.,* **-mimed, miming.** *n.* **1.** expression through movement and gesture only. **2.** drama using movement and no speech. —*v.t.* **3.** express in pantomime; mime.

păn'trȳ, *n.,* *pl.* **-tries.** small supply room or closet off a kitchen.

pănts, *n. pl.* trousers.

păp, *n.* soft food for babies or the infirm.

pä'pȧ, *n.* father.

pā'pȧ·cȳ, *n.* office of the pope. —**pa'pal,** *adj.*

pȧ·pä'yȧ, *n.* tropical tree with yellow-black edible fruit.

pā'pêr, *n.* **1.** fibrous compound made in sheets to receive writing, etc. **2.** scholarly essay. **3.** newspaper. **4. papers,** documents. —*v.t.* **5.** decorate with wallpaper.

pā'pêr·băck'', *n.* inexpensive book with paper cover.

pā''piêr-mȧ·che', *n.* molding material made of wet paper pulp and glue.

pȧ·pĭl'lȧ, *n.,* *pl.* **-pillaē,** *n.* small protuberance concerned with the senses, e.g. taste buds.

pā'pĭst, *n. Disparaging.* Roman Catholic. —**pa'pism,** *n.* —**pa·pis'ti·cal, pa·pis'tic,** *adj.*

pă·pōose', *n.* Native American baby.

păp·rĭ'kȧ, *n.* red spice made from sweet peppers.

pȧ·pȳ'rŭs, *n.* plant from the Nile from which the Egyptians prepared paper-like material.

pâr, *n.* **1.** equality in level or value. **2.** accepted stan dard; average.

păr'ȧ·ble, *n.* story conveying a moral.

păr'ȧ·chūte'', *n.,* *v.,* **-chuted, -chuting,** *n.* **1.** umbrellalike device used for descents from aircraft. —*v.i.* **2.** jump with a parachute. —*v.t.* **3.** send by parachute.

pȧ·rāde', *n.,* *v.,* **-raded, -rading.** *n.* **1.** ostentatious display. **2.** ceremonial procession or march. —*v.t.* **3.** display ostentatiously. —*v.i.* **4.** march in a parade.

păr'ȧ·dĭgm, *n.* ideal; model.

păr'ȧ·dīse'', *n.* **1.** heaven. **2.** Garden of Eden.

păr'ȧ·dŏx'', *n.* true statement that seems to contradict itself. —**par''a·dox'i·cal,** *adj.*

păr'ȧf·fĭn, *n.* waxy substance used in candles and to seal jars.

păr'ȧ·gŏn'', *n.* model of perfection.

păr'ȧ·grăph'', *n.* **1.** subdivision of a writing that contains one or more sentences. —*v.t.* **2.** divide into paragraphs.

păr'ȧ·kēet'', *n.* any of numerous slender, small parrots.

păr'ȧl·lăx'', *n.* apparent displacement of an object seen from different positions.

păr'ȧl·lĕl'', *adj.,* *n.,* *v.t.* **-leled, -leling.** *adj.* **1.** lying or moving in the same direction but equidistant at all points. **2.** essentially similar or comparable. —*n.* **3.** anything parallel. **4.** counterpart. **5.** similarity. —*v.t.* **6.** compare. **7.** be parallel to.

păr''ȧl·lĕl'ȯ·grăm'', *n.* quadrilateral with parallel opposite sides.

pȧ·răl'ȳ·sĭs, *n.,* *pl.* **-ses,** loss of voluntary muscular control. —**par''a·lyt'ic,** *n.,* *adj.* —**par'a·lyze'',** *v.t.*

păr'ȧ·mŏunt'', *adj.* superior; predominant.

păr'ȧ·môur'', *n.* extra-marital lover.

păr''ȧ·nōī'ȧ, *n.* mental disorder characterized by delusions. —**par'a·noid'',** *n.,* *adj.* —**par''a·noi'ac,** *n.,* *adj.*

păr'ȧ·pĕt, *n.* protecting wall or railing.

păr''ȧ·phêr·nāl'ĭȧ, *n. pl.* **1.** personal belongings. **2.** equipment.

păr'ȧ·phrāse'', *v.t.,* **-phrased, -phrasing,** *n.* *v.t.* **1.** restate in other words. —*n.* **2.** restatement in different words.

păr''ȧ·plē'gĭ·ȧ, *n.* paralysis of the lower half of the body. —**par''a·pleg'ic,** *n.*

păr'ȧ·sīte'', *n.* **1.** organism which lives in or on another. **2.** person who depends on or exploits another. —**par''a·sit'ic,** *adj.*

păr'ȧ·sŏl'', *n.* sun umbrella.

păr′à·trōōps, *n. pl.* soldiers who parachute from planes. —par′à·trooper, *n.*

pâr′bōĭl′′, *v.t.* boil partly.

pâr′cĕl, *n.*, *v.t.*, **-celed, -celing.** *n.* **1.** wrapped package, esp. for mailing. **2.** lot, esp. for sale. **3.** tract of land. —*v.t.* **4.** divide.

pârch, *v.t.* **1.** dry by heat. —*v.i.* **2.** suffer from heat or thirst.

pârch′mĕnt, *n.* skin of sheep or goat prepared for writing on.

pâr′dŏn, *n.* **1.** official release from penalty or punishment. **2.** indulgence, forgiveness. —*v.t.* **3.** grant pardon to. —par′don·a·ble, *adj.*

pāre, *v.t.* **pared, paring. 1.** trim off the outside part or skin of. **2.** reduce.

păr′′ė·gŏr′ĭc, *n.* soothing medicine, esp. to control diarrhea.

păr′ĕnt, *n.* mother or father. —pa·ren′ tal, *adj.* —par′ent hood′′. *n.*

păr′ĕnt·âge, *n.* descent, origin, or lineage.

pà·rĕn′thė·sĭs, *n.*, *pl.* **-ses. 1.** punctuation marks, (or), used to enclose parenthetic material. **2.** matter interpolated in writing to modify or explain the idea. —par′′en·thet′ic, par′′en·thet′i· cal, *adj.*

pâr·fāit′, *n.* frozen, layered dessert.

pă·rī′àh, *n.* outcast.

păr′ĭ·mū′tū·ėl, *n.* system of betting in which winners share the winnings and the management takes a percentage.

păr′ĭsh, *n.* **1.** ecclesiastical district under one pastor. **2.** local church community. —pa·rish′ion·er, *n.*

păr′ĭ·tў, *n.* equality; equivalence.

pârk, *n.* **1.** land set aside as a recreation area or game preserve. **2.** site for athletic events. —*v.t.*, *v.i.* **3.** halt for an extended period.

pâr′kà, *n.* hooded, cold-weather coat.

pârk′wāy′′, *n.* highway with landscaped median strip.

pâr′lànce, *n.* manner of speaking; idiom.

pâr′lāy, *n.* **1.** bet of previous winnings along with the original sum betted. —*v.t.* **2.** bet as a parlay.

pâr′lēy, *n.*, *pl.* **-leys,** *v.i.*, **-leyed, -leying.** *n.* **1.** informal conference, esp. to settle differences. —*v.i.* **2.** hold a parley.

pâr′lià·mėnt, *n.* national legislative body. —par′′lia·men·tar′i·an, *n.* —par′′lia·men′ta·ry, *adj.*

pâr′lŏr, *n.* room for entertaining.

pà·rō′chĭ·àl, *adj.* **1.** pertaining to a parish. **2.** narrow or limited in scope. —pa·ro′chi·al·ism, *n.*

păr′ò·dў, *n.*, *pl.* **-dies,** *v.t.*, **-died, -dying.** *n.* **1.** satiric or humorous imitation. —*v.t.* **2.** ridicule, travesty. —par′ o·dist, *n.* —pa·rod′ic, *adj.*

pà·rōle′, *n.*, *v.t.*, **-roled, -roling.** *n.* **1.** conditional early release from prison. —*v.t.* **2.** put on parole.

păr·ŏx′ўsm (par′ok siz′′im), *n.* sudden, sharp attack; convulsion, fit.

par·quet (par kā′), *n.* floor with an inlaid design, esp. in wood.

păr′rĭ·cīde, *n.* killing of a parent or close relative.

păr′rŏt, *n.* **1.** hook-billed tropical bird capable of talking. —*v.t.* **2.** repeat or imitate unthinkingly.

păr′rў, *v.t.*, **-ried, -rying,** *n.*, *pl.* **-ries.** *v.t.* **1.** evade, avoid. —*n.* **2.** act or instance of parrying.

pâr′sĭ·mō′′nў, *n.* extreme frugality or cheapness. —par′′si·mo′ni·ous, *adj.*

pârs′lēy, *n.* garden herb used as garnish or seasoning.

pârs′nĭp, *n.* plant with long, white edible root.

pâr′sŏn, *n.* clergyman, esp. Protestant.

pâr′sŏn·âge, *n.* house for a parson.

pârt, *n.* **1.** portion or division. **2.** spare or replacement piece for a machine. **3.** function, duty, job. **4.** role in drama, etc. —*v.t.* **5.** divide. —*v.i.* **6.** dissolve a relationship.

pâr·tāke′, *v.i.*, **-took -taken, -taking.** *v.i.* **1.** participate. **2.** receive or take a portion.

pâr′tiàl, *adj.* **1.** favoring one over another; biased. **2.** especially fond. **3.** affecting a part only. —par·tial′i·ty, *n.* —par′tial·ly, *adv.*

pâr·tĭc′ĭ·pāte′′, *v.i.*, **-pated, -pating.** take part; share. —par·tic′i·pant, *n.* —par·tic′′i·pa′tion, *n.*

pâr′tĭ·cĭ·ple, *n.* adjective based on a verb. —par′′ti·cip′i·al, *adj.*

pâr′tĭ·cle, *n.* **1.** very small piece or amount. **2.** small, functional word, e.g. a preposition, etc.

pâr·tĭc′ū·làr, *adj.* **1.** pertaining to a specific person or thing. **2.** distinctive, special. **3.** attentive to details; fastidious. —*n.* **4.** detail. —**par·tic′u·lar·ly,** *adv.*

pârt′ĭng, *n.* **1.** separation, division. **2.** departure. —*adj.* **3.** done, etc. in farewell.

pâr′tĭ·sån, *n.* **1.** person who takes a side in a controversy. **2.** guerrilla.

pâr·tĭ′tion, *n.* **1.** division into parts. **2.** divider. —*v.t.* **3.** divide into parts.

pârt′lў, *adv.* in some measure; not fully.

pârt′nêr, *n.* **1.** associate; colleague. **2.** spouse. **3.** joint owner. —**part′ner·ship′′,** *n.*

pâr′trĭdge, *n.* any of various game birds.

pâr′tў, *n., pl.* **-ties.** *n.* **1.** social gathering. **2.** group of people with common political interests and opinions. **3.** person or group concerned in a specific action; participant. **4.** group engaged in a special task.

păss, *v.t.* **1.** go past. **2.** hand over; serve. **3.** spend, as time. **4.** approve or ratify. **5.** succeed at, as a test. —*v.i.* **6.** go past. **7.** come to an end. **8.** go from place to place. **9.** be approved or ratified. —*n.* **10.** situation. **11.** paper granting admission, leave, etc. **12.** route, as between mountains. **13.** motion of the hands.

păss′a·ble, *adj.* **1.** able to be passed or crossed. **2.** good enough; tolerable. —**pass′ab·ly,** *adv.*

păs′såge, *n.* **1.** right or freedom to pass. **2.** means of passing. **3.** transportation, esp. ship passage. **4.** act or instance of passing. **5.** enactment. —**pas′sage·way′′,** *n.*

păss′book′′, *n.* bankbook, esp. for savings account.

pas′sèn·gêr, *n.* traveler, esp. on a vehicle.

păs·sé′, *adj.* out of date; old fashioned.

păs′sĭng, *adj.* **1.** transitory; fleeting. —*n.* **2.** act of a person who passes, esp. in death.

păs′sion, *n.* **1.** strong feeling or emotion. **2.** love, esp. sexual desire. **3.** anger; rage. **4. the Passion,** sufferings of Christ. —**pas′sion·ate, pas′sion·less,** *adj.* —**pas′sion·ate·ly,** *adv.*

păs′sĭve, *n.* **1.** inactive; not in action. **2.** acted upon. **3.** submissive, meek; patient. —**pas·siv′i·ty, pas′sive·ness,** *n.* —**pas′sive·ly,** *adv.*

Păss′ō′′vêr, *n.* Jewish holiday celebrating the Hebrews' liberation from slavery in Egypt.

păss′pôrt′′, *n.* official document carried by a foreign traveler.

păst, *adj.* **1.** gone by or elapsed. **2.** pertaining to an earlier time or age. **3.** *Grammar.* pertaining to a verb tense expressing time gone by. —*n.* **4.** time gone by. **5.** past tense. **6.** secret past life. —*prep., adv.* **7.** beyond.

pâs′tå, *n.* food, esp. Italian, prepared from flour and egg dough.

pâste, *n., v.t.,* **pasted, pasting.** *n.* **1.** soft mixture, esp. for sticking things together. **2.** shiny glass used in imitation gems. —*v.t.* **3.** fasten with paste. —**pas·ty,** *adj.*

pâste′bôard′′, *n.* board made of sheets of paper pasted together.

păs·tĕl′, *n.* **1.** light or pale color. **2.** drawing or painting in pastel.

păs′têrn, *n.* part of a horse's foot between the fetlock and the hoof joint.

păs′têur·īze′′, *v.t.,* **-ized, -izing.** heat to destroy harmful bacteria. —**pas′teur·i·za′tion,** *n.*

păs·tĭche (pas tēsh′), *n.* artistic composition composed of selections or motifs from other works.

păs′tīme′′, *n.* diversion; hobby.

păs′tör, *n.* clergyman serving a local parish or church.

păs′tö·rål, *adj.* **1.** pertaining to shepherds or the rural life. **2.** pertaining to a golden age. **3.** pertaining to pastors.

pās′trў, *n.* sweet baked goods.

păs′tûre, *n., v.t.,* **-tured, -turing.** *n.* **1.** grassy land used for grazing animals. —*v.t.* **2.** feed by allowing to graze.

păt, *n., adj., v.i.,* **patted, patting.** *n.* **1.** light stroke with the flat of the hand. **2.** flat piece of butter, etc. —*adj.* **3.** glib. **4.** perfectly learned. —*v.i.* **5.** place the flat of the hand on lightly.

pătch, *n.* **1.** piece used to cover or repair a worn spot. **2.** a small area distinct from that around it. —*v.t.* **3.** mend or cover with a patch. **4.** repair hastily. —**patch′work′′,** *n., adj.* —**patch′y,** *adj.*

pāte, *n.* head, esp. the crown.

på·tĕl′là, *n., pl.* **-tellae.** kneecap.

păt′ën, *n.* plate, esp. one used in the Eucharist.

păt'ĕnt, *n.* **1.** certificate of exclusive rights to an invention. —*v.t.* **2.** secure a patent on. —*adj.* **3.** something protected by a patent. **4.** evident; obvious.

pȧ·têr'nȧl, *adj.* **1.** fatherly. **2.** related through or derived from a father.

pȧ·têr'nȧl·ĭsm, *n.* benevolent or fatherly administration. —**pa·ter"nal·is'tic,** *adj.*

pȧ·têr'nĭ·tÿ, *n.* fatherhood.

păth, *n.* **1.** narrow road. **2.** course of action. —**path'way",** *n.*

pȧ·thĕt'ĭc, *adj.* **1.** evoking pity. **2.** miserably inadequate. —**pa·thet'i·cal·ly,** *adv.*

pă·thŏl'ȯ·gÿ, *n.* **1.** study of the nature of a disease. **2.** characteristics of disease. —**path"o·log'i·cal,** *adj.* —**pa·thol'o·gist,** *n.*

pā'thȯs, *n.* element evoking pity or compassion.

pā'tĭėnt, *n.* **1.** person under the care of a doctor. —*adj.* **2.** enduring without complaint. —**pa'tience,** *n.* —**pa'tient·ly,** *adv.*

pȧ'tĭ·nȧ, *n.* green film formed on copper and bronze.

pă'tĭ·ō', *n., pl.* **patios.** open courtyard.

pā'trĭ·ârch", *n.* **1.** father or founder, e.g. of a tribe or institution. **2.** venerable old man; father. **3.** ecclesiastical dignitary. —**pa'tri·ar"chal,** *adj.* —**pa'tri·ar"chy,** *n.*

pȧ·trĭ'cĭȧn, *adj.* **1.** aristocratic; of high birth. *n.* **2.** aristocrat.

păt'rĭ·mō'nÿ, *n.* inherited estate.

pā'trĭ·ȯt, *n.* person who loves and supports his country. —**pa"tri·ot'ic,** *adj.* —**pa'tri·ot"ism,** *n.*

pȧ·trōl', *n., v.t.,* **-trolled, -trolling.** *n.* **1.** guard making a round. —*v.t.* **2.** guard with a patrol. **3.** pass along regularly. —**pa·trol'man,** *n.*

pā'trȯn, *n.* **1.** influential or wealthy supporter. **2.** customer or client.

pā'trȯn·age, *n.* **1.** support by a patron. **2.** support of a business by customers. **3.** personal control of appointments to government jobs.

pā'trȯn·īze", *v.t.,* **-ized, -izing. 1.** be a customer of. **2.** treat with condescension.

păt'têr, *v.i.* **1.** make a succession of light tapping sounds. **2.** talk glibly or nonsensically. **3.** walk quickly and lightly.

—*n.* **4.** glib, rapid speech. **5.** quick pattering sound.

păt'têrn, *n.* **1.** decorative design. **2.** ideal model. **3.** model for making or copying. —*v.t.* **4.** make after a pattern.

păt'tÿ, *n., pl.* **-ties. 1.** little pie. **2.** flat, round cake of chopped food, e.g. hamburger.

pau'cĭ·tÿ, *n.* scarcity.

paunch, *n.* belly, esp. when large. —**paunch'y,** *adj.*

pau'pêr, *n.* poor person.

pause, *n.* **1.** temporary stop. —*v.i.* **2.** stop temporarily.

pāve, *v.t.,* **paved, paving.** cover with hard material, as a road. —**pave'ment,** *n.*

pȧ·vĭl'ĭȯn, *n.* **1.** light, open structure for entertainment or shelter. **2.** large tent.

paw, *n.* **1.** animal foot with nails or claws. —*v.t., v.i.* **2.** scrape or strike as if with paws.

pawn, *v.t.* **1.** pledge or stake. **2.** deposit as security for a loan. —*n.* **3.** state of being pawned. **4.** chess piece of the lowest value.

pawn'brō"kêr, *n.* person who lends money on pledged goods.

pāy, *v.,* **paid, paying,** *n. v.t.* **1.** give money to in return for goods or services. **2.** satisfy, as a debt. —*v.i.* **3.** give money in exchange. **4.** yield a profit. **5.** undergo punishment. —*n.* **6.** wages or salary. **7.** paid employment. **8.** profit. —**pay·ee',** *n.* —**pay'er,** *n.* —**pay'ment,** *n.*

pāy'a·ble, *adj.* **1.** to be paid. **2.** able to be paid.

pāy'-ȯff, *n.* **1.** final payment. **2.** final consequence.

pēa, *n.* round, edible vegetable seed.

pēace, *n.* **1.** calm and quiet. **2.** state of accord. **3.** freedom from troubling emotions or thoughts. —**peace'a·ble, peace'ful,** *adj.* —**peace'time",** *n.*

pēach, *n.* sweet juicy fruit.

pēa'cŏck", *n.* male peafowl with long, brilliant tail feathers.

pēa'fŏwl", *n.* large domesticated Asiatic pheasant.

pēa'hĕn", *n.* female peafowl.

pēak, *n.* **1.** pointed top. **2.** top of a mountain or hill.

pēaked, *adj.* **1.** pointed. **2.** (pē'kid) pale, sickly.

pēal, *n*. **1.** loud, prolonged ringing of bells. **2.** set of tuned bells. **3.** any loud, prolonged series of sounds. —*v.i.* **4.** sound in a peal.

pēa'nŭt'', *n*. pod or edible seed of an annual herb.

pear, *n*. fleshy fruit related to the apple.

pêarl, *n*. hard, lustrous gem formed within the shell of an oyster. —**pearl'y**, *adj*.

pĕas'ȧnt, *n*. poor farm worker.

pēat, *n*. highly organic soil dried for use as fuel.

pĕb'ble, *n*. small stone. —**peb'bly**, *adj*.

pē·cȧn', *n*. smooth-shelled nut from the hickory tree.

pĕc''cȧ·dĭl'lō, *n*., *pl.* **-loes, -los**, slight or minor offense.

pĕc'cȧ·rȳ, *n*. small piglike animal.

pĕck, *v.t.*, *v.i.* **1.** jab repeatedly with a beak. —*v.t.* **3.** dig with such jabs. —*n*. **3.** dry measure of eight quarts.

pĕc'tĭn, *n*. plant substance used to thicken jellies, etc.

pĕc'ū·lāte'', *v.t.*, **-lated, -lating**, embezzle. —**pec''u·la'tion**, *n*.

pē·cū'liȧr, *adj*. **1.** strange, odd. **2.** unique. **3.** distinctive, characteristic. —**pe·cu''li·ar'i·ty**, *n*. —**pe·cul'iar·ly**, *adv*.

pē·cū'nĭ·ār''ȳ, *adj*. pertaining to money; monetary.

pĕd'ȧ·gŏgue'', *n*. teacher; scholar. Also, **ped'a·gog''**, —**ped'a·go''gy**, *n*. —**ped''a·gog'ic, ped''a·gog'i·cal**, *adj*.

pĕd'ȧl, *n*. **1.** lever worked by the foot. —*v.t.*, *v.i.* **2.** move by means of pedals.

pĕd'ȧnt, *n*. **1.** person who makes a display of his learning. **2.** unimaginative adherent to the letter of a doctrine. —**pe·dan'tic**, *adj*. —**ped'an·try**, *n*.

pĕd'dle, *v.t.*, *v.i.*, **-dled, -dling**. sell on the street or road. —**ped'dler**, *n*.

pĕd'ĕs·tȧl, *n*. base for a statue, etc.

pė·dĕs'trĭ·ȧn, *n*. **1.** walker. —*adj*. **2.** prosaic; commonplace.

pē''dĭ·ăt'rĭcs, *n*. study of care and diseases of children. —**pe'di·a·tri''cian**, *n*. —**pe''di·at'ric**, *adj*.

pĕd'ĭ·grēe'', *n*. **1.** certificate of ancestry. **2.** ancestry, esp. when distinguished. —**ped'i·greed''**, *adj*.

pĕd'ĭ·mėnt, *n*. decorative triangular gable.

pēek, *v.i.* **1.** glance furtively. —*n*. **2.** brief or furtive glance.

pēel, *v.t.* **1.** strip or remove. —*n*. **2.** skin of fruit or vegetable. —**peel'ing**, *n*.

pēen, *n*. wedge or ball-shaped end of a hammer.

pēep, *v.i.* **1.** peek. **2.** utter a faint, shrill cry. —*n*. **3.** quick look or glance. **4.** faint sound.

pēer, *v.i.* **1.** look intently or searchingly. —*n*. **2.** equal in rank or abilities. **3.** nobleman. —**peer'age**, *n*.

pēer'lėss, *adj*. without equal, supreme.

pēeve, *n.*, *v.t.*, **peeved, peeving**, *v.t.* **1.** annoy, irritate. —*n*. **2.** source of annoyance. **3.** complaint. —**peev'ish**, *adj*.

pĕg, *n.*, *v.t.*, **pegged, pegging**. *n*. **1.** small hook, pin or fastener, esp. one fitting into a hole. —*v.t.* **2.** fasten with pegs.

pė·jō'rȧ·tĭve, *adj*. disparaging, negative.

pē'kōe, *n*. black Oriental tea.

pĕlf, *n*. money; riches.

pĕl'ĭ·cȧn, *n*. large bird with a pouched lower bill.

pėl·lâ'grȧ, *n*. chronic disease caused by inadequate diet.

pĕl'lėt, *n*. small ball.

pĕll'-mĕll', *adv*. in a disorderly or hasty manner.

pĕl·lū'cĭd, *adj*. clear or limpid; transparent.

pĕlt, *n*. **1.** animal hide, esp. with fur. —*v.t.* **2.** attack with blows or missiles. —*v.i.* **3.** beat relentlessly, as rain.

pĕl'vĭs, *n*. basinlike bone in the lower part of the trunk. —**pel'vic**, *adj*.

pĕn, *n.*, *v.t.*, **penned, penning**. *n*. **1.** instrument for writing with ink. **2.** small enclosure for animals or storage. —*v.t.* **3.** write. **4.** enclose.

pē'nȧl, *adj*. pertaining to punishment. —**pe'nal·ize''**, *v.t.*

pĕn'ȧl·tȳ, *n.*, *pl.* **-ties. 1.** punishment. **2.** disadvantage; hardship.

pĕn'ȧnce, *n*. **1.** self-imposed punishment for sin. **2.** sacrament of confession of sin.

pĕn'chȧnt, *n*. strong inclination; liking.

pĕn'cĭl, *n*. **1.** cylindrical implement containing graphite for writing, etc. —*v.t.* **2.** paint, draw, or write.

pĕnd'ȧnt, *n*. **1.** hanging ornament, e.g.

an earring. **2.** duplicate or balancing feature.

pĕnd′ent, *adj.* hanging; overhanging.

pĕnd′ĭng, *adj.* **1.** undecided; imminent. —*prep.* **2.** while awaiting; until.

pĕn′dū·lŭm, *n.* freely swinging suspended weight.

pĕn′e·trāte″, *v.t.* **-trated, -trating. 1.** enter. **2.** permeate. **3.** understand. **4.** affect deeply. —**pen′e·tra·ble,** *adj.* —**pen″e·tra′tion,** *n.*

pĕn′guĭn, *n.* short-legged, flightless aquatic bird.

pĕn″ĭ·cĭl′lĭn, *n.* antibiotic produced by certain molds.

pĕn·ĭn′sū·là, *n.* land body surrounded by water on three sides.

pē′nĭs, *n.* male organ of copulation and urination.

pĕn′ĭ·tĕnt, *adj.* **1.** feeling repentance. —*n.* **2.** repentant person. —**pen′i·tence,** *n.* —**pen″i·ten′tial,** *adj.*

pĕn″ĭ·tĕn′tià·rў, *n.* prison.

pĕn′knife″, *n.* small pocketknife; jackknife.

pĕn′màn, *n., pl.* **-men.** person skilled in using a pen. —**pen′man·ship″,** *n.*

pĕn′nànt, *n.* **1.** small flag for signaling. **2.** flag of championship.

pĕn′nў, *n., pl.* **-nies.** smallest denomination of U.S. currency. —**pen′ni·less,** *adj.*

pè·nŏl′ò·gў, *n.* study of criminal punishment. —**pe·nol′o·gist,** *n.* —**pe″no·log′i·cal,** *adj.*

pĕn′sion, *n.* **1.** fixed, periodic payment to a retiree. —*v.t.* **2.** give a pension to. **pen′sion·er,** *n.*

pĕn′sĭve, *adj.* sadly or dreamily thoughtful; quiet.

pĕnt, *adj.* confined; shut up.

pĕn′tà·gŏn″, *n.* polygon of five sides.

pĕn·tăm′e·têr, *n.* verse line of five metrical feet.

Pĕn′ta·teūch″, *n.* first five books of the Old Testament.

pĕnt′hŏŭse″, *n.* habitable structure on the roof of a building.

pĕnt′-ŭp′, *adj.* confined, as emotions.

pĕn·ŭl′tĭ·màte, *adj.* next to the last.

pè·nŭm′brà, *n.* partial shadow. —**pe·num′bral,** *adj.*

pē·nū′rĭ·oŭs, *adj.* **1.** miserly; stingy. **2.** impoverished. —**pen′u·ry,** *n.*

pē′ŏn, *n.* unskilled worker, esp. one in bondage. —**pe′on·age,** *n.*

pē′ò·nў, *n., pl.* **-nies.** perennial garden plant with large colorful flowers.

pēo′ple, *n., v.t.,* **-pled, -pling.** *n.* **1.** humanity generally. **2.** random group of persons. **3. peoples,** national, cultural, or racial group. —*v.t.* **4.** populate.

pĕp, *Informal. n.* **1.** energy, vigor. —*v.t.* **2. pep up,** make lively; energize. —**pep′py,** *adj.*

pĕp′pêr, *n.* **1.** pungent condiment from an East Indian plant. **2.** hot or mild fruit used as a condiment vegetable. —*v.t.* **3.** season with pepper. **4.** pelt with missiles. **5.** sprinkle as with pepper. —**pep′per·y,** *adj.*

pĕp′pêr·mĭnt″, *n.* aromatic herb used as a flavoring.

pĕp′sĭn, *n.* stomach enzyme which digests proteins.

pĕp′tĭc, *adj.* pertaining to digestion; digestive.

pêr, *prep.* thought; by means of; according to.

pêr·ăm′bū·lāte″, *v.i.,* **-ated, -ating.** walk about; stroll. —**per·am″bu·la′tion,** *n.*

pêr·cāle′, *n.* smooth, closely woven cotton.

pêr·cēive′, *v.t.* **1.** become aware of. **2.** apprehend or understand. —**per·ceiv′a·ble, per·cep′ti·ble,** *adj.* —**per·cep′tion,** *n.*

pêr·cĕnt′, *n.* part in a hundred.

pêr·cĕnt′àge, *n.* **1.** proportion per hundred. **2.** allowance, commission, or rate of interest.

pêr·cĕp′tĭve, *adj.* **1.** pertaining to perception. **2.** understanding; discerning.

pêrch, *n.* **1.** roost for birds. **2.** high spot. **3.** freshwater food fish. —*v.t., v.i.* **4.** set or rest as on a perch.

pêr·chănce′, *adv.* perhaps.

pêr′cò·lāte″, *v.t., v.i.* **-lated, -lating.** filter. —**per″co·la′tion,** *n.*

pêr·cŭs′sion, *n.* **1.** hard, sharp impact. **2.** musical instruments plucked or struck. —**per·cus′sive,** *adj.*

pêr dĭ′ĕm, by the day.

pêr·dĭ′tion, *n.* damnation.

pĕr″′e·grĭ·nā′tion, *n.* travel from one place to another. —**per′e·gri·nate″,** *v.i.*

pêr·ĕmp′tò·rў, *adj.* **1.** giving no opportunity to refuse or deny. 2. imperative. —per·emp'to·ri·ly, *adv.*

pê·rĕn'nĭ·ȧl, *adj.* 1. enduring. 2. lasting more than two years. —*n.* 3. plant growing every year. —per·en·ni'al·ly, *adv.*

pêr'fĕct, *adj.* 1. flawless and complete. 2. unmodified. 3. *Grammar.* denoting completed action. —*v.t.* (pər fekt'). 4. make perfect. —per'fect·ly, *adj.* —per·fec'tion, *n.*

pêr·fĕc'tion·ĭst, *n.* person who demands perfection.

pêr'fĭ·dȳ, *n., pl.* -dies, treachery; faithlessness. —per·fid'i·ous, *adj.*

pêr'fȯ·rāte'', *v.t.,* -rated, -rating. pierce through.

pêr·fôrce', *adv.* necessarily.

pêr·fôrm', *v.t.* 1. carry out; execute. 2. enact, play, etc. for an audience. —*v.i.* 3. appear in a play, concert, etc. —per·form'ance, *n.* —per·form'er, *n.*

pêr·fūme', *n., v.t.,* -fumed, -fuming, *n.* 1. sweet odor; fragrance. 2. sweet-smelling liquid for scenting. —*v.t.* 3. scent.

pêr·fŭnc'tö·rȳ, *adj.* routine and unenthusiastic. —per·func'to·ri·ly, *adv.* —per·func'to·ri·ness, *n.*

pêr·hăps', *adv.* maybe, possibly.

pĕr'ĭ·gēe, *n.* nearest point of an orbit to the earth.

pĕr'ĭ·hė'li·ȯn, *n.* nearest point of an orbit to the sun.

pêr'ĭl, *n.* 1. danger. 2. source of danger. —per'il·ous, *adj.*

pè·rĭm'ė·têr, *n.* outer boundary.

pē''rĭ·ŏd, *n.* 1. division or extent of time. 2. end; stop. 3. punctuation point at the end of a declarative sentence.

pē''rĭ·ŏd'ĭc, *adj.* intermittently or regularly recurring.

pē''rĭ·ŏd'ĭ·căl, *n.* publication appearing at regular intervals. —pe''ri·od'i·cal·ly, *adv.*

pè·rĭph'êr·ȳ, *n., pl.* -eries. 1. boundary of a rounded figure. 2. outer limits; border. —pe·riph'er·al, *adj.*

pĕr'ĭ·scōpe, *n.* optical instrument for viewing around an obstruction with prisms or mirrors.

pĕr'ĭsh, *v.i.* 1. die, esp. from privation or violence. 2. decay. —per'ish·a·ble, *adj.*

pêr''ĭ·tȯ·nī'tĭs, *n.* inflammation of the abdominal lining.

pêr'ĭ·wĭn''kle, *n.* 1. edible snail. 2. trailing evergreen plant.

pêr'jûre, *v.t.,* -jured, -juring. make guilty of perjury. —per'jur·er, *n.* —per'jured, *adj.*

pêr'jû·rȳ, *n., pl.* -ries. 1. lying under oath. 2. lie so uttered. —per·ju'ri·ous, *adj.*

pêrk, *v.i.* 1. become lively or vigorous. —*v.t.* 2. raise jauntily, as the head. —perk'y, *adj.*

pêr'mȧ·nĕnt, *adj.* existing always. —per'ma·nen·cy, *n.* —per'ma·nent·ly, *adj.*

pêr'mē·āte'', *v.,* -ated, -ating. *v.t.* 1. penetrate. 2. be diffused through. —*v.i.* 3. become diffused. —per''me·a'tion, *n.* —per'me·a·ble, *adj.*

pêr·mĭs'sĭve, *adj.* 1. granting permission. 2. indulgent; lenient.

pêr·mĭt *v.t.,* -mitted, -mitting, *n. v.t.* (pər mit'). 1. allow. 2. tolerate. 3. give opportunity for. —*n.* (pər'mit) 4. written permission; license. —per·mis'sion, *n.* —per·mis'si·ble, *adj.*

pêr''mū·tā'tion, *n.* change; alteration.

pêr·nĭ'cioŭs, *adj.* injurious; hurtful.

pêr''ō·rā'tion, *n.* concluding part of a speech.

pêr·ŏx'īde, *n.* 1. oxide containing a large proportion of oxygen. —*v.t.* 2. bleach with a peroxide, esp. the hair.

pêr''pĕn·dĭc'ū·làr, *adj.* 1. vertical. 2. meeting another line at a right angle. —*n.* 3. perpendicular plane or line.

pêr'pė·trāte'', *v.t.,* -trated, -trating, commit; be guilty of. —per''pe·tra'tion, *n.* —per'pe·tra''tor, *n.*

pêr·pĕt'ū·ȧl, *adj.* 1. permanent. 2. unceasing; constant. —per·pet'u·al·ly, *adv.* —per·pet'u·ate'' *v.t.* —per·pet''u·a'tion, *n.*

pêr''pė·tū'ĭ·tȳ, *n.* endless duration.

pêr·plĕx', *v.t.* bewilder. —per·plex'i·ty, *n.*

pêr'quĭs·ĭte, *n.* benefit added to regular salary.

pèr se', by, of, or in itself.

pêr'sė·cūte, *v.t.,* -cuted, -cuting. continually harass or oppress. —per''se·cu'tion, *n.* —per'se·cu·tor, *n.*

pêr''sė·vēre', *v.t.,* -vered, -vering. persist in spite of obstacles. —per″se·ver′ance, *n*.

pêr·sĭm′mŏn, *n*. astringent, edible North American fruit.

pêr·sĭst′, *v.i.* 1. continue resolutely. 2. last; endure. —per·sist′ence, *n*. —per·sist′ent, *adj.* —per·sist′ent·ly, *adv.*

pêr′sŏn, *n*. 1. human being; individual. 2. personality. 3. one's body.

pêr′sŏn·a·ble, *adj.* 1. pleasing in appearance. 2. sociable.

pêr′sŏn·āge, *n*. person of distinction or note.

pêr′sŏn·ăl, *adj.* 1. pertaining to one individual. 2. pertaining to the body and its care, clothing, etc. —per′son·al·ly, *adv.* —per′son·al·ize″, *v.t.*

pêr″sŏn·ăl′ĭ·tỹ, *n., pl.* -ties. 1. distinctive personal character. 2. personally disparaging remark. 3. notable person.

pêr·sō′nà nŏn grā′tà, unwelcome or unacceptable person.

pêr·sŏn′ĭ·fỹ, *v.t.*, -fied, -fying. 1. attribute personal character to. 2. embody; typify. —per·son″i·fi·ca′tion, *n*.

pêr″sŏn·nĕl′, *n*. employees of an organization.

pêr·spĕc′tĭve, *n*. 1. technique of three-dimensional representation. 2. extended view. 3. basis for interpretation.

pêr″spĭ·cā′cioŭs, *adj.* acutely perceptive; discerning. —per″spi·cac′i·ty, *n*.

pêr·spīre′, *v.i.* sweat. —per″spi·ra′tion, *n*.

pêr·suāde′, *v.t.*, -suaded, -suading. 1. prevail on by argument. 2. induce belief in; convince. —per·sua′sive, *adj.*

pêr·suā′sion, *n*. 1. process or act of persuading. 2. conviction or belief, opinion.

pêrt, *adj.* 1. bold; saucy; impudent. 2. lively, sprightly.

pêr·tāin′, *v.t.* have reference to; relate.

pêr″tĭ·nā′cioŭs, *adj.* holding firmly to an opinion or purpose. —per′ti·nac′i·ty, *n*.

pêr′tĭ·nĕnt, *adj.* relevant; applicable. —per′ti·nence, per′ti·nen·cy, *n*.

pêr·tûrb′, *v.t.* greatly disturb in mind; upset. —per·tur·ba′tion, *n*.

pè·rūse′, *v.t.* read or survey, esp. with thoroughness. —pe·ru′sal, *n*.

pêr·vāde′, *v.t.* -vaded, -vading. extend or spread throughout; permeate. —per·va′sive, *adj.*

pêr·vêrse′, *adj.* 1. abnormal; corrupt. 2. stubbornly contrary; obstinate. —per·verse′ly, *adv.* —per·ver′si·ty, *n*.

pêr·vêrt′, *n*. 1. perverted person, esp. sexually. —*v.t.* 2. deviate from the proper or right course of action. 3. misapply; misconstrue; distort. —per·ver′sion, *n*.

pe′sō, *n*. monetary unit of Mexico, etc.

pĕs′sĭ·mĭsm″, *n*. disposition toward the least favorable interpretation or expectation. —pes′si·mist, *n*. —pes′si·mis′tic, *adj.*

pĕst, *n*. troublesome person or thing; nuisance.

pĕs′têr, *v.t.* annoy.

pĕs′tĭ·cīde″, *n*. insecticide.

pĕs′tĭ·lĕnce, *n*. deadly epidemic or disease; plague. —pes′ti·lent, *adj.*

pĕs′tle, *n*. implement for grinding or crushing (with a mortar).

pĕt, *n., adj., v.t.*, petted, petting. *n*. 1. tamed animal kept for pleasure. 2. darling; favorite. —*v.t.* 3. indulge; pamper. 4. stroke or fondle affectionately. —*adj.* 5. treated lovingly.

pĕt′ăl, *n*. colored leaf of a flower.

pĕ·tīte′, *adj.* small or tiny: used in reference to women.

pĕ·tĭ′tion, *n*. 1. request or entreaty, esp. when written. —*v.i.* 2. present a petition; ask for. —pe·ti′tion·er, *n*.

pĕt′rĕl, *n*. small sea bird.

pĕt′rĭ·fỹ″, *v.*, -fied, -fying. *v.t.* 1. turn into stone; stiffen. 2. paralyze or stupefy with horror, wonder, etc. —*v.i.* 3. become petrified.

pĕt″rō·chĕm′ĭ·căl, *n*. chemical derived from petroleum.

pè·trō′lē·ŭm, *n*. natural oily liquid found underground.

pè·trŏl′o·gỹ, *n*. study of rocks.

pĕt′tĭ·cōat″, *n*. skirt worn under a dress.

pĕt′tĭsh, *adj.* peevish; petulant.

pĕt′tỹ, *adj.* -tier, -tiest. 1. of little importance; trivial. 2. narrow-minded; mean. —pet′ti·ness, *n*.

pĕt′ū·lànt, *adj.* marked by impatient irritation; irritable, peevish.

pè·tū′nià, *n*. annual garden plant with bright funnel-shaped flowers.

pēw, *n*. enclosed church bench.

pē′wēe, *n*. any of various small birds.

pĕw'têr, *n.* alloy composed primarily of tin.

pey·ō'tē, *n.* hallucinogenic drug derived from the mescal cactus.

phā'lănx, *n., pl.* -lanxes, -langes, **1.** body or group in formation, e.g. troops. **2.** any of the bones of the fingers or toes of mammals.

phăl'lŭs, *n., pl.* phalli. **1.** penis. **2.** symbolic representation of the penis. —phal'lic, *adj.*

phăn'tăsm, *n.* apparition; illusion.

phăn·tăs''mȧ·gō'rïȧ, *n.* succession of imagined things.

phăn'tóm, *n.* insubstantial image; dreamlike apparition.

Phăr·aōh (fa'ro), *n.* ancient Egyptian ruler.

phăr'ĭ·sēe'', *n.* **1.** self-righteous person. **2.** member of early Jewish sect.

phär''mȧ·ceū'tĭ·cȧl, *adj.* of or pertaining to pharmacy. Also, phar''ma·ceu'tic.

phär''mȧ·cŏl'ȯ·gȳ, *n.* study of drugs, esp. for medicial use. —phar''ma·col'o·gist, *n.*

phär'mȧ·cȳ, *n., pl.* -cies. **1.** practice of preparing medicines. **2.** drug store. —phar'ma·cist, *n.*

phăr'ynx, *n., pl.* -ynges, -rynxes. cavity that connects mouth and nasal passages with the esophagus. —pha·ryn'ge·al, *adj.*

phāse, *n.* **1.** stage of a process. **2.** aspect. —*v.t.* **3.** introduce or withdraw in stages.

phĕas'ȧnt, *n.* large, long-tailed, brightly colored game bird.

phē''nȯ·bâr'bĭ·tŏl, *n.* white powder used as sedative and hypnotic.

phė·nŏm'ė·nȧl, *n.* **1.** amazing. **2.** pertaining to phenomena.

phė·nŏm'ė·nŏn, *n., pl.* -na, -nons. **1.** apparent occurrence, circumstance, or fact. **2.** extraordinary person or thing.

phī'ȧl, *n.* vial.

phĭ'lȧn'dêr, *v.i.* (of a man) make love with no serious intentions. —phi·lan'der·er, *n.*

phĭ·lăn'thrȯ·pȳ, *n., pl.* -pies. **1.** love of mankind. **2.** charitable act, work, or organization. —phil''an·throp'ic, phil''an·throp'i·cal, *adj.* —phi·lan'thro·pist, *n.*

phĭ·lăt'é·lȳ, *n.* collection and study of postage stamps. —phi·lat'e·list, *n.*

phĭl''hâr·mŏn'ĭc, *adj.* music-loving.

phĭ·lĭs'tïne, *n.* person indifferent to cultural matters.

phĭ·lŏl'ȯ·gȳ, *n.* linguistics. —phi·lol'o·gist, *n.*

phĭ·lŏs'ȯ·phêr, *n.* **1.** reflective thinker. **2.** scholar trained in philosophy. **3.** person who meets difficulties calmly.

phĭ·lŏs'ȯ·phȳ, *n., pl.* -phies. **1.** study of the fundamental truths of life and the universe. **2.** system of philosophical concepts. —phil''o·soph'i·cal, phil''o·soph'ic, *adj.* —phi·los'o·phize'', *v.i.*

phlĕg·mă'tĭc, *adj.* stolid, impassive; apathetic.

phlĕgm, *n.* thick mucus secreted in the nose and throat.

phlŏx, *n.* garden plant with colorful flowers.

phō'bĭ·ȧ, *n.* persistent and irrational morbid fear.

phoē'bē, *n.* small eastern American bird.

phoē'nĭx, *n.* mythical bird said to rise from its own ashes.

phōne, *n., v.t.,* phoned, phoning. *n.* **1.** telephone. —*v.t.* **2.** make a phone call to.

phȯ·nĕt'ĭcs, *n.* study of speech sounds. —pho·net'ic, *adj.*

phō'nȯ·grăph'', *n.* machine for playing records.

phō'nȳ, *n., adj.,* -nier, -niest, *Informal.* *n.* **1.** fake person or thing. —*adj.* **2.** fake; counterfeit.

phŏs'phāte, *n.* chemical salt often used in fertilizers.

phŏs''phô·rĕs'cĕnce, *n.* luminescence without sensible heat. —phos''pho·res'cent, *adj.*

phŏs'phô·rŭs, *n.* solid nonmetallic element found in bones, nerves, etc. —phos·phor'ic, phos'pho·rous, *adj.*

phō'tō, *n., pl.* -tos. photograph.

phō''tō·é·lĕc'trĭc, *adj.* pertaining to electric effects resulting from light.

phō'tō·ĕn·grāv''ĭng, *n.* process of producing an etched printing plate from a photograph or drawing. —pho'to·en·grave'', *v.t.*

phō''tō·gĕn'ĭc, *adj.* suitable for being photographed.

phō′tȯ·grăph″, *n.* **1.** picture taken by photography. —*v.i.* **2.** take a photograph. —**pho·tog′ra·pher**, *n.*

phō·tŏg′rȧ·phȳ, *n.* process of producing images on treated surfaces by the action of light. —**pho″to·graph′ic**, *adj.*

phō″tō·sĕn′sĭ·tĭve, *adj.* sensitive or sensitized to light.

phō″tō·sȳn′thė·sĭs, *n.* process by which chlorophyll-containing plants exposed to sunlight produce carbohydrates.

phrāse, *n.*, *v.t.*, **phrased, phrasing.** *n.* **1.** sequence of words conveying a thought. **2.** brief expression or remark. **3.** unit of musical composition. —*v.t.* **4.** express in a certain way.

phrā″sē·ŏl′ȯ·gȳ, *n.* **1.** manner of speaking. **2.** collective expressions or phrases.

phrė·nĕ′tĭc, *adj.* delirious.

phrė·nŏl′ȯ·gȳ, *n.* study that infers personal characteristics from the shape of the skull. —**phre·nol′o·gist**, *n.*

phȳ′lŭm, *n.*, *pl.* **-la.** major division of plant and animal classes.

phys′ĭc, *n.* medicine, esp. a purgative.

phys′i·căl, *adj.* **1.** pertaining to the body. **2.** pertaining to matter or the material world. **3.** pertaining to physics. —*n.* **4.** medical examination. —**phys′i·cal·ly**, *adv.*

phy·si′cian, *n.* medical doctor.

phys′ĭcs, *n.* science dealing with motion, matter, energy, and force. —**phys′i·cist**, *n.*

phys″ĭ·ŏg′nȯ·mȳ, *n.*, *pl.* **-mies.** facial appearance.

phys″ĭ·ŏg′rȧ·phȳ, *n.* science of the earth's surface.

phys″ĭ·ŏl′ȯ·gȳ, *n.* science of the functioning of living matter and beings. —**phys″i·o·log′i·cal**, *adj.* —**phys″i·ol′o·gist**, *n.*

phys″ĭ·ō·thĕr′ȧ·pȳ, *n.* treatment of disease by physical means, e.g. exercise, massage, etc.

phy·sïque′, *n.* physical constitution of the body; build.

pī, *n.* Greek letter π, symbol for the value 3.1416, ratio of circumference to diameter.

pī″ȧ·nĭs′sĭ·mō, *adj.*, *adv.* *Music.* very soft.

pi·ăn′ō, *n.*, *pl.* **-anos**, *adj.*, *adv.* *n.* **1.** Also, **pi·an″o for′te**, percussive, musical keyboard instrument with steel strings struck by hammers. —*adj.* **2.** soft. —*adv.* **3.** softly. —**pi·an′ist**, *n.*

pī·ăz′zȧ, *n.* veranda or porch.

pī′cȧ, *n.* measure of printing type equal to about a sixth of an inch.

pĭc″ȧ·yūne′, *adj.* insignificant; trivial; petty.

pĭc′cȧ·lĭl″lĭ, *n.* spicy vegetable relish.

pĭc′cȯ·lō″, *n.*, *pl.* **-los**, small shrill flute.

pĭck, *v.t.* **1.** choose or select. **2.** gather, e.g. flowers. **3.** separate or pull apart. **4.** pierce with a pointed instrument. **5.** provoke, e.g. pick a fight. —*n.* **6.** choice; selection. **7.** Also, **pick′ax**, **pick′axe**, sharp tool for breaking rock. —**pick′er**, *n.*

pĭck′êr·ėl, *n.* small pike.

pĭck′ĕt, *n.* **1.** protestor stationed by a striking labor union. **2.** body or group of soldiers on lookout. **3.** pointed fence with pickets. —*v.i.* **4.** serve as a picket.

pĭck′ĭngs, *n.* **1.** gleanings. **2.** rewards; spoils.

pĭck′le, *n.*, *v.t.*, **-led, -ling.** *n.* **1.** cucumber cured in spiced vinegar. **2.** any food preserved in a pickling solution. **3.** *Informal.* difficult predicament; bind. —*v.t.* **4.** preserve in brine or vinegar.

pĭck′pŏck″ĕt, *n.* thief who steals from pockets.

pĭck′ŭp, *n.* **1.** acceleration; energy. **2.** revival of action. **3.** small open-body truck for hauling.

pĭck′ȳ, *adj.* fussy, finicky.

pĭc′nĭc, *n.*, *v.i.*, **-nicked, -nicking.** *n.* **1.** outing with an outdoor meal. —*v.t.* go on a picnic. —**pic′nick·er**, *n.*

pĭc′tûre, *n.*, *v.t.*, **-tured, -turing.** *n.* **1.** painting, drawing, photograph, etc. **2.** motion picture. —*v.t.* **3.** represent in a picture. **4.** conceive; visualize. —**pic·tor′i·al**, *adj.*

pĭc″tûr·ĕsque′, *adj.* **1.** charming; quaint. **2.** striking; vivid.

pīe, *n.* baked dish of pastry crust and filling, e.g. meat, fruit, etc.

pīe′bäld″, *adj.* marked by patches of different colors.

pīēce, *n.*, *v.t.*, **pieced, piecing.** *n.* **1.** part or single portion. **2.** artistic creation. **3.** firearm. —*v.t.* **4.** join or repair from pieces.

piece′meal″, *adv.* **1.** piece by piece. **2.** into fragments.

pied, *adj.* many-colored; variegated.

pier, *n.* **1.** massive support. **2.** structure loading and unloading vessels.

pierce, *v.t.*, **pierced, piercing, 1.** penetrate into or through. **2.** make a hole into.

pi′e·ty, *n.* religious dutifulness; devoutness.

pig, *n.* **1.** swine, esp. young. **2.** oblong metal casting.

pi′geon, *n.* short-legged, stout-bodied bird.

pi′geon·hole″, *n., v.t.*, **-holed, -holing.** *n.* **1.** small compartment, e.g. in a desk. —*v.t.* **2.** place in a pigeonhole; classify.

pig′ment, *n.* coloring matter. —**pig″men·ta′tion**, *n.*

pig′tail, *n.* tight braid of hair.

pike, *n.* **1.** large, slender freshwater fish. **2.** long wooden spear. **3.** highway.

pik′er, *n. Informal.* person who does things in a small or cheap way.

pi′laf″, *n.* seasoned rice dish.

pi·las′ter, *n.* column that projects slightly from a wall.

pile, *n., v.t.*, **piled, piling.** *n.* **1.** heap. **2.** support driven into the ground. **3.** short standing fibers, as in a rug. **4.** nuclear reactor. **5. piles,** hemorrhoids. —*v.t.* **6.** put in a pile. —*v.t., v.i.* **7.** accumulate.

pil′fer, *v.i., v.t.* steal.

pil′grim, *n.* traveler in foreign lands, esp. to a holy place. —**pil′grim·age,** *n.*

pill, *n.* medicine in tablet or capsule form.

pil′lage, *v.t.*, **-laged, -laging.** loot; plunder.

pil′lar, *n.* masonry column.

pill′box″, *n.* **1.** low shelter against gunfire. **2.** small container for pills.

pil′lo·ry, *n., pl.* **-ries.** wooden frame with head and arm holes for public punishment.

pil′low, *n.* cushion filled with feathers, etc. for support, esp. of the head. —**pil′low·case″**, *n.*

pi′lot, *n.* **1.** person who guides a ship or airplane. —*v.t.* **2.** steer; guide. —*adj.* **3.** experimental.

pi·men′to, *n., pl.* **-tos. 1.** dried fruit of a tropical tree; allspice. **2.** pimiento.

pi·mien′to, *n., pl.* **-tos.** sweet, red, garden pepper.

pimp, *n.* person who finds clients for a prostitute.

pim′ple, *n.* small, inflamed swelling on the skin. —**pim′ply**, *adj.*

pin, *n., v.t.*, **pinned, pinning.** *n.* **1.** slender, pointed fastener. **2.** piece of jewelry fastened to a garment. **3.** wooden target piece in bowling. —*v.t.* **4.** fasten with a pin. **5.** hold tight; bind.

pin′a·fore″, *n.* sleeveless dress or apron, esp. for a child.

pince′-nez″, *n.* eyeglasses held on the nose by a pinching spring.

pin′cers, *n.* gripping tool with two handles.

pinch, *v.t.* **1.** squeeze, e.g. with the thumb and forefinger. **2.** economize. **3.** steal. **4.** arrest. —*n.* **5.** act or instance of pinching. **6.** tiny amount.

pinch′hit″, *v.i.*, **-hit, -hitting.** substitute for someone else. —**pinch″hit′ter**, *n.*

pine, *v.i.*, **pined, pining,** *n. v.i.* **1.** yearn, esp. painfully. **2.** gradually fail in health from grief. —*n.* **3.** cone-bearing evergreen tree with needle-like leaves.

pine′ap″ple, *n.* tropical plant with a juicy, edible fruit.

pin′feath″er, *n.* feather just beginning to develop.

pin′ion, *n.* **1.** end of a bird's wing. **2.** small gear wheel. —*v.t.* **3.** restrain; bind.

pink, *n.* **1.** light red. **2.** colorful, showy garden flower. **3.** highest condition of health. —*adj.* **4.** of the color pink.

pin′na·cle, *n.* highest part or position.

pi·noch′le″, *n.* game played with forty-eight cards.

pint, *n.* **1.** unit of liquid measure equal to 16 fluid ounces or half a quart. **2.** unit of dry measure equal to half a quart.

pin′to, *n., pl.* **-tos. 1.** horse with white and brown patches. **2.** mottled.

pin′up″, *n.* picture of a beautiful man or woman, esp. unclothed.

pin′wheel″, *n.* toy with a wheel that spins on the end of a stick.

pi″o·neer′, *n.* **1.** early settler or adventurer. **2.** first person to do something. —*v.i.* **3.** prepare a way for others.

pi′ous, *adj.* **1.** devout. **2.** sacred. —**pi′ous·ly**, *adv.* —**pi′ous·ness**, *n.*

pipe, *n., v.t.*, **piped, piping.** *n.* **1.** tube for carrying gas, water, etc. **2.** tube with a bowl at one end for smoking tobacco. **3.** tube used in a musical instrument. —*v.t.* **4.** carry by pipe. —**pi′per,** *n.* —**pipe′line′′,** *n.*

pip′ing, *n.* **1.** pipes; plumbing. **2.** music of pipes. **3.** material to trim edges.

pip′pin, *n.* kind of yellowish apple.

pi′quant, *adj.* **1.** pleasantly sharp; pungent. **2.** provocative; charming. —**pi′quan·cy,** *n.*

pique, *n.*, *v.t.*, **-piqued, piquing.** *n.* **1.** irritation; resentment. —*v.t.* **2.** arouse resentment in, esp. by wounding pride. **3.** provoke or incite.

pi′ra·cy, *n.*, *pl.* **-cies. 1.** robbery at sea or in the air. **2.** unauthorized use of copyrighted or patented material. —**pi′rate,** *n.*, *v.t.*

pir′′ou·ette′, *v.i.*, **-etted, -etting.** *n.* *v.i.* **1.** whirl about on one foot or on the toes, esp. in ballet. —*n.* **2.** such a movement.

pis′′ca·tô·ri·al, *adj.* pertaining to fishing.

pis·tä′chi·ō′′, *n.*, *pl.* **-os.** nut with an edible greenish seed.

pis′til, *n.* seed-bearing organ in a flower.

pis′tol, *n.* small hand-carried firearm.

pis′ton, *n.* reciprocating disk moved by the pressure of steam, combustion gas, etc. in a cylinder.

pit, *n.*, *v.t.*, **pitted, pitting.** *n.* **1.** hole in the ground. **2.** cavity or hollow in the body. **3.** front part of the main floor in a theater. **4.** stone or seed of a fruit. —*v.t.* **5.** set against another. **6.** remove the pit from.

pitch, *v.t.* **1.** set up, as a tent. **2.** throw or toss. **3.** set at a certain level or point. —*v.i.* **4.** fall or plunge. —*n.* **5.** height. **6.** slope. **7.** musical tone. **8.** sticky substance from coal tar or pine bark. **9.** act or instance of pitching.

pitch′blende′′, *n.* mineral that is the principal source of radium and uranium.

pitch′êr, *n.* **1.** spouted container for liquids. **2.** one who pitches.

pitch′fôrk′′, *n.* large, sharp-pointed fork for pitching hay.

pit′e·ous, *adj.* pitiful; pathetic.

pit′fäll′′, *n.* snare; hidden difficulty.

pith, *n.* **1.** loose spongy tissue. **2.** essence; gist. —**pith′y,** *adj.*

pit′i·a·ble, *adj.* **1.** deserving pity. **2.** contemptible. —**pit′i·a·bly,** *adv.*

pit′i·fŭl, *adj.* **1.** deserving pity. **2.** feeling pity. —**pit′i·ful·ly,** *adv.* —**pit′i·ful·ness,** *n.*

pit′tànce, *n.* small portion or amount.

pi·tū′i·tär′′y̆, *n.* pertaining to a gland at the base of the brain.

pit̆y̆, *n.*, *pl.* **pities,** *v.t.*, **pitied, pitying.** *n.* **1.** sympathy for wretchedness. **2.** cause for regret. —*v.t.* **3.** feel pity for. —**pit′i·less,** *adj.* —**pit′i·less·ly,** *adv.*

piv′ot, *n.* **1.** point or object for turning. —*v.i.* **2.** turn around a point.

pix′y̆, *n.*, *pl.* **pixies.** fairy; mischievous sprite. Also, **pix′ie.**

piz′zà, *n.* flat pie covered with a spiced mixture of tomato sauce, cheese, etc.

plăc′ärd, *n.* posted public notice.

plā′cāte, *v.t.*, **-cated, -cating.** appease; pacify. —**pla′ca·ble,** *adj.* —**pla·ca′tion,** *n.*

plăce, *n.*, *v.t.*, **placed, placing.** *n.* **1.** particular point in space. **2.** function. **3.** social position. **4.** stead; lieu. —*v.t.* **5.** put in a place. **6.** identify; recognize. —**place′ment,** *n.*

plà·cĕn′tà, *n.* uterine organ which nourishes the fetus.

plăc′êr, *n.* gravel containing gold particles.

plăc′ĭd, *adj.* serene; peaceful. —**plac′id·ly,** *adv.* —**pla·cid′i·ty,** *n.*

plăck′et, *n.* slit in a garment.

plā′gĭ·a·rīze′′, *v.t.*, **-rized, -rizing.** appropriate wrongfully, as another's writings. —**pla′gi·a·rism′′,** *n.* —**pla′gi·a·rist,** *n.*

plāgue, *n.*, *v.t.*, **plagued, plaguing.** *n.* **1.** pestilence. **2.** affliction; vexation; irritation. —*v.t.* **3.** trouble; annoy.

plăid, *n.* **1.** woolen garment with a pattern of multi-colored crossbars. —*adj.* **2.** such a pattern.

plāin, *adj.* **1.** evident; obvious. **2.** candid. **3.** unpretentious. **4.** simple, uncomplicated. **5.** homely. —*n.* **6.** flat, open area or space of ground. —**plain′ly,** *adv.*

plāin′tiff, *n.* complaining party in a civil case.

plāin′tive, *n.* melancholy, sad.

plāit, *n.*, *v.t.* **1.** braid. **2.** pleat.

plăn, *n.*, *v.t.*, **planned, planning.** *n.* **1.** drawing or diagram. **2.** intended scheme or method. —*v.t.* **3.** make a plan of. —**plan'ner**, *n.*

plāne, *n., adj., v.*, **planed, planing**. *n.* **1.** flat surface. **2.** level, e.g. of experience, attainment, etc. **3.** airplane. **4.** bladed tool for smoothing wood. —*adj.* **5.** flat, level. **6.** smooth or shape with a plane. —*v.i.* **7.** glide.

plăn'ĕt, *n.* solid celestial body that revolves around the sun. —**plan'e·tar''y**, *n.*

plăn''ė·tār''ĭ·ŭm, *n.* optical device which projects images of celestial bodies on a dome.

plănk, *n.* long slab of lumber.

plănt, *n.* **1.** any of the vegetable group of organisms. **2.** buildings and equipment of a business. —*v.t.* **3.** put in the ground to grow. **4.** put plants in. —**plant'er**, *n.*

plăn·tā'tion, *n.* estate esp. for farming, etc.

plăque, *n.* decorative or commemorative tablet.

plăs'mà, *n.* liquid element of blood or lymph.

plăs'têr, *n.* **1.** composition applied to walls, etc. **2.** medicinal dressing. —*v.t.* **3.** treat or cover with plaster.

plăs'tĭc, *n.* **1.** molded synthetic material. —*adj.* **2.** capable of being molded. **3.** characterized or produced by molding. —**plas·tic'i·ty**, *n.*

plāte, *n., v.t.*, **plated, plating**. *n.* **1.** thin, flat piece of material. **2.** shallow dish from which food is served and eaten. **3.** silver or gold ware. **4.** denture. —*v.t.* **5.** coat with metal.

pla·teau (plă·tō'), *n.* large, raised plain.

plăt'fôrm, *n.* **1.** raised floor area. **2.** declaration of political principles.

plăt'ĭ·nŭm, *n.* valuable, silver-white metallic element.

plăt'ĭ·tūde'', *n.* trite, pompous, or self-righteous remark. —**plat''i·tu'di·nous**, *adj.*

plà·tŏn'ĭc, *adj.* **1.** spiritual; idealistic. **2.** pertaining to close, non-sexual love.

plà·tōōn', *n.* small military unit.

plăt'têr, *n.* large, shallow serving dish.

plăt'y·pŭs, *n.* small Australian aquatic mammal.

plau'dĭt, *n.* burst of applause.

plau'sĭ·ble, *adj.* seemingly true or believable. —**plau''si·bil'i·ty**, *n.* **plau'si·bly**, *adv.*

plāy, *n.* **1.** dramatic composition. **2.** recreational activity. **3.** fun; pleasure. **4.** maneuver, as in sports. **5.** free motion. —*v.t.* **6.** participate in a play or game. **7.** perform on a musical instrument. —*v.i.* **8.** amuse oneself. **9.** move freely. —**play'er**, *n.* —**play'ful**, *adj.*

plāy'pĕn, *n.* portable enclosed play area for a baby.

plāy'thĭng, *n.* toy.

plāy'wrĭght, *n.* writer of plays.

plä'zà, *n.* **1.** public square. **2.** shopping center.

plēa, *n.* **1.** appeal. **2.** acknowledgment or denial of guilt.

plēad, *v.*, **pleaded** or **pled, pleading**. *v.i.* **1.** appeal earnestly. **2.** make allegations in court. **3.** argue a case in court. —*v.t.* **4.** allege in excuse or justification.

plĕas'ànt, *adj.* agreeable; pleasing. —**pleas'ant·ly**, *adv.*

plĕas'àn·trÿ, *n., pl.* **-tries.** humorous or agreeable remark.

plēase, *v.*, **pleased, pleasing**. *v.t.* **1.** give satisfaction or pleasure to. —*v.i.* **2.** give pleasure. —*interj.* **3.** will you kindly? —**pleas'ing·ly**, *adv.*

plĕas'ûre, *n.* **1.** enjoyment. **2.** will or desire. —**pleas'ur·a·ble**, *adj.*

plēat, *n.* **1.** double fold in cloth. —*v.t.* **2.** fold in pleats.

plē·bē·iàn, *adj.* **1.** of or pertaining to the common people. **2.** common; vulgar. —*n.* **3.** plebeian person.

plĕb''ĭ·scīte', *n.* direct vote by the people.

plĕc'trŭm, *n.* pick for a guitar, etc.

plĕdge, *n., v.*, **pledged, pledging**. *n.* **1.** solemn promise or oath. **2.** property given in security for a loan. —*v.t.* **3.** bind or vow by a pledge. **4.** stake.

plē'nà·rÿ, *adj.* full; complete.

plĕn''ĭ·pô·tĕn'tĭ·ār''ÿ, *n., pl.* **-aries.** diplomat having full authority.

plĕn'ĭ·tūde'', *n.* fullness.

plĕn'tÿ, *n.* abundant supply. —**plen'te·ous, plen'ti·ful**, *adj.*

plĕth'ó·rà, *n.* profuseness.

pleu'rĭ·sÿ, *n.* inflammation of chest and lung membranes.

plĕx'ŭs, *n.* **1.** network of nerves or blood vessels. **2.** intricate network of component parts.

plī'à·ble, *adj.* **1.** flexible or easily bent.

2. easily influenced; adaptable. —**pli"**
a·bil'i·ty, *n.*

pli'ant, *adj.* pliable. —**pli'an·cy,** *n.*

pli'êrs, *n. pl.* small pincers for grabbing, bending, etc.

plĭght, *n.* **1.** predicament. —*v.t.* **2.** promise in marriage.

plŏd, *v.i.,* **plodded, plodding, 1.** walk slowly or heavily. **2.** work laboriously; drudge. —**plod'der,** *n.*

plŏt, *n., v.,* **plotted, plotting.** *n.* **1.** secret scheme. **2.** outline of a novel, etc. **3.** piece of land. —*v.t.* **4.** plan secretly. **5.** mark on a map, esp. position or course. —*v.i.* **6.** make secret plans; conspire. —**plot'ter,** *n.*

plŏv'êr, *n.* shore bird related to the sandpiper.

plow, *n.* **1.** implement for dividing soil. **2.** scraping implement for removing snow. —*v.t.* **3.** turn or furrow with or as with a plow. —*v.i.* **4.** move slowly or forcefully. Also, **plough.** —**plow'man,** *n.*

plow'shāre", *n.* blade of a plow.

plŏy, *n.* trick intended to trap or embarrass; tactic.

plŭck, *v.t.* **1.** pull things from. **2.** pull suddenly or forcefully. —*n.* **3.** courage.

plŭg, *n., v.,* **plugged, plugging.** *n.* **1.** object for stopping a hole. **2.** device on an electrical cord which makes the connection in the socket. **3.** *Informal.* endorsement or advertisement. —*v.t.* **4.** stop or close with a plug; insert.

plŭm, *n.* sweet, juicy fruit.

plŭm'age, *n.* feathers of a bird; finery, esp. in dress.

plŭmb, *n.* **1.** heavy weight on a measuring line. —*adv.* **2.** vertically. **3.** fully. —*adj.* **4.** vertical. —*v.t.* **5.** measure the depth of.

plŭmb'ĭng, *n.* system of water pipes. —**plumb'er,** *n.*

plūme, *n.* **1.** feather, esp. a large, conspicuous one. **2.** ornamental tuft.

plŭm'mĕt, *n.* **1.** plumb on a line. —*v.i.* **2.** plunge.

plŭmp, *adj.* **1.** fat; chubby. —*v.i.* **2.** drop or fall heavily **3.** favor something strongly.

plŭn'dêr, *v.t.* **1.** rob or pillage. —*n.* **2.** act or instance of plundering. **3.** loot; spoils.

plŭnge, *v.,* **plunged, plunging.** *n. v.t.* **1.** thrust, as into liquid. **2.** thrust into a

condition or predicament. —*v.i.* **3.** rush; dash. **4.** pitch forward. —*n.* **5.** dive or fall.

plū'rál, *adj.* denoting more than one.

plū·răl'ĭ·tў, *n.* **1.** majority. **2.** number of votes for a leading candidate over the number for a rival.

plŭs, *prep.* **1.** increased by. —*n.* **2.** mathematical sign for addition or for a positive number. **3.** something additional. —*adj.* **4.** pertaining to addition. **5.** positive.

plŭsh, *n.* **1.** long-piled fabric. —*adj.* **2.** fancy. —**plush'y,** *adj.*

plū·tŏc'rá·cў, *n., pl.* **-cies. 1.** rule by or power of the wealthy. **2.** controlling wealthy group. —**plu'to·crat",** *n.*

plū·tō'nĭ·ŭm, *n.* radioactive element.

plў, *v.,* **plied, plying,** *n., pl.* **plies.** *v.t.* **1.** work at or with. **2.** attempt to persuade. —*v.t., v.i.* **3.** travel regularly. —*n.* **4.** thickness or layer.

plў'wood, *n.* sheeting of thin plies of wood glued together.

pneŭ·măt'ĭc, *adj.* pertaining to, or using air or wind.

pneŭ·mō'nià, *n.* inflamed lung disease.

pōach, *v.i.* **1.** trespass to hunt or fish illegally. —*v.t.* **2.** cook in hot but not boiling water. —**poach'er,** *n.*

pŏck, *n.* mark on the skin; scar, esp. from smallpox.

pŏck'ĕt, *n.* **1.** pouch in a garment. **2.** cavity. **3.** isolated group or area. —*v.t.* **4.** put in one's pocket. **5.** take possession of.

pŏck'ĕt·book", *n.* purse; handbag.

pŏd, *n.* vegetable seed covering.

pō·dī'à·trў, *n.* medical treatment of the foot. —**po·di'a·trist,** *n.*

pō'dĭ·ŭm, *n.* small platform.

pō'ĕm, *n.* composition in verse.

pō'ĕt·rў, *n.* rhythmical verse composition. —**po'et,** *fem.,* **po'et·ess,** *n.* —**po·et'ic, po·et'i·cal,** *adj.*

pō'grŏm, *n.* organized massacre.

poign·ant (poin'yənt), *adj.* deeply moving. —**poign'an·cy,** *n.*

poīn·sĕt'tĭ·à, *n.* tropical plant with scarlet flowers.

poīnt, *n.* **1.** sharp end. **2.** dot. **3.** specific time or position. **4.** individual detail or idea. **5.** reason or meaning. —*v.i.* **6.** indicate a direction. —*v.i.* **7.** direct or turn. —**point'less,** *adj.*

poĭnt'-blănk', *adj*. **1.** direct; plain. —*adv*. **2.** directly.

poĭnt'êr, *n*. **1.** something that points or indicates. **2.** breed of hunting dog.

poīse, *n*., *v*., poised, poising. *n*. **1.** balance; composure. —*v.i*. **2.** be balanced. **3.** hover, e.g. a bird in the air. —*v.t*. **4.** balance.

poĭ'sŏn, *n*. **1.** substance that kills or harms. —*v.t*. **2.** administer poison to. **3.** corrupt. —poi'son·ous, *adj*.

pōke, *v*., poked, poking. *n*. *v.i*., *v.t*., *n*. thrust.

pŏk'êr, *n*. **1.** metal rod for poking fires. **2.** card game.

pō'lår, *adj*. pertaining to a pole of the earth, a magnet, etc.

pōle, *n*. **1.** long, slender, round object. **2.** end of an axis. **3.** terminal of a battery. **4.** area where magnetism is concentrated.

pōle'căt'', *n*. skunk.

pò·lĕm'ĭcs, *n*. art of argument. —po·lem'ic, *adj*.

pò·līce', *n*., *v.t*., -liced, -licing. *n*. **1.** governmental organization for enforcing the law. —*v.t*. **2.** control or regulate. —po·lice'man, *fem*., po·lice'wom''an, *n*.

pŏl'ĭ·cÿ, *n*., *pl*. -cies. **1.** course of principle action. **2.** insurance contract.

pŏl''ĭ·ō·mȳ''e·lī'tĭs, *n*. infantile spinal paralysis. Also, po'li·o.

pŏl'ĭsh, *v.t*. **1.** make smooth and glossy. **2.** refine in behavior. **3.** bring to a perfected state. —*n*. **4.** polishing material. **5.** gloss. **6.** refinement.

pŏ''lĭt·bū''rō, *n*. primary governing body of a Communist country.

pò·līte', *adj*. **1.** marked by good manners. **2.** cultivated. —po·lite'ly, *adv*. —po·lite'ness, *n*.

pŏl'ĭ·tĭc, *adj*. **1.** expedient. **2.** political.

pŏl'ĭ·tĭcs, *n*. **1.** theory and conduct of government. **2.** political affairs and methods. —po·lit'i·cal, *adj*. —pol''i·ti'cian, *n*.

pōl'kå, *n*. lively dance, eastern European in origin.

pŏll, *n*. **1.** casting of votes. **2.** total of votes. **3.** place of voting. **4.** solicitation of opinion. —*v.t*. **5.** receive votes. **6.** question regarding opinions.

pŏl'lĕn, *n*. spores of a seed plant. —pol'li·nate'', *v.t*. —pol''li·na'tion, *n*.

pol·lūte', *v.t*., -luted, -luting. make impure; contaminate. —pol·lu'tion, *n*.

pō'lō, *n*. ball game played on horseback.

pŏl''ò·nāise', *n*. slow dance from Poland.

pò·lō'nĭ·ŭm, *n*. radioactive metallic element.

pōl'têr·geīst'', *n*. mischievous ghost or spirit.

pŏl·trōōn', *n*. coward.

pŏl'ÿ·ăn''drÿ, *n*. marriage to more than one husband at a time.

pò·lÿg'å·mÿ, *n*. marriage to more than one spouse at a time. —po·lyg'a·mist, *n*. —po·lyg'a·mous, *adj*.

pŏl'ÿ·glŏt'', *adj*. **1.** knowing a number of languages. **2.** made up of several languages.

pŏl'ÿ·gŏn'', *n*. closed plane figures with three or more sides. —po·lyg'o·nal, *adj*.

pŏl'ÿ·grăph, *n*. a lie detector.

pŏl''ÿ·hē'drŏn, *n*., *pl*. -drons, -dra. closed solid figure.

pŏl'ÿ·mêr, *n*. chemical compound of large molecules formed by smaller but similar molecules.

pŏl'ÿp, *n*. **1.** projecting growth from a mucous membrane surface. **2.** small aquatic organism.

pò·lÿ'phò·nÿ, *n*. musical composition with independent melodic lines. —pol''y·phon'ic, *adj*.

pŏl''ÿ·sÿl·lăb'ĭc, *adj*. having many syllables.

pŏl'ÿ·thē''ĭsm, *n*. belief in more than one god. —pol'y·the''ist, *n*. —pol''y·the'is·tic, *adj*.

pŏmė'grăn''åte, *n*. tropical red fruit with edible seeds.

pòm'mĕl, *n*., *v.t*., -eled, -eling. *n*. **1.** knob, e.g. on a sword hilt. —*v.t*. **2.** beat or strike repeatedly.

pŏmp, *n*. stately display.

pŏm'på·dôur'', *n*. hair style with hair brushed high over the forehead.

pŏm'pŏn, *n*. ornamental ball or tuft.

pŏmp'oŭs, *adj*. **1.** pretentiously self-important; ostentatious. **2.** excessively dignified. —pom·pos'i·ty, *n*. —pomp'ous·ly, *adv*.

pŏn'chō, *n*., *pl*. -chos. *n*. blanket-like cloak with an opening for the head.

pŏnd, *n*. small body of water.

pŏn'dêr, *v.i*., *v.t*. consider deeply.

pŏn′dêr·oŭs, *adj.* **1.** heavy. **2.** lacking grace.

pōne, *n.* oval-shaped cornmeal biscuit.

pŏn′iàrd, *n.* dagger.

pŏn′tĭff, *n.* bishop or head priest, esp. a pope. —pon·tĭf′i·cal, *adj.*

pŏn·tĭf′ĭ·cāte, *v.i.*, -cated, -cating. speak dogmatically.

pŏn·tōōn′, *n.* flat-bottomed boat used esp. in construction.

pō′nÿ, *n.*, *pl.* -nies. young horse.

pōō′dle, *n.* curly-haired breed of dog.

pōōl, *n.* **1.** small, still body of fresh water. **2.** group of available workers, automobiles, etc. **3.** game similar to billiards. —*v.t.* **4.** put into a common fund or effort.

pōōp, *n.* upper deck at the stern of a ship.

pôor, *adj.* **1.** having little money. **2.** lacking. **3.** inferior. —*n.* **4.** poor people. —poor′ly, *adv.*

pŏp, *v.*, popped, popping, *n. v.i.*, *v.t.* **1.** burst with a quick, explosive sound. —*v.i.* **2.** bulge, as of the eyes. —*n.* **3.** sound of popping. **4.** carbonated soft drink.

pŏp′côrn″, *n.* Indian corn whose kernels open in a soft, starchy mass when heated.

pōpe, *n. Often cap.* head of the Roman Catholic Church.

pŏp′làr, *n.* any of various quick-growing trees.

pŏp′lĭn, *n.* ribbed, plain-woven fabric.

pŏp′ō″vêr, *n.* very light biscuit.

pŏp′pÿ, *n.*, *pl.* -pies. herb with a showy flower, one type of which yields opium.

pŏp′u·làce, *n.* people; general public.

pŏp′u·làr, *adj.* **1.** pertaining to the general public. **2.** widely liked or approved. —pop′u·lar·ly, *adv.* —pop″u·lar′i·ty, *n.* —pop′u·lar·ize, *v.t.*

pŏp′u·lāte″, *v.t.*, -lated, -lating. **1.** inhabit. **2.** furnish with inhabitants.

pŏp″′u·lā′tion, *n.* **1.** number of people. **2.** body of inhabitants.

pŏp′u·loŭs, *adj.* having many people.

pôr′cè·làin, *n.* shiny ceramic ware.

pôrch, *n.* open, often roofed, appendage to a building; veranda.

pôr′cīne, *adj.* of or suggesting swine.

pôr′cū·pīne″, *n.* rodent covered with stiff, sharp quills.

pôre, *v.i.*, pored, poring, *n. v.i.* **1.** med-itate or read attentively. —*n.* **2.** minute opening in the skin.

pôr′gÿ, *n.* salt-water food fish.

pôrk, *n.* flesh of swine used as food.

pôr·nŏg′rà·phÿ, *n.* erotic writing or art intended for sexual excitement. —por″no·graph′ic, *adj.*

pô′roŭs, *adj.* permeable to liquids and air.

pôr′pòise, *n.* any of several aquatic mammals including the common dolphin.

pôr′rĭdge, *n.* cereal boiled in milk or water.

pôr′rĭn·gêr, *n.* low dish, often with a handle.

pôrt, *n.* **1.** loading and unloading place for ships and aircraft. **2.** when facing the bow, the left side of a ship. **3.** a sweet, red wine. **4.** (computers) point at which peripheral components can be connected.

pôrt′à·ble, *adj.* easily carried; small. —port″a·bil′i·ty, *n.*

pôr′tàge, *n.* carrying of goods and boats overland.

pôr′tàl, *n.* gate or door.

pôr·tĕnd′, *v.t.* **1.** indicate in advance. **2.** indicate; signify.

pôr′tĕnt, *n.* **1.** omen. **2.** ominous significance. —por·ten′tous, *adj.*

pôr′têr, *n.* **1.** doorman. **2.** baggage carrier.

pôr′têr·hoŭse″, *n.* choice cut of beefsteak with a large tenderloin.

pôrt·fō′lĭ·ō″, *n.* **1.** portable case for documents. **2.** office and duties of a government minister. **3.** securities and stocks held by an investor. **4.** samples of work, esp. art.

pôrt′hōle″, *n.* window, esp. round, in the side of a plane or ship.

pôr′tĭ·cō″, *n.*, *pl.* -coes or -cos. roof supported by a colonnade; porch.

pôr′tion, *n.* **1.** part or share. **2.** personal fate. —*v.t.* **3.** divide into portions.

pôrt′lÿ, *adj.* fat; chubby.

pôr′traĭt, *n.* picture or description of a person. —por′traĭ·ture, *n.*

pôr·trāy′, *v.t.* **1.** depict or represent in a portrait. **2.** represent dramatically. —por·tray′al, *n.*

pōr·tù·lăc′à, *n.* tropical herb with showy flowers.

pōse, *v.*, posed, posing. *n. v.i.* **1.** hold a

position. **2.** assume a character or attitude. —*v.t.* **3.** propound or state. —*n.* **4.** fixed position. **5.** assumed character. —**po'ser**, *n*.

po·sǐ'tion, *n*. **1.** location. **2.** posture. **3.** opinion on an issue. **4.** job. —*v.t.* **5.** place.

pŏs'ǐ·tǐve, *adj.* **1.** affirmative. **2.** certain. **3.** with light and shade as in the original. **4.** numerically greater than zero. **5.** electrical charge with more protons than electrons. **6.** showing the presence of something tested for. —*n.* **7.** something positive. —**pos'i·tive·ly**, *adv.* —**pos'i·tive·ness**, *n*.

pŏs'sē, *n.* group or persons assisting a law enforcement officer.

po·sěss', *v.t.* **1.** have or own. **2.** dominate. —**pos·ses'sive**, *adj.* —**pos·ses'sion**, *n.* —**pos·ses'sor**, *n*.

pŏs'sǐ·ble, *adj.* capable of existing or happening. —**pos'sibly**, *adv.* —**pos'' si·bil'i·ty**, *n*.

pŏs'sǔm, *n.* oppossum.

pŏst, *n.* **1.** upright column or pole. **2.** appointed job, station, or task. **3.** permanent military station. —*v.t.* **4.** put up, as a public announcement. **5.** assign to a place. **6.** enter in a ledger. **7.** mail.

pŏst'áge, *n.* **1.** charge for mailing. **2.** stamps, etc. for mailing.

pŏst'ál, *adj.* pertaining to mail.

pŏst'cârd, *n.* message card mailed without an envelope.

pŏst'êr, *n.* public advertisement.

pŏs·tē'rǐ·ör, *adj.* **1.** situated behind. **2.** later in time. —*n.* **3.** buttocks, rump.

pŏs·tĕr'ǐ·tў, *n.* **1.** descendants. **2.** succeeding or future generations.

pŏs'tĕrn, *n.* **1.** back door or gate. **2.** private entrance.

pŏst'hāste', *adv.* as quickly as possible.

pŏst'hǔ·moüs, *adj.* **1.** published after the death of the author. **2.** born after the death of the father. —**post'hu·mous· ly**, *adv.*

pŏst'mǎn, *n.* mailman.

pŏst'mârk'', *n.* **1.** postal mark indicating a time and place of reception by a post office. —*v.t.* **2.** put a postmark on.

pŏst'măs''têr, *n.* manager of a post office.

pŏst-môr'tĕm, *adj.* **1.** following death. —*n.* **2.** examination of a corpse.

pŏst'ôf''fĭce, *n.* government agency that handles mail.

pŏst·ŏp'êr·à·tǐve, *adj.* following a surgical operation.

pŏst'pāid', *adj., adv.* with postage prepaid.

pŏst·pōne', *v.t.*, -poned, -poning. delay, as action. —**post·pone'ment**, *n*.

pŏst'scrǐpt'', *n.* note added to a finished letter.

pŏs·tū·lāte, *v.t.*, -lated, -lating, *n. v.t.* (pos'tyoō lāt) **1.** assume as true. —*n.* (pos'tyoō let) **2.** postulated proposition.

pŏs'tûre, *n., v.*, -tured, -turing. *n.* **1.** position of the body. **2.** attitude on a given subject. —*v.i.* **3.** affect an attitude. —*v.t.* **4.** place in a specific position.

pŏst'wâr', *adj.* after a war.

pō'sў, *n., pl.* -sies. small bouquet.

pŏt, *n., v.t.*, potted, potting. *n.* **1.** deep, round container. —*v.t.* **2.** put or plant in a pot.

pŏ'tà·ble, *adj.* drinkable.

pŏt'ǎsh'', *n.* potassium carbonate, esp. from wood ashes.

po·tǎs'sǐ·ǔm, *n.* silver, metallic, chemical element used in glass, fertilizer, etc.

pō·tā'tion, *n.* drink, esp. alcoholic.

po·tā'tō, *n., pl.* -toes. edible tuber of a common vegetable plant.

pō'tĕnt, *adj.* **1.** powerful. **2.** sexually capable. —**po'tence, po'ten·cy**, *n*.

pō'tĕn·tāte'', *n.* sovereign; ruler.

po·tĕn'tiàl, *adj.* **1.** possible; capable of being realized. —*n.* **2.** possible ability. —**po·ten''ti·al'i·ty**, *n.* —**po·ten'tial· ly**, *adv.*

pō'tion, *n.* drink, esp. a medicinal one.

pot·pour·ri (pō''pə rē'), *n.* **1.** miscellaneous collection. **2.** flower petals and spices used for scent.

pŏt'têr, *n.* maker of earthenware.

pŏt'têr·ў, *n.* **1.** dishes, pots, mugs, etc. made of baked clay. **2.** place where earthenware is made.

poüch, *n.* **1.** sack or bag. **2.** baglike part of a marsupial.

poul'trў, *n.* domestic fowl, e.g. chicken.

poünce, *v.i.* pounced, pouncing. swoop down suddenly.

poünd, *n.* **1.** unit of avoirdupois weight equal to 16 ounces or troy weight equal to 12 ounces. **2.** British monetary unit.

3. enclosure for stray dogs, etc. —*v.t.* **4.** strike forcefully and repeatedly. **5.** crush or compact by pounding. —*v.i.* **6.** throb or beat violently, as the heart.

pŏund′cāke′′, *n.* rich, sweet cake.

pôur, *v.t.* **1.** cause to flow. —*v.i.* **2.** rain heavily. —*n.* **3.** act or instance of pouring.

pŏut, *v.i.* **1.** look sullen; act hurt. —*n.* **2.** sullen mood, look or behavior.

pŏv′êr·tў, *n.* **1.** lack of money. **2.** deficiency.

pŏw′dêr, *n.* **1.** dry substance of very fine particles. —*v.t.* **2.** reduce to powder. **3.** apply powder to. —**pow′der·y,** *adj.*

pŏw′êr, *n.* **1.** ability to act. **2.** personal ability. **3.** authority. **4.** influential person, nation, etc. **5.** physical force. **6.** magnifying capacity of a lens. —**pow′er·ful,** *adj.* —**pow′er·ful·ly,** *adv.* —**pow′er·less,** *adj.*

pŏw′wŏw′′, *n.* **1.** Native American conference. **2.** a meeting.

pŏx, *n.* any disease marked by skin pustules.

prăc′tǐ·cà·ble, *adj.* feasible.

prăc′tǐ·càl, *adj.* **1.** pertaining to practice. **2.** useful. **3.** aware of realities. **4.** virtual. —**prac′′ti·cal′i·ty,** *n.* —**prac′ti·cal·ly,** *adv.*

prăc′tǐce, *n.,* *v.,* **-ticed, -ticing.** *n.* **1.** custom. **2.** actual performance. **3.** repeated exercise. **4.** professional activity. —*v.i.,* *v.t.* **5.** Also, **prac′tise,** perform habitually or repeatedly. —**prac′ticed,** *adj.*

prăc·tǐ′tion·êr, *n.* person who practices a profession.

prăg·mă′tǐc, *adj.* concerned with practical values and consequences. —**prag′ma·tist,** *n.* —**prag′ma·tism,** *n.*

prāi′riē, *n.* flat, treeless, rolling grassland.

prāise, *n.,* *v.t.,* **praised, praising.** *n.* **1.** expressed approval. **2.** homage. —*v.t.* **3.** express approval of. **4.** worship. —**praise′wor′′thy,** *adj.*

prănce, *v.i.,* **pranced, prancing. 1.** spring on the hind legs. **2.** swagger.

prănk, *n.* mischievous trick. —**prank′ster,** *n.*

prāte, *v.,* **prated, prating.** *v.i.,* *v.t.* talk excessively and foolishly.

prăt′tle, *v.i.,* **-tled, -tling.** *n.* *v.i.* **1.** chat-ter childishly or foolishly. —*n.* **2.** chatter. —**prat′tler,** *n.*

prawn, *n.* large, edible, shrimplike shellfish.

prāy, *v.i.* **1.** petition or worship a divinity. **2.** implore. **3.** ask earnestly for.

prăyêr, *n.* **1.** act of addressing a divinity. —*v.t.* **2.** earnest request. —**prayer′ful,** *adj.*

prēach, *v.t.* **1.** advocate. —*v.i.* **2.** give a sermon. —**preach′er,** *n.*

prē′ăm′′ble, *n.* introductory section.

prè·cār′ĭ·oŭs, *adj.* risky. —**pre·car′i·ous·ly,** *adv.*

prè·caŭ′tion, *n.* caution beforehand. —**pre·cau′tion·ar′′y,** *adj.*

prè·cēde′, *v.,* **-ceded, -ceding.** *v.i.,* *v.t.* go before. —**pre·ced′ence,** *n.*

prĕc′e·dènt, *n.* past occurrence or principle used as an example or justification.

prē′cĕpt, *n.* principle or rule of conduct.

prē·cĕp′tŏr, *n.* teacher or tutor.

prē′cĭnct, *n.* administrative district.

prē′cioŭs, *adj.* **1.** valuable. **2.** cherished. **3.** overly refined. —**pre′cious·ly,** *adv.*

prĕc′ĭ·pĭce, *n.* steep cliff.

prè·cĭp′ĭ·tāte′′, *v.t.,* **-tated, -tating.** *adj.,* *n.* *v.t.* **1.** throw down violently. **2.** hasten in occurring. **3.** separate from a solution. **4.** condense. —*adj.* **5.** hasty; rash; headlong. —*n.* **6.** condensed moisture. —**pre·cip′′i·ta′tion,** *n.*

prè·cĭp′ĭ·toŭs, *adj.* **1.** steep. **2.** precipitate.

prè·cīse′, *adj.* **1.** specific. **2.** scrupulous; strict. —**pre·ci′sion, pre·cise′ness,** *n.* —**pre·cise′ly,** *adv.*

prē·cis (prā sē′), *n.* concise summary.

prè·clūde′, *v.t.,* **-cluded, -cluding.** exclude the possibility of. —**pre·clu′sion,** *n.* —**pre·clu′sive,** *adj.*

prè·cō′cioŭs, *adj.* advanced in development, esp. of the mind. —**pre·coc′i·ty,** *n.*

prē′′còn·cēive′, *v.t.* form an idea or opinion of in advance. —**pre′′con·cep′tion,** *n.*

prē′′cûr′sŏr, *n.* **1.** forerunner. **2.** harbinger.

prĕd′e·cĕs′′sŏr, *n.* person or thing that precedes another.

prē·dĕs′′tǐ·nā′tion, *n.* determination in advance of actions and consequences; fate. —**pre·des′tine,** *v.t.*

prĕ·dĭc'á·mĕnt, *n*. difficult or dangerous situation.

prĕd'ĭ·cāte'', *v.t.*, -cated, -cating, *n*. *v.t*. **1**. declare; assume. **2**. base on an assumption. —*n*. (pred'ǝk ǝt) **3**. *Grammar*. part of a sentence or clause expressing what is said of its subject. —pred''i·ca'tion, *n*.

prè·dĭct', *v.t.*, tell in advance. —pre·dic' tion, *n*. —pre·dict'a·ble, *adj*.

prĕ''dĭ·lĕc'tion, *n*. preference; inclination.

prè·dŏm'ĭ·nāte'', *v.*, -nated, -nating. *v.i.* **1**. be stronger or more numerous. —*v.t.* **2**. master. —pre·dom'i·nance, *n*. —pre·dom'i·nant, *adj*. —pre·dom'i·nant·ly, *adv*.

prē·ĕm'ĭ·nĕnt, *adj*. outstanding; superior. —pre·em'i·nent·ly, *adv*. —pre· em'i·nence, *n*.

prĕ''ĕmpt', *v.t.* **1**. acquire before others do. **2**. settle on to establish the right of purchase.

prēen, *v.t.* **1**. trim with the beak, as a bird. —*v.i.* **2**. fuss over one's appearance.

prē·făb'rĭ·cāte'', *v.t.*, -cated, -cating. assemble from large, previously finished, components.

prĕf'·ace, *n., v.t.*, -aced, -acing. *n*. **1**. introductory text. —*v.t.* **2**. serve as a preface to. —pref'a·to''ry, *adj*.

prē'fĕct, *n*. magistrate; high official.

prè·fêr', *v.t.*, -ferred, -ferring. **1**. like better or favor more than others. **2**. present, as an accusation. —pref'er·a· ble, *adj*. —pref'er·a·bly, *adv*. —pref' er·ence, *n*. —pref''er·en'tial, *adj*.

prè·fêr'mĕnt, *n*. promotion; advancement.

prē'fĭx, *n*. **1**. qualifying beginning of a word. —*v.t.* **2**. put before.

prĕg'nànt, *adj*. **1**. being with child. **2**. significant; meaningful. —preg'nan· cy, *n*.

prē·hĕn'sīle, *adj*. able to grasp.

prē''hĭs·tôr'ĭc, *adj*. pertaining to the time before recorded history.

prĕj'ū·dĭce, *n., v.t.*, -diced, -dicing. *n*. **1**. opinion without adequate basis. **2**. disadvantage or injury. —*v.t.* **3**. influence or affect with prejudice. —prej'' u·di'cial, *adj*.

prĕl'áte, *n*. high church official.

prè·lĭm'ĭ·năr''ȳ, *adj., pl*. -naries. *adj*. **1**. introductory. —*n*. **2**. introductory feature.

prē'lūde, *n*. preliminary to a larger work.

prē'má·tûre'', *adj*. **1**. born or happening too early. **2**. overly hasty. —pre'' ma·ture'ly, *adv*. —pre''ma·tur'i·ty, *n*.

prē·mĕd'ĭ''tāte, *v.*, -tated, -tating. *v.i., v.t*. plan or consider beforehand. —pre''med·i·ta'tion, *n*.

prè·mĭer', *n*. **1**. chief officer, esp. a prime minister. —*adj*. **2**. first in rank.

prè·mière', *n*. first public performance.

prĕm'īse, *n*. **1**. basis of an argument or conclusion. **2**. premises, building and grounds; property.

prē'mĭ·ŭm, *n*. **1**. prize. **2**. high evaluation. **3**. bonus. **4**. cost of an insurance policy.

prē''mŏ·nĭ'tion, *n*. foreboding; presentiment. —pre·mon'i·to''ry, *adv*.

prē·nā'tàl, *adj*. prior to birth.

prē·ŏc'cū·pīed'', *adj*. completely engrossed. —pre·oc'cu·py'', *v.t.* —pre· oc''cu·pa'tion, *n*.

prē·pāre', *v.*, -pared, -paring. *v.t.* **1**. put in readiness. **2**. manufacture. —*v.i.* **3**. get or put oneself in readiness. —prep''a·ra'tion, *n*. —pre·par'a· to''ry, *adj*. —pre·par'ed·ness, *n*.

prè·pŏn'dêr·ànt, *adj*. superior in numbers, strength, etc. —pre·pon'der· ance, *n*.

prĕp''ò·sĭ'tion, *n*. word or words placed before a noun or adjective to form a modifying phrase. —prep''o·si'tion· al, *adj*.

prē''pòs·sĕss'ĭng, *adj*. impressing favorably.

prè·pŏs'têr·oŭs, *adj*. absurd.

prē·rĕq'uĭ·sĭte, *n*. something required beforehand; condition.

prè·rŏg'á·tĭve, *n*. special power, right, or privilege.

prĕs'áge, *v.t.*, -aged, -aging. **1**. foreshadow. **2**. predict.

prĕs''bȳ·tē'rĭ·àn, *adj*. **1**. of or pertaining to the principle of church government by a presbytery. **2**. pertaining to a Protestant church with this form of government. —*n*. **3**. member of a Presbyterian church.

prĕs'bȳ·tĕr''ȳ, *n., pl*. -teries, group of church elders and ministers.

pre·sci·ence (pre'shē əns, presh'əns), *n*. foreknowledge; foresight. —**pre'sci·ent**, *adj*.

prè·scrībe', *v.t.*, -scribed, -scribing. order for use, or adoption. —**pre·scrip'tion**, *n*. —**pre·scrip'tive**, *adj*.

près'ėnce, *n*. **1**. state of being present. **2**. vicinity or view. **3**. figure or bearing of a person.

près'ėnt, *adj*. **1**. being or happening now. **2**. being in a specific place. **3**. *Grammar*. denoting state or action now taking place. —*n*. **4**. present time. **5**. present tense. **6**. gift. —*v.t.* (pri zent') **7**. give, bring, or offer. **8**. furnish or allow. **9**. introduce or make public. —**pres''en·ta'tion**, *n*.

prè·sĕnt'à·ble, *adj*. suitable in appearance, manners, etc. —**pre·sent'ab·ly**, *adv*.

prè·sĕn'tĭ·mėnt, *n*. premonition.

près'ėnt·lў, *adv*. **1**. soon. **2**. at present; now.

prè·sêrve', *v.t.*, -served, -serving, *n. v.t.* **1**. keep safe. **2**. keep in good condition. **3**. prepare for storage, as food. —*n*. **4**. **preserves**, preserved fruit. **5**. sanctuary for game animals. —**pres''er·va'tion**, *n*. —**pre·serv'a·tive**, *n., adj*.

prè·sīde', *v.i.*, -sided, -siding. act as chairman; be at the head of.

près'ĭ·dėnt, *n*. **1**. chief officer of a corporation. **2**. highest elected official. —**pres'i·den·cy**, *n*. —**pres''i·den'tial**, *adj*.

prè·sĭd'ĭ·ŭm, *n*. major administrative committee of a communist state.

près̆s, *v.t.* **1**. act against with weight or force. **2**. urge forcefully. **3**. oppress. **4**. iron, as clothing. —*v.i.* **5**. move or push forcefully. —*n*. **6**. journalism. **7**. machine for printing. **8**. urgency.

près̆s'ĭng, *adj*. urgent.

près̆s'sûre, *n*. **1**. exertion of force. **2**. compulsion toward a certain action or decision. **3**. urgency.

près''tĭ·dĭg''ĭ·tā'tion, *n*. sleight of hand. —**pres''ti·dig'i·ta''tor**, *n*.

près̆s'tĭge (pres tēzh'), *n*. respected standing or reputation. —**pres·tig'ious**, *adj*.

près̆s'tō, *adv*. quickly.

prè·sūme', *v.*, -sumed, -suming. *v.t.* **1**. take for granted. —*v.i.* **2**. act with un-

warranted boldness. —**pre·sum'a·ble**, *adj*. —**pre·sum'a·bly**, *adv*.

prè·sŭmp'tion, *n*. **1**. assumption. **2**. unwarranted boldness. —**pre·sump'tive**, *adj*. —**pre·sump'tu·ous**, *adj*.

prē''sŭp·pōse', *v.t.*, -posed, -posing. **1**. suppose beforehand. **2**. require beforehand as a condition.

prè·tĕnd', *v.t.* **1**. imagine as a fantasy. **2**. profess or appear falsely. —*v.i.* **3**. make believe. **4**. make a claim. —**pre·ten'der**, *n*. —**pre·tense'**, *n*.

prè·tĕn'sion, *n*. **1**. ostentation; self-importance. **2**. act or instance of alleging or pretending. —**pre·ten'tious**, *adj*. —**pre·ten'tious·ly**, *adv*.

prē''têr·năt'ŭ·ràl, *adj*. **1**. supernatural. **2**. abnormal or exceptional.

prē'tĕxt, *n*. ostensible or false reason; excuse.

prĕt'tў, *adj.*, -tier, -tiest, *adv. adj.* **1**. pleasingly attractive. —*adv*. **2**. moderately. —**pret'ti·fy''**, *v.t.* —**pret'ti·ly**, *adv*. —**pret'ti·ness**, *n*.

prĕt'zėl, *n*. brittle, salted cracker, usually twisted.

prè·vāil', *v.i.* **1**. be widespread. **2**. prove superior in force, etc. **3**. succeed in persuasion. —**prev'a·lent**, *adj*. —**prev'a·lence**, *n*.

prè·văr'ĭ·cāte'', *v.i.*, -cated, -cating. speak falsely; lie. —**pre·var''i·ca'tion**, *n*.

prè·vĕnt', *v.t.* stop; hinder. —**pre·vent'a·ble**, **pre·vent'i·ble**, *adj*. —**pre·ven'tion**, *n*. —**pre·ven'tive**, **pre·vent'a·tive**, *adj*.

prē'viēw'', *n*. **1**. advance showing, as of a motion picture. —*v.t.* **2**. show or view in advance.

prē'vĭ·oŭs, *adj*. happening or going earlier. —**pre'vi·ous·ly**, *adj*.

prey, *n*. **1**. animal hunted for food. **2**. victim. —*v.i.* **3**. search for prey. **4**. have an oppressive effect.

prīce, *n., v.t.*, priced, pricing. *n*. **1**. amount for which something is sold. **2**. value. —*v.t.* **3**. set a price on. **4**. check or ask the price of.

prīce'lėss, *adj*. invaluable; beyond any price.

prĭck, *n*. **1**. puncture or cut from a thorn, needle, etc. —*v.t.* **2**. pierce or stab lightly.

prĭck'lў, *adj*. sharp; scratchy.

prīde, *n.*, *v.t.*, **prided, priding.** *n.* **1.** high opinion of one's worth. **2.** self-respect. **3.** person or object one is proud of. **4.** a group of lions. —*v.t.* **5.** give pride to.

priēst, *n.* **1.** clergyman; person authorized to perform religious ceremonies. **2.** Also, *fem.*, **priest′ess,** one who performs religious rites. —**priest′hood,** *n.* —**priest′ly,** *adj.*

prĭg, *n.* self-righteous person. —**prig′gish,** *adj.*

prĭm, *adj.* rigidly proper. —**prim′ly,** *adv.*

prī′′mȧ·dŏn′nȧ, *n.* **1.** principal female opera singer. **2.** *Informal.* temperamental or vain person.

prī′mȧl, *adj.* **1.** primitive; original. **2.** most important; basic.

prī′mā′′rў, *adj.*, *n.*, *pl.* **-ries.** *adj.* **1.** first in rank or importance. **2.** first in time. —*n.* **3.** preliminary election. —**pri·mar′i·ly,** *adv.*

prī′māte, *n.* **1.** any of the order of mammals that includes man. **2.** high church official.

prīme, *adj.*, *n.*, *v.t.*, **primed, priming.** *adj.* **1.** first in rank, value, etc. **2.** original. —*n.* **3.** best part or period. —*v.t.* **4.** prepare.

prim′ȇr, *n.* **1.** elementary or basic book. **2.** (prī′mər) material for preparing a surface.

prī·mē′vȧl, *adj.* pertaining to the earliest ages.

prim′i·tĭve, *adj.* **1.** earliest. **2.** simple; crude. —*n.* **3.** naive work of art. —**prim′i·tive·ly,** *adv.* —**prim′i·tive·ness,** *n.*

prĭmp, *v.t.*, *v.i.* dress or adorn oneself fastidiously.

prĭm′rōse′′, *n.* colorful perennial garden flower.

prĭnce, *n.* **1.** son of royalty. **2.** ruler. Also, *fem.*, **prin′cess.**

prĭnce′lў, *adj.* lavish.

prĭn′cĭ·pȧl, *adj.* **1.** most important. —*n.* **2.** leader. **3.** head of a school. **4.** capital sum. —**prin′ci·pal·ly,** *adv.*

prĭn′′cĭ·păl′i·tў, *n.*, *pl.* **-ties.** state governed by a prince.

prĭn′cĭ·ple, *n.* **1.** rule of action, conduct, or belief. **2.** adherence to rules of conduct. **3.** scientific law.

prĭnt, *v.t.* **1.** reproduce from inked type.

2. produce a photographic positive from. —*v.i.* **3.** draw letters or characters. —*n.* **4.** state of being printed. **5.** printed lettering. **6.** printed picture. —**print′er,** *n.*

prĭnt′ȇr, *n.* **1.** one who prints. **2.** (computers) device for transcribing data to paper.

prĭnt′ōut, *n.*, *v.* (computers) data transcribed onto paper.

prī′ŏr, *adj.* **1.** earlier. —*adv.* **2.** previously. —*n.* **3.** Also, *fem.*, **pri′or·ess,** head of a religious house. —**pri′o·ry,** *n.*

prī·ôr′ĭ·tў, *n.*, *pl.* **-ties. 1.** state of being earlier in time. **2.** precedence in order, privilege, etc.

prĭsm, *n.* three-sided glass object that breaks light into its spectrum. —**pris·mat′ic,** *adj.*

prĭs′ŏn, *n.* jail; building for confining criminals. —**pris′on·er,** *n.*

prĭs′tĭne, *adj.* unspoiled; pure.

prī′vȧte, *adj.* **1.** belonging to a specific person or group. **2.** confidential. —*n.* **3.** lowest soldier. —**pri′vate·ly,** *adv.* —**pri′va·cy,** *n.*

prī′′vȧ·tēer′, *n.* private ship commissioned for warfare.

prī·vā′tion, *n.* **1.** deprivation. **2.** lack; want; need.

prĭv′ĭ·lĕge, *n.* special advantage. —**priv′i·leged,** *adj.*

prĭv′ў, *adj.*, *n.*, *pl.* **privies.** *adj.* **1.** admitted to a secret. **2.** private; personal. —*n.* **3.** outhouse; outdoor toilet.

prīze, *n.*, *v.t.*, **prized, prizing.** *n.* **1.** reward for victory. **2.** something desirable. —*v.t.* **3.** value or esteem highly.

prō, *n.*, *pl.* **pros,** *adv.*, *adj.* *n.* **1.** *Informal.* professional. —*adv.*, *adj.* **2.** in favor.

prŏb′ȧ·ble, *adj.* **1.** likely to happen, etc. **2.** giving ground for belief. —**prob′a·bly,** *adv.* —**prob′′a·bil′i·ty,** *n.*

prō′bāte, *n.*, *adj.*, *v.t.*, **-bated, -bating.** *n.* **1.** certification of a will. —*adj.* **2.** of or pertaining to probate. —*v.t.* **3.** establish the validity of.

prō·bā′tion, *n.* act or instance of testing. —**pro·ba′tion·ar′′y,** *adj.*

prōbe, *v.t.*, **probed, probing.** *n.* *v.t.* **1.** search into thoroughly. —*n.* **2.** surgical instrument for examining wounds, etc.

prŏb′lĕm, *n.* question or situation involving difficulty. —**prob''lem·at'i· cal,** *adj.*

prō·bŏs'cĭs, *n., pl.* **-ces.** flexible snout, e.g. an elephant's trunk.

prō·cēed', *v.i.* **1.** go onward. **2.** continue an action. **3.** issue forth. —*n.* **4. proceeds,** revenue from selling. —**pro·ce' dure,** *n.* —**pro·ce'du·ral,** *adj.*

prō·cēed'ĭng, *n.* **1.** action or conduct. **2. proceedings, a.** records of a meeting, etc. **b.** legal action.

prŏ'cĕss, *n.* **1.** series of actions ending in a result. **2.** continuous action. **3.** legal summons. —*v.t.* **4.** treat or prepare by a specific process.

prō·cĕs'sion, *n.* parade.

prō·cĕs'siŏn·ăl, *n.* **1.** hymn for a procession. **2.** hymnbook.

prō-chōĭce, *adj.* supporting legalized abortion.

prō·clāim', *v.t.* **1.** announce publicly. **2.** reveal conspicuously. —**proc''la·ma' tion,** *n.*

prō·clĭv'ĭ·tÿ, *n., pl.* **-ties.** natural tendency or inclination.

prō·crăs'tĭ·nāte'', *v.,* **-nated, -nating.** *v.i., v.t.* put off to another time. —**pro· cras''ti·na'tion,** *n.* —**pro·cras'ti· na''tor,** *n.*

prō·cūre', *v. t.,* **-cured, -curing. 1.** obtain. **2.** bring about. —**pro·cure'ment,** *n.*

prŏd, *v.t.,* **prodded, prodding,** *n. v.t.* **1.** poke; jab. **2.** goad; incite. —*n.* **3.** poke. **4.** pointed instrument.

prŏd'ĭ·găl, *adj.* **1.** recklessly extravagant. **2.** lavish. —**prod''i·gal'i·ty,** *n.*

prō·dĭ'giŏŭs, *adj.* **1.** wonderful. **2.** huge. —**pro·di'gious·ly,** *adv.*

prŏd'ĭ·gÿ, *n., pl.* **-gies.** very talented young person.

prō·dūce', *v.,* **-duced, -ducing,** *v.t.* **1.** bring into existence. **2.** give birth to or bear. **3.** exhibit. —*n.* (prō'dōōs) **4.** product. **5.** fresh fruit and vegetables. —**pro·duc'er,** *n.* —**pro·duc'tion,** *n.* —**pro·duc'tive,** *adj.* —**pro''duc·tiv'i· ty, pro·duc'tive·ness,** *adj.* —**pro'' duc·tiv'i·ty, pro·duc'tive·ness,** *n.*

prō-fămĭlÿ, *adj.* anti-abortion; pro-life.

prō·fāne', *adj., v.t.,* **-faned, -faning.** *adj.* **1.** secular. **2.** impure; foul. **3.** irreverent; disrespectful. —*v.t.* **4.** treat with irreverence.

prō·făn'ĭ·tÿ, *n.* **1.** sacrilege. **2.** cursing.

prō·fĕss', *v.t.* **1.** claim of oneself. **2.** affirm allegiance to or faith in.

prō·fĕs'sion, *n.* **1.** learned occupation. **2.** act or instance of professing.

prō·fĕs'siŏn·ăl, *adj.* **1.** pursuing a profession. **2.** pertaining to a profession. **3.** meeting the standards of a profession. —*n.* **4.** professional person. —**pro·fes' sion·al·ly,** *adv.* —**pro·fes'sion·al'' ism,** *n.*

prō·fĕs'sör, *n.* college teacher of the highest rank. —**pro''fes·sor'i·al,** *adj.*

prŏf'fêr, *v.t., n.* offer.

prō·fī'ciĕnt, *adj.* skillful; learned. —**pro·fi'cient·ly,** *adv.* —**pro·fi'cien· cy,** *n.*

prō'fīle, *n.* **1.** side view. **2.** succinct sketch of a person. —*v.t.* **3.** do a biographical profile of.

prŏf'ĭt, *n.* **1.** gain from a business deal. **2.** net gain from business. **3.** benefit. —*v.i.* **4.** gain a profit. **5.** take advantage. —**prof'it·a·ble,** *adj.* —**prof'it·a· bly,** *adv.*

prŏf''ĭt·ēer', *n.* **1.** person who takes an unreasonably large profit. —*v.i.* **2.** act as a profiteer.

prŏf'lĭ·gāte, *adj.* **1.** licentious. **2.** extravagant. —*n.* **3.** profligate person. —**prof'li·ga·cy,** *n.*

prō·fŏund', *adj.* **1.** characterized by deep thought. **2.** deeply felt. **3.** deep. —**pro· found'ly,** *adv.* —**pro·fun'di·ty,** *n.*

prō·fūse', *adj.* **1.** plentiful. **2.** lavish. —**pro·fuse'ly,** *adv.* —**pro·fus'ion, pro·fuse'ness,** *n.*

prō·gĕn'ĭ·tör, *n.* forefather; precursor.

prŏg'ė·nÿ, *n., pl.* **-nies.** children; descendants.

prŏg·nō'sĭs, *n., pl.* **-noses.** forecast of the course of a disease.

prŏg·nŏs'tĭ·cāte'', *v.,* **-cated, -cating.** *v.t.* **1.** predict; presage. —*v.i.* **2.** prophesy. —**prog·nos''ti·ca'tion,** *n.*

prō'grăm, *n.* **1.** plan; method. **2.** list of subjects or events. **3.** (computers) a set of instructions to perform specific operations to data. —*v.* **4.** create a computer program. —**pro''gram·ming,** *n.*

prŏg·rĕss, *n.* (prog'res) **1.** advancement. **2.** improvement. —*v.i.* (pro gres') **3.** advance. **4.** improve. —**pro·gres'sion,** *n.* —**pro·gres'sive,** *adj.* —**pro·gres' sive·ly,** *adv.*

prō·hĭb'ĭt, *v.t.* **1.** forbid. **2.** prevent.

—pro·hib'i·tive, *adj.* —pro''hi·bi'tion, *n.* —pro''hi·bi'tion·ist, *n.*

prŏj'ĕct, *n.* **1.** plan; scheme. —*v.t.* (prō jekt') **2.** plan or intend. **3.** throw or impel forward. **4.** cast on a surface, as an image. —*v.i.* **5.** protrude. —pro·jec'tion, *n.* —pro·jec'tor, *n.*

prŏ·jĕc'tĭle, *n.* missile from a gun.

prō''lė·tär'ĭ·ăt, *n.* working class. —pro''le·tar'i·an, *n.*, *adj.*

prō·lĭf'ĕr·āte'', *v.*, -ated, ating. *v.i.*, *v.t.* **1.** grow rapidly by multiplication. **2.** spread rapidly. —pro·lif''er·a'tion, *n.*

prō·lĭf'ĭc, *adj.* productive.

prō'lŏgue, *n.* introduction to a play, novel, etc. Also, pro'log.

prō·lŏng', *v.t.* lengthen, esp. in duration.

prŏm'ė·nāde', *n.*, *v.*, -naded, -nading. *n.* **1.** leisurely walk. **2.** place for strolling. —*v.i.* **3.** take a promenade. —*v.t.* **4.** promenade on or through.

prŏm'ĭ·nėnt, *adj.* **1.** conspicuous. **2.** distinguished. —prom'i·nence, *n.* —prom'i·nent·ly, *adv.*

prō·mĭs·cū'oŭs, *adj.* indiscriminate. —pro''mis·cu'i·ty, *n.* —pro·mis'cu·ous·ly, *adv.*

prŏm'īse, *n.*, *v.t.*, -ised, -ising. *n.* **1.** assurance to do or not to do something. **2.** indication of future improvement or success. —*v.t.* **3.** make a promise. —*v.i.* **4.** give grounds for hope. —prom'is·ing, *adj.*

prŏm'īs·sô''rў, *adj.* containing a promise.

prŏm'ŏn·tô''rў, *n.*, *pl.* -ries. high land mass jutting into the sea.

prō·mōte', *v.t.* **1.** advance in rank or position. **2.** further the growth or progress of. —pro·mo'ter, *n.* —pro·mo'tion, *n.*

prŏmpt, *adj.* **1.** ready to act. **2.** quick or punctual. —*v.t.* **3.** induce to action. —prompt'ly, *adv.*

prō·mŭl'gāte, *v.t.*, -gated, -gating. proclaim publicly. —pro''mul·ga'tion, *n.*

prōne, *adj.* **1.** inclined; liable. **2.** lying face downward.

prŏng, *n.* pointed projection.

prō'noŭn'', *n.* word used as a substitute for a noun.

prō·noŭnce', *v.*, -nounced, -nouncing. *v.t.* **1.** utter; deliver. **2.** declare to be.

—*v.i.* **3.** articulate words or phrases. —pro·nounce'ment, *n.*

prō·noŭnced', *adj.* strongly marked or apparent.

prō·nŭn''cĭ·ā'tion, *n.* act or manner of speaking.

proof, *n.* **1.** evidence demonstrating a fact. **2.** standardized strength for liquor. **3.** preliminary printing, for inspection. —*adj.* **4.** impervious; invulnerable.

proof'read'', *v.t.*, -read, -reading. read to check for errors. —proof'read''er, *n.*

prŏp, *n.*, *v.t.*, propped, propping. *n.* **1.** rigid support. **2.** emotional support. **3.** any object used in a stage play. —*v.t.* **4.** support; strengthen.

prŏp'à·găn·dà, *n.* assertions, etc. intended to help or oppose a cause. —prop''a·gan'dist, *n.* —prop''a·gan·dis'tic, *adj.* —prop''a·gan·dize, *v.t.*, *v.i.*

prŏp'à·gāte'', *v.*, -gated, -gating. *v.t.*, *v.i.* **1.** reproduce; breed. —*v.t.* **2.** transmit, as ideas. —prop''a·ga'tion, *n.*

prō·pĕl'lêr, *n.* screwlike propelling device.

prō·pĕn'sĭ'tў, *n.* inclination; tendency.

prŏp'êr, *adj.* **1.** suitable. **2.** correct. **3.** *Grammar.* indicating a specific person, place, or thing. —prop'er·ly, *adv.*

prŏp'êr·tў, *n.*, *pl.* -ties. **1.** possessions. **2.** attribute.

prŏph·ė·sў (pro'fə sī), *v.*, -sied, -sying. *v.t.* **1.** foretell; predict. —*v.i.* **2.** speak by divine inspiration. —proph'e·cy, *n.*

prŏph'ĕt, *n.* **1.** utterer of divine revelations. **2.** person who prophesies the future. Also, *fem.*, proph'et·ess. —pro·phet'ic, *adj.* —pro·phet'i·cal·ly, *adv.*

prō''phy·lăx'ĭs, *n.* prevention of or protection from disease. —pro''phy·lac'tic, *adj.*

prō·pĭn'quĭ'tў, *n.* kinship; nearness.

prō·pĭ'tĭ·āte'', *v.t.*, -ated, -ating. make favorable; appease.

prō·pĭ'tioŭs, *adj.* favorable; auspicious. —pro·pi'tious·ly, *adv.*

prō·pō'nėnt, *n.* advocate; backer.

prō·pôr'tion, *n.* **1.** quantitative relation. **2.** due relationship. **3.** proportions, dimensions. —*v.t.* **4.** put in due proportion. —pro·por'tion·al, pro·por'tion·ate, *adj.*

pró·pōse', *v.*, **-posed, -posing.** *v.t.* **1.** suggest or offer. **2.** intend. —*v.i.* **3.** suggest marriage. —**prop''o·si'tion**, *n.* —**pro·pos'al**, *n.*

pró·poūnd', *v.t.* offer for consideration.

pró·prī'é·tôr, *n.* manager or owner. —**pro·pri'e·tor·ship''**, *n.* —**pro·pri'e·tar''y**, *adj.*

pró·prī'é·tỹ, *n., pl.* **-ties. 1.** respectability. **2.** suitability.

pró·pŭl'sion, *n.* propelling force.

prō·rāte', *v.*, **-rated, -rating.** *v.i.*, *v.t.* distribute or divide proportionately.

prō·sā'ĭc, *adj.* commonplace; dull.

prōse, *n.* ordinary language of speech and writing.

prŏs'é·cūte'', *v.t.*, **-cuted, -cuting. 1.** begin legal proceedings against. **2.** continue to completion. —**pros''e·cu'tion**, *n.* —**pros''e·cu'tor**, *n.*

prŏs'é·lўte'', *n.* convert.

prŏs'pĕct, *n.* **1.** likelihood, esp. of success. **2.** view. **3.** potential customer or buyer. —*v.i.* **4.** search or explore, e.g. for gold. —**pros·pec'tive**, *adj.* —**pros'pec·tor**, *n.*

prō·spĕc'tŭs, *n.* description of a new venture, etc. for prospective buyers.

prŏs'pêr, *v.i.* be successful. —**pros·per'i·ty**, *n.* —**pros'per·ous**, *adj.* —**pros'per·ous·ly**, *adv.*

prŏs'tāte, *n.* gland at the base of the male bladder.

prŏs'tī·tūte'', *n.*, *v.t.*, **-tuted, -tuting.** *n.* **1.** person who engages in sexual intercourse for pay. —*v.t.* **2.** misuse, as talent. —**pros''ti·tu'tion**, *n.*

prŏs'trāte, *v.t.*, **-trated, -trating**, *adj.* *v.t.* **1.** lay flat. **2.** exhaust of strength. —*adj.* **3.** lying. **4.** without strength. —**pros·tra'tion**, *n.*

prŏs'ў, *adj.*, **prosier, prosiest.** dull; uninteresting.

pró·tĕct', *v.t.* defend or preserve. —**pro·tec'tion**, *n.* —**pro·tec'tive**, *adj.* —**pro·tec'tive·ly**, *adv.* —**pro·tec'tor**, *n.*

pró·tĕc'tôr·àte, *n.* protection and partial control of one state by another.

prō·té·gé (prō'tə zhā''), *n.* person under patronage. Also, *fem.*, **pro'té·gée''.**

prō·tē·in, *n.* nitrogenous compound essential for life processes present in living matter.

prō'tĕst, *n.* **1.** objection. —*v.i.*, *v.t.* **2.** make an objection. —*v.t.* **3.** declare solemnly. —**pro''tes·ta'tion**, *n.* —**pro·tes'ter**, *n.*

Prŏt'és·tànt, *n.* western Christian not belonging to the Roman Catholic Church. —**Prot'es·tant·ism''**, *n.*

prō'tò·cŏl, *n.* code of etiquette, esp. diplomatic.

prō'tŏn, *n.* elementary atomic particle carrying a positive charge.

prō'tò·plăsm'', *n.* basic protein substance of living matter.

prō'tò·tўpe'', *n.* model; first specimen.

prō·trăct', *v.t.* lengthen; prolong. —**pro·trac'tion**, *n.*

prō·trăc'tòr, *n.* instrument for measuring angles.

prō·trūde', *v.i.*, **-truded, -truding.** project. —**pro·tru'sion**, *n.* —**pro·tru'sive**, *adj.*

prō·tū'bêr·ànt, *adj.* bulging out. —**pro·tu'ber·ance**, *n.*

proūd, *adj.* **1.** having self-respect. **2.** feeling honored. **3.** arrogant. **4.** glorious. —**proud'ly**, *adv.*

prove (prōōv), *v.*, **proved, proving**, *v.t.* **1.** establish the truth of. **2.** test. —*v.i.* **3.** turn out. —**prov'a·ble**, *adj.*

prŏv'én·dêr, *n.* food.

prŏv'êrb, *n.* wise popular saying. —**pro·ver'bi·al**, *adj.*

pró·vīde', *v.*, **-vided, -viding.** *v.t.* **1.** supply; equip. **2.** yield. —*v.i.* **3.** prepare beforehand. —**pro·vi'der**, *n.*

pró·vī'dĕd, *conj.* if; on condition that.

prŏv'ī·dĕnce, *n.* **1.** divine care or guidance. **2.** economy. —**prov''i·den'tial**, *adj.* —**prov'i·dent**, *adj.*

prŏv'ĭnce, *n.* **1.** administrative district. **2.** personal area of operations or expertise.

pró·vĭn'ciàl, *adj.* **1.** of a province. **2.** narrow-mindedly local.

pró·vī'sion, *n.* **1.** stipulation. **2.** act or instance of providing. **3.** prearrangement. **4. provisions**, food supply; goods. —*v.t.* **5.** supply with provisions.

pró·vī'sion·àl, *adj.* temporary; conditional.

pró·vī'sō, *n., pl.* **-sos, -soes.** stipulation.

pró·vōke', *v.t.*, **-voked, -voking. 1.** exasperate. **2.** call into being or effect. —**prov''o·ca'tion**, *n.* —**pro·voc'a·tive**, *adj.* —**pro·voc'a·tive·ly**, *adv.*

prō′vōst, *n.* high official, esp. of a university.

prow, *n.* bow of a ship or airplane.

prow′ess, *n.* **1.** bravery; strength, esp. military. **2.** extraordinary ability.

prowl, *v.i.* roam about or search stealthily. **—prowl′er,** *n.*

prŏx·īm′ĭ·tÿ, *n.* nearness.

prŏx′ÿ, *n., pl.* **proxies. 1.** agent. **2.** authority to act or vote for another.

prūde, *n.* extremely modest person. **—prud′ish,** *adj.*

prū′dénce, *n.* **1.** caution. **2.** practical wisdom. **—pru′dent,** *adj.*

prūne, *v.t.,* **pruned, pruning.** *n. v.t.* **1.** cut off; trim. **—n. 2.** dried plum.

prū′rĭ·ėnt, *adj.* having lewd thoughts. **—pru′ri·ence,** *n.*

prÿ, *v.,* **pried, prying.** *n. v.i.* **1.** inquire unjustifiably into another's affairs. **—v.i. 2.** move by leverage. **—n. 3.** act or instance of prying. **4.** lever.

psälm (sahm), *n.* sacred song or poem.

pseū′dō·nÿm, *n.* assumed or false name.

psèū·dō (sōō′dō), *adj.* false; spurious.

psÿ·chė·dĕl′ĭc (si′′kə del′ik), *adj.* **1.** pertaining to intense hallucinatory effects. **—n. 2.** hallucination-producing drug.

psy·che (si′kē), *n.* human self or soul.

psÿ·chī′á·trÿ, *n.* science of healing mental disorders. **—psy·chi′a·trist,** *n.* **—psy′′chi·at′ric,** *adj.*

psÿ′chĭc, *n.* **1.** medium or clairvoyant. **—adj.** Also, **psy′chi·cal. 2.** pertaining to the psyche. **3.** supernatural.

psÿ′′chō·á·nǎl′ÿ·sĭs, *n.* detailed study and treatment of neuroses. **—psy′′cho·an′a·lyst,** *n.* **—psy′′cho·an′a·lyze,** *v.t.* **—psy′′cho·an′′a·lyt′ic,** *adj.*

psÿ·chŏl′ō·gÿ, *n.* **1.** study of the mind and behavior. **2.** mental and behavioral constitution. **—psy′′cho·log′i·cal,** *adj.* **—psy·chol′o·gist,** *n.*

psÿ′′chō·neū·rō′sĭs, *n., pl.* **-ses.** emotional disorder or disease. **—psy′′cho·neu·rot′ic,** *adj.*

psÿ′chȯ·păth′′, *n.* mentally ill person. **—psy′′cho·path′ic,** *adj.* **—psy·chop′a·thy,** *n.*

psÿ·chō′sĭs, *n., pl.* **-ses.** mental disease marked by loss of contact with reality. **—psy·chot′ic,** *n., adj.*

psÿ′′chō·sō·mǎt′ĭc, *adj.* pertaining to physical effects caused by mental states.

psÿ′′chō·thĕr′á·pÿ, *n.* treatment of mental and emotional disorders. **—psy′′cho·ther′a·pist,** *n.*

ptō·māine (tō′mān), *n.* substance produced by bacteria in decaying matter.

pŭb, *n. British.* bar; tavern.

pū·bêr·tÿ (pyōō′bər tē), *n.* sexual maturity.

pŭb′lĭc, *adj.* **1.** of or for all people. **2.** known by or knowable to all. **—n. 3.** people generally. **—pub′lic·ly,** *adv.*

pŭb′′lĭ·cā′tion, *n.* **1.** act or instance of publishing. **2.** published work.

pŭb·lĭc′ĭ·tÿ, *n.* **1.** public attention or notice. **2.** material claiming public attention.

pŭb′lĭ·cīze′′, *v.t.,* **-cized, -cizing.** bring to public attention or notice.

pŭb′lĭsh, *v.t.* **1.** print or issue for distribution. **2.** announce publicly. **—pub′lish·er,** *n.*

pŭck′êr, *v.t., v.i., n.* curl; wrinkle.

pŭd′dĭng, *n.* soft, sweet dessert.

pŭd′dle, *n.* small pool of water.

pŭdg′ÿ, *adj.,* **pudgier, pudgiest.** short and fat; chubby. **—pudg′i·ness,** *n.*

pueb·lo (pweb′lō), *n.* **1.** adobe Indian village of U.S. Southwest. **2. Pueblo,** Southwestern U.S. Indian people.

pu·er·ile (pōō′ər il), *adj.* silly; childish. **—pu′′er·il′i·ty,** *n.*

pu·er·per·al (pōō ur′pər əl), *adj.* pertaining to childbirth.

pŭff, *n.* **1.** short quick gust, e.g. of wind. **2.** anything soft and light. **3.** light piece of pastry. **—v.i. 4.** blow or breathe in puffs. **5.** become inflated or swollen. **—v.t. 6.** blow or puff on.

pŭf′fĭn, *n.* sea bird.

pŭg, *n.* small short-haired dog.

pū′gĭl·ĭsm′′, *n.* boxing. **—pu′gil·ist,** *n.*

pŭg·nā′cĭoŭs, *adj.* fond of fighting; belligerent. **—pug·nac′i·ty,** *n.*

pūke, *v.,* **puked, puking.** *v.i., v.t.* vomit.

pŭl′chrĭ·tūde′′, *n.* beauty.

pŭll, *v.t.* **1.** move toward or after one. **2.** strain by pulling. **3.** select from a group. **—v.i. 4.** attempt to move toward one. **5.** move oneself. **—n. 6.** act or instance of pulling. **7.** something to pull on. **8.** *Informal.* influence.

pŭl′lėt, *n.* young hen.

pŭl′lēy, *n., pl.* **-leys.** wheel with a rim grooved for a rope.

pŭl′mò·nār′′ў, *adj.* of the lungs.

pŭlp, *n.* 1. soft, fleshy material. —*v.t.* 2. crush or grind to pulp. —*v.i.* 3. become pulp. —**pulp′y,** *adj.*

pŭl′pĭt, *n.* raised platform or lectern used by a clergyman.

pŭl′sāte, *v.i.,* **-sated, -sating** throb; quiver. —**pul·sa′tion,** *n.*

pŭlse, *n.* 1. regular throb of the arteries produced by the heart. —*v.i.* 2. throb regularly.

pŭl′vêr·īze′′, *v.,* **-ized, -izing.** *v.t.* 1. reduce to powder or dust. 2. completely crush. —*v.i.* 3. become reduced to dust. —**pul′′ver·i·za′tion,** *n.*

pū′mȧ, *n.* cougar.

pŭm′ĭce, *n.* porous volcanic glass.

pŭm′měl, *v.t.* beat; thrash.

pŭmp, *n.* 1. device for applying force to liquids and gases. 2. low shoe. —*v.t.* 3. move with a pump. 4. inflate. 5. attempt to wheedle information from.

pŭm′′pêr·nĭck′ĕl, *n.* hard rye bread.

pŭmp′kĭn, *n.* large orange fruit that grows on a vine.

pŭn, *n., v.i.,* **punned, punning.** *n.* 1. play with similar-sounding words with different meanings. —*v.i.* 2. make a pun.

pŭnch, *n.* 1. quick blow, esp. with the fist. 2. piercing or sinking implement. 3. sweet mixed beverage. —*v.t.* 4. hit. 5. perforate. —**punch′er,** *n.*

pŭnc·tĭl′ĭ·oŭs, *adj.* adhering to correct procedure.

pŭnc′tū·ȧl, *adj.* on time; prompt. —**punc′′tu·al′i·ty,** *n.* —**punc′tu·al·ly,** *adv.*

pŭnc′tū·āte′′, *v.t.,* **-ated, -ating.** 1. mark with commas, periods, etc. 2. mark or interrupt periodically. 3. give emphasis to. —**punc′′tu·a′tion,** *n.*

pŭnc′tûre, *v.t.,* **-tured, -turing.** *n. v.t.* 1. pierce with a pointed object. —*n.* 2. act or instance of puncturing.

pŭn′dĭt, *n.* expert.

pŭn′gĕnt, *v.t.* 1. sharp of taste. 2. biting. —**pun′gen·cy,** *n.* —**pun′gent·ly,** *adv.*

pŭn′ĭsh, *v.t.* 1. subject to penalty or revenge. 2. inflict a penalty for. —**pun′ish·a·ble,** *adj.* —**pun′ish·ment,** *n.*

pū′nǐ·tǐve, *adj.* punishing.

pŭnt, *n.* 1. flat-bottomed shallow boat.

2. kick in football. —*v.i.* 3. kick in midair.

pū′nў, *adj.* **-nier, -niest.** small; slight; weak.

pŭp, *n.* young dog. Also, **pup′py.**

pū′pȧ, *n., pl.* **-pae, -pas.** insect halfway between larva and adult.

pū′pĭl, *n.* 1. student. 2. dark opening in the iris of the eye.

pŭp′pĕt, *n.* 1. small figure moved by hand or by wires. 2. supposedly autonomous party obeying another. —**pup′′pe·teer′,** *n.*

pûr′chȧse, *v.t.,* **-chased, -chasing,** *n. v.t.* 1. buy. —*n.* 2. act or instance of purchasing. 3. thing purchased. 4. leverage. —**pur′chas·er,** *n.*

pūre, *adj.,* **purer, purest.** 1. unmixed or unpolluted. 2. absolute. 3. abstract. 4. innocent. —**pure′ly,** *adv.*

pu·ree (pyōō rā′), *n.* cooked and sieved food.

pûr′gȧ·tô′′rў, *n., pl.* **-ries.** 1. temporary punishment. 2. place for purification from sin after death.

pûrge, *v.t.,* **purged, purging.** *n. v.t.* 1. cleanse; purify. 2. rid; remove. 3. eliminate or kill for political reasons. —*n.* 4. act or instance of purging. —**pur′ga′tion,** *n.* —**pur′ga·tive,** *adj., n.*

pū′rĭ·fў, *v.,* **-fied, -fying.** *v.t.* 1. make pure. 2. free from sin or guilt. —*v.i.* 3. become pure. —**pu′′ri·fi·ca′tion,** *n.*

pū′rĭ·tȧn, *n.* 1. member of a strict religious group. 2. adherent to an unusually strict moral code. —**pu′ri·tan′i·cal,** *adj.*

pū′rĭ·tў, *n.* quality or condition of being pure.

pûrl, *v.t., v.i.* knit with an inverted stitch.

pur·lieu (par′lōō), *n.* bordering or outlying district.

pûr·loĭn′, *v.t.* steal.

pûr′ple, *n.* 1. bluish-red color. —*adj.* 2. of the color purple.

pur·port, *v.t.* (pər′′port′). 1. claim or profess. 2. express; imply. —*n.* 3. (pər′port) significance.

pûr′pòse, *n., v.t.,* **-posed, -posing.** *n.* 1. intention; object. —*v.t.* 2. intend. —**pur′pose·ful,** *adj.* —**pur′pose·less,** *adj.*

pûr′pòse·lў, *adv.* intentionally.

pûrr, *n.* 1. soft continuous sound made by a cat. —*v.i.* 2. make this sound.

pûrse, *n.*, *v.t.*, **pursed, pursing.** *n.* **1.** small bag for money. **2.** sum of money offered as a prize. —*v.t.* **3.** pucker.

pûrs'ẽr, *n.* financial officer of a ship.

pûr·su'ȧnt, *adv.* according.

pûr·sue', *v.t.*, **-sued, -suing. 1.** chase. **2.** proceed with. —**pur·su'ance**, *n.* —**pur·su'er**, *n.*

pûr·sūit', *n.* **1.** act or instance of pursuing. **2.** occupation; calling.

pū·rū·lènt (pyōōr'ə lənt), *adj.* containing pus. —**pu'ru·lence**, *n.*

pûr'vey, *v.t.* furnish; supply. —**pur·vey' ance**, *n.* —**pur·vey'or**, *n.*

pûs, *n.* yellowish fluid found in sores.

pûsh, *v.t.* **1.** press against to move. **2.** urge; press. —*v.i.* **3.** move with force. —*n.* **4.** act or instance of pushing. —**push'er**, *n.*

pŭsh'ÿ, *adj.*, **-ier, -iest.** aggressive.

pū·sĭl·lăn''ĭ·mŏŭs, *adj.* cowardly.

pŭss'ÿ, *n.*, *pl.* **-sies.** cat. Also, **puss.**

pŭss'ÿ-fŏŏt, *v.i.* act stealthily.

pŭssÿ wĭllŏw, *n.* small American willow tree.

pŭs'tūle, *n.* pus-filled pimple.

pŭt, *v.*, **put, putting.** *v.t.* **1.** carry to a specified place. **2.** cause to be in a specified condition. **3.** present for consideration. **4.** hurl overhand. **5. put off,** postpone. **6. put out, a.** extinguish. **b.** trouble. —*v.i.* **7. put up with,** tolerate.

pū'tȧ·tĭve, *adj.* reputed; supposed.

pū''trė·fÿ'', *v.*, **-fied, -fying.** *v.i.*, *v.t.* decay; rot. —**pu''tre·fac'tion**, *n.*

pū'trĭd, *adj.* **1.** rotten; decayed. **2.** corrupt; vile.

pŭtt, *v.t. Golf.* **1.** hit gently. —*n.* **2.** act or instance of putting.

pŭt'têr, *v.i.* **1.** be active without effect. —*n.* **2.** golf club for putting.

pŭt'tÿ, *n.*, *v.t.*, **-tied, -tying.** *n.* **1.** cement of linseed oil and whiting. —*v.t.* **2.** secure with putty.

pŭz'zle, *n.*, *v.*, **-zled, -zling.** *n.* **1.** device or problem posing difficulties. —*v.t.* **2.** mystify; perplex. —*v.i.* **3.** attempt to study or figure out a problem.

pÿg'mÿ, *n.*, *pl.* **-mies.** dwarf.

pÿ''lŏn, *n.* **1.** support tower. **2.** cone-shaped road marker.

pÿ''ŏr·rhē'ȧ, *n.* disease of the gums.

pÿr'ȧ·mĭd, *n.* **1.** structure or form with triangular sides. —*v.t.* **2.** increase gradually. —**py·ram'i·dal**, *adj.*

pÿre, *n.* heap of material for burning a corpse.

pÿ'rīte, *n.* yellow sulfur and iron.

pÿ''ró·mā'nĭ·ȧ, *n.* mania for starting fires. —**py''ro·ma'ni·ac''**, *n.*

pÿ''rō·tĕch'nĭcs, *n.* **1.** fireworks. **2.** display of virtuosity. —**pyro·tech'nic**, *adj.*

pÿ'thŏn, *n.* large constricting snake.

Q

Q, q, *n.* seventeenth letter of the English alphabet.

quăck, *n.* **1.** fraudulent doctor. **2.** sound of a duck. —*v.i.* **3.** utter a quack. —**quack'er·y**, *n.*

quăd'răn''gle, *n.* **1.** closed figure with four angles. **2.** enclosed four-sided yard. —**quad·ran'gu·lar**, *adj.*

quăd'rȧnt, *n.* **1.** arc of 90°. **2.** instrument for measuring altitudes.

quăd''rȧ·phŏn'ĭc, *adj.* of a sound system using four independent speakers.

quăd''rĭ·lăt'êr·ȧl, *adj.* **1.** four-sided. —*n.* **2.** plane figure with four sides.

quä·drōōn'', *n.* a person of one-quarter black ancestry.

quăd'rū·pĕd'', *n.* animal with four feet.

quăd'rū·ple, *adj.*, *v.*, **-pled, -pling.** *adj.* **1.** fourfold. **2.** having four parts. —*v.t.*, *v.i.* **3.** multiply by four.

quăd'rū'plĕt, *n.* one of four children born together.

quăd·rū'plĭ·cāte, *n.* any of four copies.

quaff (kwof), *v.t.* drink with gusto.

quăg'mīre'', *n.* boggy area.

qua·hog (quo'hog), *n.* edible American clam.

quăil, *n.*, *pl.* **quails, quail**, *v.i.* *n.* **1.** game bird. —*v.i.* **2.** lose heart or courage.

quăint, *adj.* pleasingly odd or old-fashioned. —**quaint'ness**, *n.* —**quaint'ly**, *adv.*

quăke, *v.i.*, **quaked, quaking**, *n.* *v.i.* **1.** tremble or shake. —*n.* **2.** earthquake.

Quăk'êr, *n.* member of the Society of Friends.

quăl'ĭ·fÿ'', *v.*, **-fied, -fying.** *v.t.* **1.** make eligible or capable. **2.** modify. —*v.i.* **3.**

be qualified. —**qual''i·fi·ca'tion,** *n.* —**qual'i·fied'',** *adj.*

quäl'i·tÿ, *n., pl.* **-ties. 1.** essential characteristic. **2.** degree of merit. **3.** excellence. —**qual'i·ta''tive,** *adj.*

qualm (kwahlm), *n.* **1.** misgiving. **2.** sick feeling.

quän'da·rÿ, *n., pl.* **-ries.** perplexed state.

quän'ti·tÿ, *n., pl.* **-ties. 1.** amount or number. **2.** large or considerable amount. —**quan'ti·ta''tive,** *adj.*

quâr'án·tïne'', *n., v.t.,* **-tined, -tining.** *n.* **1.** isolation of suspected disease bearers. —*v.t.* **2.** put in quarantine.

quâr'rel, *n.* **1.** angry argument; fight. —*v.i.* **2.** have a quarrel. —**quar'rel·some,** *adj.*

quâr'rÿ, *n., pl.* **-ries,** *v.t.,* **-ried, -rying.** *n.* **1.** place from which stone is extracted. **2.** object of pursuit; prey. —*v.t.* **3.** get or take from a quarry.

quârt, *n.* unit of measure equal to one fourth of a gallon.

quâr'têr, *n.* **1.** fourth part. **2.** coin with the value of 25 cents. **3. quarters,** lodgings. **4.** mercy. —*v.t.* **5.** divide into quarters. **6.** lodge. —*adj.* **7.** being a quarter.

quâr'têr·bǎck'', *n.* position in football.

quâr'têr·lÿ, *adj., n., pl.* **-lies.** *adj.* **1.** occurring every three months. —*n.* **2.** periodical published four times a year.

quâr'têr·mǎs''têr, *n.* **1.** army officer who oversees supplies, etc. **2.** petty officer in charge of a ship's signals, steering, etc.

quâr·tĕt', *n.* **1.** group of four, esp. musicians. **2.** composition for four instruments. Also, **quar·tette'.**

quâr'tō, *n.* book printed on sheets folded into quarters.

quârtz, *n.* common shiny crystalline mineral.

quäsh, *v.t.* **1.** put down completely. **2.** invalidate.

quä·sī (kwah'sī), *adj.* **1.** resembling. —*adv.* **2.** seemingly.

quät'rāin, *n.* four-line verse unit.

quä'vêr, *v.i.* **1.** tremble. **2.** speak or sing tremulously. —*n.* **3.** quavering tone.

quay (kē), *n.* pier; wharf.

quēa'sÿ, *adj.,* **-sier, -siest. 1.** nauseous. **2.** uneasy.

quēen, *n.* **1.** female sovereign. **2.** spouse of a king. **3.** fertile female of bees.

quēer, *adj.* peculiar. —**queer'ly,** *adv.* —**queer'ness,** *n.*

quĕll, *v.t.* **1.** subdue. **2.** pacify.

quĕnch, *v.t.* **1.** slake, as thirst. **2.** extinguish. **3.** cool by immersion.

quĕr'ù·loŭs, *adj.* peevish.

quē'rÿ, *n., pl.* **-ries,** *v.t.,* **-ried, -rying.** *n.* **1.** question; inquiry. —*v.t.* **2.** inquire regarding.

quĕst, *n., v.i.* search.

quĕs'tion, *n.* **1.** interrogative sentence. **2.** problem or issue. —*v.t.* **3.** ask questions of. **4.** challenge; doubt. —**ques'tion·a·ble,** *adj.* —**ques'tion·er,** *n.*

quĕs''tion·nāire', *n.* set or list of questions.

queue (kyōō), *n., v.,* **queued, queuing.** *n.* **1.** line of waiting persons. **2.** braid of hair at the back of the head. —*v.t., v.i.* **3.** form in a line.

quïb'ble, *v.i.,* **-bled, -bling,** *n. v.i.* **1.** speak evasively. **2.** cavil; carp. —*n.* **3.** act or instance of quibbling.

quiche (kēsh), *n.* French tart filled with egg, cheese, etc.

quǐck, *adj.* **1.** prompt. **2.** intelligent. **3.** speedy. —*n.* **4.** living persons. **5.** vital part. —**quick'ly,** *adv.* —**quick'ness,** *n.*

quǐck'ĕn, *v.t.* **1.** hasten. —*v.i.* **2.** become alive or sensitive.

quǐck'sǎnd'', *n.* watery, soft mass of sand that yields under weight.

quǐck'sǐl''vêr, *n.* mercury.

quǐd, *n.* cut something chewable, esp. tobacco.

qui·es·cent (kwē·es'ent), *adj.* inactive. —**qui·es'cence,** *n.*

quī'ĕt, *adj.* **1.** at rest. **2.** silent. **3.** restrained. —*v.t.* **4.** make quiet. —*v.i.* **5.** become quiet. —*n.* **6.** silence; tranquillity. —**qui'et·ly,** *adv.* —**qui'et·ness,** *n.* —**qui'e·tude'',** *n.*

qui·e·tus (kwī ēt'əs), *n.* **1.** final settlement. **2.** death.

quĭll, *n.* **1.** large stiff feather. **2.** bristle or spine.

quĭlt, *n.* lined and padded bedcovering.

quĭnce, *n.* hard yellowish fruit.

quī'nīne, *n.* bitter saltlike substance used medically.

quǐn·tĕs'sĕnce, *n.* **1.** purest essence. **2.**

completely typical example. **—quin″ tes·sen′tial,** *adj.*
quĭn·tĕt′, *n.* **1.** group of five, esp. musicians. **2.** composition for five instruments. Also, **quin·tette′.**
quĭn·tŭ′ple, *adj., v.,* **-pled, -pling.** *adj.* **1.** fivefold. **2.** having five parts. *—v.t., v.i.* **3.** multiply by five.
quĭn′tŭ·plėt, *n.* **1.** one of five children born together. **2.** group of five.
quĭp, *n., v.i.,* **quipped, quipping.** *n.* **1.** sarcastic or clever remark. *—v.i.* **2.** make a quip.
quīre, *n.* set of 24 sheets of paper.
quîrk, *n.* peculiarity.
quĭs′lĭng, *n.* traitor.
quĭt, *v.,* **quitted, quitting.** *v.t., v.i.* **1.** discontinue. *—v.t.* **2.** leave. **3.** abandon. **—quit′ter,** *n.*
quīte, *adv.* **1.** completely. **2.** positively.
quĭts, *adj.* on equal terms.
quĭt′tance, *n.* **1.** recompense. **2.** discharge from obligation or debt.
quĭv′êr, *v.t., v.i.* **1.** tremble; shake. *—n.* **2.** case for arrows.
quĭx·ŏt′ĭc, *adj.* foolishly idealistic.
quĭz, *v.t.,* **quizzed, quizzing** *n. v.t.* **1.** give a brief test to. **2.** question closely. *—n.* **3.** test or questioning.
quĭz′zĭ·cal, *adj.* **1.** comically odd. **2.** questioning. **3.** chaffing. **—quiz′zi·cal·ly,** *adv.*
quoĭt, *n.* flat ring used in throwing games.
quŏn′dam, *adj.* former.
quô′rŭm, *n.* sufficient number of attending members.
quō′ta, *n.* assigned share or number.
quō·tā′tion, *n.* **1.** word-for-word citation. **2.** specified price.
quō·tā′tion mârks, *n.* pair of punctuation marks, “ ”, used to mark the beginning and end of a direct quotation.
quōte, *v.t.,* **quoted, quoting,** *n. v.t.* **1.** repeat verbatim. **2.** cite as evidence. **3.** state, as a price. *—n.* **4.** quotation. **—quot′a·ble,** *adj.*
quōth, *v.t. Archaic.* said.
quō′tient, *n. Math.* number of times one number contains another.

R

R, r, *n.* eighteenth letter of the English alphabet.
răb′bet, *n., v.t.,* **-beted, -beting.** *n.* **1.** L-shaped notch on the end of timber, etc. *—v.t.* **2.** cut a rabbet on. **3.** join with rabbets.
răb′bī, *n., pl.* **-bis.** Jewish preacher. **—rab·bin′ic, rab·bin′i·cal,** *adj.*
răb′bĭt, *n.* small long-eared mammal.
răb′ble, *n.* mob.
răb′ĭd, *adj.* **1.** irrationally extreme. **2.** having rabies.
rā′biēs, *n.* infectious disease transmitted by animal bites.
răc·cōōn′, *n.* small nocturnal mammal.
rāce, *n., v.,* **raced, racing.** *n.* **1.** contest of speed. **2.** group of persons with a common origin. *—v.i.* **3.** participate in a race. **4.** move quickly. *—v.t.* **5.** cause to move quickly.
rā′cial, *adj.* concerning race or the differences between races. **—rac′ism,** *n.*
răck, *n.* **1.** framework for storage. **2.** barlike gear engaging a pinion. *—v.t.* **3.** torture. **4.** strain.
răck″et, *n.* **1.** noise; commotion. **2.** dishonest or illegal activity. **3.** cross-stringed light bat, used esp. in tennis.
răck″e·tēer′, *n.* gangster.
rac·on·teur (rak″on·tur′) *n.* storyteller.
răc′ȳ, *adj.,* **-ier, -iest. 1.** lively. **2.** risqué.
rā′dâr, *n.* device using radio waves to locate objects.
rā′dĭ·al, *adj.* pertaining to rays or a radius.
rā′dĭ·ant, *adj.* **1.** bright; shiny. **2.** emitting light. **—ra′di·ance,** *n.*
rā′dĭ·āte″, *v.,* **-ated, -ating.** *v.i.* **1.** move or spread like rays from a center. *—v.t.* **2.** emit, as rays.
rā′dĭ·ā″tŏr, *n.* convection heater.
răd′ĭ·cal, *adj.* **1.** fundamental. **2.** favoring drastic or extreme change. *—n.* **3.** person with radical ideas. **—rad′i·cal·ism″,** *n.*
rā′dĭ·ō″, *n.* **1.** wireless transmission of sound by electromagnetic waves. **2.** device for receiving radio transmissions.
rā″dĭ·ō·ăc′tĭve, *adj.* emitting nuclear radiation.

răd′ĭsh, *n.* edible root of a garden plant.

rā′dĭ·ŭm, *n.* radioactive metallic element.

rā′dĭ·ŭs, *n.*, *pl.* **-dii, -diuses. 1.** straight line to an arc from its center. **2.** forearm bone.

răf′fle, *n.*, *v.t.*, **-fled, -fling.** *n.* **1.** lottery for which chances are sold. —*v.t.* **2.** dispose of by raffle.

răft, *n.* floating platform.

răf′têr, *n.* roof beam.

răg, *n.* torn or waste piece of cloth. —**rag′ged,** *adj.*

răg′a·mŭf′′fĭn, *n.* scruffy child.

rāge, *n.*, *v.i.*, **raged, raging.** *n.* **1.** violent anger. **2.** popular vogue. —*v.i.* **3.** be violently angry. **4.** proceed or prevail with violence.

răg′lăn, *n.* loose overcoat with shoulders continuing from the sleeves.

ra·gout (ra gōō′), *n.* stew.

răg′tīme′′, *n.* syncopated American popular music.

răg′wēed′′, *n.* weed whose pollen causes hay fever.

rāid, *n.* **1.** sudden attack. —*v.t.* **2.** attack suddenly.

rāil, *n.* **1.** horizontal bar or beam. **2.** guide for a wheel of a railroad car. **3.** railroad. **4.** wading bird. —*v.i.* **5.** complain bitterly.

rāil′ĭng, *n.* barrier of uprights and rails.

rāil′lêr·ў, *n.* banter; ridicule.

rāil′rōad′′, *n.* **1.** road of rails on which trains run. —*v.t.* **2.** transport by railroad. **3.** *Informal.* convict wrongly an innocent person.

rāin, *n.* **1.** condensed water falling in drops from the clouds. **2.** rainstorm. —*v.i.* **3.** fall as rain. —*v.t.* **4.** give abundantly; shower. —**rain′y,** *adj.* —**rain′fall′′,** *n.*

rāin′bōw′′, *n.* colored arc of sunlight refracted through raindrops.

rāin′cōat′′, *n.* water-repellent overcoat.

rāise, *v.t.*, **raised, raising.** *n.* *v.t.* **1.** lift. **2.** set upright. **3.** solicit and collect. **4.** grow. **5.** bring up. **6.** call to attention. —*n.* **7.** increase in salary.

rāi′sĭn, *n.* sweet dried grape.

râ′jäh, *n.* oriental prince or king. Also, **ra′ja.**

rāke, *n.*, *v.t.*, **raked, raking.** *n.* **1.** pronged implement for collecting leaves, etc. **2.** libertine. **3.** slope. —*v.t.* **4.** smooth, collect, etc. with a rake.

rāk′ĭsh, *adj.* jaunty.

răl′lў, *v.*, **-lied, -lying,** *n.*, *pl.* **-lies.** *v.t.*, *v.i.* **1.** gather. —*v.t.* **2.** reorganize. **3.** tease. —*v.i.* **4.** recover strength. —*n.* **5.** gathering. **6.** recovery of strength.

răm, *n.*, *v.t.*, **rammed, ramming.** *n.* **1.** male sheep. **2.** device for battering, crushing, etc. —*v.t.* **3.** run into forcibly.

răm′ble, *v.i.*, **-bled, -bling,** *n.* *v.i.* **1.** wander leisurely. **2.** talk discursively. —*n.* **3.** leisurely stroll.

răm′ĭ·fў′′, *v.*, **-fied, -fying.** *v.t.*, *v.i.* branch out.

rămp, *n.* sloping road or walk.

răm′pāge, *n.*, *v.i.*, **-paged, -paging.** *n.* **1.** violent behavior. —*v.i.* **2.** rush about furiously.

rămp′ănt, *adj.* **1.** unchecked; raging. **2.** standing on the hind legs.

răm′pârt, *n.* mound of earth erected as a defense; parapet.

răm′shăck′′le, *adj.* shaky; rickety.

rănch, *n.* large stock farm.

răn·cĭd (ran′sid), *adj.* stale; spoiled. —**ran·cid′i·ty,** *n.*

răn′côr, *n.* resentment. —**ran′cor·ous,** *adj.*

răn′dŏm, *adj.* without pattern or aim.

rānge, *n.*, *v.*, **ranged, ranging.** *n.* **1.** extent. **2.** row. **3.** mountain chain. **4.** grazing area. **5.** distance of gunfire, reach, etc. **6.** shooting ground. **7.** stove. —*v.t.* **8.** put in a row. **9.** pass over. —*v.i.* **10.** have a range.

rāng′êr, *n.* warden or trooper policing a rural area.

rănk, *n.* **1.** group, class, or standing. **2.** high position. **3.** row. **4. ranks,** ordinary troops. —*v.t.* **5.** arrange in formation. —*v.i.* **6.** have a specified standing. —*adj.* **7.** excessively grown. **8.** offensively strong in taste or smell. **9.** utter.

răn′kle, *v.*, **-kled, -kling.** *v.t.* **1.** cause long-lasting resentment in. —*v.i.* **2.** cause long-lasting resentment.

răn′săck, *v.t.* **1.** search thoroughly. **2.** plunder; pillage.

răn′sŏm, *n.* **1.** price deemed for return of a prisoner. —*v.t.* **2.** redeem for money.

rănt, *v.i.* **1.** speak violently or wildly. —*n.* **2.** violent or extravagant speech.

răp, *v.t.*, **rapped, rapping.** *n.* *v.t.* **1.** strike sharply. —*n.* **2.** quick, sharp blow. **3.** *Informal.* blame; responsibility. **4.** musical talk or patter.

rà·pā′cious, *adj.* predatory.

rāpe, *n., v.t.,* **raped, raping.** *n.* **1.** forced sexual violation. —*v.t.* **2.** commit rape on. **3.** seize and carry off by force. —**ra′pist,** *n.*

răp′ĭd, *adj.* **1.** speedy. —*n.* **2.** **rapids,** fast-moving sections of a river. —**ra·pid′i·ty,** *n.*

ra·pi·er (rā′pē ər), *n.* small narrow sword.

rap·ine (rap′in), *n.* plunder.

răpt, *adj.* engrossed.

răp′tûre, *n.* ecstatic or beatific joy. —**rap′tur·ous,** *adj.*

rāre, *adj.,* **rarer, rarest. 1.** unusual. **2.** thin. **3.** not completely cooked. —**rar′i·ty,** *n.*

rār′e·fȳ″, *v.,* **-fied, -fying.** *v.t., v.i.* thin. —**rar″e·fac′tion,** *n.*

răs′căl, *n.* unscrupulous person. —**ras·cal′i·ty,** *n.*

răsh, *adj.* **1.** unreasonably hasty. —*n.* **2.** skin irritation.

răsh′êr, *n.* thin slice of ham or bacon.

răsp, *v.t.* **1.** scrape or grate. **2.** talk with a grating sound. —*n.* **3.** rasping sound. **4.** coarse file.

răsp′bĕr″rȳ, *n., pl.* **-ries.** juicy small red or black fruit.

răt, *n.* long-tailed rodent larger than a mouse.

rătch′ĕt, *n.* gear controlled by a pawl.

rāte, *n., v.,* **rated, rating.** *n.* **1.** fixed relation between variables. —*v.t.* **2.** establish a rate for. **3.** judge to be as specified. —*v.i.* **4.** have a specified value.

răth′êr, *adv.* **1.** to a certain extent. **2.** on the contrary. **3.** in preference.

răt′i·fȳ″, *v.t.,* **-fied, -fying.** approve formally.

ră′tion, *n.* **1.** limited allotment. —*v.t.* **2.** put on a ration.

ră′tion·ăl, *adj.* **1.** reasonable. **2.** sane. —**ra″tion·al′i·ty,** *n.*

ră′tion·āle, *n.* rational basis.

ră′tion·ăl·īze″, *v.t.,* **-ized, -izing. 1.** attempt to justify with reasons. **2.** make methodical. —**ra″tion·al·i·za′tion,** *n.*

ra·tio (rā′shō), *n.* relation of quantities.

răt·tăn′, *n.* hollow stem of a climbing palm.

răt′tle, *v.,* **-tled, -tling,** *n.* *v.i.* **1.** make successive short sharp noises. **2.** chatter. —*v.t.* **3.** confuse; disconcert. —*n.* **4.** rattling sounds. **5.** child's toy that rattles.

răt′tle·snāke″, *n.* poisonous American snake.

rau′coŭs, *adj.* harsh; hoarse.

răv′āge, *n., v.t., v.i.,* **-aged, -aging.** ruin; pillage.

rāve, *v.i.,* **raved, raving.** *n.* *v.i.* **1.** talk wildly. —*n.* **2.** *Informal.* unequivocally favorable review.

răv′ĕl, *v.t.* **1.** disengage the threads of. **2.** solve; make clear. —*v.i.* **3.** fray. **4.** become tangled.

rā′vĕn, *n.* large glossy black bird.

răv′ĕn·oŭs, *adj.* exceedingly hungry.

rà·vīne′, *n.* narrow valley.

răv′ĭsh, *v.t.* **1.** transport or fill with joy. **2.** rape.

rāw, *adj.* **1.** in a natural state; naked. **2.** uncooked. **3.** untrained; young.

rāw′hīde″, *n.* untanned hide.

rāy, *n.* **1.** narrow beam of light. **2.** glimpse. **3.** radiating line. **4.** flat ocean fish.

rāy′ŏn, *n.* synthetic silk-like fabric.

rāze, *v.t.,* **razed, razing.** demolish.

rā′zŏr, *n.* sharp instrument for shaving.

rē-, prefix meaning "again." **reaccustom, reacquaint, reacquire, readapt, reaffirm, realign, reappear, reapply, reappoint, reappraisal, rearrange, reassemble, reassert, reassess, reassign, rebind, rebutton, recheck, recommence, reconnect, reconquer, recopy, rededicate, redefine, redevelop, rediscover, redo, reelect, reemerge, reemphasize, reerect, reestablish, reevaluate, reexperience, refill, reformulate, refurnish, regrow, reheat, reignite, reinsert, reinterpret, rekindle, remarry, rename, renumber, reoccur, reorient, replant, replay, reread, resell, resupply, retake, retell, retest, retrain, retransmit, retype, reusable, reuse, reunion, reunite, reverify, rewarm, rewin, rework, rewrap.**

rē, *prep.* in the affair of.

rēach, *v.t.* **1.** arrive at. **2.** extend. **3.** be able to touch. **4.** communicate with.

—*v.i.* **5.** extend the hand. —*n.* **6.** act, instance, or extent of reaching.

rē·āct′, *v.i.* **1.** act in response. **2.** interact.

rē·āc′tion, *n.* **1.** action in response. **2.** extreme political conservatism. —**re·ac′tion·ar″y**, *adj.*, *n.*

rĕad′ĭng, *n.* interpretation of a play or musical composition.

rĕad′ÿ, *adj.*, *v.t.*, **readied, readying**, *n. adj.* **1.** prepared. **2.** willing. **3.** imminent. —*v.t.* **4.** make ready. —*n.* **5.** state of readiness. —**read′i·ly**, *adv.* —**read′i·ness**, *n.*

rē′ăl, *adj.* **1.** not false; genuine. **2.** not imaginary or ideal. —**re·al′i·ty**, *n.* —**re′al·ly**, *adv.*

rēal éstāte, *n.* property, esp. land with buildings. Also, **re′al·ty.**

rē′ăl·ĭsm, *n.* **1.** close imitation of reality. **2.** acceptance of actual conditions. —**re′al·ist**, *n.* —**re″al·is′tic**, *adj.*

rē′ăl·īze″, *v.t.* **1.** understand completely. **2.** bring into actuality. **3.** obtain as a profit. —**re″al·i·za′tion**, *n.*

rĕalm, *n.* **1.** special field of expertise. **2.** kingdom.

rē′ăl·tör, *n.* agent selling real estate.

rēam, *n.* **1.** twenty quires of paper. —*v.t.* **2.** make or enlarge by a rotary tool.

rēap, *v.t.* **1.** harvest. **2.** get as a reward. —**reap′er**, *n.*

rēar, *n.* **1.** back part. **2.** backside. —*adj.* **3.** pertaining to the rear. —*v.t.* **4.** raise; erect. **5.** bring up to maturity. —*v.i.* **6.** rise on the rear legs.

rēa′sòn, *n.* **1.** cause or justification. **2.** objectivity; logic. **3.** sanity. —*v.i.* **4.** think or argue logically. —*v.t.* **5.** infer or conclude. —**rea′son·a·ble**, *adj.* —**rea′son·a·bly**, *adv.*

rē″ás·sure′, *v.t.*, **-sured, -suring.** restore the confidence of. —**re″as·sur′ance**, *n.*

rē′bāte, *v.t.*, **-bated, -bating.** *n. v.t.* **1.** refund after payment. —*n.* **2.** amount rebated.

re·bel, *v.i.*, **-belled, -belling**, *n.*, *v.* (rē bel′). **1.** arise against authority. —*n.* (reb′əl). **2.** person who rebels. —**re·bel′lion**, *n.* —**re·bel′lious**, *adj.*

rē·bŏund, *v.i.* (rē bownd′) **1.** bounce back after impact. —*n.* (rē′bownd) **2.** act or instance of rebounding.

rė·bŭff′, *n.* **1.** blunt rejection or refusal. —*v.t.* **2.** reject curtly.

rė·būke′, *v.t.*, **-buked, -buking**, *n.* reprimand.

rē′bŭs, *n.* combination of pictures whose names combine to form a word or phrase.

rė·bŭt′, *v.t.*, **-butted, -butting.** refute. —**re·but′tal**, *n.*

rė·căl′cĭ·tránt (rē kal′sə trənt), *adj.* stubborn; refractory. —**re·cal′ci·trance**, *n.*

rė·căll′, *v.t.* **1.** remember. **2.** withdraw. **3.** call or summon back. —*n.* **4.** act or instance of recalling. **5.** memory.

rė·cănt′, *v.t.*, *v.i.* retract; renounce. —**re″can·ta′tion**, *n.*

rė″cà·pĭt′ū·lāte, *v.* **-lated, -lating.** *v.t.*, *v.i.* restate briefly; sum up. —**re″ca·pit″u·la′tion**, *n.*

rė·cēde′, *v.i.*, **-ceded, -ceding. 1.** move back. **2.** diminish.

rė·cēipt′, *n.* **1.** act or instance of receiving. **2.** document acknowledging payment or delivery. **3. receipts**, income.

rė·cēive′, *v.t.*, **-ceived, -ceiving. 1.** take when offered or sent. **2.** sustain; experience. **3.** welcome. —**re·ceiv′a·ble**, *adj.*

rė·cēiv′êr, *n.* **1.** person or thing that receives. **2.** apparatus receiving radio signals. **3.** administrator of property in litigation. —**re·ceiv′er·ship**, *n.*

rē′cĕnt, *adj.* not long past. —**re′cen·cy**, *n.*

rė·cĕp′tà·cle, *n.* container.

rė·cĕp′tion, *n.* **1.** act or instance of receiving. **2.** formal social function. **3.** quality of radio signals, etc. as received.

rė·cĕp′tĭve, *adj.* **1.** ready to consider new ideas. **2.** amenable.

rē·cĕss′, *n.* **1.** pause in work. **2.** hollowed-out space. **3. recesses**, inner areas. —*v.i.* **4.** pause in work.

rė·cĕs′sion, *n.* **1.** withdrawal. **2.** economic decline.

rė·cĕs′sion·ál, *n.* hymn sung during the withdrawal of clergy.

rĕc′ĭ·pē″, *n.* method or formula, esp. in cooking.

rė·cĭp′ĭ·ėnt, *n.* receiver.

rė·cĭp′rò·cál, *adj.* **1.** mutual. —*n.* **2.** counterpart.

rė·cĭp′rò·cāte″, *v.*, **-cated, -cating.** *v.t.*, *v.i.* **1.** give, receive, etc. in return. **2.**

move back and forth. —rec''i·proc'i·ty, *n*.

rė·cī'tȧl, *n*. **1.** account or narration. **2.** performance of music.

rė·cīte', *v.t.*, -cited, -citing. **1.** repeat from memory. **2.** narrate; read aloud. —rec''i·ta'tion, *n*.

rĕck'lėss, *adj*. foolhardy, careless.

rĕck'ȯn, *v.t.* **1.** calculate. **2.** esteem. **3.** *Dialect.* believe; suppose. —*v.i.* **4.** deal; cope.

rĕck'ȯn·ĭng, *n*. **1.** computation. **2.** settling of accounts. **3.** accounting.

rė·clāim', *v.t.* **1.** make usable. **2.** make reusable. **3.** redeem from vice, etc. —rec''la·ma'tion, *n*.

rė·clīne', *v.*, -clined, -clining. *v.i.*, *v.t.* lie or lay back.

rė'clūse, *n*. person who lives in seclusion. —re·clu'sive, *adj*.

rė·cŏg'nĭ·zȧnce, *n*. formal pledge of action.

rĕc'ȯg·nīze'', *v.t.*, -nized, -nizing. **1.** identify from memory. **2.** be aware of. **3.** acknowledge formally. —rec''og·ni'tion, *n*.

rė·coīl', *v.i.* **1.** draw or shrink back. **2.** spring back. —*n*. **3.** act or instance of recoiling.

rĕc''ȯl·lĕct', *v.t.*, *v.i.* remember. —rec''ol·lec'tion, *n*.

rĕc''ȯm·mĕnd', *v.t.* **1.** speak favorably of. **2.** advise. —rec''om·men·da'tion, *n*.

rĕc'ȯm·pĕnse'', *v.t.*, -pensed, -pensing, *n*. *v.t.* **1.** reward or compensate. —*n*. **2.** reward or compensation.

rĕc'ȯn·cīle', *v.t.*, -ciled, -ciling. **1.** return to harmony. **2.** make compatible. **3.** settle amicably. **4.** make acquiescent. —rec''on·cil'a·ble, *adj*. —rec''on·cil''i·a'tion, *n*.

rē''cȯn·noī'tėr, *v.t.*, *v.i.* search or scout. —re·con'nais·sance, *n*.

re·cord, *v.t.* (rē kord') **1.** make a written account of. **2.** put in reproducible form. —*n*. (rek 'ərd) **3.** written account. **4.** disk for sound reproduction. **5.** best performance. —*adj*. **6.** being the best to date.

re·count, *v.t.* **1.** narrate. **2.** count again. —*n*. **3.** (rē'kownt). second count.

re·coup (ri kōōp'), *v.t.* recover; make up.

rē'côurse, *n*. **1.** appeal for help. **2.** possible source of help.

rė·cŏv'êr, *v.t.* **1.** get back. **2.** salvage. —*v.i.* **3.** regain health. **4.** regain composure. —re·cov'er·a·ble, *adj*. —re·cov'er·y, *n*.

rĕc''rē·ā'tion, *n*. refreshing occupation. —rec''re·a'tion·al, *adj*.

rė·crĭm'ĭ·nāte'', *v.i.*, -nated, -nating. make an accusation in return.

rė·crūit', *n*. **1.** newly enlisted person. —*v.t.* **2.** enlist. —re·cruit'ment, *n*.

rĕc'tăn·gle, *n*. parallelogram with four right angles. —rec·tan'gu·lar, *adj*.

rĕc'tĭ·fÿ'', *v.t.*, -fied, -fying. correct. —rec''ti·fi'a·ble, *adj*. —rec''ti·fi·ca'tion, *n*.

rĕc''tĭ·lĭn'ē·ȧr, *adj*. **1.** forming a straight line. **2.** bounded by straight lines.

rĕc'tĭ·tūde'', *n*. moral uprightness.

rĕc'tȯr, *n*. **1.** clergyman in charge of a parish. **2.** head of certain universities and colleges.

rĕc'tȯ·rÿ, *n*. parsonage.

rĕc'tŭm, *n*. terminal part of the large intestine. —rec'tal, *adj*.

rė·cŭm'bėnt, *adj*. lying down. —re·cum'ben·cy, *n*.

rė·cū'pêr·āte'', *v.i.*, -ated, -ating. regain health. —re·cu'per·a·tive, *adj*.

rė·cûr', *v.i.*, -curred, -curring. **1.** occur again or repeatedly. **2.** return to one's thoughts. —re·cur'rence, *n*. —re·cur'rent, *adj*. —re·cur'rent·ly, *adv*.

rė·cÿ'cle, *v.t.* convert into reusable material.

rĕd, *n.*, *adj.*, redder, reddest. *n*. **1.** color of blood. **2. Red,** *Informal.* Communist. —*adj*. **3.** of or pertaining to red. —red'den, *v.t.*, *v.i.*

rė·dēem', *v.t.* **1.** recover. **2.** pay off. **3.** exchange for premiums. **4.** deliver from sin. **5.** fulfill, as a promise. —re·demp'tion, *n*.

Rė·dēem'êr, *n*. Jesus Christ.

rĕd'-lĕt'têr, *adj*. memorable.

rĕd'ȯ·lėnt, *adj*. **1.** odorous. **2.** suggestive. —red'o·lence, *n*.

rė·dōubt'à·ble, *adj*. formidable.

rė·dŏund', *v.i.* occur as a consequence.

re·dress, *v.t.* (rē dres') **1.** right, as a wrong. —*n*. (rē'dres) **2.** act or instance of redressing.

rĕd tāpe, bureaucratic procedures.

rė·dūce', *v.*, -duced, -ducing. *v.t.* **1.** lessen. **2.** alter. **3.** lower in rank, etc. **4.**

subdue. —*v.i.* **5.** act so as to lose weight. —**re·duc'i·ble,** *adj.* —**re·duc'tion,** *n.*

re·dŭn'dănt, *adj.* **1.** excess; surplus. **2.** repetitive. —**re·dun'dance, re·dun'dan·cy,** *n.*

rĕd'wood'', *n.* huge California evergreen tree.

rēed, *n.* **1.** tall marsh grass. **2.** vibrating part of the mouthpiece on certain wind instruments. —**reed'y,** *adj.*

rēef, *n.* **1.** ridge near the surface of a body of water. **2.** part of a sail. —*v.t.* **3.** shorten, as a sail.

rēef'êr, *n.* **1.** short jacket or coat. **2.** *Informal.* marijuana cigarette.

rēek, *v.i.* **1.** smell strongly. —*n.* **2.** strong or foul smell.

rēel, *n.* **1.** revolving drum for winding. **2.** lively dance. —*v.t.* **3.** wind on a reel. —*v.i.* **4.** stagger or sway. **5.** whirl.

re·fĕc'to·rÿ, *n.* dining hall.

re·fêr', *v.,* **-ferred, -ferring.** *v.i.* **1.** allude. **2.** look for information. —*v.t.* **3.** direct for help or information. **4.** submit for arbitration. —**re'fer·a·ble,** *adj.* —**re·fer'ral,** *n.*

rĕf'êr·ēe', *n.* **1.** arbiter. *v.t., v.i.* **2.** arbitrate.

rĕf'êr·ĕnce, *n.* **1.** act or instance of referring. **2.** something referred to. **3.** recommendation. **4.** person giving a recommendation.

rĕf''êr·ĕn'dŭm, *n.* submission of a proposed law for citizen approval.

re·fīne', *v.t.,* **-fined, -fining. 1.** free from impurities. **2.** make cultured. —**re·fine'ment,** *n.*

re·fīn'êr·ÿ, *n., pl.* **-eries.** factory for refining, esp. petroleum.

re·flĕct', *v.t.* **1.** return, as images, light, etc. **2.** think about. —**re·flec'tion,** *n.* —**re·flec'tive,** *adj.* —**re·flec'tor,** *n.*

rē'flĕx, *adj.* **1.** denoting involuntary reaction. —*n.* **2.** involuntary reaction.

re·flĕx'īve, *adj.* **1.** having the same subject and object as a verb. **2.** used as the object of a reflexive verb, as a pronoun.

re·fôrm', *n.* **1.** correction of wrongs. —*v.t.* **2.** correct the wrongs of. —*v.i.* **3.** correct one's wrongdoing. —**ref''or·ma'tion,** *n.*

re·fôrm'à·tô''rÿ, *n., pl.* **-ries.** penal institution for minors.

re·frăc'tion, *n.* bending of light or heat rays in passing from one medium to another. —**re·fract',** *v.t.* —**re·frac'tive,** *adj.* —**re·frac'tor,** *n.*

re·frāin', *v.i.* **1.** hold back; forbear. —*n.* **2.** recurring passage in a song or poem.

re·frĕsh', *v.t.* **1.** revive after stress. **2.** quicken; stimulate. —**re·fresh'ment,** *n.*

re·frĭg'êr·āte'', *v.t.,* **-ated, -ating.** keep or make cold. —**re·frig'er·ant,** *n.* —**re·frig'er·a''tor,** *n.*

rĕf'ūge, *n.* shelter from danger.

rĕf''ū·gēe', *n.* seeker of refuge.

re·fund, *v.t.* (re fund') **1.** repay. —*n.* **2.** (rē'fund). repayment.

rē·fûr'bĭsh, *v.t.* renovate.

re·fuse, *v.t.,* **-fused, -fusing.** *n.* *v.t.* (rē fyōoz') **1.** decline. **2.** decline to accept. **3.** deny, as a request. —*n.* (ref'yōoz). **4.** rubbish. —**re·fus'al,** *n.*

re·fūte', *v.t.,* **-futed, -futing.** prove wrong or false. —**ref'u·ta·ble,** *adj.* —**ref''u·ta'tion,** *n.*

rē·gāin', *v.t.* **1.** get again. **2.** return to again.

rē'gàl, *adj.* royal.

re·gāle', *v.t.,* **-galed, -galing.** entertain lavishly.

re·gā'lĭ·à, *n. pl.* royal or official insignia.

re·gârd', *v.t.* **1.** look on. **2.** consider. **3.** concern; relate to. **4.** hold in respect. —*n.* **5.** look; gaze. **6.** relation. **7.** affection and respect. **8.** particular point. **9.** **regards,** good wishes.

re·gârd'lĕss, *adj.* **1.** careless. —*adv.* **2.** anyway.

re·gät'tà, *n.* boat race.

re·gĕn'êr·āte'', *v.t., adj.* **-ated, -ating.** *v.t.* **1.** produce anew. **2.** reform. **3.** *Biol.* regrow. —*adj.* **4.** renewed; reformed. —**re·gen'er·a·tive,** *adj.*

rē'gĕnt, *n.* **1.** appointed substitute for a monarch. **2.** member of a governing board. —**re'gen·cy,** *n.*

re·gīme', *n.* **1.** system of government, etc. **2.** period of rule. Also, **ré·gime'.**

rĕg'ĭ·mĕn, *n.* **1.** government; rule. **2.** *Medicine.* system of diet, etc.

rĕg'ĭ·mĕnt, *n.* (rej'ə mənt). **1.** army unit of two or more battalions. —*v.t.* (rej'ə ment'') **2.** subject to strict discipline. —**reg''i·men'tal,** *adj.* —**reg''i·men'ta·tion,** *n.*

rē′gion, *n.* part of the earth's surface. —**re′gion·al**, *adj.*

rē′gion·al·ĭsm, *n.* **1.** sponsorship of or adherence to regional culture. **2.** regional peculiarity.

rĕg′ĭs·têr, *n.* **1.** written record, list, etc. **2.** cash register. **3.** device for regulating the passage of air. **4.** *Music.* range. —*v.t.*, *v.i.* **5.** enroll. —*v.t.* **6.** show, as on the face. —*v.i.* **7.** make an impression. —**reg′is·trant**, *n.* —**reg′′is·tra′tion**, *n.* —**reg′is·try**, *n.*

rĕg′ĭs·trâr′′, *n.* official record keeper.

rė·grĕss′, *v.i.* **1.** go back. **2.** revert. —*n.* **3.** going back. —**re·gres′sion**, *n.* —**re·gres′sive**, *adj.*

rė·grĕt′, *v.t.*, **-gretted, -gretting**, *n. v.t.* **1.** feel sorry about. —*n.* **2.** sorrow or remorse. —**re·gret′ful**, *adj.* —**re·gret′ta·ble**, *adj.*

rĕg′u·lår, *adj.* **1.** customary. **2.** consistent. **3.** symmetrical. **4.** permanent, as an army. **5.** *Informal.* **a.** complete. **b.** likeable. —*n.* **6.** someone regularly seen. **7.** regular soldier. —**reg′′u·lar′i·ty**, *n.* —**reg′u·lar·ize′′**, *v.t.*

rĕg′u·lāte′′, *v.t.*, **-lated, -lating. 1.** control by rule. **2.** make regular. —**reg′u·la′′tor**, *n.* —**reg′u·la·to′′ry**, *adj.* —**reg′u·la′′tive**, *adj.*

rė·gûr′gĭ·tāte′′, *v.*, **-tated, -tating**. *v.i.*, *v.t.* belch or vomit.

rē′′hȧ·bĭl′ĭ·tāte′′, *v.t.*, **-tated, -tating**. restore to a former good condition. —**re′′ha·bil′i·ta′′tive**, *adj.*

rē·hăsh′, *v.t.* **1.** work over again. —*n.* **2.** rchashing.

rė·hêarse′, *v.*, **-hearsed, -hearsing**. *v.t.*, *v.i.* practice for a performance. —**re·hears′al**, *n.*

reign (rān), *n.* **1.** royal power. **2.** period of rule. —*v.i.* **3.** rule as a monarch. **4.** prevail.

rē′′im·bûrse′, *v.t.*, **-bursed, -bursing**. pay back. —**re′′im·burse′ment**, *n.*

rein (rān), strap for controlling a horse.

rē′′in·câr·nā′tion, *n.* rebirth in a new body.

rein′dēer′′, *n.*, *pl.* **-deer.** large northern deer.

rē′′in·fôrce′, *v.t.*, **-forced, -forcing**. strengthen. —**re′′in·force′ment**, *n.*

rē′′in·stāte′, *v.t.*, **-stated, -stating**. restore to a former state. —**re′′in·state′ment**, *n.*

rē·ĭt′êr·āte′′, *v.t.*, **-ated, -ating**. say or do again. —**re·it′er·a′′tive**, *adj.*

rė·jĕct′, *v.t.* **1.** refuse to accept. **2.** discard. —*n.* (rē′jekt). **3.** rejected person or thing. —**re·jec′tion**, *n.*

rė·joīce′, *v.*, **-joiced, -joicing**. *v.t.* **1.** gladden. —*v.i.* **2.** feel joy. —**re·joic′ing**, *n.*

rė·joīn′, *v.t.*, *v.i.* **1.** join again. **2.** answer.

rė·joīn′dêr, *n.* **1.** reply. **2.** *Law.* defendant's response.

rė·ju′vė·nāte′′, *v.t.*, **-nated, -nating**. make young again.

rē·lăpse′, *v.i.*, **-lapsed, -lapsing**, *n. v.i.* **1.** fall into a former state. —*n.* **2.** act or instance of relapsing.

rė·lāte′, *v.*, **-lated, -lating**. *v.t.* **1.** tell; narrate. **2.** connect; associate. —*v.i.* **3.** have a relation.

rė·lā′tion, *n.* **1.** narrative. **2.** connection; association. **3.** connection by blood or marriage. —**re·la′tion·ship′′**, *n.*

rĕl′å·tĭve, *adj.* **1.** comparative. **2.** related to each other. —*n.* **3.** person related by blood or marriage.

rĕl′′à·tĭv′ĭ·tў, *n.* **1.** interdependence. **2.** *Physics.* theory of the relative character of position, motion, etc. and the interdependence of time and space.

rė·lăx′, *v.t.*, *v.i.* rest, as from work or tension. —**re′′lax·a′tion**, *n.*

re·lay *n.* (rē′lā) **1.** relief crew or team. **2.** race in which team members run individual portions. —*v.t.* (rē′lā; also ri lā′) **3.** send by relay or relays. **4.** lay again.

rė·lēase′, *v.t.*, **-leased, -leasing**, *n. v.t.* **1.** free. **2.** let go of. **3.** license for publication. —*n.* **4.** act or instance of releasing. **5.** communication, etc. **6.** *Law.* surrender, as of a claim.

rĕl′ė·gāte′′, *v.t.*, **-gated, -gating. 1.** consign to a lesser place or position. **2.** refer for decision.

rė·lĕnt′, *v.i.* become less severe, cruel, etc. —**re·lent′less**, *adj.*

rĕl′ė·vȧnt, *adj.* relating to the matter at hand. —**rel′e·vance, rel′e·van·cy**, *n.*

rē·lī′ȧ·ble, *adj.* dependable. —**re·li′′a·bil′i·ty**, *n.*

rē·lī′ȧnce, *n.* **1.** trust; confidence. **2.** something relied on. —**re·li′ant**, *adj.*

rĕl′ĭc, *n.* **1.** survival from the past. **2.** souvenir.

re·lief', *n*. **1.** release from pain, discomfort, etc. **2.** means of such relief. **3.** sculptured surface. **4.** projection from a background.

re·lieve', *v.t.*, **-lieved, -lieving. 1.** ease, as from pain or discomfort. **2.** vary. **3.** release from duty.

re·li'gion, *n*. **1.** belief in a divine being or beings. **2.** specific form of belief and practice. —**re·li'gious**, *adj*.

re·lin'quish, *v.t.* **1.** give up. **2.** renounce, as a right. —**re·lin'quish·ment**, *n*.

rel'ish, *n*. **1.** zest. **2.** condiment. **3.** appetizing flavor. —*v.t.* **4.** take pleasure in.

re·live', *v.t.*, **-lived, -living.** experience again in the imagination.

re·lo'cate, *v.*, **-cated, -cating.** *v.t., v.i.* settle in a new location.

re·luc'tant, *adj.* unwilling. —**re·luc'tance**, *n*.

re·ly', *v.i.*, **-lied, -lying.** depend; trust.

re·main', *v.i.* **1.** stay behind. **2.** endure; persist. **3.** continue as before. —*n*. **4.** **remains, a.** remainder. **b.** corpse. —**re·main'der**, *n*.

re·mand', *v.t.* send back or consign again.

re·mark', *v.t., v.i., n.* **1.** comment. —*v.t., n.* **2.** notice.

re·mark'a·ble, *adj.* worthy of notice or comment.

rem'e·dy, *n., v.t.*, **-died, -dying.** *n.* **1.** medicine or treatment. **2.** something that corrects wrong. —*v.t.* **3.** cure; correct. —**re·me'di·al**, *adj*.

re·mem'ber, *v.t.* **1.** recall to mind. **2.** not forget. **3.** carry greetings from. —**re·mem'brance**, *n*.

re·mind', *v.t.* cause to remember. —**re·mind'er**, *n*.

rem''i·nisce', *v.i.*, **-nisced, -niscing.** discuss or think about the past. —**rem''i·nis'cence**, *n*. —**rem''i·nis'cent**, *adj*.

re·miss', *adj.* careless; slack.

re·mis'sion, *n*. **1.** forgiveness. **2.** diminution, as of disease.

re·mit', *v.t.*, **-mitted, -mitting. 1.** forgive. **2.** refrain from imposing. **3.** relax; abate. **4.** send in payment. —**re·mit'tance**, *n*.

rem'nant, *n*. something left over.

re·mod'el, *v.t.*, **-eled, -eling.** make over; rebuild.

re·mon'strate, *v.*, **-strated, -strating.** *v.t., v.i.* protest; object. —**re·mon'strance**, *n*.

re·morse', *n*. mental anguish from guilt. —**re·morse'ful**, *adj*. —**re·morse'less**, *adj*.

re·mote', *adj.*, **-moter, -motest. 1.** distant. **2.** slight.

re·move', *v.*, **-moved, -moving.** *n. v.t.* **1.** move from a place. **2.** dismiss, as from office. —*v.i.* **3.** change residence. —*n*. **4.** interval; step. —**re·mov'a·ble**, *adj*. —**re·mov'al**, *n*.

re·mu'ner·ate'', *v.t.*, **-ated, -ating.** pay; recompense. —**re·mu'ner·a''tive**, *adj*.

ren'ais·sance'', *n*. **1.** rebirth. **2. Renaissance,** revival of classical learning in Europe.

re'nal, *adj.* pertaining to the kidneys.

re·nas'cence, *n*. rebirth; revival.

rend, *v.*, **rent, rending.** *v.t., v.i.* split apart by force.

ren'der, *v.t.* **1.** give in return. **2.** submit. **3.** state, as a decision. **4.** furnish. **5.** express or interpret. **6.** translate.

ren·dez·vous (ran'dā voo''), *n., pl.* **-vous. 1.** meeting place. **2.** appointment to meet.

ren·di'tion, *n*. rendering; performance.

ren'e·gade'', *n*. deserter of a cause.

re·nege', *v.i.*, **-neged, -neging.** *Informal.* go back on one's word.

re·new', *v.t.* **1.** make new. **2.** revive. —**re·new'al**, *n*.

re·nounce', *v.t.*, **-nounced, -nouncing.** give up formally. —**re·nun''ci·a'tion, re·nounce'ment**, *n*.

ren'o·vate'', *v.t.* **-vated, -vating.** make as if new.

re·nown', *n*. great reputation. —**re·nowned'**, *adj*.

rent, *n*. **1.** Also, **rent'al,** payment for temporary use. **2.** tear; rip. —*v.t.* **3.** use by paying. **4.** grant temporarily for payment.

re·pair', *v.t.* **1.** return to good condition. **2.** set right. —*v.i.* **3.** go. —*n*. **4.** act or instance of repairing. **5.** good condition. —**rep'a·ra·ble, re·pair'a·ble**, *adj*.

rep''a·rā'tion, *n*. **1.** amends for injury. **2. reparations,** compensation for war damage.

rep''ar·tee', *n*. clever, quick-witted talk.

re·past', *n*. meal.

re·pā′tri·āte″, *v.*, -ated, -ating. *v.t.*, *v.i.* return to one's country.

re·pāy′, *v.t.* -paid, -paying. pay back. —re·pay′ment, *n.*

re·pēal′, *v.t.* **1.** revoke. —*n.* **2.** revocation.

re·pēat′, *v.t.*, *v.i.* **1.** say or do again. —*n.* **2.** act or instance of repeating. —rep″e·ti′tion, *n.* —rep″e·ti′tious, *adj.*

re·pĕl′, *v.t.*, -pelled, -pelling. **1.** drive back. **2.** disgust. —re·pel′lent, *adj.*, *n.*

re·pĕnt′, *v.t.*, *v.i.* regret as wrong or mistaken. —re·pent′ance, *n.* —re·pent′ant, *adj.*

re″·pêr·cŭs′sion, *n.* **1.** indirect result. **2.** reverberation. —re″per·cus′sive, *adj.*

rep′er·toire (rĕp′êr·twär″), *n.* stock of songs, plays, etc. performed. Also, rep′er·to″ry, *n.*

re·plāce′, *v.t.*, -placed, -placing. **1.** put back in place. **2.** substitute for. —re·place′a·ble, *adj.* —re·place′ment, *n.*

re·plĕn′ĭsh, *v.t.* make full again. —re·plen′ish·ment, *n.*

re·plēte′, *adj.* plentifully filled. —re·ple′tion, *n.*

rĕp′li·cà, *n.* copy. —rep′li·cate. *v.t.*

re·plȳ′, *v.* -plied, -plying, *n.*, *pl.* -plies. *v.t.*, *v.i.*, *n.* answer.

re·pôrt′, *n.* **1.** statement. **2.** rumor. **3.** explosive noise. —*v.t.* **4.** give an account of. **5.** inform against. —*v.i.* **6.** make a report. **7.** present oneself.

re·pōse′, *v.t.*, -posed, -posing, *n.* *v.t.* **1.** rest or sleep. **2.** place. **3.** depend. —*n.* **4.** rest or sleep. **5.** tranquillity.

re·pŏs′ĭ·tôr″ÿ, *n.*, *pl.* -tories. place of storage.

rĕp″re·hĕnd′, *v.t.* rebuke. —rep″re·hen′si·ble, *adj.* —rep″re·hen′sion, *n.*

rĕp″re·sĕnt′, *v.t.* **1.** exemplify. **2.** portray. **3.** act or speak for. —rep″re·sen·ta′tion, *n.*

rĕp″re·sĕn′ta·tĭve, *adj.* **1.** serving as an example. **2.** acting or speaking for others. —*n.* **3.** person who represents. **4.** elected legislator.

re·prĕss′, *v.t.* restrain; check. —re·pres′sive, *adj.* —re·pres′sion, *n.*

re·priēve′, *v.t.*, -prieved, -prieving. *n.* *v.t.* **1.** relieve temporarily. —*n.* **2.** temporary delay; respite.

rĕp′rĭ·mănd″, *n.* **1.** severe or formal rebuke. —*v.t.* **2.** rebuke; censure.

re·prīs′àl, *n.* retaliation.

re·prōach′, *v.t.* **1.** scold for a fault; blame. —*n.* **2.** discredit. —re·proach′ful, *adj.*

rĕp′ro·bāte″, *n.*, *adj.*, *v.t.*, -bated, -bating. *n.* **1.** depraved person. —*adj.* **2.** depraved. —*v.t.* **3.** condemn.

re″·pro·dūce′, *v.t.*, -duced, -ducing. **1.** copy; duplicate. **2.** produce by propagation. —re″pro·duc′tion, *n.* —re″pro·duc′tive, *adj.*

re·prōof′, *n.* rebuke; censure.

re·prove′, *v.t.*, -proved, -proving. rebuke; censure. —re·prov′al, *n.*

rĕp′tīle, *n.* cold-blooded vertebrate. —rep·til′i·an, *adj.*

re·pŭb′lĭc, *n.* state governed by elected legislators.

re·pŭb′lĭ·càn, *adj.* **1.** pertaining to or favoring a republic. —*n.* **2.** **Republican,** member of the Republican party. **3.** partisan of a republican form of government. —re·pub′li·can·ism, *n.*

re·pū′dĭ·āte″, *v.t.*, -ated, -ating. disown; disavow.

re·pŭg′nànt, *adj.* distasteful. —re·pug′nance, *n.*

re·pŭlse′, *v.t.*, -pulsed, -pulsing, *n.* *v.t.* **1.** drive back, as an attack. **2.** reject; rebuff. —*n.* **3.** act or instance of repulsing. —re·pul′sion, *n.*

re·pŭl′sĭve, *adj.* disgusting.

rĕp′ū·tà·ble, *adj.* of good reputation.

rĕp″ū·tā′tion, *n.* **1.** estimation of a person or thing. **2.** fame.

re·pūte′, *n.* *v.t.*, -puted, -puting. *n.* **1.** reputation. —*v.t.* **2.** consider or regard.

re·quĕst′, *v.t.* **1.** ask for. —*n.* **2.** act or instance of requesting. **3.** something requested.

rĕ′quĭ·ĕm, *n.* service for the dead.

re·quīre′, *v.t.*, -quired, -quiring. **1.** need. **2.** demand. —re·quire′ment, *n.*

rĕq′uĭ·sĭte, *n.* **1.** something necessary. —*adj.* **2.** required; necessary.

rĕq″uĭ·sī′tion, *n.* **1.** act or instance of requiring. **2.** formal order for goods, etc. —*v.t.* **3.** take by authority.

re·quīte′, *v.t.*, -quited, -quiting. repay; return. —re·quit′al, *n.*

re·scĭnd′, *v.t.* revoke; annul.

rĕs′cūe, *v.t.*, -cued, -cuing, *n.* *v.t.* **1.**

free or save. —*n.* **2.** act or instance of rescuing.

re·search', *n.* **1.** careful investigation. —*v.t.* **2.** do research on or in.

re·sem'ble, *v.t.*, **-bled, -bling.** be like or similar to. —**re·sem'blance**, *n.*

re·sent', *v.t.* feel indignant at. —**re·sent'ful**, *adj.* —**re·sent'ment**, *n.*

res''er·va'tion, *n.* **1.** act or instance of reserving. **2.** advance request for accommodation. **3.** public land for Native Americans.

re·serve', *v.t.*, **-served, -serving,** *n. v.t.* **1.** keep back; set aside. —*n.* **2.** something reserved. **3.** reticence, as about feelings. **4.** inactive troops subject to call. **5.** reserved district.

re·serv'ist, *n.* member of a military reserve.

res'er·voir'' (rĕz'er vwar''), *n.* storage place for water.

re·side', *v.i.*, **-sided, -siding. 1.** dwell. **2.** be present.

res'i·dence, *n.* **1.** dwelling place. **2.** act or instance of residing. —**res'i·dent**, *n., adj.* —**res''i·den'tial**, *adj.*

res'i·due'', *n.* remainder. —**re·sid'u·al**, *adj.*

re·sign', *v.i.* **1.** give up a job or duty. —*v.t.* **2.** give up. **3.** yield or submit.

res''ig·na'tion, *n.* **1.** act or instance of resigning. **2.** submission, as to the inevitable.

re·signed', *adj.* reluctantly submissive.

re·sil'i·ent, *adj.* elastic; buoyant. —**re·sil'i·ence**, *n.*

res'in, *n.* substance exuded by certain plants. —**res'in·ous**, *adj.*

re·sist', *v.t., v.i.* withstand; oppose. —**re·sist'ance**, *n.*

res'o·lute'', *adj.* firm in purpose; determined.

res''o·lu'tion, *n.* **1.** formal expression of opinion. **2.** decision. **3.** firmness of purpose.

re·solve', *v.,* **-solved, -solving,** *n. v.t., v.i.* **1.** decide; determine. —*v.t.* **2.** analyze. **3.** solve. **4.** dispel, as fear. —*n.* **5.** determination.

res'o·nant, *adj.* **1.** resounding. **2.** vibrant; sonorous. —**res'o·nance**, *n.* —**res'o·nate''**, *v.t., v.i.* —**res'o·na''tor**, *n.*

re·sort', *v.i.* **1.** have recourse. —*n.* **2.** public place, as for recreation. **3.** recourse.

re·sound', *v.i.* reverberate; ring out. —**re·sound'ing**, *adj.*

re'source'', *n.* **1.** source of help or support. **2.** resources, money; means.

re·source'ful, *adj.* clever; able.

re·spect', *n.* **1.** esteem; honor. **2.** consideration. **3.** detail. **4.** deference; regard. —*v.t.* **5.** show consideration for. **6.** hold in honor. —**re·spect'a·ble**, *adj.* —**re·spect'ful**, *adj.*

re·spect'ing, *prep.* concerning.

re·spec'tive, *adj.* relating to each of several.

res'pi·ra''tor, *n.* apparatus for artificial breathing.

re·spire', *v.,* **-spired, -spiring.** *v.t., v.i.* breathe. —**res''pi·ra'tion**, *n.* —**re·spir'a·to''ry**, *adj.*

res'pite, *n.* temporary relief.

re·splend'ent, *adj.* shining brightly. —**re·splend'ence**, *n.*

re·spond', *v.i.* **1.** answer. **2.** react.

re·spond'ent, *n. Law.* defendant.

re·sponse', *n.* reply. —**re·spon'sive**, *adj.*

re·spon''si·bil'i·ty, *n., pl.* **-ties. 1.** state of being responsible. **2.** obligation.

re·spon'si·ble, *adj.* **1.** accountable. **2.** reliable. **3.** distinguishing between right and wrong. —**re·spon'si·bly**, *adv.*

rest, *n.* **1.** sleep; repose. **2.** inactivity after work. **3.** support; base. **4.** *Music.* silent interval. —*v.i.* **5.** be at rest. **6.** lay. **7.** lie. —*v.t.* **8.** cause to rest. **9.** base. —**rest'ful**, *adj.* —**rest'less**, *adj.*

res'tau·rant, *n.* public eating place.

res''tau·ra·teur', *n.* proprietor of a restaurant.

res''ti·tu'tion, *n.* **1.** return of something taken away. **2.** reparation.

res'tive, *adj.* **1.** balky; stubborn. **2.** restless.

re·store', *v.t.,* **-stored, -storing. 1.** return to a former state. **2.** give back. —**res''to·ra'tion**, *n.* —**re·stor'a·tive**, *adj.*

re·strain', *v.t.* **1.** hold back; check. **2.** confine.

re·straint', *n.* **1.** control of emotions, etc. **2.** confinement. **3.** something that restrains.

re·strict', *v.t.* limit; confine. —**re·stric'**

tion, *n.* —re·stric′tive, *adj.* —re·strict′ed, *adj.*

re·sult′, *n.* **1.** consequence; outcome. —*v.i.* **2.** follow as a consequence. —re·sult′ant, *adj., n.*

re·sume′, *v.t.,* -sumed, -suming. **1.** continue. **2.** take again. —re·sump′tion, *n.*

ré·su·mé′, *n.* summary, as of work experience.

re·sur′gent, *adj.* tending to rise again. —re·sur′gence, *n.*

res′′ur·rect′, *v.t.* raise from the dead. —res′′ur·rec′tion, *n.*

re·sus′ci·tate′′, *v.,* -tated, -tating. *v.t., v.i.* revive from unconsciousness. —re·sus′′ci·ta′tion, *n.* —re·sus′ci·ta′′tor, *n.*

re′tail, *n.* **1.** sale of consumer goods. —*v.t., v.i.* **2.** sell at retail.

re·tain′, *v.t.* **1.** keep; hold. **2.** hire by a retainer.

re·tain′er, *n.* **1.** fee for continuing services. **2.** servant.

re·tal′i·ate′, *v.i.,* -ated, -ating. give like for like, esp. in revenge. —re·tal′i·a·to′′ry, *adj.*

re·tard′, *v.t.* hinder; slow. —re·tar·da′tion, *n.* —re·tard′ant, *n.*

re·tard′ed, *adj.* limited or slow in mental development.

retch, *v.i.* try to vomit.

re·ten′tion, *n.* **1.** act or instance of retaining. **2.** power of remembering. —re·ten′tive, *adj.*

ret′i·cent, *adj.* disposed to silence; taciturn. —ret′i·cence, *n.*

ret′i·na, *n.* coating of the posterior interior of the eyeball.

ret′i·nue′′, *n.* group of attendants.

re·tire′, *v.,* -tired, -tiring. *v.i., v.t.* **1.** withdraw. **2.** withdraw from working life. —*v.i.* **3.** go to bed. —*v.t.* **4.** pay off, as bonds. —re·tir′′ee′, *n.* —re·tire′ment, *n.*

re·tir′ing, *adj.* shy; reserved.

re·tort′, *v.t., v.i.* **1.** answer smartly or wittily. —*n.* **2.** quick, witty answer.

re·touch′, *v.t.* touch up or improve, as a photograph.

re·tract′, *v.t., v.i.* withdraw. —re·tract′a·ble, *adj.* —re·trac′tion, *n.*

re·treat′, *n.* **1.** withdrawal, as from danger. **2.** secluded place. —*v.i.* **3.** withdraw.

re·trench′, *v.t., v.i.* cut down as an economy. —re·trench′ment, *n.*

ret′′ri·bu′tion, *n.* retaliation; punishment. —re·trib′u·tive, *adj.*

re·trieve′, *v.t.,* -trieved, -trieving. **1.** regain. **2.** recover. **3.** make good, as a mistake. —re·triev′al, *n.*

ret′′ro·ac′tive, *adj.* valid for some past period.

ret′ro·grade′′, *adj., v.i.,* -graded, -grading. *adj.* **1.** directed backward; reversed. —*v.i.* **2.** go backward. **3.** degenerate. —ret′′ro·gres′sion, *n.* —ret′′ro·gres′sive, *adj.*

ret′ro·spect′′, *n.* look to the past. —ret′′ro·spec′tive, *adj.* —ret′′ro·spec′tion, *n.*

re·turn′, *v.i.* **1.** go back. **2.** reply. —*v.t.* **3.** put back. **4.** repay. **5.** elect or reelect. **6.** yield, as a profit. —*n.* **7.** act or instance of returning. **8.** recurrence. **9.** repayment; yield. **10.** report; response. —re·turn′a·ble, *adj.*

rev, *v.t.,* revved, revving, *n. Informal. v.t.* **1.** increase the speed of, as a motor. —*n.* **2.** revolution, as of a machine.

re·vamp′, *v.t.* redo; revise.

re·veal′, *v.t.* **1.** disclose. **2.** manifest.

rev·eil·le (rev′ə lē), *n. Military.* signal for awakening.

rev′el, *v.i.,* -eled, -eling, *n. v.i.* **1.** take great delight. **2.** make merry. —*n.* **3.** merrymaking. —rev′el·ry, *n.*

rev′′e·la′tion, *n.* **1.** act or instance of revealing. **2. Revelation,** last book of the New Testament.

re·venge′, *n., v.t.,* -venged, -venging. *n.* **1.** retaliation. **2.** vindictiveness. —*v.t.* **3.** take revenge for. —re·venge′ful, *adj.*

rev′e·nue′′, *n.* income, as from taxes.

re·ver′ber·ate′′, *v.,* -ated, -ating. *v.t., v.i.* reecho; resound.

re·vere′, *v.t.,* -vered, -vering. regard with deep respect, love, etc.

rev′er·ence, *n., v.t.,* -enced, -encing. *n.* **1.** deep respect. —*v.t.* **2.** revere; honor. —rev′er·ent, rev′′er·en′tial, *adj.*

rev′er·end, *adj.* **1.** worthy of reverence. **2. Reverend,** title of respect for a clergyman.

rev′er·ie, *n., pl.* -ies. daydreaming; deep musings. Also, rev′er·y.

re·verse′, *adj., n., v.,* -versed, -versing. *adj.* **1.** turned backward. **2.** making an opposite motion. —*n*. **3.** opposite; contrary. **4.** misfortune. —*v.t.* **5.** turn back or in an opposite direction. **6.** exchange; transpose. —*v.i.* **7.** move in an opposite direction. **—re·vers'i·ble,** *adj*.

rè·vêrt', *v.i.* return as to a former way or state, etc. **—re·ver'sion,** *n*.

rè·view', *n*. **1.** reexamination. **2.** general survey or report. **3.** critical writing. —*v.t.* **4.** reexamine. **5.** look back on. **6.** write a review of. **7.** inspect formally.

rè·vile', *v.t.*, **-viled, -viling.** speak abusively. **—re·vile'ment,** *n*.

rè·vise', *v.t.*, **-vised, -vising.** amend. **—re·vi'sion,** *n*.

rè·viv'àl, *n*. **1.** return to life, use, etc. **2.** emotional religious meeting. **—re·viv'al·ist,** *n*.

rè·vive', *v.*, **-vived, -viving.** *v.i.*, *v.t.* return to consciousness or effectiveness.

rè·võke', *v.t.*, **-voked, -voking.** repeal or nullify. **—rev'o·ca·ble,** *adj.* **—rev''o·ca'tion,** *n*.

rè·võlt', *n*. **1.** uprising; rebellion. —*v.i.* **2.** rebel. —*v.t.* **3.** disgust.

rĕv''ò·lū'tion, *n*. **1.** war against one's government. **2.** complete change. **3.** rotation. **—rev''o·lu'tion·ar''y,** *adj., n*. **—rev''o·lu'tion·ist,** *n*.

rĕv''ò·lū'tiòn·īze'', *v.t.*, **-ized, -izing.** change completely or radically.

rè·võlve', *v.*, **-volved, -volving.** *v.t.* **1.** cause to rotate. —*v.i.* **2.** rotate.

rè·võlv'êr, *n*. pistol with a revolving magazine.

rè·vūe', *n*. light musical show.

rè·vŭl'sion, *n*. **1.** violent change of feeling. **2.** disgust.

rè·ward', *n*. **1.** grateful gift or payment. —*v.t.* **2.** give a reward to.

rhăp'sò·dÿ, *n., pl.* **-dies. 1.** free, irregular musical composition. **2.** emotional ecstasy. **—rhap·sod'ic,** *adj*.

rhē'ō·stăt'', *n*. device for varying an electric current.

rhē'sŭs, *n*. monkey of India.

rhĕt'ò·rĭc, *n*. **1.** art of using language effectively. **2.** exaggerated speech. **—rhe·tor'i·cal,** *adj*.

rheū'mà·tĭsm'', *n*. painful condition of the muscles and joints. **—rheu·mat'ic,** *adj*.

rhīne'stōne'', *n*. imitation diamond.

rhī·nŏc'êr·ŏs, *n*. massive, thick-skinned mammal with a horned snout.

rhō''dò·dĕn'dron, *n*. evergreen shrub with pink, white, or purple flowers.

rhŏm'bŭs, *n., pl.* **-buses, -bi.** equilateral parallelogram with oblique angles.

rhū'bârb, *n*. edible plant with long, thick stalks.

rhȳme, *n., v.*, **rhymed, rhyming.** *n*. **1.** similarity of sound at verse ends. **2.** poetry with such similarity. —*v.i.*, *v.t.* **3.** compose in rhyme.

rhȳthm, *n*. regular recurrence of stress, as in poetry or music. **—rhyth'mic,** *adj*.

rĭb, *n., v.t.*, **ribbed, ribbing.** *n*. **1.** one of the curved bones around the chest cavity. **2.** rib-like structure. —*v.t.* **3.** reinforce with ribs. **4.** *Informal.* tease.

rĭb'àld, *adj*. indecent or vulgar in language. **—rib'ald·ry,** *n*.

rĭb'bòn, *n*. narrow strip of fabric.

rī'bō·flā''vĭn, *n*. component of the vitamin B complex found in milk, eggs, meat, etc.

rīce, *n*. edible cereal of warm climates.

rĭch, *adj*. **1.** having much wealth. **2.** abundant; abounding. **3.** full of desirable qualities or resources. **4.** appetizing but hard to digest. **5.** mellow. —*n*. **6.** the rich, people of wealth. **7.** riches, wealth. **—rich'ly,** *adv.* **—rich'ness,** *n*.

rĭck, *n*. stack of hay, straw, etc.

rĭck'ĕts, *n*. nutritional deficiency disease of childhood characterized by bone deformities.

rĭck'ĕt·ÿ, *adj*. shaky; feeble.

rĭck'shaw, *n*. carriage pulled by a man. Also, **rick'sha.**

rĭc·o·chet (rĭk'ə shā''), *n., v.i.*, **-cheted, -cheting.** *n*. **1.** rebound of an object from a hard surface. —*v.i.* **2.** rebound.

rĭd, *v.t.*, **rid** or **ridded, ridding.** free; clear. **—rid'dance,** *n*.

rĭd'dle, *n., v.*, **-dled, -dling.** *n*. **1.** puzzle; enigma. **2.** coarse sieve. —*v.t.* **3.** pierce with holes. **4.** sift through a riddle. **5.** permeate.

rīde, *v.*, **rode, ridden, riding.** *n. v.t.* **1.** be carried on or within. **2.** be carried over or through. —*v.i.* **3.** be carried. **4.** depend (on). **5.** be at anchor. —*n*. **6.** act or instance of riding.

rīd'êr, *n*. **1.** person who rides. **2.** addition to a document.

ridge, *n.*, *v.*, **ridged, ridging.** *n.* **1.** narrow, raised edge. **2.** sharp crest or elevation of land. —*v.t.*, *v.i.* **3.** form into a ridge.

rid'i·cule'', *n.*, *v.t.*, **-culed, -culing.** *n.* **1.** derision. —*v.t.* **2.** make fun of; mock. —**ri·dic'u·lous**, *adj.*

rife, *adj.* **1.** widespread. **2.** abundant.

riff'räff'', *n. pl.* worthless people.

ri'fle, *n.*, *v.t.*, **-fled, -fling.** *n.* **1.** shoulder gun with a rifled barrel. —*v.t.* **2.** ransack and rob. **3.** cut spiral grooves in, as a gun barrel. —**ri'fle·man**, *n.*

rift, *n.*, *v.t.*, *v.i.* split.

rig, *v.t.*, **rigged, rigging**, *n. v.t.* **1.** equip, as for sailing. **2.** manipulate. —*n.* **3.** arrangement of the sails, etc. on a ship. **4.** equipment. **5.** tractor-trailer.

rig'à·mà·rôle'', *n.* complicated, often meaningless, procedure or talk. Also, **rig'ma·role''**.

rig'ging, *n.* ropes and other tackle for a ship, crane, etc.

right, *adj.* **1.** good; virtuous. **2.** correct. **3.** suitable. **4.** opposite to left. **5.** straight. —*n.* **6.** what is right, just, etc. **7.** lawful power or privilege. **8.** *Politics.* conservative. —*adv.* **9.** properly. —*v.t.* **10.** correct; put in order. **11.** set upright.

right angle, 90-degree angle.

righ'teoŭs, *adj.* **1.** virtuous; blameless. **2.** just; worthy.

right'fŭl, *adj.* just; legitimate.

right'ist, *n.*, *adj.* conservative in politics.

right'-wing', *adj.* politically conservative.

rig'ĭd, *adj.* **1.** stiff; unyielding. **2.** strict. —**rig'id·ness, ri·gid'i·ty**, *n.*

rig'ör, *n.* **1.** strictness. **2.** hardship. —**rig'or·ous**, *adj.*

ri'gör môr'tĭs, stiffening of the muscles after death.

rile, *v.t.*, **riled, riling.** *Informal.* anger; irritate.

rill, *n.* small stream.

rim, *n.*, *v.t.*, **rimmed, rimming.** *n.* **1.** edge; border; margin. —*v.t.* **2.** furnish with a rim.

rime, *n.*, *v.*, **rimed, riming.** *n.* **1.** rhyme. **2.** hoarfrost —*v.t.*, *v.i.* **3.** form a rhyme.

rind, *n.* hard outer coating, as of cheese or fruit.

ring, *n.*, *v.*, **rang, rung, ringing.** *n.* **1.** sound of a bell. **2.** finger band. **3.** circular object or area. **4.** group of conspirators. **5.** telephone call. —*v.t.* **6.** sound, as a bell. **7.** call by telephone. **8.** encircle. —*v.i.* **9.** resound. **10.** sound clearly. **11.** seem to be true or false.

ring'êr, *n.* **1.** person who rings bells. **2.** *Informal.* **a.** fraudulent substitute. **b.** identical-seeming person or thing.

ring'lēad'êr, *n.* person who leads others in mischief.

ring'lĕt, *n.* **1.** little ring. **2.** curl of hair.

ring'wörm'', *n.* contagious fungous skin disease.

rink, *n.* area for skating.

rinse, *v.t.*, **rinsed, rinsing**, *n. v.t.* **1.** wash lightly, as to remove soap. —*n.* **2.** act or instance of rinsing. **3.** solution for rinsing.

ri'ŏt, *n.* **1.** act of mob violence. —*v.i.* **2.** take part in a riot. —**ri'ot·ous**, *adj.*

rĭp, *v.t.*, *v.i.*, **ripped, ripping**, *n.* tear.

ripe, *adj.*, **riper, ripest.** fully aged or developed. —**rip'en**, *v.i.*, *v.t.*

rĭp'ple, *v.*, **-pled, -pling**, *n. v.i.*, *v.t.* **1.** form in little waves. —*n.* **2.** little wave.

rĭp'-rôar'ĭng, *adj. Informal.* lively and boisterous.

rĭp'sǎw'', *n.* saw for cutting wood along the grain.

rīse, *v.i.*, **rose, risen, rising**, *n. v.i.* **1.** get up. **2.** rebel. **3.** ascend. **4.** begin. **5.** increase in amount, degree, etc. **6.** originate. —*n.* **7.** act or instance of rising. **8.** small hill. **9.** increase. **10.** advance in rank, power, etc.

rĭs''ĭ·bĭl'ĭ·ty, *n.*, *pl.* **-ties.** ability to laugh.

rĭs'ĭ·ble, *adj.* causing laughter; ridiculous.

rĭsk, *n.* **1.** chance of defeat, injury, loss, etc. —*v.t.* **2.** expose to risk. **3.** incur the risk of. —**risk'y**, *adj.*

rĭs·qué', *adj.* suggestive of indecency.

rīte, *n.* ceremonial act.

rĭt'ū·àl, *n.* **1.** set form for rites. —*adj.* **2.** according to a ritual. —**rit'u·al·ism''**, *n.* —**rit'u·al·ist**, *n.* —**rit''u·al·is'tic**, *adj.*

rī'vàl, *n.*, *adj.*, *v.t.*, **-valed, -valing.** *n.* **1.** competitor. **2.** equal. —*adj.* **3.** competing. —*v.t.* **4.** compete with. **5.** equal. —**ri'val·ry**, *n.*

rīve, *v.t.*, *v.i.*, **rived, rived** or **riven, riving.** **1.** tear apart. **2.** split.

rĭv′êr, *n.* large natural stream of water.

rĭv′ĕt, *n.* **1.** metal bolt forged tight after insertion. —*v.t.* **2.** fasten with rivets.

rĭv′ū·lĕt, *n.* small brook.

rōach, *n.* cockroach.

rōad, *n.* way for travel. —**road′side″**, *n., adj.* —**road′way″**, *n.*

rōam, *v.i.* wander.

rōan, *n.* horse with white or gray spots.

rôar, *v.i.* **1.** emit a bellow. —*n.* **2.** act or instance of roaring.

rōast, *v.t.* **1.** cook with dry heat. —*n.* **2.** roasted piece of meat.

rŏb, *v.t.*, **robbed, robbing.** take from without right. —**rob′ber·y,** *n.*

rōbe, *n., v.t.*, **robed, robing.** *n.* **1.** long, loose piece of clothing. —*v.t.* **2.** clothe in a robe.

rŏb′ĭn, *n.* bird with a red breast.

rō′bŏt, *n.* man-like machine.

rō·bŭst′, *adj.* vigorous.

rŏck, *n.* **1.** piece of stone. —*v.i.*, *v.t.* **2.** swing back and forth. —**rock′y,** *adj.*

rŏck′êr, *n.* curved base for rocking objects.

rŏck′ĕt, *n.* object propelled by reactive thrust. —**rock′et·ry,** *n.*

rŏck ′n′ rōll, *n., adj.* a form of popular music originating in the U.S. and characterized by a distinct beat. Also, **rock.**

rŏd, *n.* **1.** round, slender object. **2.** five-and-a-half linear yards.

rō′dĕnt, *n.* gnawing mammal.

rō′dē·ō″, *n., pl.* **-os.** cowboy show.

rōe, *n.* fish eggs.

rōgue, *n.* rascal. —**ro′guish,** *adj.* —**ro′guer·y,** *n.*

rōĭl, *v.t.* soil. —**roil′y,** *adj.*

rōĭs′têr, *v.i.* carouse.

rōle, *n.* character assumed. Also, **rôle.**

rōll, *v.i.* **1.** move like a ball, or as if on wheels. **2.** revolve; turn over and over. **3.** move like waves; billow. —*v.t.* **4.** cause to roll. **5.** move on wheels. **6.** shape into a round or cylindrical form. **7.** smooth or flatten with a cylinder, as metal. —*n.* **8.** act or instance of rolling. **9.** a cylinder, as of paper, wire, etc. **10.** list of names. **11.** small loaf of bread.

rŏl′lĭck·ĭng, *adj.* jolly; boisterous.

rō·māine′, *n.* type of lettuce.

rō·măn′ à clĕf″, *n.* novel that disguises real people and events.

rō·mănce′, *n.* **1.** love affair. **2.** fanciful

story. **3.** realm of fantasy. —**ro·man′tic,** *adj.* —**ro·man′ti·cal·ly,** *adv.*

Rōmàn nūmêràls, I for 1, V for 5, X for 10, L for 50, C for 100, D for 500, M for 1,000.

rō·măn′tĭ·cĭsm, *n.* romantic artistic movement. —**ro·man′ti·cist,** *n., adj.*

rŏmp, *v.i.* **1.** play boisterously. —*n.* **2.** act or instance of romping.

rŏmp′êrs, *n. pl.* loose overall for a child.

rōof, *n., pl.* **roofs,** *v.t. n.* **1.** covering for a building. —*v.t.* **2.** furnish with a roof. —**roof′ing,** *n.* —**roof′less,** *adj.* —**roof′top″,** *n.*

rŏŏk, *n.* **1.** castle-like chesspiece. —*v.t.* **2.** *Informal.* cheat.

rŏŏk′iē, *n. Informal.* raw recruit.

rŏŏm, *n.* **1.** space. **2.** fully enclosed space in a building. —*v.i.* **3.** lodge. —**room′ful″,** *n.* —**room′mate″,** *n.* —**room′y,** *adj.*

rŏŏst, *n., v.i.* perch.

rŏŏst′êr, *n.* male chicken.

rŏŏt, *n.* **1.** buried part of a plant. **2.** similar part of a tooth, hair, etc. **3.** basic cause. —*v.t.* **4.** plant. **5.** dig. —*v.i.* **6.** grow roots. **7.** cheer.

rōpe, *n., v.t.*, **roped, roping.** *n.* **1.** length composed of strands used for pulling or binding. —*v.t.* **2.** tie with rope.

rō′sà·rȳ, *n., pl.* **-ries. 1.** chain of beads used by Roman Catholics to count prayers said. **2.** series of prayers.

rōse, *n.* flowers with thorns and scented petals. —**rose′bud″,** *n.* —**rose′bush″,** *n.*

rō·sé, *n.* pink light wine.

rō′sē·āte, *adj.* **1.** rose-colored. **2.** brightly promising.

rōse′mār″ÿ, *n.* leaves of an evergreen shrub, used in cooking.

rō·sĕtte′, *n.* round ornament.

rōse′wōōd″, *n.* reddish wood used in cabinetmaking.

rŏs′ĭn, *n.* solid substance remaining after distilling turpentine, used esp. for treating bows of violins, etc.

rŏs′têr, *n.* list.

rŏs′trŭm, *n., pl.* **-trums, -tra.** speaker's platform.

rōs′ÿ, *adj.* **-ier, -iest. 1.** pink. **2.** optimistic; promising. —**ros′i·ly,** *adv.*

rŏt, *v.*, **rotted, rotting,** *n.* decay. —**rot′ten,** *adj.*

rō′ta·rÿ, *adj.* rotating as a whole or in part.

rō′tāte″, *v.,* -tated, -tating. *v.t., v.i.* **1.** turn around a point. —*v.t.* **2.** assign regular turns to. —**ro′ta·to″ry,** *adj.*

rōte, *n.* memorization.

rō′tŏr, *n.* rotating part of a machine.

rō′tŭnd′, *adj.* plump. —**ro·tun′di·ty,** *n.*

rō·tŭn′dȧ, *n.* round hall.

rou·é′, *n.* dissipated man.

roūge, *n.* red cosmetic or polishing powder.

roūgh, *adj.* **1.** unfinished. **2.** violent. **3.** *Informal.* troublesome. —**rough′en,** *v.t., v.i.*

roūgh′ȧge, *n.* coarse food.

roūgh′hoŭse″, *n.* *Informal.* violent amusement or fight.

roūgh′nĕck″, *n.* *Informal.* boisterous or violent person.

roū·lĕtte′, *n.* gambling wheel.

roŭnd, *adj.* **1.** curved, or with a curved exterior. **2.** approximate. —*n.* **3.** repeated series. **4.** single shot. —*adv., prep.* **5.** around. —*v.t.* **6.** make round. **7.** go around.

roŭnd′a·bŏut″, *adj.* indirect.

roŭnd′lÿ, *adv.* **1.** in a round way. **2.** thoroughly.

roŭnd′ŭp″, *n.* **1.** gathering of cattle. **2.** summary.

roūse, *v.,* roused, rousing. *v.t., v.i.* **1.** awaken. —*v.t.* **2.** excite.

roŭt, *v.t.* **1.** put to flight. **2.** gouge. —*n.* **3.** disorderly flight.

roūte, *n., v.t.,* routed, routing. *n.* **1.** course of travel. —*v.t.* **2.** assign a route to.

roū·tïne′, *n.* **1.** standard course of action. —*adj.* **2.** ordinary; customary.

rōve, *v.i.,* roved, roving. wander.

rōw, *v.,* rowed, rowing. *n. v.t., v.i.* **1.** move with oars. —*n.* **2.** group in a line. **3.** rŏw, fight; quarrel. —**row′boat″,** *n.*

rŏw′dÿ, *adj.,* -dier, -diest, *n., pl.* -dies. *adj.* **1.** boisterous or violent. —*n.* **2.** rowdy person.

rŏy′ȧl, *adj.* **1.** pertaining to kings or queens. —*n.* **2.** sail above a top gallant. —**roy′al·ist,** *n.*

rŏy′ȧl·tÿ, *n., pl.* -ties. **1.** kings and queens. **2.** fee to an author, patentee, etc.

R.S.V.P., *French.* Abbr. for *répondez s'il vous plaît:* please send an answer.

rŭb, *v.,* rubbed, rubbing, *n. v.t.* **1.** apply friction to. **2.** apply with friction. —*v.i.* **3.** apply friction. —*n.* **4.** act or instance of rubbing. **5.** source of difficulty.

rŭb′bêr, *n.* **1.** resilient substance. **2.** decisive game. —**rub′ber·ize″,** *v.t.* —**rub′ber·y,** *adj.*

rŭb′bĭsh, **1.** cast-off material. **2.** worthless speech, etc.

rŭb′ble, *n.* broken stone or masonry.

rŭb′ĭ·cŭnd, *adj.* ruddy.

rŭb′rĭc, *n.* note to a text.

rū′bÿ, *n., pl.* -bies. deep red precious stone.

rŭck′ŭs, *n.* *Informal.* disturbance.

rŭd′dêr, *n.* steering device.

rŭd′dÿ, *adj.,* -dier, -diest. reddish. —**rud′di·ness,** *n.*

rūde, *adj.* ruder, rudest. **1.** offensive in manner. **2.** rough; rugged.

rū′dĭ·mĕnt, *n.* basic principle, etc. —**ru″di·men′ta·ry,** *adj.*

rūe, *v.t.,* rued, ruing. *n. v.t.* **1.** feel remorse or regret for. —*n.* **2.** remorse or regret. —**rue′ful,** *adj.*

rŭf′fĭ·ȧn, *n.* hoodlum.

rŭf′fle, *v.t.,* -fled, -fling. **1.** disturb the surface of. **2.** disturb the calm of.

rŭg, *n.* floor cloth.

rŭg′gĕd, *adj.* **1.** rough in surface or outline. **2.** harsh.

rŭin, *n.* **1.** Also, **ruins,** remains of something destroyed or injured. **2.** downfall. **3.** source of one's downfall. —*v.t.* **4.** bring to ruin. —**ru″in·a′tion,** *n.* —**ru′in·ous,** *adj.*

rūle, *n., v.,* ruled, ruling. *n.* **1.** principle or law. **2.** government; dominion. **3.** measuring stick. —*v.t., v.i.* **4.** govern. —*v.t.* **5.** make a formal authoritative decision. —**rul′ing,** *n., adj.*

rūl′êr, *n.* **1.** sovereign. **2.** measuring stick.

rŭm, *n.* alcoholic liquor made from sugar.

rŭm′bȧ, *n.* Cuban dance.

rŭm′ble, *v.i.,* -bled, -bling, *n. v.i.* **1.** dull continuous noise. —*n.* **2.** act or instance of rumbling.

rū′mĭ·nāte″, *v.i.,* -nated, -nating. **1.** chew the cud. **2.** muse; meditate. —**ru′mi·nant,** *adj., n.*

rŭm′mȧge, *v.,* -maged, -maging. *v.t., v.i.* search thoroughly.

rū′mör, *n.* **1.** unconfirmed popular report. —*v.t.* **2.** tell in a rumor.

rŭmp, *n.* hindquarters.

rŭm′ple, *v.t.*, **-pled, -pling.** muss.

rŭm′pŭs, *n.* disorderly or noisy activity.

rŭn, *v.*, **ran, run, running,** *n.*, *v.i.* **1.** move quickly on the feet. **2.** be in motion; operate. **3.** flow. —*v.t.* **4.** operate or manage. **5.** drive. —*n.* **6.** act or instance of running. **7.** route or journey. **8.** series. **9.** brook.

rŭn′a·roūnd′′, *n. Informal.* evasive treatment.

rŭn′a·wāy′′, *n.*, *adj.* fugitive.

rŭn′-dōwn′′, *adj.* **1.** without energy. **2.** out of repair. **3.** (of a clock, etc.) needing to be wound up.

rŭn′dōwn′′, *n.* summary.

rŭng, *n.* rodlike crosspiece.

rŭn′lĕt, *n.* small stream. Also, **run′nel.**

rŭn′nêr, *n.* **1.** person who runs. **2.** long foot or slide, as on a sled, etc. **3.** long rug.

rŭn′nêr-ŭp′, *n.*, *pl.* **-ners-up.** second-best racer or performer.

rŭn′nĭng, *n.* **1.** competitive condition. —*adj.* **2.** operating. **3.** (of measurement) linear. **4.** continuous.

rŭn′-ŏf-thė-mĭll′, *adj.* not special.

rŭnt, *n.* stunted creature. —**runt′y**, *adj.*

rŭn′wāy′′, *n.* strip, pavement, etc. for running, esp. by airplanes landing or taking-off.

rŭp′tûre, *n.*, *v.*, **-tured, -turing.** *n.* **1.** hernia. **2.** break. —*v.t.* **3.** cause a rupture. —*v.i.* **4.** undergo a rupture.

rūr′ål, *adj.* pertaining to the country.

rūse, *n.* trick.

rŭsh, *v.i.* **1.** hurry. —*v.t.* **2.** charge; attack with speed. —*n.* **3.** hurry. **4.** grasslike marsh plant.

rŭs′sĕt, *n.* reddish brown.

rŭst, *n.* **1.** coating of oxydized iron or steel. **2.** plant fungus disease. —*v.i.* **3.** have rust. —*v.t.* **4.** cause to rust. —**rust′y**, *adj.*

rŭs′tĭc, *adj.* **1.** rural. —*n.* **2.** rural person.

rŭs′tle, *v.*, **-tled, -tling**, *n.* *v.i.* **1.** make a soft, whispering sound. —*v.t.* **2.** steal, as cattle. —*n.* **3.** rustling sound.

rŭt, *n.*, *v.t.*, **rutted, rutting.** *n.* **1.** worn track. **2.** fixed routine. —*v.t.* **3.** make ruts in. —**rut′ty**, *adj.*

rū′′tȧ·bā′gȧ, *n.* type of turnip.

rūth′lĕss, *adj.* without compunction or compassion.

rȳe, *n.* **1.** edible grain. **2.** whiskey distilled from this.

S

S, s, *n.* nineteenth letter of the English alphabet.

Săb′bȧth, *n.* day of worship and rest.

sā′bêr, *n.* singled-edged curved sword. Also, **sa′bre.**

sā′ble, *n.* weasellike mammal with dark-brown fur.

săb′o·tâge′′, *n.*, *v.t.* **-taged, -taging.** *n.* **1.** intentional damage to equipment. —*v.t.* **2.** damage intentionally. —**sab′o·teur′′.**

săc, *n.* baglike part of the body.

săc·chȧ·rīne, *adj.* **1.** too sweet, as in manner. —*n.* **2.** saccharin.

săc·chȧ·rĭn, *n.* sugar substitute.

sac·er·do·tal (sas′′ər dō′təl, sak′′ər dō′təl), *adj.* pertaining to or suggesting priests.

sa·chet (sa chā′), *n.* bag of scented powder.

săck, *n.* **1.** bag, esp. a large, strong one. **2.** plunder. —*v.t.* **3.** put into a sack or sacks. **4.** plunder.

săck′clŏth, *n.* coarse cloth worn by penitents.

săc′rȧ·mĕnt, *n.* **1.** ceremony or act regarded as sacred. **2. Sacrament,** Eucharist. —**sac′′ra·men′tal**, *adj.*

sā′crĕd, *adj.* **1.** holy. **2.** safe from attack, ridicule, etc. **3.** binding, as a promise. —**sa′cred·ly**, *adv.* —**sa′cred·ness**, *n.*

săc′rĭ·fīce, *n.*, *v.*, **-ficed, -ficing.** *n.* **1.** offer of something valuable to a deity. **2.** intentional loss of one thing to gain another. —*v.t.* **3.** offer or lose in a sacrifice. —*v.i.* **4.** make a sacrifice. —**sac′′ri·fi′cial**, *adj.*

săc′rĭ·lĕge, *n.* violation or mockery of something sacred. —**sac′′ri·le′gious**, *adj.*

săc′rĭs·tȧn, *n.* person in charge of a sacristy.

săc′rĭs·tȳ, *n.*, *pl.* **-ties.** place for keeping the sacred vessels, etc. of a church.

săc′rō·sănct, *adj.* sacred.

săd, *adj.*, sadder, saddest. low in spirits; melancholy. —sad′ly, *adv.* —sad′ness, *n.* —sad′den, *v.t.*, *v.i.*

săd′dle, *n.*, *v.t.*, -dled, -dling. *n.* 1. seat for the rider of a horse, bicycle, etc. —*v.t.* 2. put a saddle on. 3. impose a burden on. —sad′dle·bag, *n.*

săd′ĭsm, *n.* practice of cruelty for pleasure. —sad′ist, *n.* —sa·dis′tic, *adj.*

sa·fa·ri (sə fah′rē), *n.* journey, esp. in Central Africa, for hunting or exploration.

sāfe, *adj.* safer, safest. *n.* *adj.* 1. free from danger or risk. —*n.* 2. container protecting against theft, fire, etc. —safe′ly, *adv.* —safe′ty, *n.*

sāfe′guârd, *v.t.* 1. protect from danger. —*n.* 2. something protective.

săg, *v.i.*, sagged, sagging, *n.* *v.i.* 1. bend or hang downwards where not supported; droop. —*n.* 2. distortion caused by sagging.

sâ′gà, *n.* Nordic heroic legend.

sà·gă′cĭ·tў, *n.* wisdom. —sa·ga′cious, *adj.* —sa·ga′cious·ly, *adv.*

sāge, *n.*, *adj.*, sager, sagest. *n.* 1. wise and learned person. 2. seasoning herb. —*adj.* 3. wise. —sage′ly, *adv.* —sage′ness, *n.*

sa·hib (sah′ēb), *n.* respectful term for a European, used in the Indian subcontinent.

said, *adj.* previously mentioned.

sāil, *n.* 1. area of cloth used to drive a ship or boat by the force of moving air. 2. excursion in a ship or boat so driven. —*v.i.* 3. make such an excursion or excursions. 4. depart in a ship.

sāil′bōat′′, *n.* boat moved by sails.

sāil′fĭsh, *n.* large fish with saillike dorsal fin.

sāil′ör, *n.* 1. member of a ship's crew. 2. enlisted man in a navy.

sāint, *n.* 1. person officially venerated by a church. 2. person leading a religious or upright life. —saint′hood, *n.* —saint′ly, *adj.*

sāke, *n.* 1. benefit. 2. purpose. 3. (sak′ē) Japanese rice wine.

sāl′à·ble, *adj.* able to be sold. Also, sale′a·ble.

sà·lā·cioŭs, *adj.* obscene; lewd.

săl′ăd, *n.* dish mainly of raw vegetables or fruits.

săl′à·măn′′dêr, *n.* small, tailed amphibian.

sà·lâ′mĭ, *n.* spiced sausage.

săl′à·rў, *n.*, *pl.* -ries. regular payment for a permanent employee. —sal′a·ried, *adj.*

sāle, *n.* 1. act or occasion of selling. 2. demands for something sold. 3. offer of goods at reduced prices. —sales′clerk′′, *n.* —sale′room′′, sales′room′′, *n.*

sāles′măn, *n.* man who sells merchandise, etc. Also, *fem.*, sales′wom′′an, sales′la′′dy, sales′girl′′.

sā′lĭent, *adj.* 1. outstanding. 2. projecting. —*n.* 3. area that projects. —sa′li·ent·ly, *adv.* —sa′li·ence, *n.*

sā·lĭne (sā′lĭn), *adj.* salty. —sa·lin′i·ty, *n.*

sà·lī′và, *n.* fluid secreted in mouth by glands to aid digestion. —sa′li·va′′ry, *adj.*

săl′lōw, *adj.* with a sickly, yellowish complexion.

săl′lў, *n.*, *pl.* -lies, *v.i.*, -lied, -lying. *n.* 1. counterattack from a fortified position. 2. witticism. —*v.i.* 3. emerge briskly.

săl′mŏn, *n.* edible fish with pink flesh.

sà·lŏn′, *n.* 1. room for conversation. 2. art gallery.

sà·lōōn′, *n.* 1. place where liquor is served. 2. public room, esp. on a ship.

sălt, *n.* 1. sodium chloride. 2. *Chemistry.* compound derived from an acid. 3. wit; piquancy. —*v.t.* 4. treat with salt. —salt′y, *adj.* —salt′shak′′er, *n.*

sălt′·ĭne′, *n.* salted cracker.

sălt′′pē′têr, *n.* potassium nitrate. Also, salt′′pe′tre.

sà·lū′brĭ·oŭs, *adj.* promoting health. —sa·lu′bri·ous·ly, *adv.*

săl′ū·tàr′′ў, *adj.* beneficial.

săl′′ū·tā′tion, *n.* 1. greeting. 2. opening phrase of a letter, naming the addressee.

sà·lūte′, *n.*, *v.* -luted, -luting. *n.* 1. act expressing respect or attention in military etiquette. 2. greeting. 3. firing of cannons, etc. as a sign of welcome. —*v.t.* 4. recognize with a salute. —*v.i.* 5. perform a salute.

săl′văge, *v.t.*, -vaged, -vaging, *n.* *v.t.* 1. rescue from loss, as a ship. 2. gather for reuse, as discarded material. —*n.* **3.** salvaged material.

săl·vā′tion, *n.* act of saving or state of being saved, as from damnation or destruction.

sălve, *n., v.t.,* **salved, salving.** *n.* **1.** soothing or healing ointment. —*v.t.* **2.** cover with salve.

săl′vō, *n., pl.* **-vos, -voes.** discharge of many guns, etc. in rapid succession.

sāme, *adj.* **1.** identical. **2.** without change. **3.** previously mentioned. —*n.* **4.** same thing or person. —**same′ness,** *n.*

săm′ȯ·vâr, *n.* metal tea urn.

săm′păn, *n.* sculled Chinese or Japanese boat.

săm′ple, *n., adj., v.t.,* **-pled, -pling.** *n.* **1.** something representing more or others of its kind. —*adj.* **2.** serving as a sample. —*v.t.* **3.** take a sample of.

săm′plêr, *n.* piece of needlework demonstrating skill.

săn″à·tô′rĭ·ŭm, *n.* sanitarium.

sănc′tĭ·fȳ, *v.t.,* **-fied, -fying. 1.** make sacred. **2.** free of sin. —**sanc″ti·fi·ca′tion,** *n.*

sănc′tĭ·mō″nȳ, *n.* showy or false piety. —**sanc″ti·mo′ni·ous,** *adj.*

sănc′tion, *n.* **1.** permission or support. **2.** non-belligerent measure against a nation by other nations. —*v.t.* **3.** authorize.

sănc′tĭ·tȳ, *n.* holiness or sacredness.

sănc′tū·ār″ȳ, *n., pl.* **-aries. 1.** consecrated place. **2.** place of refuge.

sănc′tŭm, *n.* consecrated place.

sănd, *n.* **1.** fine pieces of rock. **2. sands,** sandy area. —*v.t.* **3.** rub with sandpaper. —**sand′er,** *n.* —**sand′storm″,** *n.*

săn′dàl, *n.* open shoe secured by straps.

săn′dàl·wŏŏd, *n.* aromatic Asiatic wood.

sănd′bâr″, *n.* low island of sand.

sănd′pā″pêr, *n.* **1.** sand-coated paper for smoothing or reducing surfaces. —*v.t.* **2.** rub with sandpaper.

sănd′pīp″êr, *n.* small shore bird.

sănd′stōne, *n.* stone made of sand naturally cemented together.

sănd′wĭch, *n.* **1.** bread, roll, etc. in two slices with meat, etc. between them. —*v.t.* **2.** insert.

sănd′ȳ, *adj.,* **ier, -iest. 1.** abounding in sand. **2.** colored like sand.

sāne, *adj.,* **saner, sanest.** mentally sound. —**sane′ly,** *adv.*

sang-froid (säh″frwah′), *n.* control of one's emotions.

săn′guĭ·nār″ȳ, *adj.* **1.** bloody. **2.** bloodthirsty.

săn′guĭne, *adj.* optimistic.

săn″ĭ·tār″ĭ·ŭm, *n.* place for the recovery of health.

săn′ĭ·tār′ȳ, *adj.* **1.** free of harmful bacteria, etc. **2.** pertaining to health.

săn″ĭ·tā′tion, *n.* provisions against disease.

săn′ĭ·tȳ, *n.* mental soundness.

săp, *n., v.t.,* **sapped, sapping,** *n.* **1.** juice of a tree, etc. **2.** *Informal.* fool. —*v.t.* **3.** weaken.

sā′pĭ·ėnt, *adj.* wise; knowing. —**sa′pi·ence,** *n.*

săp′lĭng, *n.* young tree.

săp′phīre, *n.* blue gemstone.

săp′sŭck″êr, *n.* variety of woodpecker.

sâr′căsm, *n.* **1.** making of agreeably worded but harshly intended remarks. **2.** such a remark. —**sar·cas′tic,** *adj.* —**sar·cas′ti·cal·ly,** *adv.*

sâr·cŏph′à·gŭs, *n., pl.* **-gi.** stone coffin.

sâr′dĭne′, *n.* trade name for a small canned ocean fish.

sâr·dŏn′ĭc, *adj.* bitterly sarcastic. —**sar·don′i·cal·ly,** *adv.*

sar·sa·pa·ril·la (sas″pə ril′ə, sahrs″pə ril′ə), *n.* tropical vine with fragrant roots.

sâr·tô′rĭ·àl, *adj.* pertaining to tailors or tailoring.

săsh, *n.* **1.** cloth band worn over the upper part of the body or around the waist. **2.** frame for window glass.

săs′sà·frăs, *n.* American tree with aromatic bark at the roots.

Sā′tàn, *n.* the Devil. —**sa·tan′ic,** *adj.*

sătch′ėl, *n.* small cloth suitcase or bag.

sāte, *v.t.,* **sated, sating.** satisfy fully or to excess, as an appetite.

să·tēen′, *n.* satinlike cotton fabric.

săt′ėl·līte, *n.* **1.** heavenly body moving around a planet. **2.** organization, etc. dominated or controlled by another.

sa·ti·ate (sā′shē āt), *v.t.,* **-ated, -ating.** glut. —**sa″ti·a′tion, sa·ti′e·ty,** *n.*

săt′ĭn, *n.* glossy fabric or silk or a silk substitute. —**sa′tin·y,** *adj.*

săt′īre, *n.* **1.** sarcasm or ridicule in the exposure of wrongful actions or atti-

tudes. **2.** story, etc. using these means.
—sa·tir′i·cal, sa·tir′ic, *adj.* —sa·tir′
i·cal·ly, *adv.* —sat′ir·ist, *n.*

săt′ir·īze, *v.t.*, -ized, -izing. portray satirically.

săt′ĭs·fȳ, *v.t.*, -fied, -fying. **1.** fulfill the wishes or needs of. **2.** convince. **3.** pay, as a debt. —sat′′is·fac′tion, *n.* —sat′′ is·fac′to·ry, *adj.*

săt′ū·rāte, *v.t.*, -rated, -rating. cause complete absorption by. —sat′′u·ra′ tion, *n.*

Săt′ûr·dāy, *n.* seventh day of the week.

Săt′ûrn, *n.* second-largest planet in the solar system.

sat·ur·nine (sat′ər nīn′′), *adj.* gloomy.

sā′tyr, *n.* **1.** classical forest deity. **2.** lecherous man.

sauce, *n.* **1.** liquid for flavoring or cooking. **2.** semiliquid stewed fruit.

sauce′păn′′, *n.* small, handled cooking pot.

sau′cêr, *n.* small dish.

sau′cy̆, *adj.*, -cier, -ciest. impudent. —sau′ci·ness, *n.* —sau′ci·ly, *adv.*

sauer′kraut′′, *n.* chopped fermented cabbage.

sau′nà, *n.* Finnish hot-air bath.

saun′têr, *v.i.*, *n.* stroll.

sau′sàge, *n.* minced and seasoned meat, often in a casing.

sâu·têrne, *n.* sweet white wine.

sau·té, *v.t.*, -téed, téeing. fry quickly in a little fat.

săv′àge, *adj.* **1.** uncivilized. **2.** fierce or harsh. —*n.* **3.** uncivilized person. —sav′age·ly, *adv.* —sav′age·ry, *n.*

sà·vânt (sa vahnt′), *n.* learned person.

sāve, *v.t.*, saved, saving, *prep.*, *conj.* *v.t.* **1.** keep from harm. **2.** keep for future use. **3.** keep from being wasted. **4.** keep from sin or its consequences. —*prep.*, *conj.* **5.** except.

sāv′ĭng, *adj.* **1.** redeeming. **2.** thrifty. —*n.* **3.** economy. **4.** savings, money saved. —*prep.* **5.** with the exception of.

sāv′iôr, **1.** rescuer. **2. the Savior,** Christ. Also, sav′iour.

sa·voir-faire (sav′′wahr fār′), *n.* skill in human relations.

sā′vör, *n.*, *v.t.* taste or smell. Also, sa′ vour.

sā′vör·y̆, *adj.* pleasant-tasting or smelling.

sāw, *n.*, *v.t.*, sawed, sawing. *n.* **1.** cutting

tool with a row of teeth. **2.** saying or proverb. —*v.i.* **3.** cut with a saw. —saw′ mill′′, *n.* —saw′yer, *n.*

săx′ò·phōne, *n.* keyed metal reed instrument. —sax′o·phon′′ist, *n.*

sāy, *v.t.*, said, saying, *n.* *v.t.* **1.** speak. **2.** declare to be true. —*n.* **3.** chance to speak.

sāy′ĭng, *n.* proverb.

scăb, *n.*, *v.i.*, scabbed, scabbing. *n.* **1.** crust over a healing wound or sore. **2.** worker who replaces a striking worker. —*v.i.* **3.** form a scab. —scab′by, *adj.*

scăb′bård, *n.* sword sheath.

scā′bĭes, *n.* itching skin disease.

scăf′fōld, *n.* **1.** Also, scaf′fold·ing, temporary platform. **2.** platform for execution of condemned persons.

scăl′à·wăg′′, *n.* scoundrel.

scăld, *v.t.* **1.** burn with hot fluid. **2.** heat almost to boiling. —*n.* **3.** burn made by hot fluid.

scāle, *n.*, *v.t.*, scaled, scaling. *n.* **1.** platelike portion of the covering of a fish, snake, etc. **2.** flake or layer of material. **3.** Also, scales, weighing device. **4.** range of musical tones. **5.** system of relations, as of actual size to represented size or of different degrees of a thing. —*v.t.* **6.** remove scales from. **7.** climb. **8.** determine the relative size of. —scal′y, *adj.*

scăl′liòn, *n.* any of several varieties of small onion.

scăl·lŏp, *n.* **1.** bivalve mollusk. **2.** any of the curves forming part of a decorative border. —*v.t.* **3.** decorate with scallops.

scălp, *n.* **1.** hair and skin covering the top of the head. —*v.t.* **2.** take a scalp from, esp. as a trophy.

scăl′pėl, *n.* surgical knife.

scăm, *n.* con game; deception practiced to defraud.

scămp, *n.* rascal; imp.

scăm′pêr, *v.i.* **1.** run quickly. —*n.* **2.** fast run.

scăn, *v.t.*, scanned, scanning. **1.** examine in detail. **2.** examine quickly. **3.** analyze the rhythmic pattern of.

scăn′dàl, *n.* **1.** malicious gossip. **2.** disgraceful occurrence or situation. —scan′dal·ous, *adj.*

scăn′dàl·īze, *v.t.*, -ized, -izing. shock with a scandal.

scănt, *adj.* scarcely sufficient. Also,

scant'y. —scant'i·ly, *adv.* **—scant'i·ness,** *n.*

scape'goat, *n.* person blamed for the misdeeds of others.

scape'grace, *n.* rascal.

scap'u·la, *n., pl.* **-lae, -las.** shoulder blade. —**scap'u·lar,** *adj.*

scar, *n., v.t.,* **scarred, scarring.** *n.* **1.** mark left by a cut. —*v.t.* **2.** cut so as to make a scar.

scar'ab, *n.* carved image of a beetle.

scarce, *adj.,* **scarcer, scarcest.** not plentiful or common. —**scarc'i·ty, scarce'ness,** *n.*

scarce'ly, *adv.* **1.** only just; barely. **2.** hardly.

scare, *n., v.t.,* **scared, scaring,** *v.t.* **1.** frighten. —*v.i.* **2.** become frightened. —*n.* **3.** frightening occurrence.

scare'crow'', *n.* device to frighten birds from a planted field.

scarf, *n., pl.* **scarfs, scarves.** length of cloth for warming the neck and chest.

scar'i·fy, *v.t.,* **-fied, -fying.** scratch or cut.

scar'let, *adj., n.* bright red.

scar'let fever, contagious disease marked by fever and scarlet rash.

scat, *v.i.,* **scatted, scatting.** *Informal.* run away.

scath'ing, *adj.* bitterly harsh, as something said or written. —**scath'ing·ly,** *adv.*

scat'ter, *v.t.* **1.** throw in all directions. —*v.i.* **2.** move away rapidly in all directions.

scav'enge, *v.,* **-enged, -enging.** *v.t.* **1.** clean out. —*v.i.* **2.** search for refuse that can be eaten or reused. —**scav'en·ger,** *n.*

sce·nar'i·o, *n.* story outline, esp. in the motion pictures.

scene, *n.* **1.** what is seen from a certain place. **2.** location of an action. **3.** subdivision of a dramatic act. **4.** emotional display in public. —**scen'ic,** *adj.*

scen'er·y, *n.* **1.** pleasant outdoor scene. **2.** painted canvases, etc. representing the scene of a dramatic action.

scent, *n.* **1.** distinctive smell. **2.** trail left by something with such a smell. **3.** perfume. **4.** sense of smell. —*v.t.* **5.** smell. **6.** perfume.

scep'ter, *n.* short staff symbolizing royal power. Also, **scep'tre.**

scep'tic, *n.* skeptic.

sched'ule, *n., v.t.,* **-uled, -uling.** *n.* **1.** list of the times of planned actions or events. **2.** any orderly list. —*v.t.* **3.** put on a schedule.

scheme, *n., v.i.,* **schemed, scheming.** *n.* **1.** plan or design. **2.** plot; intrigue. —*v.i.* **3.** plot to do or attain something. —**schem'er,** *n.*

schism (siz'əm), *n.* division, as between factions in an organization. —**schis·mat'ic,** *adj., n.*

schist (shist), *n.* layered crystalline rock.

schiz·o·phre·ni·a (skit''zə frē'nē ə), *n.* mental disorder. —**schiz''o·phre'nic schiz'oid,** *adj.*

schle·miel', *n. Yiddish.* a person who is a habitual failure.

schlock, *Yiddish. n.* **1.** inferior goods or materials. —*adj.* **2.** inferior in material or workmanship.

schmaltz, *n. Informal.* sentimental art.

schol'ar, *n.* **1.** person who studies to acquire knowledge. **2.** school pupil.

schol'ar·ly, *adj.* pertaining to or in the manner of scholars.

schol'ar·ship, *n.* **1.** activities and accomplishments of scholars. **2.** grant of money to make school attendance possible.

scho·las'tic, *adj.* pertaining to education.

school, *n.* **1.** place or institution for education or training. **2.** educational activity. **3.** group with a common set of beliefs or practices. **4.** group of fish, etc. —*v.t.* **5.** educate or train. —**school' book,** *n.* —**school'boy,** *n.* —**school' girl,** *n.* —**school'mate,** *n.* —**school' house,** *n.* —**school'room,** *n.* —**school' teach·er,** *n.*

schoon'er, *n.* fore-and-aft rigged sailing vessel with two or more masts, including a foremast.

schwa (shwah), *n.* unstressed vowel sound, e.g. the *o* in *factor,* represented by the symbol ə.

sci·at·i·ca (sî at'ik ə), *n.* neuralgia of the hip and thigh —**sci·at'ic,** *adj.*

sci'ence, *n.* **1.** systematic acquisition of knowledge, esp. knowledge that can be measured precisely. **2.** precise method or skill. —**sci''en·tif'ic,** *adj.* —**sci''en·tif'i·cal·ly,** *adv.* —**sci'en·tist,** *n.*

scin·til'la, *n.* glimmering; trace.

scin′til·late, *v.i.* -lated, -lating. sparkle. —**scin″til·la′tion,** *n.*

sci·on (sī′ən), *n.* **1.** descendant. **2.** plant shoot or bud, esp. for grafting.

scis′sörs, *n.* instrument for cutting by means of two moving blades.

scle·rō′sis, *n.* hardening of body tissue. —**scle·rot′ic,** *adj.*

scöff, *n., v.i.* jeer. —**scof′fer,** *n.*

scōld, *v.t.* **1.** reproach at length. —*n.* **2.** person who scolds.

scönce, *n.* wall bracket for lights.

scöne, *n.* flat biscuit.

scoōp, *n.* **1.** device for digging deeply. **2.** act or instance of scooping. **3.** amount held by a scoop. **4.** *Informal.* prior publication of news. —*v.t.* **5.** remove or empty with a scoop. **6.** *Informal.* get the better of by publishing news first.

scoōt, *v.i.* go quickly.

scoōt′êr, *n.* small, low-built two-wheeled vehicle.

scōpe, *n.* range of responsibility or possibility for action.

scörch, *v.t.* **1.** burn on the surface. —*n.* **2.** surface burn.

scöre, *n., v.,* **scored, scoring.** *n.* **1.** total, as of points in a game. **2.** *Informal.* **know the score,** know the actual situation. **3.** long, shallow cut. **4.** group of twenty. **5.** musical arrangement. —*v.t.* **6.** add, as points in a game. **7.** mark with a long, shallow cut. —*v.t.* **8.** gain points, as in a game.

scörn, *n.* **1.** contempt. **2.** derision. —*v.t.* **3.** treat with scorn. —**scorn′ful,** *adj.* —**scorn′ful·ly,** *adv.*

scôr′pï·òn, *n.* poisonous, long-tailed, eight-legged animal.

Scötch, *n.* malted-barley whisky made in Scotland.

scötch, *v.t.* make ineffective.

scoūn′drèl, *n.* rascal.

scoūr, *v.t.* **1.** clean with a steady rubbing action. **2.** go over repeatedly, as during a search.

scoûrge (skərj), *n., v.t.,* **scourged, scourging.** *n.* **1.** whip. **2.** major affliction. —*v.t.* **3.** beat with a whip. **4.** punish or harass severely.

scoūt, *n.* **1.** person sent to explore or search. —*v.t.* **2.** reject as absurd. —*v.i.* **3.** act as a scout.

scöw, *n.* flat-bottomed barge or boat.

scöwl, *v.t.,* **1.** frown angrily. —*n.* **2.** angry frown.

scräb′ble, *v.i.,* -bled, -bling. **1.** scratch or scrape with the hands. **2.** struggle without dignity.

scräg′glÿ, *adj.,* -glier, -gliest. ragged.

scräg·gÿ, *adj.* -gier, -giest. scrawny.

scräm′ble, *v.,* -bled, -bling, *n. v.t.* **1.** mix up; confuse. —*v.i.* **2.** move in short, rapid steps. —*n.* **3.** scrambling motion or gait. **4.** undignified struggle, as for something of value.

scräp, *n., adj., v.t.,* **scrapped, scrapping.** *n.* **1.** small piece. **2.** refuse material, esp. when reclaimable. **3.** *Informal.* fight. —*adj.* **4.** in the form of scrap. —*v.t.* **5.** make into scrap. **6.** discard. —**scrap′heap,** *n.*

scräp′boōk, *n.* album for printed and written material, etc.

scräpe, *v.,* **scraped, scraping,** *n. v.t.* **1.** rub against roughly. **2.** remove by rough rubbing. **3.** get by tedious labor. —*v.i.* **4.** rub roughly against something. —*n.* **5.** act of scraping. **6.** area scraped. **7.** dangerous situation. —**scrap′er,** *n.*

scräp′ple, *n.* fried dish of meal and meat scraps.

scrätch, *v.t.* **1.** make a long, shallow cut in. **2.** cross out; eliminate. —*n.* **3.** long, shallow cut. **4. from scratch,** from the beginning. **5. up to scratch,** up to standard.

scrätch′ÿ, *adj.,* -ier, -iest. suggesting scratching, esp. in sound.

scräwl, *v.t., v.i.* **1.** write with a bad hand. —*n.* **2.** writing in a bad hand.

scräwn′ÿ, *adj.,* -nier, -niest. disagreeably thin.

scrëam, *n.* **1.** loud, high-pitched cry. —*v.i.* **2.** utter such a cry.

scrëech, *n.* **1.** harsh screamlike sound. —*v.i.* **2.** utter such sounds.

scrëen, *n.* **1.** flat object or surface for division, protection, or concealment. **2.** surface on which motion pictures, television programs, etc. are projected. **3. the screen,** motion-picture industry. —*v.t.* **4.** enclose or protect with or as if with a screen. **5.** sift through a screen. **6.** investigate for suitability.

scrëw, *n.* **1.** simple machine for fastening, moving, etc., in the form of an inclined plane wound around an axis. **2.** propeller. —*v.t.* **3.** fasten with screws.

4. turn as one does a screw. —**screw'driv''er,** n.

scrĭb'ble, v., -bled, -bling, n. v.t., v.i. 1. write hastily and carelessly. —n. 2. hasty or careless writing.

scrībe, n. Archaic. writer or clerk.

scrĭm'màge, n., v.i. -maged, -maging. n. 1. play in football. —v.i. 2. take part in a scrimmage.

scrĭmp, v.i. save; economize.

scrĭp, n. certificate used in place of money.

scrĭpt, n. 1. handwriting. 2. manuscript, esp. of a play, etc.

Scrĭp'tûre, n. 1. portion or portions of the Bible. 2. **the Scriptures,** the Bible. —scrip'tur·al, adj.

scrŏf'ŭ·là, n. tuberculosis of the lymph glands.

scrōll, n. 1. roll of paper, etc. bearing writing or print. 2. spiral ornamental motif. —v. 3. (computers) to move the display on a monitor so that other data can be read.

scrō'tŭm, n. baglike skin enclosure for testicles.

scrōunge, v., scrounged, scrounging. v.t. 1. Informal. beg or steal in a minor way. —v.i. 2. Informal. look for something desired.

scrŭb, v.t., scrubbed, scrubbing, n., adj., v.t. 1. wash with a vigorous rubbing action. 2. Informal. eliminate; cross off. —n. 3. stunted trees or shrubbery. —adj. 4. inferior.

scrŭff, n. nape of the neck.

scrŭ'ple, n. prompting of the conscience.

scrŭ'pü·loŭs, adj. 1. conscientious. 2. careful. —scru'pu·lous·ly adv.

scrŭ'tĭ·nīze, v.t., -nized, -nizing. examine carefully. —scru'ti·ny, n.

scŭd, v.i., scudded, scudding. move rapidly.

scŭff, v.t. 1. wear by rubbing or scraping. —v.t., v.i. 2. shuffle, as the feet.

scŭf'fle, v.i., -fled, -fling, n., v.i. 1. fight confusedly at close quarters. —n. 2. confused fight at close quarters.

scŭll, n. 1. oar used at a boat's stern. 2. racing rowboat. —v.t., v.i. 3. move with a scull.

scŭl'lêr·ÿ, n. room for cleaning dishes, kitchen utensils, etc.

scŭlp'tûre, n. 1. art of composing in three dimensions. 2. example of this art. —sculp'tur·al, adj. —sculp'tor, n., fem., sculp'tress.

scŭm, n. 1. film on a liquid surface. 2. rabble. —scum'my, adj.

scŭp'pêr, n. drainage opening in a deck or flat roof.

scûrf, n. flecks of dead skin.

scûr'rĭl·oŭs, adj. grossly insulting. —scur'ril·ous·ly, adv. —scur·ril'i·ty, scur'ril·lous·ness, n.

scûr'rÿ, v.i., -ried, -rying, n., pl. -ries. v.i. 1. move hastily. —n. 2. hasty movement.

scûr'vÿ, n. disease due to vitamin deficiency.

scŭt'tle, n., v., -tled, -tling. n. 1. hatchlike opening in a deck or roof. 2. coal bucket. —v.t. 3. sink intentionally. —v.i. 4. scurry.

scȳthe, n. mowing instrument with curved blade and long handle.

sēa, n. 1. part of an ocean, esp. one partly bounded by land. 2. **the sea,** the oceans. 3. large inland body of water. 4. relative turbulence of ocean water at a given time. —sea'board'', sea'coast'', n.

sēa'fār''ĭng, n. activity of one who travels on or works at sea. —sea'far''er, n.

sēa'gō''ĭng, adj. pertaining to or suitable for travel on the sea.

sēa hôrse, semitropical fish with head of horselike form.

sēal, n. 1. device for giving official character to or preventing tampering with a document, locked space, etc. 2. stamp used to shape such a device. 3. device to prevent passage of air, etc. 4. fourflippered sea mammal. —v.t. 5. put seal on. 6. enclose with a seal.

sēa'līŏn, large seal.

sēam, n. 1. line of junction. 2. mineral stratum. —v.t. 3. join at or with a seam. —seam'less, adj.

sēa'màn, n., pl. -men. sailor. —sea'man·ship'', n.

sēam'strèss, n. sewing woman.

sēam'ÿ, adj. seamier, seamiest. 1. having seams. 2. less attractive; sordid.

se·ance (sā'ahns), n. meeting for communication with the dead.

sēa'plāne, n. airplane able to land on water.

sēa'pôrt'', n. port fronting on an ocean.

sēar, *v.t.* **1.** burn the surface of. **2.** wither.

sêarch, *n.* **1.** methodical attempt to find something. —*v.t.* **2.** examine in making a search. —*v.i.* **3.** hunt. —**search′er**, *n.*

sêarch′ĭng, *adj.* deep and perceptive, as an investigation.

sêarch′līght, *n.* directed light for distinguishing objects in the dark.

sēa′shĕll′′, *n.* shell of saltwater mollusk.

sēa′shôre′′, *n.* shore of an ocean. Also, **sea′side′′**.

sēa′sĭck′′, *adj.* sick from the motion of a ship. —**sea′sick′′ness**, *n.*

sēa′sŏn, *n.* **1.** quarter of the year beginning at a solstice or equinox. **2.** appropriate time. —*v.t.* **3.** flavor with salt, spices, herbs, etc. **4.** prepare for use by aging or exposure to weather. —**sea′son·al**, *adj.*

sēa′sŏn·a·ble, *adj.* coming at the appropriate time.

sēa′sŏn·ĭng, *n.* flavoring of salt, spices, herbs, etc.

sēat, *n.* **1.** place for sitting. **2.** place of governmental activities, residence, etc. **3.** location. **4.** place in a legislature, etc. —*v.t.* **5.** put onto a seat. **6.** install in a seat.

sēa′wāy′′, *n.* **1.** inland waterway to the sea. **2.** area of open sea.

sēa′wēed′′, *n.* ocean plant.

sēa′wôr′′thy̆, *adj.* suitable for navigation at sea.

se·ba·ceous (si bā′shəs), *adj.* fatty.

se·cēde′, *v.i.*, **-ceded, -ceding.** withdraw from a political state, etc. —**se·ces′sion**, *n.*

se·clūde′, *v.t.*, **-cluded, -cluding.** isolate, esp. from society or activity. —**se·clu′sion**, *n.*

sĕc′ŏnd, *adj.* **1.** next after the first. —*n.* **2.** sixtieth of a minute. **3.** person serving as an assistant or witness. **4.** **seconds**, goods rejected for ordinary sale. —*v.t.* **5.** approve. —*adv.* **6.** as a second point. —**sec′ond·ly**, *adv.*

sĕc′ŏnd·ār·y̆, *adv.* **1.** forming a second stage or phase. **2.** of a second level of importance. —**sec′on·dar′′i·ly**, *adv.*

sĕc′ŏnd-hănd′, *adj.* **1.** belonging or offered to a new owner. **2.** not original.

sē′crĕt, *n.* **1.** something not to be known by everyone. **2.** hidden cause or reason. —*adj.* **3.** hidden or not to be known by everyone. —**se′cret·ly**, *adv.* —**se′cre·cy**, *n.*

sĕc′′rė·tār′ĭ·ăt, *n.* group of administrative officials.

sĕc′rė·tār′′y̆, *n.*, *pl.* **-taries. 1.** assistant to a businessman, official, etc. **2.** head of a government department. **3.** writing desk. —**sec′′re·tar′i·al**, *adj.*

se·crēte′, *v.t.*, **-creted, -creting. 1.** produce and release substances, as a gland. **2.** hide. —**se·cre′tion**, *n.* —**se·cre′to·ry**, *adj.*

sē′crė·tĭve, *adj.* **1.** reluctant to reveal information. **2.** pertaining to secretion. —**se′cre·tive·ly**, *adv.* —**se′cre·tive·ness**, *n.*

sĕct, *n.* religious group.

sĕc·tār′ĭ·ăn, *adj.* **1.** pertaining to separate sects. —*n.* **2.** member of a sect.

sĕc′tion, *n.* **1.** separate part. **2.** act or instance of dividing. **3.** view of a thing as if divided. —*v.t.* **4.** divide. —**sec′tion·al**, *adj.*

sĕc′tör, *n.* **1.** *Geometry.* plane figure formed of a segment of a circle and two of its radii. **2.** area, esp. of military operation.

sĕc′ū·lăr, *adj.* not religious. —**sec′u·lar·ize**, *v.t.*

se·cūre′, *adj.*, *v.t.*, **-cured, -curing.** *adj.* **1.** safe or certain. **2.** firmly in place. —*v.t.* **3.** make secure. **4.** obtain. —**se·cure′ly**, *adv.*

se·cūr′ĭ·ty̆, *n.*, *pl.* **-ties. 1.** state of being secure. **2.** protection or precaution. **3.** pledge on a loan, etc. **4.** **securities**, bonds, stocks, etc.

se·dăn′, *n.* closed automobile with front and rear seats.

se·dāte′, *n.* quiet in manner. *v.* apply (or administer) a sedative.

sĕd′a·tĭve, *n.* **1.** medicine to relieve pain or nervousness. —*adj.* **2.** relieving pain or nervousness. —**se·da′tion**, *n.*

sĕd′ĕn·tār′′y̆, *adj.* not physically active.

Se·der (sā′dər′′), *n.* Jewish home ceremony at Passover.

sĕd′′ĭ·mĕnt, *n.* matter falling to the bottom of a body of liquid.

se·dĭ′tion, *n.* incitement to rebellion. —**se·di′tious**, *adj.*

se·dūce′, *v.t.*, **-duced, -ducing. 1.** tempt or induce to commit a wrong. **2.** induce to perform a sexual act. —**se·duc′er,**

fem., **se·duc'tress**, *n.* —**se·duc'tion**, *n.*

se·dŭc'tĭve, *adj.* tempting; attractive.

sĕd'ū·loŭs, *adj.* diligent.

sēe, *v.*, saw, seen, seeing, *n. v.t.* **1.** sense with the eyes. **2.** realize or understand. **3.** make sure. **4.** escort. —*v.i.* **5.** have use of the eyes. **6.** find out or understand. **7.** attend, as to a task. **8.** bishopric.

sēed, *n., pl.* seeds, seed, *v.t. n.* **1.** thing from which a plant grows. **2.** offspring. —*v.t.* **3.** sow seed in. **4.** remove seeds from. —**seed'less**, *adj.*

sēed'lĭng, *n.* new growth from a seed.

sēed'ÿ, *adj.* seedier, seediest. **1.** having seeds. **2.** shabby.

sēe'ĭng, *conj.* in view of the fact.

sēek, *v.t.*, sought, seeking. **1.** look for. **2.** intend and attempt. —**seek'er**, *n.*

sēem, *v.t., v.i.* give the effect of being or acting in some specified way.

sēem'ĭng, *adj.* apparent. —**seem'ing·ly**, *adv.*

sēem'lÿ, *adj.*, -lier, -liest. proper in appearance or effect. —**seem'li·ness**, *n.*

sēep, *v.i.* ooze. —**seep'age**, *n.*

sēer, *n.* person who professes to foresee the future. Also, *fem.*, **seer'ess**.

sēer'sŭck''êr, *n.* crinkled striped fabric.

sēe'sāw'', *n.* recreation of swinging up and down on a balanced plank.

sēethe, *v.*, seethed, seething. *v.t., v.i.* boil.

sĕg'mènt, *n.* **1.** portion. —*v.t.* **2.** divide into portions. —**seg''men'tal**, *adj.* —**seg''men·ta'tion**, *n.*

sĕg'rè·gāte, *v.t.*, -gated, -gating. keep apart from others. —**seg''re·ga'tion**, *n.*

seine (sān), *n.* **1.** weighted fishing net. —*v.t., v.i.* **2.** fish with such a net.

seis·mic (sīz'mĭk), *adj.* pertaining to or affected by earth tremors.

seīs'mò·grăph, *n.* device for measuring earth tremors.

sēize, *v.t.*, seized, seizing. **1.** take by authority or force. **2.** grasp, as an idea.

sēiz'ûre, *n.* **1.** taking by authority or force. **2.** attack of illness.

sĕl'dòm, *adv.* rarely.

se·lĕct', *v.t.* **1.** choose. —*adj.* **2.** selected; choice. —**se·lec'tion**, *n.*

se·lĕc'tĭve, *adj.* **1.** pertaining to selection. **2.** careful in selecting.

se·lĕct'măn, *n.* New England town officer.

sĕlf, *n.* **1.** one's own person. **2.** one's own well-being. —*adj.* **3.** of the same kind.

sĕlf''-às·sūr'ànce, *n.* self-confidence. —**self''-as·sured'**, *adj.*

sĕlf'-cĕn·tēred, *adj.* seeing all things in reference to one's self or self-interest.

sĕlf'-còn·cēit', *n.* excessively good opinion of oneself.

sĕlf''-cŏn'fĭ·dènce, *n.* confidence in one's own ability, rightness, etc. —**self''-con'fi·dent**, *adj.*

sĕlf''-cŏn'scioŭs, *adj.* excessively aware of the impression one may be making.

sĕlf''-còn·tāined', *adj.* **1.** complete in itself. **2.** reserved in manner.

sĕlf''-còn·trōl', *n.* ability to restrain one's impulses or expressions of emotion.

sĕlf''-dè·nī'àl, *n.* readiness to forgo gratifications to further a cause, help another, etc. —**self''-de·ny'ing**, *adj.*

sĕlf'-ès·tēem', *n.* good opinion of one's self.

sĕlf'-ĕv'ĭdènt, *adj.* evident without further proof or explanation

sĕlf'-ĕx·plăn'à·tò''rÿ, *adj.* needing no explanation; obvious.

sĕlf''-ĭm·pôrt'ànt, *adj.* seeming to have an excessive idea of one's own importance.

sĕlf''-ĭn'têr·èst, *n.* concern for one's own well-being.

sĕlf'ĭsh, *adj.* acting for or thinking of one's own well-being alone. —**self'ish·ly**, *adv.* —**self'ish·ness**, *n.*

sĕlf'lèss, *n.* self-sacrificing.

sĕlf'-māde', *n.* prosperous, famous, or powerful through one's own efforts.

sĕlf''-pòs·sĕs'sion, *n.* self-control. —**self''-pos·sessed'**, *adj.*

sĕlf''-rē·lī'ànce, *n.* reliance on one's own resources. —**self''-re·li'ant**, *adj.*

sĕlf'-rè·spĕct', *n.* respect for one's own dignity, rights, etc. —**self'-re·spect'ing**, *adj.*

sĕlf''-rīgh'teoŭs, *adj.* conceitedly sure of one's righteousness.

sĕlf'sāme'', *adj.* identical.

sĕlf''-săt'ĭs·fīed, *adj.* satisfied with one's own personality, accomplishments, etc. —**self'-sat''is·fac'tion**, *n.*

self-sēek'ĭng, *adj.* motivated by self-interest.

sĕlf'-stȳled', *adj.* called by oneself.

sĕlf''-sŭf·fī'ciėnt, *adj.* able to depend on one's own resources. **—self''-suf·fi'cien·cy,** *n.*

sĕll, *v.t.,* **sold, selling. 1.** exchange for money. **2.** offer for sale. **—v.i. 3.** attract the buying public. **—sel'ler,** *n.*

sĕlt'zêr, *n.* carbonated water.

sĕl'vȧge, *n.* woven edge on a length of cloth. Also, **sel'vedge.**

sè·măn'tĭcs, *n.* study of word meanings. **—se·man'tic,** *adj.*

sĕm'ȧ·phôre'', *n.* signal using different positions of arms or flags.

sĕm'blȧnce, *n.* **1.** seeming state. **2.** resemblance.

sē'mėn, *n.* fluid containing sperm.

sè·mĕs'têr, *n.* unit consisting of half a school year.

sĕ'mĭ·cîr''cle, *n.* half a circle. **—se''mi·cir'cu·lar,** *adj.*

sĕm'ĭ·cōl''ŏn, *n.* punctuation mark of the form ; that is used to divide clauses of a sentence.

sĕm''ĭ·còn·dŭc'tör, *n.* a material used to modify electrical current, used in solid-state circuitry.

sĕm'ĭ·när'', *n.* academic class with a format of discussion or research.

sĕm'ĭ·när''ÿ, *n., pl.* **-naries. 1.** school for divinity students. **2.** school for young women. **—sem'i·nar'i·an,** *n.*

sĕm''ĭ·prĕ'ciȯŭs, *adj.* not considered precious, as certain decorative stones used as gems.

sĕn'ȧte, *n.* **1.** senior legislative body. **2. the senate,** upper legislative house in the United States or Canada. **—sen'a·tor,** *n.* **—sen''a·tor'i·al,** *adj.*

sĕnd, *v.,* **sent, sending.** *v.t.* **1.** cause to go. **—v.i. 2.** send for, cause to come. **—send'er,** *n.*

sē'nīle, *adj.* decrepit, esp. mentally, in old age. **—se·nil'i·ty,** *n.*

sēn'iȯr, *adj.* **1.** older. **2.** higher in authority. **3.** having more years of employment or service. **4.** in the last year of school. **—n. 5.** senior person. **—sen·ior'i·ty,** *n.*

sě·ñôr', *n., pl.* **-nores.** *Spanish.* Mr. or Sir.

sě·ñô'rȧ, *n., pl.* **-noras.** *Spanish.* Mrs. or Madam.

sě·ñô·rĭ'tȧ, *n., pl.* **-ritas.** *Spanish.* Miss.

sĕn·sā'tion, *n.* **1.** use of the senses. **2.** experience obtained through the senses. **3.** intuition or feeling. **4.** something causing excited public interest.

sĕn·sā'tión·ȧl, *adj.* causing or intended to cause excited public interest. **—sen·sa'tion·al·ly,** *adv.* **—sen·sa'tion·al·ism,** *n.*

sĕnse, *n., v.t.,* **sensed, sensing.** *n.* **1.** sight, hearing, touch, taste, or smell. **2.** impression obtained through one of these. **3.** intuition regarding a situation. **4.** Often, **senses,** reason. **5.** meaning. **—v.t. 6.** perceive by or as if by one of the senses.

sĕnse'lèss, *adj.* **1.** unreasonable. **2.** unconscious.

sĕn''sĭ·bĭl'ĭ·tÿ, *n., pl.* **-ties. 1.** ability to sense or be aware of things. **2.** Often, **sensibilities,** emotional sensitivity.

sĕn'sĭ·ble, *n.* **1.** reasonable. **2.** perceptible through the senses. **3.** aware. **—sen'si·bly,** *adv.*

sĕn'sĭ·tĭve, *n.* **1.** able to sense or register objects, data, etc. in small amounts. **2.** easily disturbed. **—sen''si·tiv'i·ty,** *n.*

sĕn'sĭ·tīze, *v.t.,* **-tized, -tizing.** make sensitive.

sĕn'sȯ·rÿ, *adj.* pertaining to the senses.

sĕn'sŭ·ȧl, *adj.* **1.** given to the pleasures of the senses. **2.** pertaining to such pleasure. **—sen'su·al·ism,** *n* **—sen'su·al·ist,** *n.*

sĕn'sŭ·ȯŭs, *n.* **1.** pertaining to the senses. **2.** pleasing to the senses or emotions. **—sen''su·ous·ly,** *adv.* **—sen'su·ous·ness,** *n.*

sĕn'tĕnce, *n., v.t.,* **-tenced, -tencing.** *n.* **1.** unit of prose writing expressing one thought. **2.** legal decision, esp. regarding a punishment. **3.** punishment, esp. a term of imprisonment. **—v.t. 4.** determine the punishment of.

sĕn''tĕn'tiȯŭs, *adj.* tiresomely opinionated or voluble on matters of right and wrong.

sĕn'tiėnt, *adj.* having feeling or perception. **—sen'tience,** *n.*

sĕn'tĭ·mėnt, *n.* **1.** personal feeling. **2.** statement of such feeling. **3.** opinion.

sĕn''tĭ·mĕn'tȧl, *adj.* characterized by love, pity, etc., esp. to an unreasonable extent. **—sen''ti·men''tal'i·ty,** *n.* **—sen''ti·men'tal·ism,** *n.* **—sen''ti·men'tal·ist,** *n.*

sĕn′tĭ·nĕl, *n.* guard.

sĕn′trў, *n., pl.* **-tries.** soldier on guard duty.

sĕp′a·rāte, *v.,* **-rated, -rating,** *adj. v.t., v.i.* **1.** part. —*adj.* (sep′ərət) **2.** unconnected; individual. —**sep′a·rate·ly,** *adv.* —**sep′′a·ra′tion,** *n.* —**sep′a·ra·ble,** *adj.* —**sep′a·ra′′tor,** *n.*

sē′pĭ·å, *n.* dark brown.

sēp′sĭs, *n.* infection of the blood. —**sep′tic,** *adj.*

Sĕp·tĕm′bĕr, *n.* ninth month.

sĕp′tĭc, *adj.* **1.** pertaining to putrefaction. **2.** pertaining to sepsis.

sĕp′′tū·å·gė·nār′ĭ·ån, *n.* person in his or her seventies.

sĕp′ŭl·chêr, *n.* tomb. Also, **sep′ul·chre.**

sė·pŭl′chrål, *adj.* **1.** lugubrious or gloomy. **2.** pertaining to sepulchers.

sē′quėl, *n.* **1.** event that follows. **2.** story continuing the subject of a previous one.

sē′quènce, *n.* **1.** succession or series. **2.** consequence. **3.** episode in a motion picture or television program.

sė·quĕs′têr, *v.t.* **1.** set apart. **2.** seize or impound. —**se′′ques·tra′tion,** *n.*

sē′quĭn, *n.* small glittering disk sewn to a costume.

sĕr′åph, *n., pl.* **-aphs, -aphim.** angel of the highest order. —**se·raph′ic,** *adj.*

sēre, *adj.* withered.

sĕr′ė·nāde′′, *n., v.t.,* **-naded, -nading.** *n.* **1.** musical composition for outdoor evening performance. —*v.t.* **2.** perform a serenade for.

sė·rēne′, *adj.* **1.** calm. **2.** fair, as the weather. —**se·ren′i·ty,** *n.* —**se·rene′ly,** *adv.*

sêrf, *n.* person in bondage to a landlord. —**serf′dom,** *n.*

sêrge, *n.* twilled fabric.

ser·geant (sar′gent), *n.* highest noncommissioned army officer.

sē′rĭ·ål, *adj.* **1.** forming part of a series. —*n.* **2.** story appearing in installments. —**se′ri·al·ly,** *adv.*

sē′riēs, *n., pl.* **-ries.** group of things coming after the other.

sē′rĭ·oŭs, *adj.* **1.** solemn. **2.** earnest, sincere. **3.** important. —**se′ri·ous·ly,** *adv.* —**se′ri·ous·ness,** *n.*

sêr′môn, *n.* speech to a religious congregation.

sêr′pĕnt, *n.* any large snake.

sêr·pĕn·tĭne, *adj.* winding in snakelike loops.

sĕr′rāt·ĕd, *adj.* resembling sawteeth in outline. —**ser·ra′tion,** *n.*

sē′rŭm, *n.* liquid part of the blood, sometimes used in inoculation.

sêr′vånt, *n.* person hired to work in a household.

sêrve, *v.,* **served, serving.** *v.t.* **1.** act in the service of. **2.** be of use to. **3.** present for consumption, as food or drink. **4.** undergo, as a prison sentence. —*v.i.* **5.** act in the service of a person, organization, or cause. **6.** suffice.

sêr′vĭce, *n., v.t.,* **-viced, -vicing.** *n.* **1.** activity on behalf of a person, organization, or cause. **2.** employment as a domestic worker. **3.** military organization or the military. **4.** favor. **5.** session of public worship. **6.** set of matched dishes, eating implements, etc. —*v.t.* **7.** supply, maintain, or repair.

sêr′vĭce·å·ble, *adj.* useful.

sêr′vĭce·măn′′, *n.* **1.** member of an armed force. **2.** person who maintains, repairs, or fuels machinery.

sêr′vīle, *adj.* slavelike; obsequious. —**ser·vil′i·ty,** *n.*

sêr′vĭ·tūde, *n.* bondage.

sēs′å·mē, *n.* East Indian plant yielding oil and edible seeds.

sĕs′′quĭ·cĕn·tĕn′nĭ·ål, *n.* **1.** one hundred fiftieth anniversary. —*adj.* **2.** pertaining to such an anniversary.

sĕs′sion, *n.* **1.** occasion of the gathering of members of a group. **2. in session,** formally convened.

sĕt, *v.,* **set, setting,** *n., adj. v.t.* **1.** place or put. **2.** put in proper or specified order or condition. **3.** place before others, as an example, problem, etc. —*v.i.* **4.** become fixed or firm. **5.** go below the horizon, as a star or planet. **6. set out** or **off,** begin to travel. —*n.* **7.** apparatus. **8.** complete group or collection. **9.** television or radio receiver. **10.** arrangement of theatrical scenery. —*adj.* **11.** firm or fixed. **12.** determined. **13.** prearranged.

sĕt′băck′′, *n.* temporary defeat or hindrance.

sĕt·tēe′, *n.* sofa or bench with a back.

sĕt′têr, *n.* hunting dog.

set'ting, *n.* **1.** locale of a story. **2.** environment. **3.** music of a song.

set'tle, *v.,* **-tled, -tling.** *v.t.* **1.** resolve, as a dispute. **2.** free from disturbance. **3.** pay, as a debt. **4.** set in a position of rest. **5.** colonize. —*v.i.* **6.** fall gently into a position of rest. **7.** reach an agreement or compromise. **8.** take up residence. —**set'tler,** *n.* —**set'tle·ment,** *n.*

sev'en, *n., adj.* one plus six.

sev''en·teen', *n., adj.* seven plus ten. —**sev''en·teenth',** *adj.*

sev'en''ty, *n., adj.* seven times ten. —**sev'en·ti''eth,** *adj.*

sev'er, *v.t.* cut off or separate. —**sev'er·ance,** *n.*

sev'er·al, *adj.* **1.** a few. **2.** individual. **3.** respective. —**sev'er·al·ly,** *adv.*

se·vere', *adj.* **1.** sternly demanding. **2.** harsh or violent. **3.** seriously bad. **4.** austerely simple. —**se·vere'ly,** *adv.* —**se·ver'i·ty,** *n.*

sew (sō), *v.t.,* **sewed, sewed** or **sewn, sewing.** join with thread. —**sew'er,** *n.*

sew'age, *n.* waste material in sewers. Also, **sew'er·age.**

sew'er, *n.* covered channel for waste.

sex, *n.* **1.** individual nature as determined by the reproductive system. **2.** either of two divisions of a species as so determined. **3.** activities, thoughts, etc. as influenced by the reproductive system. —**sex'u·al,** *adj.* —**sex'u·al·ly,** *adv.*

sex'is·m, *n.* discrimination on the basis of sex.

sex'tant, *n.* navigational instrument using the elevation of the sun.

sex·tet', *n.* **1.** group of six, esp. musicians. **2.** musical composition for six instruments. Also, **sex·tette'.**

sex'ton, *n.* caretaker of a church.

sex'tu·ple, *adj.* occurring six times.

shab'by, *adj.,* **-bier, -biest. 1.** worn and untidy-looking. **2.** mean. —**shab'bi·ness,** *n.* —**shab'bi·ly,** *adv.*

shack, *n.* shanty.

shack'le, *n., v.t.,* **-led, -ling.** *n.* **1.** Usually, **shackles,** chains for binding prisoners. **2.** binding part of a padlock. —*v.t.* **3.** bind with or as with shackles.

shad, *n., pl.* **shads, shad.** herringlike fish spawning in rivers.

shade, *n., v.t.,* **shaded, shading.** *n.* **1.** area sheltered from direct light. **2.** device for cutting off direct light. **3.** variety of color or tone. **4.** slight degree. **5.** soul of a dead person. —*v.t.* **6.** shelter from direct light. **7.** vary, as a color or tone.

shad'ow, *n.* **1.** darkness of a shaded area. **2.** slight remnant or trace. —*v.t.* **3.** shade. **4.** follow secretly. —**shad'ow·y,** *adj.*

shad'y, *adj.* **1.** in the shade. **2.** *Informal.* to be suspected.

shaft, *n.* **1.** long, cylindrical object for support, rotation, etc. **2.** beam of light. **3.** narrow vertical space.

shag, *n.* long, rough hair, fur, or nap. —**shag'gy,** *adj.*

shah, *n.* former sovereign of Iran.

shake, *v.,* **shook, shaken, shaking,** *n.* *v.t.,* **1.** cause to move rapidly back and forth. **2.** upset emotionally. —*v.i.* **3.** move rapidly back and forth. —*n.* **4.** act or instance of shaking. **5.** wood shingle.

shak'er, *n.* **1.** device for sprinkling seasoning. **2. Shaker,** member of an American celibate religious sect.

shak'y, *adj.,* **-kier, -kiest. 1.** unstable. **2.** tending to shake. **3.** of doubtful validity. —**shak'i·ly,** *adv.* —**shak'i·ness,** *n.*

shale, *n.* layered rock of hardened clay.

shall, *v.* am, is, or are going to.

shal'lot, *n.* onionlike plant used in cooking.

shal'low, *adj.* **1.** not deep. **2.** without depth of thought or feeling.

sham, *adj., n., v.t.,* **shammed, shamming.** *adj.* **1.** false; imitation. —*n.* **2.** something false or imitative. —*v.t.* **3.** pretend; feign.

sham'ble, *v.i.,* **-bled, -bling.** *n.* *v.i.* **1.** walk draggingly or awkwardly. —*n.* **2. shambles, a.** scene of disorder. **b.** slaughterhouse. **3.** shambling gait.

shame, *n., v.t.,* **shamed, shaming.** *n.* **1.** painful sense of guilt or inadequacy. **2.** disgrace. **3.** deplorable situation. —*v.t.* **4.** put to shame. —**shame'ful,** *adj.* —**shame'less,** *adj.*

shame'faced, *adj.* showing embarrassment. —**shame'fac'ed·ly,** *adv.*

sham·poo', *v.t.,* **-pooed, -pooing,** *n.* *v.t.* **1.** wash with soap, as the hair or a carpet. —*n.* **2.** soap, etc. used for shampooing.

sham'rock, *n.* cloverlike plant with a triple leaf: symbol of Ireland.

shăng′haī, *v.t.*, **-haied, -haiing.** abduct for work on a ship.

shănk, *n.* **1.** lower leg above the ankle. **2.** shaft of a hand tool between the handle and working end.

shăn′tŭng, *n.* textured silk.

shăn′tў, *n.*, *pl.* **-ties.** roughly built wooden house.

shāpe, *n.*, *v.t.*, **shaped, shaping.** *n.* **1.** form. **2.** *Informal.* condition. —*v.t.* **3.** give form to. —**shape′less**, *adj.*

shāpe′lў, *adj.* handsome in form. —**shape′li·ness**, *n.*

shāre, *n.*, *v.t.* **shared, sharing.** *n.* **1.** rightful or predetermined portion. —*v.t.* **2.** divide into such portions. **3.** use or experience together.

shârk, *n.* **1.** large predatory fish. **2.** person who preys on others.

shârp, *adj.* **1.** having or as if having a cutting point or edge. **2.** clearly defined. **3.** shrewd. **4.** alert. **5.** abrupt. **6.** *Music.* raised in pitch. —*adv.* **7.** punctually. —*n.* **8.** a semitone higher than a stated tone. —**sharp′en·er**, *n.* —**sharp′ly**, *adv.* —**sharp′ness**, *n.* —**sharp′en**, *v.t.*

shârp′êr, *n.* swindler.

shârp′shōōt′′êr, *n.* good marksman.

shăt′têr, *v.t.*, *v.i.* break in small pieces.

shāve, *v.t.*, **shaved, shaved** or **shaven, shaving,** *n.* *v.t.* **1.** cut the hair off with a razor. **2.** remove with a razor. **3.** cut in thin layers with a tool. —*n.* **4.** act or instance of being shaved.

shāv′ĭng, *n.* thin layer of material shaved from a larger piece.

shāwl, *n.* cloth covering head and shoulders.

shē, *pron.* woman or female previously mentioned.

shēaf, *n.*, *pl.* **sheaves.** bundle.

shēar, *v.t.*, **sheared, sheared** or **shorn, shearing,** *n.* *v.t.* **1.** divide as with the motion of one blade across another. —*n.* **2.** device for shearing.

shēars, *n. pl.* large scissors.

shēath, *n.*, *pl.* **sheaths.** closely fitting case or cover.

shēathe, *v.t.*, **sheathed, sheathing.** put into a sheath.

shĕd, *v.t.*, **shed, shedding,** *n.* *v.t.* leave or cast off. **2.** pour forth, as light. —*n.* **3.** rough shelter.

shēen, *n.* dull reflection.

shēep, *n.*, *pl.* **sheep.** mammal yielding fleece and mutton.

shēep′ĭsh, *adj.* bashful or embarrassed.

shēer, *adj.* **1.** absolute; utter. **2.** very steep or perpendicular. **3.** transparent, as a fabric. —*v.i.* **4.** swerve.

shēet, *n.* **1.** broad, thin piece of material. **2.** cloth used to cover a mattress or a sleeper. **3.** rope for controlling the position of a sail.

shēik, *n.* Arab chief.

shĕk′ĕl, *n.* ancient Hebrew coin.

shĕlf, *n.*, *pl.* **shelves. 1.** horizontal ledge or slab of supporting objects. **2.** ledge, as of rock.

shĕll, *n.* **1.** hard outer covering. **2.** shotgun cartridge. **3.** explosive artillery missile. **4.** racing rowboat. —*v.t.* **5.** separate from its shell. **6.** bombard with shells.

shĕl·lăc′, *n.* **1.** varnish containing a certain resin. **2.** the resin itself. —*v.t.* **3.** varnish with shellac.

shĕll′fĭsh′′, *n.* any aquatic animal with a shell.

shĕl′têr, *n.* **1.** something serving as a protection, as against the weather. —*v.t.* **2.** protect. —*v.i.* **3.** take shelter.

shĕlve, *v.*, **shelved, shelving. 1.** put on a shelf. **2.** postpone action or decision on. **3.** provide with shelves. —*v.i.* **4.** slope.

shĕp′hêrd, *n.* **1.** Also, *fem.*, **shep′herd·ess,** person who leads and guards sheep. —*v.t.* **2.** escort with close vigilance.

shêr′bĕt, *n.* frozen dessert of water, gelatin, flavoring, and sometimes milk.

shĕr′ĭff, *n.* county police officer.

shĕr′rў, *n.*, *pl.* **-ries.** Spanish fortified wine.

shiēld, *n.* **1.** piece of armor worn on the arm. **2.** any defensive device. —*v.t.* **3.** protect or hide.

shĭft, *v.t.*, *v.i.* **1.** move from place to place. **2.** change, as one's place. **3.** change, as the gears of a motor vehicle. —*n.* **4.** act or instance of shifting. **5.** lever for changing gears in a motor vehicle. **6.** daily period of labor.

shĭft′lĕss, *n.* lazy or feeble.

shĭft′ў, *adj.*, **shiftier, shiftiest.** tricky; unreliable. —**shift′i·ly**, *adv.* —**shift′i·ness**, *n.*

shĭl′lĭng, *n.* former British coin, one-twentieth of a pound.

shĭl′lȳ-shăl′lȳ, *v.i.*, **-lied, -lying.** hesitate or quarrel over trifles.

shĭm, *n.* thin piece for raising an object or filling a gap.

shĭm′mêr, *v.i.* **1.** glow or appear in a flickering, unsteady way. —*n.* **2.** effect given in so doing. —shim′mer·y, *adj.*

shĭn, *n.* front of the shank of the leg.

shīne, *v.*, shone or, for *v.t.*, shined, shining, *n. v.i.* **1.** emit or reflect strong light. **2.** gain distinction. —*v.t.* **3.** polish to a high gloss. —*n.* **4.** shining light. —shin′y, *adj.*

shĭn′gle, *n.* **1.** thin plate of wood or other material used on houses as a roof covering or siding. **2.** shingles. virus disease with blisters as a symptom. —*v.t.* **3.** cover with shingles.

shĭn′nȳ, *n.* street hockey.

shĭp, *n.*, *v.*, shipped, shipping. *n.* **1.** large ocean-going vessel. **2.** sailing vessel square-rigged on all of at least three masts. —*v.t.* **3.** send by a foreign carrier. —*v.i.* **4.** engage to work on a voyage. —ship′mate′′, *n.* —ship′ment, *n.* —ship′per, *n.*

shĭp′pĭng, *n.* vessels, esp. merchant ships.

shĭp′shāpe′′, *adj.*, *adv.* in good order.

shĭp′wrĕck′′, *n.* destruction of a ship from running aground.

shĭp′yârd′′, *n.* place for building or repairing ships.

shīre, *n.* British county.

shîrk, *v.t.* **1.** evade, as an obligation. —*n.* **2.** person who shirks something. —shirk′er, *n.*

shîrr, *v.t.* gather on parallel strands for decorative effect, as curtain material.

shîrt, *n.* a long- or short-sleeved upper garment usually having a front opening, collar and cuffs, worn esp. by men.

shĭv′êr, *v.i.* **1.** tremble. —*v.t.* **2.** smash to pieces. —*n.* **3.** trembling movement. **4.** broken fragment. —shiv′er·y, *adj.*

shōal, *n.* **1.** area of shallow water. **2.** large number of fish.

shōat, *n.* young pig.

shŏck, *n.* **1.** violent impact. **2.** violent emotional disturbance. **3.** bodily disturbance caused by loss of blood circulation, a current of electricity passing through the body, etc. **4.** stack of sheaves of grain. **5.** tangled mass, as of hair. —*v.t.* **6.** disturb with a shock. —shock′ing, *adj.*

shŏd′dȳ, *adj.* poor in quality. —shod′di· ness, *n.*

shoe (shōō), *n.*, *v.t.*, shod, shoeing. *n.* **1.** protective covering for the foot. **2.** something suggesting this. —*v.t.* **3.** provide with shoes. —shoe′lace′′, shoe′string′′, *n.* —shoe′mak′′er, *n.*

shoe′hôrn′′, *n.* device to assist slipping the foot into a shoe.

shōōt, *v.t.* **1.** send a missile from. **2.** hit with a missile. **3.** emit rapidly, as a missile. —*v.i.* **4.** use a gun, bow, etc. **5.** grow or sprout. —*n.* **6.** sporting event with shooting. **7.** young plant growth. —shoot′er, *n.*

shŏp, *n.*, *v.i.*, shopped, shopping. *n.* **1.** store, esp. a small specialized one. **2.** industrial workroom. —*v.i.* **3.** look for or make purchases. —shop′per, *n.* —shop′keep′′er, *n.*

shŏp′lĭft′′êr, *n.* person who steals from shops.

shôre, *n.*, *v.t.*, shored, shoring. *n.* **1.** land bordering a body of water. **2.** seacoast. **3.** prop. —*v.t.* **4.** prop.

shôrt, *n.* **1.** not tall or long. **2.** abrupt in manner. **3.** scanty, as a supply. **4.** below the required amount. **5.** flaky, as pastry. —*adv.* **6.** abruptly. —*n.* **7.** short circuit. **8.** shorts, short-legged pants or underpants. —*v.t.* **9.** create a short circuit in. —short′ly, *adv.* —short′ness, *n.* short′en, *v.t.*

shôrt′àge, *n.* short supply.

shôrt cĭrcuĭt, deviation of current in an electrical circuit rendering it useless.

shôrt′còm′′ĭng, *n.* fault or inadequacy.

shôrt′cŭt′′, *n.* shorter way than the usual.

shôrt′ĕn·ĭng, *n.* greasy substance for making pastry short.

shôrt′hănd′′, *n.* system of writing for fast note-taking.

shôrt′-līved′′, *adj.* not living or existing long.

shôrt′-sīght′′ĕd, *adj.* without foresight.

shŏt, *n.*, *pl.* shots or (for 3) shot. **1.** discharge of a missile. **2.** range of a gun, bow, etc. **3.** *Often pl.* missiles, esp. shotgun pellets or cannonballs. **4.** iron ball for hurling in athletic contests. **5.** marksman.

shŏt´gŭn, *n.* gun firing shells filled with metal pellets.

should (shŏŏd), *v.* **1.** ought to. **2.** were to. **3.** past tense of *shall.*

shŏul´der, *n.* **1.** part of the human body between the upper arms and neck. **2.** corresponding area in animals. **3.** unpaved strip alongside a road. —*v.t.* **4.** push with the shoulder. **5.** take up and carry.

shŏut, *n.* **1.** very loud call or voice. —*v.i.* **2.** give such a call. —*v.t.* **3.** utter in such a voice.

shŏve, *v.,* **shoved, shoving,** *n. v.t., v.i.* **1.** push vigorously. —*n.* **2.** vigorous push.

shŏv´el, *n.* **1.** hand tool or machine for scooping up material. —*v.t.* **2.** raise or move with a shovel. **3.** clear with a shovel.

shōw, *v.,* **showed, shown** or **showed, showing,** *n. v.t.* **1.** display. **2.** guide. **3.** prove or demonstrate. —*v.i.* **4.** be visible or apparent. —*n.* **5.** entertainment. **6.** exhibit. **7.** ostentation. —**show´boat´´,** *n.* —**show´case´´,** *n.* —**show´man,** *n.* —**show´piece,** *n.* —**show´room,** *n.*

shōw´dōwn´´, *n.* **1.** confrontation, as between enemies. **2.** climactic event.

shōw´êr, *n.* **1.** brief rainstorm. **2.** bath in which water is sprayed from above. **3.** large number of small objects dropped or hurled. —*v.t.* **4.** bestow liberally. —*v.i.* **5.** rain briefly.

shōw´ôff´´, *n.* vain, ostentatious person.

shōw´ÿ, *adj.,* **-ier, -iest.** attracting attention, esp. through gaudiness.

shrăp´nel, *n.* small fragments hurled by the bursting of an artillery shell.

shrĕd, *n., v.t.,* **shredded, shredding.** *n.* **1.** torn strip. **2.** bit, as of doubt or evidence. —*v.t.* **3.** tear into shreds.

shrĕw, *n.* **1.** small mouselike mammal. **2.** quarrelsome woman. —**shrew´ish,** *adj.*

shrĕwd, *adj.* clever in dealing with or understanding others. —**shrewd´ly,** *adv.* —**shrewd´ness,** *n.*

shriēk, *n.* **1.** loud, shrill cry. —*v.i.* **2.** utter such a cry.

shrīke, *n.* bird of prey.

shrĭll, *adj.* high-pitched. —**shril´ly,** *adv.* **shrill´ness,** *n.*

shrĭmp, *n.* small, long-tailed shellfish.

shrīne, *n.* sacred place.

shrĭnk, *v.,* **shrank** or **shrunk, shrunk** or **shrunken, shrinking.** *v.i.* **1.** become smaller. **2.** draw back, as in fear. —*v.t.* **3.** cause to shrink. —**shrink´age,** *n.*

shrĭvel, *v.i.* shrink and become wrinkled.

shrŏud, *n.* **1.** wrapping for a corpse. **2.** line steadying a ship's mast. —*v.t.* **3.** wrap or conceal.

shrŭb, *n.* small, treelike plant. —**shrub´ber·y,** *n.*

shrŭg, *n., v.,* **shrugged, shrugging.** *n.* **1.** movement of raising both shoulders. —*v.i.* **2.** make such a movement. —*v.t.* **3.** move in shrugging.

shŭck, *n., v.t.* husk or shell.

shŭd´dêr, *v.i.* **1.** tremble violently and briefly. —*n.* **2.** act or instance of shuddering.

shŭf´fle, *v.i.,* **-fled, -fling,** *n. v.i.* **1.** walk with feet scraping the ground. **2.** mix, as playing cards. —*n.* **3.** shuffling gait.

shŭf´fle·bôard´´, *n.* game played by shoving wooden disks along a marked surface.

shŭn, *v.t.,* **shunned, shunning.** avoid.

shŭnt, *v.t.* **1.** divert. **2.** move, as cars in a railroad yard.

shŭt, *v.,* **shut, shutting,** *adj. v.t.* **1.** close. **2.** keep in or out. —*v.i.* **3.** be closed. —*adj.* **4.** closed.

shŭt´têr, *n.* **1.** cover for a window opening. **2.** device for timed exposure of film in a camera.

shŭt´tle, *v.i.,* **-tled, -tling,** *n. v.i.* **1.** go short distances back and forth. —*n.* **2.** device on a loom for moving warp thread back and forth. **3.** public transit vehicle that runs between two closely spaced terminals.

shÿ, *adj.,* **shier, shiest,** *v.,* **shied, shying,** *n., pl.* **shies.** *adj.* **1.** timid in the presence of others. **2.** lacking by a specified number. —*v.t.* **3.** toss, esp. with a sideways motion. —*v.i.* **4.** start with surprise, as a horse. —*n.* **5.** act or instance of shying. —**shy´ly,** *adv.* —**shy´ness,** *n.*

sĭb´lĭng, *n.* brother or sister.

sĭc, *v.t.,* **sicked, sicking,** *adv. v.t.* **1.** urge to an attack. —*adv.* **2.** *Latin.* thus; (it is written).

sĭck, *adj.* **1.** not in health. **2.** suffering nausea. **3.** disgusted or upset. **4.** *Informal.* mentally warped. —*n.* **5.** sick

people. —**sick'ness,** *n.* —**sick'en,** *v.t.,*
v.i.

sick'le, *n.* crescent-shaped tool for mowing.

sick'ly, *adj.,* **-lier, -liest.** not healthy or robust.

side, *n., adj., v.i.,* **sided, siding.** *n.* **1.** area of someone or something to the right or left of the face or front. **2.** direction or location to the right or left. **3.** any direction or location from a central point. **4.** line or surface defining a form. **5.** aspect. **6.** person or group in a dispute or conflict. **7.** opinion or cause of such a person or group. —*adj.* **8.** pertaining to a side direction or location. **9.** of secondary importance. —*v.i.* **10.** ally oneself.

side'bôard'', *n.* article of furniture for dishes, silver, and napkins.

side'bûrns'', *n. pl.* whiskers down the sides of the face.

side'lĭne'', *n.* secondary source of income.

side'lŏng'', *adj., adv.* to the side.

sĭ·dē'rē·ăl, *adj.* pertaining to stars.

side'shōw'', *n.* minor entertainment at a circus.

side'stĕp'', *v.t.,* **-stepped, -stepping.** evade by or as if by stepping sideways.

side'swīpe'', *v.t.,* **-swiped, -swiping.** brush the side of in passing.

side'trăck'', *v.t.* divert or distract from accomplishing a purpose.

side'wälk'', *n.* walk beside a roadway.

side'wāys'', *adv., adj.* **1.** with a side foremost. **2.** to or from one side. Also, **side'wise''.**

sīd'ĭng, *n.* short track for trains halted beside a through track.

sīdle, *v.i.,* **-dled, -dling.** move sideways.

SIDS, sudden infant death syndrome, unexplained death of baby while asleep.

siēge, *n.* prolonged attack on a fortified place.

sĭ·ĕn'nȧ, *n.* reddish- or yellowish-brown.

sĭ·ĕs'tȧ, *n.* brief daytime nap.

sīeve, *n., v.t.,* **sieved, sieving.** *n.* **1.** strainer of wire mesh. —*v.t.* **2.** run through or separate with a sieve.

sĭft, *v.t.* separate with a sieve. —**sift'er,** *n.*

sīgh, *v.i.* **1.** release pent-up breath in re-

action to grief, annoyance, etc. —*n.* **2.** such a release of breath.

sīght, *n.* **1.** sense perceived by the eyes. **2.** something seen. **3.** something remarkable to see. **4.** range of distances one's eyes can see clearly. **5.** aiming device for shooting or bombing. —*v.t.* **6.** discover with the eye. **7.** aim with a sight. —**sight'less,** *adj.*

sīght'ly, *adj.,* **-lier, -liest.** pleasing to see.

sīgn, *n.* **1.** indication. **2.** written, printed, or hand-given symbol. **3.** display surface containing such symbols or writing. —*v.t.* **4.** put a signature on. —**sign'er,** *n.*

sĭg'nȧl, *n., adj., v.t.,* **-naled, -naling.** *n.* **1.** device presenting a message in symbols. **2.** message so presented. —*adj.* **3.** acting as a signal. **4.** marked. —*v.t.* **5.** indicate through a signal. **6.** communicate through a signal. —**sig'nal·er,** *n.* —**sig'nal·man,** *n.* —**sig'nal·ly,** *adv.*

sĭg'nȧl·īze'', *v.t.,* **-ized, -izing.** call attention to or make noteworthy.

sĭg'nȧ·tô''rў, *n., pl.* **-ries.** signer, esp. of a document.

sĭg'nȧ·tûre, *n.* **1.** one's name in one's handwriting. **2.** *Music.* sign indicating key and tempo.

sĭg'nĕt, *n.* letter seal, often mounted on a ring.

sĭg·nĭf'ĭ·cȧnce, *n.* **1.** meaning. **2.** importance. —**sig·nif'i·cant,** *adj.*

sĭg·nĭ·fŷ'', *v.t..* **-fied, -fying.** **1.** mean. **2.** indicate. —**sig''ni·fi·ca'tion,** *n.*

sī'lĕnce, *n., v.t.,* **-lenced, lencing.** *n.* **1.** absence of noise, conversation, or sound. **2.** absence of information or communication. —*v.t.* **3.** make silent. **4.** put out of action, as enemy guns. —**si'lent,** *adj.* —**si'lent·ly,** *adv.*

sĭl·hŏu·ĕtte (sil''ŏŏ et'), *n., v.t.,* **-etted, -etting** *n.* **1.** outline figure, usually filled in with black. —*v.t.* **2.** cause to appear in outline against a lighter background.

sĭl'ĭ·cȧ, *n.* hard, glassy substance appearing in sand, quartz, etc.

sĭl'ĭ·cŏn, *n.* nonmetallic element appearing in various compounds.

sĭlk, *n.* cloth made of fiber spun by silkworms.

sĭlk'ĕn, *adj.* **1.** made of silk. **2.** suggesting silk in smoothness. Also, **silk'y.**

silk'worm'', *n.* moth caterpillar whose cocoons provide silk fiber.

sill, *n.* horizontal structural member, esp. below a wall or opening.

sil'ly, *adj.*, **-lier, -liest. 1.** foolish or stupid. **2.** unreasonable. —**sil'li·ness**, *n.*

sī'lō, *n.* airtight place for storing fodder.

silt, *n.* **1.** fine earth, etc. deposited by running water. —*v.t.* **2.** fill or clog with silt.

sil'vêr, *n.* **1.** white noble metallic element. **2.** coins, utensils, etc. customarily made of silver. **3.** lustrous whitish gray. —*adj.* **4.** made of or colored silver. **5.** pertaining to a twenty-fifth wedding anniversary. **6.** eloquent, as the tongue. —**sil'ver·y**, *adj.* —**sil'ver·smith''**, *n.*

sil'vêr·wāre'', *n.* tableware traditionally made of silver.

sim'i·àn, *adj.* **1.** pertaining to or suggesting apes and monkeys. —*n.* **2.** ape or monkey.

sim'i·làr, *adj.* of the same sort. —**sim'i·lar·ly**, *adv.* —**sim''i·lar'i·ty**, *n.*

sim'i·lē'', *n.* expression comparing one thing to another.

si·mil'i·tūde'', *n.* likeness.

sim'mêr, *v.t.*, *v.i.* almost boil.

sī''mŭl·tā'nē·oŭs, *adj.* at the very same time. —**si''mul·ta'ne·ous·ly**, *adv.*

sī'mȯ·nÿ, *n.* profiting financially from religion.

sim'pêr, *v.i.* **1.** smile foolishly or affectedly. —*n.* **2.** foolish or affected smile.

sim'ple, *adj.*, **-pler, -plest. 1.** of the most basic kind. **2.** readily understood or mastered. **3.** low in intelligence. —**sim'ply**, *adv.* —**sim·plic'i·ty**, *n.*

sim'ple-mīnd'ĕd, *adj.* foolish; low in intelligence.

sim'ple·tòn, *n.* foolish or naive person.

sim'pli·fȳ, *v.t.*, **-fied, -fying.** make easier to understand or master. —**sim''pli·fi·ca'tion**, *n.*

sim·plis'tĭc, *adj.* unrealistically over-simplified.

sim'ū·lāte, *v.t.*, **-lated, -lating. 1.** pretend; feign. **2.** imitate closely. —**sim''u·la'tion**, *n.*

sin, *n.*, *v.i.*, **sinned, sinning.** *n.* **1.** violation of religious law. —*v.i.* **2.** commit such a violation. —**sin'ful**, *adj.* **sin'ful·ly**, *adv.* —**sin'ful·ness**, *n.*

since, *conj.* **1.** during the time after. **2.** because or inasmuch as. —*adv.* **3.** from that time on. **4.** at some time afterwards.

sin·cēre', *adj.*, **-cerer, -cerest.** genuine; honest and unaffected. —**sin·cere'ly**, *adv.* —**sin·cer'i·ty**, *n.*

si·ne·cure (sī'ne kyōōr''), *n.* salaried job requiring no serious work.

sin'ew, *n.* **1.** tendon. **2.** muscular strength. —**sin'ew·y**, *adj.*

sing, *v.*, **sang** or **sung, sung, singing.** *v.i.* **1.** make musical sounds with the voice. —*v.t.* **2.** render by singing. —**sing'er**, *n.*

singe, *v.t.*, **singed, singeing.** burn on the surface.

sin'gle, *adj.*, *v.t.*, **-gled, -gling**, *n. adj.* **1.** alone or unique. **2.** unmarried. —*v.t.* **3. single out,** select. —*n.* **4.** something single. —**sin'gly**, *adv.*

sing'sŏng'', *adj.* monotonously rhythmical.

sin'gū·làr, *adj.* **1.** peculiar or extraordinary. **2.** unique. **3.** *Grammar.* pertaining to one person or thing. —*n.* **4.** *Grammar.* singular number of a word. —**sin'gu·lar·ly**, *adv.* —**sin''gu·lar'i·ty**, *n.*

sin'ĭs·têr, *adj.* evilly threatening.

sink, *v.*, **sank** or **sunk, sunk** or **sunken, sinking**, *n. v.i.* **1.** descend beneath a surface. **2.** pass into a depressed state. —*v.t.* **3.** cause to descend or penetrate beneath a surface. —*n.* **4.** basin with a drain. —**sink'er**, *n.*

sin'nêr, *n.* person who sins.

sin'ū·oŭs, *adj.* meandering; serpentine.

sī'nŭs, *n.* cavity, esp. one in the skull opening into the nasal passages.

sip, *v.*, **sipped, sipping**, *n. v.t.* **1.** drink in tiny amounts. —*n.* **2.** act or instance of sipping. **3.** amount sipped at a time.

sī'phòn, *n.* **1.** curved tube for sucking liquids automatically from place to place. —*v.t.* **2.** pass through a siphon.

sîr, *n.* **1.** formal term used in addressing a man. **2.** title given a British knight or baronet.

sīre, *n.*, *v.t.*, **sired, siring.** *n.* **1.** male parent, esp. of an animal. **2.** formal term used in addressing a king. —*v.t.* **3.** beget.

sī'rėn, *n.* **1.** mythical sea nymph luring sailors with singing to shipwreck. **2.**

horn with a wavering tone used on emergency vehicles.

sîr′loĭn, *n*. cut of beef at the loin end by the rump.

sîr′ŭp, *n*. syrup.

sī′sȧl, *n*. plant fiber used for ropes, etc.

sĭs′sȳ, *n*. *Informal*. **1.** timid or unmanly male. **2.** nickname for a sister.

sĭs′tẽr, *n*. **1.** daughter of one's own parents. **2.** nun. —**sis′ter·ly**, *adj*.

sĭs′têr·hōŏd′′, *n*. **1.** organization of nuns. **2.** condition of being a sister.

sĭs′têr-ĭn-lāw′′, *n*., *pl*. **sisters-in-law. 1.** sister of a spouse. **2.** wife of a brother.

sĭt, *v*., **sat, sitting.** *v.i.* **1.** rest on the behind. **2.** be located. **3.** pose, as for a portrait. **4.** be in session, as a court. —*v.t.* **5.** seat. —**sit′ter**, *n*.

sīte, *n*. location, as of a building.

sĭt′tĭng, *n*. session.

sĭt′ū·āte′′, *v.t.*, **-ated, -ating.** place or locate.

sĭt′′ū·ā′tion, *n*. **1.** location. **2.** condition or predicament. **3.** job.

sĭx, *n*., *adj*. one plus five. —**sixth**, *adj*.

sĭx′′tēen′, *n*., *adj*. six plus ten. —**six·teenth′**, *adj*.

sĭx′tȳ, *n*., *adj*. six times ten. —**six′ti·eth**, *adj*.

sīz′à·ble, *adj*. fairly large. Also, **size′a·ble.**

sīze, *n*., *v.t.*, **sized, sizing.** *n*. **1.** area, volume, number, etc. by which something is measured or graded. **2.** Also, **siz′ing**, pasty substance used to coat or fill cloth, paper, etc. —*v.t.* **3.** size up, measure or appraise intuitively. **4.** treat with sizing.

sĭz′zle, *v.i.*, **-zled, -zling**, *n*. *v.i.* **1.** hiss or crackle, as from being fried. —*n*. **2.** hissing or crackling, as from being fried.

skāte, *n*., *v.i.*, **skated, skating.** *n*. **1.** piece of footwear for gliding across ice. **2.** roller skate. **3.** flat-bodied fish of the ray family. —*v.i.* **4.** go on skates. —**skat′er**, *n*.

skein (skān), *n*. coil of yarn or thread.

skĕl′ė·tȯn, *n*. **1.** bone structure of an animal. **2.** structural frame. —**skel′e·tal**, *adj*.

skĕp′tĭc, *n*. doubter. —**skep′ti·cal**, *adj*. —**skep′ti·cal·ly**, *adv*. —**skep′ti·cism′′**, *n*.

skĕtch, *n*. **1.** rough drawing. **2.** brief outline. —*v.t.* **3.** make a sketch of.

skĕtch′ȳ, *adj*. vague or without detail. —**sketch′i·ly**, *adv*.

skēw, *v.t.*, *v.i.* **1.** slant. —*adj*. **2.** aslant.

skēw′êr, *n*. **1.** needle for holding pieces of meat together. —*v.t.* **2.** pierce with or as if with a skewer.

skī, *n*., *pl*. **skis**, *vi.*, **skied, skiing**. *n*. **1.** long flat runner for gliding or walking on snow. —*v.i.* **2.** glide on skis. —**ski′er**, *n*.

skĭd, *v.*, **skidded, skidding**, *n*. *v.i.*, *v.t.* **1.** slide, by accident or intention. —*n*. **2.** object or surface on which objects are skidded. **3.** skidding motion.

skĭff, *n*. rowboat.

skĭll, *n*. practiced ability. —**skilled**, *adj*. —**skill′ful**, *adj*. —**skill′ful·ly**, *adv*.

skĭl′lėt, *n*. frying pan.

skĭm, *v.*, **skimmed, skimming**. *v.t.* **1.** remove from a liquid surface. —*v.i.* **2.** move lightly across a surface.

skĭmp, *v.i.* economize; scrimp.

skĭmp′ȳ, *adj*., **skimpier, skimpiest.** scant.

skĭn, *n.*, *v.t.*, **skinned, skinning**. *n*. **1.** outer covering of an animal body. —*v.t.* **2.** remove skin or hide from. —**skin′ner**, *n*. —**skin′′less**, *adj*.

skĭn′flĭnt′′, *n*. miserly person.

skĭn′nȳ, *adj*. thin of body.

skĭp, *v.*, **skipped, skipping**, *n*. *v.i.* **1.** jump lightly. —*v.t.* **2.** omit. —*n*. **3.** light jump.

skĭp′pêr, *n*. ship or boat captain.

skîr′mĭsh, *n*. **1.** brief, minor battle. —*v.i.* **2.** have a skirmish.

skîrt, *n*. **1.** open-bottomed garment fastened around the waist. **2.** Often, **skirts**, portion of a coat, dress, etc. that falls below the waist. —*v.t.* **3.** pass around the border of. **4.** evade, as subject of controversy.

skĭt, *n*. brief comic play.

skĭt′tĭsh, *adj*. readily excited or frightened.

skŭl′′dŭg′gêr·ȳ, *n*. treacherous intrigue.

skŭlk, *v.i.* lurk.

skŭll, *n*. bony shell of a head.

skŭnk, *n*. small mammal defending itself with foul-smelling liquid.

skȳ, *n.*, *pl*. **skies. 1.** part of the atmosphere visible from the earth. **2.** condition of this at a certain place and time.

skȳ′līght″, *n.* window in the surface of a roof or ceiling.

skȳ′līne″, *n.* silhouette of a city against the horizon.

skȳ′rŏck″ėt, *n.* **1.** firework rising high before exploding. —*v.i.* **2.** rise rapidly.

skȳ′scrāp″êr, *n.* very tall building, esp. one for offices.

slăb, *n.* flat, fairly thick piece of material.

slăck, *adj.* **1.** loose. **2.** inactive. **3.** lazy or indifferent. —*n.* **4.** slack part. **5.** period of inactivity. —*v.t.*, *v.i.* **6.** slacken. —**slack′ly**, *adv.* —**slack′ness**, *n.*

slăck′ėn, *v.t.*, *v.i.* **1.** make or become slack. **2.** lessen in intensity or vigor.

slăcks, *n. pl.* loosely fitting trousers.

slăg, *n.* molten waste from smelting.

slāke, *v.t.*, **slaked, slaking. 1.** quench with a drink. **2.** pour water on, as quicklime.

slăm, *v.t.*, **slammed, slamming**, *n. v.t.* **1.** push violently and noisily into place. —*n.* **2.** act of pushing thus.

slăn′dêr, *n.* **1.** maliciously untrue statement or statements about someone. —*v.t.* **2.** utter such statements about. —**slan′der·ous**, *adj.*

slăng, *n.* highly informal speech. —**slang′y**, *adj.*

slănt, *v.t.*, *v.i.* **1.** move or head diagonally. —*n.* **2.** diagonal movement or heading. **3.** attitude or opinion.

slăp, *v.t.*, **slapped, slapping**, *n. v.t.* **1.** hit with a flat object, esp. the hand. **2.** put together, etc. in haste. —*n.* **3.** act or instance of slapping.

slăsh, *v.t.* **1.** cut deeply with a long, sweeping motion. —*n.* **2.** long, deep cut.

slăt, *n.* thin board.

slāte, *n.*, *v.t.*, **slated, slating.** *n.* **1.** stone that can be cleaved into thin pieces. **2.** list of candidates. —*v.t.* **3.** cover with slate. **4.** intend for nomination, promotion, dismissal, etc.

slăt′têrn, *n.* slovenly woman.

slăugh′têr, *n.* **1.** mass killing; massacre. **2.** killing of animals for meat. —*v.t.* **3.** submit to slaughter. —**slaugh′ter·house″**, *n.*

slāve, *n.*, *v.i.*, **slaved, slaving.** *n.* **1.** person treated as the property of another. —*v.i.* **2.** drudge. —**slav′ery**, *n.*

slav·er (slāhv′ər), *v.i.* drool.

slāv′ĭsh, *adj.* in the manner of a slave, esp. in lacking originality or initiative.

slăw, *n.* coleslaw.

slāy, *v.t.*, **slew, slain, slaying.** kill. —**slay′er**, *n.*

slēa′zȳ, *adj.*, **-zier, -ziest.** shoddy.

slĕd, *n.*, *v.i.*, **sledded, sledding.** *n.* **1.** vehicle for gliding across snow or ice. —*v.i.* **2.** travel by sled.

slĕdge, *n.*, *v.t.*, **sledged, sledging.** *n.* **1.** sledlike vehicle. **2.** Also, **sledge′hammer**, heavy hammer. —*v.t.* **3.** transport by sledge.

slēek, *adj.* **1.** smooth or glossy. —*v.t.* **2.** make smooth. —**sleek′ly**, *adv.* —**sleek′ness**, *n.*

slēep, *n.*, *v.i.*, **slept, sleeping.** *n.* **1.** periodic state of unconscious rest. —*v.i.* **2.** be in such a state. —**sleep′y**, *adj* —**sleep′less**, *adj.*

slēep′êr, *n.* **1.** sleeping person. **2.** sill-like timber. **3.** railroad car with berths.

slēet, *n.* rain frozen in fine particles.

slēeve, *n.* part of a shirt or coat covering an arm.

sleigh (slā), *n.* horse-drawn light sled.

sleight óf hănd, rapid, secret hand movements for creating illusions.

slĕn′dêr, *adj.* **1.** attractively thin. **2.** meager, as means of livelihood. —**slen′der·ness**, *n.*

slēuth, *n. Informal.* detective.

slīce, *n.*, *v.t.*, **sliced, slicing.** *n.* **1.** thin piece cut from a larger one. —*v.t.* **2.** cut as a slice. **3.** cut slices from. —**slic′er**, *n.*

slĭck, *adj.* **1.** smooth or slippery. **2.** cunning. —*n.* **3.** area of floating oil. —*v.t.* **4.** make smooth.

slĭck′êr, *n.* raincoat with a slick outer surface.

slīde, *v.*, **slid, sliding**, *n. v.t.*, *v.i.* **1.** move with surface contact between the object moving and something else. —*n.* **2.** act or instance of sliding. **3.** object or surface used in sliding. **4.** fall of earth, rock, etc. down a slope. **5.** transparent plate used with a microscope, magic lantern, etc.

slĭght, *adj.* **1.** unimportantly little. **2.** slender. —*v.t.*, *n.* **3.** snub. —**slight′ly**, *adv.* —**slight′ness**, *n.* —**slight′ing·ly**, *adv.*

slī′lȳ, *adv.* slyly.

slǐm, *adj.*, **slimmer, slimmest. 1.** slender. **2.** small in amount or size. —**slim'ness**, *n.*

slǐme, *n.* semi-liquid, sticky matter.

slǐm'ÿ, *adj.*, **slimier, slimiest. 1.** of the nature of slime. **2.** disgustingly wheedling.

slǐng, *n.*, *v.t.*, **slung, slinging.** *n.* **1.** flexible device for hurling missiles. **2.** suspended cloth support. —*v.t.* **3.** hurl or throw. **4.** put in a sling.

slǐnk, *v.i.*, **slunk, slinking.** walk furtively.

slǐp, *v.*, **slipped, slipping,** *n. v.t., v.i.* **1.** slide smoothly. **2.** escape. —*v.i.* **3.** loose grip or footing. **4.** make a mistake. —*n.* **5.** act or instance of slipping. **6.** underskirt. **7.** space between piers for a ship.

slǐp'pêr, *n.* soft unlaced shoe for household wear.

slǐp'pêr·ÿ, *adj.*, **-ier, -iest. 1.** allowing slipping. **2.** cunning and unreliable.

slǐp'shŏd'', *adj.* careless.

slǐt, *n., v.t.*, **slitted, slitting.** *n.* **1.** long, deep opening. —*v.t.* **2.** cut with slits.

slǐth'êr, *v.i.* slide with a side-to-side motion.

slǐv'êr, *n., v.t.* splinter.

slŏb, *n. Informal.* uncouth or clumsy person.

slŏb'bêr, *v.i., n.* drool.

slŏg, *v.i.*, **slogged, slogging.** advance heavily or with difficulty; plod.

slō'găn, *n.* motto.

sloop, *n.* one-masted sailing vessel.

slŏp, *v.*, **slopped, slopping,** *n. v.t., v.i.* **1.** spill or toss carelessly, as a liquid. —*n.* **2.** something slopped. **3.** swill.

slōpe, *n., v.*, **sloped, sloping.** *n.* **1.** angled rise or descent. —*v.t.* **2.** cause to rise or descend in a slope. —*v.i.* **3.** form a slope.

slŏp'pÿ, *adj.* **1.** untidy. **2.** carelessly done. —**slop'pi·ly**, *adv.* —**slop'pi·ness**, *n.*

slŏsh, *v.t.* splash or slop.

slŏt, *n.* narrow opening.

slŏth, *n.* **1.** South American arboreal mammal. **2.** laziness. —**sloth'ful**, *adj.*

slŏuch, *v.i.* **1.** have a drooping posture. —*n.* **2.** drooping posture. **3.** incompetent or lazy person. —**slouch'y**, *adj.*

slough, *n.* **1.** (sloo or slō) muddy or marshy area. **2.** (sluf) dead, cast-off

skin. —*v.t.* **3.** cast off. —*v.i.* **4.** be cast off, as dead skin.

slov·en (sluv'ən), *n.* untidy or careless person. —**slov'en·ly**, *adj.*

slōw, *adj.* **1.** moving or acting without speed. **2.** not learning or understanding readily. **3.** behind the correct or appointed time. **4.** lacking in activity or vigor. —*adv.* **5.** slowly. —*v.t.* **6.** cause to move or act slowly. —*v.i.* **7.** move or act slowly. —**slow'ly**, *adv.* —**slow'ness**, *n.*

slŭdge, *n.* semi-liquid sediment.

slūe, *v.*, **slued, sluing.** *v.t., v.i.* turn or swerve.

slŭg, *v.t.*, **slugged, slugging,** *n. v.t.* **1.** hit, esp. with the fists. —*n.* **2.** crawling mollusk leaving a slimy trail. **3.** bullet. **4.** false coin.

slŭg'gàrd, *n.* lazy person.

slŭg'gǐsh, *adj.* abnormally slow or lacking in vigor. —**slug'gish·ly**, *adv.* —**slug'gish·ness**, *n.*

slūice, *n.* **1.** artificial channel controlled by a gate. **2.** Also, **sluice gate,** gate controlling this channel.

slŭm, *n.* squalid home or residential area.

slŭm'bêr, *v.i.* **1.** sleep deeply. —*n.* **2.** deep sleep.

slŭmp, *v.i.* **1.** drop or sag heavily. —*n.* **2.** act or instance of slumping.

slûr, *v.t.*, **slurred, slurring,** *n. v.t.* **1.** say indistinctly. **2.** disparage. —*n.* **3.** indistinct speech. **4.** disparaging remark.

slŭsh, *n.* melting snow. —**slush'y**, *adj.*

slŭt, *n.* immoral or slatternly woman.

slÿ, *adj.*, **slyer** or **slier, slyest** or **sliest. 1.** cunning; tricky. **2.** gently mischievous. —**sly'ly, sli'ly**, *adv.* —**sly'ness**, *n.*

smǎck, *v.t.* **1.** separate noisily, as the lips. **2.** slap. —*v.i.* **3.** have a taste or suggestion. —*n.* **4.** act or instance of smacking. **5.** taste or suggestion. **6.** fishing boat.

smǎll, *adj.* **1.** little. **2.** of no great importance, value, etc. **3.** petty or mean. —*adv.* **4.** into small pieces. —*n.* **5.** narrow part, esp. of the back. —**small'ness**, *n.*

smǎll'pŏx'', *n.* contagious disease with fever and pustules as symptoms.

smârt, *adj.* **1.** severe, as a blow. **2.** intelligent or clever. **3.** briskly efficient. **4.** in style. —*n.* **5.** sharp, stinging pain. —*v.i.* **6.** feel such a pain. —**smart'ly**, *adv.* —**smart'ness**, *n.* —**smart'en**, *v.t.*

smăsh, *v.t.* **1.** break into fragments. —*n.* **2.** act or instance of smashing. **3.** serious automobile accident.

smăt'têr·ĭng, *n.* slight knowledge.

smēar, *v.t.* **1.** rub with greasy clinging material. **2.** slander. —*n.* **3.** smeared area. **4.** slander.

smĕll, *n.* **1.** sense perceived by the nose and olfactory organs. **2.** odor. —*v.t.* **3.** sense with the nose and olfactory organs. —*v.i.* **4.** have an odor.

smĕlt, *n., pl.* **smelts, smelt,** *v.t. n.* **1.** small northern salt-water fish. —*v.t.* **2.** melt or fuse so as to extract metal. **3.** extract from ore by melting or fusing. —**smelt'er,** *n.*

smīle, *v.i.,* **smiled, smiling,** *n. v.i.* **1.** assume a look of pleasure, etc. by upturning the corners of the mouth. **2.** look favorably. —*n.* **3.** smiling appearance.

smîrch, *v.t.* **1.** stain or soil. —*n.* **2.** stain.

smîrk, *v.i.* **1.** have an affected or self-satisfied smile. —*n.* **2.** such a smile.

smīte, *v.t.,* **smote, smitten** or **smiting.** *Archaic.* **1.** hit; strike. **2.** overcome with charm.

smĭth, *n.* metalworker.

smĭth'ÿ, *n., pl.* **smithies.** blacksmith's shop.

smŏck, *n.* loose garment covering the whole body.

smŏg, *n.* fog with smoke.

smōke, *n., v.,* **smoked, smoking.** *n.* **1.** unconsumed material emitted by a fire. —*v.i.* **2.** inhale and exhale smoke from smoldering tobacco, etc. —*v.t.* **3.** burn in order to inhale and exhale the smoke. **4.** treat with smoke. —**smok'y,** *adj.* —**smoke'stack'',** *n.*

smōk'êr, *n.* **1.** person who smokes. **2.** railroad car or compartment where smoking is permitted.

smōl'dêr, *v.i.* **1.** burn flamelessly. **2.** exist partly suppressed. Also, **smoul'der.**

smōōth, *adj.* **1.** without unevenness. **2.** without difficulty. **3.** without harsh or disturbing qualities. **4.** ingratiating. —*v.t.* **5.** make smooth. —**smooth'ly,** *adv.* —**smooth'ness,** *n.*

smŏth'êr, *v.t.* **1.** suffocate. **2.** cover completely.

smŭdge, *n., v.t.,* **smudged, smudging.** *n.* **1.** spot of smoke, dirt, ink, etc. —*v.t.* **2.** stain or treat with smoke, dirt, ink, etc.

smŭg, *adj.* excessively self-satisfied. —**smug'ly,** *adv.* —**smug'ness,** *n.*

smŭg'gle, *v.t.,* **-gled, -gling.** bring in or out secretly in violation of laws or regulations. —**smug'gler,** *n.*

smŭt, *n.* **1.** soot or smudge. **2.** obscenity. **3.** fungous plant disease. —**smut'ty,** *adj.*

snăck, *n.* small meal.

snăg, *n., v.,* **snagged, snagging.** *n.* **1.** projection that catches or tears. **2.** obstacle. —*v.t.* **3.** catch or damage, as with a snag.

snāil, *n.* crawling mollusk with a shell.

snāke, *n., v.i.* **snaked, snaking.** *n.* **1.** scaly reptile without limbs. —*v.i.* **2.** move or lie sinuously.

snăp, *v.,* **snapped, snapping,** *n., adj. v.i.* **1.** make a sharp clicking sound. **2.** go into or out of a close-fitting socket. **3.** break abruptly. **4.** bite. **5.** speak crossly and abruptly. —*v.t.* **6.** cause to snap. **7.** photograph. —*n.* **8.** act or instance of snapping. **9.** fastener that snaps shut. —*adj.* **10.** hasty, as a judgment.

snăp'drăg''ŏn, *n.* plant with flowers in spikes.

snăp'pĭsh, *adj.* short-tempered.

snăp'pÿ, *adj.* quick.

snăp'shŏt'', *n.* uncomposed photograph from a small, hand-held camera.

snāre, *n., v.t.,* **snared, snaring.** trap.

snârl, *v.i.* **1.** growl. —*v.t.* **2.** tangle.

snătch, *v.t.* **1.** grab. —*v.i.* **2.** reach suddenly or eagerly. —*n.* **3.** act or instance of snatching. **4.** fragment.

snēak, *v.i.* **1.** go furtively. —*v.t.* **2.** bring in or out furtively. —*n.* **3.** furtive, dishonest person. —**sneak'y,** *adj.*

snēak'êr, *n.* low, soft-soled shoe.

snēer, *v.i.* **1.** express contempt. —*n.* **2.** expression of contempt.

snēeze, *v.i.,* **sneezed, sneezing,** *n. v.i.* **1.** expel breath explosively and involuntarily. —*n.* **2.** act or instance of sneezing.

snĭck'êr, *n.* **1.** contemptuous, high-pitched laugh. —*v.i.* **2.** give such a laugh. Also, **snig'ger.**

snīde, *adj.* malicious, as a remark.

snĭff, *v.i.* **1.** inhale quickly through the

nose. **2.** exhale loudly through the nose. —*n.* **3.** act or instance of sniffing.

snif'fle, *v.i.* **1.** inhale through the nose. —*n.* **2. sniffles,** *Informal.* mild cold symptoms.

snip, *v.t.,* **snipped, snipping,** *n. v.t.* **1.** cut as with scissors. —*n.* **2.** snipped-off fragment. **3. snips,** shears.

snipe, *n., v.i.,* **sniped, sniping.** *n.* **1.** wading bird. —*v.i.* **2.** shoot from a hidden position. —**snip'er,** *n.*

snip'pet, *n.* small piece, as of information.

sniv'el, *v.i.* plead, complain, etc. in a whining tone.

snob, *n.* person with ostentatious likes and dislikes based on pretentious standards of excellence. —**snob'bish,** *adj.* —**snob'ber·y,** *n.*

snood, *n.* net covering the back of a woman's hair.

snoop, *Informal. v.i.* **1.** seek information furtively. —*n.* **2.** Also, **snoop'er,** person who snoops.

snooze, *v.i.,* **snoozed, snoozing,** *n.* nap.

snore, *v.i.,* **snored, snoring,** *n. v.i.* **1.** breathe noisily while sleeping. —*n.* **2.** sound of such breathing.

snor'kel, *n.* ventilating tube for a submarine, etc. under water.

snort, *n.* **1.** loud exhalation through the nose. —*v.i.* **2.** give such an exhalation.

snot, *n. Informal.* mucus from the nose.

snout, *n.* protruding front of an animal head.

snow, *n.* **1.** precipitation frozen in crystalline flakes. —*v.i.* **2.** precipitate snow. —**snow'drift'',** *n.* —**snow' fall'',** *n.* —**snow'flake'',** *n.* —**snow' storm'',** *n.* —**snow'y,** *adj.*

snow'ball'', *n.* **1.** ball of compacted snow. —*v.i.* **2.** increase with gathering speed.

snow'shoe'', *n.* webbed flat frame for supporting the foot on snow.

snub, *v.t.,* **snubbed, snubbing,** *n., adj. v.t.* **1.** refuse attention or respect to. —*n.* **2.** act or instance of snubbing. —*adj.* **3.** short and upturned, as a nose.

snuff, *v.t.* **1.** trim, as a burned wick. **2.** extinguish or eliminate. —*n.* **3.** powdered tobacco.

snuf'fle, *v.i.,* **-fled, -fling.** sniffle.

snug, *adj.,* **snugger, snuggest. 1.** cozy. **2.** neat. **3.** tight in fit. —**snug'ly,** *adv.*

snug'gle, *v.i.* **-gled, -gling.** cuddle or nestle.

so, *adv.* **1.** as stated or indicated. **2.** to such an extent. **3.** *Informal.* very; very much. **4.** in this way. —*conj.* **5.** therefore. **6.** in order that. —*adj.* **7.** true.

soak, *v.t.* **1.** cover with a liquid. **2.** absorb. —*v.i.* **3.** become absorbed. —*n.* **4.** act or instance of soaking.

soap, *n.* **1.** substance used in washing. —*v.t.* **2.** cover with soap. —**soap'y,** *adj.*

soar, *v.i.* **1.** rise into the air. **2.** glide or hover in the air.

sob, *v.i.,* **sobbed, sobbing,** *n. v.i.* **1.** weep convulsively. —*n.* **2.** sound of sobbing.

so'ber, *adj.* **1.** not drunk. **2.** serious or quiet. —*v.t.* **3.** make sober. **4.** cause grave feelings in. —**so'ber·ly,** *adv.* —**so''bri'e·ty, so'ber·ness,** *n.*

so-called, *adj.* called thus; used esp. when so named without justification.

soc'cer, *n.* a variety of football played without using the hands and arms.

so'cia·ble, *adj.* friendly; gregarious. —**so'cia·bly,** *adv.* —**so''cia·bil'i·ty,** *n.*

so'cial, *adj.* **1.** pertaining to society. **2.** sociable. —**so'cial·ly,** *adv.*

so'cial·ism, *n.* theory advocating public ownership of means of production, with work and products shared. —**so''cial· ist,** *n.* —**so''cial·is'tic,** *adj.* —**so'' cial·ize',** *v.t.*

so'cial·ite'', *n.* person in fashionable society.

so·ci'e·ty, *n., pl.* **-ties. 1.** group sharing a common culture, location, etc. **2.** human beings, in their relations with one another. **3.** world of the upper class. **4.** organization, esp. a professional or public-service one.

so''ci·ol'o·gy, *n.* study of society. —**so'' ci·o·log'i·cal,** *adj.* —**so''ci·ol'o·gist,** *n.*

sock, *n.* **1.** short stocking. —*v.t.* **2.** *Informal.* hit.

sock'et, *n.* a hollow part in which something is inserted and held.

sod, *n.* earth with growing grass.

so'da, *n.* **1.** drink with soda water. **2.** mixture of soda water, ice cream, and flavoring. **3.** chemical containing sodium.

so·dăl'ĭ·tỹ, *n.*, *pl.* -ties. Catholic religious or charitable society.

sŏdà wâtêr, *n.* water charged with carbon dioxide.

sŏd'dĕn, *n.* 1. stupefied. 2. soggy.

sō'dĭ·ŭm, *n.* alkaline chemical element.

sŏd·ó·mỹ *n.* abnormal sexual intercourse. —sod'o·mite, *n.*

sō'fà, *n.* wide, upholstered seat with a back and arms.

sŏft, *adj.* 1. yielding readily to pressure. 2. gentle. 3. quiet. 4. weak. 5. nonalcoholic. 6. permitting lathering, as water. —soft'ly, *adv.* —soft'ness, *n.* —soft'en, *v.t.*, *v.i.*

sŏft'băll'', *n.* baseball-like game using a softer ball.

sŏft'wāre, *n.* (computers) programming enabling a system to function.

sŏg'gỹ, *adj.* moist and heavy with absorbed liquid.

sōil, *v.t.* 1. dirty. —*n.* 2. earth. 3. sewage.

sō'joŭrn, *v.i.* 1. stay briefly. —*n.* 2. brief stay.

sŏl'àce *n.* comfort in unhappiness.

sō'làr, *adj.* pertaining to the sun.

sŏl'dêr, *n.* 1. alloy with low melting point for joining or patching metal. —*v.t.* 2. treat with solder.

sŏl'diêr, *n.* 1. member of an army. —*v.i.* 2. live as a soldier. —sol'dier·ly, *adj.* —sol'dier·y, *n.*

sōle, *n.*, *v.t.*, soled, soling, *adj.* *n.* 1. saltwater flatfish. 2. wearing surface on the bottom of a shoe. —*v.t.* 3. fit with soles. —*adj.* 4. single; only. —sole'ly, *adv.*

sŏl'ĕmn, *adj.* 1. serious; earnest. 2. formal. 3. sacred. —sol'emn·ly, *adv.* —so·lem'ni·ty, *n.*

sŏl'ĕm·nīze, *v.t.*, -nized, -nizing. observe or put into effect with a ceremony. —sol''em·ni·za'tion, *n.*

so·lĭc'ĭ·tör, *n.* 1. person who solicits. 2. English lawyer other than a barrister.

so·lĭc'ĭ·toŭs, *adj.* showing friendly concern. —so·lic'i·tous·ly, *adv.* —so·lic'i·tude'', *n.*

so·lĭc'ĭt, *v.t.* 1. request. 2. canvass for. —so·li''ci·ta'tion, *n.*

sŏl'ĭd, *adj.* 1. pertaining to or existing in three dimensions. 2. firm; substantial. 3. not hollow. 4. dense. 5. reliable. 6. entire. —*n.* 7. three-dimensional object. 8. non-fluid material. —sol'id·ly,

adv. —so·lid'i·ty, *n.* —so·lid'i·fy'', *v.t.*, *v.i.*

sŏl''ĭ·dăr'ĭ·tỹ, *n.* unity of purpose, resolve, etc.

sŏl''ĭd-stāte', *adj.* designating electronic circuitry that uses solid semiconductors, as transistors, to control current.

so·lĭl'o·quỹ, *n.*, *pl.* -quies. speech made to or as if to oneself. —so·lil'o·quize, *v.i.*

sŏl'ĭ·tāire'', *n.* 1. card game for one. 2. single gemstone in a setting.

sŏl'ĭ·tär''ỹ, *adj.* 1. single. 2. alone. 3. isolated.

sŏl'ĭ·tūde, *n.* state of being alone or isolated.

sō'lō, *n.* performance by one person, esp. in music or aviation. —so'lo·ist, *n.*

sŏl'stĭce, *n.* point when the sun is furthest from the equator; beginning of summer or winter.

sŏl'ū·ble, *adj.* able to be dissolved. —sol''u·bil'i·ty, *n.*

so·lū'tion, *n.* 1. means of solving a problem. 2. dispersal of one material in another. 3. material, usually a liquid, that results from this.

sŏlve, *v.t.*, solved, solving. explain or find means to overcome, as a problem. —solv'a·ble, *adj.*

sŏl'vĕnt, *n.* 1. material that dissolves another. —*adj.* 2. able to dissolve something. 3. able to meet one's debts. —sol'ven·cy, *n.*

sŏm'bêr, *adj.* gloomy. Also, som'bre. —som'ber·ly, *adv.*

sòm·brĕ'rō, *n.* broad-brimmed hat worn in Hispanic countries.

sòme, *adj.* 1. indefinite amount or number of. 2. certain unknown or unspecified. —*pron.* 3. unknown or unspecified number.

sòme'bŏdỹ'', *pron.* unspecified person. Also, some'one''.

sòme'hōw'', *adv.* in some way. Also, some'way''.

sòm'êr·säult'', *n.* 1. overturn forward or backward of a crouched person. —*v.i.* 2. execute a somersault.

sòme'thĭng, *n.* thing not specified.

sòme'tīme'', *adv.* 1. at an indefinite time. —*adj.* 2. *Archaic.* former.

sòme'tīmes'', *adv.* now and then.

sòme'whât'', *adv.* to some extent.

sòme'whère'', *adv.* at or to an unspecified place.

sŏm·năm'bū·lĭsm, *n.* sleepwalking. —som·nam'bu·list, *n.*

sŏm'nò·lėnt, *adj.* drowsy. —som'no·lence, *n.*

sòn, *n.* male offspring.

sò·nä'tà, *n.* instrumental musical composition.

sŏng, *n.* vocal musical composition.

sŏn'ĭc, *adj.* pertaining to sound.

sòn'-ĭn-lāw, *n.*, *pl.* sons-in-law. husband of one's daughter.

sŏn'nėt, *n.* poem with fourteen lines.

sò·nô'roŭs, *adj.* deep or rich in sound. —so·no'rous·ly, *adv.* —so·nor'i·ty, *n.*

soōn, *adv.* after a short time.

soōt, *n.* black particles in smoke. —soot'y, *adj.*

soōthe, *v.t.*, soothed, soothing. 1. free of agitation or annoyance. 2. relieve, as pain.

soōth'sāy''êr, *n.* person who claims to know the future.

sŏp, *n.* 1. morsel dipped in liquid. 2. something that appeases. —*v.t.*, *v.i.* 3. soak. —*v.t.* 4. absorb.

sò·phĭs'tĭ·cāte'', *v.t.* 1. make sophisticated. —*n.* 2. sophisticated person.

sò·phĭs'tĭ·cāt''ėd, *adj.* 1. acquainted with the ways of society. 2. technologically advanced. —so·phis''ti·ca'tion, *n.*

sŏph'ĭs·trў, *n.* specious, unsound reasoning. —soph'ist, *n.*

sŏph'ò·môre'', *n.* second-year secondary or college student.

sŏph'ò·môr'ĭc, *adj.* intellectually immature.

sŏ''pò·rĭf'ĭc, *adj.* 1. sleep-inducing. —*n.* 2. soporific drug.

sò·prăn'ō, *n.* singer in the highest vocal range.

sôr'cêr·êr, *n.* magician. Also, *fem.,* sor'cer·ess. —sor'cer·y, *n.*

sôr'dĭd, *adj.* 1. disgustingly mean or ignoble. 2. filthy.

sôre, *adj.*, sorer, sorest, *n. adj.* 1. aching or tender. 2. grieving. 3. causing trouble or annoyance. 4. *Informal.* angry. —*n.* 5. sore place on the body. —sore'ly, *adv.* —sore'ness, *n.*

sôr·ghum (sor'gəm), *n.* cereal grass made into syrup, etc.

sò·rôr'ĭ·tў, *n.*, *pl.* -ties. women's organization, esp. in a college.

sôr'rėl, *n.* 1. reddish-brown. 2. horse of this color. 3. plant with sour-tasting leaves.

sŏr'rōw, *n.* 1. great unhappiness or regret. —*v.i.* 2. feel sorrow. —sor'row·ful, *adj.* —sor'row·ful·ly, *adv.*

sŏr'rў, *adj.* 1. feeling regret. 2. feeling pity. 3. miserable.

sôrt, *n.* 1. type; classification. 2. quality. —*v.t.* 3. arrange by type.

sôr'tiè, *n.* 1. swift counterattack, as from a besieged place. 2. aerial combat mission.

SOS, call for help.

sō'-sō', *adj.* 1. not especially good or bad. —*adv.* 2. not especially well or badly.

sŏt, *n.* drunkard.

soŭf·flé', *n.* light, puffy baked dish.

sough (sōw, sŭf), *v.i.* rustle or sigh, as the wind.

soul, *n.* 1. non-material aspect of a person. 2. emotional or moral aspect of the personality. 3. feeling or sensitivity. 4. essence. 5. human being. —soul'ful, *adj.* —soul'less, *adj.*

soūnd, *n.* 1. air vibrations perceptible in part to the ear. 2. tone or noise that is heard. 3. inlet or channel of sea water. —*v.t.* 4. cause to make a sound. 5. measure the depth of. 6. determine the attitude or opinion of. —*v.i.* 7. make a sound. 8. seem. 9. sound like, imply. —*adj.* 10. healthy. 11. reasonable. 12. reliable. —sound'less, *adj.* —sound'proof'', *adj.* —sound'ly, *adv.* —sound'ness, *n.*

soŭp, *n.* savory, mainly liquid food.

soŭr, *adj.* 1. acid-tasting. 2. fermented beyond the normal state. 3. ill-tempered. —*v.i.* 4. become sour. —sour'ly, *adv.* —sour'ness, *n.*

sôurce, *n.* origin.

soūse, *v.t.*, soused, sousing. *n. v.t.* 1. immerse or steep. 2. pickle. —*n.* 3. pickled food. 4. act or instance of sousing.

soūth, *n.* 1. direction of the South Pole. 2. region located in this direction. —*adj.*, *adv.* 3. to or toward the south. 4. from the south, as a wind. —south'ward, *adv.*, *adj.* south'ern, *adj.* —south'ern·er, *n.* —south'er·ly, *adj.*, *adv.*

sŏŭth''ēast', *n.* direction halfway between south and east. —**south''east'**, *adj., adv.*

sŏŭth''wĕst', *n.* direction halfway between south and west. —**south''west'**, *adj., adv.*

sou·ve·nir (sōō'və nēr), *n.* thing to remember a place, event, etc. by.

sov·er·eign (sov'rən), *n.* **1.** monarch. **2.** former British gold coin. —*adj.* **3.** having supreme political power. **4.** politically independent. —**sov'er·eign·ty,** *n.*

sō'vĭ·ĕt, *adj.* **1.** Soviet, pertaining to the Soviet Union. —*n.* **2.** former Russian governmental council.

sŏw, *v.t.* **1.** plant, as seed. —*n.* **2.** sŏw, female hog. —**sow'er,** *n.*

sŏy'bēan'', *n.* plant grown for its seeds.

spä, *n.* resort with mineral springs.

spāce, *n., v.t.,* **spaced, spacing.** *n.* **1.** limitless three-dimensional expanse. **2.** specific area within this. **3.** outer space. **4.** distance. —*v.t.* **5.** separate, esp. at regular intervals.

spāce'crăft'', *n.* vehicle for exploration of outer space.

spāce'flīght'', *n.* flight through outer space.

spāce'shĭp'', *n.* vehicle for travel in outer space.

spāce'wälk'', *n.* personal movement away from a spacecraft in outer space.

spā'cioŭs, *adj.* amply extensive.

spāde, *n., v.t.,* **spaded, spading.** *n.* **1.** shovel with long shaftlike handle. **2.** spades, black suit of playing cards. —*v.t.* **3.** dig with a spade.

spá·ghĕt'tĭ, *n.* stringy pasta, usually served with a sauce.

spăn, *n., v.t.,* **spanned, spanning.** *n.* **1.** something between two supports. **2.** distance between the thumb and little finger, when extended. **3.** duration. **4.** pair of harnessed animals. —*v.t.* **5.** cross.

spăn'gle, *n., v.t.,* **-gled, -gling.** *n.* **1.** glittering decoration. —*v.t.* **2.** decorate with spangles.

spăn'iĕl, *n.* short-legged, long-eared dog.

spănk, *v.t.* slap on the behind.

spănk'ĭng, *adj.* brisk.

spâr, *v.i.,* **sparred, sparring,** *n.* *v.i.* **1.** box with the fists. —*n.* **2.** pole. **3.** crystalline rock.

spāre, *v.t.,* **spared, sparing,** *adj.,* **sparer, sparest.** *v.t.* **1.** use or spend with restraint. **2.** prevent from occurring, being known, etc., as something unpleasant. **3.** treat leniently. **4.** give without inconvenience. —*adj.* **5.** in reserve; extra. **6.** gaunt; lean.

spāre'rĭb'', *n.* pork rib cut at the thin end.

spârk, *n.* **1.** glowing, burning piece of matter from a fire. **2.** electric flash. **3.** trace, as of life.

spâr'kle, *v.i.,* **-kled, -kling,** *n.* *v.i.* **1.** emit or reflect small flashes of light. **2.** effervesce, as wine. **3.** glitter, as eyes. —*n.* **4.** act or instance of sparkling.

spâr'rŏw, *n.* bird of the finch family.

spârse, *adj.,* **sparser, sparsest. 1.** scattered. **2.** scanty. —**sparse'ly,** *adv.* —**sparse'ness, spars'i·ty,** *n.*

Spâr'tàn, *adj.* austere; disciplined.

spăsm, *n.* sudden and involuntary contraction of the muscles.

spăs·mŏd'ĭc, *adj.* **1.** in spasms. **2.** at unpredictable intervals. —**spas·mod'i·cal·ly,** *adv.*

spăs'tĭc, *adj.* characterized by spasms.

spăt, *n. Informal.* quarrel about a small matter.

spā'tiàl, *adj.* pertaining to space.

spăt'têr, *v.t.* splash, esp. in small amounts over a wide area.

spat·u·la (spach'ə lə), *n.* broad-bladed device for handling foods, etc.

spăwn, *n.* **1.** eggs of some animals, esp. fish and mollusks. —*v.t.* **2.** originate in abundance. —*v.i.* **3.** lay spawn.

spēak, *v.,* **spoke, spoken, speaking.** *v.i.* **1.** communicate with the voice. **2.** give a speech or lecture. —*v.t.* **3.** present by means of the voice. **4.** use in speaking, as a language.

spēak'êr, *n.* **1.** person who speaks. **2.** president of a legislature. **3.** loudspeaker.

spēar, *n.* **1.** long-handled, pointed weapon for hurling or thrusting. —*v.t.* **2.** wound with a spear. —**spear'head,** *n.*

spēar'mĭnt'', *n.* fragrant mint used as flavoring.

spē'ciàl, *adj.* **1.** distinct from all others. **2.** remarkable. —**spe'cial·ly,** *adv.*

spē'ciàl·īze, *v.i.,* **-ized, -izing.** study,

work, or trade in a special area. **—spe'**
cial·ist, *n.*

spē'ciàl·tȳ, *n., pl.* **-ties.** area of speciali-
zation.

spē'ciēs, *n.* group of fundamentally identical plants or animals.

spe·cie (spē'shē), *n.* coins.

spė·cif'ĭc, *adj.* **1.** detailed. **2.** exact. **3.**
characteristic.

spē'cĭ·fȳ'', *v.t.,* **-fied, -fying.** state or demand specifically.

spĕc'ĭ·mèn, *n.* typical example.

spē'cioŭs, *adj.* falsely seeming good or
valid. **—spe'cious·ly,** *adv.* **—spe'**
cious·ness, *n.*

spĕck, *n.* **1.** small particle or spot. **—***v.t.*
2. mark with specks.

spĕck'le, *n., v.t.,* **-led, -ling.** *n.* **1.** small
spot. **—***v.t.* **2.** mark with speckles.

spĕc'tà·cle, *n.* **1.** marvelous event or
sight. **2.** grandiose public entertainment. **3.** spectacles, eyeglasses.

spĕc·tăc'ū·làr, *adj.* marvelous or grandiose in appearance, etc.

spĕc'tā·tör, *n.* person who sees an event
or view.

spĕc'têr, *n.* ghost; apparition. Also,
spec'tre. —spec'tral, *adj.*

spĕc'trŏ·scōpe, *n.* instrument for producing and analyzing spectra. **—spec''**
tro·scop'ic, *adj.*

spĕc'trŭm, *n., pl.* **-tra, -trums.** group
of color bands produced when light is
dispersed by a prism.

spĕc'ū·lāte, *v.i.,* **-lated, -lating. 1.**
think contemplatively. **2.** undertake a
business risk in the hope of large profits. **—spec''u·la'tion,** *n.* **—spec''u·la·**
tive, *adj.* **—spec''u·la'tor,** *n.*

spēech, *n.* **1.** ability to speak. **2.** way of
speaking. **3.** something spoken. **4.** talk
to an audience. **—speech'less,** *adj.*

spēed, *n., v.,* **sped** or **speeded, speed-**
ing. *n.* **1.** swiftness of motion or action.
2. rate of motion or action. **—***v.t.* **3.** increase the speed of. **—***v.i.* **4.** move
swiftly. **5.** drive with excessive speed.
—speed'y, *adj.* **—speed'i·ly,** *adv.*
—speed'er, *n.*

spéed·ŏm'ė·têr, *n.* speed-registering device.

spĕll, *v.,* **spelled** or **spelt, spelling,** *n. v.t.*
1. name the letters of. **2.** comprise the
letters of. **3.** take over from, as in a
shared task. **—***v.i.* **4.** name the letters

forming ordinary words. **—***n.* **5.** en-
chantment. **6.** period of time.

spĕll'bŏund'', *adj.* entranced.

spĕnd, *v.t.,* **spent, spending. 1.** pay. **2.**
pass, as a period of time. **3.** use up or
exhaust. **—spend'er,** *n.*

spĕnd'thrĭft'', *n.* spender to excess.

spĕnt, *adj.* **1.** exhausted. **2.** used up or
worn out.

spêrm, *n.* male germ cell carried by semen. **—sper·mat'ic,** *adj.*

spĕw, *v.t., v.i.* vomit or pour with force.

sphēre, *n.* **1.** round solid with all radii
equal; ball. **2.** area of influence, activity, knowledge, etc. **—spher'i·cal,** *adj.*

sphēr'ŏĭd, *n.* approximately spherical
solid.

sphĭnx, *n. Classical mythology.* creature
with a human head and the body of a
lion.

spīce, *n., v.t.,* **spiced, spicing.** *n.* **1.** aromatic plant substance for seasoning,
preservation, etc. **—***v.t.* **2.** season or
treat with spice. **—spic'y,** *adj.*

spī'dêr, *n.* eight-legged predatory arachnid that captures insects in a web.
—spi'der·y, *adj.*

spĭg'ŏt, *n.* faucet.

spīke, *n., v.t.,* **spiked, spiking.** *n.* **1.**
large hammer-driven fastener. **2.**
pointed feature. **3.** long stalk bearing
grains or blossoms. **—***v.t.* **4.** fasten with
spikes. **5.** frustrate; thwart.

spĭll, *v.,* **spilled** or **spilt, spilling.** *v.t.* **1.**
lose, as from the tipping of a container.
2. shed, as blood. **—***v.i.* **3.** be lost, as
over the rim of a container.

spĭll'wāy'', *n.* channel letting excess water escape.

spĭn, *v.,* **spun, spinning,** *n. v.t.* **1.** make
from twisted yarn. **2.** make into yarn or
thread. **3.** make from secretions, as a
spider web. **—***v.t., v.i.* **4.** whirl. **—***n.* **5.**
whirling motion. **6.** *Informal.* brief
ride. **—spin'ner,** *n.*

spĭn'àch, *n.* plant with dark-green edible
leaves.

spĭn'dle, *n.* **1.** rod used in spinning
thread. **2.** any slender round rod.

spĭn'dlĭng, *adj.* lanky. Also, **spin'dly.**

spĭn'drĭft'', *n.* spray from wave crests.

spīne, *n.* **1.** Also called **spinal column.**
backbone; vertebrae. **2.** thorn. **—spin'**
al, *adj.* **—spin'y,** *adj.*

spīne'lĕss, *adj.* without courage.

spĭn'ĕt, *n*. small upright piano.

spĭn'stêr, *n*. unmarried woman past the normal marriageable age.

spī'rȧl, *n*. **1.** flat curve with steadily increasing radius. —*adj.* **2.** formed along such a curve. —*v.i.* **3.** move in such a curve. —spi'ral·ly, *adj.*

spīre, *n*. tall pyramidal structure forming the roof of a tower.

spĭr'ĭt, *n*. **1.** spiritual part of a person; soul. **2.** ghost. **3.** mood, sentiment, or intent. **4.** vigor or courage. **5.** spirits, **a.** state of mind. **b.** distilled alcoholic liquor. **6.** Holy Ghost. —*v.t.* **7.** smuggle. —spir'it·ed, *adj.* —spir'it·less, *adj.*

spĭr'ĭt·ū·ȧl, *adj.* **1.** pertaining to religion. **2.** pertaining to the soul. **3.** concerned with matters of the soul. —*n.* **4.** Negro religious song. —spir'it·u·al·ly, *adv.* —spir''it·u·al'i·ty, *n*.

spĭr'ĭt·ŭ·ȧl·ĭsm'', *n*. belief that the living and the dead can communicate. —spir'it·u·al·ist, *n*. —spir''it·u·al·is'tic, *adj.*

spĭr'ĭt·ū·oŭs, *adj.* alcoholic and distilled.

spĭt, *v.*, spat, spit, or (for 2) spitted, spitting, *n. v.t.* **1.** eject from the mouth. **2.** skewer. —*v.i.* **3.** eject saliva from the mouth. —*n.* **4.** saliva. **5.** long skewer. **6.** small peninsula.

spīte, *n.*, *v.t.*, spited, spiting. *n*. **1.** small-minded hostility or vengefulness. **2.** in spite of, notwithstanding. —*v.t.* **3.** offend or hurt out of spite. —spite'ful, *adj.* —spite'ful·ly, *adv.* —spite'ful·ness, *n*.

spĭt'tle, *n*. saliva.

spĭt·tōōn', *n*. receptacle for spit.

splăsh, *v.t.* **1.** cause to fly in various directions, as a liquid. —*v.i.* **2.** fly in various directions, as a liquid. —*n.* **3.** act, instance, or sound of splashing.

splăt·ter, *v.i.* be splashed.

splāy, *v.t.*, *v.i.* **1.** spread apart. —*adj.* **2.** spreading apart.

splēen, *n*. **1.** organ for modifying the blood structure. **2.** anger or irritation. —sple·net'ic, *adj.*

splĕn'dĭd, *adj.* **1.** magnificent. **2.** excellent. —splen'did·ly, *adv.* —splen'dor, *n*.

splīce, *v.t.*, spliced, splicing, *n. v.t.* **1.** join into a single piece. —*n.* **2.** joint created by splicing.

splĭnt, *n*. **1.** temporary reinforcement for a broken bone. **2.** thin slip of wood forming part of a basket.

splĭn'têr, *n*. **1.** sharp, broken fragment. —*v.t.*, *v.i.* **2.** break into splinters.

splĭt, *v.*, split, splitting, *n.*, *adj. v.t.*, *v.i.* **1.** break or pull in two. —*v.t.* **2.** share or divide. —*n.* **3.** act or instance of splitting. —*adj.* **4.** having been split.

splŏtch, *n.*, *v.t.* spot or stain. —splotch'y, *adj.*

splûrge, *v.i.*, splurged, splurging, *n*. *v.i.* **1.** spend money lavishly and showily. —*n.* **2.** act or instance of splurging.

splŭt'têr, *v.i.* **1.** babble, as with confusion or rage. —*n.* **2.** spluttering speech.

spoĭl, *v.*, spoiled or spoilt, spoiling, *n*. *v.t.* **1.** ruin. **2.** damage the character of with indulgence. —*v.i.* **3.** become unfit to eat, drink, or use. —*n.* **4.** spoils, loot. —spoil'er, *n*. —spoil'age, *n*.

spōke, *n*. shaft between the hub and rim of a wheel.

spōkes'mȧn, *n*. person who speaks for a group.

spō''li·ā'tion, *n*. looting.

spónge, *n.*, *v.*, sponged, sponging. *n*. marine animal. **2.** skeleton of this animal or an imitation in plastic, used to absorb water. —*v.t.* **3.** wipe with a sponge. —*v.i.* **4.** *Informal.* live at the expense of others. —spong'y, *adj.*

spóng'êr, *n*. *Informal.* one who lives at the expense of others.

spŏn'sôr, *n*. **1.** person who undertakes responsibility for another. **2.** godparent. **3.** advertiser who buys television or radio time. —*v.t.* **4.** act as sponsor for.

spŏn·tā'nē·oŭs, *adj.* **1.** occurring without an external cause. **2.** lively and natural in manner. —spon·ta'ne·ous·ly, *adv.* —spon''ta·ne'i·ty, spon·ta'ne·ous ness, *n*.

spōōk, *n*. *Informal.* ghost. —spook'y, *adj.*

spōōl, *n*. small drum on which thread, film, recording tape, etc. is wound.

spōōn, *n*. **1.** utensil for handling or stirring liquids or food. —*v.t.* **2.** handle or serve with a spoon.

spōōr, *n*. trail of animal scent.

spô·răd'ĭc, *adj.* occasional. —spo·rad'i·cal·ly, *adv.*

spôre, *n*. seedlike body from which fungi, mosses, etc. grow.

spôrt, *n*. 1. recreation involving bodily activity. 2. amusement. 3. plant or animal of abnormal form. —*v.i.* 4. play vigorously. —**sports'man**, *n*. —**sports'man·ship''**, *n*. —**sports'man·ly**, *adj*.

spôr'tĭve, *adj*. playful. —**spor'tive·ly**, *adv*. —**spor'tive·ness**, *n*.

spŏt, *n*., *v.t.*, **spotted**, **spotting**, *adj*. *n*. 1. round mark. 2. place. —*v.t.* 3. mark with spots. 4. notice. —*adj*. 5. immediate. 6. random, as a survey. —**spot'less**, *adj*. —**spot'ty**, *adj*. —**spot'ter**, *n*.

spôuse, *n*. husband or wife.

spôut, *n*. 1. channel for discharging liquids, grain, etc. —*v.t.* 2. emit with force. 3. recite enthusiastically.

sprâin, *v.t.* 1. injure by wrenching muscles or ligaments. —*n*. 2. injury so produced.

sprăt, *n*. small fish of the herring family.

sprăwl, *v.i.* 1. stretch out in an ungraceful way. —*n*. 2. act or instance of sprawling.

sprăy, *n*. 1. liquid driven in fine particles. 2. device for shooting such liquid. 3. small branch with flowers or leaves. —*v.t.* 4. drive as a spray. 5. apply spray to. —**spray'er**, *n*.

sprĕad, *v.*, **spread**, **spreading**, *n*. *v.t.*, *v.i.* 1. extend. 2. scatter or disperse. —*v.t.* 3. cover or apply thinly. —*n*. 4. extent. 5. distribution. 6. cloth for covering a bed. 7. soft food eaten with breadstuffs. —**spread'er**, *n*.

sprēe, *n*. occasion of uninhibited activity.

sprĭg, *n*. twig or spray.

spright'lў, *adj.*, **-lier**, **-liest**. lively. —**spright'li·ness**, *n*.

sprĭng, *n.*, *v.*, **sprang** or **sprung**, **sprung**, **springing**, *adj*. *n*. 1. season between winter and summer, beginning at the vernal equinox. 2. stream emerging from the earth. 3. resilient elastic device, e.g. a wire coil. 4. jump. —*v.i.* 5. jump. 6. arise or emerge. —*v.t.* 7. cause to act suddenly. 8. disclose suddenly. —**spring'time**, *n*. —**spring'y**, *adj*.

sprĭn'kle, *v.*, **-kled**, **-kling**, *n*. *v.t.* 1. scatter thinly. —*v.i.* 2. rain lightly. —*n*. 3. act or instance of sprinkling. 4. something sprinkled. —**sprink'ler**, *n*.

sprĭnt, *n*. 1. short run. —*v.i.* 2. make a short run. —**sprint'er**, *n*.

sprīte, *n*. elf or fairy.

sprŏck'ĕt, *n*. gear tooth engaging with a chain.

sprŏut, *v.i.* 1. begin to grow or send forth shoots. —*n*. 2. shoot that has sprouted.

sprūce, *n.*, *adj.*, **sprucer**, **spruciest**, *v.t.*, *n*. 1. coniferous evergreen. —*adj*. 2. tidy; neat. —*v.t.* 3. make tidy.

sprў, *adj.*, **sprier** or **spryer**, **spriest** or **spryest**. active; lively. —**spry'ly**, *adv*. —**spry'ness**, *n*.

spŭd, *n*. 1. type of spade. 2. *Informal*. potato.

spūme, *n*. foam.

spŭnk, *n*. *Informal*. courage. —**spunk'y**, *adj*.

spŭr, *n.*, *v.t.*, **spurred**, **spurring**. *n*. 1. sharp device for urging on a horse. 2. short extension. —*v.t.* 3. urge on.

spŭr'ĭ·oŭs, *adj*. false; fraudulent. —**spur'i·ous·ly**, *adv*. —**spur'i·ous·ness**, *n*.

spŭrn, *v.t.* reject with scorn.

spŭrt, *v.t.*, *v.i.* 1. shoot forth, as a liquid. —*v.i.* 2. have a sudden, short increase of energy or activity. —*n*. 3. act or instance of spurting.

spŭt'nĭk, *n*. man-made satellite.

spŭt'têr, *v.t.* 1. eject in drops or particles. —*v.i.* 2. splutter. —*n*. 3. act, instance, or sound of sputtering.

spū'tŭm *n*. saliva, etc. ejected from the mouth.

spў, *n.*, *pl.* **spies**, *v.* **spied**, **spying**. *n*. 1. person who attempts to obtain secret information. —*v.t.* 2. notice, esp. at a distance. —*v.i.* 3. act as a spy.

squăb, *n*. young pigeon.

squăb'ble, *n.*, *v.i.*, **-bled**, **-bling**. quarrel over trifles.

squăd, *n*. small group, as of soldiers.

squăd'rŏn, *n*. military unit of airplanes, ships, or cavalry.

squăl'ĭd, *adj*. 1. dirty or nasty. 2. in miserable condition. —**squal'id·ly**, *adv*. —**squal'id·ness**, *n*. —**squal'or**, *n*.

squăll, *n*. 1. strong, brief storm or gust of wind. —*v.i.* 2. weep loudly. —**squall'y**, *adj*.

squân'dêr, *v.t.* spend or use up wastefully.

squāre, *n.*, *adj.*, **squarer**, **squarest**, *v.t.*, **squared**, **squaring**. *n*. 1. right-angled figure with four equal sides. **2.** paved public area. **3.** tool for laying out or checking angled lines. **4.** *Math.* product of a number multiplied by itself. —*adj.* **5.** formed like a square. **6.** of an area equal to linear measure squared. **7.** honest or substantial. —*adv.* **8.** fairly; straightforwardly. —*v.t.* **9.** make square. **10.** *Math.* multiply by itself. —*v.i.* **11.** be consistent. —**square′ly,** *adv.*

squāre′-rĭgged′, *adj.* with sails rigged athwart the vessel. —**square′-rig′ger,** *n.*

squâsh, *v.t.* **1.** crush. —*n.* **2.** game played with rackets. **3.** gourdlike fruit.

squât, *v.i.,* **squatted** or **squat, squat- ting,** *n., adj. v.i.* **1.** crouch with the legs doubled under the body. **2.** settle without authority. —*n.* **3.** squatting position. —*adj.* **4.** Also, **squat′ty,** short and broad of figure. —**squat′ter,** *n.*

squaw̆, *n.* American Indian woman.

squaw̆k, *n.* **1.** loud, harsh cry. —*v.i.* **2.** utter a squawk.

squēak, *n.* **1.** shrill noise. —*v.i.* **2.** make squeaks. —**squeak′y,** *adj.*

squēal, *n.* **1.** shrill cry. —*v.i.* **2.** make squeals.

squēam′ĭsh, *adj.* **1.** easily disgusted. **2.** prudish. —**squeam′ish·ly,** *adv.* —**squeam′ish·ness,** *n.*

squēe′gēe, *n.* flat-bladed cleaner for plate glass.

squēeze, *v.t.,* **squeezed, squeezing,** *n.* *v.t.* **1.** press from both sides. **2.** cram. —*n.* **3.** act or instance of squeezing. **4.** hug.

squĕlch, *v.t.* **1.** silence with a crushing remark. —*n.* **2.** crushing remark.

squĭd, *n.* ten-armed sea mollusk.

squĭnt, *v.i.* **1.** see through partly-closed eyes. **2.** be cross-eyed. —*n.* **3.** act or instance of squinting.

squīre, *n., v.t.,* **squired, squiring.** *n.* **1.** country gentleman. **2.** gentleman escorting a lady. —*v.t.* **3.** escort.

squîrm, *v.i., n.* wriggle.

squîr′rĕl, *n.* bushy-tailed rodent living in trees.

squîrt, *v.t., v.i.* **1.** shoot, as a liquid. —*n.* **2.** jet of liquid. **3.** device for squirting.

stăb, *v.t.,* **stabbed, stabbing,** *n. v.t.* **1.** wound with a knife, etc. —*n.* **2.** wound or thrust from such a weapon.

stā′bil·īze, *v.t.,* **-lized, -lizing.** cause to be or remain stable. —**sta′bi·liz′′er,** *n.* —**sta′′bi·li·za′tion,** *n.*

stā′ble, *n., v.t.,* **-bled, -bling,** *adj. n.* **1.** Also, **stables,** accommodation for animals, esp. horses. —*v.t.* **2.** put into a stable, as a horse. —*adj.* **3.** resistant to displacement or change. —**sta·bil′i·ty,** *n.*

stăc·câ′tō, *adj. Music.* separated by brief silences.

stăck, *n.* **1.** orderly pile. **2.** Often, **stacks,** storage space for library books. **3.** chimney or funnel. —*v.t.* **4.** gather into stacks.

stā′dĭ·ŭm, *n., pl.* **-diums, -dia.** outdoor arena for spectator sports.

stăff, *n., pl.* **staves** or **staffs** (for 1), **staffs** (for 1, 3), *v.t. n.* **1.** stick carried in the hand. **2.** group of employees, esp. in administrative jobs. **3.** *Music.* group of five horizontal lines used in musical notation. —*v.t.* **4.** provide or work as a staff for.

stăg, *n.* **1.** adult male deer. —*adj.* **2.** for men only.

stāge, *n., v.t.,* **staged, staging.** *n.* **1.** distinct phase of a process, journey, etc. **2.** performers' platform. **3.** theatrical profession. —*v.t.* **4.** present on a stage. **5.** divide into phases.

stāge′cōach′′, *n.* horse-drawn coach for long-distance travel.

stăg′gêr, *v.i.* **1.** walk or stand unsteadily. —*v.t.* **2.** cause to stagger or falter. **3.** schedule over a range of times. —*n.* **4.** staggering gait.

stăg′ĭng, *n.* scaffolding.

stăg′nànt, *adj.* **1.** not flowing, as a body of water. **2.** undesirably inactive. —**stag′nate,** *v.i.* —**stag′′na′tion,** *n.*

stāid, *adj.* sober and quiet; sedate. —**staid′ly,** *adv.* —**staid′ness,** *n.*

stāin, *n.* **1.** discoloration. **2.** dye applied to wood or other materials. —*v.t.* **3.** discolor. **4.** apply dye to.

stāir, *n.* tall flight of steps. Also, **stairs, stair′way′′.** —**stair′well′′,** *n.*

stāir′cāse′′, *n.* interior stair.

stāke, *n., v.t.,* **staked, staking.** *n.* **1.** upright post. **2.** something wagered. **3. stakes,** something to be gained through risk. **4. at stake,** in danger of loss. —*v.t.* **5.** mark or secure with a stake. **6.** wager.

stá·lăc′tīte, *n*. icicle-like deposit of lime on a cave roof.

stá·lăg′mīte, *n*. conical deposit of lime on a cave floor.

stāle, *adj.*, staler, stalest, *v.i. adj.* 1. no longer fresh. —*v.i.* 2. become stale. —stale′ness, *n*.

stāle′māte″, *n*. 1. *Chess*. situation making a move impossible. 2. deadlock. —*v.t.* 3. halt through a stalemate.

stălk, *v.t.* 1. pursue stealthily. —*v.i.* 2. walk proudly or deliberately. —*n*. 3. plant stem.

stăll, *n*. 1. compartment. 2. stop because of malfunctioning. 3. *Informal*. pretext for delay. —*v.t.* 4. put or keep in a stall. 5. *Informal*. delay or keep waiting. —*v.i.* 6. stop because of malfunctioning.

stăl′lión, *n*. ungelded male horse.

stăl′wàrt, *adj.* 1. reliable through bravery, vigor, or faithfulness. —*n*. 2. stalwart person.

stăm′ĭ·nà, *n*. enduring vigor.

stăm′mêr, *v.i.* 1. speak with involuntary repetitions or pauses. —*n*. 2. stammering way of speaking.

stămp, *v.t.* 1. step on forcefully. 2. form or print with a stamp. 3. affix a stamp to. —*n*. 4. act or instance of stamping. 5. descending device for printing, embossing, cutting, etc. 6. adhesive paper proving payment of postage, etc. 7. type of personal character.

stăm″pēde′, *n*., *v.*, -peded, -peding. *n*. 1. mass flight, as of frightened cattle. —*v.i.* 2. flee in a stampede. —*v.t.* 3. cause to stampede.

stănce, *n*. 1. position of a standing person. 2. attitude or policy.

stânch, *adj.* 1. (stonch) stalwart. —*v.t.* 2. (stanch) stop from escaping, as blood. 3. stop from bleeding. —stanch′ly, *adv.* —stanch′ness, *n*.

stăn′chión, *n*. structural post.

stănd, *v.*, stood, standing, *n. v.i.* 1. be or become upright on the feet. 2. be located, as a tall object. 3. halt or refrain from moving. 4. take a position, as in a controversy. 5. have toleration. —*v.t.* 6. cause to be upright. 7. endure or tolerate. —*n*. 8. small platform or table. 9. small sales booth. 10. position, as in a controversy. 11. halt. 12. area of trees.

stăn′dàrd, *n*. 1. basis for evaluation or

measurement. 2. upright support. 3. military or personal flag. —*adj.* 4. of the normal or typical sort.

stăn′dàrd·īze, *v.*, -ized, -izing. *v.t.*, *v.i.* conform to a standard. —stan″dard·i·za′tion, *n*.

stănd′-bȳ, *n.*, *pl.* -bys, *adj. n*. 1. possible substitute. —*adj.* 2. for emergency use.

stănd′ĭng, *n*. 1. status. 2. duration. —*adj.* 3. upright. 4. permanent. 5. fixed in place. 6. stagnant.

stănd′poīnt″, *n*. viewpoint.

stăn′zà, *n*. set of verses.

stā′ple, *n.*, *v.t.*, -pled, -pling, *adj. n*. 1. fastener of bent wire or bar stock. 2. main or standard commodity. 3. textile fiber. —*v.t.* 4. fasten with staples. —*adj.* 5. main or standard. —sta′pler, *n*.

stâr, *n.*, *adj.*, *v.*, starred, starring. *n*. 1. heavenly body of incandescent gas. 2. figure with radiating points. 3. prominent or leading performer or player. —*v.t.* 4. have in a leading role. 5. mark with a star. —*v.i.* 6. have a leading role. —star′ry, *adj.*

stâr′board″, *Nautical*. *n*. 1. right-hand side, facing forward. —*adj.* 2. located on this side. —*adv.* 3. toward this side.

stârch, *n*. 1. tasteless vegetable substance found in potatoes, flour, etc. and used for stiffening. —*v.t.* 2. treat with starch. —starch′y, *adj.*

stāre, *v.i.*, stared, staring, *n. v.i.* 1. gaze with fixed, open eyes. —*n*. 2. act or instance of staring.

stâr′fĭsh″, *n*. star-shaped sea animal.

stârk, *adj.* 1. outright. 2. bleak. 3. stiff. —*adv.* 4. utterly.

stâr′lĭng, *n*. small bird of European origin.

stârt, *v.t.*, *v.i.* 1. begin. —*v.t.* 2. knock loose. —*v.i.* 3. jump with surprise. 4. move or arise suddenly. —*n*. 5. beginning. 6. sudden movement from surprise. 7. lead in a race or pursuit. —start′er, *n*.

stâr′tle, *v.t.*, -tled, -tling. disturb with sudden surprise.

stârve, *v.*, starved, starving. *v.t.* 1. kill or trouble with hunger. —*v.i.* 2. die or be troubled from hunger. —star″va′tion, *n*.

stāte, *n.*, *adj.*, *v.t.*, stated, stating. *n*. 1. condition. 2. politically autonomous or semi-autonomous region. **3.** civil government. **4.** pomp. —*adj.* **5.** formally conducted. —*v.t.* **7.** declare. —**state'hood''**, *n.*

stāte′hoūse'', *n.* U.S. state capitol.

stāte′lў, *adj.*, **-lier, -liest.** dignified. —**state′li·ness**, *n.*

stāte′mėnt, *n.* **1.** declaration. **2.** financial account or bill.

stāte-ȯf-thē-ârt, *adj.* of or pertaining to the highest level of technological achievement to date.

stāte′roōm'', *n.* private cabin on a ship.

stātes′man, *n.* person wise in government. —**states′man·ship**, *n.*

stăt′ĭc, *adj.* **1.** not moving. —*n.* **2.** unmoving electrical charges. **3.** radio interference caused by such charges.

stā′tion, *n.* **1.** building where a train, bus, etc. stops or originates. **2.** place for sending broadcasts. **3.** place of duty. **4.** place where one stops. **5.** position, as in society. —*v.t.* **5.** assign to a place.

stā′tion·ār''ў, *adj.* **1.** not in motion. **2.** not moving to another place.

stā′tion·ĕr, *n.* seller of paper and writing materials. —**sta′tion·er''y**, *n.*

stà·tĭs′tĭcs, *n.* collection and analysis of numerical data. —**sta·tis′ti·cal**, *adj.* —**sta·tis′ti·cal·ly**, *adv.* —**sta''tis·ti′cian**, *n.*

stăt′ū·ār''ў, *n.* statues collectively.

stăt′ūe, *n.* three-dimensional sculpture of a human or animal.

stăt′ū·ėsque′, *adj.* like a statue, esp. in posture.

stăt′''ū·ĕtte′, *n.* small statue.

stăt′ûre, *n.* **1.** tallness. **2.** eminence or achievement.

stătŭs quō, *Latin.* present condition.

sta·tus (stā′təs, stă′təs), *n.* **1.** position, as in society. **2.** state or condition.

stăt′ūte, *n.* law; ordinance. —**stat′u·to''ry**, *adj.*

stāunch, *n.*, *adj.* stanch.

stāve, *n.*, *v.t.*, **staved** or (for 3) **stove, staving.** *n.* **1.** curved board forming part of a barrel side. **2.** *Music.* staff. —*v.t.* **3.** break in or crush. **4.** repel.

stāy, *v.*, **stayed, staying.** *n.* *v.i.* **1.** remain or continue. —*v.t.* **2.** halt or delay. **3.** support or prop. —*n.* **4.** temporary residence. **5.** halt or delay. **6.** support or prop. **7.** fore-and-aft line supporting a mast.

stĕad, *n.* **1. in one′s stead,** in place of one. **2. in good stead,** advantageously.

stĕad′făst'', *adj.* **1.** unchanging. **2.** loyal or determined. —**stead′fast''ly**, *adv.* —**stead′fast''ness**, *n.*

stĕad′ў, *adj.*, **steadier, steadiest,** *v.*, **steadied, steadying.** *adj.* **1.** firm; unwavering. **2.** regular; unvarying. **3.** reliable. —*v.t.*, *v.i.* **4.** make or become steady. —**stead′i·ly**, *adv.*

stĕāk, *n.* slice of meat or fish for broiling or frying.

stĕal, *v.*, **stole, stolen, stealing.** *v.t.* **1.** take without right. —*v.i.* **2.** move silently.

stĕalth, *n.* secret activity. —**stealth′y**, *adj.* —**stealth′i·ly**, *adv.*

stĕam, *n.* **1.** gaseous or vaporized water. —*v.t.* **2.** treat with steam. —*v.i.* **3.** turn into or give off steam. —*adj.* **4.** working by steam. **5.** carrying steam. —**steam′y**, *adj.* —**steam′boat''**, *n* —**steam′ship''**, *n.*

stĕam′êr, *n.* **1.** vehicle operated by steam, esp. a ship or automobile. **2.** device for treating with steam.

stēed, *n.* riding horse.

stēel, *n.* **1.** iron alloyed with carbon. —*adj.* **2.** made of or resembling steel. —*v.t.* **3.** make resolute or courageous. —**steel′y**, *adj.*

stēel′yârd'', *n.* scale with a weighted arm.

stēep, *adj.* **1.** far from horizontal. —*v.t.* **2.** soak. **3.** absorb. —**steep′ly**, *adv.* —**steep′ness**, *n.*

stēe′ple, *n.* **1.** tall tower with a spire. **2.** spire.

stēe′ple·chāse'', *n.* horse race over obstacles.

stēer, *v.t.* **1.** direct or guide. —*n.* **2.** castrated bull.

stēer′ȧge, *n.* cheap, cabinless passenger accommodations on a ship.

stein, *n.* beer mug, esp. one of earthenware.

stĕl′lȧr, *adj.* pertaining to or suggesting stars.

stĕm, *n.*, *v.*, **stemmed, stemming.** *n.* **1.** support of a plant, leaf, or fruit. **2.** single support, as of a glass. **3.** uninflected part of a word. **4.** extreme forepart of a ship′s bow. —*v.t.* **5.** take the stem from. **6.** check, as liquid. **7.** make headway against. —*v.i.* **8.** be derived or originate.

stěnch, *n.* stink.

stěn'cĭl, *n., v.t.,* **-ciled, -ciling.** *n.* **1.** pierced sheet allowing paint or ink to mark an underlying surface. —*v.t.* **2.** paint or ink with a stencil.

stě·nŏg'rȧ·phў, *n.* shorthand writing. —**sten''o·graph'ic**, *adj.* —**ste·nog'ra·pher**, *n.*

stěn·tô'ri·ȧn, *adj.* very loud of voice.

stěp, *n., v.i.* **stepped, stepping.** *n.* **1.** movement of the walking foot. **2.** gait. **3.** raised surfaee on which one walks upwards. **4.** stage of a process. —*v.i.* **5.** walk. **6.** press down with the foot.

stěp-, by the remarriage of a parent: a prefix.

stěp'lăd''dêr, *n.* ladder with steps.

stěppe, *n.* plain, esp. in southeast Europe or Asia.

stěr'ē·ō, *n.* device for playing recorded or broadcast music in stereophonic sound.

stěr''ē·ȯ·phŏn'ĭc, *adj.* pertaining to realistic sound reproduction through two or more loudspeakers.

stěr'ē·ȯ·scōpe'', *n.* viewer using twin pictures and two eyepieces for a realistic effect.

stěr'ē·ȯ·tӯpe'', *n., v.t.,* **-typed, -typing.** *n.* **1.** process for casting printing plates. **2.** unimaginative or oversimplified conception. —*v.t.* **3.** reproduce by the stereotype process. **4.** conceive as a stereotype.

stěr'ĭle, *adj.* **1.** free of microbes. **2.** barren. **3.** uncreative or unimaginative. —**ster·il'i·ty**, *n.*

stěr'ĭ·līze'', *v.t.,* **-lized, -lizing.** make sterile. —**ster''i·liz''er**, *n.* —**ster''i·li·za'tion**, *n.*

stěr'lĭng, *adj.* **1.** composed of 92.5° silver. **2.** in British money. **3.** fine; noble.

stêrn, *adj.* **1.** grimly strict. —*n.* **2.** after end of a ship. —**stern'ly**, *adv.* —**stern'ness**, *n.*

stêr'nŭm, *n.* breastbone.

stěth'ȯ·scōpe'', *n.* instrument for listening to body sounds.

stē've·dôre'', *n.* handler of ship's cargoes.

stēw, *n.* **1.** dish of simmered food. —*v.t.* **2.** simmer to cook.

stēw'ȧrd, *n.* **1.** business manager, esp. on an estate. **2.** person in charge of food, supplies, and services. **3.** attendant. Also, *fem.,* **stew'ard·ess.**

stĭck, *v.,* **stuck, sticking,** *n. v.t.* **1.** pierce. **2.** thrust. **3.** cause to adhere. —*v.i.* **4.** fail to move properly. **5.** adhere. **6.** project. **7.** remain. —*n.* **8.** length of wood. **9.** short length. **10.** lever. **11.** walking cane.

stĭck'êr, *n.* **1.** person or thing that sticks. **2.** adhesive label.

stĭck'lêr, *n.* person who insists on something.

stĭck'ў, *adj.,* **stickier, stickiest. 1.** adhesive. **2.** *Informal.* **a.** muggy. **b.** troublesome or difficult.

stiff, *adj.* **1.** unbending. **2.** not moving easily. **3.** formal or distant in manner. —**stiff'ly**, *adv.* —**stiff'ness**, *n.* —**stif'fen**, *v.t., v.i.*

stī'fle, *v.,* **-fled, -fling.** *v.t.* **1.** smother. **2.** suppress. —*v.i.* **3.** suffer from lack of air.

stĭg'mȧ, *n., pl.* **-mata, -mas.** mark or indication of disrepute. —**stig'ma·tize''**, *v.t.*

stīle, *n.* **1.** steps over a fence. **2.** upright framing member.

stĭ·lĕt'tō, *n.* Italian dagger.

stĭll, *adj.* **1.** motionless or silent. **2.** tranquil. **3.** not sparkling, as wine. —*adv.* **4.** up to an indicated time. **5.** even more or even less. —*adv., conj.* **6.** nevertheless. —*v.t., v.i.* **7.** make or become still. —*n.* **8.** distillation apparatus. —**still'ness**, *n.*

stĭll'bôrn'', *adj.* **1.** born dead. **2.** abortive.

stĭlt, *n.* pole serving as an extension of the legs.

stĭlt'ĕd, *adj.* affectedly dignified.

stĭm'ū·lāte, *v.t.,* **-lated, -lating. 1.** cause to be active or more active. **2.** inspire. —**stim''u·la'tion**, *n.* —**stim'u·la·tive**, *adj.* —**stim'u·lant**, *n.*

stĭm'ū·lŭs, *n., pl.* **-li.** something stimulating.

stĭng, *v.t.,* **stung, stinging.** *n. v.t.* **1.** inflict a small, painful wound or blow. **2.** annoy or goad severely. —*n.* **3.** wound from stinging. **4.** sharp part for stinging. **5.** undercover operation run by a law enforcement agency to catch suspected criminals.

stĭn'gў, *adj.* characteristic of or suggest-

ing miserliness. —**stin'gi·ly,** *adv.*
—**stin'gi·ness,** *n.*

stink, *v.i.* **stank** or **stunk, stunk, stinking,** *n. v.i.* **1.** have a bad smell. —*n.* **2.** bad smell.

stint, *v.t.* **1.** limit. **2.** limit oneself. —*n.* **3.** limitation. **4.** task or work period.

sti'pend, *n.* regular payment.

stip'ple, *v.t.,* **-pled, -pling,** *n. v.t.* **1.** paint in small dots. —*n.* **2.** texture of small dots.

stip'u·late, *v.t.,* **-lated, -lating.** require as a condition. —**stip''u·la'tion,** *n.*

stir, *v.t.* **stirred, stirring,** *n. v.t.* **1.** mix by moving. **2.** move. **3.** rouse. —*n.* **4.** public excitement or commotion.

stir'ring, *adj.* **1.** exciting. **2.** active.

stir'rup, *n.* foothold hanging from a saddle.

stitch, *n.* **1.** single repeated operation in sewing, knitting, etc. **2.** sharp pain. —*v.t.* **3.** sew.

stock, *n.* **1.** goods, materials, etc. on hand. **2.** cattle. **3.** any of various parts of guns, implements, etc. **4.** ancestry. **5.** soup or stew base. **6.** dividend-bearing shares. —*adj.* **7.** standard; uniform. —*v.t.* **8.** keep for sale or use. **9.** supply with stock. **10.** supply with live fish, as a pond. —**stock'brok''er,** *n.* —**stock'hold''er,** *n.* —**stock'pile'',** *n.* —**stock'yard'',** *n.*

stock·ade', *n.,* *v.t.,* **-aded, -ading.** *n.* **1.** barrier of upright stakes. —*v.t.* **2.** put a stockade around.

stock'ing, *n.* clothing for the foot and lower parts of the leg.

stock'y, *adj.* broad and short of figure.

stodg'y, *adj.,* **stodgier, stodgiest.** heavy and boring. —**stodg'i·ly,** *adv.* —**stodg'i·ness,** *n.*

sto'ic, *n.* **1.** person who maintains indifference to pain or sorrow. —*adj.* **2.** Also, **sto'i·cal,** characteristic of a stoic. —**sto'i·cal·ly,** *adv.* —**sto'i·cism,** *n.*

stoke, *v.t.,* **stoked, stoking.** keep burning by adding fuel. —**stok'er,** *n.*

stole, *n.* scarflike garment worn behind the neck and over the shoulders.

stol'id, *adj.* showing no liveliness. —**stol'id·ly,** *adv.* —**sto·lid'i·ty,** *n.*

stom'ach, *n.* **1.** organ of digestion. **2.** tolerance. —*v.t.* **3.** take into the stomach.

4. tolerate. —**sto·mach'ic,** *adj.* —**stom'ach·ache'',** *n.*

stone, *n.,* *pl.* **stones,** *adj.,* *v.t.,* **stoned, stoning.** *n.* **1.** hard mineral substance. **2.** small piece of this. **3.** gem. **4.** pit of a fruit. **5.** hard object formed in a digestive organ. —*adj.* **6.** made of stone. —*v.t.* **7.** attack with stones. **8.** pit, as a fruit. —**ston'y,** *adj.*

stooge, *n. Informal.* **1.** comedian's assistant. **2.** underling or henchman.

stool, *n.* armless, backless seat.

stoop, *v.i.* **1.** bend forward. **2.** demean oneself. —*n.* **3.** bent posture. **4.** small porch.

stop, *v.,* **stopped, stopping,** *n. v.t.* **1.** prevent from starting or going on. **2.** clog or plug. —*v.i.* **3.** act or move no further or not at all. **4.** stay briefly. —*n.* **5.** act, instance, or place of stopping. **6.** device for controlling tone in a musical instrument. —**stop'page,** *n.*

stop'gap', *n., adj.* makeshift.

stop'ov·er, *n.* brief pause during a journey.

stop'per, *n.* **1.** plug, as for a bottle. —*v.t.* **2.** close with a stopper. Also, **stop'ple.**

stop'watch'', *n.* watch for measuring elapsed time.

stor'age, *n.* **1.** act or instance of storing. **2.** condition of being stored.

store, *n.,* *v.t.,* **stored, storing.** *n.* **1.** place for the sale of goods. **2.** place of storage. **3. stores,** supplies. **4. in store,** waiting in the future. —*v.t.* **5.** accumulate and save. **6.** put away for future use. —**store'front,** *n.* —**store'house'',** *n.* —**store'keep''er,** *n.* —**store'room,''** *n.*

stork, *n.* long-billed, long-legged wading bird.

storm, *n.* **1.** high wind, often with rain, snow, etc. **2.** sudden attack. —*v.t.* **3.** attack suddenly and violently. —*v.i.* **4.** blow as a storm. **5.** rage. —**storm'y,** *adj.* —**storm'i·ly,** *adv.*

sto'ry, *n.,* *pl.* **-ries.** **1.** account of events, often fictitious. **2.** newspaper report. **3.** *Informal.* lie. **4.** level in a building.

stoup (stoōp), *n.* basin for holy water.

stout, *adj.* **1.** sturdy. **2.** courageous; resolute. **3.** heavy-set. —*n.* **4.** dark, sweet, beerlike drink. —**stout'ly,** *adv.* —**stout'ness,** *n.*

stove, *n.* device for heating or cooking.

stōw, *v.t.* **1.** put in storage, as on a ship. —*v.i.* **2. stow away**, hide on a ship for a free passage. —**stow'age**, *n.* —**stow'a·way''**, *n.*

străd'dle, *v.t.*, **-dled, -dling**, *n. v.t.* **1.** stand over or mount with a leg on each side. —*n.* **2.** straddling posture.

strāfe, *v.t.*, **strafed, strafing.** fire down upon from an aircraft.

străg'gle, *v.i.*, **-gled, -gling.** stray or fall behind. —**strag'gler**, *n.*

straight, *adj.* **1.** from point to point in the shortest way; direct. **2.** unmodified or undiluted. **3.** in good order or condition. **4.** honest or unevasive. —*adv.* **5.** directly. **6.** without modification. **7.** honestly; without evasion. **8.** so as to be clearly understood. —**straight'ness**, *n.* —**straight'en**, *v.t.*, *v.i.*

straight'a·wāy, *n.* **1.** straight part of racetrack, etc. —*adv.* **2.** Also, **straight'way''**, at once.

straight''fôr'ward, *adj.* unevasive; honest.

strāin, *v.t.* **1.** tax the strength of. **2.** injure or distort through force. **3.** run through a filter or sieve. —*n.* **4.** major effort or burden. **5.** injury from straining. **6.** trying experience. **7.** melody. **8.** chain of ancestors or descendants. **9.** heredity. —**strain'er**, *n.*

strāit, *n.* **1.** narrow natural waterway. **2. straits**, difficulties.

strāit'ën, *v.t.* make narrow or meager.

strănd, *n.* **1.** length of fiber for twisting into rope. **2.** length of hair. **3.** river or ocean shore. —*v.t.* **4.** run aground. **5.** put in a helpless position.

strānge, *adj.*, **stranger, strangest. 1.** strikingly unfamiliar; odd. **2.** not known to one. —**strange'ly**, *adv.* —**strange'ness**, *n.*

strān'gêr, *n.* unfamiliar person.

strān'gle, *v.*, **-gled, -gling.** *v.t.* **1.** kill by choking. —*v.i.* **2.** choke. —**stran'gler**, *n.* —**stran''gu·la'tion**, *n.*

străp, *n.*, *v.t.*, **strapped, strapping.** *n.* **1.** band for fastening. —*v.t.* **2.** fasten with a strap.

stra·ta·gem (stra'tə jəm), *n.* plot; trick.

strà·tēg'ĭc, *adj.* **1.** pertaining to strategy. **2.** important in a strategy.

străt'è·gÿ, *n.*, *pl.* **-gies. 1.** art of planning military operations. **2.** stratagem or series of stratagems. —**strat'e·gist**, *n.*

străt'ĭ·fÿ, *v.*, **-fied, -fying.** *v.t.*, *v.i.* form in layers. —**strat''i·fi·ca'tion**, *n.*

străt'o·sphēre'', *n.* atmospheric zone 6 to 15 miles above the earth. —**strat''o·spher'ic**, *adj.*

strā'tŭm, *n.*, *pl.* **-ta, -tums.** layers, as of rock.

straw, *n.* **1.** stalk of threshed grain. **2.** quantity of such stalks. **3.** tube for sucking liquids.

straw'bĕr''rÿ, *n.*, *pl.* **-ries.** red fruit of a vinelike plant.

strāy, *v.i.* **1.** wander aimlessly. **2.** wander away. —*adj.* **3.** passing or occurring by chance. —*n.* **4.** animal that strays.

strēak, *n.* **1.** long mark. **2.** trait of character. **3.** brief period, as of luck. —*v.t.* **4.** mark with streaks. —*v.i.* **5.** move swiftly. **6.** run naked through a public place. —**streak'ing**, *n.*

strēam, *n.* **1.** body of running water. **2.** steady flow. —*v.i.* **3.** flow quickly and steadily. **4.** run with moisture.

strēam'êr, *n.* long, narrow flag or piece of bunting.

strēam'līne'', *v.t.* **1.** make with a form minimizing air or water resistance. **2.** purge of unnecessary elements.

strēet, *n.* road in an urban area.

strēet'câr'', *n.* rail car for transportation along streets.

strĕngth, *n.* **1.** power of the muscles. **2.** resistance to force. **3.** ability of the mind. **4.** purity.

strĕngth'ën, *v.t.*, *v.i.* make or become stronger.

strĕn'ū·oŭs, *adj.* **1.** involving great effort. **2.** vigorous.

strĕss, *n.* **1.** emphasis. **2.** difficulties. **3.** force causing a strain. —*v.t.* **4.** put a stress on.

strĕtch, *v.t.*, *v.i.* **1.** extend or spread. **2.** strain, as a muscle. **3.** pull taut. —*n.* **4.** act or instance of stretching. **5.** unbroken extent.

strĕtch'êr, *n.* **1.** device for carrying a sick person lying down. **2.** device for stretching.

strĕw, *v.t.*, **strewed, strewed** or **strewn, strewing.** scatter.

strī'āt·ėd, *adj.* with closely-spaced grooves or furrows. —**stri'a'tion**, *n.*

strĭct, *adj.* **1.** demanding exact conformity. **2.** conforming exactly. —**strict'ly**, *adv.* —**strict'ness**, *n.*

stric′tûre, *n.* adverse criticism.

strīde, *v.i.,* **strode, stridden, striding,** *n. v.i.* **1.** walk with long steps. —*n.* **2.** long step. **3.** distance covered by such a step.

strī′dènt, *adj.* loud and harsh.

strīfe, *n.* conflict.

strīke, *v.,* **struck, struck** or **stricken, striking,** *n. v.t.* **1.** hit. **2.** make an impression on. **3.** afflict. **4.** discover, as a mineral. **5.** ignite, as a match. —*v.i.* **6.** stop work to enforce demands. —*n.* **7.** act or instance of striking. **8.** *Baseball.* failure to bat. **9.** *Bowling.* perfect score with the first bowl. —**strik′er,** *n.*

strīk′ĭng, *adj.* remarkable.

strĭng, *n., v.t.,* **strung, stringing.** *n.* **1.** thin cord. **2.** cord on a musical instrument. **3. strings,** musical instruments using such cords. **4.** series or row. —*v.t.* **5.** furnish with strings. **6.** hang from a cord. **7.** set in a series or row. —**stringed,** *adj.* —**string′y,** *adj.*

strĭng bēan, bean with edible pods.

strĭn′gènt, *adj.* very strict. -**strin′gent·ly,** *adv.* —**strin′gen·cy,** *n.*

strĭp, *n., v.t.,* **stripped, stripping.** *n.* **1.** long narrow piece. —*v.t.* **2.** remove the clothing or covering from. **3.** remove from an underlying surface. **4.** steal or confiscate the possessions of.

strīpe, *n.* **1.** long, broad mark. **2.** sort or kind. —*v.t.* **3.** mark with stripes.

strĭp′lĭng, *n.* boy.

strīve, *v.i.,* **strove, striven, striving.** try hard; strain.

strōke, *v.t.,* **stroked, stroking,** *n. v.t.* **1.** rub or graze gently. —*n.* **2.** act or instance of stroking. **3.** blow. **4.** single movement that is repeated. **5.** sudden attack of illness, esp. apoplexy. **6.** sudden occasion, as of luck. **7.** line made by a pen or pencil. **8.** way of swimming.

strōll, *v.i.* **1.** walk idly. **2.** wander. —**strol′ler,** *n.*

strŏng, *adj.* having strength. —**strong′ly,** *adv.*

strŏng′hōld′′, *n.* place secure against attack.

strŏp, *n., v.t.,* **stropped, stropping.** *n.* **1.** leather strap for sharpening. —*v.t.* **2.** sharpen with a strop.

strŭc′tûre, *n.* **1.** part of a building giving strength. **2.** something built. **3.** basic form, as of a composition. —**struc′tur·al,** *adj.* —**struc′tur·al·ly,** *adv.*

strŭg′gle, *v.i.,* **-gled, -gling,** *n. v.i.* **1.** strive. **2.** fight. —*n.* **3.** strenuous effort. **4.** fight.

strŭm, *v.t.* **strummed, strumming.** play lightly or carelessly, as a piano or plucked string instrument.

strŭt, *v.i.,* **strutted, strutting,** *n. v.i.* **1.** walk affectedly. —*n.* **2.** act or instance of struggling. **3.** postlike brace.

strych·nine (strik′nin), *n.* poisonous alkaloid.

stŭb, *n., v.t.,* **stubbed, stubbing.** *n.* **1.** short remnant. **2.** stump. —*v.t.* **3.** ram against something, esp. a toe.

stŭb′ble, *n.* **1.** plant stalks mown short. **2.** short growth of beard.

stŭb′bŏrn, *adj.* refusing to obey, give up, etc. —**stub′born·ly,** *adv.* —**stub′born·ness,** *n.*

stŭc′cō, *n., pl.* **-coes, cos,** *v.t.,* **-coed, -coing.** *n.* **1.** coarse exterior plaster. **2.** fine interior plaster. —*v.t.* **3.** cover with stucco.

stŭd, *n., v.t.,* **studded, studding.** *n.* **1.** projecting feature. **2.** upright wall-framing member. **3.** buttonlike fastener. **4.** collection of horses. **5.** male animal, esp. a horse, for breeding. —*v.t.* **6.** furnish or sprinkle with or as if with studs.

stū′dènt, *n.* person who studies.

stŭd′iēd, *adj.* intentional.

stū′dĭ·ō, *n.* **1.** artist's workplace. **2.** room for television or radio performers. **3.** place for television or radio performers. **4.** place for making motion pictures.

stū′dĭ·oŭs, *adj.* studying diligently. —**stu′di·ous·ly,** *adv.*

stŭd̄ÿ, *n., pl.* **studies,** *v.t.,* **studied, studying.** *n.* **1.** methodical acquisition of skill or knowledge. **2.** subject of such activity. **3.** room for reading or writing. **4.** deep thought. —*v.t.* **5.** make a subject of study.

stŭff, *n.* **1.** material. **2.** assorted or worthless objects or materials. —*v.t.* **3.** fill under pressure.

stŭff′ĭng, *n.* material stuffed into a hollow object.

stŭff′ÿ, *adj.,* **stuffier, stuffiest. 1.** dull and formal. **2.** lacking fresh air.

stul′ti·fȳ, *v.t.*, **-fied, -fying.** cause to seem foolish.

stŭm′ble, *v.i.*, **-bled, -bling.** trip and begin to fall.

stŭmp, *n.* **1.** remnant of something cut off. —*v.t.* **2.** baffle. —*v.i.* **3.** walk ponderously. **4.** travel on a political campaign.

stŭn, *v.t.*, **stunned, stunning. 1.** halt with amazement. **2.** knock unconscious.

stŭnt, *n.* **1.** act displaying skill. —*v.t.* **2.** hinder in growing.

stū′pe·fȳ, *v.t.*, **-fied, -fying. 1.** put in a stupor. **2.** amaze. —**stu′′pe·fac′tion**, *n.*

stū·pĕn′doŭs, *adj.* astounding.

stū′pĭd, *adj.* **1.** low in intelligence. **2.** pointless. —**stu·pid′ly**, *adv.* —**stu·pid′i·ty**, *n.*

stū′pŏr, *n.* unconscious or semiconscious state.

stûr′dȳ, *n.* **1.** strong. **2.** vigorous. —**stur′di·ly**, *adv.* —**stur′di·ness**, *n.*

stûr′geȯn, *n.* large fish whose roe is caviar.

stŭt′têr, *v.i.*, *n.* stammer.

stȳ, *n.*, *pl.* **sties. 1.** pig shelter. **2.** swollen inflammation of the eyelid.

stȳle, *n.*, *v.t.*, **styled, styling.** *n.* **1.** manner of artistic composition, writing, living, etc. **2.** kind or variety. **3.** elegance. **4.** formal name. —*v.t.* **5.** apply a style to. —**sty·lis′tic**, *adj.*

stȳl′ĭsh, *adj.* in style; elegant.

stȳl′ĭst, *n.* artist as a possessor as a style.

stȳ′lŭs, *n.* **1.** pointed writing instrument. **2.** phonograph needle.

stȳ′miĕ, *v.t.*, **-mied, -mying.** hinder.

stȳp′tĭc, *adj.* stopping the flow of blood.

suâve (swahv), *adj.* smoothly polite. —**suave′ly**, *adv.* —**suav′i·ty, suave′ness**, *n.*

sŭb′cȯm·mĭt′′tēe, *n.* committee reporting to a committee.

sŭb·cȯn′scioŭs, *n.* **1.** part of the mind beyond consciousness. —*adj.* **2.** pertaining to this part of the mind. —**sub·con′scious·ly**, *adv.*

sŭb·cȯn′ti·nėnt, *n.* large land mass within a continent.

sŭb′di·vīde′′, *v.t.*, **-vided, -viding.** divide still further. —**sub′di·vi′′sion**, *n.*

sŭb·dūe′, *v.t.*, **-dued, -duing. 1.** overcome. **2.** lower in intensity.

sŭb′jĕct, *n.* **1.** thing thought, written, etc. about. **2.** person or thing acted upon. **3.** person ruled by a government. **4.** *Grammar.* person or thing about which a sentence tells. —*adj.* **5.** being a subject. **6.** exposed to a specified treatment. —*v.t.* **7.** **sŭb·jĕct′**, submit to a specified treatment. —**sub·jec′tion**, *n.*

sŭb·jĕc′tĭve, *adj.* existing or originating in one person's mind. —**sub·jec′tive·ly**, *adv.* —**sub′′jec·tiv′i·ty**, *n.*

sŭb·joȋn′, *v.t.* added at the end.

sŭb′ju·gāte′′, *v.t.*, **-gated, -gating.** conquer. —**sub′′ju·ga′tion**, *n.*

sŭb·jŭnc′tĭve, *Grammar.* *adj.* **1.** pertaining to a verbal mode of possibility, etc. —*n.* **2.** subjunctive mode.

sŭb·lēase, *n.*, *v.t.*, **-leased, -leasing.** *n.* **1.** lease from a tenant. —*v.t.* **2.** rent with such a lease.

sŭb·lĕt′, *v.t.*, **-letted, -letting.** sublease.

sŭb·li·māte′, *v.t.*, **-mated, -mating.** *n.* *v.t.* **1.** divert into a more acceptable form. **2.** sublime. —*n.* (sub′lə mət) **3.** product of subliming. —**sub′′li·ma′tion**, *n.*

sŭb·līme′, *adj.*, *n.*, *v.t.*, **-limed, -liming.** *adj.* **1.** noble and exalted. —*n.* **2.** realm of sublime things. —*v.t.* **3.** vaporize, then solidify. —**sub·lime′ly**, *adv.* —**sub·lim′i·ty**, *n.*

sŭb′ma·rïne′′, *n.* **1.** underwater vessel. —*adj.* **2.** undersea. **3.** pertaining to submarines.

sŭb·mêrge′, *v.*, **-merged, -merging.** *v.i.* sink into a liquid. —**sub·mer′gence**, *n.*

sŭb·mêrse′, *v.t.*, **-mersed, -mersing.** submerge. —**sub·mer′sion**, *n.* —**sub·mers′i·ble**, *adj.*

sŭb·mĭt′, *v.*, **-mitted, -mitting.** *v.t.* **1.** offer, as in surrender. **2.** offer for consideration. **3.** subject to a specified treatment. —*v.i.* **4.** surrender or yield oneself. —**sub·mis′sion**, *n.* —**sub·mis′sive**, *adj.*

sŭb·ôr′di·nāte′′, *v.t.* **-ated, -ating,** *adj.*, *n.*, *v.t.* **1.** subject to the will of another. —*adj.* (sub ôr′də nət) **2.** lower in rank or importance. —*n.* **3.** someone or something subordinate. —**sub·or′′di·na′tion**, *n.*

sŭb·ôrn′, *v.t.* induce to commit a wrong.

sub·poe·na (sə pē′nə), *n.*, *v.t.*, **-naed,**

-naeing. *n.* **1.** summons to court. —*v.t.* **2.** serve with such a summons.

sub·scribe', *v.,* **-scribed, -scribing.** *v.i.* **1.** pay for continued supply of a periodical, service, etc. **2.** promise to contribute money. **3.** agree. —*v.t.* **4.** sign. —**sub·scrib'er,** *n.* —**sub·scrip'tion,** *n.*

sub·se·quent, *adj.* occurring after. —**sub'se·quent·ly,** *adv.*

sub·sêr'vi·ent, *adj.* **1.** servile. **2.** subordinate. —**sub·ser'vi·ence,** *n.* —**sub·ser'vi·ent·ly,** *adv.*

sub·side', *v.i.,* **-sided, -siding. 1.** settle or sink. **2.** die down. —**sub·sid'ence,** *n.*

sub·sid'i·ar''y, *adj., n., pl.* **-ries.** *adj.* **1.** subordinate or auxiliary. —*n.* **2.** subsidiary entity.

sub'si·dy, *n., pl.* **-dies.** monetary aid, esp. from a government. —**sub'si·dize'',** *v.t.*

sub·sist', *v.i.* **1.** exist. **2.** maintain one's existence. —**sub·sist'ence,** *n.*

sub'stance, *n.* **1.** material. **2.** essential part or aspect. **3.** basic meaning.

sub·stan'tial, *adj.* **1.** solid. **2.** considerable in amount. **3.** material. **4.** essential. **5.** important in the community. —**sub·stan'tial·ly,** *adv.*

sub·stan'ti·ate, *v.t.,* **-ated, -ating.** show to be true. —**sub·stan''ti·a'tion,** *n.*

sub'stan·tive, *n.* **1.** noun or word used as a noun. —*adj.* **2.** having substance

sub'sti·tute, *v.,* **-tuted, -tuting.** *n. v.t., v.i.* **1.** put or act in another's place. —*n.* **2.** person or thing that substitutes. —**sub''sti·tu'tion,** *n.*

sub'têr·fuge'', *n.* evasive trick or trickery.

sub''têr·rā'nē·an, *adj.* underground.

sub'tle, *adj.* **1.** highly sensitive. **2.** scarcely perceived. **3.** cunning. —**sub'tly,** *adv.* —**sub'tle·ty,** *n.*

sub·tract', *v.t.* remove, as one quantity from another. —**sub·trac'tion,** *n.*

sub·trop'i·cal, *adj.* close to the tropics.

sub'urb, *n.* community adjoining or dependent on a city. —**sub·ur'ban,** *adj.*

sub·vêrt', *v.t.* undermine or corrupt. —**sub·ver'sion,** *n.* —**sub·ver'sive,** *adj., n.*

sub'wāy'', *n.* **1.** underground railroad. **2.** pedestrian underpass.

suc·ceed', *v.i.* **1.** obtain good results. **2.** attain success. —*v.t.* **3.** follow in an office, inheritance, etc.

suc·cess', *n.* **1.** favorable outcome of an attempt. **2.** commonly sought goals. **3.** person or thing that attains success. —**suc·cess'ful,** *adj.*

suc·ces'sion, *n.* **1.** sequential order of things. **2.** act of succeeding another. —**suc·ces'sive,** *adj.* —**suc·ces'sive·ly,** *adv.* —**suc·ces'sor,** *n.*

suc·cinct (suk sinkt'), *adj.* restricted to essential information. —**suc·cinct'ly,** *adv.* —**suc·cinct'ness,** *n.*

suc'cör, *n., v.t.* help in need.

suc'co·tash, *n.* corn and lima beans cooked together.

suc'cu·lent, *adj.* juicy. —**suc'cu·lence,** *n.*

suc·cumb', *v.i.* **1.** yield. **2.** die.

such, *adj.* **1.** of the kind mentioned. **2.** so much of. —*adv.* **3.** so greatly. —*pron.* **4.** the kind mentioned. **5.** such a person or thing.

suck, *v.t.* **1.** draw by suction. **2.** absorb by capillarity. **3.** lick and absorb.

suck'êr, *n.* **1.** person or thing that sucks. **2.** fresh-water fish. **3.** lollipop. **4.** *Informal.* person easily cheated.

suck'le, *v.t.,* **-led, -ling.** feed at the breast.

suck'ling, *n.* unweaned child or animal.

suc'tion, *n.* forcing of a fluid into a vacuum by atmospheric pressure.

sud'den, *adj.* quick and unexpected. —**sud'den·ly,** *adv.* —**sud'den·ness,** *n.*

suds, *n. pl.* **1.** fine soap bubbles. **2.** soapy water.

sue, *v.,* **sued, suing.** *v.t.,* **1.** claim damages from in court. —*v.i.* **2.** make an appeal.

suede (swād), *n.* soft leather with a nap.

su'et, *n.* hard animal fat.

suf'fêr, *v.t.* **1.** undergo. **2.** permit or tolerate. —**suf'fer·er,** *n.*

suf'fêr·ance, *n.* **1.** tacit permission. **2.** endurance.

suf·fice', *v.i.,* **-ficing.** be enough.

suf·fi'cient, *adj.* enough. **-suf·fi'cient·ly,** *adv.* —**suf·fi'cien·cy,** *n.*

suf'fix, *n. Grammar.* ending added to a word to give a new meaning.

suf'fo·cate, *v.,* **-cated, -cating.** *v.t., v.i.* cut off or be without air for breathing. —**suf''fo·ca'tion,** *n.*

suf'frage, *n.* right to vote.

sŭf·fūse′, *v.t.* spread light, color, etc. over.

sŭg′ar, *n.* **1.** sweet carbohydrate. —*v.t.* **2.** add sugar to. —**sug′ar·y**, *adj.*

sŭg·gĕst′, *v.t.* **1.** offer as advice. **2.** propose. **3.** imply. —**sug·ges′tion**, *n.*

sŭg·gĕs′tĭve, *adj.* full of implication, esp. of impropriety.

sū′ĭ·cīde″, *n.* **1.** willful killing of oneself. **2.** person who kills himself willfully. —**su″i·cid′al**, *adj.*

sūit, *n.* **1.** complete set of clothes. **2.** lawsuit. **3.** appeal. **4.** playing cards with a common symbol. —*v.t.* **5.** satisfy; please. **6.** adapt. **7.** clothe.

sūit′a·ble, *adj.* right; appropriate. —**suit′a·bly**, *adv.*

sūit′cāse″, *n.* travel case for clothes, etc.

suite (swēt), *n.* **1.** apartment of connected rooms. **2.** set of musical compositions.

sūit′ör, *n.* wooer.

sŭl′fāte, *n.* salt of sulfuric acid.

sŭl·fūr′ĭc, *adj.* pertaining to or containing sulfur. Also, **sul′fur·ous**.

sŭlk, *v.i.* **1.** be angry and aloof. —*n.* **2.** fit of sulking. —**sulk′y**, *adj.*

sŭl′lėn, *adj.* **1.** quietly resentful. **2.** gloomy. —**sul′len·ly**, *adv.* —**sul′len·ness**, *n.*

sŭl′lỹ, *v.t.*, -**lied**, -**lying**. **1.** disgrace. **2.** soil or pollute.

sŭl′phŭr, *n.* sulfur.

sŭl′tàn, *n.* Muslim ruler.

sŭl′trỹ, *adj.*, -**trier**, -**triest**. **1.** hot and humid. **2.** sexually inviting. —**sul′tri·ness**, *n.*

sŭm, *n.*, *v.t.*, **summed, summing**. *n.* **1.** number obtained by addition. **2. in sum**, as a summary. —*v.t.* **3.** add up. **4.** summarize.

sū′măc, *n.* small tree. Also, **su′mach**.

sŭm′ma·rīze, *v.t.*, -**rized**, -**rizing**. present in a summary.

sŭm′ma·rỹ, *n.*, *pl.* -**ries**, *adj.* *n.* **1.** presentation of essential information only. —*adj.* **2.** without formalities or preliminaries. —**sum·ma′ri·ly**, *adv.*

sŭm·mā′tion, *n.* concluding summary.

sŭm′mêr, *n.* **1.** season between spring and autumn, beginning at the summer solstice. —*v.i.* **2.** spend the summer. —**sum′mer·y**, *adj.*

sŭm′mĭt, *n.* highest point.

sŭm′mŏn, *v.t.* order or ask to come.

sŭm′mŏns, *n.* **1.** order to appear in court. **2.** order or request to come.

sŭmp, *n.* pit for collecting ground water.

sŭmp′tū·oŭs, *adj.* costly and luxurious. —**sump′tu·ous·ly**, *adv.* —**sump′tu·ous·ness**, *n.*

sŭn, *n.*, *v.t.*, **sunned, sunning**. *n.* **1.** star of the solar system. **2.** rays from this star. —*v.t.* **3.** expose to the sun. —**sun′ny**, *adj.* —**sun′beam″**, *n.* —**sun′light″**, *n.* —**sun′lit″**, *adj.*

sŭn′bāthe″, *v.i.*, -**bathed**, -**bathing**. lie down to receive solar rays. —**sun′bath**, *n.*

sŭn′bûrn″, *n.*, *v.t.*, -**burned**, -**burning**. burn from or with the rays of the sun.

sŭn′dāe, *n.* ice cream topped with flavored syrup.

Sŭn′dāy, *n.* first day of the week.

sŭn′dī″al, *n.* instrument telling time by the shadow of a pointer.

sŭn′dŏwn″, *n.* time of sunset.

sun·dry (sun′drē), *adj.* various.

sŭn′flŏw″êr, *n.* tall plant with large, yellow-petaled blossoms.

sŭn′glăss″ės, *n.*, *pl.* spectacles tinted to weaken the sun's rays.

sŭn′lămp″, *n.* ultraviolet lamp.

sŭn′rīse″, *n.* rise of the sun above the horizon.

sŭn′sĕt″, *n.* descent of the sun below the horizon.

sŭn′shīne, *n.* rays of the sun.

sŭn′strōke″, *n.* collapse from overexposure to the sun.

sŭn′tăn″, *n.* darkening of the skin resulting from sunbathing.

sŭp, *v.i.*, **supped, supping**. have supper.

sū·pêrb′, *adj.* admirably excellent. —**su·perb′ly**, *adv.*

su·per·cil·i·ous (soō″pər sil′e əs), *adj.* proudly contemptuous. —**su″per·cil′i·ous·ly**, *adv.* —**su″per·cil′i·ous·ness**, *n.*

sū″pêr·fī′ciál, *adj.* **1.** on the surface only. **2.** lacking depth of thought or feeling. —**su″per·fi′cial·ly**, *adv.* —**su″per·fi·ci·al′i·ty**, *n.*

sū·pêr′flū·oŭs, *adj.* **1.** more than is useful. **2.** redundant; useless. —**su·per′flu·ous·ly**, *adv.* —**su″per·flu′i·ty**, *n.*

sū″pêr·hū′màn, *adj.* beyond ordinary human limitations.

sū″pêr·ĭm·pōse′, *v.t.*, -**posed**, -**posing**. place over something else.

su'pêr·ĭn·těnd'', *v.t.* supervise. —su'' per·in·ten'dence, *n.* —su''per·in· ten'dent, *n., adj.* —su''per·in·ten' den·cy, *n.*

su·pē'rĭ·ōr, *adj.* **1.** better. **2.** excellent. **3.** proud; haughty. **4.** higher in position. —*n.* **5.** superior person. **6.** head of a religious community. —su·pe''ri·or'i· ty, *n.*

su·pêr'lȧ·tǐve, *adj.* **1.** of the highest excellence. **2.** *Grammar.* denoting the extreme in a comparison. —*n.* **3.** something superlative. —su·per'la· tive·ly, *adv.*

su''pêr·năt'ū·rȧl, *adj.* **1.** outside the laws of nature. —*n.* **2.** realm of things outside such laws. —su''per·nat'u· ral·ly, *adv.*

su''pêr·nū'mêr·ār·ÿ, *adj., n., pl.* -ries. *adj.* **1.** extra; nonessential. —*n.* **2.** something supernumerary. **3.** nonspeaking actor.

su·pêr·scrībe'', *v.t.,* -scribed, -scribing. write over. —su''per·scrip' tion, *n.*

su''pêr·sēde', *v.t.,* -seded, -seding. replace, esp. in importance or function.

su''pêr·sŏn'ĭc, *adj.* pertaining to speeds faster than that of sound.

su''pêr·stǐ'tion, *n.* unconfirmed belief, esp. in the supernatural. —su''per·sti' tious, *adj.* —su''per·sti'tious·ly, *adv.*

su'pêr·struc''tûre, *n.* upper structure.

su''pêr·vēne', *v.i.,* -vened, -vening. **1.** arrive or occur in addition. **2.** occur afterward. —su''per·ven'tion, *n.*

su'pêr·vīse'', *v.t.,* -vised, -vising. direct and inspect. —su'per·vis''or, *n.* —su''per·vi'so·ry, *adj.* —su''per·vi' sion, *n.*

su'pīne, *adj.* **1.** lying on the back. **2.** wrongly passive. —su'pine·ly, *adv.*

sŭp'pêr, *n.* late dinner.

sŭp·plănt', *v.t.* replace, as in favor or function.

sŭp'ple, *adj.,* -pler, -plest. flexible. —sup'ple·ly, *adv.* —sup'ple·ness, *n.*

sŭp'plė·mėnt, *n.* **1.** desirable addition. —*v.t.* (sup'pləment'') **2.** give a supplement to. —sup''ple·men'tal, sup'' ple·men'ta·ry, *adj.*

sŭp'plĭ·cāte'', *v.t.,* -cated, -cating. implore. —sup''pli·ca'tion, *n.* —sup'' pli·ant, sup'pli·cant, *n.*

sŭp·plÿ', *v.t.,* -plied, plying, *n., pl.*

-plies. *v.t.* **1.** provide, as goods. **2.** fill, as a need. —*n.* **3.** act or instance of supplying. **4.** something supplied. **5.** stock, as of goods. —sup·pli'er, *n.*

sŭp·pôrt', *v.t.* **1.** hold up. **2.** provide a livelihood for. **3.** endure. **4.** be loyal to. **5.** confirm. —*n.* **6.** someone or something that supports.

sŭp·pōse', *v.t.,* -posed, -posing. **1.** assume as true. **2.** expect to act as stated. —sup·pos'ed·ly, *adv.* —sup''po·si' tion, *n.*

sŭp·prĕss', *v.t.* **1.** force into inaction. **2.** kept from being known or apparent. —sup·pres'sion, *n.*

sup·pu·rate (sup'yə rāt), *v.i.,* -rated, -rating. form pus. —sup''pu·ra'tion, *n.*

sŭ·prēme', *adj.* highest or greatest. —su· preme'ly, *adv.* —su·prem'a·cy, *n.*

sur·charge, *n., v.t.,* -charged, -charging. *n.* (sər'chahrj) **1.** added or excessive charge. —*v.t.* (sər chahrj') **2.** impose a surcharge on.

sure (shōōr), *adj.,* surer, surest. **1.** convinced; positive. **2.** reliant. **3.** reliable. **4.** unerring. **5.** *Informal.* yes, indeed. —sure'ly, *adv.*

sure·ty (shōōr'i tē, shōōr'tē), *n., pl.* -ties. **1.** certainty. **2.** security against risk. **3.** guarantor.

sûrf, *n.* waves breaking against land, shoals, etc.

sûr'fȧce, *n., adj., v.,* -faced, -facing. *n.* **1.** outer area. **2.** upper area of a body of water. **3.** outer appearance. —*adj.* **4.** apparent; specious. —*v.t.* **5.** finish or dress the surface of. —*v.i.* **6.** come to the surface, as of a body of water.

sur·feit (sər'fit), *n.* **1.** excess, as of eating or drinking. **2.** revulsion from such excess. —*v.t.* **3.** cause to feel such revulsion.

sûrge, *v.i.* surged, surging, *n.* *v.i.* **1.** move in a sudden swell. **2.** gather volume or force suddenly. —*n.* **3.** act or instance of surging.

sûr'gèon, *n.* practitioner of surgery.

sûr'gêr·ÿ, *n., pl.* -ries. **1.** treatment of illness by physical rather than chemical means. **2.** place where such treatment is given. —sur'gi·cal, *adj.* —sur'gi·cal· ly, *adv.*

sûr'lÿ, *adj.* -lier, -liest. sullenly illtempered. —sur'li·ness, *n.*

sûr·mīse′, *v.t.*, -mised, -mising, *n.* guess.

sûr·mount′, *v.t.* **1.** get or be on top of. **2.** overcome, as an obstacle. —**sur·mount′a·ble**, *adj.*

sûr′nāme″, *n.* last name; family name.

sûr·pǎss′, *v.t.* **1.** be superior to. **2.** exceed.

sûr·plǐce, *n.* loose-fitting robe.

sûr′plǔs, *adj.* **1.** beyond the needed amount. —*n.* **2.** surplus amount.

sûr·prīse′, *n.*, *v.t.*, -prised, -prising. *n.* **1.** emotion on encountering the unexpected. **2.** unexpected occurrence. —*v.t.* **3.** fill with surprise. **4.** attack, etc. when not expected.

sûr·rěn′dêr, *v.t.* **1.** give up. —*v.i.* **2.** yield to superior force. —*n.* **3.** act or instance of surrendering.

sûr″rěp·tī′tioŭs, *adj.* stealthy. —**sur″rep·ti′tious·ly**, *adv.*

sûr′rȯ·gāte″, *n.* **1.** substitute. **2.** judge for legacies and estates.

sûr·rōund′, *v.t.* enclose or be close to on all sides. —**surrounding**, *adj.*

sûr·rōund′ǐngs, *n. pl.* things all around; environment.

sûr′tǎx″, *n.* tax added to a tax.

sûr·veil′lǎnce, *n.* close observation.

sur·vey, *v.t.*, *n.*, *pl.* -veys. *v.t.* (sər vā′) **1.** measure or evaluate precisely. **2.** view. —*n.* (sər′vā) **3.** act or instance of surveying. **4.** general summary. —**sur′vey′or**, *n.*

sûr·vīve′, *v.*, -vived, -viving. *v.i.* **1.** remain alive. —*v.t.* **2.** outlive. —**sur·viv′or**, *n.* —**sur·viv′al**, *n.*

sŭs·cěp·tī′ble, *adj.* easily affected. —**sus·cep″ti·bil′i·ty**, *n.*

sŭs·pěct′, *v.t.* **1.** regard without trust. **2.** guess. —*n.* (sus′pekt) **3.** suspected person. —*adj.* **4.** to be regarded without trust.

sŭs·pěnd′, *v.t.* **1.** hang. **2.** postpone. **3.** dismiss or expel temporarily.

sŭs·pěn′dêrs, *n. pl.* straps for holding up the trousers.

sŭs·pěnse′, *n.* anxiety due to uncertainty.

sŭs·pěn′sion, *n.* **1.** act or instance of suspending. **2.** postponement. **3.** distribution of particles throughout a fluid.

sŭs·pī′cion, *n.* **1.** feeling of one who suspects. **2.** state of being suspected. **3.** trace.

sŭs·pī′cioŭs, *adj.* **1.** having suspicions.

2. arousing suspicion. —**sus·pi′cious·ly**, *adv.*

sŭs·tāin′, *v.t.* **1.** maintain; continue. **2.** support. **3.** endure. **4.** suffer. —**sus·tain′er**, *n.*

sŭs′tė·nȧnce, *n.* **1.** means of existence. **2.** act or instance of sustaining.

sū·tûre, *n.*, *v.t.*, -tured, -turing. *n.* **1.** line of junction. **2.** means by which a wound is sewn. —*v.t.* **3.** join with a suture.

svělte, *adj.* slender.

swâb, *n.*, *v.t.*, swabbed, swabbing. *n.* **1.** absorbent wiping device. —*v.t.* **2.** wipe with a swab.

swǎg′gêr, *v.i.* **1.** walk arrogantly. —*n.* **2.** swaggering gait.

swāle, *n.* **1.** low, marshy area. **2.** valley-like area between slopes.

swǎl′lōw, *v.t.* **1.** take down the throat. **2.** suppress, as an emotion. **3.** *Informal.* accept foolishly as true. —*n.* **4.** small, forked-tailed bird. **5.** act or instance of swallowing.

swǎmp, *n.* **1.** area of wet land and water vegetation. —*v.t.* **2.** drench. **3.** overload, as with work. —**swamp′y**, *adj.*

swǎn, *n.* large, long-necked water bird.

swâp, *v.t.*, swapped, swapping, *n.* *Informal.* exchange.

swârm, *n.* **1.** large, unorganized group. —*v.i.* **2.** move in a swarm.

swârth′y, *adj.*, -ier, -iest. rather dark-skinned. —**swarth′i·ness**, *n.*

swâsh′bŭck″lǐng, *adj.* showily brave or belligerent.

swâs′tǐ·kȧ, *n.* cross with end pieces forming right angles: in one form the Nazi symbol.

swǎt, *v.t.*, swatted, swatting, *n.* *Informal.* *v.t.* **1.** hit sharply. —*n.* **2.** act or instance of swatting. —**swat′ter**, *n.*

swâth, *n.* mown pathlike area.

swāy, *v.i.* **1.** move unsteadily from side to side. —*v.t.* **2.** influence through argument. —*n.* **3.** act or instance of swaying. **4.** domination.

sweār, *v.*, swore, sworn, swearing. *v.t.* **1.** affirm with an oath. **2.** bind with an oath. —*v.i.* **3.** utter profanity.

swēat, *v.i.*, sweat or sweated, sweating, *n.* *v.i.* **1.** pass moisture through the pores. **2.** accumulate surface moisture. —*n.* **3.** sweated body moisture. **4.** sweating condition. —**sweat′y**, *adj.*

swĕat'ẽr, *n.* knitted garment covering the area from waist to neck.

swēep, *v.,* **swept, sweeping.** *v.t.* **1.** free of loose dirt, etc., esp. with brushing motions. **2.** free of enemies or rivals. —*v.i.* **3.** move swiftly and continuously. —*n.* **4.** act or instance of sweeping. **5.** scope.

swēep'stākes'', *n.* race for a prize given by the competitors.

swēet, *adj.* **1.** somewhat sugarlike in taste. **2.** agreeable, esp. to the senses. **3.** gentle. —*n.* **4.** piece of candy, etc. —**sweet'ly,** *adv.* —**sweet'ness,** *n.* —**sweet'en,** *v.t., v.i.*

swēet'heârt'', *n.* loved one.

swēet'pēa, *n.* fragrant, flowering climbing plant.

swēet pόtātό, trailing plant with sweet, edible orange root.

swĕll, *v.,* **swelled, swelled** or **swollen, swelling,** *n., adj. v.t., v.i.* **1.** expand beyond natural size from pressure. —*n.* **2.** act or instance of swelling. **3.** large rounded ocean wave or waves. —*adj.* **4.** *Informal.* excellent.

swĕl'tẽr, *v.i.* suffer from heat.

swẽrve, *v.,* **swerved, swerving,** *n. v.t., v.i.* **1.** turn suddenly aside. —*n.* **2.** act or instance of swerving.

swĭft, *adj.* **1.** quick or prompt. **2.** fast. —*n.* **3.** fast, swallowlike bird. —**swift'ly,** *adv.* —**swift'ness,** *n.*

swĭg, *n., v.t.* **swigged, swigging.** *Informal. n.* **1.** swallow. —*v.t.* **2.** drink in swallows.

swĭll, *v.t.* **1.** drink greedily. —*n.* **2.** liquified garbage used as pig food.

swĭm, *v.i.,* **swam, swum, swimming,** *n. v.i.* **1.** move through water by actions of the body. **2.** be drenched or immersed. **3.** be confused or dizzy. —*n.* **4.** occasion of swimming. —**swim'mer,** *n.*

swĭn'dle, *v.t.,* **-dled, -dling,** *n. v.t.* **1.** cheat. **2.** fraud. —**swin'dler,** *n.*

swīne, *n.,* pl. swine. pig or hog.

swĭng, *v.,* **swung, swinging,** *n. v.t., v.i.* **1.** move back and forth through part of a circle. **2.** move one way in a circular path. —*n.* **3.** suspended seat for swinging. **4.** swinging blow. **5.** act, example, or magnitude of swinging.

swīpe, *v.t.,* **swiped, swiping,** *n. Informal. v.t.* **1.** steal. **2.** hit with a swinging blow. —*n.* **3.** act or instance of swiping.

swîrl, *v.t., v.i., n.* whirl.

swĭsh, *v.t., v.i.* **1.** whirl through the air with a sound. —*n.* **2.** sound of such whirling.

swĭtch, *n.* **1.** change. **2.** device for controlling electric current. **3.** device for directing train movements. **4.** rodlike whip. —*v.t.* **5.** change or exchange. **6.** control or direct with a switch. **7.** beat with a switch. —**switch'board'',** *n.*

swĭv'ẽl, *n.* **1.** rotating support. —*v.t., v.i.* **2.** turn on or as if on a swivel.

swōōn, *n., v.i.* faint.

swōōp, *v.i.* **1.** descend speedily, as a bird of prey. —*n.* **2.** act or instance of swooping.

swôrd'fĭsh'', *n.* large salt-water fish with swordlike upper jawbone.

swôrd, *n.* long, sharp-pointed or -bladed weapon. —**sword'play,''** *n.* —**swords'man,** *n.*

syb'ȧ·rīte'', *n.* lover of luxury. —**syb''a·rit'ic,** *adj.*

syc'ȧ·môre'', *n.* plane tree.

syc·ȯ·phȧnt, (sĭk'ə fənt), *n.* flatterer and parasite. —**syc'o·phan·cy,** *n.*

syl'lȧ·ble, *n.* individual sound that is part of a spoken word. —**syl·lab'ic,** *adj.*

syl'lȧ·bŭs, *n.,* pl. **-buses, -bi.** academic course outline.

sylph, *n.* graceful, slender woman.

syl'vȧn, *adj.* **1.** pertaining to forests. **2.** forested.

symˈbȯl, *n.* **1.** something representing another thing. **2.** sign representing instructions or orders. —**sym·bol'ic, sym·bol'i·cal,** *adj.* —**sym·bol'i·cal·ly,** *adv.* —**sym'bol·ize'',** *v.t.*

sym'bȯl·ĭsm, *n.* group of symbols.

sym'mė·trў, *n.,* pl. **-tries. 1.** mirror-image uniformity on opposite sides. **2.** harmony of arrangement. —**sym·met'ric, sym·met'ri·cal,** *adj.* —**sym·met'ri·cal·ly,** *adv.*

sym'pȧ·thīze'', *v.i.,* **-thized, -thizing. 1.** be in sympathy. **2.** express sympathy. —**sym''pa·thiz'er,** *n.*

sym'pȧ·thў, *n.,* pl. **-thies. 1.** oneness of feeling or opinion. **2.** regret for another's unhappiness. **3.** loyalty. —**sym''pa·thet'ic,** *adj.* —**sym''pa·thet'i·cal·ly,** *adv.*

sym'phò·nỹ, *n., pl.* -nies. major orchestral composition. —sym·phon'ic, *adj.*

sym·pō'sǐ·ŭm, *n., pl.* -siums, -sia. 1. formal discussion by experts. 2. collection of papers on a topic.

symp'tom, *n.* characteristic indication, esp. of an illness. —symp''to·mat'ic, *adj.*

syn'à·gŏgue'', *n.* congregation or house of Jewish worship.

syn'chrò·nīze'', *v.t.*. -nized, -nizing. 1. cause to occur at the same time or rate of speed. 2. cause to register the same time. —syn''chro·ni·za'tion, *n.* —syn'chro·nous, *adj.*

syn'cò·pāte'', *v.t.*, -pated, -pating. *Music.* stress the normally unaccented beat. —syn''co·pa'tion, *n.*

syn'dǐ·càte, *n., v.t.*, -cated, -cating. *n.* 1. organization of independent organizations for a major effort. 2. organization selling material to newspapers. —*v.t.* (sin'di kāt'') 3. sell as a syndicate to newspapers. —syn''di·ca'tion, *n.*

syn'drōme'', *n.* group of symptoms of a given illness.

syn'fûèl, *n.* synthetic fuel.

syn'òd, *n.* ecclesiastical council.

syn'ò·nỹm, *n.* different word of similar meaning. —syn·on'y·mous, *adj.* —syn·on'y·mous'ly, *adv.*

syn·ŏp'sǐs, *n., pl.* -ses. summary; brief outline.

syn'tăx, *n.* arrangement of words, as in a sentence.

syn'thè·sǐs, *n., pl.* -ses. combination of different parts to form a whole.

syn'thè·sīze'', *v.t.*, -sized, -sizing. make into or as a synthesis.

syn·thĕt'ǐc, *adj.* 1. imitating a natural material, esp. in composition. 2. pertaining to synthesis. —syn·thet'i·cal·ly, *adv.*

syph'ǐ·lǐs, *n.* a venereal disease. —syph''i·lit'ic, *adj., n.*

sўr·īnge', *n.* plunger-operated device for drawing up and ejecting fluids.

sў'rŭp, *n.* heavy, sweet liquid, esp. one of sugar and water. —syr'up·y, *adj.*

sўs'tèm, *n.* 1. order or method. 2. coordinated arrangement of working elements. —sys''tem·at'ic, *adj.* —sys''tem·at'i·cal·ly, *adv.*

sўs'tèm·à·tīze'', *v.t.*, -tized, -tizing. arrange according to a system.

sys·to·le (sis'tə lē), *n.* rhythmic contraction of the heart. —sys·tol'ic, *adj.*

T

T, t, *n.* twentieth letter of the English alphabet.

tăb, *n.* 1. extension for pulling. 2. bill of charges.

tăb'bỹ, *n., pl.* -bies. house cat.

tăb'êr·năc''le, *n.* place of worship.

tā'ble, *n., v.t.*, -bled, -bling. *n.* 1. piece of furniture with a broad horizontal surface. 2. orderly arrangement of data. —*v.t.* 3. postpone, as legislation. —ta'ble·cloth'', *n.* —ta'ble·ware'', *n.*

tăb'leau, *n., pl.* -leaux. picture: scene.

ta·ble d'hôte (tah''bəl dōt'), *n.* fixed-price meal.

tā'ble·lănd'', *n.* plateau.

tā'ble·spoōn'', *n.* spoon of one half a fluid ounce. —ta'ble·spoon''ful, *n.*

tăb'lĕt, *n.* 1. slab for writing or lettering. 2. pill. 3. pad of paper.

tăb'loīd, *n.* small-format newspaper.

tă·boo', *n., pl.* -boos, *adj., v.t.*, -booed, -booing. *n.* 1. prohibition, as by society. —*adj.* 2. prohibited. —*v.t.* 3. prohibit. Also, ta·bu'.

tăb'ū·làr, *adj.* in table form.

tăb'ū·lāte'', *v.t.*, -lated, -lating. arrange in a table. —tab''u·la'tion, *n.* —tab'u·la''tor, *n.*

tăc'ǐt, *adj.* understood though not stated. —tac'it·ly, *adv.*

tăc'ǐ·tûrn'', *adj.* choosing to speak little. —tac''i·turn'i·ty, *n.*

tăck, *n.* 1. short, pointed fastener. 2. change of course. —*v.t.* 3. fasten with tacks. 4. cause to change course. —*v.i.* 5. change course.

tăck'le, *n., v.t.*, -led, -ling. *n.* 1. equipment. 2. system of ropes and pulleys. 3. felling, as in football, by grasping the legs. —*v.t.* 4. undertake. 5. fell with a tackle.

tăck'ỹ, *adj.*, -ier, -iest. 1. sticky. 2. *Informal.* of poor quality.

tâ'cō, *n.* folded and filled fried tortilla.

tăct, *n.* sense of how not to offend. —tact'ful, *adj.* —tact'less, *adj.*

tăc'tĭcs, *n.* **1.** science of maneuvering armed forces. **2.** connivance; artifice. —**tac·ti·cal,** *adj.* —**tac·ti·cian,** *n.*

tăc'tĭle, *adj.* pertaining to touch. —**tac·til'i·ty,** *n.*

tăd'pōle'', *n.* larva of a frog or toad.

tăf'fe·tà, *n.* stiff silky fabric.

tăf'fy, *n.* chewy candy.

tăg, *n., v.,* **tagged, tagging.** *n.* **1.** label attached with a cord. **2.** chasing game. —*v.t.* **3.** apply a tag to. —*v.i.* **4.** follow closely.

tāil, *n.* **1.** distinct hindmost extremity of an animal. **2.** feature similar in shape or location, as on a vehicle. —**tail' gate'',** *n.* —**tail'light'',** *n.* —**tail' less'',** *adj.*

tāil'ör, *n.* **1.** maker of clothes. —*v.t.* **2.** make as a tailor does.

tāil'spĭn'', *n.* winding plunge of an airplane.

tāint, *v.t.* **1.** pollute or poison. —*n.* **2.** trace of pollution.

tāke, *v.,* **took, taken, taking.** *v.t.* **1.** carry. **2.** escort. **3.** accept. **4.** seize. **5.** make use of. **6.** select. **7.** require. **8.** react to. **9.** assume. **10.** engage in. —*v.i.* **11.** be effective.

tāke'ŏff'', *n.* beginning of a flight.

tāke'ō''vêr, *n.* assumption of control.

tāk'ĭng, *adj.* **1.** attractive. —*n.* **2.** takings, profits.

tălc, *n.* soft mineral. Also, **tal'cum.**

tāle, *n.* **1.** narrative. **2.** piece of gossip. **3.** lie. —**tale'bear''er,** *n.*

tăl'ĕnt, *n.* **1.** personal ability. **2.** person or persons of talent. —**tal'ent·ed,** *adj.*

tāles'màn, *n.* person called for jury duty.

tăl'ĭs·màn, *n.* object warding off evil.

tălk, *v.i.* **1.** speak words. **2.** confer. **3.** gossip. —*v.t.* **4.** persuade. —*n.* **5.** conversation. **6.** speech. **7.** gossip or rumor.

tălk'à·tĭve, *adj.* loving to talk.

tălk'ĭng-to'', *n. Informal.* scolding.

tăll, *adj.* **1.** very high. **2.** of a specified height.

tăl'lōw, *n.* solid animal fat.

tăl'lў, *n., pl.* **-lies,** *v.,* **-lied, -lying.** *n.* **1.** sum. **2.** account; score. —*v.t.* **3.** add up. —*v.i.* **4.** correspond.

Tăl'mŭd, *n.* compilation of Hebrew law. —**Tal·mud'ic,** *adj.*

tăl'ón, *n.* bird claw.

tà·mä'lē, *n.* Mexican dish of meat, red peppers, and corn meal in corn husks.

tăm'bóu·rĭne'', *n.* shallow drumlike instrument.

tāme, *adj.,* **tamer, tamest,** *v.t.,* **tamed, taming.** *adj.* **1.** obedient to a master. **2.** without spirit. —*v.t.* **3.** make tame. —**tame'ly,** *adv.* —**tame'ness,** *n.* —**tam'a·ble, tame'a·ble,** *adj.* —**tam'er,** *n.*

tămp, *v.t.* pack or drive with gentle blows.

tăm'pêr, *v.i.* interfere wrongly.

tăn, *n., adj.,* **tanner, tannest,** *v.t.,* **tanned, tanning.** *n.* **1.** yellow-brown. **2.** suntan. —*adj.* **3.** yellow-brown. —*v.t.* **4.** convert into leather.

tăn'à·gêr, *n.* small, colorful American songbird.

tăn'dĕm, *adv., adj.* with one behind the other.

tăng, *n.* penetrating flavor. —**tang'y,** *adj.*

tăn'gĕnt, *n.* line touching a curve. —**tan·gen·tial,** *adj.* —**tan'gen·cy,** *n.*

tăn''gêr·ïne', *n.* type of orange.

tăn'gĭ·ble, *adj.* **1.** able to be touched. **2.** able to be defined. —**tan''gi·bil'i·ty,** *n.*

tăn'gle, *v.,* **-gled, -gling,** *n., v.t.* **1.** intertwine in a disorderly way. —*n.* **2.** tangled state.

tăn'gō, *n., pl.* **-gos.** South American dance.

tănk, *n.* **1.** container for fluids. **2.** armored fighting vehicle. —**tank'ful,** *n.*

tănk'ärd, *n.* tall mug with a side handle.

tănk'êr, *n.* ship carrying liquids in bulk.

tăn'nêr, *n.* maker of leather. —**tan'ner·y,** *n.*

tăn''tà·līze'', *v.t.,* **-lized, -lizing.** torment with gratification withheld. —**tan''tal·i·za'tion,** *n.*

tăn'tà·mŏunt'', *adj.* equivalent.

tăn'trŭm, *n.* outburst of rage.

tăp, *v.,* **tapped, tapping,** *n. v.t., v.i.* **1.** strike lightly. —*v.t.* **2.** draw off or upon. —*n.* **3.** light blow. **4.** valve or plug.

tăp dănce, dance with light taps of the foot. —**tap'-dance'',** *v.i.*

tāpe, *n., v.t.,* **taped, taping.** *n.* **1.** thin, flat, long strip. —*v.t.* **2.** bind with tape. **3.** record on tape.

tā'pêr, *n.* **1.** convergence of sides or

edges. —*v.t., v.i.* **2.** decrease steadily in thickness. **3.** candle.

tăp'ĕs·trў, *n., pl.* **-tries.** *n.* woven decorative panel.

tāpe'wŏrm'', *n.* flat parasitic worm.

tăp''ĭ·ō'cà, *n.* starchy substance from cassava roots.

tăp'rōōt'', *n.* single, deep-going root.

tăps, *n. Military.* bugle call signifying retirement for the night and also played after military funerals.

tär, *n., v.t.,* **tarred, tarring.** *n.* **1.** thick black liquid distilled from wood, coal, etc. —*v.t.* **2.** coat with tar.

tà·răn'tū·là, *n.* large, hairy spider.

tär'dў, *adj.,* **-dier, -diest.** behind the expected time. —**tar'di·ly,** *adv.* —**tar'di·ness,** *n.*

tāre, *n.* **1.** container weight. **2.** weed.

tär'gĕt, *n.* something aimed at.

tär'ĭff, *n.* **1.** tax on imports or exports. **2.** price or charge.

tär'nĭsh, *v.t.* **1.** spoil the luster of. —*v.i.* **2.** become tarnished. —*n.* **3.** tarnished state.

tä'rōt, *n.* set of fortune-telling cards.

tär·pău'lĭn, *n.* waterproof cloth cover.

tär'pŏn, *n.* large west Atlantic game fish.

tăr'rà·gŏn, *n.* seasoning of fragrant leaves.

tar·ry, *v.i.,* **-ried, -rying,** *adj. v.i.* (tar'ē) **1.** linger. —*adj.* (tahr'ē) **2.** covered with or suggesting tar.

tärt, *adj.* **1.** acid, as to the taste. —*n.* **2.** small pie.

tär'tàn, *n.* plaid cloth pattern of crisscrossed bands of color.

tär'tàr, *n.* **1.** potassium salt used as a condiment. **2.** deposit on the teeth. —**tar·tar'ic,** *adj.*

tăsk, *n.* **1.** something to be done. —*v.t.* **2.** burden.

tăsk'măs''tĕr, *n.* person who exacts work of others.

tăs'sĕl, *n.* ornamental gathering of hanging threads.

tāste, *v.,* **tasted, tasting,** *n. v.t.* **1.** sense with the tongue. **2.** experience. —*v.i.* **3.** have a specific flavor. —*n.* **4.** sense operating through the tongue. **5.** flavor. **6.** sense of what is appropriate or seemly. **7.** liking. —**tast'er,** *n.* —**taste'less,** *adj.*

tāste'fŭl, *adj.* in good taste.

tāst'ў, *adj.,* **-ier, -iest.** good-tasting. —**tast'i·ness,** *n.*

tăt'tĕr, *n.* **1.** ragged fragment. —*v.t.* **2.** reduce to tatters. —**tat'tered,** *adj.*

tăt'tle, *v.i.,* **-tled, -tling.** gossip.

tăt'tle·tāle'', *n.* betrayer of secrets.

tăt·tōō', *v.t.,* **-tooed, -tooing,** *n., pl.* **-toos.** *v.t.* **1.** mark with pigments under the skin. —*n.* **2.** tattooed design. **3.** military drum or bugle signal.

tāunt, *v.t.* **1.** mock. —*n.* **2.** mocking remark.

tāut, *adj.* tight or tense. —**taut'ly,** *adv.* —**taut'ness,** *n.*

tāu·tŏl'ō·gў, *n., pl.* **-gies.** useless repetition of an idea in a logical argument. —**tau''to·log'i·cal,** *adj.*

tăv'ĕrn, *n.* public drinking place.

tāw'drў, *adj.,* **-drier, -driest.** cheap and showy. —**taw'dri·ly,** *adv.* —**taw'dri·ness,** *n.*

tāw'nў, *adj.,* **-nier, -niest.** tan.

tăx, *n.* **1.** money exacted by a government. **2.** demand on resources. —*v.t.* **3.** exact a tax on or from. **4.** accuse. —**tax'a·ble,** *adj.* —**tax·a'tion,** *n.* —**tax'pay''er,** *n.*

tăx'ĭ, *n., pl.* **-is,** *v.i.,* **-ied, -iing** or **-ying.** *n.* **1.** Also, **tax'i·cab'',** hired vehicle with metered charges. —*v.i.* **2.** travel by taxi. **3.** move without flying, as an airplane.

tăx'ĭ·dêr''mў, *n.* art of simulating animals using their skins. —**tax''i·der'mist,** *n.*

tēa, *n.* **1.** drink made from the dried leaves of a shrub grown in Asia. **2.** drink made from other leaves and flowers. **3.** meal, etc. at which tea is served. —**tea'cup'',** *n.* —**tea'ket''tle,** *n.* —**tea'pot'',** *n.*

tēach, *v.,* **taught, teaching.** *v.t.* **1.** inform on a subject. **2.** inform students regarding. —*v.i.* **3.** be a teacher. —**teach'a·ble,** *adj.* —**teach'er,** *n.*

tēak, *n.* brown East Indian hardwood.

tēal, *n., pl.* **teals, teal. 1.** freshwater duck. **2.** color of green.

tēam, *n.* **1.** group of animals or persons acting together. —*v.i.* **2.** join or act in a team. —**team'mate'',** *n.* —**team'work'',** *n.*

tear, *v.,* **tore, torn, tearing,** *n., v.t.* (ter) **1.** pull apart by force. **2.** make by piercing or rending. **3.** lacerate or harass.

—*v.i.* **4.** be torn. **5.** hurry. —*n.* **6.** torn place. **7** (tēr) liquid from the weeping eye. —**tear′drop″**, *n.* —**tear′ful**, *adj.*

tēase, *v.t.*, **teased, teasing. 1.** bother with gentle malice. **2.** comb.

tēa′spoon″, *n.* spoon holding one and a third fluid drams. —**tea′spoon·ful″**, *n.*

tēat, *n.* nipple.

tĕch′nǐ·cal, *n.* **1.** pertaining to technology. **2.** pertaining to technique. **3.** pertaining to specific details. —**tech′ni·cal·ly**, *adv.* —**tech″ni·cal′i·ty**, *n.* —**tech·ni′cian**, *n.*

tĕch·nǐque′, *n.* **1.** working method. **2.** proficiency. Also, **tech′nic.**

tĕch·nŏc′rå·cȳ, *n.* government by technical experts.

tĕch·nŏl′ò·gȳ, *n.*, *pl.* **-gies.** application of science, esp. to industry. —**tech″no·log′i·cal**, *adj.*

tē′dǐ·ŭm, *n.* wearisome or boring quality or state. —**te′di·ous**, *adj.*

tēe, *n.* stand for a golf ball being driven.

tēem, *v.i.* swarm.

tēen′-āge′, *adj.* pertaining to the teens as an age. Also, **teen′age″**. —**teen′ ag″er**, *n.*

tēens, *n. pl.* **1.** years of life between 13 and 19. **2.** numbers in a series between 10 and 19.

tēe′nȳ, *adj.*, **-nier, -niest.** *Informal.* tiny.

tēethe, *v.i.*, **teethed, teething.** grow teeth.

tēe·tō′tål·êr, *n.* total abstainer from alcohol. Also, **tee·to′tal·ler.**

tĕl′ė·căst″, *v.t.*, **-cast** or **-casted, -casting**, *n.* broadcast via television. —**tel′e·cast″er**, *n.*

tĕl′ė·grăph″, *n.* **1.** apparatus sending messages in code by electrical impulses. —*v.t.* **2.** reach by telegraph. **3.** send by telegraph. —**tel″e·graph′ic**, *adj.* —**te·leg′ra·phy**, *n.* —**te·leg′ra·pher**, *n.* —**tel′e·gram″**, *n.*

tė·lĕp′å·thȳ, *n.* extra-sensory communication. —**tel″e·path′ic**, *adj.* —**te·lep′a·thist**, *n.*

tĕl′ė·phōne″, *n.*, *v.t.*, **-phoned, -phoning**, *n.* **1.** device for transmitting personal spoken messages. —*v.t.* **2.** reach by telephone. **3.** transmit by telephone. —**tel″e·phon′ic**, *adj.*

tĕl′ė·scōpe″, *n.*, *v.*, **-scoped, -scoping**, *n.* **1.** device for magnifying distant images. —*v.t.*, *v.i.* **2.** slide lengthwise into one another. —**tel″e·scop′ic**, *adj.*

tĕl″ė·tȳpe′wrīt″êr, *n.* telegraphic apparatus sending and receiving typed messages.

tĕl′ė·vīse″, *v.t.*, **-vised, -vising.** transmit by television.

tĕl′ė·vĭ″sion, *n.* **1.** method of transmitting images by radio waves and electrical impulses. **2.** industry using this method. **3.** television receiving set.

tĕll, *v.*, **told, telling.** *v.t.* **1.** inform. **2.** recount. **3.** order. **4.** distinguish; recognize. —*v.i.* **5.** give a narrative. **6.** have an effect. —**tel′ling**, *adj.* —**tel′ling·ly**, *adv.*

tĕll′êr, *n.* **1.** narrator. **2.** bank clerk.

tĕll′tāle″, *adj.* secret-revealing.

tė·mĕr′ǐ·tȳ, *n.* audacity.

tĕm′pêr, *n.* **1.** mood. **2.** anger. **3.** control of one's anger. **4.** hardness and flexibility, as of steel. —*v.t.* **5.** moderate. **6.** give toughness to.

tĕm′pêr·à, *n.* paint with egg, glue, etc.

tĕm′pêr·à·mėnt, *n.* natural mental disposition. —**tem″per·a·men′tal**, *adj.*

tĕm′pêr·ánce, *n.* moderation, esp. in drinking.

tĕm′pêr·åte, *adj.* **1.** moderate. **2. Temperate,** situated between a tropic and the Arctic or Antarctic Circle.

tĕm′pêr·à·tûre, *n.* **1.** relative heat. **2.** condition of excessive body heat.

tĕm′pêred, *adj.* **1.** modified. **2.** having a specified temperament.

tĕm′pĕst, *n.* violent storm. —**tem·pes·tu′ous**, *adj.*

tĕm′plāte, *n.* pattern for forming.

tĕm′ple, *n.* **1.** place of worship. **2.** area to either side of the brow.

tĕm′pō, *n.*, *pl.* **-pos, -pi.** rate of speed, as for music.

tĕm′pó·rål, *adj.* **1.** worldly, not spiritual. **2.** pertaining to time.

tĕm′pó·rār″ȳ, *adj.* for a limited time. —**tem″po·rar′i·ly**, *adv.*

tĕm′pó·rīze″, *v.i.*, **-rized, -rizing.** evade argument or time requirements. —**tem″po·ri·za′tion**, *n.*

tĕmpt, *v.t.* create an appetite or inclination in. —**temp·ta′tion**, *n.* —**tempt′er**, *fem.*, **tempt′ress**, *n.*

tĕn, *n.* nine plus one.

tĕn′á·ble, *adj.* defensible, as an argu-

ment. —ten″a·bil′i·ty, *n*. —ten′a·
bly, *adv*.

tĕ·nā′cioŭs, *adj*. 1. holding firmly. 2.
stubborn. —te·na′cious·ly, *adv*. —te·
nac′i·ty, *n*.

tĕn′ànt, *n*. renter of building space or
land. —ten′an·cy, *n*.

tĕnd, *v.i*. 1. have a tendency. —*v.t*. 2.
manage or care for.

tĕn′dèn·cÿ, *n*., *pl*. -cies. mild predomi-
nance of a certain result, preference,
etc.

tĕn·dĕn′tioŭs, *adj*. expressed with a
bias. —ten·den′tious·ly, *adv*.

tĕn′dĕr, *adj*. 1. soft. 2. warmly affectionate. 3. feeling pain readily. —*n*. 4.
person who tends. 5. railroad car for
fuel. 6. something offered in payment.
—*v.t*. 7. offer. —ten′der·ly, *adv*.
—ten′der·ness, *n*. —ten′der·heart′
ed, *adj*. —ten′der·ize″, *v.t*.

tĕn′dĕr·fŏŏt″, *n*., *pl*. -foots, -feet. new-
comer to out-of-door pursuits.

tĕn′dĕr·lŏīn″, *n*. 1. tenderest cut of beef
or pork loin. 2. graft-ridden city neighborhood.

tĕn′dòn, *n*. muscle attachment.

tĕn′drĭl, *n*. attachment on a climbing
plant.

tĕn′é·mėnt, *n*. 1. shabby apartment
building. 2. apartment in such a building.

tĕn′ĕt, *n*. doctrine accepted as truth.

tĕnnĭs, *n*. game played with rackets and a
ball.

tĕn′òn, *n*. end of a rail, etc., held in the
mortise of another such piece.

tĕn′ör, *n*. 1. highest male singing voice.
2. gist.

tĕn′pĭns″, *n*. bowling game.

tĕnse, *adj*., tenser, tensest, *v*., tensed,
tensing, *n*. *adj*. 1. taut. 2. nervous:
strained. —*v.t*. 3. make tense. —*v.i*. 4.
become tense. —*n*. 5. *Grammar*. expression of past, present, future, etc.
—tense′ly, *adv*. —ten′sion, tense′
ness, ten′si·ty, *n*.

tĕn′sĭle, *adj*. capable of being stretched.

tĕnt, *n*. 1. fabric shelter spread over
poles. —*v.i*. 2. lodge in a tent.

tĕn′tà·cle, *n*. grasping or feeling attachment of an invertebrate.

tĕn′tà·tĭve, *adj*. made or done as a trial.
—ten′ta·tive·ly, *adv*.

tĕn′têr·hŏŏk″, *n*. on tenterhooks, in
suspense.

tĕnth, *adj*. 1. following nine others. —*n*.
2. one of ten equal parts.

tĕn′ū·oŭs, *adj*. 1. thin. 2. insubstantial.
—ten′u·ous·ly, *adv*. —ten·u′i·ty, ten′
u·ous·ness, *n*.

tĕn′ûre, *n*. 1. right to continuing employment. 2. occupation, as of public
office.

tē′pēe, *n*. conical tent of American Indi-
ans.

tĕp′ĭd, *adj*. lukewarm. —te·pid′ity, tep′
id·ness, *n*. —tep′id·ly, *adv*.

tè·quï′là, *n*. Mexican distilled liquor.

têrm, *n*. 1. word with a specific meaning.
2. period of activity. 3. terms, a. requirements of an agreement. b. basis of
a relationship.

têr′mĭn·àl, *n*. 1. station at the end of a
railroad, etc. 2. electrical connecting
point. 3. (computers) work station for
data processing. —*adj*. 4. coming at the
end. 5. causing death. —ter″min·al·
ly′, *adv*.

têr′mĭ·nāte″, *v*., -nated, -nating. *v.t*.,
v.i. finish. —ter′mi·na·ble, *adj*.
—ter″mi·na′tion, *n*.

têr″mĭ·nŏl′o·gÿ, *n*., *pl*. -gies. employment of terms.

têr′mĭ·nŭs, *n*., *pl*. -nì, -nuses. 1. end or
limit. 2. station at the end of a railroad,
etc.

têr′mīte, *n*. wood-eating insect.

têrn, *n*. gull-like bird.

tĕr′ràce, *n*., *v.t*., -raced, -racing. *n*. 1.
raised outdoor platform. —*v.t*. 2. form
in terraces.

tĕr′rà cŏt′tà, earthenware material used
in building and decoration.

tĕrrà fĭr′mà, dry land.

têr·rāin′, *n*. land with its natural features.

tĕr′rà·pĭn, *n*. type of turtle.

tèr·rār′ĭ·ŭm, *n*., *pl*. -iums, -ia. glass
box for growing small plants and animals.

tèr·rĕs′trĭ·àl, *adj*. pertaining to the
earth.

tĕr′rĭ·ble, *adj*. 1. bad; poor. 2. awesome.

tĕr′rĭ·blÿ, *adv*. 1. in a terrible manner. 2.
Informal. extremely.

tĕr′rĭ·êr, *n*. small hunting dog.

tĕr·rĭf'ĭc, *adj.* **1.** awesome in force. **2.** *Informal.* very good.

tĕr'rĭ·fȳ'', *v.t.,* **-fied, -fying.** fill with terror.

tĕr'rĭ·tô''rȳ, *n., pl.* **-ries. 1.** region without full political status. **2.** distinct area of land. **—ter''ri·to'ri·al,** *adj.*

tĕr'rör, *n.* **1.** great fear. **2.** cause of such fear.

tĕr'rör·ĭsm, *n.* use of terror to enforce demands. **—ter'ror·ist,** *n., adj.,* **—ter''ror·is'tic,** *adj.*

tĕr'rör·īze'', *v.t.,* **-ized, -izing.** intimidate with terror. **—ter''ror·i·za'tion,** *n.*

têrse, *adj.,* **terser, tersest.** short-spoken; concise. **—terse'ly,** *adv.* **—terse'ness,** *n.*

tĕr'tĭ·ār''y̆, *adj.* third in order.

tĕst, *n.* **1.** act or event that reveals qualities, accomplishments, illnesses, etc. **—v.t. 2.** subject to a test. **—v.t. 3.** perform a test. **—test'er,** *n.*

tĕs'tà·mĕnt, *n.* **1.** *Law.* will. **2.** part of the Bible. **—tes''ta·men'ta·ry,** *adj.*

tĕs'tā·tör, *n.* maker of a will.

tĕs'tĭ·cle, *n.* male sex gland.

tĕs'tĭ·fȳ'', *v.,* **-fied, -fying.** *v.t., v.i.* bear witness.

tĕs''tĭ·mō'nĭ·ȧl, *adj.* **1.** expressing gratitude. **—n. 2.** recommendation.

tĕs'tĭ·mō''nȳ, *n., pl.* **-nies.** declaration.

tĕs'tȳ, *adj.,* **-tier, -tiest.** irritable. **—tes'ti·ly,** *adv.* **—tes'ti·ness,** *n.*

tĕt'à·nŭs, *n.* acute spasmodic disease.

tête-a-tête, *n.* intimate conversation.

tĕth'êr, *n.* **1.** long tying rope. **—v.t. 2.** fasten with a tether.

tĕt''rȧ·hē'dron, *n., pl.* **-drons, -dra.** four-sided solid.

tĕxt, *n.* **1.** written matter. **2.** textbook. **—tex'tu·al,** *adj.*

tĕxt'bōōk'', *n.* school book.

tĕx'tĭle, *n.* cloth.

tĕx'tûre, *n.* surface quality. **—tex'tur·al,** *adj.*

thăn, *conj.* introduces a basis of comparison.

thănk, *v.t.* express gratitude to. **—thank'ful,** *adj.* **—thank'ful·ly,** *adv.* **thank'less,** *adj.* **—thank'less·ly,** *adv.*

thănks, *n.* **1.** gratitude. **—interj. 2.** I thank you.

thănks'gĭv''ĭng, *n.* **1.** expression of thanks to God. **2. Thanksgiving,** U.S. holiday.

thăt, *pron., adj., pl.* **those,** *conj. pron., adj.* **1.** the one. **2.** the other. **—pron. 3.** which. **—conj. 4.** (used to introduce noun and adverbial clauses). **—adv. 5.** to such an extent.

thătch, *n.* **1.** roof surface of straw, reeds, etc. **—v.t. 2.** cover with such a surface.

thaw, *v.i.* **1.** warm above freezing. **—n. 2.** state of thawing.

thė, *def. article.* (refers to a particular person, thing, or type.)

thē·ȧ·têr, *n.* **1.** place for plays, etc. **2.** theatrical profession. Also, **the'a·tre.** **—the·at'ri·cal,** *adj.* **—the·at'ri·cal·ly,** *adv.*

thĕft, *n.* stealing.

thĕir, *adj.* pertaining to them.

thĕirs, *pron.* something pertaining to them.

thĕm, *pron.* objective of they.

thēme, *n.* **1.** subject. **2.** basic melody. **—the·mat'ic,** *adj.*

thĕm·sĕlves', *pron.* **1.** (intensive and reflexive of they). **2.** their true selves.

thĕn, *adv.* **1.** at that time. **2.** and after. **3.** in that case. **—n. 4.** that time.

thĕnce, *adv.* from there or then.

thĕnce''fôrth', *adv.* from then on. Also, **thence''for'ward.**

thē·ŏc'rȧ·cȳ, *n., pl.* **-cies.** rule by priests. **—the''o·crat'ic,** *adj.*

thē·ŏl'ó·gȳ, *n., pl.* **-gies.** study of religious doctrine. **—the''o·log'i·cal,** *adj.* **—the''o·lo'gian,** *n.*

thē'ó·rĕm, *n.* something to be proved.

thē'ó·rȳ, *n., pl.* **-ies. 1.** statement of a possible truth. **2.** untried assumption. **—the''o·ret'i·cal,** *adj.* **—the''o·ret'i·cal·ly,** *adv.* **—the'o·rize,''** *v.i.* **—the'o·rist,** *n.*

thē·ŏs'ó·phȳ, *n.* mystical religion. **—the''o·soph'ic,** *adj.* **—the·os'o·phist,** *n.*

thĕr''ȧ·peū'tĭc, *adj.* aiding health. **—ther''a·peu'tics,** *n.*

thĕr'ȧ·pȳ, *n., pl.* **-pies.** healing process. **—ther'a·pist,** *n.*

thĕre, *adv.* **1.** at or to that place. **2.** in that respect. **3.** used to introduce expressions of existence or nonexistence.

thĕre'ȧf'têr, *adv.* from then on.

thĕre'bȳ, *adv.* in connection with that.

thĕre'fôre'', *adj.* for this reason.

thĕre·ĭn′, *adv*. in that.

thĕre·ŏf′, *adv*. of that.

thĕre·ŏn′, *adv*. **1**. on that. **2**. just afterward.

thĕre·to′, *adv*. to that place.

thĕre′ŭp·ŏn′, *adv*. **1**. just afterward. **2**. in consequence.

thêr′màl, *adj*. pertaining to heat.

thêr·mŏm′ė·têr, *n*. heat-measuring device.

thêr′′mō·nū′clē·àr, *adj*. pertaining to atomic fusion at high heat.

thêr′mòs, *n*. heat-insulated bottle.

thêr′mó·stăt′′, *n*. heating control.

thė·saū′rŭs, *n*., *pl*. -**ri**, -**ruses**. *n*. book of synonyms and antonyms.

thē′sĭs, *n*., *pl*. -**ses**. **1**. belief to be defended. **2**. research paper.

thĕs′pĭ·àn, *n*. **1**. actor or actress. —*adj*. **2**. pertaining to the theater.

they, *n*. plural of *he, she,* or *it*.

thĭck, *n*. **1**. deep from front to back. **2**. dense. —**thick′ly**, *adv*. —**thick′ness**, *n*. —**thick′en**, *v.t., v.i*.

thĭck′ĕt, *n*. thick clump of shrubbery.

thĭck′sĕt′, *adj*. stout.

thĭck′-skĭnned′, *adj*. coarse; insensitive.

thiĕf, *n*., *pl*. **thieves**. person who steals. —**thiev′er·y**, *n*. —**thiev′ish**, *adj*.

thĭgh, *n*. upper leg. —**thigh′bone′′**, *n*.

thĭm′ble, *n*. fingertip protector.

thĭn, *adj*., **thinner, thinnest,** *v.t*., **thinned, thinning.** *adj*. **1**. shallow from front to back. **2**. not dense; meager. —*v.t*. **3**. make thin. —**thin′ly**, *adv*. —**thin′ness**, *n*. —**thin′ner**, *n*.

thĭng, *n*. inanimate entity.

thĭnk, *v*., **thought, thinking.** *v.t*. **1**. have in the mind. **2**. believe. —*v.i*. **3**. employ the mind. —**think′er**, *n*.

thĭn′-skĭnned′, *adj*. sensitive to insult.

thĭrd, *adj*. **1**. being number three. —*n*. **2**. one of three equal parts.

thĭrst, *n*. desire to absorb liquids. —**thirst′y**, *adj*. —**thirst′i·ly**, *adv*.

thĭr·tēen′, *adj*., *n*. ten plus three. —**thirteenth′′**, *adj*.

thĭr′tў, *adj*., *n*. three times ten. —**thir′ti·eth**, *adj*., *n*.

thĭs, *pron*., *adj*., *pl*. **these**, *adv. pron*., *adj*. **1**. designating something near at hand. —*adv*. **2**. to this extent.

thĭs′tle, *n*. prickly plant.

thĭth′êr, *adv*. to that place.

thŏng, *n*. small flexible strap.

thô′răx, *n*., *pl*. -**raxes**, -**races**. center of the body. —**tho·rac′ic**, *adj*.

thôrn, *n*. spike of a plant stalk. —**thorn′y**, *adj*.

thŏr′ōugh, *adj*. complete in every detail. —**thor′ough·ly**, *adv*. —**thor′ough·ness**, *n*.

thŏr′ōugh·brĕd′′, *adj*. pedigreed.

thŏr′ōugh·fāre′′, *n*. way through.

thŏr′ōugh·gō′ĭng, *adj*. thorough.

thōu, *pron*. *Archaic*. you.

thōugh, *conj*. **1**. despite the fact that. —*adv*. **2**. however.

thŏught, *n*. **1**. thinking process. **2**. something thought. **3**. something to consider. —**thought′ful**, *adj*. —**thought′ful·ly**, *adv*. —**thought′ful·ness**, *n*. —**thought′less**, *adj*. —**thought′less·ly**, *adv*. **thought′less·ness**, *n*.

thōu′sànd, *adj*., *n*. ten times one hundred. —**thou′sandth**, *adj*., *n*.

thrăsh, *v.t*. beat vigorously.

thrĕad, *n*. **1**. length of spun fiber. **2**. ridge on a screw. —*v.t*. **3**. put a thread through.

thrĕad′bāre′′, *adj*. worn thin.

thrĕat, *n*. warning of revenge or danger.

thrĕat′ĕn, *v.t*. make or constitute a threat against.

thrēe, *n*. two plus one.

thrĕsh, *v.t*. separate from husks. —**thresh′er**, *n*.

thrĕsh′ōld, *n*. doorway pavement.

thrīce, *adv*. three times.

thrĭft, *n*. saving of money, etc.

thrĭft′ў, *adj*., -**ier**, -**iest**. characterized by thrift. —**thrift′i·ly**, *adv*.

thrĭll, *v.t*. **1**. excite emotionally. —*v.i*. **2**. be excited emotionally. —*n*. **3**. act or instance of thrilling.

thrīve, *v.i*., **thrived** or **throve, thrived** or **thriven, thriving.** be prosperous or healthy.

thrōat, *n*. interior of the neck.

thrŏb, *v.i*., **throbbed, throbbing.** *n*., *v.i*. **1**. beat, as the heart or pulse, with more than usual force. —*n*. **2**. act or instance of throbbing.

thrōe, *n*. pang.

thrŏm·bō′sĭs, *n*. clotting of blood.

thrōne, *n*. chair of state.

thrŏng, *n*., *v.i*. crowd.

thrŏt′tle, *n*., *v.t*., -**tled**, -**tling**. *n*. **1**. valve. *v.t*. **2**. squeeze and choke.

throügh, *prep.* **1.** from end to end of. **2.** by means of. —*adv.* **3.** from end to end. —*adj.* **4.** from end to end. **5.** finished.

throügh·oūt', *prep.* **1.** in every part of. —*adv.* **2.** in every part.

thrōw, *v.t.*, threw, thrown, *n.*, *v.t.* **1.** propel unsupported. **2.** send forcefully. —*n.* **3.** act or instance of throwing. **4.** distance of throwing. —throw'er, *n.*

throw'băck'', *n.* reversion.

thrū, *prep.*, *adv.*, *adj.* through.

thrŭsh, *n.* songbird.

thrŭst, *v.*, thrust, thrusting, *n.* *v.t.*, *v.i.*, *n.* push.

thŭd, *v.i.*, thudded, thudding, *n.* boom with a dull sound.

thŭg, *n.* hoodlum.

thŭmb, *n.* **1.** innermost hand digit. —*v.t.* **2.** move with the thumb.

thŭmb'tăck'', *n.* broad-headed tack.

thŭmp. *n.* **1.** heavy blow. **2.** sound produced by such a blow.

thŭn'dêr, *n.* **1.** sound following lightning. —*v.t.* **2.** say loudly or vehemently. —thun'der·ous, *adj.* —thun'der·bolt'', *n.* —thun'der·clap'', *n.* —thun'der·cloud'', *n.* —thun'der·show''er, *n.* —thun'der·storm'', *n.*

thŭn'dêr·strŭck'', *adj.* stupefied with amazement. Also, thun'der·strick'' en.

Thûrs'dāy, *n.* fifth day of the week.

thŭs, *adv.* **1.** in this way. **2.** to this extent. **3.** therefore.

thwart, *v.t.* obstruct.

thȳ, *adj. Archaic.* your.

thyme (tīm), *n.* herb plant used for seasoning.

thȳ'rōīd glănd, ductless gland regulating growth.

thȳ·sĕlf', *pron. Archaic.* yourself.

ti·är'à, *n.* woman's decorative coronet.

tĭc, *n.* repeated muscular spasm.

tĭck, *n.* **1.** sound of a mechanical clock. **2.** bloodsucking insect. **3.** mattress cloth. —*v.i.* **4.** make a ticking sound. —tick' er, *n.*

tĭck'ĕt, *n.* **1.** paper giving admission. **2.** list of candidates.

tĭck'le, *v.*, -led, -ling. *v.t.* **1.** cause to twitch by light stroking. **2.** amuse. —*v.i.* **3.** cause tickling.

tĭck'lĭsh, *adj.* **1.** susceptible to tickling. **2.** needing caution.

tĭd'bĭt'', small morsel.

tīde, *n.* periodic fluctation of sea level. —tid'al, *adj.* —tide'wa''ter, *n.*, *adj.*

tī'dĭngs, *n. pl.* news.

tī'dȳ, *adj.*, -dier, -diest, *v.t.*, -died, -dying. *adj.* **1.** orderly. —*v.t.* **2.** make orderly. —ti'di·ness, *n.* —ti·di·ly, *adv.*

tīe, *v.t.*, tied, tying, *n.* *v.t.* **1.** fasten with ropes, etc. **2.** equal in scoring. —*n.* **3.** something that ties. **4.** something that prevents spreading. **5.** equal score. **6.** necktie.

tiēr, *n.* horizontal row.

tīe'-ŭp'', *n.* stoppage.

tĭff, *n.* slight quarrel.

tī'gêr, *n.* large catlike African and south Asian animal. Also, *fem.*, ti'gress.

tīght, *adj.* **1.** preventing movement. **2.** fully stretched. —*adv.* **3.** securely. —*n.* **4.** tights, tight-fitting hose. —tight'ly, *adv.* —tight'ness, *n.* —tight'en, *v.t.*, *v.i.* —tight'-fit'ting, *adj.*

tīght''-fĭst'ĕd, *adj.* stingy.

tīght'rōpe'', *n.* taut rope for balancing acrobats.

tīle, *n.*, *v.t.*, tiled, tiling. *n.* **1.** thin piece of material, originally baked earth. —*v.t.* **2.** furnish with tiles. —til'ing, *n.*

tĭll, *prep.*, *conj.* **1.** until. —*v.t.* **2.** prepare for growing crops. —*n.* **3.** money drawer. —till'age, *n.*

tĭl'lêr, *n.* steering lever.

tĭlt, *v.t.*, *v.i.* **1.** slant from an upright position. —*n.* **2.** act or instance of tilting.

tĭm'bêr, *n.* **1.** cut wood. **2.** trees collectively. —tim'bered, *adj.*

tim·bre (tam'bər), *n.* distinctive quality of sound.

tīme, *n.*, *v.t.*, timed, timing. *n.* **1.** past, present, and future. **2.** Often, times, period of occurrence. **3.** instance. —*prep.* **4.** times, multiplied by. —*v.t.* **5.** determine the time or duration of. —tim'er, *n.*

tīme'-hŏn'ōred, *adj.* honored because of long duration or usage.

tīme'lĕss, *adj.* eternal.

tīme'lȳ, *adj.*, -lier, -liest. coming at the right time. —time'li·ness, *n.*

tīme'piēce'', *n.* clock or watch.

tīme'sêrv''êr, *n.* exploiter of popular trends. —time'serv''ing, *n.*, *adj.*

tīme'tā''ble, *n.* schedule of times.

tīme'wôrn'', *adj.* worn or hackneyed by long use.

tĭm′ĭd, *adj.* lacking self-confidence. —**tim′id·ly,** *adv.* —**ti·mid′i·ty,** *n.*

tĭm′ĭng, *n.* performance with regard to time.

tĭm′ŏr·oŭs, *adj.* fearful. —**tim′or·ous·ly,** *adv.*

tĭm′ó·thÿ, *n.* grass used for hay.

tĭm′pà·nĭ, *n. pl.* kettledrums. —**tim′pa·nist,** *n.*

tĭn, *n., v.t.,* **tinned, tinning.** *n.* **1.** white metallic element. —*v.t.* **2.** plate with tin. —**tin′foil″,** *n.* —**tin′smith″,** *n.*

tĭnc′tûre, *n.* **1.** tinge. **2.** medicine in alcohol.

tĭn′dêr, *n.* dry flammable material. —**tin′der·box″.**

tĭne, *n.* fork prong.

tĭnge, *n., v.t.,* **tinged, tingeing** or **tinging.** *n.* **1.** slight color or trace. —*v.t.* **2.** give a tinge to.

tĭn′gle, *v.i.,* **-gled, -gling.** feel a slight prickle.

tĭn′kêr, *v.i.* work inexpertly.

tĭn′kle, *v.i.,* **-kled, -kling,** *n. v.i.* **1.** ring lightly. —*n.* **2.** light ringing sound.

tĭn′sèl, *n.* metal foil.

tĭnt, *n.* **1.** light color or shade. —*v.t.* **2.** give a tint to.

tī′nÿ, *adj.,* **-nier, -niest.** very small.

tĭp, *n., v.,* **tipped, tipping.** *n.* **1.** outermost point. **2.** reward for a service. —*v.t., v.i.* **3.** overturn. —*v.t.* **4.** give a tip to. —**tip′per,** *n.*

tĭp′sÿ, *adj.,* **-sier, -siest.** intoxicated. —**tip′si·ly,** *adv.*

tĭp′tŏe″, *v.i.,* **-toed, -toing.** walk on the balls of the feet.

tĭp′tŏp″, *adj.* **1.** highest. **2.** best.

tī′rāde, *n.* vehement speech.

tīre, *v.,* **tired, tiring,** *n. v.t.* **1.** make tired. —*v.i.* **2.** become tired. —*n.* **3.** wearing surface of a wheel.

tīred, *adj.* without strength because of exertion. —**tired′ly,** *adv.*

tīre′lèss, *adj.* without becoming tired. —**tire′less·ly,** *adv.*

tīre′sóme, *adj.* annoying; tedious. —**tire′some·ly,** *adv.* —**tire′some·ness,** *n.*

tĭs′sûe, *n.* **1.** thin cloth or paper. **2.** organic matter.

tī′tàn, *n.* giant. —**ti·tan′ic,** *adj.*

tĭt′ĭl·lāte″, *v.t.,* **-lated, -lating.** excite pleasantly. —**tit″il·la′tion,** *n.*

tī′tle, *n., v.t.,* **-tled, -tling.** *n.* **1.** formal name. **2.** right of ownership. —*v.t.* **3.** give a title to. —**ti′tled,** *adj.*

tĭt′têr, *v.i.,* *n.* giggle.

tĭt′tle, *n.* minute amount.

tĭt′ù·làr, *adj.* **1.** having a title. **2.** in name only. —**tit′u·lar·ly,** *adv.*

tĭz′zÿ, *n., pl.* **-zies.** *Informal.* excited state.

to, *prep.* **1.** as far as. **2.** in the direction of. **3.** until; before. **4.** being supported or held by. **5.** along with. **6.** in compassion or equivalence with.

tōad, *n.* froglike animal.

tōad′stool″, *n.* inedible mushroom.

tōast, *n.* **1.** browned sliced bread. **2.** drink in honor of someone. —*v.t.* **3.** brown with heat. **4.** drink in honor of. —**toast′er,** *n.* —**toast′mas″ter,** *n.*

tò·băc′cō, *n., pl.* **-cos.** leaves prepared for smoking, chewing, etc. —**to·bac′co·nist,** *n.*

tò·bŏg′gàn, *n.* **1.** long, flat sled. —*v.i.* **2.** coast on such a sled.

tò·dāy, *adv.* **1.** on the present day. —*n.* **2.** present day. **3.** modern times.

tŏd′dle, *n., v.i.,* **-dled, -dling.** *n.* **1.** unsteady walk. —*v.i.* **2.** walk in a toddle.

tŏd′dÿ, *n., pl.* **-dies.** hot alcoholic drink.

tōe, *n.* foot digit. —**toed,** *adj.* —**toe′nail″,** *n.*

tò·gĕth′êr, *adv.* one with another.

tōĭl, *n., v.i.* labor. —**toil′er,** *n.* —**toil′some,** *adj.*

toī′lét, *n.* **1.** dress and grooming. **2.** place or fixture for excretion.

toīl′et·rÿ, *n., pl.* **-ries.** aid to grooming.

tōĭls, *n. pl.* snare.

tō′kèn, *n.* **1.** souvenir. **2.** indication. **3.** metal disk used in payment. —*adj.* **4.** intended as a gesture.

tŏl′êr·ánce, *n.* **1.** patience or understanding. **2.** permissible deviation. **3.** resistance to poison, etc. —**tol′er·ant,** *adj.*

tŏl′êr·āte″, *v.t.,* **-ated, -ating. 1.** be patient with. **2.** endure. —**tol″er·a′tion,** *n.* —**tol′er·a·ble,** *adj.* —**tol′er·a·bly,** *adv.*

tŏll, *n.* **1.** tariff. *v.t., v.i.* **2.** ring solemnly. —**toll′gate″,** *n.*

tŏm, *adj.* male.

tŏm′à·hăwk″, *n.* Native American ax.

tò·mā′tō, *n., pl.* **-toes.** juicy red or yellow vegetable.

tomb, *n.* burial place. —**tomb'stone,''** *n.*

tŏm'bŏy'', *n.* boyish girl.

tò·mŏr'rōw, *n.*, *adv.* day after this.

tŏm'-tŏm'', *n.* hand drum.

tŏn, *n.* U.S. unit of 2,000 pounds.

tōne, *n.* **1.** sound of a certain pitch. **2.** shade of color. **3.** air or appearance. —**ton'al,** *adj.* —**to·nal'i·ity,** *n.* —**tone'deaf'',** *adj.*

tŏngs, *n. pl.* pincers.

tòngue, *n.* **1.** flexible licking and tasting organ in the mouth. **2.** language. **3.** projection.

tóngue'-lăsh''ĭng, *n.* severe scolding.

tòngue'-tīed'', *adj.* rendered speechless.

tŏn'ĭc, *n.* **1.** invigorating medicine. **2.** *Music.* keynote.

tò'nīght', *n.*, *adv.* this night.

tòn'nàge, *n.* shipping, esp. in terms of cargo capacity.

tŏn'sĭl, *n.* oval growth at the back of the throat. —**ton''sil·li'tis,** *n.*

tŏn·sô'rĭ·àl, *adj.* pertaining to barbering.

tōō, *adv.* **1.** also. **2.** excessively.

tōōl, *n.* **1.** object for shaping, fastening, etc. **2.** something or someone used. —*v.t.* **3.** shape with a tool.

tōōt, *v.i.* **1.** give a shrill whistle. —*n.* **2.** shrill whistle.

tōōth, *n.*, *pl.* **teeth. 1.** hard white growth used for biting. **2.** similar object in a gear, etc. —**tooth'ache'',** *n.* —**tooth' brush'',** *n.* —**toothed,** *adj.* —**tooth' less,** *adj.* —**tooth'pick'',** *n.* —**tooth'y,** *adj.*

tōōth'sòme, *adj.* tasty.

tŏp, *n.*, *v.t.*, **topped, topping.** *n.* **1.** uppermost point or part. **2.** spinning toy. —*v.t.* **3.** put a top on. **4.** remove a top from. **5.** surpass.

tō'păz, *n.* yellow gem.

tŏp'cōat'', *n.* light overcoat.

tŏp'-dräw'ėr, *adj.* *Informal.* first-rate. Also, **top'-flight', top'-notch'.**

tŏp'-hĕav''ÿ, *adj.* liable to tip.

tŏp'ĭc, *n.* subject of discussion. —**top'i·cal,** *adj.*

tŏp'mōst'', *adj.* at the very top.

tŏp'nŏtch', *adj.* *Informal.* among the best.

tò·pŏg'rá·phÿ, *n.*, *pl.* **-phies. 1.** study of the earth's surface. **2.** terrain. —**top''**

o·graph'i·cal, top''o·graph'ic, *adj.* —**to·pog'ra·pher,** *n.*

tŏp'pĭng, *n.* something put on top.

tŏp'ple, *v.,* **-pled, -pling.** *v.t.,* *v.i.* overturn.

tŏp'sāil'', *n. Nautical.* second sail up.

tŏp'sōil'', *n.* fertile surface soil.

tŏp'sÿ-tûr'vÿ, *adv.,* *adj.* in disorder.

Tō'ràh, *n.* Hebrew scriptures.

tôrch, *n.* flame-bearing object. —**torch' light'',** *n.,* *adj.*

tôr'ē·à·dôr'', *n.* bullfighter.

tor·ment, *v.t.* (tor ment') **1.** harass or torture. —*n.* (tor'ment) **2.** tormented state. **3.** something that torments. —**tor·men'tor, tor·men'ter,** *n.*

tôr·nā'dō, *n.,* *pl.* **-does, -dos.** violent whirlwind.

tôr·pē'dō, *n.,* *pl.* **-does,** *v.t.,* **-does, -doing.** *n.* **1.** explosive water projectile. —*v.t.* **2.** hit with a torpedo.

tôr'pĭd, *adj.* without energy. —**tor'pid· ly,** *adv.* —**tor'por, tor·pid'i·ty,** *n*

tôrque, *n.* twisting force.

tôr'rėnt, *n.* rush of fluid. —**tor·ren' tial,** *adj.*

tôr'rĭd, *adj.* **1.** hot. **2. Torrid,** between the tropics on either side of the equator.

tôr'sion, *n.* twisting. —**tor'sion·al,** *adj.*

tôr'sō, *n.,* *pl.* **-sos.** trunk of the human body.

tôrt, *n. Law.* basis of a civil suit.

tor'til·la (tôr tē'yà), *n.* flat Mexican cake of corn meal.

tôr'toise, *n.* land turtle.

tôr'tū·oŭs, *adj.* winding; involved. —**tor'tu·ous·ly,** *adv.* —**tor'tu·ous· ness,** *n.*

tôr'tûre, *n.,* *v.t.,* **-tured, -turing.** *n.* **1.** application of severe pain, etc. —*v.t.* **2.** subject to torture. —**tor'tur·er,** *n.*

tŏss, *v.t.* **1.** throw lightly. **2.** jerk upward. —*n.* **3.** act or instance of tossing.

tŏss'ŭp'', *n.* even chance.

tŏt, *n.* small child.

tō'tàl, *adj.* **1.** being a sum. **2.** complete. —*n.* **3.** sum. —**to'tal·ly,** *adv.* —**to·tal' i·ty,** *n.*

tō·tǎl''ĭ·tār'ĭ·àn·ĭsm, *n.* absolute control by one political group. —**to·tal''i· tar'i·an,** *n.,* *adj.*

tōte, *v.t.,* **toted, toting.** carry.

tō'tėm, *n.* natural object used as a clan symbol. —**to·tem'ic,** *adj.*

tŏt'têr, *v.i.* walk unsteadily.

toŭch, *v.t.* **1.** tap, pat, or feel. **2.** move emotionally. —*n.* **3.** act or instance of touching. **4.** distinctive manner. **5.** slight amount. —**touch′ing,** *adj.* —**touch′ing·ly,** *adv.*

toŭch ănd gō, precarious situation.

toŭch′dōwn, *n.* football score.

toŭched, *adj.* **1.** emotionally moved. **2.** insane.

toŭch′stōne″, *n.* test of genuineness or worth.

toŭch′ÿ, *adj.,* **-ier, -iest.** readily hurt or annoyed. —**touch′i·ness,** *n.*

toŭgh, *adj.* **1.** resistant to injury. **2.** enduring. **3.** brutal. **4.** difficult. —**tough′ness,** *n.* —**tough′en,** *v.t., v.i.*

tou·pee (tōō pa′), *n.* small wig worn esp. by men.

toŭr, *n.* **1.** trip with many stops. —*v.t.* **2.** make a tour through.

toŭr dė fôrce, *n., pl.* **tours de force.** example of high skill.

toŭr′ĭst, *n.* person on a pleasure tour. —**tour′ism,** *n.*

toŭr′nȧ·mėnt, *n.* **1.** knightly contest. **2.** series of athletic contests.

toûr′nĭ·qŭet, *n.* twisted device to stop bleeding.

tŏu′sle, *v.t.,* **-sled, -sling.** muss.

tōŭt, *Informal. v.t.* **1.** praise highly. **2.** sell bets. —*n.* **3.** person who touts.

tōw, *v.t.* **1.** pull with a line. —*n.* **2.** act or instance of towing. —**tow′line″,** **tow′rope″,** *n.* —**tow′path″,** *n.*

tō·wȧrd′, *prep.* in the direction of. Also, **to·wards′.**

tŏw′ėl, *n.* drying cloth.

tōw′ėr, *n.* **1.** tall construction. —*v.i.* **2.** stand high.

tōw′ėr·ing, *adj.* **1.** standing high. **2.** violent.

tōwn, *n.* **1.** large community. **2.** urban center. —**towns′man,** *n.* —**towns′-peo″ple,** *n., pl.*

tōwn′shĭp″, *n.* unit of local government.

tŏx′ĭc, *adj.* poisonous. —**tox·ic′i·ty,** *n.*

tŏx″ĭ·cŏl′ó·gÿ, *n.* study of poisons. —**tox″i·col′o·gist,** *n.*

tŏx′ĭn, *n.* poison from organisms.

tōÿ, *n.* **1.** something to play with. —*v.i.* **2.** play; trifle.

trāce, *n., v.t.,* **traced, tracing.** *n.* **1.** faint sign or trail. —*v.t.* **2.** follow the trail of. **3.** copy by following the lines of. —**trace′a·ble,** *adj.* —**trac′er,** *n.* —**trac′ing,** *n.*

trăc′ėr·ÿ, *n., pl.* **-ies.** decorative frame in a window.

trăck, *n.* **1.** trail or trace. **2.** pair of rails, etc. used as a guide. —*v.t.* **3.** follow or trace. —**track′less,** *adj.*

trăct, *n.* **1.** expanse of land. **2.** series of bodily organs. **3.** religious leaflet.

trăc′tȧ·ble, *adj.* readily managed. —**trac′ta·bly,** *adv.* —**trac″ta·bil′i·ty,** *n.*

trăc′tion, *n.* **1.** pulling effort. **2.** friction between a foot or wheel and a surface.

trăc′tör, *n.* pulling vehicle.

trāde, *v.,* **traded, trading,** *n. v.t.* **1.** exchange. —*v.t.* **2.** have business dealings. **3.** make an exchange. —*n.* **4.** buying and selling. **5.** skilled occupation. **6.** swap. —**trad′er,** *n.*

trāde′-ĭn″, *n.* return of a used object in partial payment for a new one.

trāde′mârk″, *n.* symbol of a business or product.

trāde′ôff″, *n.* sacrifice of one advantage for another.

trādes′mȧn, *n.* **1.** skilled worker. **2.** merchant.

trāde wĭnd, tropical wind blowing toward the equator.

trȧ·dī′tion, *n.* long-accepted custom or belief. —**tra·di′tion·al,** *adj.* —**tra·di′tion·al·ly,** *adv.* —**tra·di′tion·al·ist,** *n., adj.*

trȧ·dūce′, *v.t.,* **-duced, -ducing.** slander.

trăf′fĭc, *n., v.i.,* **-ficked, -ficking.** *n.* **1.** movement along roadways. **2.** commerce. —*v.i.* **3.** have dealings. —**traf′fick·er,** *n.*

trăg′ė·dÿ, *n., pl.* **-ies. 1.** drama ending unhappily. **2.** disastrous event. —**tra·ge′di·an,** *n., fem.,* **tra·ge′di·enne″.** —**trag′ĭc, trag′i·cal,** *adj.* —**trag′i·cal·ly,** *adv.*

trāil, *n.* **1.** mark left in passing. **2.** route, esp. in wild country. —*v.t.* **3.** trace. **4.** drag. —*v.i.* **5.** drag or grow along the ground.

trāil′ẽr, *n.* vehicle pulled by another.

trāin, *n.* **1.** string of railroad cars. **2.** trailing skirt or cape. **3.** connected series. **4.** procession. —*v.t.* **5.** educate for a purpose. **6.** exercise for sports.

—train·ee', *n.* —train'er, *n.* —train'ing, *n.*

träipse, *v.i.* traipsed, traipsing. *Informal.* walk.

trait, *n.* distinctive quality.

trai'tor, *n.* betrayer. —trai'tor·ous, *adj.*

trà·jĕc'to·rÿ, *n., pl.* -ries. path of a missile.

trăm, *n.* car on rails.

trăm'mèl, *n.* 1. Usually trammels, hindrance or restraint. —*v.t.* 2. hinder or restrain.

trămp, *v.i.* 1. walk heavily. 2. travel on foot. —*n.* 3. vagrant. 4. hike. 5. unscheduled freighter.

trăm'ple, *v.,* -pled, -pling. *v.i.* 1. tread heavily. —*v.t.* 2. crush under foot.

tram·po·line (tram'pə lēn''), *n.* stretched horizontal sheet used by gymnasts.

trănce, *n.* sleeplike or abstracted state.

trăn'quĭl, *adj.* serene; relaxed. —tran'quil·ly, *adv.* —tran·quil'i·ty, *n.* —tran'quil·ize'', *v.t.* —tran'quil·iz''er, *n.*

trăns·ăct', *v.t.* complete, as a business deal. —trans·ac'tion, *n.* —trans·ac'tor, *n.*

trăns''àt·lăn'tĭc, *adj.* 1. from across the Atlantic Ocean. 2. across the Atlantic Ocean.

trăn·scĕnd', *v.t.* 1. go outside the limits of. 2. surpass. —tran·scend'ent, *adj.*

trăn''scèn·dĕn'tàl, *adj.* beyond the limits of the apparent world. —tran''scen·den'tal·ism, *n.* —tran''scen·den·tal·ist, *n., adj.*

trăns''cŏn·tĭ·nĕn'tàl, *adj.* across a continent.

trăn·scrībe', *v.t.,* -scribed, -scribing. copy elsewhere or in another medium.

trăn'scrĭpt, *n.* copy of a document.

trăn·scrĭp'tion, *n.* 1. transcript. 2. arrangement of a musical score. 3. radio or television recording.

trăn'sĕpt, *n.* arm of a church crossing the nave.

trăns'fêr, *v.,* -ferred, -ferring, *n. v.t., v.i.* 1. move to another place. —*n.* 2. act or instance of transferring. 3. authorization for transferring. —trans·fer'a·ble, *adj.* —trans·fer'ence, *n.*

trăns·fĭg'ûre, *v.t.,* -ured, -uring. make glorious. —trans·fig''u·ra'tion, *n.*

trăns·fĭx', *v.t.* 1. pierce. 2. halt in one's tracks.

trăns·fôrm', *v.t., v.i.* change in nature. —trans''for·ma'tion, *n.* —trans·form'er, *n.*

trăns·fūse', *v.t.,* -fused, -fusing. 1. instill. 2. admit to a blood vessel. —trans·fu'sion, *n.*

trăns·grĕss', *v.t.* 1. sin against. 2. go beyond. —trans·gres'sion, *n.* —trans·gres'sor, *n.*

trăn'sìent, *adj.* 1. temporary. —*n.* 2. temporary lodger. —tran'sient·ly, *adv.* —tran'science, tran'scien·cy, *n.*

trăn·sĭs'tor, *n.* device controlling electrical current flow. —tran·sis'tor·ize'', *v.t.*

trăn'sĭt, *n.* 1. movement from place to place. 2. public transportation.

trăn·sĭ'tion, *n.* gradual change of nature or condition. —tran·si'tion·al, *adj.*

trăn'sĭ·tĭve, *adj. Grammar.* taking a direct object.

trăn'sĭ·tô''rÿ, *adj.* impermanent. —tran'si·to''ri·ness, *n.*

trăns·lāte', *v.t.,* -lated, -lating. 1. alter in language. 2. alter in condition. —trans·la'tion, *n.* —trans·la'tor, *n.* —trans·lat'a·ble, *adj.*

trăns·lĭt'êr·āte'', *v.t.,* -ated, -ating. put into a different alphabet, etc. —trans·lit''er·a'tion, *n.*

trăns·lū'cĕnt, *adj.* passing light but not images. —trans·lu'cence, trans·lu'cen·cy, *n.*

trăns·mī'grāte, *v.i.,* -grated, -grating. enter a new body after death. —trans''mi·gra'tion, *n.*

trăns·mĭs'sìon, *n.* 1. act or instance of transmitting. 2. something transmitted. 3. gear assembly.

trăns·mĭt', *v.t.,* -mitted, -mitting. 1. convey through a medium. 2. send out in radio waves. 3. hand down, as to a new generation. —trans·mit'tal, trans·mit'tance, *n.* —trans·mit'ti·ble, trans·mit'ta·ble, *adj.* —trans·mit'ter, *n.*

trăns·mūte, *v.t.,* -muted, -muting. alter in nature. —trans''mu·ta'tion, *n.* —trans·mut'a·ble, *adj.*

trăns''ō·cē·ăn'ĭc, *adj.* across the ocean.

trăn'sòm, *n.* 1. crosspiece. 2. window over a door.

trăns''pà·cĭf'ĭc, *adj.* 1. from across the

Pacific Ocean. **2.** across the Pacific Ocean.

trăns·pār′ėnt, *adj.* **1.** passing light and images. **2.** obvious. **—trans·par′ent·ly,** *adv.* **—trans·par′en·cy,** *n.*

trăn·spīre′, *v.i.,* **-spired, -spiring. 1.** become known. **2.** *Informal.* occur. **—tran′′spi·ra′tion,** *n.*

trăns·plănt′, *v.t.* **1.** plant in a new place. **2.** graft surgically. **—n. 3.** act or instance of transplanting. **—trans′′planta′tion,** *n.*

trăns·pôrt′, *v.t.* **1.** carry. **—n.** (trans′port) **2.** transportation. **3.** state of rapture. **4.** carrier for troops. **—trans′′por·ta′tion,** *n.*

trăns·pōse′, *v.,* **-posed, -posing.** *v.t., v.i.* change in order or position. **—trans′′po·si′tion,** *n.*

trăns·sĕx′ū·ȧl, *n.* person who identifies with or undergoes surgery to become the opposite sex.

trăns·shĭp′, *v.t.,* **-shipped, -shipping.** put on a new conveyance. **—trans·ship′ment,** *n.*

trăns·vêrse′, *adj.* crosswise. **—trans·verse′ly,** *adv.*

trăns·vĕs′tīte, *n.* dresser in clothes of the opposite sex.

trăp, *n., v.t.,* **trapped, trapping.** *n.* **1.** device for catching animals. **2.** trick for detection or capture. **—v.t. 3.** catch. **4.** adorn. **—trap′per,** *n.* **—trap′pings,** *n. pl.*

trăp′dôor′, *n.* horizontal door.

trȧ·pēze′, *n.* swing with a bar.

trăp′ė·zoĭd′′, *n.* four-sided figure with two parallel sides. **—trap′′e·zoi′dal,** *adj.*

trăsh, *n.* discarded matter. **—trash′y,** *adj.*

trau̇′mȧ, *n., pl.* **-mas, -mata.** bodily or emotional shock. **—trau·mat′ic,** *adj.* **—trau′ma·tize′′,** *v.t.*

trȧ·vāil, *n.* agony.

trăv′ėl, *v.i.,* **-eled** or **-elled, -eling** or **-elling,** *n. v.i.* **1.** go on a journey. **—n. 2.** traveling, esp. for pleasure. **—trav′el·er, trav′el·ler,** *n.*

trăv·êrse′, *v.t.,* **-ersed, -ersing.** pass across.

trăv′ės·tŷ, *n., pl.* **-ties,** *v.t.,* **-tied, -tying.** *n.* **1.** mocking imitation. **—v.t. 2.** make a travesty of.

trăwl, *n.* **1.** dragged fish net. **—v.i. 2.** use a trawl. **—trawl′er,** *n.*

trāy, *n.* shallow, broad receptacle.

trēach′êr·ÿ, *n., pl.* **-ies.** betrayal of trust. **—treach′er·ous,** *adj.*

trĕad, *v.,* **trod, trodden, treading.** *v.i.* **1.** walk deliberately. **—v.t. 2.** press, make, etc. by treading. **—n. 3.** manner of treading. **4.** step. **5.** surface of a wheel, tire, etc. that touches the ground.

trēa′dle, *n.* foot-operated lever.

trēa′sȯn, *n.* betrayal of one's country. **—trea′son·a·ble, trea′son·ous,** *adj.*

trĕas′ūre, *n., v.t.,* **-ured, -uring.** *n.* **1.** precious possession. **—v.t. 2.** regard as a treasure.

trĕas′ûr·êr, *n.* handler of funds.

trĕas′ûre-trōve′′, *n.* discovered treasure.

trĕas′ûr·ÿ, *n., pl.* **-ies.** department or place for storing money.

trĕat, *v.t.* **1.** act toward as specified. **2.** handle as specified. **3.** give medical care to. **4.** have as a guest. **—n. 5.** something offered a guest. **6.** source of pleasure. **—treat′ment,** *n.*

trēa′tīse, *n.* paper on a subject.

trēa′tŷ, *n., pl.* **-ties.** agreement between nations.

trĕ′ble, *adj., v.t.,* **-bled, -bling.** *adj.* **1.** triple. **2.** high-pitched. **—v.t. 3.** multiply by three. **—treb′ly,** *adv.*

trēe, *n., v.t.,* **treed, treeing.** *n.* **1.** tall plant with a woody stem and branches. **—v.t. 2.** chase up a tree. **—tree′less,** *adj.*

trĕk, *v.i.,* **trekked, trekking,** *n. v.i.* **1.** travel with difficulty. **—n. 2.** long, difficult journey.

trĕl′lĭs, *n.* frame for climbing plants.

trĕm′ble, *v.i.,* **-bled, -bling. 1.** shiver. **2.** be in fear or awe.

trė·mĕn′doŭs, *adj.* huge. **—tre·men′dous·ly,** *adv.*

trĕm′ȯ·lō′′, *n., pl.* **-os.** wavering of a musical tone.

trĕm′ȯr, *n.* quiver.

trĕm′ū·loŭs, *adj.* timid.

trĕnch, *n.* deep, narrow ditch.

trĕnch′ȧnt, *adj.* incisive.

trĕnd, *n.* current style or tendency.

trĕp′′ĭ·dā′tion, *n.* fear and doubt.

trĕs′pȧss, *v.i.* **1.** enter property without right. **—n. 2.** sin. **—tres′pas·ser,** *n.*

trĕss, *n.* lock of hair.

trĕs'tle, *n.* **1.** transverse frame. **2.** viaduct on framed towers.

trī'ăd, *n.* group of three.

trī'ăl, *n.* **1.** test, as for value. **2.** annoyance or source of annoyance. **3.** examination in a law court.

trī'ăn·gle, *n.* three-sided figure. —tri·an'gu·lar, *adj.*

trībe, *n.* group of related persons under one leader. —trib'al, *adj.* —tribes'man, *n.*

trĭb''ū·lā'tion, *n.* distress.

trī·bŭ'năl, *n.* court of justice.

trĭb'ūne, *n.* speaking platform.

trĭb'ū·tār''ÿ, *adj., n., pl.* -ies. *adj.* **1.** paying tribute. **2.** flowing into a larger stream. —*n.* **3.** tributary stream or river.

trĭb'ūte, *n.* **1.** compulsory payment. **2.** expression of gratitude or honor.

trīce, *n.* instant.

trĭck, *n.* **1.** cunning or treacherous act. —*v.t.* **2.** cheat. —trick'er·y, *n.* —trick'ster, *n.*

trĭck'le, *v.i.,* -led, -ling. flow in a thin, slow stream.

trĭck'ÿ, *adj.,* -ier, -iest. **1.** treacherous; wily. **2.** challenging the skill or cunning.

trī'cy·cle, *n.* three-wheeled vehicle.

trī'dĕnt, *n.* three-pronged spear.

trīed, *adj.* proved, esp. as trustworthy.

trī'fle, *n., v.i.,* -fled, -fling. *n.* **1.** something of little importance. —*v.i.* **2.** talk or act frivolously. —tri'fler, *n.*

trī'flĭng, *adj.* unimportant; insignificant.

trī'fō''căls, *n.* spectacles with three focuses.

trĭg'gĕr, *n.* **1.** lever for firing a gun. —*v.t.* **2.** precipitate; cause to happen.

trĭg''ò·nŏm'ĕ·trÿ, *n.* mathematics based on the triangle. —trig''o·no·met'ric, *adj.*

trĭll, *n.* **1.** high, warbling sound. —*v.i.* **2.** emit a trill.

trĭl'liŏn, *n.* one thousand billion.

trĭl'ò·gÿ, *n., pl.* -gies. trio of related novels, etc.

trĭm, *v.t.,* trimmed, trimming, *n., adj.,* trimmer, trimmest. *v.t.* **1.** make neat. **2.** decorate. **3.** balance. —*n.* **4.** good condition. —*adj.* **5.** neat. —trim'lÿ, *adv.* —trim'mer, *n.*

trī·mĕs'têr, *n.* three months.

trĭm'mĭng, *n.* something added, as a decoration.

trĭn'ĭ·tÿ, *n., pl.* -ties. **1.** set of three. **2.** the Trinity, God as Father, Son, and Holy Spirit.

trĭn'kĕt, *n.* small ornament.

tri·o (trē'ō), *n., pl.* -os. group of three.

trĭp, *v.,* tripped, tripping, *n. v.i.* **1.** stumble and lose balance. —*v.t.* **2.** cause to stumble. **3.** set in motion. —*n.* **4.** act or instance of tripping. **5.** journey.

trī·pâr'tīte, *adj.* in three parts.

trīpe, *n.* **1.** edible part of an animal stomach. **2.** *Informal.* drivel.

trĭp'hăm''mêr, *n.* heavy mechanical hammer.

trī'ple, *adj., v.,* -pled, -pling. *adj.* **1.** in three parts. **2.** three times normal size. —*v.t., v.i.* **3.** multiply three times. —tri'plÿ, *adv.*

trī'plĕt, *n.* one of three siblings born at the same time.

trĭp'lĭ·cāte, *n.* threefold form.

trī'pŏd, *n.* three-legged support.

trī·sĕct', *v.t.* divide in three. —tri·sec'tion, *n.*

trīte, *adj.,* triter, tritest. overly familiar. —trite'lÿ, *adv.* —trite'ness, *n.*

trī'ŭmph, *n.* **1.** victory. **2.** delight in victory. —*v.i.* **3.** be victorious. —tri·um'phal, *adj.* —tri·um'phant, *adj.*

trī·ŭm'vĭ·răte, *n.* trio in power.

trĭv'ĕt, *n.* stand for hot things.

trĭv'ĭ·ă, *n., pl.* trivial things.

trĭv'ĭ·ăl, *adj.* petty and unimportant. —triv''i·al'i·ty, *n.* —triv''i·al·ly, *adv.*

trŏll, *n.* supernatural cave dweller.

trŏl'lēy, *n., pl.* -leys. **1.** raised structure for collecting electricity. **2.** streetcar with such a structure. **3.** wheeled container.

trŏm·bōne', brass musical instrument. —trom·bon'ist, *n.*

trōōp, *n.* **1.** uniformed group. —*v.i.* **2.** move in a group. —troop'er, *n.*

trō'phÿ, *n., pl.* -phies. memento of victory.

trŏp'ĭc, *n.* **1.** boundary of the Torrid Zone. **2.** tropics, Torrid Zone or nearby areas. —*adj.* **3.** Also, trop'i·cal, pertaining to the Torrid Zone.

trō'pĭsm, *n. Biology.* response, as in growth, to stimuli.

trŏt, *v.i.*, trotted, trotting, *n. v.i.* **1.** run at moderate speed. —*n.* **2.** trotting gait. —trot'ter, *n.*

troū'bå·dôur'', *n.* medieval singer.

troŭ'ble, *n.*, *v.*, -bled, -bling. *n.* **1.** worry or exertion. **2.** source of these. —*v.t.* **3.** cause trouble to. —*v.i.* **4.** go to trouble. —trou'ble·some, *adj.* —trou'ble·mak''er, *n.*

trŏugh, *n.* long, open container.

troŭnce, *v.t.*, trounced, trouncing. beat.

troūpe, *n.* group of performers. —troup'er, *n.*

troū'sêrs, *n. pl.* pants.

troŭs'seau, *n.*, *pl.* -seaux, -seaus. bride's clothing, etc.

trŏut, *n.*, *pl.* trout, trouts. edible freshwater fish.

trŏw'ĕl, *n.* spreading or scooping hand tool.

trŏy, *adj.* pertaining to a jeweler's weight with a twelve-ounce pound.

trū'ånt, *n.* unauthorized absentee from school. —tru'an·cy, *n.*

trūce, *n.* temporary suspension of hostilities.

trŭck, *n.* **1.** freight motor vehicle. **2.** hand cart for loads. —*v.t.* **3.** carry by truck. —truck'er, *n.*

trŭck'le, *v.i.*, -led, -ling. be servilely submissive.

trŭc'ū·lĕnt, *adj.* fierce. —truc'u·lent·ly, *adv.* —truc'u·lence, *n.*

trŭdge, *v.i.*, trudged, trudging, *n. v.i.* **1.** walk laboriously. —*n.* **2.** laborious walk.

trūe, *adj.*, truer, truest. **1.** according with truth. **2.** faithful. —tru'ly, *adv.* —true'ness, *n.*

trū'ĭsm, *n.* tritely true statement.

trŭmp, *n.* highest-ranking card.

trŭmp'êr·ÿ, *n.*, *pl.* -ies. worthlessly pretentious things.

trŭm'pĕt, *n.* brass musical wind instrument. —trum'pet·er, *n.*

trŭn'cāte, *v.t.*, -cated, -cating. remove part of. —trun·ca'tion, *n.*

trŭn'cheŏn, *n.* club.

trŭn'dle, *v.t.*, -dled, -dling. roll out or along.

trŭnk, *n.* **1.** large piece of luggage. **2.** main stem of a tree. **3.** body apart from head and limbs.

trŭss, *n.* **1.** frame of triangular parts. **2.** support for the ruptured. —*v.t.* **3.** bind up. **4.** support with a truss.

trŭst, *n.* **1.** reliance; faith. **2.** custody. **3.** monopolistic combination. —*v.t.* **4.** have reliance or faith in. —trust'ful, trust'ing, *adj.* —trust'worth''y, trust'y, *adj.*

trŭst·ee', *n.* person to whom property is entrusted. —trus·tee'ship, *n.*

trŭst'ÿ, *adj.*, -ier, -iest. trustworthy.

trūth, *n.* **1.** that which is actually so. **2.** accuracy. —truth'ful, *adj.* —truth'ful·ly, *adv.* —truth'ful·ness, *n.*

trÿ, *v.t.*, tried, trying, *n. v.t* **1.** attempt. **2.** test. **3.** examine in a court of law. **4.** annoy or afflict. —*n.* **5.** attempt or test. —try'ing, *adj.*

trÿ'ōut'', *n. Informal.* test operation.

trÿst, *n.* lovers' appointment.

tsâr, *n.* Slavic emperor, variant of czar.

tŭb, *n.* broad, deep vessel.

tū'bå, *n.* large brass wind musical instrument.

tŭb'bÿ, *adj.*, -bier, -biest. chubby.

tūbe, *n.* hollow cylinder. —tub'ing, *n.* —tub'u·lar, *adj.*

tū'bêr, *n.* swelling part of an underground plant stem. —tu'ber·ous, *adj.*

tū·bêr''cū·lō'sĭs, *n.* illness with swelling lesions. —tu·ber'cu·lar, tu·ber'cu·lous, *adj.*

Tūes'dāy, *n.* third day of the week.

tŭft, *n.* cluster of fibers, threads, etc.

tŭg, *v.t.*, tugged, tugging, *n. v.t.* **1.** pull forcefully. —*n.* **2.** act or instance of tugging. —tug'boat'', *n.*

tū·ī'tion, *n.* fee for teaching.

tū'lĭp, *n.* plant with a cup-shaped flower.

tŭm'ble, *v.i.*, -bled, -bling. **1.** fall or roll helplessly. **2.** perform acrobatics on a flat surface.

tŭm'blêr, *n.* **1.** drinking glass. **2.** acrobat who tumbles.

tū'mĭd, *adj.* swollen.

tŭm'mÿ, *n.*, *pl.* -mies. *Informal.* stomach.

tū'mör, *n.* abnormal growth.

tū'mŭlt, *n.* commotion. —tu·mul'tu·ous, *adj.*

tŭn, *n.* large cask.

tū'nà, *n.*, *pl.* -na, nas. large ocean fish.

tŭn'drå, *n.* barren Arctic plain.

tūne, *n.*, *v.t.*, -tuned, tuning. *n.* 1. melody. 2. harmony. —*v.t.* 3. put in tune. —tune'ful, *adj.* —tune'less, *adj.*

tūn'ĭc, *adj.* jacket, often belted.

tŭn'nĕl, *n.*, *v.i.*, -neled, -neling. *n.* 1. route cut underground. —*v.i.* 2. dig a route.

tûr'băn, *n.* headdress of wound cloth.

tûr'bĭd, *adj.* cloudy or muddy. —tur·bid'i·ty, *n.*

tûr'bīne, *n.* rotary engine driven by the passing of a fluid.

tûr'bō·jĕt'', *n.* jet engine using turbine-compressed air.

tûr'bū·lĕnt, *adj.* in disturbed motion. —tur'bu·lence, *n.*

tŭ·rēen', *n.* covered soup container.

tûrf, *n.* earth held by grass roots. —turf'y, *adj.*

tûr'gĭd, *adj.* pompously or excessively worded. —tur'gid·ly, *adv.* —tur·gid'i·ty, tur·gid·ness, *n.*

tûr'kĕy, *n.* large North American fowl.

tûr'mŏĭl, *n.* confused activity.

tûrn, *v.t.*, *v.i.* 1. change in direction. 2. change in nature. —*n.* 3. curve. 4. loop. 5. place in a sequence. 6. act toward another. —turn'ing, *n.*

tûrn'à·bŏut'', *n.* reversal of conditions.

tûrn'cōat'', *n.* renegade.

tûr'nĭp, *n.* edible root.

tûrn'ŏut'', *n.* attendance at a meeting.

tûrn'ō''vèr, *n.* 1. rate of sale, replacement, etc. 2. baked dish of crust folded over filling.

tûrn'pīke'', *n.* toll road.

tûrn'stīle'', *n.* rotating gate.

tûrn'tā''ble, *n.* rotating platform.

tûr'pèn·tīne'', *n.* oil from coniferous trees.

tûr'pĭ·tūde'', *n.* vileness.

tûr'quoĭse, *n.* greenish-blue stone.

tûr'rĕt, *n.* 1. small tower. 2. housing for cannon.

tûr'tle, *n.* shell-encased reptile.

tŭsk, *n.* long, projected tooth.

tŭs'sle, *n.*, *v.i.*, -sled, -sling. struggle.

tū'tè·làge, *n.* 1. guardianship. 2. education. —tu'te·lar, tu'te·lar''y, *adj.*

tū'tör, *n.* 1. private teacher. —*v.t.* 2. teach privately. —tu·to'ri·al, *adj.*, *n.*

tŭx·ē'dō, *n.* semiformal evening suit.

TV, television.

twăng, *n.* 1. sound of a plucked string. 2. nasal accent.

twēak, *v.t.*, *n.* pinch with a twist.

twēed, *n.* rough woolen cloth.

twēet, *n.*, *v.i.* chirp.

twēez'êrs, *n. pl.* small pincers.

twĕlve, *n.*, *adj.* ten plus two. —twelfth, *adj.*, *n.*

twĕn'tў, *adj.*, *n.* two times ten. —twen'ti·eth, *adj.*

twīce, *adv.* two times.

twĭd'dle, *v.t.*, -dled, -dling. play with absently.

twĭg, *n.* tiny plant branch.

twī'līght'', *n.* half-light, as between day and night.

twĭll, *n.* cloth with a diagonal pattern.

twĭn, *n.* 1. one of two siblings born at the same time. 2. exact match. —*adj.* 3. matching another or each other exactly.

twīne, *n.*, *v.*, twined, twining. *n.* 1. string. —*v.t.*, *v.i.* 2. twist together.

twīnge, *n.* stab of pain.

twĭn'kle, *v.i.*, -kled, -kling, *n.* *v.i.* 1. gleam intermittently. 2. show amusement. —*n.* 3. act or instance of twinkling.

twĭn'klĭng, *n.* instant.

twîrl, *v.t.*, *v.i.* rotate rapidly.

twīst, *v.t.* 1. wind around, rotate, or bend into a helical form. 2. distort the actuality of. —*v.i.* 3. assume a twisted form. 4. squirm. —*n.* 5. act or instance of twisting.

twĭt, *v.t.*, twitted, twitting. address teasingly.

twĭtch, *v.i.* 1. jerk spasmodically. 2. pluck. —*n.* 3. spasmodic jerk.

twĭt'têr, *v.i.* chirp rapidly.

two, *n.*, *adj.* one plus one. —two'fold'', *adj.*, *adv.* —two'some, *n.*

two'-ĕdged', *adj.* interpretable two ways.

tў·cōōn', *n.* man of great wealth and power.

tўpe, *n.*, *v.t.*, typed, typing. *n.* 1. variety; sort. 2. reproducible characters used in printing. —*v.t.* 3. classify. 4. produce with a typewriter.

tўpe'wrīt''êr, *n.* machine for producing letters by mechanical means.

tў'phoĭd, *n.* acute infectious disease.

tў·phoōn', *n.* violent storm of the west Pacific Ocean.

tў'phŭs, *n.* acute infectious disease.

tўp'ĭ·căl, *n.* 1. representative of a type. 2. customary. —typ'i·cal·ly, *adv.*

tўp′ĭ·fỹ″, *v.t.,* **-fied, -fying.** be typical of.

tўp′ĭst, *n.* user of typewriters.

tỹ·pŏg′rȧ·phỹ, *n.* art of composing and printing with type. **—ty″po·graph′ic,** *adj.* **—ty·pog′ra·pher,** *n.*

tỹ′rȧnt, *n.* harsh, arbitrary ruler. **—tyr′an·ny,** *n.* **—ty·ran′ni·cal,** *adj.* **—tyr′an·nize″,** *v.i., v.t.*

tỹ′rō, *n., pl.* **-ros.** beginner; novice.

U

U, u, *n.* twenty-first letter of the English alphabet.

ū·bĭq′uĭ·tỹ, *n.* presence everywhere simultaneously. **—u·biq′ui·tous,** *adj.*

ŭd′dêr, *n.* mammary gland of a cow.

ŭg′lỹ, *adj.,* **-lier, -liest. 1.** unattractive. **2.** discomforting: difficult. **—ug′li·ness,** *n.*

ū·kāse′, *n.* arbitrary command.

ŭl′cêr, *n.* open break in tissue. **—ul′cer·ous,** *adj.* **—ul′cer·ate″,** *v.i., v.t.*

ŭl′nȧ, *n.* large bone of the forearm. **—ul′nar,** *adj.*

ŭl·tē′rĭ·ör, *adj.* **1.** further; beyond. **2.** concealed; disguised.

ŭl′tĭ·mȧte, *adj.* **1.** final; conclusive. **2.** fundamental; basic. **—ul′ti·mate·ly,** *adv.*

ŭl″tĭ·mā′tŭm, *n., pl.* **-matums, -mata.** final, decisive demand.

ŭl′tĭ·mō, *adj.* of or occurring in the preceding month.

ŭl′trȧ·līght, *n.* miniature aircraft for solo, powered flight.

ŭl″trȧ·mȧ·rīne′, *adj.* deep blue.

ŭl″trȧ·vī′ȯ·lĕt, *adj.* beyond the visible spectrum at its violet end.

ŭm′bĕl, *n.* cluster of flowers with the stalks having a common center.

ŭm′bêr, *n.* reddish brown.

ŭm·bĭl′ĭ·cŭs, *n.* navel. **—um·bil′i·cal,** *adj.*

ŭm′brȧge, *n.* resentment; pique.

ŭm·brĕl′lȧ, *n.* collapsible device with a fabric-covered frame, carried for protection against the weather.

ŭm′pīre, *n., v.t.,* **-pired, -piring.** *n.* **1.** final authority; judge. **—v.t. 2.** to serve as umpire for.

ŭn-, prefix indicating "not." **unable, unassuming, unavoidable, unaware, unbalanced, unbend, unborn, unbridled, uncertain, uncivil, unclean, unclothe, uncommon, unconcern, unconscious, uncork, undeniable, undeclared, undress, undue, unduly, uneasy, unequal, unerring, unexpected, unfailing, unfaithful, unfasten, unfit, unfold, unfortunate, unfriendly, ungodly, unhinge, unholy, unlike, unlock, unnatural, unpack, unroll, unscrew, unsettle, unshackle, unsightly, untangle, untouchable, untrue, untruth, untypical, unusual, unveil, unwell, unwind, unwise, unyoke.**

ū″năn′ĭ·moŭs, *adj.* totally agreed. **—u·na·nim′i·ty,** *n.* **—u″nan′i·mous·ly,** *adv.*

ŭn″ȧ·wāres′, *adv.* not aware.

ŭn·bȯ′sȯm, *v.t.* disclose; reveal.

ŭn·cälled′-fôr″, *adj.* unwarranted; unneeded.

ŭn·căn′nỹ, *adj.* unnatural; eerie.

ŭn′cle, *n.* brother of one's mother or father, or husband of one's aunt.

Ŭncle Săm, the United States.

ŭn·cŏn′scion·ȧ·ble, *adj.* excessive; unreasonable. **—un·con′scion·a·bly,** *adv.*

ŭn·coûth′, *adj.* lacking grace; clumsy.

ŭnc′tion, *n.* consecration with oil.

ŭnc′tū·oŭs, *adj.* **1.** oily. **2.** unpleasantly suave.

ŭn′dêr, *prep., adj., adv.* **1.** below; beneath. **2.** less than. **—adj. 3.** lower.

ŭn′dêr·brŭsh″, *n.* low-growing forest shrubs and grass.

ŭn′dêr·cȯv″êr, *adj.* disguised; secret.

ŭn′dêr·cŭt″, *v.t.,* **-cut, -cutting.** offer at a lower price than.

ŭn′dêr·dŏg″, *n.* predicted loser.

ŭn″dêr·ĕs′tĭ·māte″, *v.t.,* **-ated, -ating.** value or estimate too low.

ŭn″dêr·gō′, *v.t.* **-went, -gone, -going.** endure; experience.

ŭn·dêr·grăd′ū·ȧte, *n.* college student working toward a bachelor's degree.

ŭn′dêr·grȯûnd″, *adj.* **1.** below the ground. **2.** secret; confidential. **—adv. 3.** below the ground. **—n. 4.** secret army of resistance.

ŭn′dêr·hănd″, *adj.* secret; sly. Also, un′der·hand″ed.

ŭn′dêr·mīne″, *v.t.* -mined, -mining. weaken; sabotage.

ŭn·dêr·nēath′, *prep.*, *adv.* beneath.

ŭn·dêr·stănd′, *v.t.*, *v.i.* -stood, -standing. *v.t.* 1. comprehend; take the meaning of. —*v.i.* 2. sympathize. —un·der·stand′ing, *n.*, *adj.*

ŭn·dêr·stood′, *adj.* assumed; agreed upon.

ŭn′dêr·stŭd·ў, *n.*, *pl.* -dies. performer on call for emergencies.

ŭn·dêr·tāke′, *v.t.*, -took, -taken. 1. set about; enter upon. 2. accept as an obligation.

ŭn′dêr·tāk″êr, *n.* director of funerals.

ŭn′dêr·wörld″, *n.* world of criminals.

ŭn′dêr·wrīte″, *v.t.* -wrote, -written, -writing. accept, as an expense or liability. —un′der·writ″er, *n.*

ŭn″do′, *v.t.* -did, -done, -doing. 1. unfasten. 2. nullify. 3. ruin.

ŭn′dū·lāte″, *v.t.*, *v.i.*, -lated, -lating. 1. move or form in waves. 2. fluctuate in pitch and cadence. —un″du·la′tion, *n.*

ŭn·êarth′, *v.t.* discover; reveal.

ŭn′guĕnt, *n.* ointment; salve.

u·ni·corn (yōō′ ni korn), *n.* mythical horselike animal with a single horn.

ū′nĭ·fôrm″, *adj.* 1. alike; similar. *n.* 2. distinctive or stylized dress for a particular group. —*v.t.* 3. clothe with a uniform. —u·ni·form′i·ty, *n.*

ū′nĭ·fў″, *v.t.* -fied, -fying. make into a whole; unite. —u″ni·fi·ca′tion, *n.*

ŭ·nĭ·lăt′êr·al, *adj.* one-sided.

ŭn′iŏn, *n.* 1. act or instance of uniting. 2. labor group organized for mutual aid. —un′ion·ize″, *v.t.*, *v.i.*

Ūniŏn Jăck, British flag.

ū″nīque′, *adj.* 1. single; only. 2. rare; unusual. —u·nique′ly, *adv.*

ū′nĭ·sŏn″, *n.* agreement; harmony.

ū′nĭt, *n.* single amount, item, etc.

ū·nīte′, *v.t.*, *v.i.*, -nited, -niting. join into one group or entity.

ū′nĭ·tў, *n.* 1. state of being united; oneness. 2. agreement.

ū″nĭ·vêr′sal, *adj.* including all. —u″ni·ver·sal′i·ty, *n.*

ū′nĭ·vêrse″, *n.* entirety of physical creation.

ū″nĭ·vêr′sĭ·tў, *n.*, *pl.* -ties. large institution of higher learning.

ŭn·kĕmpt′, *adj.* untidy; shabby; messy.

ŭn·lĕss′, *conj.*, *prep.* if not; except.

ŭn·răv′el, *v.t.* 1. disentangle; undo. 2. solve.

ŭn·rĕst′, *n.* 1. uneasy state. 2. discontent.

ŭn·rū′lў, *adj.* undisciplined; rebellious. —un·rul′i·ness, *n.*

ŭn·tīe′, *v.t.*, -tied, -tying. loosen or undo.

ŭn·tĭl′, *conj.*, *prep.* 1. up to the time when. 2. before.

ŭn′to, *prep.* Archaic. to.

ŭn·tōld′, *adj.* vast; incalculable.

ŭn·tó·ward′, *adj.* 1. improper. 2. adverse.

ŭn·wiēld′ў, *adj.* awkward; bulky.

ŭn·wĭt′tĭng, *adj.* unintentional; inadvertent. —un·wit′ting·ly, *adv.*

ŭn·wŏnt″ĕd, *adj.* not usual; uncharacteristic.

ŭp, *adv.*, *adj.*, *prep.*, *v.t.*, -ped, -ping. *adv.* 1. to a higher level or location. 2. straight; erectly. 3. at bat. 4. awake; out of bed. 5. (computers) operating. —*prep.* 6. to a higher level or place in or on. —*v.t.* 7. increase.

ŭp·brāid′, *v.t.* scold; chide.

ŭp·hēav′al, *n.* turmoil; unrest; agitation.

ŭp·hōld′, *v.t.* -held, -holding. support; advocate.

ŭp·hōl′stêr, *v.t.* furnish with padding and fabric covering. —up·hol′ster·er, *n.*

ŭp′kēep′, *n.* maintenance; support.

ŭp·lĭft′, *v.t.* 1. elevate; exalt. —*n.* 2. edification.

ŭp·ŏn′, *prep.* on; onto.

ŭp′pêr, *adj.* higher. —up′per·most″, *adj.*

ŭp′rīs″ĭng, *n.* rebellion; revolt.

ŭp′rōar″, *n.* tumult; din.

ŭp·rōōt″, *v.t.* 1. to pull up by the roots. 2. displace from a home or homeland.

ŭp·sĕt′, *v.*, -set, -setting, *adj.*, *n.* *v.t.* (up set′) 1. overturn. 2. defeat. 3. put in confusion or distress. —*v.i.* 4. be overturned. —*adj.* 5. distressed in mind. —*n.* (up′set″) 6. act or instance of upsetting.

ŭp′shŏt, *n.* final result.

ŭp″stāirs′, *adj.* 1. situated on an upper

floor. —*adv.* **2.** to or on an upper floor. —*n.* **3.** floor above a ground floor.

ŭp′stärt″, *n.* person of recent power or wealth.

ŭp′-tò-dāte′, *adj.* latest; modern; current.

ŭp′wård, *adv.* **1.** Also, **up′wards,** to a higher level or place. —*adj.* **2.** toward a higher level or place.

ū·rā′nĭ·ŭm, *n.* radioactive metallic element used as a source for atomic energy.

ûr′bàn, *adj.* pertaining to cities.

ûr·bāne′, *adj.* sophisticated; polite. —**ur·ban′i·ty,** *n.*

ûr′chĭn, *n.* unkempt child; ragamuffin.

ûrge, *v.t.,* **urged, urging,** *n. v.t.* **1.** advocate. **2.** implore. —*n.* **3.** impulse; desire; longing.

ûr′gènt, *adj.* pressing; vital; crucial. —**ur′gen·cy,** *n.* —**ur′gent·ly,** *adv.*

ū′rĭ·nāte″, *v.i.* **-nated, -nating.** pass urine. —**u″ri·na′tion,** *n.*

ū′rĭne, *n.* fluid waste from kidneys.

ûrn, *n.* vase.

ŭs, *pron.* objective case of we.

ūs′àge, *n.* **1.** custom. **2.** treatment; handling.

use, *v.t.,* **used, using,** *n. v.t.* (yōoz) **1.** employ or engage for a purpose. **2.** expend; consume. **3.** behave toward; treat. **4.** do regularly. **5.** accustom; habituate. —*n.* (yōos) **6.** application; employment. **7.** value; service. —**us′a·ble,** *adj.* —**use′ful,** *adj.* —**use′less,** *adj.*

ūs′êr-frĭĕnd′lў, *adj.* (computers) designed for ease of use.

ŭsh′êr, *n., v.t.* escort; guide.

ū′sū·àl, *adj.* **1.** habitual; customary. **2.** ordinary; common. —**u′su·al·ly,** *adv.*

ū·sûrp′, *v.t.* take or assume without right. —**u·surp′er,** *n.*

ū′sū·rў, *n.* lending of money at excessive interest. —**u′sur·er,** *n.*

ū·tĕn′sĭl, *n.* implement or vessel useful esp. in the kitchen.

ū′têr·ŭs, *n.* female bodily organ in which fetuses develop.

ū·tĭl″ĭ·tār′ĭ·àn, *adj.* practical; useful; functional.

ū·tĭl′ĭ·tў, *n., pl.* **-ties. 1.** usefulness; function. **2.** service provided for public use.

ū′tĭ·līze, *v.t.,* **-lized, -lizing.** make use of. —**u″ti·li·za′tion,** *n.*

ŭt′mōst″, *adj.* **1.** furthest. **2.** greatest.

ū·tŏ′pĭ·àn, *adj.* impossibly ideal.

ŭt′têr, *v.t.* **1.** say; speak; enunciate. —*adj.* **2.** total; complete. —**ut′ter·ance,** *n.* —**ut′ter·ly,** *adv.*

ū′vū·là, *n.* fleshy pendant lobe of the soft palate.

ux·o·ri·ous (ōok sōr′i əs), *adj.* excessively fond of one's wife.

V

V, v, *n.* twenty-second letter of the English alphabet.

vā′càn·cў, *n., pl.* **-cies. 1.** state of being vacant. **2.** void. **3.** available rental space.

vā′cànt″, *adj.* **1.** empty; uninhabited. **2.** stupid; foolish. **3.** expressionless. —**va′cant″ly,** *adv.*

vā′cāte″, *v.,* **-cated, -cating.** *v.t.* **1.** deprive of an occupant or incumbent. **2.** leave. **3.** void; annul. —*v.i.* **4.** vacate a tenancy, office, or post.

vā·cā′tion, *n.* **1.** respite from duty or occupation. **2.** period of rest and relaxation. —*v.i.* **3.** take a vacation. —**va·ca′tion·er, va·ca′tion·ist,** *n.*

văc′cĭ·nāte″, *v.t.,* **-nated, -nating.** inoculate with serum for immunity to disease. —**vac″ci·na′tion,** *n.*

văc′cĭne, *n.* substance used for vaccinating. —**vac′ci·nal,** *adj.*

văc′ĭl·lāte″, *v.i.* **-lated, -lating. 1.** sway; oscillate; fluctuate. **2.** waver; hesitate. —**vac″il·la′tion,** *n.*

vă·cū′ĭ·tў, *n., pl.* **-ties. 1.** emptiness. **2.** emptyheadedness. —**vac′u·ous,** *adj.* —**vac′u·ous·ly,** *adv.*

văc′ū·um, *n.* **1.** space devoid of matter. —*v.t.* **2.** use a vacuum cleaner on.

văg′à·bònd″, *adj.* **1.** wandering; rootless. —*n.* **2.** person leading a vagabond life.

vā′gàr·ў, *n., pl.* **-garies.** capricious action or notion.

va·gin·a (və jī′nə), *n.* canal in the female from the vulva to the uterus. —**vag′i·nal,** *adj.*

vā′grànt, *n.* **1.** wanderer, esp. without visible means of support. —*adj.* **2.**

wandering; itinerant. **3.** random; wayward. **—va′gran·cy,** *n.*

vague, *adj.,* **vaguer, vaguest. 1.** not definite; imprecise. **2.** indistinct; blurred. **—vague′ly,** *adv.* **—vague′ness,** *n.*

vain, *adj.* **1.** futile. **2.** conceited. **—vain′ly,** *adv.*

val·ance (vāl′əns), *n.* drapery or frame disguising the top of a window.

vāle, *n.* valley.

văl·e·dĭc′tion, *n.* act of bidding farewell. **—val′′e·dic′to·ry,** *adj.*

vă′lĕnce, *n. Chemistry.* combining power of an element or radical.

văl′ĕn·tīne, *n.* **1.** sentimental greeting on St. Valentine's Day. **2.** sweetheart chosen on St. Valentine's Day.

val·et (val′it, val′ā), *n.* man's personal servant.

văl′iănt, *adj.* possessing valor; courageous. **—val′ian·tly,** *adv.*

vă′lĭd, *adj.* **1.** reasonable. **2.** having legal force. **—va·lid′i·ty,** *n.* **—val′id·ly,** *adv.* **—val′i·date,** *v.t.*

va·lise, *n.* traveling bag; suitcase.

văl′lēy, *n.* long depression between mountains, plateaus, etc.

văl′ŏr, *n.* courage; bravery. **—val′o·rous,** *adj.* **—val′o·rous′′ly,** *adv.*

văl′ū·a·ble, *adj.* **1.** having worth or usefulness. **—n. 2.** valuables, valuable possessions. **—val′u·a·bly,** *adv.*

văl·ū·ā′tion, *n.* estimated value.

văl′ūe, *n., v.t.* **-ued, -uing.** *n.* **1.** importance; worth. **2.** relative worth. **3.** basic principle. **—v.t. 4.** estimate the worth of. **5.** prize; esteem. **—val′ue·less,** *n.*

vălve, *n.* device for regulating the flow of a fluid. **—val′vu·lar,** *adj.*

vămp, *n.* **1.** uppermost front part of a shoe, etc. **2.** seductive woman. **3.** repeated introductory musical passage. **—v.i. 4.** play a musical vamp.

văm′pire′′, *n.* **1.** corpse believed to rise and suck the blood of sleepers at night. **2.** Also, **vampire bat,** South American bat subsisting on blood.

văn, *n.* **1.** foremost part; vanguard. **2.** enclosed truck.

văn′dăl, *n.* person who willfully damages property. **—van′dal·ism,** *n.* **—van′dal·ize,** *v.t.*

Văn·dȳke′, *n.* short, pointed, trimmed beard.

vāne, *n.* blade rotated by moving air, steam, etc.

văn′guârd′′, *n.* **1.** advance troops. **2.** forefront of an action, movement, or cause.

va·nĭl′là, *n.* extract of a tropical American orchid used in cookery.

văn′ĭsh, *v.i.* disappear.

văn′i·tў, *n., pl.* **-ties.** inflated pride; conceit.

văn′quĭsh, *v.t.* defeat; conquer.

văn′tàge, *n.* position giving strategic advantage.

vă′pĭd, *adj.* dull; uninteresting; flat. **—vap′id·ly,** *adv.* **—va·pid′i·ty,** *n.*

vā′pŏr, *n.* gaseous substance, as steam or mist. **—va′por·ous,** *adj.*

vā′pŏr·īze′′, *v.,* **-ized, -izing.** *v.t., v.i.* turn into vapor. **—va′′por·i·za′tion,** *n.* **—va′por·i′′zer,** *n.*

vār′i·à·ble, *adj.* **1.** changeable; fluctuating. **2.** inconstant; fickle. **—var′′i·a·bil′i·ty,** *n.* **—var′i·a·bly,** *adv.*

vār′i·ănce, *n.* **1.** divergence. **2.** disagreement.

vār′i·ănt, *adj.* **1.** varying. **2.** altered in form. **—n. 3.** variant form or structure.

vār′′i·ā′tion, *n.* **1.** change; alteration. **2.** degree of change. **3.** elaboration of a musical theme. **—var′′i·a′tion·al,** *adj.* **—var′′i·a′tion·al·ly,** *adv.*

vār′i·e·gāte′′, *v.t.,* **-gated, -gating. 1.** add different colors to; dapple. **2.** add variety to. **—var′′i·e·gat′ed,** *adj.* **—var′′i·e·ga′tion,** *n.*

va·rī′e·tў, *n., pl.* **-ties. 1.** diversity. **2.** assortment. **3.** category; kind; type. **—va·ri′e·tal,** *adj.*

va·rī′ō·là, *n.* smallpox; cowpox.

vār′i·oŭs, *adj.* **1.** several. **2.** diverse; different. **—var′i·ous·ly,** *adv.*

vâr′nĭsh, *n.* **1.** resinous liquid preparation drying to a hard, glossy surface. **2.** outward appearance; gloss. **—v.t. 3.** apply varnish to. **4.** gloss over; conceal.

vār′ў, *v.,* **varied, varying.** *v.t., v.i.* **1.** change; fluctuate. **2.** differ. **—var′i·ance,** *n.*

vāse, *n.* ornamental vessel often used to hold flowers.

văs′sal, *n.* **1.** landholder subservient to a feudal lord. **2.** person under domination of another. **—vas′sal·age,** *n.*

văst, *adj.* enormous; huge; immense. **—vast′ly,** *adv.* **—vast′ness,** *n.*

văt, *n*. large vessel for holding fluids.

vaude'vĭlle, *n*. stage entertainment with a series of acts. —**vaude·vil'lian**, *n*.

vault, *n*. **1**. arched structure forming a ceiling. **2**. space covered by such a structure. **3**. burial chamber. **4**. room or container for valuables. —*v.t.* **5**. form or cover with a vault. **6**. leap over. —*v.i.* **7**. perform a leap; jump.

vaunt, *v.i.* **1**. brag; boast. —*v.t.* **2**. call attention to boastfully. —*n*. **3**. boast.

VCR, video cassette recorder.

vēal, *n*. flesh of a young calf.

vēer, *v.i.* **1**. change direction or course. —*n*. **2**. act or instance of veering.

věg'è·tà·ble, *n*. **1**. partly edible plant. —*adj*. Also, **veg'e·tal**. **2**. being a vegetable. **3**. pertaining to plants.

věg''è·tār'ĭ·àn, *n*. **1**. abstainer from meat. —*adj*. **2**. advocating the exclusion of meat in the diet. **3**. consisting solely of vegetables. —**veg''e·tar'i·an·ism**, *n*.

věg'è·tāte'', *v.i.*, **-tated, -tating**. **1**. grow in the manner of a plant. **2**. lead a passive life. —**veg'e·ta''tive**, *adj*.

vē'hè·mènt, *adj*. **1**. passionate; emotional; fervid. **2**. violent. —**ve'he·ment·ly**, *adj*. —**ve'he·mence**, *n*.

vē'hĭ·cle, *n*. **1**. inert medium containing an active agent. **2**. means of transporting or conveying. —**ve·hic'u·lar**, *adj*.

veil, *n*. **1**. net-like cloth for covering the face. **2**. outer covering of a nun's headdress. **3**. screen; cover-up. —*v.t.* **4**. cover with or as if with a veil.

vein, *n*. **1**. tubular vessel conveying blood within the body. **2**. tubular thickening in an insect wing or a leaf. **3**. stratum of mineral, ore, or ice. **4**. spirit; mood —*v.t.* **5**. pattern with or as if with veins.

věl'lŭm, *n*. parchment.

vè·lŏc'ĭ·tў, *n*., *pl*. **-ties**. speed.

věl'vèt, *n*. fabric with a thick, short, soft pile. —**vel'vet·y**, *adj*.

vē'nàl, *adj*. open to bribery or corruption; mercenary. —**ve'nal·ly**, *adv*. —**ve·nal'i·ty**, *n*.

vĕnd, *v.t.* sell; peddle. —**ven'dor**, *n*.

vè·nēer', *n*. **1**. facing of fine material. **2**. outer appearance. —*v.t.* **3**. cover with or as with a veneer.

věn'ĕr·à·ble, *adj*. worthy of or commanding reverence. —**ven·er·a·bil'i·ty**, *n*.

věn'êr·āte'', *v.t.*, **-ated, -ating**. respect deeply; worship; revere. —**ven''er·a'tion**, *n*.

vè·nē'rē·àl, *adj*. relating to or resulting from sexual activity.

věnge'ànce, *n*. retaliation; retribution.

věnge'fŭl, *adj*. seeking revenge; vindictive. —**venge'ful·ly**, *adv*.

vē'nĭ·àl, *adj*. pardonable; forgivable. —**ve'ni·al·ly**, *adv*.

věn'ĭ·sòn, *n*. deer meat.

věn'òm, *n*. **1**. poisonous secretion. **2**. malice; spite. —**ven'om·ous**, *adj*.

věnt, *n*. **1**. means of outlet or escape. —*v.t.* **2**. provide or serve as a vent. **3**. give free expression to.

věn'tĭ·lāte, *v.t.*, **-ated, -ating**. **1**. provide with or expose to fresh air. **2**. express openly and freely. —**ven·ti·la'tion**, *n*.

věn·trĭl'ŏ·quĭsm, *n*. technique of projecting the voice so that it seems to emanate from a source other than the speaker. —**ven·tril'o·quist**, *n*.

věn'tûre, *v.t.*, **-tured, -turing**, *n*. *v.t.* **1**. expose to hazard; risk. **2**. offer at risk of rejection. —*n*. **3**. challenging or risky undertaking. —**ven'ture·some, ven'tur·ous**, *adj*.

Vē'nŭs, *n*. **1**. goddess of love. **2**. second planet in distance from the sun.

vè·rā'ciŏus, *adj*. openly honest; truthful. —**ve·ra'cious·ly**, *adj*. —**ve·rac'i·ty**, *n*.

vè·răn'dà, *n*. an open portico attached to a building; porch. Also, **ve·ran'dah**.

vêrb, *n*. *Grammar*. part of speech indicating action, occurrence, being, etc.

vêr'bàl, *adj*. **1**. relating to or formed of words. **2**. oral; spoken. **3**. relating to or constituting a verb or form of a verb. —**ver'bal·ly**, *adv*.

vêr'bàl·īze'', *v*., **-ized, -izing**. *v.t.* **1**. express in words. —*v.i.* **2**. speak in words. —**ver''bal·i·za'tion**, *n*.

vêr·bā'tĭm, *adv*. word for word; literally.

vêr'bĭ·àge, *n*. excess of words.

vêr·bōse', *adj*. wordy; loquacious. —**ver·bose'ness, ver·bos'i·ty**, *n*.

vêr'dànt, *adj*. green. —**ver'dant·ly**, *adj*. —**ver'dan·cy**, *n*.

vêr'dĭct, *n*. decision.

vêr'dūre, *n*. **1**. greenery. **2**. greenness.

vêrge, *n*., *v.i.*, **verged, verging**. *n*. **1**.

margin; edge. —*v.i.* **2.** border; surround. **3.** tend; incline.

vĕr′ĭ·fy̆, *v.t.,* **-fied, -fying.** prove or ascertain the correctness of. —**ver·i·fi′a·ble,** *adj.* —**ver·i·fi·ca′tion,** *n.*

vĕr′ĭ·lў, *adv.* truly.

vĕr″ĭ·sĭm·ĭl′ĭ·tūde, *n.* appearance of truth or reality.

vĕr′ĭ·tȧ·ble, *adj.* true; genuine. —**ver′i·ta·bly,** *adj.*

vĕr′ĭ·tў, *n., pl.* **-ties.** truth.

vêr′mĭn, *n. pl.* obnoxious animals or creatures collectively. —**ver′min·ous,** *adj.*

vêr·năc′ū·lȧr, *adj.* **1.** locally native. —*n.* **2.** language characteristic, esp. of a particular group or class.

vêr′nȧl, *adj.* pertaining to spring.

vêr′sȧ·tĭle, *adj.* changing tasks or activities easily. —**ver·sa·til′i·ty,** *n.*

vêrse, *n.* **1.** poetry. **2.** part of a poem, esp. when rhymed. **3.** passage from the Bible.

vêrsed, *adj.* accomplished; skilled; knowledgeable.

vêr·sĭ·fy̆, *v.,* **-fied, -fying.** *v.t.* **1.** put into verse. —*v.i.* **2.** compose verse. —**ver″si·fi·ca′tion,** *n.* —**ver′si·fi″er,** *n.*

vêr′sĭon, *n.* **1.** account. **2.** translation.

vêr′tė·brȧ, *n., pl.* **-bras, -brae.** segment of the spinal column. —**ver′te·bral,** *adj.*

vêr′tė·brāte, *adj.* **1.** having vertebras. —*n.* **2.** creature having vertebras.

vêr′tĭ·cȧl, *adj.* **1.** perpendicular to the horizon. —*n.* **2.** vertical plane, line, etc. —**ver′ti·cal·ly,** *adv.*

vêr′tĭ·gō″, *n., pl.* **-gos.** dizziness.

vĕr′y̆, *adv., adj.,* **-ier, -iest.** *adv.* **1.** to a great extent. —*adj.* **2.** identical; actual. **3.** absolute.

vĕs′pêrs, *n. sing.* evening religious service.

vĕs′sėl, *n.* **1.** ship, boat, etc. **2.** container for fluid. **3.** channel for blood.

vĕst, *n.* **1.** sleeveless garment worn under a coat or jacket. —*v.i.* **2.** put in possession or control of. **3.** endow with authority.

vĕs′tĭ·būle, *n.* antichamber. —**ves·ti·bu·lar,** *adj.*

vĕs′tĭge, *n.* remnant; trace. —**ves·tig′i·al,** *adj.*

vĕst′mĕnt, *n.* gown; robe.

vĕst-pŏckėt, *adj.* small enough for a pocket.

vĕs′trў, *n., pl.* **-tries. 1.** auxiliary room of a church. **2.** church committee. —**ves′try·man,** *n.*

vĕt′êr·ȧn, *n.* **1.** person who has served, esp. in the military forces. —*adj.* **2.** greatly experienced.

vĕt′êr·ĭ·nār″ў, *adj., n., pl.* **-ies.** *adj.* **1.** pertaining to the healing of animals. —*n.* **2.** Also, **vet″er·i·nar′i·an,** doctor for animals.

vē′tō, *n., pl.* **-toes,** *v.t.,* **-toes, -toing.** *n.* **1.** power to reject, prohibit, or ignore. **2.** prohibition. —*v.t.* **3.** reject or prohibit by veto.

vĕx, *v.t.* **1.** irritate. **2.** trouble. —**vex″a′ti·ous,** *adj.* —**vex′ed·ly,** *adj.*

vĕxed, *adj.* controversial.

vī′ȧ, *prep.* by way of.

vī′ȧ·ble, *adj.* capable of or fit for living. —**vi′a·bly,** *adv.*

vī′ȧ·dŭct″, *n.* long road bridge.

vī′ȧnd, *n.* item of food, esp. when very choice or tasty.

vī′brȧnt, *adj.* **1.** oscillating; fluctuating. **2.** vigorous; energetic. —**vi′brant·ly,** *adj.* —**vi′bran·cy,** *n.*

vī′brāte, *v.,* **-brated, -brating.** *v.t., v.i.* **1.** move rapidly back and forth. —*v.i.* **2.** shiver. **3.** resound. —**vi·bra′tion,** *n.* —**vi′bra·to″ry,** *adj.* —**vi·bra·tor,** *n.*

vĭc′ȧr, *n.* **1.** parish priest. **2.** representative of the pope or of a bishop. **3. Vicar of Christ,** pope. —**vic′ar·ship″,** *n.*

vĭ·cār′ĭ·oŭs, *adj.* **1.** serving in the place of another. **2.** experienced in imagination only. —**vi·car′i·ous·ly,** *adv.* —**vi·car′i·ous·ness,** *n.*

vīce, *n.* **1.** moral depravity. **2.** habitual personal shortcoming.

vīce′-prĕs′ĭ·dėnt, *n.* official next in rank below president. —**vice′-pres″i·den′tial,** *adj.* —**vice″-pres′i·den·cy,** *n.*

vīce′rŏy̆, *n.* deputy sovereign; representative ruler. —**vice-re′gal,** *adj.*

vī′ce vêr′sȧ, with the order changed; conversely.

vĭ·cĭn′ĭ·tў, *n., pl.* **-ties.** local area; neighborhood.

vĭ′cioŭs, *adj.* **1.** depraved; immoral. **2.** spiteful; malicious. **3.** evil. —**vi′cious·ly,** *adv.* —**vi′cious·ness,** *n.*

vi·cis·si·tude (və sis′ə tōōd″), *n.* unpredictable change.

vĭc′tĭm, *n.* **1.** sufferer from a force or action. **2.** dupe. —vic′tim·ize″, *v.t.*

vĭc′tör, *n.* winner; conqueror.

vĭc′tö·rӯ, *n.*, *pl.* -ries. success in a contest; triumph. —vic·to′ri·ous, *adj.* —vic·to′ri·ous·ly, *adv.*

vict·ual (vĭ′təl), *n.* **1. victuals,** food. —*v.t.* **2.** provision.

vĭd′ē·ō, *n.*, *adj.* **1.** television. **2.** a short, visual performance featuring a rock music soundtrack.

vĭd″ē·ō·tāpe′, *n.* electromagnetic tape for recording visual images.

vīe, *v.i.* vied, vying. contend; compete.

vieῶ, *n.* **1.** seeing; beholding. **2.** area or range of vision. **3.** landscape. **4.** purpose. **5.** opinion; attitude. —*v.* **6.** look at; regard. —view′er, *n.* —view′less, *adj.*

vĭg′ĭl, *n.* act of keeping awake and alert.

vĭg′ĭ·lănt, *adj.* alert; keenly aware. —vig′i·lant·ly, *adv.* —vig′i·lance, *n.*

vĭg′ör, *n.* robust health, energy, or strength. —vig′or·ous, *adj.* —vig′or·ous·ly, *adv.*

vīle, *adj.*, viler, vilest. **1.** of little account; mean. **2.** nasty; contemptible. —vile′ly, *adv.* —vile′ness, *n.*

vĭl′ĭ·fӯ″, *v.t.* -fied, -fying. denounce; defame. —vil″i·fi·ca′tion, *n.*

vĭl′lȧ, *n.* country or suburban house.

vĭl′lȧge, *n.* small town; hamlet. —vil′lag·er, *n.*

vĭl′lȧin, *n.* wicked person; scoundrel. —vil′lain·ous, *adj.* —vil′lain·y, *n.*

vĭm, *n.* vigor; robustness.

vĭn′dĭ·cāte″, *v.t.* -cated, -cating. absolve from suspicion or doubt. —vin″di·ca′tion, *n.* —vin′di·ca·ble, *adj.*

vĭn·dĭc′tĭve, *adj.* holding a grudge. —vin·dic′tive·ly, *adj.* —vin·dic′tive·ness, *n.*

vīne, *n.* slender, creeping or climbing plant.

vĭn′e·gȧr, *n.* sour fermented liquid. —vin′e·gar·y, *adj.*

vīne′yȧrd, *n.* garden or plantation for the growth of vines.

vĭn′tȧge, *n.* **1.** wine extracted from a single harvest of grapes. **2.** harvest of grapes.

vī′o·lāte″, *v.t.*, -lated, -lating. **1.** break; transgress. **2.** desecrate. **3.** rape. —vi″o·la′tion, *n.* —vi′o·la″tor, *n.*

vĭ·ō′là′, *n.* string instrument with a pitch slightly below that of a violin.

vī′o·lênt, *adj.* **1.** physically aggressive. **2.** severe; turbulent. —vi′o·lent·ly, *adv.* —vi′o·lence, *n.*

vī′o·let, *n.* **1.** low-growing herb bearing purplish or bluish blossoms. **2.** bluish purple.

vī′o·lin, *n.* small, stringed musical instrument played with a bow. —vi″o·lin′ist, *n.*

vī″o·lŏn·cĕl′lō, *n.*, *pl.* -los. cello. —vi″o·lon·cel′list, *n.*

vī′pêr, *n.* **1.** venomous snake. **2.** ill-tempered, malicious person. —vi′per·ous, *adj.*

vĭ·râ′gō, *n.*, *pl.* -gos, -goes. malicious woman; shrew; witch.

vîr′gĭn, *n.* **1.** sexually inexperienced person. —*adj.* **2.** being a virgin. **3.** unexplored, unexploited, etc. —vir′gin·al, *adj.*

vĭr′īle, *adj.* **1.** capable of siring offspring. **2.** vigorous; manly; potent. —vi·ril′i·ty, *n.*

vîr′tū·ȧl, *adj.* so in effect. —vir′tu·al·ly, *adv.*

vîr′tūe, *n.* **1.** morality. **2.** chastity. **3.** merit. —vir′tu·ous, *adj.* —vir′tu·ous·ly, *adv.* —vir′tu·ous·ness, *n.*

vîr″tū·ō′sō, *n.*, *pl.* -sos, -si. musician, etc., of outstanding skill. —vir″tu·os′i·ty, *n.*

vĭr′ū·lênt, *adj.* **1.** poisonous; deadly. **2.** hostile. —vir′u·lence, vir′u·len·cy, *n.* —vir′u·lent·ly, *adv.*

vī′rŭs, *adj.* infectious agency. —vi′ral, *adj.* —vi′ral·ly, *adv.*

vĭs′ȧge, *n.* **1.** face. **2.** aspect; look.

vī·sȧ, *n.* endorsement to a passport.

vĭs·cêr·ȧ, *n.* *pl.* internal bodily organs. —vis′cer·al, *adj.*

vĭs·cĭd, *adj.* sticky to the touch; tacky. Also, vis′cous. —vis·cos′i·ty, *n.*

vīse, *n.* holding tool attached to a work bench, etc.

vĭs′ĭ·ble, *adj.* **1.** capable of being seen. **2.** perceptible. —vis′i·bly, *adv.* —vis·i·bil′i·ty, *n.*

vī′siŏn, *n.* **1.** sense of sight. **2.** supernatural apprehension. **3.** foresight. —vi′sion·al, *adj.*

vĭ′siŏn·ȧr″ӯ, *adj.* **1.** fanciful. **2.** apprehended by or as by supernatural means. **3.** unreal; fancied. —*n.* **4.** person seeing visions. **5.** impractical person; dreamer.

vĭs′ĭt, *v.t.* **1.** go to and stay briefly at. **2.** afflict. —*n.* **3.** brief stay, esp. as a guest. —vis′i·tor, *n.* —vis′i·tant, *adj.* —vis″i·ta′tion, *n.*

vī′sör, *n.* forward projecting part, as of a helmet or cap.

vĭs′tà, *n.* panoramic view.

vĭs′ū·ăl, *adj.* pertaining to sight. —vis′u·al·ly, *adj.*

vĭs′ū·à·līze″, *v.t.,* -ized, -izing. obtain or create a picture or conception of. —vis″u·al·i·za′tion, *n.*

vī′tàl, *adj.* **1.** pertaining to life or existence. **2.** extremely important. **3.** full of exuberance, creativity, etc. —vi′tal·ly, *adv.* —vi·tal′i·ty, *n.*

vī′tà·mĭn, *n.* organic substance vital in small quantities to proper nutrition. —vi″ta·min′ic, *adj.*

vi·ti·ate (vish′i āt″), *v.t.,* -ated, -ating. **1.** impair. **2.** invalidate; negate. —vi″ti·a′tion, *n.*

vĭt′rē·oŭs, *adj.* glazed or glassy.

vĭt′rĭ·ŏl, *n.* sulfuric acid.

vĭt″rĭ·ŏl′ĭc, *adj.* **1.** pertaining to vitriol. **2.** caustic, as criticism.

vī·tū′pêr·āte″, *v.t.,* -ated, -ating. **1.** criticize harshly or abusively. **2.** revile. —vi·tu″per·a′tion, *n.* —vi·tu′per·a·tive, *adj.*

vī·vā′cioŭs, *adj.* animated; lively. —vi·va′cious·ly, *adj.* —vi·vac′i·ty, vi·va′cious·ness, *n.*

vĭv′ĭd, *adj.* **1.** bright; brilliant. **2.** intense. —viv′id·ly, *adj.* —viv′id·ness, *n.*

vĭv′ĭ·sĕct″, *v.t.* dissect while alive. —viv″i·sec′tion, *n.* —viv″i·sec′tion·ist, *n.*

vĭx′èn, *n.* **1.** female fox. **2.** mischievous girl or woman.

vō·căb′ū·lär·ÿ, *n.,* *pl.* -ies. **1.** stock of words used by a person, people, or group. **2.** collection of words in alphabetical order.

vō′càl, *adj.* **1.** pertaining to the voice. **2.** pertaining to singing. **3.** articulate; outspoken. —vo′cal·ly, *adj.* —vo′cal·ize, *v.t., v.i.* —vo″cal·i·za′tion, *n.*

vō·cā′tion, *n.* profession; occupation. —vo·ca′tion·al, *adj.*

vōc′ā·tĭve, *adj.* **1.** relating to a grammat-

ical case indicating person or thing addressed. —*n.* **2.** vocative case.

vō·cĭf′·êr·āte, *v.,* -ated, -ating. *v.i., v.t.* shout. —vo·cif″er·a′tion, *n.* —vo·cif″er·ous, *adj.*

vōgue, *n.* **1.** fashion; trend. **2.** popular favor or approval.

voīce, *n.,* *v.t.* **voiced, voicing.** *n.* **1.** sound uttered through the mouth. **2.** singing or speaking voice. **3.** expression. **4.** choice. **5.** right to express one's opinion. **6.** *Grammar.* verbal inflection indicating whether subject is acting or acted upon. —*v.t.* **7.** express; declare. —voice′less, *adj.*

voīd, *adj.* **1.** without legal power. **2.** useless; fruitless. **3.** empty; hollow. —*n.* **4.** empty or hollow space. —*v.t.* **5.** cancel; invalidate. —void′a·ble, *adj.* —void′ance, *n.*

vŏl′à·tĭle, *adj.* **1.** evaporating rapidly. **2.** energetic; lively. **3.** tending to erupt into violence. —vol·a·til′i·ty, *n.*

vŏl·cā′nō, *n.,* *pl.* -noes, -nos. mountain that ejects molten lava, rock, and steam. —vol·can′ic, *adj.* —vol·can′i·cal·ly, *adv.*

vō·lī′tion, *n.* **1.** power of choosing or determining; will. **2.** act of willing. —vo·li′tion·al, *adj.*

vŏl′lēy, *n.,* *pl.* -leys, *v.t. n.* **1.** simultaneous discharge of a number of missiles. —*v.t.* **2.** fire in a volley.

vōlt, *n.* unit of electromotive force.

vŏl′ù·ble, *adj.* fluent; talkative. —vol′u·bly, *adv.* —vol·u·bil′i·ty, *n.*

vŏl′ūme, *n.* **1.** size in three dimensions. **2.** quantity; mass. **3.** degree of loudness. **4.** book.

vò·lū′mĭ·noŭs, *adj.* **1.** great in size or degree. **2.** consisting of or filling many books. —vo·lu′min·ous·ly, *adv.*

vŏl′ŭn·tār″ÿ, *adj.* **1.** performed or acted on by choice. **2.** controlled by the will. —vol″un·tar′i·ly, *adv.*

vŏl″ŭn·tēer′, *v.t.* **1.** offer freely or spontaneously. —*v.i.* **2.** volunteer oneself. —*n.* **3.** person who volunteers.

vò·lŭp′tū·oŭs, *adj.* sensuous; sensual; luxurious. —vo·lup′tu·ous·ly, *adv.* —vo·lup′tu·ous·ness, *n.*

vōm′ĭt, *v.i.* **1.** disgorge the contents of the stomach through the mouth. —*v.t.* **2.** eject with force. —*n.* **3.** matter ejected by vomiting.

vô·rā′cioŭs, *adj*. ravenous; greedy. —vo· ra′cious·ly, *adv*. —vo·ra′ci·ty, vo·ra′ cious·ness, *n*.

vôr′tĕx, *n*., *pl*. -tices, -texes. whirling mass drawing objects to a central cavity.

vōte, *n*., *v*., voted, voting. *n*. 1. formal expression of opinion or choice, as by ballot. 2. right to such opinion or choice. 3. votes collectively. —*v.t*. 4. express or endorse by vote. —*v.i*. 5. cast one's vote. —vot′er, *n*.

vŏuch, *v.i*. 1. give a guarantee or surety. 2. give personal assurance.

vŏuch′êr, *n*. 1. person who vouches. 2. document certifying the occurrence of a transaction.

vōuch·sāfe′, *v.t*., -safed, -safing. permit; grant; allow.

vōw, *n*. 1. pledge; solemn promise. —*v.t*. 2. promise solemnly; swear. —*v.i*. 3. make a vow.

vōw′el, *n*. 1. speech sound made with the central part of the breath channel unblocked. 2. letter representing a vowel: *a, e, i, o, u* and sometimes *y*.

vŏy′ȧge, *n*., *v*., -aged, -aging. *n*. 1. an extended journey, esp. by sea. —*v.i*. 2. make a journey; travel. —*v.t*. 3. traverse; sail. —voy′ag·er, *n*.

vŭl′căn·īze′′, *v.t*., -ized, -izing. treat crude or synthetic rubber chemically to give it elasticity and strength. —vul′′ can·i·za′tion, *n*. —vul′can·i′′ zer, *n*.

vŭl′gȧr, *adj*. 1. lacking taste or breeding; unrefined. 2. ordinary; plebian. 3. ostentatiously showy. 4. indecent; obscene. 5. vernacular. —vul′gar·ly, *adv*. —vul·gar′i·ty, vul′gar· ness, *n*.

vŭl′nêr·a·ble, *adj*. 1. capable of being physically or emotionally wounded. 2. open to damage or attack. —vul′ner·a· bly, *adv*. —vul′′ner·a·bil′i·ty, *n*.

vŭl′tûre, *n*. 1. large bird subsisting chiefly on carrion. 2. predatory or rapacious person. —vul′tur·ous, *adj*.

vŭl′vȧ, *n*., *pl*. -vas, -vae. external female genital organs. —vul′val, vul′var, *adj*.

vȳ′ĭng, *adj*. competing; competitive.

W

W, w, *n*. twenty-third letter of the English alphabet.

wăck′ў, *adj*. -ier, -iest. *Informal*. odd, erratic, crazy. —wack′i·ly, *adv*. —wack′i·ness, *n*.

wâd′dle, *v.i*., -dled, -dling, *n*. *v.i*. 1. walk like a duck. —*n*. 2. waddling gait.

wāde, *v*., waded, wading. *v.i*. 1. walk through water. —*v.t*. 2. cross by wading. —wad′er, *n*.

wā′fêr, *n*. 1. thin, crisp cracker or cookie. 2. thin disk of bread used in the Eucharist.

wâf′fle, *n*. crisp batter cake baked in a double griddle.

wâft, *v.t*., *v.i*. float through air or over water.

wăg, *v*., wagged, wagging, *n*. *v.t*., *v.i*. 1. shake in an arc. —*n*. 2. wit, joker. —wag′ger·y, *n*. —wag′gish, *adj*.

wāge, *n*., *pl*. wages, *v.t*., waged, waging. *n*. 1. pay. —*v.t*. 2. carry on, as war.

wā′gêr, *n*., *v.t*., *v.i*. bet.

wăg′gle, *v*., -gled, -gling. *n*. *v.t*., *v.i*. 1. shake. —*n*. 2. shake.

wăg′ŏn, *n*. four-wheeled draft freight vehicle.

wāif, *n*. homeless child or animal.

wāil, *v.i*., *v.t*. 1. cry mournfully. —*n*. 2. mournful cry. —wail′er, *n*.

wāin′scŏt, *n*. 1. woodwork along an interior wall. —*v.t*. 2. line with woodwork.

wāist, *n*. part of the body between ribs and hips. —waist′band′′, *n*. —waist′ line′′, *n*.

wāit, *v.i*. 1. stop briefly; pause. 2. be in expectation. 3. be patient. 4. remain undone. 5. serve food, etc. —*n*. 6. act, instance, or period of waiting. 7. in wait, in ambush.

wāit′êr, *n*. 1. person who waits. 2. Also, *fem*., wait′ress, server of diners.

wāive, *v.t*., waived, waiving. give up; relinquish.

wāiv′êr, *n*. document that relinquishes.

wāke, *v*., waked, or woke, woken, waking, *n*. *v.i*. 1. awake. 2. be alert. —*v.t*. 3. arouse. —*n*. 4. vigil, as over a corpse. —wake′ful, *adj*. —wake′ful· ly, *adv*. —wake′ful·ness, *n*.

wāle, *n*., *v.t*., waled, waling. *n*. 1. welt as from a whip. —*v.t*. 2. mark with wales.

wälk, *v.i.* **1.** go on foot. —*v.t.* **2.** cause to walk. **3.** accompany on foot. —*n.* **4.** act or instance of walking. **5.** place for walking. —**walk′er,** *n.*

wälk′ie-tälk′ie, *n.* portable two-way radio.

wäll, *n.* **1.** upright enclosure. —*v.t.* **2.** enclose or separate.

wäll′bôard′′, *n.* light material for covering interior walls or ceilings.

wäl′lĕt, *n.* pocket case for money, cards, etc.

wäll′flow′′êr, *n. Informal.* **1.** girl onlooker at a party. **2.** sweet-scented flowering plant that sometimes grows on walls.

wäl′lŏp, *v.t.* **1.** beat or thrash. —*n.* **2.** powerful blow.

wäl′lōw, *v.i.* **1.** roll about, as in mud. **2.** indulge oneself. —*n.* **3.** muddy area.

wäll′pā′′pêr, *n.* **1.** decorative paper for interior walls. —*v.t.* **2.** put wallpaper on.

Wäll Strēet, U.S. financial world.

wäl′nŭt′′, *n.* edible nut from a northern tree.

wäl′rŭs, *n.* large sea mammal with two tusks.

wältz, *n.* **1.** dance in three-quarter time. —*v.i.* **2.** dance a waltz. —*v.t.* **3.** *Informal.* lead briskly. —**waltz′er,** *n.*

wäm′pŭm, *n.* shell beads used by Native Americans as money or ornaments.

wän, *adj.,* **wanner, wannest.** pale or sick-looking. —**wan′ly,** *adv.*

wänd, *n.* rod with supposed magical power.

wän′der, *v.i.* **1.** move about aimlessly. **2.** stray. —*v.t.* **3.** travel over. —**wan′der·er,** *n.*

wän′dêr·lŭst′′, *n.* desire to wander or travel.

wāne, *v.i., n.,* **wane, waning.** *v.i.* **1.** grow dim, as the moon's light. **2.** decline in strength or power. —*n.* **3.** decrease or decline.

wăn′gle, *v.t.,* **-gled, -gling.** *Informal.* get by scheming or persuasion.

wänt, *v.t.* **1.** wish for. **2.** desire, crave, demand. —*v.i.* **3.** be lacking or deficient. —*n.* **4.** something needed. **5.** deficiency or lack. —**want′ing,** *adj., prep.*

wän′tŏn, *adj.* **1.** gratuitous. **2.** sexually loose. —*n.* **3.** lascivious woman. —*v.t.* **4.** squander. —**wan′ton·ly,** *adv.* —**wan′ton·ness,** *n.*

wâp′ĭ·tĭ, *n., pl.* **-tis, -ti.** elk with wide antlers.

wâr, *n., v.i.,* **warred, warring.** *n.* **1.** armed conflict, as between nations. **2.** hostility or struggle. —*v.i.* **3.** be in conflict. —**war′fare′′,** *n.* —**war′like,** *adj.*

wâr′ble, *v.,* **-bled, -bling.** *n. v.t., v.i.* **1.** sing with trills, as a bird. —*n.* **2.** warbling. —**war′bler,** *n.*

wârd, *n.* **1.** administrative division of a city. **2.** division of a hospital. **3.** person under the care of a guardian. —*v.t.* **4.** repel or avert.

wâr′dĕn, *n.* **1.** chief officer of a prison. **2.** person in charge of others or things, keeper.

wârd′êr, *n.* guard.

wârd′rōbe′′, *n.* **1.** collection for clothes. **2.** closet of clothes.

wârd′rōōm′′, *n.* living and dining area for commissioned officers on a warship.

wāre, *n.* goods for sale.

wāre′hōuse′′, *n., v.t.,* **-housed, -housing.** *n.* **1.** storage building. —*v.t.* **2.** store in a warehouse.

wâr′hĕad′′, *n.* explosive front part of a bomb, missile, or torpedo.

wâr′hôrse′′, *n.* **1.** veteran of many conflicts. **2.** overfamiliar concert number.

wâr′lŏck′′, *n.* male with magical power; sorcerer.

wâr′lôrd′′, *n.* military ruler.

wârm, *adj.* **1.** having or giving moderate heat. **2.** friendly or affectionate. **3.** irritated or angry. —*v.t., v.i.* **4.** heat moderately. —**warm′ly,** *adv.* —**warmth, warm′ness,** *n.* —**warm′ish,** *adj.*

wârm′heârt′ĕd, *adj.* friendly; sympathetic.

war·mon·ger (wor′mun′′gər), *n.* inciter of war.

wârn, *v.t.* give notice of danger, caution. —**warn′ing,** *n., adj.*

wârp, *n.* **1.** distortion. **2.** lengthwise threads in cloth. —*v.t., v.i.* **3.** distort.

wâr′rănt, *n.* **1.** authorization, as by law. **2.** guarantee. —*v.t.* **3.** authorize. **4.** guarantee. —**war′rant·a·ble,** *adj.*

wâr′răn·tў, *n., pl.* **-ties.** guarantee on something sold.

wâr′rĭ·ŏr, *n.* soldier.

wârt, *n.* small hard protuberance on the skin. —**wart'y**, *adj.*

wār' y̆, *adj.*, **warier, wariest.** cautious; watchful. —**war'i·ly**, *adv.* —**war'i·ness**, *n.*

wăs, *v.* 1st and 3rd person singular, past indicative of be.

wâsh, *v.t.* **1.** clean with or in water or a solution. **2.** flow over. —*v.i.* **3.** wash oneself. **4.** undergo washing. —*n.* **5.** washing, as of clothes. **6.** current behind a moving ship or plane. —**wash'a·ble**, *adj.* —**wash'board'**, *n.* —**wash'bowl'**, *n.* —**wash'cloth'**, *n.* —**wash'stand'**, *n.*

wâsh'ĕr, *n.* **1.** washing machine. **2.** pierced disk for tightening a joint to prevent leakage, etc.

wâsh'out'', *n.* **1.** washing away of earth, soil, etc. **2.** *Informal.* failure.

WASP, *n.* white Anglo-Saxon Protestant. Also, **W.A.S.P., Wasp.**

wâsp, *n.* stinging insect. —**wasp'ish**, *adj.*

was'sail (wos'əl), *n.* **1.** drinking or toasting a person's health, as with a spiced ale. **2.** drinking festivity. **3.** hot drink made with beer, wine, or cider and spices. —*v.i.*, *v.t.* **4.** toast.

wâste, *v.*, **wasted, wasting**, *n.*, *adj.* *v.t.* **1.** use up needlessly. **2.** ruin. —*v.i.* **3.** be used up gradually. —*n.* **4.** needless consumption or expenditure. **5.** unused remains. **6.** neglect. **7.** ruin. —*adj.* **8.** unused. —**waste'bas'ket**, *n.* —**waste'ful**, *adj.* —**waste'pa'per**, *n.*

wast·rel (wās'trəl), *n.* wasteful person; spendthrift.

wâtch, *v.i.* **1.** observe; be on the alert. —*v.t.* **2.** observe. **3.** guard or tend. —*n.* **4.** period of watching; observation. **5.** small timepiece worn on the person. —**watch'band**, *n.* —**watch'dog**, *n.* —**watch'ful**, *adj.* —**watch'man**, *n.* —**watch'tow'er**, *n.*

wâtch'wôrd'', *n.* **1.** password. **2.** motto; slogan.

wä'tẽr, *n.* **1.** colorless, odorless liquid forming rain, rivers, etc. —*v.t.* **2.** supply with water. —*v.i.* **3.** discharge water or tears. —**wa'ter·y**, *adj.*

wä'tẽr·bĕd'', *n.* heavy water-filled bag used as a bed.

wätẽr clŏsẽt, toilet.

wä'tẽr·cŏl''ŏr, *n.* **1.** pigment mixed with water. **2.** painting with such pigments.

wä'tẽr·côurse'', *n.* channel for water, as a river, canal, etc.

wä'tẽr·fäll'', *n.* steep fall of water, as over a precipice.

wä'tẽr·fōwl'', *n.* water bird.

wätẽr glăss, drinking glass.

wätẽr lĭl'y̆, aquatic plant with floating leaves and flowers.

wä'tẽr·lŏgged'', *adj.* saturated with water.

wä'tẽr·mârk'', *n.* **1.** mark showing height of water, as of a river, etc. **2.** manufacturer's impression on paper. —*v.t.* **3.** mark with a watermark.

wä'tẽr·mĕl''ŏn, *n.* large fruit with juicy, red pulp.

wä'tẽr·prōof'', *adj.* **1.** impervious to water. —*v.t.* **2.** make waterproof.

wä'tẽr·shĕd'', *adj.* **1.** ridge between two drainage areas. **2.** drainage area

wä'tẽr·skī'', *v.*, **-skied, -skiing**, *n.* *v.i.* **1.** skim over water on ski-like boards drawn by a line attached to a speedboat. —*n.* **2.** short, broad board for water-skiing.

wä'tẽr·spōut'', *n.* **1.** pipe for discharging water. **2.** tubelike column of air and water occurring over water.

wätẽr tāble, *n.* level below which the ground is saturated.

wä'tẽr·whēel'', *n.* mill wheel moved by water.

wâ'tẽr·wŏrks'', *n.* plant for supplying water.

wătt, *n.* unit of electric power. —**watt'age**, *n.*

wăt'tle, *n.* **1.** stakes interwoven with twigs, as for fences, walls, etc. **2.** fleshy skin hanging from the throat or chin.

wāve, *n.*, *v.*, **waved, waving.** *n.* **1.** ridge along the ocean's surface. **2.** undulation. **3.** movement back and forth, as of a hand or flag. —*v.i.*, *v.t.* **4.** move to and fro. —*v.i.* **5.** signal with the hand. —**wav'y**, *adj.*

wā'vẽr, *v.i.* **1.** hesitate. **2.** sway. —*n.* **3.** wavering.

WAVES, *n.* W(omen) A(ccepted for) V(oluntary) E(mergency) S(ervice); women in the U.S. Navy.

wăx, *n.* **1.** readily melted, molded, and burned substance. —*v.t.* **2.** treat with wax. —*v.i.* **3.** increase, as the moon. **4.**

Archaic. become. —**wax'en**, *adj*. —wax'er, *n*. —wax'y, *adj*.

wăx'wĭng'', *n*. crested bird with scarlet wings' ends.

wāy, *n*. **1**. manner, custom, or fashion. **2**. plan. **3**. direction or route. **4**. ways, tracks for launching a ship.

wāy'fār''êr, *n*. traveler or rover.

wāy''lāy', *v.t.*, -laid, -laying. lie in wait for; ambush.

wāy'wàrd, *adj*. **1**. willful. **2**. capricious. —way'ward·ness, *n*.

wē, *pron*. nominative plural of *I*.

wĕak, *adj*. **1**. not strong physically. **2**. lacking moral or mental strength. **3**. easily broken. —**weak'ly**, *adj.*, *adv*. —**weak'en**, *v.t.*, *v.i.* —**weak'ling**, *n*. —**weak'ness**, *n*.

wĕalth, *n*. **1**. abundance of money or property. **2**. large and valuable amount. —wealth'y, *adj*.

wēan, *v.t.* **1**. accustom to food other than mother's milk. **2**. cure of a dependency or delusion.

wĕap'ŏn, *n*. instrument for fighting. —weap'on·ry, *n*.

weār, *v.*, -wore, worn, wearing. *v.t.* **1**. have on the body, as clothing. **2**. diminish by use. —*v.i.* **3**. deteriorate as through use. —*n.* **4**. diminution or impairment through use. **5**. clothing. —wear'a·ble, *adj*. —wear'er, *n*.

wēa'rĭ·sòme, *adj*. tiresome.

wēar'ў̆, *adj.*, -rier, -riest, *v.t.*, -rying, -ried. *adj.* **1**. very tired. **2**. causing fatigue. —*v.t.* **3**. tire. —**wear'i·ly**, *adv*. —wear'i·ness, *n*.

wēa'sèl, *n*. small, flesh-eating mammal.

wĕath'êr, *n*. **1**. condition of the sky. **2**. storms, rains, etc. —*v.t.* **3**. withstand. **4**. expose to the weather. —*adj.* **5**. toward the wind.

wĕath'êr·bēat''èn, *adj*. showing the effect of weather.

wēave, *v.*, wove, woven or weaved, weaving, *n.* *v.t.* **1**. interlace threads, etc., as on a loom. **2**. construct, as in the mind. —*v.i.* **3**. become interlaced. —*n.* **4**. type of weaving. —weav'er, *n*.

wĕb, *n.*, *v.t.*, webbed, webbing. *n.* **1**. something woven. **2**. network spun by spiders. **3**. trap. —*v.t.* **4**. join or cover, as by or with a web. —**webbed**, *adj*. —web'bing, *n*.

wĕb'fŏŏt'', *n.*, *pl.* -feet. foot with webbed toes. —**web'-foot''ed**, **web'-toed''**, *adj*.

wĕd, *v.*, wedded, wedded or wed, wedding. *v.t.*, *v.i.* **1**. marry. **2**. join. —wed'ding, *n*.

wĕdge, *n.*, *v.*, wedged, wedging. *n.* **1**. object with two faces meet at a sharp angle. —*v.t.* **2**. force or fix with a wedge. —*v.i.* **3**. become wedged.

wĕd'lŏck, *n*. state of marriage.

Wĕdnes'dāy, *n*. fourth day of the week.

wēe, *adj*. tiny.

wēed, *n*. **1**. useless plant. —*v.i.* **2**. free from weeds. —**weed'er**, *n*. —weed'y, *adj*.

wēek, *n*. **1**. period of seven days, esp. starting from Sunday. **2**. working days of the week.

wēek'dāy'', *n*. **1**. any day except Saturday or Sunday. —*adj.* **2**. pertaining to such days.

wēek'ĕnd'', *n*. Saturday and Sunday.

wēek'lў̆, *adj.*, *adv.*, *n.*, *pl.* -lies. *adj.* **1**. appearing or occurring once a week. **2**. lasting a week. —*adv.* **3**. every week. —*n.* **4**. weekly periodical.

wēep, *v.i.*, wept, weeping. mourn or shed tears. —weep'er, *n*.

wēe'vĭl, *n*. beetle destructive to grain, fruit, etc.

weigh, *v.t.* **1**. measure the heaviness of. **2**. consider carefully. —*v.i.* **3**. have significance. **4**. be a burden. —**weigh'er**, *n*.

weight, *n*. **1**. heaviness or pressure. **2**. burden, influence, or importance. —*v.t.* **3**. burden. —**weight'y**, *adj*. —weight'i·ness, *n*.

weird, *adj*. strange, uncanny, or queer. —**weird'ly**, *adv*. —weird'ness, *n*.

wĕl'còme, *n.*, *v.t.*, -comed, -coming, *adj.* *n.* **1**. friendly greeting. —*v.t.* **2**. greet with pleasure. —*adj.* **3**. happily or readily received. **4**. freely permitted.

wĕld, *v.t.* **1**. unite, as by heat or pressure. —*n.* **2**. welded joint. —**weld'er**, *n*.

wĕl'fāre'', *n*. **1**. well-being. **2**. aid for the poor.

wĕll, *adv.*, better, best, *adj.*, *n.*, *v.i.*, *interj. adv.* **1**. in a benevolent, good, or thorough manner. —*adj.* **2**. in good health. **3**. suitable. —*n.* **4**. opening in the earth as a source of water, oil, etc. —*v.i.* **5**. flow or gush. —*interj.* **6**. (exclamation denoting surprise or introducing a sentence).

wĕll- prefix meaning "in a good or thorough manner." **well-accomplished, well-adjusted, well-aimed, well-argued, well-armed, well-arranged, well-attended, well-aware, well-behaved, well-built, well-considered, well-contented, well-controlled, well-developed, well-disciplined, well-documented, well-earned, well-educated, well-equipped, well-governed, well-hidden, well-justified, well-kept, well-liked, well-loved, well-managed, well-planned, well-prepared, well-protected, well-qualified, well-regulated, well-remembered, well-respected, well-satisfied, well-secured, well-situated, well-spent, well-stated, well-suited, well-taught, well-trained, well-traveled, well-treated, well-understood, well-used.**

wĕll'-bē·ĭng, *n.* state of being well and happy.

wĕll'-brĕd', *adj.* with good manners.

wĕll'-ĕs·tăb'lĭshed, *adj.* settled; firmly in place.

wĕll'-foŭnd'ĕd, *adj.* based on good reason. Also, **well'-ground'ed,** *adj.*

wĕll'hĕad'', *n.* fountainhead; source.

wĕll'-măn'nêred, *adj.* polite; courteous.

wĕll'-mēan'ĭng, *adj.* having good intentions. —**well'-meant',** *adj.*

wĕll'-nīgh', *adv.* almost.

wĕll'-ôff', *adj.* **1.** in a good condition. **2.** prosperous.

wĕll'-prē·sĕrved', *adj.* **1.** in good condition. **2.** youthful for one's age.

wĕll'-roŭnd'ĕd, *adj.* **1.** having varied abilities. **2.** well-diversified.

wĕll'-spō'kĕn, *adj.* speaking well or pleasantly.

wĕll'sprĭng'', *n.* source.

wĕll'-tȯ-dō', *adj.* wealthy.

wĕll'-wĭsh''êr, *n.* person who wishes well to another.

wĕlt, *n.* **1.** ridge or wale on the body from a blow. **2.** leather strip on the seam of a shoe. —*v.t.* **3.** beat soundly.

wĕlt'êr, *v.i.* **1.** roll or heave, as waves. **2.** wallow. —*n.* **3.** jumble or muddle.

wĕn, *n.* skin cyst or tumor.

wĕnch, *n.* **1.** young woman. **2.** strumpet.

—*v.i.* **3.** associated with promiscuous women.

wĕnt, *v.i.* past form of *go.*

wēre, *v.* past plural form of *be.*

wēre'wŏlf'', *n., pl.* **-wolves.** person changed into a wolf.

wĕst, *n.* **1.** compass point to the left of north. **2.** direction of such point. **3.** Also, **West,** the Occident. —*adj., adv.* **4.** toward or from the west. —**west'ern,** *adj.* —**west'ern·er,** *n.*

wĕst'êr·lў, *adj., adv.* **1.** from the west, as wind. **2.** toward the west.

wĕst'êrn·īze'', *v.t.,* **-ized, -izing.** make Occidental in culture.

wĕst'wȧrd, *adj.* **1.** toward the west. —*adv.* **2.** Also, **west'wards, toward the west.** —*n.* **3.** westward direction.

wĕt, *adj.,* **wetter, wettest,** *n., v. adj.* **1.** covered with water or liquid. —*n.* **2.** water or moisture. —*v.t.* **3.** make wet. —*v.i.* **4.** become wet. —**wet'ness,** *n.*

whăck, *Informal. v.t., v.i.* **1.** slap or strike. —*n.* **2.** sharp blow.

whāle, *n., v.i.,* **whaled, whaling.** *n.* **1.** large sea mammal. —*v.i.* **2.** hunt whales. —**whal'er,** *n.*

whāle'bōne'', *n.* elastic material in the upper jaw of some whales.

whȧrf, *n., pl.* **wharves.** pier or quay.

whăt, *pron., pl.* **what,** *adj., adv., interj. pron.* **1.** which one? **2.** that which. —*adj.* **3.** which kind of. —*adv.* **4.** how? **5.** partly. —*interj.* **6.** (exclamation of surprise).

whăt·ĕv'êr, *pron.* **1.** anything that. —*adj.* **2.** of any kind.

whăt'nŏt'', *n.* open cupboard, as for bric-a-brac.

wheăl, *n.* small swelling, as from an insect bite.

wheăt, *n.* cereal grass used in flour, etc.

whee'dle, *v.t.,* **-dled, -dling.** persuade by coaxing.

wheel, *n.* **1.** rotating disk that transmits power or facilities movement. —*v.t., v.i.* **2.** move on wheels. **3.** revolve.

wheel'bar''rȯw, *n.* one-wheeled container for moving loads.

wheel'bāse'', *n.* distance between the front and rear wheel hubs of an automobile.

wheel'êr-dēal'êr, *n. Informal.* person skillful in business deals.

wheeze, *v.i.,* **wheezed, wheezing.** *n. v.i.*

1. breathe with a whistling sound. —*n.*
2. a wheezing sound. —**wheez′y,** *adj.*

whĕlm, *v.t.* 1. submerge. 2. overwhelm.

whĕlp, *n.* 1. young of a dog, bear, etc. —*v.t., v.i.* 2. give birth to.

whĕn, *adv.* 1. at what time? —*conj.* 2. at the time that. —*pron.* 3. what or which time.

whĕnce, *adv.* from what place, cause, etc.

whĕn·ĕv′êr, *adv.* 1. when. —*conj.* 2. at whatever time.

whĕre, *adv.* 1. at what place? 2. in what way? —*conj.* 3. at which place; wherever. —*pron.* 4. the place at which.

whĕre′a·bōuts′′, *adv.* 1. where. —*n.* 2. location.

whĕre·ăs′, *conj.* 1. considering that. 2. on the contrary.

whĕre′fōre′′, *adv., conj.* for what.

whĕre·ĭn′, *conj.* in which.

whĕre′′ŭp·ŏn′, *conj.* upon which.

whĕre′wĭth·äl′′, *n.* means.

whĕr′·rў, *n., pl.* **-ries.** light rowboat.

whĕt, *v.t.*, **whetted, whetting.** 1. sharpen. 2. stimulate, as the appetite. —**whet′stone′′,** *n.*

whĕth′êr, *conj.* 1. if it is so that. 2. if either.

whĕy, *n.* water part of curdled milk.

whĭch, *pron.* 1. what one? 2. that. —*adj.* 3. what one.

whĭch·ĕv′êr, *pron., adj.* 1. any. 2. regardless of which.

whĭff, *n.* light odor or puff.

whĭf′fle·trēe′′, *n.* crossbar to which harness traces are fastened.

whīle, *n., conj., v.t.*, **whiled, whiling.** *n.* 1. time. —*conj.* 2. during the time that. 3. although. —*v.t.* 4. spend pleasantly, as time.

whĭm, *n.* sudden fancy; caprice. —**whim′si·cal,** *adj.* —**whim′sy,** *n.*

whīne, *v.i.*, **whined, whining.** 1. complain childishly. 2. make a high-pitched, nasal sound. —**whin′ing·ly,** *adv.* —**whin′y,** *adj.*

whĭn′nў, *v.i.*, **-nied, -nying,** *n., pl.* **-nies.** neigh.

whĭp, *v.*, **whipped, whipping,** *n. v.t.* 1. strike or lash. —*v.i.* 2. move quickly. —*n.* 3. instrument for whipping.

whĭp′cōrd′′, *n.* hard, braided cord.

whĭp′lăsh′′, *n.* neck injury from jerking of the head as in an automobile accident.

whĭp′pêr·snăp′′pêr, *n.* presumptuous person.

whĭp′pėt, *n.* fast dog.

whĭp′pōor·wĭll′′, *n.* gray bird with nocturnal cry.

whĭr, *v.*, **whirred, whirring,** *n. v.i., v.t., n.* hum or buzz. Also, **whirr.**

whĭrl, *v.i., v.t.* 1. move or revolve rapidly. —*n.* 2. whirling movement. 3. uproar or confusion.

whĭrl′pōōl′′, *n.* whirling current of water.

whĭrl′wĭnd′′, *n.* whirling current of air.

whĭsk, *v.t., v.i.* 1. brush with a quick motion. —*n.* 2. act or instance of whisking. —**whisk′broom′′,** *n.*

whĭsk′êr, *n.* 1. a facial hair. 2. long bristle, as on a cat.

whĭs′kėy, *n., pl.* **-keys, -kies.** liquor distilled from fermented grain. Also, **whis′ky.**

whĭs′pêr, *v.i., v.t.* 1. speak softly. 2. make a low rustling. —*n.* 3. act or instance of whispering.

whĭst, *n.* card game.

whĭs′tle, *v.i.*, **-tled, -tling,** *n. v.i.* 1. make a high-pitched sound through pursed lips. —*n.* 2. act or instance of whistling. 3. noise-making device using steam or air.

whĭt, *n.* small bit.

whīte, *adj.* 1. of the color of snow. 2. pale. 3. pure. —*n.* 4. opposite to black. 5. Caucasoid. —**white′ness,** *n.* —**whit′ish,** *adj.* —**whit′en,** *v.t., v.i.*

whīte ĕlêphánt, 1. albino elephant. 2. awkward, useless possession.

whīte′fĭsh′′, *n.* edible lake fish.

Whīte Hōuse, 1. residence of the U.S. president. 2. executive branch of the U.S. government.

whīte līe, small, pardonable lie.

whīte slāve, woman forced into prostitution. —**white slavery.**

whīte′wăsh′′, *n.* 1. mixture for whitening walls. —*v.t.* 2. apply whitewash to. 3. *Informal.* conceal the guilt of.

whĭth′êr, *adv., conj. Archaic.* to what place.

whīt′ĭng, *n.* 1. food fish. 2. chalk for paints.

whĭt′lōw, *n.* inflammation of a finger or toe.

whǐt′tle, *v.,* -tled, -tling. *v.t., v.i.* **1.** cut or carve, as from wood. —*v.t.* **2.** reduce the amount of.

whǐz, *v.i.,* whizzed, whizzing, *n. v.i.* **1.** make a buzzing sound in motion. —*n.* **2.** such a sound. **3.** *Informal.* expert. Also, **whizz.**

who, *pron.* **1.** which person? **2.** person that.

whōa, *interj.* stop!

who·ěv′ẽr, *pron.* anyone that.

whōle, *adj.* **1.** entire. **2.** intact. **3.** *Math.* not a fraction. —*n.* **4.** all the amount. —**whole′ly,** *adv.* —**whole′ness,** *n.*

whōle′heârt′ěd, *adj.* enthusiastic; dedicated. —**whole′heart′ed·ly,** *adv.*

whōle′sāle′′, *n., adj., v.,* -saled, -saling. *n.* **1.** sale of goods in quantity, as to retailers. —*adj.* **2.** selling by wholesale. —*v.t., v.i.* **3.** sell wholesale. —**whole′sal′er,** *n.*

whōle′sŏme, *adj.* healthful, salutary. —**whole′some·ly,** *adv.* —**whole′some·ness,** *n.*

whom, *pron. Grammar.* objective case of who.

whōōp, *n.* **1.** shout of joy. **2.** sound in whooping cough. —*v.t., v.i.* **3.** utter with whooping.

whŏp′pêr, *n. Informal.* **1.** something unusually large. **2.** outrageous lie. —**whop′ping,** *adj.*

whôre, *n., v.i.,* whored, whoring. *n.* **1.** prostitute. —*v.i.* **2.** consort with whores. —**whor′ish,** *adj.*

whôrl, *n.* spiral or circular arrangement.

whose, *pron. Grammar.* possessive case of who.

who′sŏ·ěv′ẽr, *pron.* whoever.

whȳ, *adv., n., pl.* whys, *interj. adv.* **1.** for what reason or cause. —*n.* **2.** reason, cause, or purpose. —*interj.* **3.** exclamation of surprise.

wǐck, *n.* length of fiber that absorbs fuel to burn.

wǐck′ěd, *adj.* **1.** bad, evil. **2.** mischievous. —**wick′ed·ly,** *adv.* —**wick′ed·ness,** *n.*

wǐck′êr, *n.* **1.** flexible twig. —*adj.* **2.** made of wicker. —**wick′er·work′′,** *n.*

wǐck′ět, *n.* **1.** small gate. **2.** upright frame used in cricket or croquet.

wīde, *adj.,* wider, widest. *adj.* **1.** broad. —*adv.* **2.** far. —**wide′ly,** *adv.* —**wide′ness,** *n.* —**wid′en,** *v.t., v.i.* —**wide′spread′,** *adj.*

wīde′-à·wāke′, *adj.* alert.

wǐdg′eȯn, *n.* fresh-water wild duck. Also, **wig′eon.**

wǐd′ōw, *n.* **1.** unmarried woman whose husband has died. —*v.t.* **2.** make into a widow. Also, *masc.,* **wid′ow·er.** —**wid′ow·hood′′,** *n.*

wǐdth, *n.* breadth.

wiěld, *v.t.* **1.** handle or manage. **2.** exercise, as authority or power. —**wield′er,** *n.*

wiē′nêr, *n.* frankfurter. Also, *Informal,* **wee′nie** or **wie′nie.**

wīfe, *n., pl.* wives. married woman. —**wife′less,** *adj.* —**wife′ly,** *adj.*

wǐg, *n., v.,* wigged, wigging. *n.* **1.** artificial hair piece. —*v.t.* **2.** furnish with a wig.

wǐg′gle, *v.,* -gled, -gling, *n. v.i., v.t.* **1.** move with quick motions from side to side. —*n.* **2.** act or instance of wiggling. —**wig′gly,** *adj.*

wǐg′wǎg′′, *v.,* -wagged, -wagging, *n. v.t., v.i.* **1.** signal with swung flags. —*n.* **2.** act or instance of wigwagging.

wǐg′wăm, *n.* Native American hut.

wīld, *adj.* **1.** uncivilized. **2.** uncontrollable. **3.** lacking restraint; dissolute. —*n.* **4.** desolate region. —**wild′ly,** *adv.* —**wild′ness,** *n.*

wīld′căt′′, *n., v.,* -catted, -catting. *n.* **1.** large, fierce feline. **2.** savage person. **3.** exploratory oil or gas well. —*v.i., v.t.* **4.** search for oil or gas.

wǐl′dêr·ness, *n.* uninhabited region.

wīld′-gōōse′chāse, search for a nonexistent thing.

wīle, *n., v.t.,* wiled, wiling. *n.* **1.** sly trick. —*v.t.* **2.** beguile. **3.** wile away, pass leisurely, as time.

wǐll, *n., v.,* willed, willing. *n.* **1.** power of conscious choice or action. **2.** determination. **3.** disposition toward another. **4.** legal document of one's wishes after death. —*v.i., v.t.* **5.** desire, wish or want. **6.** bequeath by a will. —*auxiliary v.* **7.** am, is, or are about to. **8.** am, is, or are willing to. **9.** am, is, or are expected to. —**will·a·ble,** *adj.*

wǐll′fŭl, *adj.* **1.** intentional. **2.** stubborn. Also, **wil′ful.** —**will′ful·ly,** *adv.* —**will′ful·ness,** *n.*

wǐll′ǐng, *adj.* **1.** favorably inclined. **2.**

cheerfully done. —**will'ing·ly,** adv. —**will'ing·ness,** n.

will''-ò'-thė-wĭsp', 1. elusive light. 2. anything that deludes.

wĭl'lōw, n. slender tree with flexible limbs and narrow leaves. —**wil'low·y,** adj.

wĭl'lÿ-nĭl'lÿ, adv., adj. whether willingly or not.

wĭlt, v.i. 1. become limp or weak; droop. —v.t. 2. cause to wilt. —n. 3. wilted state.

wĭl'ÿ, adj., -lier, -liest. sly. —**wi'li·ness,** n.

wĭn, v., won, winning, n. v.i. 1. succeed. —v.t. 2. gain, as a victory, favor, etc. 3. influence. —n. 4. victory.

wĭnce, v.i., winced, wincing, n. v.i. 1. shrink, as from a blow or pain. —n. 2. act or instance of wincing.

wĭnch, n. 1. crank. 2. windlass. —v.t. 3. hoist or haul by a winch.

wĭnd, v., wound, winding, n. v.t. (wīnd) 1. turn. —v.i. 2. coil. 3. make one's way, as along a path. —n. (wind) 4. air in motion, as a gale. 5. breath. 6. intestinal gas. —**wind'er,** n. —**wind'y,** adj.

wĭnd'bȧg'', n. Informal. empty talker.

wĭnd'brēȧk'', n. shield against the wind.

wĭnd'bûrn'', n. inflammation of the skin from the wind. —**wind'burned'',** adj.

wĭnd'ėd, adj. out of breath.

wĭnd'fȧll, n. 1. unexpected good fortune. 2. something blown down by the wind.

wĭnd ĭnstrùmėnt, musical instrument sounded by the breath.

wĭnd'jȧm''mêr, n. large sailing ship.

wĭnd'lȧss, n. winch.

wĭnd'mĭll'', n. wind-driven machine.

wĭn'dōw, n. opening in a wall for light, air, etc. —**win'dow·pane'',** n. —**win'dow·sill'',** n. —window shade.

wĭndōw drĕssĭng, 1. store display. 2. specious display.

wĭnd'pīpe'', n. trachea.

wĭnd'rōw'', n. row of leaves, hay, etc.

wĭnd'shiēld'', n. glass above and across a car's dashboard.

wĭnd'ŭp'', n. 1. conclusion or end. 2. Baseball. pitcher's arm and body movements before throwing.

wĭnd'wȧrd, n. 1. direction from which the wind blows. —adj. 2. moving to windward. —adv. 3. toward the wind.

wīne, n., v., wined, wining. n. 1. fermented juice from grapes, other fruits, or plants. —v.i. 2. entertain with wine. —**win'y,** adj.

wīn'êr·ÿ, n., pl. -ies. wine-making place.

wĭng, n. 1. organ for flight of birds, insects, bats, etc. 2. supporting surface of an airplane. 3. distinct section. —v.t. 4. shoot in an arm or wing. —v.i. 5. travel on wings. —**wing'ed,** adj. —**wing'less,** adj. —**wing'like,** adj. —**wing'tip'',** n.

wĭng'spȧn'', n. distance between an airplane's wingtips.

wĭng'sprĕȧd'', n. distance between the tips of extended wings.

wĭnk, v.t., v.i. 1. close and open quickly, as one eye. 2. signal by winking. —v.i. 3. shine or twinkle. —n. 4. winking, as a signal. 5. instant.

wĭn'nêr, n. person or thing that wins.

wĭn'nĭng, adj. 1. pleasing; charming. 2. victorious. —n. 3. Often winnings, something won, as money. —**win'ning·ly,** adv.

wĭn'nōw, v.t., v.i. 1. blow away from grain. 2. separate.

wĭn·ō, n., pl. -os. Informal. alcoholic who drinks cheap wine.

wĭn'sȯme, adj. attractive. —**win'some·ly,** adv. —**win'some·ness,** n.

wĭn'têr, n. 1. cold season between autumn and spring. 2. time likc winter, as of decline, cold, etc. —v.i. 3. spend the winter. —**win'ter·time'',** n. —**win'try,** win'ter·y, adj.

wĭn'têr·grēen'', n. small evergreen aromatic shrub with white flowers.

wĭn'têr·īze'', v.t., -ized, -izing. prepare for winter.

wīpe, v.t., wiped, wiping, n., v.t. 1. clean or rub. —n. 2. act or instance of wiping. —**wip'er,** n.

wīre, n., v., wired, wiring. n. 1. string-like piece of metal. 2. Informal. telegram. —v.t. 3. install or bind with wire. —v.t., v.i. 4. telegraph.

wīre'hȧir'', n. fox terrier.

wīre'lĕss, adj. Archaic. pertaining to radio.

wīre'tȧp''pĭng, n. listening secretly to the telephone calls of others.

wir′y̆, *adj.*, **-ier, -iest.** lean and tough.

wis′dŏm, *n.* **1.** knowledge and good judgment. **2.** wise teachings.

wisdom tooth, back molar.

wise, *adj.*, **wiser, wisest. 1.** showing knowledge and judgment. **2.** erudite or informed. **3.** *Informal.* insolent. **—wise′ly,** *adv.*

wise′ā·crê, *n.* person who affects to have wisdom. Also, *Informal*, **wise guy.**

wise′crăck″, *Informal. n.* **1.** flippant remark. **—v.i. 2.** make wisecracks.

wish, *v.t.* **1.** want or desire. **—v.i. 2.** yearn. **—n. 3.** desire; longing. **—wish′er**, *n.* **—wish′ful,** *adj.* **—wish′ful·ly,** *adv.* **—wish′ful·ness,** *n.*

wish′bŏne″, *n.* forked breastbone of a bird.

wish′y̆-wăsh′y̆, *adj.* weak and vacillating.

wisp, *n.* thin film or strand. **—wisp′y,** *adj.*

wis·tē′rĭ·ȧ, *n.* climbing shrub with showy flowers.

wist′fŭl, *adj.* longing or yearning. **—wist′ful·ly,** *adv.* **—wist′ful·ness,** *n.*

wit, *n.* **1.** intelligence. **2.** cleverness of expression. **3.** person clever with words. **—wit′less**, *adj.* **—wit′less·ly,** *adv.* **—wit′ty,** *adj.* **—wit′ti·ly,** *adv.*

witch, *n.* **1.** woman with supposed supernatural power. **2.** ugly woman. **—witch′craft″,** *n.* **—witch′er·y,** *n.*

witch dŏctŏr, man who uses magic to cure sickness.

witch hāzĕl, 1. shrub with yellow leaves. **2.** liquid extracted from it.

with, *prep.* **1.** accompanied by. **2.** characterized by. **3.** against. **4.** in regard to.

with·draw′, *v.*, **-drew, -drawn, -drawing.** *v.t.* **1.** take back. **2.** retract, as a statement, etc. **—v.i. 3.** remove oneself. **—with·draw′al,** *n.*

withe, *n.* willow twig.

with′êr, *v.t., v.i.* **1.** shrivel. **—v.t. 2.** confuse and humiliate. **—with′er·ing·ly,** *adv.*

with′êrs, *n. pl.* lower nape of the neck of a sheep, horse, etc.

with·hŏld′, *v.t.*, **-held, -holding. 1.** hold back. **2.** deduct, as taxes.

with·in′, *adv.* **1.** inside; indoors. **—prep. 2.** inside. **3.** in the area of.

with·out′, *prep.* **1.** lacking; not with. **2.** outside. **—adv. 3.** outside; externally.

with·stănd′, *v.t.*, **-stood, -standing.** resist or oppose.

wit′ness, *n.* **1.** person who sees. **2.** testimony. **—v.t. 3.** see. **4.** attest.

wit′tĭ·cĭsm″, *n.* witty remark.

wit′tĭng, *adj.* knowing; intentional. **—wit′ting·ly,** *adv.*

wiz′ȧrd, *n.* magician; sorcerer. **—wiz′ard·ry,** *n.*

wiz′ĕned, *adj.* withered.

wŏb′ble, *v.*, **-bled, -bling,** *n. v.i., v.t.* **1.** shake. **—n. 2.** wobbling motion. **—wob′bly,** *adj.* **—wob′bli·ness,** *n.*

wŏe, *n.* **1.** grief. **2.** trouble. **—interj. 3.** alas! **—woe′ful,** *adj.* **—woe′ful·ly,** *adv.* **—woe′ful·ness,** *n.*

wŏe′bē·gŏne″, *adj.* showing woe. **—woe′be·gone″ness,** *n.*

wŏlf, *n.*, *pl.* **wolves. 1.** wild, doglike mammal. **2.** *Informal.* man who flirts with women. **3.** cruel person. **—v.t. 4.** devour greedily. **—wolf′hound″,** *n.* **—wolf′ish,** *adj.* **—wolf′like″,** *adj.*

wŏl″vêr·īne′, *n.* stocky, carnivorous mammal.

wŏm′ȧn, *n.*, *pl.* **women.** female human being. **—wom′an·hood″,** *n.* **—wom′an·ish,** *adj.* **—wom′an·like″,** *adj.* **—wom′an·ly,** *adj.* **—wom′an·li·ness,** *n.*

wŏm′ȧn·īze″, *v.* **-ized, -izing.** *v.t.* **1.** make effeminate. **—v.t. 2.** pursue women habitually. **—wom′an·iz″er,** *n.*

womb, *n.* **1.** uterus. **2.** source of being.

wŏn′dêr, *n.* **1.** awe or amazement. **2.** source of such an emotion. **—v.i. 3.** be curious. **4.** be filled with wonder. **—won′der·ful,** *adj.* **—won′der·ful·ly,** *adv.* **—won′der·ing·ly,** *adv.* **—won′der·ment,** *n.* **—won′drous,** *adj.* **—won′drous·ly,** *adv.*

wŏnt, *adj.* **1.** Also, **wont′ed,** accustomed. **—n. 2.** habit.

wŏn′t, *v.* contraction of *will not*.

woo, *v.i., v.t.* solicit for love or favor. **—woo′er,** *n.*

wood, *n.* **1.** hard substance beneath the bark of trees. **2.** Also, **woods**, forest. **3.** lumber. **—adj. 4.** wooden; made of wood. **—wood′en,** *adj.* **—wood′en·ness,** *n.* **—wood′craft″,** *n.* **—wood′cut″ter,** *n.* **—wood′ed,** *adj.* **—wood′pile″,** *n.* **—wood′shed″,** *n.* **—woods′**

man, *n*. —woods′y, *adj*. —wood′y, *adj*.

wŏŏd′bīne″, *n*. honeysuckle or the Virginia creeper.

wŏŏd′chŭck″, *n*. burrowing and hibernating marmot.

wŏŏd′cŏck″, *n*. snipelike game bird.

wŏŏd′cŭt″, *n*. 1. carved block of wood. 2. print from this block.

wŏŏd′ĕn, *adj*. 1. made of wood. 2. without natural feeling or expression. —wood′en·ly, *adv*.

wŏŏd′lănd″, *n*. land covered with trees.

wŏŏd′pĕck″êr, *n*. bird with a hard bill for pecking.

wŏŏd′wĭnd″, *n*. musical non-brass wind instrument.

wŏŏd′wŏrk″, *n*. 1. objects made of wood. 2. wooden fittings of a house, as doors, moldings, etc. —wood′work″er, *n*. —wood′work″ing, *n*.

wŏŏf, *n*. cross-threads of a fabric.

wŏŏf′êr, *n*. loudspeaker for reproducing low frequencies.

wŏŏl, *n*. 1. soft, curly hair, as from sheep, goats, etc. 2. yarn or garments made from such. —wool′en, wool′len, *adj*. —wool′y, wool′ly, *adj*. —wool′i·ness, wool′li·ness, *n*.

wŏŏl′găth″êr·ĭng, *n*. absentmindedness or daydreaming.

wŏŏz′y̆, *adj*., -ier, -iest. *Informal*. muddled or dizzy. —wooz′i·ly, *adv*. —wooz′i·ness, *n*.

wŏrd, *n*. 1. spoken or written sounds with meaning as a unit of language. 2. words, speech or talk. 3. promise or assurance. 4. news or information. 5. (computers) several bits of data treated as a unit. —*v.t*. 6. express in words. —word″age, *n*. —word″ing, *n*. —word″less, *adj*. —word″y, *adj*. —word″i·ness, *n*.

wŏrk, *n*., *v*., worked or wrought, working, *n*. 1. labor or toil. 2. occupation. 3. something on which one is working. —*v.i*. 4. do work. 5. act or operate. —*v.t*. 6. manage or manipulate. 7. solve. 8. cultivate, as the soil. 9. provoke or excite. —work′a·ble, *adj*. —work′bench″, *n*. —work′book″, *n*. —work′er, *n*. —work′day″, *n*. —work′ing·man″, *n*. —work′man, *n*. —work′shop″, *n*. —work′week″, *n*.

wŏrk′dāy, *n*. 1. day on which work is done. 2. part of the day one works.

wŏrk′măn·like″, *adj*. skillful.

wŏrk′măn·shĭp″, *n*. 1. workman's art or skill. 2. quality of work.

wŏrk′ŏut″, *n*. practice athletic session.

wŏrld, *n*. 1. earth; universe. 2. people; mankind. 3. part of the earth. 4. great quantity or extent. —world′wide′, *adj*.

wŏrld′ly̆, *adj*., -lier, -liest. 1. secular. 2. Also, world′ly-wise′, sophisticated. —world′li·ness, *n*.

wŏrm, *n*. 1. long, soft, legless, creeping animal. 2. something like this creature. 3. *Informal*. contemptible person. 4. worms, intestinal disease from parasitic worms. —*v.i*. 5. move or act stealthily. —*v.t*. 6. get by insidious efforts. 7. free from worms. —worm′y, *adj*. -ier, -iest. —worm′i·ness, *n*.

wŏrm′wŏŏd″, *n*. 1. bitter, strong-smelling herb. 2. something bitter or unpleasant.

wŏrn, *adj*. 1. used by wear, handling, etc. 2. exhausted; tired. —worn′-out′, *adj*.

wŏr′ry̆, *v*., -ried, -rying, *n*., *pl*. -ies. *v.i*. 1. feel anxious. —*v.t*. 2. make anxious. 3. anxiety. 4. cause of anxiety. —*n*. 3. anxiety. 4. cause of anxiety. —wor′ri·er, *n*. —wor′ri·some, *adj*.

wŏrse, *adj*. 1. bad in a greater or higher degree. 2. in poorer health. —*n*. 3. that which is worse. —*adv*. 4. in a worse manner. —wors′en, *v.t*., *v.i*.

wŏr′shĭp, *n*., *v*., -shiped, or -shipped, -shiping or -shipping. *n*. 1. reverence for a deity. 2. admiration or love. —*v.t*., *v.i*. 3. show religious reverence. —wor′ship·er, wor′ship·per, *n*. —wor′ship·ful, *adj*.

wŏrst, *adj*. 1. bad in the highest degree. 2. least well. —*n*. 3. that which is worst. —*adv*. 4. in the worst manner. —*v.t*. 5. beat; defeat.

wor·sted (wŏŏs′tĭd), *n*. 1. firmly twisted wool yarn. 2. garment made of it. —*adj*. 3. consisting of worsted.

wŏrt, *n*. infusion with malt before fermentation, as in making beer or mash.

wŏrth, *n*. 1. material value, as in money. 2. importance; value. —*adj*. 3. worthy of; justifying. 4. having equal value. —worth′less, *adj*. —worth′less·ness, *n*.

wŏrth′whīle′, *adj*. worthy of doing, etc.

wŏrth′ÿ, *adj.*, **-ier**, **-iest**. deserving. —**worth′i·ly**, *adv.* —**worth′i·ness**, *n.*

woŭld, *auxiliary v.* expressing condition, futurity, habitual action, or request.

woŭld′-bē′′, *adj.* wishing or intending to be.

woŭnd, *n.* **1.** physical injury. **2.** injury to feelings, sensibilities, etc. —*v.t.* **3.** injure. —**wound′ed**, *adj.*, *n.*, *pl.*

wrăck, *n.* ruin or destruction.

wrāith, *n.* ghost.

wrăn′gle, *v.t.*, *v.i.*, **-gled**, **-gling**, *n.* dispute.

wrăp, *v.*, **wrapped** or **wrapt**, **wrapping**, *n.* *v.t.*, *v.i.* **1.** wind or fold, as around something. —*v.t.* **2.** enclose or envelop. —*n.* **3.** outer garment wrapped around the body. —**wrap′ping**, *n.*

wrăp′pêr, *n.* **1.** person who wraps. **2.** something wrapped around as a cover.

wrăth, *n.* **1.** anger; rage. **2.** vengeance. —**wrath′ful**, *adj.* —**wrath′ful·ly**, *adv.*

wrēak, *v.t.* inflict.

wrēath, *n.*, *pl.* **wreaths.** circular formation, as of flowers, etc.

wrēathe, *v.t.*, **wreathed**, **wreathing.** **1.** form into a wreath. **2.** encircle.

wrĕck, *n.* **1.** structure or object in ruins. **2.** run-down person. —*v.t.* **3.** tear down or destroy. —**wreck′age**, *n.* —**wreck′er**, *n.*

wrĕn, *n.* small active songbird.

wrĕnch, *n.* **1.** sudden twist or pull, as to the arms, back, etc. **2.** sudden emotional strain. **3.** tool for turning bolts, etc. —*v.t.*, *v.i.* **4.** turn suddenly. —*v.t.* **5.** overstrain or injure.

wrĕst, *v.t.* **1.** pull violently. **2.** usurp. —*n.* **3.** twist.

wrĕs′tle, *v.*, **-tled**, **-tling**. *v.t.* **1.** grapple and attempt to throw down. —*v.i.* **2.** engage in wrestling. **3.** struggle. —**wrest′ler**, *n.*

wrĕtch, *n.* **1.** unhappy person. **2.** despicable person.

wrĕtch′ĕd, *adj.* **1.** pitiful. **2.** contemptible. **3.** worthless. —**wretch′ed·ly**, *adv.* —**wretch′ed·ness**, *n.*

wrĭg′gle, *v.i.*, *n.*, **-gled**, **-gling**. *v.i.* **1.** squirm; twist and turn. —*n.* **2.** act or instance of wriggling. —**wrig′gly**, *adj.*

wrĭght, *n.* carpenter.

wrĭng, *v.t.*, **wrung**, **wringing**, *n.*, *v.t.* **1.** twist; press; squeeze. —*n.* **2.** act or instance of wringing. —**wring′er**, *n.*

wrĭn′kle, *n.*, *v.*, **-kled**, **-kling**. *n.* **1.** ridge or furrow on a surface. **2.** ingenious trick or device. —*v.t.*, *v.i.* **3.** crease or furrow. —**wrin′kly**, *adj.*

wrĭst, *n.* joint between the hand and forearm. —**wrist′band′′**, *n.* —**wrist′watch′′**, *n.*

wrĭt, *n.* **1.** *Law.* formal legal order or document. **2.** something written.

wrīte, *v.*, **wrote**, **written**, **writing**. *v.i.* **1.** form letters, words, etc., as with a pen, pencil, etc. —*v.t.* **2.** compose. **3.** communicate with. —**writ′er**, *n.*

wrīthe, *v.*, **writhed**, **writhing**, *n.* *v.t.*, *v.i.* **1.** squirm, twist, or bend, as in pain. —*n.* **2.** act or instance of writhing.

wrŏng, *adj.* **1.** not right or good. **2.** not truthful or factual. **3.** inappropriate. —*n.* **4.** injustice; evil. —*v.t.* **5.** do wrong to. —**wrong′ly**, *adv.* —**wrong′ness**, *n.* —**wrong′do′′er**, *n.* —**wrong′do′′ing**, *n.* —**wrong′ful**, *adj.* —**wrong′ful·ly**, *adv.*

wrŏng′hĕad′′ĕd, *adj.* deeply erroneous.

wrŏth, *adj.* *Archaic.* angry.

wrŏught, *adj.* **1.** worked. **2.** shaped by beating.

wrŏught′-ŭp′, *adj.* upset; excited.

wrÿ, *adj.*, **wrier**, **wriest**. **1.** distorted or lopsided. **2.** misdirected or perverse. **3.** bitterly ironic. —**wry′ly**, *adv.* —**wry′ness**, *n.*

wûrst, *n.* sausage.

X

X, x, *n.* twenty-fourth letter of the English alphabet.

xē′nŏn, *n.* chemically inactive gaseous element.

xēn′′o·phō′bĭ·à, *n.* irrational fear of that which is foreign or strange. —**xen′′o·pho′bic**, *adj.*

Xmàs, *n.* Christmas.

x′-rāy, *n.* **1.** electromagnetic radiation which penetrates solids. **2.** picture made by x-rays. —*v.t.* **3.** treat or photograph with x-rays.

xȳ′lĕm, *n.* woody tissue of plants and trees.

xȳ′lȯ·phōne′′, *n*. musical instrument with wooden sounding bars struck by small hammers.

Y

Y, y, *n*. twenty-fifth letter of the English alphabet.

yächt, *n*. pleasure ship. —**yachts′man**, *n*.

yä·hōō′, *n*. coarse or rowdy person.

Yäh′weh, *n*. God of the Hebrews.

yăk, *n*. long-haired Tibetan ox.

yăm, *n*. edible potatolike root; sweet potato.

yăm′mêr, *v.i.*, -**mered**, -**mering**. **1.** complain or whine. **2.** talk persistently; chatter.

yănk, *v.t.*, *v.i.* **1.** pull strongly and abruptly. —*n*. **2.** strong, abrupt pull. **3.** **Yank**, Yankee.

Yăn′kēe, *n*. native or inhabitant of the U.S., the northeastern U.S., or New England.

yăp, *v.i.*, **yapped**, **yapping**, *n*. *v.i.* **1.** yelp; bark shrilly. —*n*. **2.** shrill bark.

yârd, *n*. **1.** linear unit of measure equal to 3 feet. **2.** open area. **3.** long spar that supports a sail.

yârd′áge, *n*. amount in yards.

yârd′stĭck′′, *n*. one-yard measuring stick.

yârn, *n*. **1.** multi-stranded thread for sweaters, etc. **2.** story; tall tale.

yăw, *v.i.* **1.** deviate from a course. —*n*. **2.** deviation.

yăwl, *n*. two-masted sailboat.

yăwn, *v.i.* **1.** involuntarily open the mouth wide as from drowsiness. —*n*. **2.** act or instance of yawning.

yeā, *adv.*, *n*. yes.

yēar, *n*. **1.** time period equal to 365 or 366 days. **2.** **years**, age. —**year′ly**, *adv.*, *adj.*

yēar′lĭng, *n*. year-old animal.

yêarn, *v.i.* **1.** desire earnestly or strongly. **2.** feel affection or tenderness. —**yearn′ing**, *n.*, *adj.*

yēast, *n*. fungous substance used to leaven bread, etc.

yĕll, *v.i.*, *n* cry; shout.

yĕl′lōw, *n*. **1.** bright color of butter, etc. —*adj*. **2.** of the color yellow. **3.** *Informal*. cowardly; chicken.

yĕl′lōw fē′vêr, *n*. tropical disease.

yĕlp, *v.i.* **1.** cry quickly or shrilly like a dog. —*n*. **2.** quick, sharp bark.

yĕn, *n*. *Informal*. desire; urge.

yeō·mȧn, *n*. **1.** naval petty officer. **2.** small independent farmer. —*adj*. **3.** valiant.

yĕs, *adv.*, *n*. expression of assent, agreement or affirmation.

yĕs′têr·dāy, *adv.*, *n*. day before today.

yĕt, *adv.* **1.** up to now. **2.** besides. **3.** nevertheless. **4.** eventually. —*conj*. **5.** but; still.

yēw, *n*. coniferous evergreen tree or bush.

yiĕld, *v.t.*, *v.i.* **1.** produce. **2.** surrender. **3.** concede. —*v.i.* **4.** give way to force. —*n*. **5.** amount produced.

yō·dĕl, *v.*, -**deled**, -**deling**, *n*. *v.t.*, *v.i.* **1.** shout or sing alternating falsetto with chest voice. —*n*. **2.** act or instance of yodeling.

yō′gȧ, *n*. **1.** Hindu philosophy teaching suppression of the body to free the soul. **2.** system of exercises for total bodily control.

yō′gĭ *n*. adherent of yoga.

yō′gûrt, *n*. fermented milk food.

yōke, *n.*, *v.*, **yoked**, **yoking**. *n*. **1.** device for joining oxen. **2.** pair, esp. of oxen. **3.** something oppressive. —*v.t.* **4.** put a yoke on.

yō′kėl, *n*. rustic; bumpkin.

yōlk, *n*. yellow part of the egg.

Yŏm Kĭp·pūr (yom kē pōōr′), *n*. Jewish Day of Atonement.

yŏn′dêr, *adj.*, *adv*. over there.

yôre, *adv.*, *adj*. *Archaic*. long ago.

yoū, *pron*. **1.** person or persons addressed. **2.** any person.

yŏung, *adj*. **1.** in the early stages of life, etc. **2.** pertaining to youth. —*n*. **3.** children; young people. —**young′ish**, *adj*.

yŏung′stêr, *n*. child; youth.

yoŭr, *adj*. pertaining to you.

yoŭrs, *pron.*, belonging to you.

yoŭr·sĕlf′, *pron.*, *pl.* -**selves**. **1.** form of you used reflexively or emphatically. **2.** your true self.

yoūth, *n*. **1.** young state. **2.** child; young person. —**youth′ful**, *adj*. —**youth′ful·ly**, *adv*. —**youth′ful·ness**, *n*.

yowl, *v.i.*, *n*. howl.

yŭc′cå, *n*. tropical American plant.
yūle, *n*. Christmas.
yūle′tīde′′, *n*. Christmas season.

Z

Z, z, *n*. twenty-sixth letter of the English alphabet.
zā′nÿ, *n*., *pl*. -nies, *adj*. *n*. **1.** clown. **2.** silly person. —*adj*. **3.** crazy; foolish.
zēal, *n*. intense or eager interest. —zeal′ous, *adj*. —zeal′ous·ly, *adv*. —zeal′ous·ness, *n*.
zēal·ót (zel′ot), *n*. enthusiast; fanatic. —zeal′ot·ry, *n*.
zē′brå, *n*. black and white striped horse-like African mammal.
Zĕn, *n*. Buddhist sect.
zē′nĭth, *n*. **1.** celestial point directly overhead. **2.** highest point.
zĕph′ÿr, *n*. mild or gentle breeze.
zĕp′pè·lĭn, *n*. large dirigible. Also, Zep′pe·lin.
zē′rō, *n*. **1.** numerical symbol, 0, denoting the absence of quantity. **2.** nothing.
zĕst, *n*. **1.** something enhancing enjoyment. **2.** enjoyment. —zest′ful, *adj*. —zest′ful·ly, *adv*.
zĭg′zăg′′, *n*., *adj*., *adv*., *v.i*., -zagged, -zagging. *n*. **1.** short sharp alternations in a line. —*adj*., *adv*. **2.** with or having

sharp back and forth turns. —*v.i*. **3.** proceed in a zigzag.
zĭnc, *n*. bluish metallic element.
zĭnc ŏx′īde, *n*. zinc and oxygen salve.
zĭng, *n*. **1.** sharp singing or whistling sound. **2.** vitality. —*v.i*. **3.** move with or make a zinging sound.
zĭn′nĭ·å, *n*. colorful annual garden flower.
Zī′ŏn·ĭsm′′, *n*. political movement for re-establishment of the Jewish Biblical homeland. —Zi′on·ist, *n*.
zĭp, *v*., zipped, zipping, *n*. *v.i*. **1.** act or move speedily or energetically. —*v.t*. **2.** fasten with a zipper. —*n*. **3.** energy.
zĭp′pêr, *n*. slide fastener with interlocking teeth.
zĭth′êr, *n*. stringed musical instrument.
zō′dĭ·ăc, *n*. imaginary heavenly region including the paths of all planets except Pluto, with divisions for the twelve constellations.
zŏm′bĭ, *n*. reanimated dead body. Also, zom′bie.
zōne, *n*., *v.t*., zoned, zoning. *n*. **1.** special area or region. —*v.t*. **2.** mark off or arrange in zones.
zōō, *n*. park where animals are exhibited.
zō·ŏl′o·gÿ, *n*. study of animals. —zo·o·log′i·cal, *adj*. —zo·ol′o·gist, *n*.
zōōm, *v.i*. **1.** move quickly with a humming sound. **2.** fly upward sharply and at great speed.
zūc·chĭ′nĭ, *n*. green cylindrical summer squash.
zÿ·gōte′, *n*. fertilized egg cell.

FOR GIFT GIVING

WEDDING ANNIVERSARY SYMBOLS

	TRADITIONAL	MODERN
1st	paper	clocks
2nd	cotton	china
3rd	leather	crystal, glass
4th	books	electrical appliances
5th	wood	silverware
6th	sugar, candy	wood
7th	wool, copper	desk sets
8th	bronze, pottery	linens, laces
9th	pottery, willow	leather
10th	tin, aluminum	diamond jewelry
11th	steel	fashion jewelry
12th	silk, linen	pearls, colored gems
13th	lace	textiles, furs
14th	ivory	gold jewelry
15th	crystal	watches
20th	china	platinum
25th	silver	silver
30th	pearl	diamond
35th	coral	jade
40th	ruby	ruby
45th	sapphire	sapphire
50th	gold	gold
55th	emerald	emerald
60th	diamond	diamond
75th	diamond	diamond

BIRTHSTONES

January	Garnet
February	Amethyst
March	Bloodstone or Aquamarine
April	Diamond
May	Emerald
June	Pearl or Alexandrite
July	Ruby
August	Sardonyx or Peridot
September	Sapphire
October	Opal or Tourmaline
November	Topaz
December	Turquoise or Zircon

WEIGHTS AND MEASURES

Cubic Measure

1.728 cubic inches	1 cubic foot
27 cubic feet	1 cubic yard
128 cubic feet	1 cord (wood)
40 cubic feet	1 ton (shipping)
2,150.42 cubic inches	1 standard bushel
231 cubic inches	1 U.S. standard gallon
1 cubic foot	about ⅘ of a bushel

Dry Measure

2 pints	1 quart
8 quarts	1 peck
4 pecks	1 bushel

Liquid Measure

4 gills	1 pint
2 pints	1 quart
4 quarts	1 gallon
31½ gallons	1 barrel

Imperial Liquid Measure

1 U.S. gallon	0.833 Imperial gallon
1 U.S. gallon	3.785 liters
1 Imperial gallon	1.201 U.S. gallons
1 Imperial gallon	4.546 liters
1 liter	0.264 U.S. gallon
1 liter	0.220 Imperial gallon

Long Measure

12 inches	1 foot
3 feet	1 yard
5½ yards	1 rod
40 rods	1 furlong
8 furlongs	1 statute mile
3 miles	1 league

Mariner's Measure

6 feet	1 fathom
120 fathoms	1 cable length
7½ cable lengths	1 mile
5,280 feet	1 statute mile
6,080.2 feet	1 nautical mile

Square Measure

144 square inches	1 square foot
9 square feet	1 square yard
30¼ square yards	1 square rod
40 square rods	1 rood
4 roods	1 acre
640 acres	1 square mile

Avoirdupois Weight

27^{11}/$_{32}$ grains	1 dram
16 drams	1 ounce
16 ounces	1 pound
25 pounds	1 quarter
4 quarters	1 cwt
2,000 pounds	1 short ton
2,240 pounds	1 long ton

Troy Weight

24 grains	1 pwt
20 pwt	1 ounce
12 ounces	1 pound

Used for weighing gold, silver and jewels

METRIC EQUIVALENTS

Linear Measure

1 centimeter		0.3937 inch
1 inch		2.54 centimeters
1 decimeter	3.937 inches	0.328 foot
1 foot		3.048 decimeters
1 meter	39.37 inches	1.0936 yards
1 yard		0.9144 meter
1 dekameter		1.9684 rods
1 rod		0.5029 dekameter
1 kilometer		0.621 mile
1 mile		1.609 kilometers

Square Measure

1 square centimeter	0.1550 square inch
1 square inch	6.452 square centimeters
1 square decimeter	0.1076 square foot
1 square foot	9.2903 square decimeters
1 square meter	1.196 square yards
1 square yard	0.8361 square meter

309

```
1 acre ............................................160 square rods
1 square rod ....................................0.00625 acre
1 hectare ........................................2.47 acres
1 acre ...........................................0.4047 hectare
1 square kilometer...............................0.386 square mile
1 square mile....................................2.59 square kilometers
```

Weights

```
1 gram...........................................0.03527 ounce
1 ounce..........................................28.35 grams
1 kilogram.......................................2.2046 pounds
1 pound..........................................0.4536 kilogram
1 metric ton ....................................0.98421 English ton
1 English ton ...................................1.016 metric tons
```

Measure of Volume

```
1 cubic centimeter ..............................0.061 cubic inch
1 cubic inch ....................................16.39 cubic centimeters
1 cubic decimeter ...............................0.0353 cubic foot
1 cubic foot ....................................28.317 cubic decimeters
1 cubic meter ...................................1.308 cubic yards
1 cubic yard ....................................0.7646 cubic meter
1 stere .........................................0.2759 cord
1 cord ..........................................3.624 steres
1 liter ............0.908 dry quart ............1.0567 liquid quarts
1 quart dry......................................1.101 liters
1 quart liquid...................................0.9463 liter
1 dekaliter .............2.6417 gallons .........1.135 pecks
1 gallon.........................................0.3785 dekaliter
1 peck ..........................................0.881 dekaliter
1 hektoliter ....................................2.8375 bushels
1 bushel.........................................0.3524 hektoliter
```

APPROXIMATE METRIC EQUIVALENTS

```
1 decimeter .....................................4 inches
1 liter .............1.06 quarts liquid ..........0.9 quart dry
1 meter .........................................1.1 yards
1 kilometer .....................................⅝ of a mile
1 hektoliter.....................................2⅝ bushels
1 hectare .......................................2½ acres
1 kilogram ......................................2⅕ pounds
1 stere, or cubic meter .........................¼ of a cord
1 metric ton ....................................2,204.6 pounds
```

States and Territories of the United States with Their Post Office Abbreviations and Capitals

Alabama (AL) .... Montgomery
Alaska (AK) .... Juneau
Arizona (AZ) .... Phoenix
Arkansas (AR) .... Little Rock
California (CA) .... Sacramento
Colorado (CO) .... Denver
Connecticut (CT) .... Hartford
Delaware (DE) .... Dover
District of Columbia (DC)
Florida (FL) .... Tallahassee
Georgia (GA) .... Atlanta
Hawaii (HI) .... Honolulu
Idaho (ID) .... Boise
Illinois (IL) .... Springfield
Indiana (IN) .... Indianapolis
Iowa (IA) .... Des Moines
Kansas (KS) .... Topeka
Kentucky (KY) .... Frankfort
Louisiana (LA) .... Baton Rouge
Maine (ME) .... Augusta
Maryland (MD) .... Annapolis
Massachusetts (MA) .... Boston
Michigan (MI) .... Lansing
Minnesota (MN) .... St. Paul
Mississippi (MI) .... Jackson
Missouri (MO) .... Jefferson City
Montana (MT) .... Helena
Nebraska (NE) .... Lincoln
Nevada (NV) .... Carson City
New Hampshire (NH) .... Concord
New Jersey (NJ) .... Trenton
New Mexico (NM) .... Santa Fe
New York (NY) .... Albany
North Carolina (NC) .... Raleigh
North Dakota (ND) .... Bismarck
Ohio (OH) .... Columbus
Oklahoma (OK) .... Oklahoma City
Oregon (OR) .... Salem
Pennsylvania (PA) .... Harrisburg
Rhode Island (RI) .... Providence
South Carolina (SC) .... Columbia
South Dakota (SD) .... Pierre
Tennessee (TN) .... Nashville
Texas (TX) .... Austin
Utah (UT) .... Salt Lake City